THE LAST CANNON SHOT

Be satisfied we will never forget our allegiance till
the last cannon which is shot on this continent in
defence of Great Britain is fired by the hand of a
French Canadian.

ETIENNE-PASCAL TACHÉ

The Last Cannon Shot

A Study of
French-Canadian Nationalism
1837-1850

JACQUES MONET, S.J.

University of Toronto Press

F
1027
M.66

58878

for

DOMINIQUE MONET

1961-

Preface

Any student who has ever written a book knows how little he could have produced without the kindness of many people. First of all, I want to thank my Superiors in the Upper Canada Province of the Jesuit Order. They not only allowed and sponsored my studies, but assumed the financial burden. I owe them far more than I can say. The publication of the manuscript was also helped by a most welcome grant from the Social Science Research Council of Canada, using funds provided by the Canada Council. There are then the alert and helpful members of the staffs of the Public Archives in Ottawa, of the Archives of the Province of Quebec, of the Bibliothèque Saint-Sulpice in Montreal, and, finally, of the Salle Gagnon at the Montreal City Library where Mlle Marie Baboyant typifies so charmingly all the qualities of the ideal librarian. Miss Francess Halpenny and Mrs. Marion Magee of the University of Toronto Press, and Mrs. Laurier LaPierre of Montreal gave me many valuable suggestions. In a special way I also want to thank Abbé Jean-Marie Beauchemin who opened the Archdiocesan Archives of Quebec for me, and Père Paul Desjardins, S.J., of the Archives of Collège Saint-Marie in Montreal, who did me favours over a period of many months.

I am highly indebted to Père Léon Pouliot, S.J., who very generously put at my disposal the result of his years of research on Bishop Bourget and the French-Canadian Catholic Church. He gave me time, and conversation, and much patience. I also owe a heavy debt to M. Fernand Ouellet, now of Carleton University in Ottawa, and to Mr. W. G. Ormsby, now of Brock University at St. Catharines. From the first I heard a great deal about Papineau; and from Mr. Ormsby I derived precious insights into the connection between *la survivance* and the Union. Dr. Ramsay Cook of the Department of History at the University of Toronto also gave me valuable advice, which I sincerely appreciate. Anyone who has read the published works of these scholars, or conversed with them, will easily recognize in the pages that follow my obligation to them.

Above all, there is Dr. J. M. S. Careless who suggested and directed my studies at the University of Toronto, smiled, encouraged, showed growing interest, read manuscripts, gave warnings, proposed improvements, and generally brought it about that I owe to him, more than to any other individual, the completion of this work.

If historical research can be said to have any effect, this may be that a new generation may learn more wisdom and respect by studying the record handed down by its forebears. In my family the next generation exists in my nephew who carries the name my grandfather taught my generation to respect. May he grow wise! And may he and his contemporaries come to understand the record handed down of how the *Canadien* people, although divided and insecure, summoned all their energies to defend their heritage; and of how they finally insured it because, although alien in language and culture, they had grasped the organic vitality of the British constitution in which freedom wears a Crown.

JACQUES MONET, S.J.

Loyola College
Montreal, P.Q.
July 25, 1966

Contents

THE LAST CANNON SHOT

Introduction

Montreal, Friday evening, April 24, 1846. The winter had been long, and the worries that came, almost with the first snowfall, had not yet disappeared. Lately the newspapers had once more begun their stories of American preparations for war. Even now, the galleries of the Assembly are crowded as members debate a new Militia bill. For a month LaFontaine and his followers have relentlessly attacked *les ministres*, but tonight promises to be the climax. For tonight *le parti Canadien* assails Colonel Gugy, the Adjutant-General, who has been distributing all the better commissions to the British.

A hush falls as Morin advances in his new Speaker's robes. First, the prayer; then the member for Kamouraska, Colonel Taché, rises. The visitors strain in the galleries lest they miss a word, for Taché is famous for his enthusiastic oratory. He begins slowly. Proudly, he recalls the exploits in which he shared in 1813. He assures the honourable members opposite that Lower Canadians stand ready to vindicate their bravery: "Our Loyalty is not one of speculation, of pounds, shillings, and pence, we do not carry it on our lips, we do not make a traffic of it. But we are in our habits, by our laws, by our religion . . . monarchists and conservatives." The galleries roar approval; the members on the left pound their desks; the Treasury benches realize that they are in for a hard evening again. Taché continues. Now he is defending his people against the calumnies of their enemies. It is equal justice he demands for them, the equal justice promised but denied for fifty years. Give them only their due, and the "light and joyous battalions of French Canada" will fly against the enemy. "Indeed"— he points to the portrait of Victoria at the far end of the chamber— "we claim to be children of the same mother as you. . . . Be satisfied we will never forget our allegiance till the last cannon which is shot on this continent in defence of Great Britain is fired by the hand of a French Canadian." The House bursts into cheers at this ringing declaration of French Canada's loyalty.

The cheers died slowly that night, and their echo reverberates to this day. Yet many in the visitors' gallery may have mused upon the speech. No one in Taché's audience could forget that a mere nine years before the French Canadians of the Richelieu and Deux-Montagnes regions, swayed by the oratory of Papineau and encouraged by the sympathy of the district of Montreal and of much of the district of Quebec, had rallied against the Crown. During November and December 1837 these "monarchists and conservatives" had fought the Queen's soldiers. They had been effectively defeated: but not before Colborne, and others acting in the name of their sovereign, had created bitter anti-British feelings, even among those French Canadians who had opposed the revolt. A year later, in November 1838, when French Canadians from across the border had returned to proclaim a republic, a second revolt had broken out. And, again, although it had been resoundingly defeated, it roused new racial rancours.

All this had occurred less than a decade ago. Yet now, in April 1846, Taché, who had himself led a minor outbreak in Montmagny, boasted of his people's loyalty to Britain, and his people cheered their approval. What a change was here!

Of what, then, did the French Canadians fashion their loyalty? What sort of nationalism allowed an erstwhile rebel to proclaim that he would be the last loyal defender of the authority he had sought to destroy? That is the question which this study seeks to answer for the decade that followed the "troubles" of 1837—a decade most critical not only for French Canada, but for the whole future of what has since become the Kingdom of Canada.

At the beginning of the 1840's, the French Canadians had come to a cross roads. Since early in the seventeenth century they had been struggling along the path mapped out by Champlain. But now they wondered. The founder of Quebec had set out to create a nation. He cherished a plan to transform New France into a self-sufficient, commercial and agricultural country. Quebec would stand as a metropolis, an emporium of trade regulating the commerce of vast hinterlands and collecting dues from every ship sailing the St. Lawrence. Champlain had caught a vision—audacious, glamorous, new. He saw to it that the land was settled and developed. He trained and instructed the first *coureurs-de-bois*. And soon, after they had learned to guard against the cold and the daily fear of the Indian, the *Canadiens* set out, as Champlain had planned, to claim their heritage. By 1712, with the colony at its peak, they had stamped on the map of North America a huge fleur-de-lis extending from Hudson Bay to New Orleans, from

Newfoundland to Lake Winnipeg. And they were exporting over 550,000 pounds of beaver pelt annually.

But as Champlain's king had failed him, his successors failed Canada. They sent out a mere handful of settlers, never enough to fulfil the great man's dreams. And although the traders—small minds that went ill with a great kingdom—built fortunes for themselves, they never succeeded in perpetuating their wealth in industrial and commercial enterprises. They spent their profits as fast as they made them. And at the Conquest in 1760, they left a ruined colony. The *Canadiens*, however, kept the vision. Seventy thousand strong, they had held a continent for forty years against a million. They had lost it; they were restricted now to the valley of the St. Lawrence. But they remained a strong-willed, irrepressible people.

The better to keep alive their nation, the French Canadians changed their ways. And by the first decade of the nineteenth century they had created a new leadership to replace the old. On the one hand, since the Loyalists and other British immigrants underscored for them the distinction of their Roman Catholic religion, they surrendered the initiative in cultural activities to their curés and priests. And after the introduction of the British parliamentary system in 1791, when the new franchise turned the habitant into the political equal of the seigneur, they gradually gave authority to a different kind of lay leader. No longer could they be an exuberant people of voyageurs opening up a continent. They were now a landed, close-knit nationality protecting its way of life under the guidance of local curés and their own elected politicians. By the 1830's, however, they faced the century of progress. Under British dominion for seventy-five years, they had indeed succeeded in saving the essentials: their ancestral lands, their French language, their Catholic faith, their time-honoured and peculiar jurisprudence, and their family traditions. But they needed more if they were to live a normal national life. The seigneurial system could no longer provide for the growing population, the economy lagged, education problems had reached such an impasse that the schools closed, and the civil code no longer corresponded to modern circumstances. Above all, the thrust of the growing professional middle class created a serious social situation of which the rebellion of 1837 was only one expression. That revolt failed. Clearly, if *la survivance* were to continue successful, new solutions were needed.

Perhaps the *Canadiens'* greatest problem was learning to live with their neighbours. Geography, economics, and history linked them to

British Upper Canada, and to that other world with joys and sorrows all its own, the English-speaking commercial class of Montreal and Quebec City. In solving this problem, the years after 1837 proved crucial. For Durham's proposal to make French Canada and English Canada one state forced the French Canadians for the first time to face the issue squarely. And the quality of their response during that decade has marked the evolution of Canadian history ever since.

The 1840's were also the critical years in the evolving partnership between both Canadas and Great Britain. For between 1838 and 1850 Great Britain and Canada together learned to solve in peace the ugly and frustrating problem of colonial liberty, and thus to bequeath to the twentieth century one of the few successful international organizations in the free world. The French Canadians probably played the leading part in the creation of this splendid prize; and although no one seems to have realized it at the time, it was, again, the quality of their nationalism in the 1840's that determined the kind of Commonwealth we know today.

By 1850 it would be clear that French Canada had succeeded in reforming its systems and institutions to meet the challenges of another century; that both French and English Canadians could live together within the bosom of a single state—and from this bicultural point of view, the protocol of 1867 was only a readjustment, not a new departure; and, finally, that it was the flexibility of British political institutions that could best reconcile Canada's autonomy and the imperial connection. In particular, the new beginnings and new dimensions of the decade made clear how truly interdependent these three—*la survivance*, the success of the Canadian experiment, and the British constitution—had become.

This, then, is a study of French-Canadian nationalism in what was probably its greatest decade. It is not however a theoretical dissertation on the "ism" as such. It is rather a study of people and events, and of the thoughts of people during those events. Indeed, it is largely a description of public opinion. Public opinion, of course, arises out of a whole complex of socio-psychological, economic, and political causes of which most of the actors on the historical stage are usually unaware. Thus an account of it may seem, at first glance, to be a superficial answer to the question posed by such a phenomenon as nationalism. Yet it is far from this. Not infrequently public opinion creates social pressures of its own, and these in turn will affect the deeper pressures that have caused it. Thus it is that a record of public opinion must precede any analysis of the so-called deeper motivations.

But more important still: it is in the description of public opinion that future generations unquestionably find the best and surest expression of what is fundamental in the heritage they have received. For it manifests its own causes as the actors themselves understood them and willed to pass them on. Thus what must first be settled upon if any "ism" is to be correctly understood is not so much the deep-set social structures, not the broadening perspective, nor yet what is perhaps the truth, but rather what the actors in the historical drama thought to be the truth.

Like their counterparts in any generation, the propertied classes of French Canada in the 1840's, the press, the priests, and the politicians probably never realized the psychological, economic, and social motivations which later analysts may find to have been the mainspring of their opinions and actions. They may not have understood, for example, that the shifts in the price of basic commodities, or the evolution of the demography of their society, or the clash of majority and minority interests were the "real" causes affecting their pattern of thought. They may not have known why they wrote and said what they did. This study would not have told them. It is not an analysis of their subconscious. It is "truer" still than that: it is a description of their thoughts and actions.

Public opinion is also reflected in the press. And it can be gained as well from a comparison of the public statements of leading figures with the opinions expressed in their private correspondence. Throughout the 1840's the two traditional estates of French-Canadian leaders, the politicians and the priests, continued to serve as the main fulcrum of the *Canadiens'* convictions. And so this investigation of French-Canadian nationalism is an account of the people's opinion as reflected not only by property and the press, but also by the writings and actions of priests and politicians.

This study also focuses closely on the verdict of the electorate. Of course, the electorate is not necessarily the people. In fact, in the French Canada of the 1840's the electorate represented only about one-eighth of the total population—the franchise being restricted, in the counties, to property owners with an income of £12 a year, or, in the cities, to those whose property brought them £5 a year, or again to those who paid £10 a year in rent. Yet the electors are often identified with the people—mainly out of convenience, and also because no one in the middle of the nineteenth century doubted for a moment that property owners truly reflected the thoughts of the public.

Throughout this study many of the terms used are employed in the sense in which they were understood by the French Canadians of the 1840's. The more important may be designated as follows: a *patriote* is one of the rebels of 1837–38, or a very close sympathizer; a *vendu* is a French Canadian who has become an ally of the British minority in Lower Canada; a Tory is an English-speaking person who is neither an Upper Canadian Reformer nor a Lower Canadian *patriote*. *La nation canadienne* is what would today be termed French Canada; a *Canadien* is a member of that nation, although like John Neilson or Wolfred Nelson his membership may be more legal than physical; and a *nationaliste* is one who seeks the advantage of the *Canadiens*. For the *Canadiens* there were no Canadians. The English-speaking community was spoken of as "les Anglais," or "les Irlandais" (the Scots having somehow got lost), or—an expression that has since disappeared—"les Bretons."

As well as their vocabulary, I will also let stand most of the contemporary French-Canadian judgments, and their highly self-centred view of Canadian affairs. Someone outside the French community might, for example, render a much less severe verdict on Sydenham, or on the riots over the Rebellion Losses bill. French-Canadian nationalism, however, was not woven out of historical verdicts, but out of the manner in which such men and their deeds appeared to the *Canadiens* at the time. And this is the nationalism that has marked us all to this day.

A threefold division has always been curiously satisfying to the human mind, and the development of French-Canadian nationalist opinion between 1837 and 1850 naturally focuses on three distinct issues: the question of accepting or rejecting the union of Lower and Upper Canada, the campaign for responsible government, and, finally, the agitation for repeal of the Union and annexation to the United States. Accordingly, this study is divided into three parts, each dealing with the *Canadien* reaction to one of these issues.

PART ONE

The Debate on the Union
1837-1842

1

The People and the Press: "Le Grand Découragement" 1837-1841

The times were hard. For three years, from mid-1837 onwards, *la nation canadienne* suffered one setback after another, each apparently worse than its predecessor. Rain and bad crops in the rest of the province added to the distress of civil war in the Richelieu and Deux-Montagnes regions. There, in November 1837, the *patriotes*, urged on by Louis-Joseph Papineau, rushed to arms, and reaped only crushing distress. At the first sign of the "troubles," Sir John Colborne had proclaimed martial law, suspended the constitution in favour of a special council made up of rabid French-baiting Tories, bureaucrats, and *vendus*, and then, at the head of a column of British regulars and their associated volunteers, had ridden off to give the rebels a stark surprise. After a victory carousal at Saint-Eustache, for example, Colborne's men tramped through the countryside looting, burning, stealing, and sending hundreds of *Canadiens* scurrying through the nights across the snow to the American border. Even *Le Populaire*, a newspaper edited by a noted *vendu*, Hyacinthe Leblanc de Marconnay, admitted that "dans un rayon de quinze milles, il n'y avait pas un bâtiment qui n'ait été saccagé et pillé par ces nouveaux vandales; Loyaux et Révolutionnaires, amis et ennemis, familles paisibles ou neutres, femmes, enfants, vieillards, ont été la proie d'une troupe de gens qui n'avaient aucun sentiment d'humanité."[1]

The countryside, never wealthy, was now almost destitute. The small village merchants were ruined by the flight, bills unpaid, of so many heads of families. Money was scarce. And in the whole bleak

[1] *Le Populaire*, déc. 1837.

province, there seemed no one to direct or console; for, as a result of the rebellion, the *Canadiens'* traditional leaders, the priests and the politicians, had lost much of their authority. And, in their mood of deep disturbance and unease, the people knew not whom to trust.

The curés and priests had hardly been expected to unravel the involved economic tangle; but many of them, especially those in the Montreal district, did not even fulfil their calling to offer spiritual consolation. The Church hierarchy had been openly impatient with its flock's patriotic preoccupations. Bishop Jacques Lartigue of Montreal, an old, sickly man with a native talent for withstanding criticism, had seen nothing but the abstract moral implications of the rejection of civil authority. To his priests, gathered on July 25, 1837, to celebrate the consecration of his young coadjutor, Bishop Ignace Bourget, he recalled that "il n'est jamais permis de se révolter contre l'autorité légitime, ni de transgresser les lois du pays."[2] Brought up on theological dicta influenced by the European aristocratic reaction to the French Revolution, he could only consider armed revolt sinful and believe that his people must be in grave fault. As rebellious activity increased, he spoke out again, and in his celebrated *mandement* of October 24, 1837, exposed the current conservative doctrine on obedience to civil authority, quoting as confirmation the recent teaching of Pope Gregory XVI to the Bishops of Poland on the outbreak of revolution there in 1830.[3] This view may or may not have influenced the rebellion, but it certainly weakened the Bishop's influence and the rapport between his priests and their people.

But the curés closest to the centres of rebel activity sided with their parishioners. Some felt that "le pasteur ne devait pas se séparer de ses ouailles";[4] others simply disagreed with the Bishop's understanding of the theory of passive resistance. At Saint-Benoît, the curé, Etienne Chartier, a handsome, distinguished, and charming man with, unfortunately, less prudence than power of independent thought, sided openly with the rebels. In 1829 he had caused a stir at the Collège de Sainte-Anne-de-la-Pocatière where, as director, he exchanged (to the thrill of the students and the horror of the old guard) the traditional rigorist discipline for the new advanced

---

[2]Quoted in Gérard Filteau, *Histoire des Patriotes* (3 vols., Montréal, 1938–42), II, 132.

[3]*Mandements, lettres pastorales, circulaires et autres documents publiés dans le diocèse de Montréal depuis son érection*, I (Montréal, 1869), 14–21.

[4]Archives de l'Archevêché de Québec (AAQ), M. Blanchet à Lord Gosford, 9 nov. 1837.

methods inspired by Lamennais.[5] And now, in direct defiance of his bishop's doctrine, he explained from the pulpit the "liberal" view of the right to revolt, lent his eloquence to the *patriote* leaders, and, footsore, tired, and hungry, joined his parishioners "la pioche à la main, le saint jour du Dimanche" to dig defensive trenches against Colborne's volunteers. On the eve of the engagement at Saint-Eustache, he held a meeting there "et encouragea les gens à la révolte."[6] Later, with a price on his head, he escaped to the United States in disguise, and, unflagging in his zeal, shared the refugees' plottings and the ban of his bishop.

The rebels may have been impressed, and so may some of their friends, but the majority of *Canadiens* knew very well that most of their priests, and especially those in command, had, willy-nilly, resisted the *patriotes'* best efforts. They knew what Bishop Lartigue thought about those they looked upon as heroes: "des mauvais sujets . . . prétendus libéraux, attachés à détruire dans nos peuples l'amour de la religion";[7] they knew, too, that Lartigue's new coadjutor, who may have been more sympathetic, was not a man to let his feelings (or common sense) interfere with the strict letter of the law. And in Quebec City, where prudent, diplomatic cordiality usually marked the close connection between church and government, the courtly, white-haired archbishop, Joseph Signay, was a close friend of the Governor General. Indeed, he was so out of touch with his people's feelings that he urged one curé to explain that Colborne's devastating march was intended not so much as a punitive measure as a gesture "pour protéger les bons et fidèles sujets."[8] Above all, the people were stung by the severity of the Church's curse. The *patriote* dead were deprived of the customary and consoling ceremonies of a Catholic funeral, a special shame in a *milieu* so sensitive to tradition; and among those who survived, "ceux qui se sont mêlés en mal de politique" found themselves deprived of the sacraments until they had performed an especially rigorous penance. No wonder the *Canadiens* wavered in confidence towards their priests.

Even before the actual outbreak, a number of curés from around Saint-Hyacinthe admitted that "il est visible que depuis un certain

[5]W. Lebon, *Histoire du Collège de Sainte-Anne-de-la-Pocatière: Le premier demi-siècle, 1827–1877* (Québec, 1948), I, 420–9.
[6]Archives de l'Archevêché de Montréal (AAM), Bourget à Chartier, 12 déc. 1837. Archives de la Province de Québec (APQ), Documents, 1837–38, 719.
[7]AAM, Lartigue à Belcourt, 24 avril 1838.
[8]AAQ, Signay à Leclerc, 25 nov. 1837.

temps le clergé perd l'attachement et la confiance des catholiques de ce diocèse parce qu'ils sont persuadés que des vues d'intérêt le fait [sic] embrasser le parti du Gouvernement. . . ."[9] And during 1837, when "les passions humaines sont tellement soulevées" that distrust and suspicion often became real hatred, Bishop Lartigue complained of "la haine que lui portaient plusieurs de ses diocésains" and other curés were, understandably, most upset about their parishioners who, like those in Chambly, jeered at them with cries of "Vive Papineau! A bas le mandement!" Some actually feared their people might go as far as the classical revolutionaries—"il faut fuir ou mourir martyr des maximes de l'Evangile, suivant l'exemple de l'ancien clergé en France et en Espagne"[10]—and they were not, perhaps, far wrong. From his camp in Vermont, Papineau wrote to his wife on December 10, 1837: "Les chances de salut sont peu nombreuses. Elles eussent été certaines si les prêtres se fussent bornés à prier. C'est leur état; ils ne font du bien que quand ils y rentrent, ils ne font que du mal quand ils en sortent. Si le pays ne les sauve pas malgré eux-mêmes, ils y souf-friront plus de mal d'ici deux ou trois ans qu'ils n'en ont infligé depuis de longues années."[11]

As far as most of the *Canadiens* were concerned, however, the *patriotes* had performed just as badly. At the first sign of danger, Papineau, the great leader, had fled across the border; so had the dour and scholarly Dr. Edmund B. O'Callaghan, the editor of the English-speaking *patriote* organ, the *Vindicator*. Louis Perrault, the owner of the *Vindicator*, had made no secret of his republican ideas and had played an important part in organizing a rebel unit in Montreal, Les Fils de la Liberté, but he too hastened to Burlington, as did Dr. Thomas Bouthillier of Saint-Hyacinthe, the commander of a picket of one hundred men at Saint-Charles. One *patriote* leader showed more cour-age: Jean-Joseph Girouard had only managed to get out of his house in Saint-Benoît minutes before Colborne arrived. With a price of £500 on his head he hid near the home of a poor habitant named Saint-Amant; but on hearing that his friend Chénier had been killed and Wolfred Nelson captured, he ordered Saint-Amant to deliver him up and claim the reward. Dr. Wolfred Nelson, perhaps Papineau's most sincere lieutenant, a learned, impetuous man with a generous heart who was known affectionately throughout the Richelieu Valley

[9]Quoted in C. P. Choquette, *Histoire du Séminaire de Saint-Hyacinthe depuis sa fondation jusqu'à nos jours*, I (Montréal, 1911), 203.

[10]AAM, Bourget à Blanchet, 21 mai 1838, à Lefebvre, 4 nov. 1838, à Mignault, 6 nov. 1838. AAQ, DM VII, 59. Bourget à Turgeon, 5 mars 1838.

[11]Quoted in J. Bruchési, "Lettres d'un exilé," *Cahiers des Dix* (1951), p. 68.

as "le loup rouge," had been captured on December 12 and con-ducted to prison in Montreal between rows of jeering, spitting, and snowball-throwing Tories.[12]

As for the most notorious of the *patriotes*, Ludger Duvernay, the editor of the famed Montreal newspaper, *La Minerve*—a braggard, a coward, a heavy drinker, yet a man who remained strangely popular —he too, with a price on his head, had managed to elude the British to join the others in Vermont. There for the next four years he tried desperately to live up to his old, dissolute standards in the only two ways he knew: by stirring up trouble and by editing a newspaper. Early in 1838 he founded the semi-masonic, strongly anti-clerical, and republican Association des Frères Chasseurs, but it never did the damage he had hoped. Later, he began the inflammatory sheet, *Le Patriote Canadien*, but it was a dismal financial failure. Duvernay had left the *Minerve* offices in charge of two of his printers, François Lemaître and James Phelan. They fought among themselves and split the equipment Duvernay had entrusted to them, each starting his own flimsy journal. Phelan edited *Le Temps*; Lemaître, *La Quotidienne*, a satirical sheet which appeared irregularly and was shut down at the outbreak of the second rebellion in November 1838 when Lemaître was discovered to be one of the leading Chasseurs.[13] Two other of Duvernay's tense young men, Jean-Baptiste Houlée and Pierre Le-febvre, also plotted revolution and, in August 1838 started to publish *Le Courrier Canadien*. But instead of overthrowing the Special Coun-cil, they took to fighting publicly with Lemaître and Phelan, each one betraying the other in turn to the secret council of the Chasseurs. In all of this, of course, they were playing true to the type of young, wide-eyed doctrinaire who, while washing the world free of all imperfection, spends most of his time attacking his fellows instead of his problems. They could hardly replace, as popular leaders, the great ones who had fled.

One newspaper that continued publication was *Le Populaire*, a sheet founded early in 1837 by one of Duvernay's bitter personal enemies, Léon Gosselin, with the specific aim of fighting the *patriotes*. For most of the French, it must accordingly have been on the side of the devil; and it hardly lived up to its name. In 1838 it was edited by Hyacinthe Leblanc de Marconnay, an interesting character who had

---

[12]A. Fauteux, *Les Patriotes de 1837–8* (Montréal, 1950), p. 253; L. O. David, *Biographies et portraits* (Montréal, 1878), p. 283.
[13]APQ, Papiers Duvernay, R.P. à ?, 1838; Girard à ?, 16 juil. 1838; Houlée à Duvernay, 8 août 1838; Lefebvre à Duvernay, 18 sept. 1838.

fled France after the July Revolution, married a French Canadian, worked for several newspapers including *La Minerve*, and now flattered himself that he led "un parti modéré qui exerce une grande influence sur les effets de la révolte."[14] But obviously neither he nor his paper offered much comfort for his adopted people.

Nor, for the moment, could the political thinkers in the old capital at Quebec. In 1838 the best known and probably most highly respected of these was Etienne Parent, the editor of *Le Canadien*. He wrote clearly and elegantly, and later lectured frequently on such varied subjects as political philosophy, progress, and the relations of church and state. As well as a distinguished *savant* he was also undoubtedly patriotic. During the "troubles" he was in prison for months, but continued to edit *Le Canadien* with materials smuggled into him each day by an assistant. This feat endeared him to the populace, but it could not make a popular leader of him. A hard, silent, moody man—Durham called him "ce petit homme dyspeptique"—his gifts were all of the mind. His eyes were bright and intense, but his presence was awkward. All his life he stuttered unpleasantly, and after his damp imprisonment he went deaf. As an intellectual (often with genius and audacity far in advance of his time) he was destined to inspire the national goals of his generation, but as a political leader he would not do.

The acknowledged monarch of the press, and certainly a writer as widely read as Parent, was John Neilson, the long-time editor of the colony's leading newspaper, the bilingual *Quebec Gazette*. A stubborn, sturdy Scot whose household's language was French, he had changed political sides ten times over and had attacked and supported both the government and the *patriotes*, but always, with calm deliberation he had pursued a steady star: the emancipation of French Canada.[15] Currently, he pressed hard against any of those in sympathy with rebellion, sat on the Special Council, and, to many, appeared only another *vendu*. As his special assistant for the French *Gazette*, Neilson had tutored Ronald MacDonald, a fellow Scot (but from Prince Edward Island) as bilingual as himself, although supremely indolent and a heavy drinker. Certainly not one to cheer the grim atmosphere.

A sign of just how grim the situation had become was the work of the silly young poet and *patriote*, Joseph-Guillaume Barthe. Between 1838 and 1840 he published almost weekly such bleak works as an

[14]Public Archives of Canada (PAC), MG 24, A 13, Bagot Papers, 10, Marconnay à Bagot, 23 oct. 1841; Filteau, *Patriotes*, II, 74.

[15]Francis J. Audet, "John Neilson," Royal Society of Canada, *Transactions*, 3rd series, XXII (1928), s. 1, 81–98.

apostrophe to Queen Victoria (*L'Aurore,* July 31, 1840) which included the lines:

> O toi ! jeune Princesse, assise sur un Trône,
> Je veux que d'heureux jours le destin te couronne,
> Que tu fasses longtemps les délices des tiens,
> Et que mille autres bras en fidèles soutiens,
> Affermisse encore ton illustre puissance:

or this (contradictory) one dedicated to the *patriotes* (*Le Fantasque,* December 26, 1838) which led to his arrest and imprisonment for three months:

> Les fils des Canadas, amans de liberté,
> Perdant leur vain espoir dans un sceptre insensé,
> Et d'un généreux sang rachetant leur patrie,
> Bravèrent dans nos champs la mitraille ennemie;
> O peuple! jette un funèbre feston
> Sur leur tombeau ... bats le mâle clairon!
> Couvre de drapeaux sombres
> Les tombeaux et leurs ombres! ...

Mercifully, however, the *Canadiens* had a chance to laugh. In August 1837 Napoléon Aubin, a clever young Frenchman who had emigrated to Canada in the early 'thirties, founded the humorous journal, *Le Fantasque.* A natural satirist, he soon became the talk of several towns. As far away as Paris, Lamennais refused to believe *Le Fantasque* was drawn up entirely by one man, thinking it impossible "qu'un homme eut autant d'esprit à lui tout seul."[16] Aubin wrote with wit and showed no mercy. And everyone enjoyed it—except perhaps the objects of his banter. Soon *Le Fantasque* was successfully competing with the well-established *Le Canadien.* For it was more than just recreation: it was the wit of Gaul to cheer the depressed and those who had failed, it was a clever retort to the Church's curse, it raised eyebrows at the fleeing *patriotes* and the frustrated leaders of opinion. Above all, it provided the laughter *la nation canadienne* needed during these bitterest years.

THE HATED GOVERNORS

Lord Durham arrived with the summer of 1838, and was greeted with enthusiasm. Papineau himself hoped much from his coming and expected from him even greater reforms than from his own defunct

[16]Quoted in A. Lusignan, *Nouvelles Soirées canadiennes,* p. 439.

Assembly.[17] The *patriote* and national historian-to-be, François-Xavier Garneau, hymned his arrival in *Le Canadien* on June 8, 1838:

> Durham ferme l'oreille aux conseils de vengeance.
> D'un peuple sans appui prends sur toi la défense.
> Oui, sois juste pour tous: mais non, ne souffre point
> Que le puissant haineux dépouille l'orphelin.
> Réforme les abus, remonte vers leur cause. . . .

The Archbishop of Quebec rejoiced that the new Governor had chosen to circulate his first proclamation by sending it to the curés throughout the province. "Je ne doute pas," he wrote to Durham's first secretary, Charles Buller, "que ce corps, à la loyauté duquel Son Excellence veut bien rendre un témoignage si flatteur, ne remplisse fidèlement les vues de Son. Ex. tant par son attachement à Sa Grandeur Souveraine que par l'intérêt pour son troupeau auquel il est uni par des liens si étroits."[18] Parent and *Le Canadien* even claimed that if the French Canadians themselves had been at liberty to select their own government, they would not have found greater friends than Durham and his entourage. Shortly afterwards, when the Governor solved what must have been a very ticklish problem, the fate of the rebel prisoners, his popularity reached its zenith. *Le Fantasque* reflected on July 7: "Tous les actes du Gouverneur sont jusqu'à présent marqués du sceau de la précision, de l'habilité, de la fermeté et de l'indépendance, et ce que l'on doit le plus admirer en eux c'est qu'ils ne se font point attendre comme sous les paresseux gouvernans dont le Canada fut si long-tems surchargé."

Aubin, however, soon shifted from praise to sarcasm. For as the reforming Governor's régime grew older, the French Canadians slowly began to suspect the great Durham, and *Le Fantasque* reflected their mistrust. One by one, throughout the summer and fall, Aubin began to mock the Governor's achievements: promises aplenty, a few new policemen in Quebec, the bribing of several newspapers, a new mast atop the dome of the ex-Assembly Hall to fly the Durham standard. The Governor had also committed the sin of arbitrary rule—without an assembly, "à la Napoléon, c'est-à-dire à cheval! au galop, ou ce qui est plus commode encore, en steamboat." Aubin invited the legislators of the world to visit Lower Canada and view the latest style in government. For although he had changed the personnel of the Special Council, Durham still ruled without consulting the people. In fact, he had probably changed the councillors, Aubin averred on July 14,

---

[17] APQ, Collection Papineau-Bourassa, 530a, Papineau à Roebuck, 17 mai 1838.
[18] AAQ, Signay à C. Buller, 4 juin 1838.

to provide fresh jobs for his friends. This, of course, was a capital sin! And worse yet was the exclusion of French Canadians from appointments. On June 16, shortly after Durham landed, Aubin had printed an open letter in which he explained that the French Canadian habitant would respect Britain's power in return for "son culte, sa chaumière et surtout la langue de ses ancêtres," and added realistically: "Accordez à son cousin de la ville de partager avec quelques autres envieux (car il en est partout) les emplois et les salaires de votre Gouvernement, afin qu'il puisse s'en faire une petite gloire auprès de ses voisins, et vous aurez son dévouement, son amour et sa vie." But Durham did not heed, if he read Le Fantasque at all. On September 1, for example, only two of thirteen appointees were French Canadians, and these were named to the rather insignificant posts of "commissaires pour la décision des petites causes"—and almost all his lists were the same.[19]

The suspicions thus aroused soon turned to certainty. Le Canadien had already pointed out that Durham consorted with Tories and Montreal merchants, that he encouraged nothing savouring of French Canada.[20] Now he named to an important post on the municipal commission the fiery Adam Thom, described in Le Populaire (November 24) as "cet ennemi irréconciliable des Canadiens . . . ce fanatique haineux, méprisé même pour la lâcheté et le sang-froid de sa violence politique." Indeed, this most notorious and fiercest of the anti-French writers was the editor of the Montreal Herald, "ce monstre altéré du sang canadien."[21] His appointment, as Archbishop Signay confided to his friend, Lord Gosford, proved a biting blow: "La confiance dans l'administration était telle [at the time of the amnesty] que toute la presse canadienne applaudit tout d'une voix, mais la position de M. Adam Thom à une des commissions établies pour aider l'administration et les incidents qui l'ont suivie nous ont amenés de nouvaux malheurs. De là le peuple a conclu qu'on en voulait à ses institutions, à ses lois, à ses usages."[22] To make things worse, the Governor sent Thom as his personal representative to a public political meeting in Montreal on October 1; Thom's speech breathed hatred, prejudice, contempt for all things French. And eight days later, in his farewell proclamation, Durham spoke for himself in an accent that recalled Thom's, declaring his aim to elevate the whole of Lower Canada to

[19]Le Fantasque, 16 juin, 14 juil., 4, 25 août, 1, 8 sept. 1838.
[20]W. Smith, "The Reception of the Durham Report in Canada," Canadian Historical Association, Report (1928), p. 41.
[21]Papiers Duvernay, 525, Dumesnil à Duvernay, 3 août 1841.
[22]AAQ, Gouvernement, V, 154, Signay à Gosford, 3 déc. 1838.

"a thoroughly British character . . . to raise the defective institutions of Lower Canada to the level of British civilization and freedom."[23] Now there could be no doubt. As some had feared all along, Durham had turned against the French.[24] *Le Canadien* warned that if any more serious troubles occurred, Durham and his deplorable policy of "anglification" would be to blame. Within eight weeks, the pace of events had indeed quickened: Durham was replaced by Colborne as administrator; four hundred *patriotes* precipitated a second rebellion; Bishop Lartigue, "déclaré dans les papiers publics comme coupable de haute trahison envers la Nation canadienne,"[25] fled from Montreal to the Séminaire de Québec; and 1200 French Canadians, led by Wolfred Nelson's brother Robert, crossed the border at Napierville where they decreed "au nom du Peuple du Bas-Canada," that "Le Bas-Canada doit prendre la forme d'un gouvernement RÉPUBLICAIN et se déclare maintenant, de fait, RÉPUBLIQUE."[26]

Colborne moved swiftly, proclaiming martial law, suspending the right of *habeas corpus*, and closing almost all the remaining French-language newspapers. He then transported the civil administration from Quebec to Montreal, crossed with his troops to Laprairie (with bagpipes playing "The Campbells are Coming"!), and put the countryside to the sword, thereby living up to his already hated reputation among the *Canadiens*. In fact the Administrator had only acted as best he could. Usually he left orders forbidding plunder and destruction, but his soldiers and volunteers promptly disobeyed—as on the infamous night of November 12, 1838, when "tout le pays en arrière de Laprairie présentait l'affreux spectacle d'une vaste nappe de flammes livides et l'on rapporte que pas une seule maison rebelle n'a été laissée debout."[27] Guilty or not, Colborne created a deep store of resentment and "wounds in the minds of the Canadians that could never be healed."[28] During the remainder of the decade editors never mentioned Colborne without referring to "maisons réduites en cendre, habitants massacrés, femmes, enfants et vieillards livrés à la fureur d'une soldatesque effrénée."[29]

[23]Quoted in M. Wade, *The French Canadians* (Toronto, 1955), p. 190.

[24]PAC, MG 24, B 14, Papiers LaFontaine, Nelson à LaFontaine, 16 juil. 1838; Papiers Duvernay, Duchesnois à Duvernay, 20 avril 1838, and Mailhiot à Duvernay, 23 août 1838.

[25]AAM, Lartigue à Provencher, 21 avril 1839.

[26]Quoted in V. Morin, "La 'république canadienne' de 1838," *Revue d'Histoire de l'Amérique française*, II (1949), 483.

[27]Quoted in Filteau, *Patriotes*, III, 187.

[28]The remark is D.-B. Viger's to S. Derbyshire. Quoted in Wade, *The French Canadians*, p. 185.

[29]*Le Canadien*, 20 nov. 1839.

Etienne Parent summed up the feelings of his compatriots in two articles published in *Le Canadien* to celebrate Colborne's departure. Colborne, he said, had failed to appreciate that the "troubles" sprang less from a desire for independence than from endless grievances against the local oligarchy and that their remedy therefore lay not in fire and fury but in wise concession. By this failure he had multiplied difficulties for his successor: "le gouvernement de Sir John a repoussé le peuple, l'a dégoûté, l'a froissé dans ses sentiments les plus délicats, l'a jeté dans le désespoir, a détruit sa confiance dans la justice des autorités, et a laissé une tâche d'Hercule au prochain administrateur." Parent's thoughts were always on a high plane. Aubin merely laughed: "Quelle différence y a-t-il entre Sir John et de la *cire jaune?*—C'est que l'une est le *grand sceau* de la Province, et qu'on dit que l'autre n'est pas le *grand sot* de la province" (*Le Fantasque*, September 17). Most *Canadiens* however would probably have spoken more like the *patriote*, Dr. Fortier, who wrote to Ludger Duvernay on hearing that Colborne had been granted a peerage: "Ils ont fait Colborne Pair—il faut se rappeler que tous les lieutenants des despotes ont été récompensés de leurs assassinats. Le duc d'Albe, le duc de Northumberland, Sir Hudson Lowe! Dieu quel *quarto*—j'oubliais Bond Head et Arthur Young—pour compléter la demi-douzaine de meurtriers."[30] "Le vieux brûlot," they called him at first, recalling his torchlight processions through the Richelieu Valley; later, when he became Baron Seaton, they pronounced it Satan. Both names endured.

Of all the misdeeds imputed to Colborne, the hardest for the French Canadians to bear were the trials and executions of the rebels, and the decree exiling fifty-eight of them to Australia as political prisoners. The trials, of which there were to be fourteen—throughout which the gibbet stood forebodingly in the square in front of the Court House—began in Montreal on November 28, 1838, and ended on the first of May following. During that time, the grimmest of so many grim months, 108 *patriotes* were tried, 99 condemned, and 12 executed in three ruthless public performances on December 21, January 18, and February 15. In the minds of most *Canadiens*, however, the banishment of the fifty-eight to Australia seems to have been still worse. Durham's measure exiling twenty-four leaders of the first rebellion had been received as a great act of mercy, but Colborne's seemed a dreadful affair. Since all newspapers were suppressed at the outset of the second rebellion—except for *Le Fantasque* which chose its words carefully until it too was closed down on January 2, 1839— the initial reaction to the edict is hard to assess. But when the presses

[30]Papiers Duvernay, 404, Fortier à Duvernay, 2 fév. 1840.

rolled again in the early spring of 1839, all the editors filled their pages with news and comments on the exiles. There could be no doubt then of their sentiments. Until the last minute they had hoped for a pardon, considering the British government too diplomatic and too honourable to permit the injustice![31]

Indeed the French Canadian's emotions had been hit hard. His way of life which rested upon the family structure and respect for the *père de famille* had been challenged by Colborne's decision. To the *Canadien* who had spent over sixty years in a society in which a trip from Saint-Eustache to Quebec City was a once-in-a-lifetime event, Australia was the end of the world. But what hurt more than the actual banishment of the exiles was the company they would have to keep. The habitant had high moral standards and was generally law-abiding; now, as *Le Canadien* noted (December 6), he saw his fellows, "de simples cultivateurs, d'humbles ouvriers, même de pauvres journaliers," sent to a penal colony, where they had to work in chain gangs, tied to push-carts, and (according to *Le Fantasque*, September 9, 1841) were regularly flogged before meals "par manière de coup d'appétit." He felt the dishonour more than the punishment.

Most important of all, the exiles served as an outlet for French-Canadian self-pity. Through all the articles, letters, descriptions, and comments on the fifty-eight Lower Canadian prisoners, the editors seldom as much as mentioned the eighty-three from Upper Canada who suffered the same fate. This self-pity flourished particularly, of course, in the existing atmosphere of oppression. The French Canadians felt deeply the government's obvious mistrust and were hurt by the open contempt of the English-speaking press. Disheartened and defeated, they had lost their vision. They were frightened. Ordinary citizens wrote of the "terreur et panique"[32] that prevented free expression: "les Tories me prescrivent à moi, sujet Anglais, de dire tout ce que je pense."[33] They considered themselves condemned "comme des animaux qu'on mène à la boucherie."[34] And the press acted with equal circumspection. Etienne Parent admitted to the French-baiting Montreal *Gazette* that fear put him at a disadvantage in answering its insults. Indeed, according to *L'Ami du Peuple* on February 20, 1839, "la Province est couverte de troupes britanniques, prêtes à faire respecter l'autorité," and all classes of society were affected. "Les

---

[31]See *Le Canadien*, 1 août 1839, and *Le Fantasque*, 1 oct. 1839.
[32]Papiers Duvernay, 299, Mailhiot à Duvernay, 14 mai 1839.
[33]*Ibid.*, Pacaud à Duvernay, 11 juin 1840.
[34]*Ibid.*, 413, Plinguet à Duvernay, 11 juin 1840.

putains (excusez, mais après tout, c'est une nouvelle)," wrote an ardent and lonely young Chasseur to Duvernay about his problems, "se plaignent amèrement de la sévérité de la police. Le gouverneur n'est pas populaire au Bordel."[35]

The French had also to endure the abuse heaped upon them by the Tory press. In *Le Canadien*, Parent explained that his people were extremely sensitive and would rather suffer material want than be the butt of the kind of insult and injury they were now forced to bear. Durham had taken advice from their enemies, the English sneered at their institutions, and now the *Gazette* even questioned their intelligence. They would much rather put up with Colborne's looting, he cried out on September 9, in a paragraph of rare emotion:

Qu'on emprisonne, qu'on exile, qu'on pille, qu'on pende ceux qu'un système abusif, pendant de longues années, a poussés au désespoir, cela peut encore se supporter; mais qu'on déverse ainsi le mépris hautement et à pleines mains sur une population malheureuse, écrasée . . . c'en est trop. . . . N'y a-t-il donc pas de justice divine, et quels crimes avons-nous donc commis contre le ciel pour qu'il nous livre à de telles souffrances, plus cruelles encore que le fer et le feu.

The times were dark and dangerous, wrote an ex-*patriote* to Duvernay: "Ce n'est plus les temps d'autrefois, mon cher Duvernay, plus de joyeuses réunions, plus d'épanchements d'amitié, d'idées et de sentiments. Un profond égoisme, une morgue insolente, un isolement complet d'une classe à l'autre, voilà ce que semblent avoir produit les évènements des trois dernières années."[36] The Bishop in Montreal agreed. He regretted that happiness had fled; "la Religion et les vieilles mœurs françaises" had disappeared forever.[37] It was against this background of disillusion and destruction, exile, contempt, and disappointment, that the French Canadians would argue the great debate over the Union.

[35]*Ibid.*, Ouimet à Duvernay, 7 août 1838.
[36]*Ibid.*, 471, Amiot à Duvernay, 3 fév. 1841.
[37]AAM, Bourget à Cabrat, 11 avril 1839.

2

"Poulet" Thomson and the Project of Union

Leaving the *Canadiens* to fire and fury and Colborne, Durham had returned to London in November 1838 to prepare his report. In it he claimed that British North America was retarded because it lacked real British political institutions and indulged in the luxury of "two nations warring in the bosom of a single state." Salvation, peace, prosperity, reform, and all other good would come if the colonies were granted responsible government, "that wise principle of our Government, which has vested the direction of the national policy, and the distribution of patronage, in the leaders of the Parliamentary majority,"[1] and if the troublesome non-British element were eliminated. He therefore advised political union of English Upper Canada and French Lower Canada into a single English-speaking province, in which the *Canadien* population would be numerically overwhelmed and gradually assimilated into the English-speaking majority. And to the new parliament of this united province, meeting in a capital moved to an English *milieu*, he urged the granting of responsible government.[2]

Durham signed his report on January 31, 1839. His recommendation about responsible government eventually became fact, but not for ten years, because at first imperial statesmen were sceptical of its value, if not satisfied that it was completely unimportant. Lord John

---

[1]Durham's *Report*, as quoted in C. W. New, *Lord Durham* (Oxford, 1929), p. 500.

[2]The term "responsible government" has held a variety of meanings. In general, it describes most of the conventions governing the relations between the Crown, its ministers, and parliament. Outside the process out of which they arose, they are illogical and unintelligible. But, properly understood, they mean, essentially, that the sovereign's public acts must be countersigned by a minister who assumes individual responsibility for them and that the cabinet of ministers is collectively responsible to the House of Commons to such a degree that when defeated in the House, it must either resign or appeal to the electorate.

Russell was to change his mind, but when speaking on a petition from the Assembly of Lower Canada in 1837, he was unconvinced:

I hold this proposition to be entirely incompatible with the relations between the mother country and the Colony. . . . That part of the constitution which requires that the ministers of the Crown shall be responsible to Parliament and shall be removable if they do not obtain the confidence of Parliament, is a condition which exists in an imperial legislature only. It is a condition which cannot be carried into effect in a colony—it is a condition which can only exist in one place, namely the seat of empire.[3]

So were his colleagues. Melbourne, then prime minister, confessed later that "the opinion of this country and this government was entirely opposed to independent responsible government."[4]

Durham's advice about union, on the other hand, received immediate attention. At the beginning of May 1839 Russell introduced a Union bill into the House of Commons, the principle was agreed upon in July, and in September, Charles Poulett Thomson received his commission to go to the Canadas "to learn their deliberate wishes and to obtain their co-operation by frank and unreserved personal intercourse."

Meanwhile the *Report* had been received in Quebec. At *Le Canadien*, Parent translated it immediately and published it in instalments throughout March and April. Although it sketched a design to crush his national culture, he agreed—surprisingly enough—with the plan for the Union, and in a remarkable series of articles, published between May and November 1839, he revealed his reasons. Since Great Britain had determined to annihilate *la nation canadienne*, his compatriots had no choice but to resign themselves "avec la meilleure grâce possible" (May 13) and try, moreover, to work sincerely within the framework of the new constitution.

Nous croyons . . . qu'il eut été d'une sage politique pour l'Angleterre de favoriser l'extension et l'affermissement dans le Bas-Canada d'une nation différente de celle des états voisins; mais les Canadiens-français . . . n'ont plus rien à attendre . . . pour leur nationalité. Que leur reste-il donc à faire pour leur propre intérêt et dans celui de leurs enfants, si ce n'est de travailler eux-mêmes de toutes leurs forces à amener une assimilation qui brise la barrière qui les sépare des populations qui les environnent de toutes parts. (October 23)

[3]Quoted in Sir Charles Lucas, ed., *The Durham Report* (3 vols., Oxford, 1912), I, 143–4, and in O. A. Kinchen, *Lord Russell's Canadian Policy* (Lubbock, Texas, 1945), pp. 33–4.
[4]Chester Martin, "Lord Durham's Report and Its Consequences," *Canadian Historical Review*, XX (1939), 178.

"Nous sommes disposés," he explained on October 23, "à apporter dans l'Union proposée toute la bonne disposition nécessaire pour rendre l'alliance aussi profitable, aussi heureuse que possible." But, as he had emphasized on May 13, the *Canadiens* must insist in return on the Union's twin, responsible government: "En nous résignant au plan de Lord Durham . . . nous entendons qu'on le suive dans toutes ses parties favorables." With and by these two, the Union and responsible government, the margin of gain was worth the loss: they could achieve at last their goal of thirty years, victory over the local oligarchy of British merchants and Tories. For by the Union they would be joined in their struggle by the Reformers of Upper Canada whose strength they needed and who also needed them. Together thus, "parlant par la même voix et à la fois, et en agissant de concert," they could force from the English politicians "un Gouvernement satisfaisant, responsable, condition indispensable de bonheur et de prospérité" (August 2). To accomplish this, assimilation, though regrettable, would not be too high a price, but "une œuvre désirable à l'accomplissement de laquelle tout le monde doit travailler cordialement" (November 4). Thus, Parent foresaw, French Canadians would gain more in political power than they would lose in cultural strength.

Parent thus urged what for latter-day *nationalistes* would be the supreme sacrifice. Yet at the same time he seemed aware that such heroism might not be necessary. Indeed, throughout these penetrating articles he emphasized that the *Canadiens'* survival as a distinct national group went hand in hand with the British connection. On May 13, he wrote: "notre 'nationalité' ne pouvait se maintenir qu'avec la tolérance sincère, sinon l'assistance active de la Grande-Bretagne." *La nation canadienne*, he explained, had received from William Pitt a constitution that made it a separate colony and permitted it to continue as a different nation. Thus segregated, and by using British institutions, the *Canadiens* had preserved and developed their own distinctive cultural patterns. Their survival still depended upon Britain's pledges that the system protecting their language, educational traditions, and religious practices would be guarded. But for this protection—for which they were bound to Britain by "les liens de l'intérêt, de l'honneur et de la reconnaissance"—they would long ago have fallen under the numbers and influence of their immediate neighbours, and inevitably lost their identity. So, to save themselves, they had twice defended Britain's empire at the price of their blood, and, more subtly, had kept Upper Canada British by setting up a rival culture to that of the merchants and Loyalists. For, as Parent saw it, the Upper Canadians and the British of Lower Canada remained attached to the mother country mainly as a lever against this majority national group foreign to their interests and mentality. "Du moment qu'elle n'aura plus à craindre ou à jalouser une nationalité française dans le Bas-Canada," he argued, the English-speaking North American population would sound the tocsin of revolt exactly as it had in 1775.

The British connection and the French-Canadian nationality were thus inextricably related: the stronger the nationality, the greater the safety of the empire, and *vice versa*. Accordingly when he recommended on November 4 that his compatriots join with the Upper Canadians to hammer out "l'établissement de bonne foi du système représentatif et ses conséquences, dont la principale est la responsabilité," he knew they would also be preserving "la connexion avec l'Empire Britannique." In this he was in agreement with the Upper Canadians who considered that Lord Durham's recommendations would save the link with Britain and prevent absorption into the United States. Without true British institutions, on the other hand, he also agreed, "les passions seront mises en jeu, et la séparation aura lieu, coûte que coûte, et très probablement au profit des Etats-Unis, qui, bon gré mal gré, entraîneront dans leur orbite ces provinces encore faibles."[5] Hence, by pressing French Canadians to accept Union-and-assimilation as the price for responsible government, Parent was also, if not prophesying, perhaps at least subtly reminding the *Canadiens* that with the full measure of British institutions they were not necessarily sacrificing anything.

At the other editorial desk in Quebec sat John Neilson, autonomy's undoubted champion. Immediately he spoke out against both of Durham's main proposals, marshalling his arguments in a series running, like Parent's, through November 1839.[6] If it were meant as a punishment for rebellion, Neilson argued, the Union was unjust. "Le rapport de Lord Durham et les fausses représentations des journaux insensés et révolutionnaires ici paraissent avoir persuadé tous les partis dans le Parlement britannique que la majorité des habitants du Bas-Canada sont des rebelles irréconciliables" (August 13). No, the vast majority of French Canadians had proclaimed their loyalty, and only eight of the thirty-nine counties had been disturbed. But even if the majority had rebelled, "la bonne conduite passée des Canadiens-français ne sera-t-elle comptée pour rien?" Scotland in 1715 and

[5]*Le Canadien*, 4 nov. 1839.
[6]Neilson's articles against the Union begin in the English *Gazette* on April 29 but not until May 14 in the French one.

Ireland in 1798, he continued (in a somewhat strange version of the facts), had not been so badly treated as the French were to be now. If, on the other hand, the Union were intended as a solution to the problem of the "two nations warring in the bosom of a single state," it would surely fail. Racial strife had not caused the "troubles," but, he claimed a bit naïvely, the agitations of "des hommes ambitieux, factieux, et mécontents" (November 28). Most of these were banished now, and the great constitution of 1791 could function smoothly.

Whatever the alleged reasons for doing so Neilson considered the very principle of changing the constitution to be wrong. The Union, by abolishing the Act of 1791 "qui garantissait tous ses droits et ses intérêts" (May 25) to the French population, would violate the special social rights repeatedly confirmed by the British, at the surrender in September 1759, by the Proclamation of 1763, and in the Quebec Act of 1774. These rights, enshrined by prescription and preserved at the price of the *Canadiens'* blood in 1775 and 1812, should not be altered lightly. Besides, he continued, the repeal of the fifty-year-old constitution in favour of one in which the French, as a group, had no part ran counter to every known British precedent. At the time of the union of England and Scotland, "l'union fut effectuée du consentement des autorités constitutionnelles des deux royaumes," and when Ireland was joined to Great Britain, "ce fut aussi du consentement de l'autorité constitutionnelle établie en Irlande" (August 13). Moreover, in both these unions, there had been no intention to submerge the interests and cultural heritage of the people. Now, however, by joining the two cultural groups into one legislative system in which each would inevitably contend to "faire et défaire l'un pour l'autre des lois qu'ils ignorent mutuellement" (June 11), this act of union threatened the whole legal system in which the tenure of property was made secure, and thus placed in jeopardy the entire amalgam of natural habits and social arrangements peculiar to the *Canadiens*.

Nor did Neilson have any patience with responsible government, the high principle for which all this was to be sacrificed. It was, he thundered, an impossible, expensive, "un-British" calculating theory borrowed from the Americans and designed only to give jobs to radicals. Clearly he did not understand what Parent meant by responsible government. He remembered only that he had heard Mackenzie, Papineau, Nelson, and the other rebels call for it. But the balanced, ordered constitution of 1791, he understood and loved; this, if allowed to function properly, he knew could work. The other was a theoretical "système de réformes, une utopsie [*sic*] aussi flatteuse que toutes les autres" (July 27), a plan by ambitious reformers "qui ont rendu au peuple canadien le même service que leurs maîtres et leurs prototypes ont rendu à la France, sans parler de la Pologne et des autres pays auxquels ils ont fait faire du *progrès* en arrière" (May 25).

What was Lord Durham thinking? How could he, or the British parliament believe in such folly? Did they think, all of a sudden, they had become

de froids philosophes qui peuvent fabriquer des constitutions de gouvernement avec des espérances illusoires, innover et changer les choses avec aussi peu de souci des conséquences que les sept ou huit fournées de feseurs [sic] de Constitutions qui se sont essayés à ce métier en France depuis cinquante ans, ou que les législateurs éclairés de la douzaine d'Etats de l'Amérique du Sud, qui après vingt années de "gouvernement responsable" n'ont d'autre loi ni constitution que *l'épée.* (November 28)

Did they not realize responsible government was an American illusion? In the United States, where it was actually practised, it provided a fancy term for what was "pourriture et corruption." Every day, Neilson averred, American newspapers "annoncent la disparition de quelqu'agent comptable, emportant avec lui sa responsabilité." What about the Indian agent in Tennessee who fled to Texas with $77,000.00 in government funds? What about the lynch laws—"il n'est pas rare d'y voir un juge assassiné ou jugé d'après le code Lynch"? What about slavery? What about the fathers "qui vendent ou laissent vendre leurs propres enfants?" What about the spoils system which bred "probablement plus de péculateurs que le vaste Empire britannique?" What about the "situation morale" produced by a "responsible government" like that of New York where, last year, there were 55 suicides, 15 murders, 6 manslaughters, 75 accidental deaths, 24 burned alive, 8 delirium tremens, 11 still births, 54 apoplexy cases, and 7 who died "pour avoir bu de l'eau froide." In Lower Canada, if it did not call forth all of this, responsible government would serve mainly to create jobs for scheming politicians "qui prétendent asseoir la société sur de nouvelles bases (c-à-d eux-mêmes)."

Finally, Neilson concluded, even if the Union and the American spoils system which went with it had been theoretically just, this particular plan which subjected the French majority to the Upper Canadian minority, which intended to move the capital from Lower to Upper Canada, and which, as became increasingly obvious as the months went by, forced Lower Canadians to take on the debt of Upper Canada, this Union bill was vicious in practice. Besides it took the British connection out of the safekeeping of "les loyaux sujets britanniques de ces provinces" and, through responsible government, handed it, at the peril of the empire, to "les hommes à livres, à sous, et à deniers."

By agreeing to co-operate with the Union, then, the *Canadiens* would sacrifice the prescribed, accumulated rights and victories of their ancestors to a chimera; they risked the constitution that guaranteed their social arrangements, their language, and their customs, for a theory, a dubious definition.

Both Neilson and Parent cared for the British connection and admired the British constitution. Both were thoroughly devoted to French Canada. But while the one looked forward, the other looked back. Neilson loved the constitution with its ordered splendour and august advantages. He had fought, along with Papineau, to make it function, then broken with his friend because he would tamper with its second chamber; now he fought the Union because it would introduce what he considered a new element. He revered the eighteenth-century constitution inasmuch as it was stable, balanced, static, and because it preserved property and the privileges of the Church, isolated the French Canadians' own separate state, and guaranteed their institutions and manners: the customs he and his household observed in his *manoir* at Cap Rouge. Parent, on the other hand, asked questions. He realized the organic vitality of a constitution that kept renewing itself. He investigated it, he understood what power it could give his countrymen, what it could offer for their development. He saw it as the key to the future. He did not revere it; he saw how it could serve. For years, he had urged that it should be allowed to evolve. Now he had faith in it, and he dared to take the risk: to sacrifice the separate state if need be in order to prepare a greater prosperity, a happier, broader, and ever-widening destiny for his people. As Neilson looked to the constitution to consolidate what had been acquired, Parent looked to it to open up the future.

In Montreal the editors reacted more cautiously to the Durham *Report.* When news of it arrived, *L'Aurore des Canadas* had been suspended since March 16, and its editor, Jean Boucher de Belleville, the author among other achievements of the revolutionary Déclaration de Saint-Ours of May 1837, imprisoned for criticisms of Colborne and the Special Council. When it did reappear in mid-July 1839 it spoke without wit or spirit, following "la règle que nous nous sommes faite de n'entrer dans aucune discussion" (August 13). About the subject which was on everyone's lips, Belleville hesitated to give a firm opinion, leaning now to approval of responsible government, then to horror at the idea of union. Once he claimed neither to approve nor to disapprove until the details were worked out. But he reprinted verbatim the long discussion which *La Gazette de Québec* had serialized, and then, on October 11, he risked a careful approbation, saying that Neilson's ideas "sont ceux de l'honnête homme qui s'indigne à l'idée d'une injustice odieuse." Concurrently, however, Belleville had been running approving accounts of the Durhamite meetings in which the Reformers of Upper Canada were pressing for the adoption of the *Report*, and finally, in the same issue that congratulated Neilson, he praised the Grand Master of the Orange Order, Ogle Gowan, whose letter on responsible government proved "une argumentation puissante, irrésistible en faveur d'un système gouvernemental réformé et qui aurait pour base le principe salutaire de la responsabilité, question qui se popularise de plus en plus dans notre sœur-province. ... Elle a été un sujet de plaisir et de satisfaction pour nous." By November Colborne had gone, and Belleville felt bolder. He agreed that "à peu près tous ceux qui n'ont pas un intérêt direct ou indirect à la continuation de l'Irresponsabilité, sont les avocats ou au moins les amis naturels du système de Responsabilité," and declared himself in agreement with *Le Canadien* (November 5). A month later an article on the Union reflected, generally, Parent's position that "un rapprochement entre les réformistes du Haut et du Bas-Canada" would best secure the final defeat of "les organes du Compact" (December 6).

L'Ami du Peuple, the other French paper in Montreal, was founded in 1832 by the merchant party and sincerely hated by all the *patriotes*. For a time during and after the failure of the rebellions, it was the only French newspaper allowed in the province, and by mid-1839 it claimed that it "voit chaque jour la liste de ses abonnés se grossir de noms" (August 21). As an organ of the Lower Canadian Tory group, it might have been expected to endorse Durham's plan. Yet it feared the possible alliance, which Parent foresaw, of the Reformers in both provinces. Accordingly it opposed the Union and underlined the practical difficulties, observing, for instance, that Durham ought to have spent more time studying the Canadian situation before recommending a union of provinces between which roads and communications were so poor (May 22).

In August 1839 Leblanc de Marconnay, out of work since *Le Populaire* closed down in 1838, took over the editorial chair at *L'Ami*, promising to offer "une politique tournée vers le plus grand bien du plus grand nombre," a policy which he defined on August 21: "Rallier les partis, concilier les divisions, appaiser les répugnances, fronder les vices, honorer la vertu . . . défendre les oppimés [*sic*], flétrir les oppresseurs, Ceci deviendra l'object [*sic*] de nos soins vigilans : ramener aux devoirs envers la religion et le trône sera le but de notre sollici- tude." Leblanc opposed the Union for reasons admittedly modelled on John Neilson's. He feared for the British connection and the separate state, identifying himself, on December 7, with "la masse attachée à la Grande-Bretagne et surtout à l'intérêt du pays, qui voit l'Union avec ses conséquences et qui la repousse"—one *conséquence*, of course, being the alliance of both Reform parties and the resulting (he thought) absorption into the United States. Like Neilson, he also considered responsible government impossible and illogical.

Whatever his theory, Leblanc also bore personal grudges against Parent and the others who accepted the Union and responsible govern- ment. He had fought them personally before the "troubles" (there was a matter of an unpaid salary and several subsequent duels) and still considered Parent "un élève de Papineau." As for the others, they were "des libéraux avec vengeance," ex-*patriotes* who advocated the Union only because they knew it could not work and would thus pro- vide them with "un nouveau motif irritant de révolte" (December 11). "Les patriotes (c'est-à-dire la queue de Papineau)," he averred on December 31, "veulent bien de l'Union à quelque prix qu'elle arrive parce qu'ils prévoient que l'issue en sera indubitablement une désunion un peu plus vive"—a not completely unreasonable opinion.

The reaction of French Canadians to Durham's proposals was not, therefore, entirely unfavourable. Indeed, only *La Gazette de Québec* was resolutely opposed. *L'Ami du Peuple*, with far less influence and edited by a noted *vendu*, had taken some months before agreeing with Neilson. *L'Aurore* had also hesitated but had finally assented to the proposals. And Parent's *Le Canadien*, the proudest and most influen- tial paper, responded with something akin to enthusiasm. Perhaps the *Canadiens* assented merely because it would bring some agreement, some decision, an end to all the strife. Perhaps they were too busy binding their wounds to worry about politics. For this summer and autumn of 1839 had been one of misery, distrust, and discouragement. One *patriote* wrote to Duvernay: "Je crois volontiers que notre automne et notre hiver passeront sans troubles, parce que c'est ma conviction intime que le pays en général désire une telle tranquillité et quelle [*sic*] est dans ses intérêts. . . . Le pays veut et a besoin de tranquillité; c'est le seul moyen de sortir de la position désavantageuse que nous occupons."[7] On November 5 *L'Aurore* declared that almost all of French Canada approved the Union; at about the same time, the new governor, Poulett Thomson, who had arrived on October 19, was writing to the Colonial Secretary that he foresaw no difficulty in winning the assent of Lower Canada: "The large majority ... of those whose opinions I have had the opportunity of learning, both of British and French origin, and of those too whose character and station entitle them to the greatest authority, advocate warmly the establishment of the union."[8]

The project of Union, then, seemed destined for success, and the French Canadians reconciled to risking their culture. (And how differently might all subsequent history have read!) But several factors militated against this success: the vicious attacks of the Lower Canadian Tory press, the violence of the anti-French spokesmen in Toronto, and especially the personality and methods of Poulett Thomson.

The Montreal Tories had never been noted for their love of French-Canadian reformers. Now, with the rebels routed in battle and the British government finally converted to their own pet project of assimilation, they could afford to print their dreams about the future. In May 1839 the *Montreal Herald* began with the calm suggestion that representation in the new Union parliament might be set at 103 to 25 in favour of the English.[9] As the summer went on, one startling suggestion followed another. By autumn, the *Montreal Gazette* had joined in with proposals such as the proscription of the French language and the limitation of the franchise to those who could read and sign their name (a suggestion that would strike the majority of the habitants off the voting lists). In another issue, the *Montreal Gazette* suggested restricting the candidates for parliament to those who could speak fluent English.[10] Clearly the Montreal press had not understood *Le Canadien's* warning (November 20) that the Union would find smooth passage only if it were based on a reasonable and fair constitution: "C'est presque une religion que les usages nationaux d'un peuple, et si l'on ne veut soulever une résistance poussée jusqu'au fanatisme, qu'on se borne à opérer sur la raison du peuple, sur le sentiment de ses intérêts."

The Upper Canadians seemed just as unreasonable. In December

[7]Papiers Duvernay, 352, Sicotte à Duvernay, 16 oct. 1839.
[8]Thomson to Russell, Nov., 1839, quoted in G. P. Scrope, *Memoir of Lord Sydenham* (London, 1844), p. 136.
[9]*Le Canadien*, 10 mai 1839.
[10]*Ibid.*, 20, 25 nov. 1839.

1839 the Governor General, who had come to Toronto especially, introduced his project of Union to the Upper Canadian legislature. The members proceeded to suggest ideas that astonished French Canada. Etienne Parent gave a regular account of the debates in *Le Canadien* throughout January 1840 with fascinated but increasing anxiety. As he saw it, the Upper Canadians seemed intent on warping the project with palpable injustice. For one thing, they wanted the capital transferred to Upper Canada for reasons hardly flattering to the French: "Il pensait," Parent related on January 3 about one of the speakers, "que cette prérogative [of the Crown in choosing the capital] devait s'exercer en faveur du Haut-Canada . . . parce que cela éloignerait les représentants Français, pendant les sessions, de leurs associés et de leurs compagnons nationaux et politiques." For another, they demonstrated an inclination towards charging their debts to the credit of Lower Canada. Again, they obviously entertained too healthy a prejudice about their own superiority over the *Canadiens*. "Nous nous attendions," Parent had commented painfully on November 20,

à trouver chez la population britannique du Haut Canada dans la personne de ses représentants, cet esprit de justice, de tolérance, de fraternité, de bienveillance avec lequel nous étions nous-mêmes disposés à entrer dans l'Union; mais que nous ont dévoilé les Débats, Résolutions, et adresses des Chambres du Haut-Canada? Justement les mêmes antipathies et jalousies nationales, la même arrogance, les mêmes prétentions à la supériorité et à l'ascendance et à la domination, qui ont caractérisé le parti soi-disant britannique dans le Bas-Canada.

Indeed, in a single day's consensus of prejudice, one speaker had opposed the Union out of fear of the influence of "tous les Notaires Publics"; a second had declared that the French would be a drain on Upper Canada's progress, the *Canadiens* having "aucun canal ni chemin de fer d'aucune importance; ils n'ont rien fait en fait d'améliorations, et du moment que nous serons unis, ils détruiront toutes les mesures que nous proposerons pour cette fin"; and another had admitted that the French formed "un peuple bon et doux" but complained nevertheless that a "nombre d'entr'eux ne savent signer leur nom et ils sont égarés par des hommes rusés et trompeurs." Above all, perhaps, most Upper Canadian representatives feared the French domination consequent upon representation by population. "Je ne puis nier," the member for Glengarry declared, as Parent reported on January 8, "et je regrette beaucoup d'être obligé d'admettre le fait, que les Canadiens Français . . . ne peuvent avec sûreté être revêtus du

droit de législation. . . . Le parti Canadien Français, avec ses sentiments actuels, aurait une majorité dans l'Assemblée Unie, . . . [mais]
une Assemblée Unie avec une telle majorité serait bientôt placée dans la
même position que l'Assemblée du Bas-Canada avant la rébellion de
1837." "Le Haut Canada," a colleague joined in, "ne pouvait jamais
prospérer uni avec le Bas-Canada; il serait accablé par une majorité
française." It would be essential at least, they all agreed, to abolish the
use of the French language and to assimilate the *Canadiens*. "La nécessité de parler l'Anglais, les forcera à l'apprendre," a member concluded
with smug, vulgar condescension, "et rien n'est plus propre à dissiper
leurs préjugés."[11]

Parent was nettled. "Il est de notre devoir," he insisted on January
10,

de signaler un fait important résultant des conditions injustes apposées à
l'Union des Canadas, et des sentiments de mépris et de méfiance contre les
Bas-Canadiens, exprimés dans le cours des débats sur la question de l'Union
dans la Chambre d'Assemblée du Haut Canada, par un grand nombre des
membres de cette Chambre; nous voulons parler d'une opposition qui se
forme et se grossit de jour en jour au sein de notre société contre le projet
d'Union."

Ready to accept assimilation as a price for responsible government, he
could not admit injustice and oppression. He concluded on January 31:
"Que doit-il arriver, lorsque les Bas-Canadiens, pour prix des énormes
sacrifices qu'on leur impose, ne doivent attendre que défiance, mépris,
et oppression, et le même esprit d'ascendance nationale qui a été la
cause de tous leurs maux passés? Il ne leur reste évidemment qu'une
marche à suivre, celle de se lever jusqu'au dernier contre le projet
de l'Union." *L'Aurore*—"cette feuille unionnaire de Montréal," as
Neilson called it—concurred. Neilson himself ran two or three I-told-
you-so columns in *La Gazette de Québec*—on January 23: "On sait
maintenant à quelles conditions la coquine qu'on veut donner pour
femme à Jean-Baptiste consent à l'épouser malgré lui." Meanwhile
Thomson had done more than his share in antagonizing the
Canadiens.

In mid-afternoon on October 19, 1839, "toute la garnison était
sur pied" in Quebec as Colborne rode out of the Château Saint-Louis
to welcome his successor, Charles Poulett Thomson. His ship, the
Pique, had docked two days earlier in the ancient harbour, but Poulett
Thomson had decided to remain aboard until Colborne arrived from
Montreal. Then, short, slender, but supremely self-confident, he

11*Ibid.*, 8, 10 jan. 1840.

stepped briskly off the gangplank and took the salute from his predecessor. After this simple ceremony, he drove to the castle to take his oath of office, receive the greetings of the Special Councillors, and issue a proclamation announcing his assumption to power. It was a dark, cool day; and in the port, berthed forebodingly beside the *Pique* the *Buffalo* waited to carry the fifty-eight exiles to Australia.

News of Thomson's appointment had reached Canada a month earlier, and with it, speculation had begun about his antecedents in trade and reform. Though the last might be reassuring, the *Canadiens* wondered about the first. *L'Ami du Peuple* asked whether Thomson was not linked to the Quebec merchants' long-time rivals, the timber interests trading with the Baltic? And even if he did overcome this personal involvement, would his business interests not incline him, in any event, to favour the local oligarchy and its French-baiting policies? "Il se propose de se guider," Parent mused uneasily in *Le Canadien* on October 18, "'sur l'opinion des hommes marquants de la race Britannique dans les deux Canadas.'" He was also the first governor of the Canadas chosen from outside the aristocracy—an unflattering gesture to a people so sensitive to appearances. And he had such a funny name! As sharp as usual, Aubin underlined this aspect on October 1 in *Le Fantasque*: "Notre nouveau Gouverneur-Général, le très-honorable POULET Thomson est maintenant attendu journellement à Québec. Je fais matin et soir des vœux pour que ce POULET-là fasse de meilleur ouvrage que les coqs-d'inde qui l'ont précédé. A en croire ces poules mouillées de journaux tories ce n'est toujours pas un aigle. Le bon Dieu bénisse tous ces oiseaux là."

Even so, the *Canadiens* decided to give the man a chance. John Neilson asked that they join in signing an address of welcome prepared by the Quebec merchants and left on display at the Court House. And, in Montreal, *L'Aurore* declared its intention to be firm but fair on October 18: "Comme nous ne voudrions pas être jugés par Mr. Thompson [*sic*] sans être entendus, il ne faut pas, non plus, le juger sans l'entendre. Espérons qu'il se montrera juste et honnête; mais qu'il le soit ou non, pour le juger donnons-lui le temps de se prononcer. Nous ne le jugerons alors [que] par ses actes et c'est le seul moyen de le juger avec justice."

"Le Soleil Levant"—so Belleville called him—arrived in Montreal on October 23 and won opinions which could have been much worse. When he held his first levee at the Château de Ramezay on October 26, he received more callers than any of his predecessors. He also made a good impression. As *L'Ami du Peuple* noted on October 30:

Son Excellence paraissait souffrante, ce qui donnait à sa figure une teinte d'austérité. Pour notre compte nous ne sommes pas trop fâchés de cette raideur; elle aura pour mérite de tenir quelque temps les partis en respect, de soustraire l'exécutif aux insinuations dont il ne manquera pas d'être l'objet. . . . Ses traits annoncent l'homme qui a l'habitude des affaires et qui n'est pas étranger à l'impassibilité qui doit distinguer les personnages revêtus de hautes fonctions. Il est âgé de 37 à 38 ans, mais la maturité de son esprit perce dans toute sa contenance. . . . L'entourage de Son Excellence avait quelque chose de brillant et le riche costume d'apparat que le Gouverneur portait était fait pour en imposer.[12]

Within weeks, however, the *Canadiens'* fears were confirmed. The Tory merchants quickly persuaded Thomson to postpone his departure for Upper Canada. And as 1839 turned into 1840 Thomson became more and more the prisoner of the Tory interests in the province. The *Canadiens* had received happy assurances that he would base his policy on the principle of "equal justice," but they gradually came to understand how wide a distinction he could draw between word and deed. By August 3, 1840, *Le Canadien* could claim ". . . dans le Bas-Canada, depuis l'administration Dalhousie, il n'y en eut pas d'aussi impopulaire que celle du gouverneur général actuel. . . . Et encore pouvons-nous dire que l'état de la Presse ne représente qu'imparfaitement l'état de mécontentement qui règne parmi le peuple, sans distinction de partie."

The *Canadiens* reacted to these developments in an unusual way. In earlier decades they had answered Governors Dalhousie and Aylmer by withholding supplies; to Gosford, Durham, and Colborne they had presented apathy and rebellion; but with Poulett Thomson "que nous maudissons tous bien sincèrement,"[13] they simply laughed.

"Notre POULET" began to figure prominently in the press; indeed, for the next two years, *Le Fantasque* hardly ever referred to the Governor General otherwise than as POULET. Aubin claimed, for example, on April 13, 1840, that it was no wonder that so many pigeons had been sighted this year over Lower Canada, for "Messieurs les pigeons, tout fier de savoir que les Canadas étaient gouvernés par un volatile, ont cru devoir venir déposer leurs hommages aux pieds ou plutôt aux pattes de notre POULET." Later on May 4,

[12]The details of Thomson's arrival were reported in *L'Ami du Peuple, Le Canadien, La Gazette de Québec, Le Fantasque,* and *L'Aurore* during October and November 1839.
[13]Papiers Duvernay, 449, Fortier à Duvernay, 12 oct., 1840.

playing upon *voler*, to fly, and *voler*, to steal, he reflected it was perfectly normal for the Governor to have advocated the Union: "Le bill d'Union dressé d'après les plans de notre gouverneur-général veut que le Bas-Canada paie les dettes du Haut. Les gens qui ne sont point versés dans les mystifications politiques appellent cela un vol. Moi, je trouve absolument rien là d'étonnant. Ne voit-on pas tous les jours des poulets essayer de voler." And, playing upon *cornichon*, a pickle, and *cornichon*, a greenhorn, he went on in the same issue: "Tous ceux qui on vu Mr. Thompson [*sic*] s'accordent à dire que c'est un POULET tout à fait appétissant. Je le crois bien, il est tout entouré de corni-chons." Aubin kept this up for eighteen months, finding even more enjoyment still in the parsimonious, vain, and unscrupulous aspects of Thomson's personality.

The Governor—"cet avare"—counted his pennies like every mer-chant, Aubin averred, on July 27, and prided himself on his domestic economy. (In fact Thomson did live very simply.) How handy, there-fore that he should only have to walk across Bonsecours Market Square to reach Government House: "Il a même été faire le marché lui-même et il aurait sans doute continué s'il n'avait su qu'on se moquait publiquement de lui." At home, he spent much of his time in the kitchen preparing the menu: "Il va goûter les sauces de ses cuisines; collationne le livre de son maître d'hôtel; fait servir à ses aides-de-camp des viandes froides afin qu'ils en mangent moins. . . . Il querellait, il y a quelque tems, son cuisinier de ce qu'il n'avait su faire que trois crèmes avec une bouteille de marasquin, disant que lui-même aurait pu en faire au moins une douzaine."[14] Aubin concluded on the advantages of being governed by a good housewife. Parsimonious, Thomson was conceited as well. Aubin refers several times to his thirst for a title. Once (July 22) he imagines the Governor writing to Melbourne: "Tâchez de me faire nommer Chevalier. Un joli *Sir* devant mon nom ferait voir que je ne suis pas un triste *sire*." Later, on August 21, *Le Canadien* too smiled at the prospect of a title for the Governor and sug-gested appropriate companions: Colborne could be created baron de Saint-Benoît, and his fellow officer, Colonel Gore, could be comte de Saint-Denis. Aubin also realized how much Thomson enjoyed cheering crowds. In one of his cleverest satires, on July 6, he pictured "le POULET" explaining, at great pains and with accents of Spanish, Italian, Arabic, and very poor French, to the confused Montreal chief of police that it was his duty to gather and pay a noise-making crew for the

[14]*Le Fantasque*, 13 avril 1840.

Governor's every appearance, just as London policemen did to celebrate the outings of the Queen. To the objection about high costs, "le POULET" answered: "*You fanatic ignorant canadian,* vous pas comprendre le spéculation. Les pauvres gens qui vont se prosterner et crier devant le reine et les grandes personnages reçoivent du Police comme j'ai dit à vos, trois ou quatre shellings. Avec cela ils vont se saouler au taverne et le Police les prend le soir et fait payer à eux cinque shellings d'amende pour les corriger de l'ivrognerie. You see! voyevous?" In this passage Aubin is also satirizing Thomson's superb confidence in the art of bribing, a characteristic *Le Canadien* also touched on later (September 6, 1841), putting in Thomson's mouth some light verse:

Membres charmants, venez à moi.
Je suis une caisse sonore
Qui s'ouvre aussitôt qu'on l'adore;
Je suis le million qui luit;
Je suis la commission même. . . .

Je suis un vieux commis de banque,
Je connais la valeur de l'or;
Je serai pour celui qui manque
De principes, un vrai trésor.

Bourgeois, conceited, and crafty, the Governor was apparently also a ladies' man—or so the French Canadians thought. *Le Fantasque* reported on August 3 that a frequent topic of conversation in the streets of Quebec during the summer of 1840 was "le célibat de monsieur Poulet Thomson." And on hearing of a palace revolution in Turkey, Aubin, on July 27, offered the exiled prime minister a new job as "premier eunuque du sérail de monsieur Poulet Thompson [*sic*]." The same type of rumour, circulating in Kingston after the vice-regal transfer there, led to this unequivocal note from *Le Fantasque* on the new capital city (September 23, 1841): "La cage de milord Poulet est située au milieu d'un petit bois . . . là aussi est son sérail, dont l'une des demoiselles *d'honneur,* dit la chronique scandaleuse de Kingston, est passée aux Etats-Unis pour de *grosses* affaires."

In April 1841, the Governor General, who had been created Baron Sydenham in September 1840, almost died of an attack of gout. *Le Canadien* noted ironically on May 14: "On a remarqué que Lord Sydenham était sujet aux attaques de goutte à peu près vers le temps où arrivent des malles d'Angleterre, ce qui semblerait signifier qu'elles lui apportent de mauvaises nouvelles sur la politique de la 'justice égale'." On April 26 Aubin had also taken advantage of this occasion to publish his version of Lord Sydenham's last will and testament. In it he is at his mocking best—and incidentally provides a good summary of French-Canadian feeling towards the Governor. "Le POULET" gives nothing to the poor, for stolen goods can only do them harm, but he bequeaths to his successor a list of the Special Councillors: "au cas d'une nouvelle suspension de la constitution, cette liste d'hommes uniques ne pourrait manquer de leur servir"; to his future biographer he gives "ma bibliothèque consistant en un dictionnaire du commerce; un traité du calcul des intérêts. . . . Je lui recommande de me flatter beaucoup dans sa description de ma vie publique parceque même avec cette précaution on la trouvera encore assez hideuse." To Colonel Gugy (a *vendu* politician and a gallant who served as another object of Aubin's satire) he donates his horses and his ladies of honour. He hesitates however to recommend a successor, for

on trouvera difficilement un homme possédant toutes les qualités requises pour continuer mon œuvre. . . . Je recommande seulement à mes successeurs . . . de se procurer de l'argent, beaucoup d'argent, toujours de l'argent; l'argent fait la force! . . . Je les prie bien d'abolir autant que possible la langue française, . . . d'attaquer tout de bon la religion catholique . . . de ne pas négliger l'emploi constant de la police; . . . ce corps nous procure un excellent canal pour l'écoulement de l'argent surabondant du coffre public.

About the same time, May 21, 1841, *Le Canadien*, less subtle, but no less emphatic, summed up its feelings: "Nous ne voyons pas quels ménagements a droit d'attendre de notre part le chef de l'administration la plus inique et la plus tyrannique qu'ait jamais eue le Bas-Canada. . . . Chacun de ses actes est une injustice ou une spoliation contre un peuple sans défense."

Laugh as they did at his person, the French Canadians nonetheless felt Thomson's measures were intolerable. They were increasingly shocked by his use of arbitrary methods to force them into the Union. He had kept Colborne's Special Council and summoned its members on such short notice that only fifteen dared to brave the November snows to Montreal. To this rump he submitted his project of Union on November 11, 1839, and ordered a vote in an *in camera* session on the thirteenth—before any of those who opposed it could discuss amendments. His terms, besides, were obviously unfair to Lower Canada. A population of 650,000 was to have in the united legislature the same representation as the upper province's 450,000, and the Upper Canadian debt of £1,200,000 (huge compared to Lower Canada's £95,000) was to be charged to both; again, the plan called for a permanent civil list to be accorded the new government, an especially sensitive item to the *Canadiens* who had, for years before the rebellions, drawn their battle line against the Tories on this very issue. And to add insult to injury, Thomson claimed in published despatches to the imperial authorities that the Special Council represented *Canadien* opinion.[15]

The *Canadiens* were thoroughly annoyed. It was one thing to agree to a measure, another to be forced to accept unjust conditions. And Poulett Thomson continued. He allowed the sale of the exiles' confiscated property, thus in the eyes of the French punishing not so much the poor exiles themselves as their poorer and innocent wives and children.[16] He was right, of course, when he wrote, referring to necessary measures like these, that "nothing but a despotism could have got them through. A House of Assembly, whether single or double, would have spent ten years at them."[17] But such a course gave a bad impression of just what was meant by the kind of responsible government the Union might bring. Obviously the government was at one with the *Canadiens'* worst enemies, with those whose ravings filled the Montreal English-speaking press and the debates in Toronto.

So Parent's compatriots, who had originally welcomed the *Report* with a minimum of prejudice, revolted at the insult of the Tories and Upper Canadians. Prepared to accept from Durham the Union and the gradual assimilation he proposed, they would not suffer the insolence of their neighbours, and the high-handed arrogance of that "POULET."[18]

[15]*Ibid.*, 27 avril 1840.
[16]*Le Canadien*, 6 déc. 1839.
[17]Thomson to ?, quoted in Scrope, *Sydenham*, p. 174.
[18]When Sydenham died, the *Canadiens* seemed to forget even the most elementary good manners. At first, they continued to laugh. On September 9, Aubin imagined Sydenham writing to Sir Robert Peel: "A propos pour comble de détresse, mon cheval est tombé, moi dessus, je me suis cassé le cou tout près de la cheville du pied. . . . Les canadiens . . . ont montré la plus vive sympathie . . . . pour mon cheval." Later, as reports from Kingston grew more serious, he stopped his banter to say very plainly on September 13, "Quant à nous, nous ne voulons malheur à personne, mais si son Excellence se cassait le col ou autre chose nous dirions: Que la volonté de Dieu soit faite. Tant pis pour lui, tant mieux pour nous."

After the Governor had died, Etienne Parent put out a single issue of *Le Canadien* with the traditional black lines of mourning, but not a single word about the Governor. On the back page of the next issue (September 29), he published a short summary of the details of the funeral in Kingston. In Montreal, *L'Aurore* came out on September 25, with black lines, but wrote bitterly: "Nos réflexions sur sa vie privée seraient . . . injustifiables aujourd'hui que la tombe le sépare de nous. Mais sa vie publique appartient à l'histoire. . . . Comme Canadiens, comme libéraux et même comme hommes, nous ne pouvons oublier ces crimes. . . . Dieu auquel il s'est recommandé en mourant . . . nous l'espérons, l'a reçu au sein de sa miséricorde infinie."

3

Politicians and Priests, I
1838-1840

THE POLITICIANS

While the *Canadien* press expressed its views, the politicians and the priests were preparing their positions. At first the *Canadiens* had no political leaders. Since the "troubles," many had fled, others were in prison or in hiding, still others, the *vendus*, busily adored what they had formerly burned.

The vast Papineau-Cherrier-Viger-Dessaulles-Lartigue family complex had been (for the moment) torn apart. The great Louis-Joseph, with his second son, Lactance, had reached Paris by various stages, distributing his immediate family at the stops along the way—his wife Julie, Gustave, and the girls in Montreal; his nephew Denis-Emery, the family philosopher, at the Collège de Saint-Hyacinthe; Amédée, his eldest son, at Saratoga to study law. His brother and business agent, Denis-Benjamin, he left in charge of the seigneury at Petite-Nation. His cousin and closest friend, Louis-Michel "le beau" Viger had retired, after nine months of imprisonment, to the more congenial world of business. Another cousin, Côme-Séraphin Cherrier, timid, hesitant, but among the more popular of the young *patriote* orators, had spent four horrible months in prison and three more under frustrating house arrest. After this he resolved never again to enter politics. Cherrier's benefactor, another cousin and one of the most remarkable men of his generation, Denis-Benjamin Viger—a scholar, a wealthy proprietor, a great lawyer, and as a politician second only to Papineau in the affections of the party—was sitting in the Montreal prison, refusing with imperturbable serenity to be set free. He had been arrested on November 4, 1838, along with practically every other *Canadien* politician in Montreal. Most had been released before Christmas, but on December 18 Viger had been told that he would not be freed unless he posted bail for future good conduct. Reasoning that to do this would imply that his previous conduct had been wrong, he had refused. And as the authorities equally refused to let him out unconditionally, he remained in prison until *habeas corpus* was restored in May 1840. He alone had been asked for such bail because he had been one of the main financial backers of most of the *patriote* press and had encouraged the rebellion by his "activité pour encourager à répandre des publications qui ont eu décidément de l'influence pour produire les derniers mouvements insurrectionnels."[1]

Among the other *patriote* leaders, Dr. O'Callaghan had fled the country for good and turned his interest to writing history. Robert Nelson, the provisional republic's president, had run to the gold mines of California in December 1838, covered with debts and ridicule; Wolfred Nelson had been exiled to Bermuda from where, by 1839, he was making his way back to the Canadian border. Jean-Joseph Girouard, released by amnesty, kept aloof. So, after two months in prison did Edouard-Raymond Fabre, the wealthy bookdealer whose back room had served for three years as headquarters for Papineau's plottings.

While most of these trusted leaders kept away or silent, the French members of the oligarchy remained—men such as Colonel Barthélémi-Conrad Gugy who had led a group of volunteers in 1837 and been rewarded with the post of magistrate in Montreal; Frédéric-Auguste Quesnel, a genial, kindly gentleman who had opposed Papineau since 1834 and considered it a point of honour to accept a seat on the Special Council; and the very wealthy Augustin Cuvillier, one of the founders of the Bank of Montreal, and a leader, on the French side, in the political crises of the 1820's who had later turned against the *patriotes* and been defeated in 1834. These *vendus* had lost most, if not all, credit with their people; so had the few chastened *patriotes* who, after helping to light the rebellion's fires, had tried to put them out. Such was that elegant man-of-the-world Charles-Clément de Sabrevois, fourth seigneur de Bleury. He had supported Papineau against the moderates, almost until he heard the sound of cannon; then he had accepted a call to the Legislative Council and sprung to the government's defence to the point of fighting six consecutive duels—the last against Ludger Duvernay. In June 1839, Bleury put the finishing touches to a manuscript against Papineau and reaped the reward for his loyalty with a sinecure in the Department of Public Works.

[1]*Mémoires relatifs à l'emprisonnement de l'Honorable D. B. Viger* (Montréal. 1840), p. 9.

Alexandre-Maurice DeLisle, Cuvillier's son-in-law, a once popular young politician, was also now the beneficiary of an official post with the hated Special Council.

But the French-Canadian political stage was not left completely vacant by the loss of exiles, prisoners, and *vendus*. Two men still worked behind the scenes, Louis-Hippolyte LaFontaine and Augustin-Norbert Morin. In 1839 circumstances and personality had made LaFontaine French Canada's main spokesman. Almost all the others were silenced, and Papineau's senior lieutenant and obvious heir, Denis-Benjamin Viger, refused to leave his prison. Also LaFontaine carried in his files a letter from Wolfred Nelson that gave him at least temporary headship of the shattered party. "Mon absence peut être facilement supportée par le pays," Nelson had written on the very day he was shipped into exile, "il lui reste dans son sein des amis pas plus sincères mais bien plus capables d'avancer son bonheur; à eux je laisse la tâche de veiller à ses intérêts, et personne, mon cher monsieur, plus que vous peut opérer son salut, et lui faire honneur."[2]

Nelson was right. LaFontaine fitted the demands of the new role. A tall portly man, he commanded respect by his presence alone, but he could impose it as well by the strength of his character. Though not the scholar Parent was, he could argue with terse, logical, unanswerable precision, and manœuvre, moreover, with sharp accuracy. He could claim none of Bleury's dash, or any of the idiosyncrasies that gave Morin's personality so much of its charm. He had none of Viger's urbanity, none of Aubin's sense of humour. But he held the highest of ideals and saw politics, not as the game that Duvernay played, but as the most serious of vocations. A man of few (if any) close friends, he loved his country not with the wild passion of Papineau but with a steady devotion.

During 1837–38, LaFontaine had finally and definitely proved his skill by managing to star on both sides. Steadily supporting Papineau until the outbreak of hostilities in November 1837, he had then travelled to Quebec with an old friend, the Montreal merchant and reformer, James Leslie, to plead with Lord Gosford to summon the Assembly.[3] Unsuccessful, he then decided to bring his request directly to the Colonial Office. He left for Europe, explaining, in a nice bit of political doubletalk, that since he could conscientiously neither take part in the rebellion nor resist it, he preferred not to witness it. In

[2]Papiers LaFontaine, W. Nelson à LaFontaine, 2 juil. 1838.
[3]*Ibid.*, LaFontaine et Leslie à Gosford, 5 déc. 1838.

Britain, he urged a constitutional solution and, on his return to America in June 1838, visited Papineau at Saratoga where he was well received. Then, as the second outbreak began, he joined Denis-Benjamin Viger, E.-R. Fabre, and all good *patriotes* in Colborne's prison. By the beginning of 1839, having thus avoided the traps of both the republicans and the *vendus*, he could claim to be both a successor of Papineau and a disciple of the British constitution. Later (as in these events too, perhaps) he could identify his country's cause with his own ambitions and find all his sins and virtues invaluable political assets. His strange mixture of ambition and stubborn idealism coincided well with the constant pressure needed to win responsible government. His cold, tense reserve made him a man of mystery, an unselfish and disinterested leader to his followers.

Where LaFontaine led, Morin followed. Indeed he seemed born to follow, just as LaFontaine was made to lead. Tall but stooped, he walked and talked slowly and softly. He looked pale; all his life he seemed to carry the stamp of his sickly and premature birth. Nor did he enjoy financial independence as LaFontaine did; he was poor and always in need of allowances from his associates. And he carried a heart as tender and pious as that of an old woman; he spent hours in church every day (his friends nicknamed him "le révérend") and he burst into tears at the sight of misery or disease. He could show little initiative, or even energy. But he was loved more than any other public figure of his time and was respected by every political group. He also enjoyed a reputation for learning and for integrity that was second to none. Like the knights of legend, he seemed without fear and beyond reproach—a precious political asset.

Understandably Morin wrote better than he spoke; back in the 1820's he had worked for a short time with Duvernay on *La Minerve*. In 1834 he had helped write the Ninety-Two Resolutions. Later, he refused to bear arms and co-operated with Durham's secretary, Charles Buller, who found him "a sincere and able collaborateur."[4] After the second rebellion he was forced into hiding, but continued his political activity, serving as LaFontaine's Quebec agent.

Now, during the spring of 1839, LaFontaine and Morin worked in silence. Indeed, in April, they had begun to count the minutes in what may well have been *la nation canadienne's* finest hour.

Like Etienne Parent (and perhaps with him) LaFontaine had thought about the Union, about his nationality, and the British connection.

[4]*Ibid.*, C. Buller to LaFontaine, Aug. 11, 1838.

And some time between the first rebellion and mid-1839, he had concluded that the Union was not an evil in itself, that the British constitution generously applied could preserve both his people's heritage and Britain's empire. When he arrived in London in January 1838, he found waiting for him a warm letter from his old associate, James Leslie, advising him to study the constitution uniting Norway and Sweden, for "a Union of the Canadas may probably be proposed and if on fair and equitable principles I see no serious objections to it. Care, however, must be taken that the representation is based upon population and that the heavy public debt of the Upper is not saddled on the Lower Province."[5] LaFontaine accordingly kept an open mind, and, going on to Paris, he wrote back from there to the English reformer, Edward Ellice, two long letters with his deductions that French-Canadian interests were best safeguarded within the framework of true British institutions. "Les Canadiens," he wrote in a paragraph which became the *leitmotif* of his pronouncements for the next decade, "sont devenus par les traités sujets Anglais. Ils doivent être traités comme tels." If the British, he explained, abandoning the "gouvernement batard [*sic*], contre nature" which flourished under the Act of 1791, allowed the constitution to develop as it should— "qu'elle marche franchement vers une politique libérale mais ferme"— he had no doubt that harmony within Canada itself, and between Canada and Britain would soon be restored. What was essential for success was not, he hinted, a particular political state (repeating here what he had several times urged before the rebellion). On the contrary, the imperial authorities must cease to consider the *Canadiens* a separate race, thus excluding them from "la grande famille." If, instead of looking upon them as "des êtres inférieurs . . . qui devraient toujours être traités comme tels," the British treated the French as another political party (in this case a majority party), they could both work in amity and peace within the British parliamentary system. With this "principe dominant de votre gouvernement constitutionnel . . . le principe démocratique, principe essentiel du gouvernement anglais" well established, French-Canadian and British interests could go forward, interacting harmoniously.[6]

LaFontaine was not telling Ellice definitely whether or not he considered the Union a fair price for responsible government, or whether his cultural heritage would be saved by the honest working of the British parliamentary system, but he did make clear his view that

[5]*Ibid.*, Leslie to LaFontaine, Jan. 6, 1838.
[6]*Ibid.*, LaFontaine à Ellice, 17, 29 avril 1838.

the solution to the *Canadien* problem was not racial but political. It was not isolation they needed, but to be treated as other British subjects. Thinking thus, he was broadminded enough to see beyond the accepted views of the leaders who had resisted the Union in 1822. Moreover, he was clever and adroit enough to appeal to the British on their own terms, basing his people's plea not on the abstract doctrine of natural rights or national self-rule, or on the difficult defence of particularist institutions, but on grounds which no British parliament could consistently refuse for long. In this he displayed his sharp sense of political realism. He was also saving his nation's heritage. For however vague his thought may still have been in these first months of 1838, he knew that if he sought first for responsible government, all other things would be added unto him. And here his mind's eye met that of the Upper Canadian Reformer, Francis Hincks.

In April 1839, a year having elapsed since his letters to Ellice, LaFontaine received from Hincks the first of some dozen letters which over the next nine months were to persuade him to accept the Union.[7] Hincks was the handsome and dark young Briton who was currently saturating Upper Canada with Durham meetings, Durham flags, and Durham songs. "Though I have not the honour of personal acquaintance with you," he began on April 12,

I should be much gratified if you would inform me candidly and confidentially how you like the report and what you think of present prospects. . . . Lord Durham ascribes to you national objects; if he is right, Union would be ruin to you, but if he is wrong and you are really desirous of liberal institutions and economical government, the Union would in my opinion give you all you could desire, as an United Parliament would have an immense Reform majority.

LaFontaine had urged that the *Canadiens'* problem was not their desire for "national objects." They wanted to be treated as a political party. Now Hincks agreed: "If we all combine as *Canadians* to promote the good of all classes in Canada there cannot be a doubt that under the new Constitution worked as Lord Durham proposes, the only party that would suffer would be the bureaucrats." LaFontaine answered quickly on April 21 that while disagreeing violently with Durham's proposals to outlaw the French language and fund Upper Canada's

[7]The Papiers LaFontaine contain some ten letters from Hincks to LaFontaine between April 12, 1839, and January 30, 1840. These contain evidence of some eight or ten having gone from LaFontaine to Hincks so that the correspondence probably went something like this: Hincks to LaFontaine, April 12, 30, May 26, Sept. 9, Oct. 9, Dec. 4, 11, 20, 1839, and Jan. 9, 30, 1850; LaFontaine to Hincks, April 21, Sept. 1, 26, Oct. 2, Nov. 1, 19, 29, Dec. 15, 1839.

debt on the united province, he did "like the principles of government laid down in the report."

Hincks might well rejoice. Thoroughly dedicated to responsible government, he knew the Colonial Secretary denied it. Furthermore, he realized from the state of politics in Upper Canada that the Reformers there were unequal to forcing imperial policy. He needed the French group and LaFontaine agreed to co-operate. As the months went on, however, Hincks found his correspondent increasingly suspicious. LaFontaine was not a man to give his confidence easily. And the autumn of 1839 brought more difficulties. Union was one thing, disgrace another. Although Hincks underlined on April 30 that no matter what the terms "a really responsible executive council would accomplish all that we want," Thomson's arbitrary methods, which gradually turned Parent and his friends against the Union, also raised suspicions in LaFontaine's mind. By September 9 Hincks had to again remind him that "Union would, I am convinced be beneficial to the French Canadians. It would remove the *pretext* of national hatred and secure the common objects of all." LaFontaine could see the point— responsible government was the guarantee that *la survivance* would be put in the hands of the *Canadiens* themselves. Yet—and his fears would be confirmed by the debates in Toronto—the Upper Canadians, supposedly so co-operative, seemed so insensitive to *Canadien* susceptibilities. Even Hincks answered (April 30) LaFontaine's grievances about French being outlawed in House debates by saying that all the French-Canadian leaders knew English and that the other members did not have the habit of speaking anyway: "as in Upper Canada they do nothing but vote."

On October 9 Hincks was forced to agree with his friend's "just indignation," and on November 14 he returned to his argument: "Be assured the Union is the only chance for us Reformers." In three letters in December he explained and encouraged, repeated and reassured. Finally, LaFontaine surrendered. He had, however, been master of the situation all along. For, whatever the pressure from Hincks, LaFontaine clearly had the choice of accepting or refusing the Union. Of course it was forced upon the French Canadians by the Colonial Office and, in this sense, neither LaFontaine nor anyone else could do anything about it. But the *Canadien* leader did not have to co-operate, to plan a party strategy that implied a willingness to make the Union work. He did agree to this. And despite the fearful bitterness and acrimony shown to his people, despite the injustice of the bill, despite Thomson, he remained faithful to his decision.

He had not made the decision lightly. Twelve years later, in a speech at a banquet in Montreal—reported in the Montreal *Gazette* of October 6, 1851—LaFontaine recalled this autumn of 1839:

After having carefully examined the rod by which it was intended to destroy my countrymen, I beseeched some of the most influential among them to permit me to use it, to save those whom it was unjustly designed to punish. ... I saw that this measure enclosed in itself the means by which the people could obtain that control upon the Government to which they have a just claim.

He consulted with influential friends and sent letters back and forth to Quebec and Three Rivers. Leslie had agreed all along. Morin and Parent, Morin's close friend, shared with him "idées communes" on the subject.[8] So did Côme-Séraphin Cherrier. And so did an old enemy, Charles Mondelet, a wealthy young lawyer who had acted as counsel for some of the *patriotes* and been arrested for his pains at the same time as LaFontaine in November 1838. During this imprisonment, LaFontaine and Mondelet, once bitter political and personal enemies, became fast friends. Dominique Mondelet, Charles' elder brother, sat on the Special Council and voted for the Union. Charles agreed with him, and in December 1839 joined LaFontaine on a trip to Quebec to confer with Parent and persuade partisans there. "LaFontaine et Chs Mondelet sont à Québec," Louis Perrault wrote to Duvernay, "ce sont des furieux en faveur de l'Union."[9]

All these negotiations were conducted in deep secrecy. "I am glad," Hincks wrote on November 14, "to see you are cautious in advocating it. I almost fear *Le Canadien* has said too much in its favour." Did they fear the Governor General might frustrate their grand design, or that the Tories in the two provinces might contrive a counterplan? They understood, perhaps, that public opinion in Lower Canada, unanimous in its disgust at the debates over the bill in Toronto, would reject outright any alliance with these same debaters. "M. Cherrier et moi," LaFontaine recalled later, "nous trouvant seuls, nous ne pûmes nous dissimuler qu'il était impossible de mouvoir et la ville et les campagnes, tant était grand le découragement où les avaient jetés les événements malheureux dont ils avaient tant souffert."[10] Did they hope that the Union might still be averted? At all events they kept their counsel: as did another powerful group that was also working behind the scenes during these months.

[8]Papiers LaFontaine, Morin à LaFontaine, 22 mars 1840.
[9]Papiers Duvernay, 385, Perrault à Duvernay, 23 déc. 1839.
[10]Speech in the House, 23 jan. 1849, quoted in Thomas Chapais, *Cours d'histoire du Canada* (Québec, 1923), VI, 306.

THE PRIESTS

Since the beginning of the "troubles," the bishops and clergy had been organizing resistance to the Union. In the diocese of Montreal where the rebellion raged and where Bishop Lartigue's *mandement* had caused such a stir, the bright young abbé, Jean-Charles Prince, superior of the Collège de Saint-Hyacinthe wrote to Bishop Lartigue at the beginning of the rebellion suggesting that

on ne saurait nier que le retard apporté par le Gouvernement à opérer certaines réformes promises, sert de prétexte à un certain nombre pour justifier les excès auxquels ils se portent; . . . [Les prêtres] supplient Votre Grandeur de trouver bon qu'une requête basée sur ces considérations soit adressée par le clergé aux trois branches du Gouvernement Impérial. . . . Cette requête ne serait qu'un acte de justice à l'égard du Peuple.[11]

Bishop Lartigue thought the idea a good one: by a petition to the imperial parliament, the clergy, while adhering strictly to the *mandement* against armed revolt, would show those who sympathized with reform that they sympathized with them. Prince drew up the document, and some priests had already signed it when Lord Gosford let the officials at the Bishop's Palace know that he thought it inopportune.[12] It was accordingly discarded.

A few weeks later, the "troubles" being (temporarily) over, rumours began circulating that as a punishment for rebellion Lower Canada would be united to the upper province. The Bishop therefore decided to turn Abbé Prince's petition into an address of loyalty and a plea against the Union. New signatures were collected, and by the end of January 1838 he was able to send it to Gosford with a reminder that the clergy's loyalty "est fondé non sur la politique mais sur la religion qui nous fait un dogme immuable de la fidélité aux Puissances établies par l'ordre de Dieu sur la société," and a prayer that the departing Governor do his utmost to prevent "l'Union des deux Provinces parce qu'elle amènerait en peu de temps pour l'Angleterre la séparation de ses colonies en Amérique."[13]

In Quebec, Archbishop Signay who had had doubts about the first petition for reform,[14] agreed wholeheartedly to oppose the Union. In January 1838 he ordered an address to be prepared by the efficient

11*Procès verbal d'une réunion du clergé au Collège Saint-Hyacinthe 4 nov. 1837*, quoted in Choquette, *Histoire du Séminaire de Saint-Hyacinthe*, I, 203.
12AAM, Bourget à Hudon, 2 déc. 1837.
13*Ibid.*, Lartigue à Gosford, fin janvier 1838.
14AAQ, Signay à Lartigue, 14 nov. 1837.

and ubiquitous Abbé Charles-Félix Cazeau, who had also been his predecessor's secretary and who was for the next generation the main power behind the episcopal throne of Quebec. By mid-February every priest in the Quebec and Three Rivers districts had signed. At the end of the month, the Archbishop sent the address to Gosford, who, on July 10, 1838, reported that he had presented both petitions against the Union to the Queen and that "Her Majesty was pleased to receive the same most graciously." He explained also that on June 21 he had presented the petitions to the House of Lords and given copies "to Mr. Labouchere who duly presented them to the House of Commons."[15]

The priests believed they had good reasons to fear a plan for Union. Like John Neilson they saw it as a threat to the British connection. It would "fortifier les rebelles en les réunissant,"[16] and many of those whom they knew to be outstanding *patriotes*—and anti-clericals— seemed to be urging the Union for the very reason that it would provide an excuse for further rebellion. Bishop Lartigue noted that "plusieurs des Patriotes qui ne veulent que le malheur de leur patrie refusent de signer contre l'Union pour le seul plaisir de faire du mal et d'envenimer les différends";[17] Archbishop Signay agreed in a letter to Lord Gosford that the radicals wanted Union "dans l'unique espoir de voir augmenter la désaffection dans le Bas-Canada, ainsi que les sympathies américaines, et de parvenir par cette voie à l'indépendance."[18] In conscience the clergy could barely tolerate such republican aims, in which they felt there would be no safety for the rights of the Church. The Union might well compromise their position anyway. "Il pourrait bien arriver (et la supposition est loin d'être chimérique)," reflected Signay, "que les prétentions déjà manifestées à diverses époques par la majorité des deux chambres d'Assemblée, fussent élevées, par la majorité de l'Assemblée des provinces réunies. Quelle digue les autorités britanniques pourraient-elles opposer à ce nouveau torrent d'autant plus formidable que le parti radical aurait très probablement en tête des hommes d'origine britannique?"[19]

The priests may or may not have known of the doings of Hincks, Leslie, LaFontaine, Morin, and the others who were preparing to fulfil the Archbishop's prediction. But if they did, they could not help noting that Hincks advocated the "voluntary principle" and the abolition of the clergy reserves in Upper Canada as much as he did

[15]*Ibid.*, A III-41, Gosford to Signay, July 10, 1838.
[16]*Ibid.*, VG X, 148, Cooke à Signay, 30 jan. 1838.
[17]*Ibid.*, DM VII, 60, Lartigue à Signay, 5 mars 1838.
[18]*Ibid.*, GV 138, Signay à Gosford, 22 fév. 1838.
[19]*Ibid.*

responsible government. They remembered too that LaFontaine was the man who had written one of those unanswerable arguments in which he specialized against the power of bishops over the curés: a "trop célèbre pamphlet" which Archbishop Signay compared to the writings of the *philosophes* against the clergy prior to 1789, and which Bishop Lartigue felt compelled to answer anonymously.[20] At all events, the priests could have had little doubt from the hatred entertained towards the Bishop of Montreal by the rebels, from the new and sinister warnings in Nelson's declaration of independence regarding the separation of church and state, and from the whole tenor of the radicals' "liberal" platform which the Pope had condemned, that if control of the state passed to an assembly of such men, the Church, for whose well-being they felt responsible before God, would fall upon evil days.

The bishops were worried, too, about the British connection. Bishop Lartigue declared: "je crains qu'on ne travaille en ce moment à séparer le Canada de la Grande-Bretagne en favorisant l'Union législative des provinces."[21] They did not fear the loss of the imperial link because (as Parent would have argued) it guaranteed French Canada's cultural survival, but rather because it was the legal "état social" against which revolt was sinful. It also embodied, as Neilson could have argued, the security of the "privilèges déjà accordés aux colonies par la Grande-Bretagne."[22] Prominent among these were the legal existence, incorporations, and rights of the Church to tithing and property, as well as the huge tangle of prescription and custom which history had woven between churchmen and government officials in New France and which the British connection had confirmed. In a letter to Gosford on February 22, 1838, Archbishop Signay emphasized that the end of the British connection would destroy the clergy as well as its means of subsistence and influence.[23]

The bishops were not playing politics; they were following what they understood to be the dogma of the Church, and their own official tradition of self-interested obeisance to the Crown. As successors of those great bishops, Briand and Plessis, they naturally attributed the Church's freedom from harassment by an heretical King of England

[20]L. H. LaFontaine, *Notes sur l'inamovibilité des curés dans le Bas-Canada* (Montréal, 1837); [J. J. Lartigue], *Remarques sur les notes de M. LaFontaine, avocat, relativement à l'inamovibilité des curés dans le Bas-Canada* (Montréal, 1837); S. Pagnuelo, *Etudes historiques et légales sur la liberté religieuse au Canada* (Montréal, 1872), p. 202. AAQ, Régistre des lettres, 18, 57, Signay à Lartigue, 4 avril 1847.

[21]AAM, Lartigue à Mgr Provencher, 21 avril 1839.

[22]*Ibid.*, Lartigue à Gosford, 12 déc. 1839.

[23]AAQ, GV 138, Signay à Gosford, 22 fév. 1838.

to their loyalty to the Crown. They were also, probably, disturbed by vague premonitions that the old ways to which they had grown accustomed were passing into history. The Union would mark the end of the courteous and courtly style of fusing the good of the throne with the good of the altar which they and the British government had so carefully devised by discreet promises and gentlemanly agreements. By moving "authority" from government to assembly, Durham's proposals would gradually but inevitably usher in the rule of public opinion, and to the bishops this could mean only complications and difficulties. They were not really aware of this; they saw it only as through a glass darkly. But in spite of themselves they were faced with a dramatic historical turn, and they feared it.

The first threat came over a matter that touched them closely: education. Shortly after the arrival of the Durham mission, the Governor General had appointed Arthur Buller, his first secretary's brilliant younger brother, to head a commission of inquiry into education and to draft a new plan. The province stood in great need of one. Since May 1836 when the Legislative Council had vetoed the Assembly's education bill, Lower Canada had had no legal school organization. Buller accordingly set to work and by November 1838 had completed the main outline of the scheme that formed Appendix D of Durham's *Report*. In it he subscribed wholeheartedly to Durham's main recommendation that "the principle of Anglification is to be unequivocally recognised and inflexibly carried out." Hence he proposed to sweep away both the *école de syndic* law of 1829, and the *écoles de fabrique* which the school law of 1824 had placed under the control of the curés. In their place, he advanced a system based on the educational laws of the United States and Prussia, a plan in which the only elementary schools would be those common to both English- and French-speaking children, and consequently interdenominational and secular.[24] Even before they were published, his proposals raised a storm.

Characteristically Bishop Lartigue led the opposition. Always an intransigent opponent of a government-controlled school system, he lost no time in expressing his opinion as soon as he heard of Buller's assignment. If the Governor intended "imposer au pays une éducation générale ou déiste," he wrote to Archbishop Signay, the bishops must not hesitate "de nous brouiller avec lui."[25] Indeed, he continued, unless the new commission intended to advise "deux bureaux *indépendants*

[24]L. P. Audet, *Le Système scolaire de la province de Québec*, VI, *La Situation Scolaire à la veille de l'Union, 1836–1840* (Québec, 1956).
[25]AAM, Lartigue à Signay, 23 juil. 1839; à Turgeon, 6 août 1839.

d'éducation catholique et d'éducation protestante, de donner dans le premier la plus grande influence au clergé," he would refuse to co-operate with Buller. He did visit Buller but did not, of course, succeed in moving him. The Archbishop of Quebec, more diplomatic and less aggressive, waited to see what Buller proposed before condemning him. He did nonetheless join in a petition to the Governor General in which he, his coadjutor, Bishop Pierre-Flavien Turgeon, and Bishop Lartigue underlined "que le Gouvernement doit se contenter de favoriser par des moyens pécuniaires et en nombre suffisant, des écoles catholiques entièrement distinctes et séparées de celles des autres dénominations religieuses, sans préjudice des secours que la loi pourrait procurer à celles-ci; et quant aux susdites écoles catholiques, les maîtres, les livres et les modes d'instruction, soient sous le contrôle de leur église."[26]

When Buller finished his scheme, he sent a draft to the Séminaire de Québec for comment. Archbishop Signay obliged in two, long, practical letters which argued that no system could work in Lower Canada unless it included Catholic schools controlled by the clergy.[27] In Montreal, meanwhile, Bishop Lartigue was shown a copy of Buller's plan by his old friend (and cousin), Jacques Viger, who had apparently been assisting Buller. Lartigue concluded that the plan "n'a ni queue ni tête et semble fait pour donner beaucoup d'argent à quelques employés."[28] The bishops, in a word, objected to any system which did not include Catholic schools set up in accordance with the prescriptions of canon and ancient French law. The bishops stood ready, therefore, when the *Report* arrived in March 1839. Lartigue called it "très dangereux pour les Catholiques"[29] and Archbishop Signay underlined "notre opposition à un semblable plan."[30] They immediately grasped (nor did it take great perception to do so) the intimate link between Buller's challenge to their control of education and Durham's over-all policy "pour nous *anglifier*, c'est-à-dire nous décatholiser par une union législative et un système d'écoles neutres."[31] They had opposed the idea of Union, indeed petitioned against it, because they cared for the British connection, because they suspected the plots of the radicals, because they feared for the special social

[26]AAQ, Requête des Evèques de Québec, de Montréal, et de Sidyme à Son Excellence le Comte de Durham, 29 oct. 1838.
[27]AAQ, Signay à A. Buller, 30 oct., 5 nov. 1839.
[28]AAM, Lartigue à Signay, 21 nov. 1839.
[29]AAM, Lartigue à Mgr l'Archevèque de Dublin, 26 avril 1839.
[30]AAQ, Signay à Provencher, 13 avril 1839.
[31]AAM, Lartigue à Griffith, 27 avril 1839.

privileges of the Church. These were weighty reasons but secular ones. Now the bishops found that the Union meant *décatholiser* and *écoles neutres*: this they must fight.

THE POLITICIANS REORGANIZE

Late in 1839 as the whole press joined in public denunciation of the Union, and the clergy resolved privately that it was a threat to the faith, *la nation canadienne*, unaware that LaFontaine had chosen his position, began to question the politicians still in the country.

Forced to declare themselves, the politicians split into three groups. One, including the older men like Quesnel and younger men who had grown disillusioned like Cherrier or Girouard, retreated to the sidelines to watch. A second group comprised those radically opposed to the Union—some desperate to prevent it and searching for any means to kill it; others, less violent, but no less determined. The third group included those who were furious over the conditions of the bill, but ready to accept the Union in principle, either because they realized the possibilities it opened to their people, or because, as rebels, they rejoiced at another reason for further agitation. Thus, in this last group, some would oppose the Union, others the Union bill.

In the anti-Union group were the young extremists, mostly *expatriotes* and junior members of the Papineau family who had not yet awakened from their dreams. One, Jacques-Alexis Plinguet, still hoped for salvation from the south: "Espérons qu'enfin la cause patriotique prévaudra en Canada, comme aux états en 1773 et nous bénirons à jamais les noms de ceux que nous auront ouvert la marche, que tous les Canadiens soient unis et les Anglais ne seront pas longtemps à nous tyranniser comme ils le font maintenant."[32] Thomas Fortier, less confident of the success of war, made no secret of his republican sympathies: "Nous agrandirons notre pavillon pour y mettre des étoiles qui ne nous auront pas coûté bien cher."[33] A third, John Ryan, returning from exile, found the Union ridiculous and prayed that "Nelson et Papineau continueront à combattre pour l'indépendance du Canada."[34] The young extremists stood as one, however, in what they did not want. The Union, to them, symbolized the worst defeat, a circumstance which only the dishonest or disloyal could accept

[32]Papiers Duvernay, 413, Plinguet à Duvernay, 11 juin 1840.
[33]*Ibid.*, 479, Fortier à Duvernay, 1 mars 1841.
[34]*Ibid.*, 407, John Ryan à Duvernay, 20 fév. 1840.

peaceably. To acquiesce, as Papineau suggested from Paris, was treachery to *la nation canadienne*, but to refuse to co-operate with the Union and patiently await "le jour indéterminé de l'émancipation" was true patriotism.[35]

The less extreme politicians who actually led the anti-Union party— Neilson in Quebec, Leblanc de Marconnay and, after his release in May 1840, Denis-Benjamin Viger in Montreal—insisted, not on vague notions of annexation or independence, but on the return of the constitution of 1791. But their patriotism was just as absolute. They shared with their younger followers a horror of the very principle of union. It spelled corruption; it had been forced on the *Canadiens* without their consent, and even Upper Canada's approval had been obtained by false promises; it declared injustice. Nor could they understand how it could be made palatable by the mere formula of responsible government. To them, responsible government was a sham. Logically it was impossible, as Amédée Papineau heard from his cousin, Denis-Emery:

Il y a une distinction qui réellement annule le gouvernement responsable parce qu'il est dit qu'il y a deux personnes distinctes dans le gouverneur le représentant de sa majesté qui à ce titre est inviolable et irresponsable au peuple mais seulement au roi, et le gouverneur proprement dit qui, lui a encore deux fonctions à remplir. Défendre les intérêts de la métropole et ceux de la colonie. Quand ils se trouveront en contact l'un à l'autre évidemment il prendra soin des premiers aux dépens des seconds.[36]

And practically, as Amédée would answer,[37] echoing his father, it was a refined method of multiplying *vendus*, men who could help themselves to government salaries and claim simultaneously to be serving the people.

On the other side stood LaFontaine and his friends whose relations with the Reformers of Upper Canada remained a secret but who made no attempt to hide their opinion that responsible government could achieve reform as well as save their nation's heritage. They had a following. From Saint-Hyacinthe, Dr. Bouthillier, partly echoing Hincks, wrote:

Je ne vois pas ce que nous aurions tant à gagner séparés du Haut-Canada. Réunis les radicaux ou réformistes du Haut et du Bas-Canada formeront un corps plus nombreux et contre lequel on ne pourra plus mettre en œuvre les

---

[35]*Ibid.*, 443–4, A. Papineau à Duvernay, 3 oct. 1840.
[36]Collection Papineau-Bourassa, D.-E. Papineau à A. Papineau, 7 juil. 1841.
[37]Papiers Duvernay, 512, A. Papineau à Duvernay, 9 juil. 1841.

préjugés d'origine, et, si l'Angleterre voulait sincèrement nous accorder le redressement des griefs, je ne vois pas pourquoi les choses n'iraient pas bien. Mais si on ne veut pas nous accorder de réformes, unis ou séparés nous ne serons ni mieux ni pis.[38]

A number of those who followed, however, did so for reasons of their own. They were the ones L'Ami du Peuple called "des libéraux avec vengeance" on January 11, 1840, and about whom Bishop Bourget wrote to Archbishop Signay: "Il est à croire que nos laïcs ne voudront point se remuer pour éviter le malheur de l'Union. Plusieurs de nos Patriotes sont sous cette impression que l'Union des deux Provinces opérera plus vite leur désunion de la mère patrie."[39]

However that may have been—and L'Ami and the Bishop may have misinterpreted others' motives—LaFontaine led a party that would fight, not against the Union, but for specific reforms of the Union bill. It was not enough, however, to convince a few friends of this policy. LaFontaine, Morin, Parent, and the others had to take action, and master the art of strategy. Thus LaFontaine set to work to convince first those opposite him on the political stage and then the mass of his compatriots.

[38]Ibid., 408, Bouthillier à Duvernay, 28 fév. 1840.
[39]AAQ, DM VII, 188, Bourget à Signay, 31 jan. 1840.

4

Politics 1840-1841

On December 22, 1839, the Upper Canadian Project of Union left Toronto for Montreal where James Stewart, chief justice of the Court of Queen's Bench for Lower Canada, fused it with the Special Council's resolutions into a draft which was sent to Westminster early in 1840. The *Canadiens* saw that now was the last opportunity to check its passing.

In Quebec it was naturally Neilson who took the lead. A select meeting was held on January 17 at the home of his most trusted political lieutenant, the notary Edouard Glackmeyer, a meeting which included such important persons as René-Edouard Caron, the wealthy, honoured, and honourable lawyer who had served and would serve again as mayor of Quebec, and Thomas Cushing Aylwin, a brilliant young bicultural orator. Here Neilson laid plans to rally the province. He proposed a series of resolutions that soon became a stirring call against the Union.[1] A week later, to an excited crowd at the Ecole des Glacis, he read the petition "contre l'Union et pour le maintien de la Constitution de 1791,"[2] and, after more speeches by Caron and Aylwin, won approval for a committee of forty notables charged with finding signatures. The committee worked well under the leadership of Glackmeyer with help from Etienne Parent and François-Xavier Garneau. Soon the trickle of signatures became a flood. By mid-April they amounted to 39,928, and, Neilson having refused, Vital Têtu, a prominent French-Canadian merchant, agreed to carry them to Westminster.[3]

Neilson had worked quickly and well. He had convinced most *Canadiens* in the district of Quebec that "il ne leur reste évidemment

[1] PAC, MG 24, B 1, Neilson Collection, X. For minutes of the meeting at Glackmeyer's see *Le Canadien*, 27 jan. 1840.
[2] *La Gazette de Québec*, 30 jan. 1840; see also 25 jan. 1840.
[3] *Le Canadien*, 3 fév., 2 mai 1840; *La Gazette de Québec*, 28 avril 1840.

qu'une marche à suivre, celle de se lever jusqu'au dernier contre le project de l'Union" (*Le Canadien*, January 31). He also had won the wholehearted support and co-operation of the clergy. Indeed he and his committee remained throughout the anti-Union campaign in close touch with the Séminaire where they had many contacts: Caron and Abbé Cazeau had long been close friends; Ronald MacDonald, once a minor cleric at the Séminaire, edited the religious columns of *La Gazette* under the general supervision of Abbé Charles-François Baillargeon, the curé of the cathedral; and Neilson himself was an old companion of the Archbishop. The day after the petition was launched, Archbishop Signay sent a circular letter to his clergy, urging them to "user prudemment de votre influence auprès de vos paroissiens, pour les engager à signer l'adresse."[4] Many curés seemed anxious to do just this. Several used the letter, meant only for private circulation, as material for their Sunday sermons; many more sent back encouraging reports.[5] After the signatures had come in, Bishop Turgeon wrote to the curés and religious communities in the name of Neilson's committee to ask for donations towards the expenses of Têtu's trip to London. He himself contributed £10, Archbishop Signay £25, and several curés sent £10 each.[6] Têtu left Quebec at the end of April. He may not have really expected that the petition would weigh much with the imperial cabinet, but there could be no doubt of how strongly the *Canadiens* opposed the Union, and of how much "Neilson est à la tête."[7]

In Montreal LaFontaine had to act with skill. He was not popular. "Il passe dans le public pour se donner des airs aristocratiques," wrote one of the radicals to Duvernay.[8] Personally he drew a mixed reception. To people like Perrault and the young extremists who noted his new-found friendship with Mondelet and the Upper Canadians—"ils voudraient voir leurs plans se réaliser afin d'être des grands hommes"[9] —he seemed mainly an ambitious *vendu*. Was he not coveting the chair which rightly belonged to the imprisoned Viger? ("Vous voyez que maître LaFontaine sait bien jouer ses cartes pour paraître chef du

---

[4]Circulaire au clergé, 25 jan. 1840, in H. Têtu, ed., *Mandements des Evêques de Québec* (Québec, 1888), III, 400. See also L. Pouliot, "Les Evêques du Bas-Canada et le projet d'Union," *Revue d'Histoire de l'Amérique française*, VIII (1954–5), 157–71.
[5]See, for example, AAQ, VG XI, 2, T. Cooke à Turgeon, 31 jan. 1840.
[6]AAM, Bourget à Turgeon, 21 mars 1840.
[7]Papiers Duvernay, 404, Fortier à Duvernay, 2 fév. 1840.
[8]*Ibid.*, 525, Dumesnil à Duvernay, 31 août 1841.
[9]*Ibid.*, 385, Perrault à Duvernay, 23 déc. 1839.

parti."[10]) To the clergy and those who followed Neilson, on the other hand, he looked like a *patriote*, as *L'Ami du Peuple* explained on July 15, 1840, "ex-rival sans énergie de Papineau," whose "conduite louvoyeuse" was just another technique to destroy the constitution of 1791 "et faire élire L.H.L. qui, j'ai peur, le sera."[11] When some Upper Canadian newspapers referred to a possible alliance with him, Leblanc de Marconnay objected in *L'Ami du Peuple* on July 15: "Nous pouvons affirmer à nos confrères du Haut-Canada que lorsqu'il faudra un chef aux Canadiens, on en choisira un qui aura montré plus de caractère que ce partisan méticuleux."

However true this was, LaFontaine could not afford to be outdone by Neilson. Having called a meeting on February 21 he kept his crowd wide awake with a vigorous attack on the suspension of the constitution, the Special Council, the forcing of the Union on Lower Canada, and finally on "tout ce qu'il y a d'humiliant, d'injuste et de tyrannique" in the Upper Canadian bill.[12] He left no doubt about his feelings towards the bill itself, but cleverly avoided an attack on the principle of union. Then Cherrier, persuaded to come out of retirement for the occasion, launched Montreal's *requête*. Unlike Neilson's, however, it won no support; indeed, it never left Montreal.

LaFontaine had planned shrewdly. He had sided with Neilson; yet he had not challenged the Union. Picking his speakers with care, he had managed to have beside him at the meeting only those who believed in responsible government: Mondelet, Cherrier, Joseph Bourret, another influential laywer prominent in the Saint-Jean-Baptiste Society before the rebellion, George-Etienne Cartier, already known as LaFontaine's *aide-de-camp*, and Morin, the only notable in Quebec who had not signed Neilson's petition. "Cette opération," Leblanc de Marconnay complained to Neilson, "est une affaire de clique, dans laquelle MM. Lafontaine [*sic*], Morin, Chs Mondelet et quelques autres exaltés cherchent à reprendre les fils des opérations de Mr Papineau."[13]

In the petition itself, LaFontaine made no clarion call. Once it was started, he contributed nothing to its success. Indeed he had made sure that most opponents of the Union would not sign it: he had refused to approve Neilson's petition because, he said, it censured the last parliament of Lower Canada. In his own *requête*, he blamed the

---

[10]*Ibid.*, 437, Perrault à Duvernay, 22 sept. 1840.
[11]*Ibid.*, 448, Gauvin à Duvernay, 9 oct. 1840.
[12]*Le Canadien*, 28 fév. 1840.
[13]Neilson Collection, X, 17–19, Marconnay à Neilson, 10 fév. 1840.

Colonial Office, and he knew that Leblanc and his friends could not assent to this. Since both *L'Ami* and *L'Aurore* sided with Neilson, LaFontaine's petition received little publicity. Nor did LaFontaine stimulate enthusiasm of his own. For one thing the people were apathetic, perhaps fearing reprisals. (Martial law still reigned.) Also there was no organization like the Quebec committee to descend on every parish, quill at the ready. And the clergy who had helped Neilson disapproved of LaFontaine and disagreed with his text. Bishop Lartigue even sent a *circulaire* to his priests telling them not to sign, or even to encourage others to sign the petition because of the "inconvenance qu'il y a d'attribuer nos malheurs aux mauvaises administrations coloniales et à celle des ministres de la reine."[14] Instead he arranged for a separate petition to be sent by the clergy on their own. As a result, LaFontaine's petition looked rather thin. Leblanc, disappointed, blamed LaFontaine outright in *L'Ami* on March 28:

La première pensée de pétitionner contre l'Union prit naissance à Québec, et nous aimerions à reconnaître que c'est là qu'on a travaillé plus généralement, plus courageusement, plus effectivement, et plus convenablement à cette grande opération patriotique; toutes les opinions ont fait sagement sacrifice de leurs vues personnelles . . . pour suivre le standard d'un général expérimenté, et qui n'a jamais déserté les champs où il s'agissait de combattre une pensée aussi préjudiciable à l'intérêt du pays comme à la domination britannique: celle d'une union des deux provinces. . . . Des démarches ont été faites à Montréal, mais elles ont été frappées de nullité dès l'origine soit par le peu de confiance que présentaient quelques uns des chefs de la mesure, soit par la présence même d'hommes qui contribuèrent à égarer le peuple et qui cherchent en vain à faire croire qu'ils ont encore du crédit auprès de ceux qu'ils trompèrent.

Leblanc's frustration proved how well LaFontaine had succeeded. He had prevented Neilson from invading the district of Montreal with real anti-Union propaganda, while, at the same time, stealing his fire. Yet he had seemed to do all he could to block the Union. The party was united; as Denis-Emery Papineau wrote to his cousin Amédée: "tous nos hommes politiques à Montréal, L.V., H.L., C.C., D.B.V., J.G., &c y sont opposés."[15] Everyone had joined the opposition.

But even more than by sponsoring a petition against the Union, LaFontaine demonstrated his solidarity with the anti-Unionists by refusing Thomson's invitation to become Solicitor General of Lower

---

[14]AAM, Circulaire au clergé, 27 fév. 1840.
[15]Collection Papineau-Bourassa, D.-E. Papineau à A. Papineau, 20 fév. 1840. The initials must stand for Louis Viger, Hippolyte LaFontaine, Côme Cherrier, Denis-Benjamin Viger, and Jean Girouard.

Canada. No doubt he acted with sincerity; in fact a year later on August 28, 1840, he explained in *L'Aurore* that "je n'entendais pas le gouvernement responsable à la manière de Son Excellence." But he knew full well that his acceptance would have alienated the Neilson-Viger group and shaken the unity of the *Canadiens* as well as his chances of influencing them in the future. So, despite Baldwin's example and the advice of Hincks, he turned down the proposal precisely for this reason—or so he must later have explained to Hincks, who answered: "I confess however that I was rather pleased to see that the Governor was willing to have acted with you, and I do not agree that you would have forged chains for yourself, if your friends could only have consented to it."[16] In other words, he had reasoned that if he wanted "his friends" eventually to consent to his own plans, he must not associate with the hated "POULET" (and thus become a *vendu*). He declined Thomson's offer but allowed the fact that he had been asked to leak out—which was poor parliamentary etiquette but excellent politics.

It was also necessary politics. For as the final debates in London over the Union began to appear in the Lower Canadian press in May 1840, the opposition to it grew increasingly fierce. Even Hincks admitted "the Bill appears to me to be abominable,"[17] while *La Gazette* in Quebec and *L'Ami* and *L'Aurore* in Montreal repeated all their old grievances.

"L'Acte du Port de Boston," Neilson intoned in *La Gazette* on May 16, "la suspension de la charte de Massachusetts Bay, et l'acte du Timbre s'élèvent tous en jugement contre l'imprudence de toucher aux constitutions établies dans les colonies de ce continent." The Union (he reiterated on May 19) was impractical: imagine forcing "les pêcheurs des bords du golfe Saint Laurent et les backwoodsmen du fond des grands lacs de se rencontrer pour délibérer en commun." And it was un-British: "TAXATION WITHOUT REPRESENTATION—ces mots sonnent dur à tout sujet britannique. La Constitution britannique, de même que la loi morale, regarde le droit de propriété comme absolu et inviolable" (July 7). In Montreal, Leblanc broadened the theme in *L'Ami du Peuple* during May and June. As "le signal de commotion future," Union threatened "l'avenir de la puissance britannique dans l'Amérique." And, as his first effort after leaving prison, Viger sent *L'Aurore* a lengthy argument based on a pamphlet he had written years before about the iniquities of the union of Belgium and Hol-

[16]Papiers LaFontaine, Hincks to LaFontaine, April 6, 1841.
[17]*Ibid.*, Hincks to LaFontaine, May 2, 1840.

land.[18] The authors of the present scheme, he argued, should at least have spared Canada the same fatal flaws: Belgium with a population twice that of Holland had equal representation, was forced to assume the Dutch debt, saw its language proscribed. Then, within fifteen years, came the revolution. Above all, the anti-*unionnaires* implied throughout, the Union must be prevented because it forced *la nation canadienne* out of its protective boundaries. On May 5 in *La Gazette* Neilson blamed Parent and *Le Canadien* for disagreeing: "Nous doutons fort que ce soit en continuant à s'associer à ce qui se passe au Haut-Canada et en Nouvelle-Ecosse que Le Canadien pourra contribuer à réparer le mal que les chefs populaires du Bas-Canada lui ont fait en s'y associant et en cherchant des appuis au dehors . . . au lieu de s'appuyer sur les droits et privilèges que leur garantissent l'ancienne constitution."

There was the rub: the Union forced "des appuis au dehors." And that was precisely Parent's reason for agreeing to it in principle; for— and during the spring of 1840 he also repeated all his old arguments— the policies of the Reformers would replace Britain's pledges as the guarantee of *Canadien* rights. "Sans parler des principes de justice et de libéralité qui doivent servir de guide aux hommes qui se sont rangés sous les bannières de la réforme," he wrote on July 6, underlining the interdependence of all British North Americans,

il se trouve que le parti réformiste du Haut-Canada, ayant à lutter contre une faction Tory extrêmement influente, aura besoin dans la législature unie de l'appui des réformistes du Bas-Canada dont la masse est française. On voit donc les réformistes du Haut-Canada rassurer la population Canadienne-Française du Bas-Canada contre la proscription dont les lois, la langue et les institutions de cette dernière sont menacées. . . . Ainsi nos enragés d'Union-aires qui avaient rêvé la dégradation, l'ilotisme du peuple Canadien, n'auront fait que donner à ce peuple de nouvaux protecteurs, un appui des plus puissants dans le parti réformiste du Haut-Canada. . . . Tout ce qui nous reste à faire, c'est d'entrer de bon cœur et de bonne foi dans l'œuvre qui doit faire, avec le temps, disparaître de notre état social ce qui nous sépare des populations qui nous environnent de toutes parts, et nous empêche de former avec elles une masse de peuple homogène, ayant une communauté d'intérêts, de vues, et d'affections, d'où résultera une grande nationalité Canadienne assez forte pour se protéger elle-même et vivre de sa propre vie. . . . Et puisque nous perdons l'appui des successeurs de Pitt, . . . cherchons des amis ailleurs, des alliés autour de nous, des alliés qui nous offrent une alliance honorable.

Parent ended on a hopeful note. But he did so alone. Neilson, Leblanc,

[18]*Considérations relatives à la dernière révolution de la Belgique.* Réimprimé d'après la publication faite de cet ouvrage en mai 1831 (Montréal, 1840) excerpts reprinted in *L'Aurore*, 16, 19 juin 1840.

and the others thought only of this last chance lost, of the petitions proved useless. It could do no good; but the less they could do about it, the more they agitated. And they found encouragement in the new life injected into L'Aurore by Viger's release, and in the founding of a new radical newspaper in Montreal.

When the law suspending habeas corpus lapsed in May 1840, Viger, after nineteen months in captivity, came out to take control of the anti-Union forces in Montreal. LaFontaine, incidentally, had seized this as another opportunity to show solidarity with Viger's friends, and, in a way, to score against the Governor. A few days before Viger would be automatically set free on habeas corpus, Thomson was due to give a ball in honour of the Queen's birthday. Realizing how much they could hurt the vice-regal vanity, the French politico-social set let it be known they would boycott the affair unless Viger was released beforehand. Whether or not he feared the snub, and the newspapers at the time thought he did, the Governor yielded. Viger was let out— apparently on his own terms. And the Château de Ramezay shone as on the grandest of its nights. Inside, rare wines flowed, while seasoned meats and sugared fruits were carried into scented salons. "Le punch à la romaine introduit par le cuisinier des Hussards," commented L'Ami du Peuple on May 27, "les glaces et autres rafraîchissemens, ainsi qu'un splendide souper furent goutés par la démocratie d'une manière toute aristocratique." Everyone was there, LaFontaine, Mondelet, Cherrier, Leblanc de Marconnay, Quesnel, Louis-Michel Viger, all turning the Governor's soirée into a success, but, especially, all demonstrating their regard for the splendid companion whom LaFontaine knew many still considered the leader of the party.

Viger was well qualified to lead. Physically, his bright, kindly eyes and imposing head of white hair made people overlook how angular were his nose and chin, and how short his stature; he projected an impression of charming, urbane distinction. Even Papineau always referred to him as Monsieur. Socially, his connections were impeccable. He was a cousin and close friend of Bishop Lartigue and liked to refer to his attachment for the Sulpicians who had educated him and for the pious practices of the Sodality of the Blessed Virgin. During his imprisonment Bishop Bourget had made it a point to visit him several times, and at the end of March 1840, Bishop Lartigue, in one of the last acts of his life, had begged Poulett Thomson for his release.[19] Politically, he could also boast a flawless background. Cultured, learned in several sciences, in history, in constitutional precedent, he had served in Lower Canada's legislature almost since its

[19]AAM, Lartigue au Gouverneur-Général, 31 mars 1840.

inception. He had seconded his cousin Papineau in all his policies, probably inspiring a number of them himself. Now, still proud in his people's service, he claimed the leadership he had inherited from Papineau and gave new enthusiasm to the anti-Union forces which LaFontaine was trying so carefully to restrain.

Viger combined in his person the qualities of both the Neilson–clerical group and the young radicals. As a wealthy landowner, and perhaps especially as a host whose refined grace and rich table had few rivals in the city, Viger was also well connected with the *haute* professional *bourgeoisie* and the prominent French families. Yet, intellectually, he almost sided with the young radicals, having easily assimilated the thought of the ages of reason and revolution. "C'est l'histoire de l'Irlande et de la Révolution française qui m'ont fait politique,"[20] he was fond of saying, and from his intellectual heights he approved many of the ideas held by liberals and nationalists. Soon after his release, Viger took over active control of *L'Aurore*, which, indeed, he had been subsidizing from his prison. For a few months, he added his own well-bred, intelligent articles to Boucher de Belleville's indifferent editorials. Then, in the autumn of 1840, he persuaded Joseph-Guillaume Barthe to stop versifying and take the editorial chair. From then on *L'Aurore* gradually waxed louder in its attacks against the Union, becoming in the Montreal area "la seule maîtresse, pour ainsi dire, des sentiments de nos habitants."[21]

While Viger thus reorganized *L'Aurore*, the young, spirited ex-Chasseurs also began a press campaign which, though it lasted a bare six or seven months, intensified the anti-Union crusade. They started *La Canadienne* which claimed on June 4, 1840, to be "un autre journal dévoué au intérêts canadiens." After its financing was taken over in November 1840 by another republican, Dr. Henri-Alphonse Gauvin, it was rechristened *Le Jean-Baptiste*. Jacques-Alexis Plinguet, an apprentice of Duvernay's, and the twenty-five-year-old Dr. Gauvin took charge. They found their inspiration mainly in the exiled Duvernay, who, in turn, readily obliged with a whole series of articles urging continued resistance. The young editors needed little urging; they all had high hopes and courage. "Il y a trop de faiblesse dans les Canadiens aujourd'hui," Plinguet wrote in a letter thanking Duvernay for an article,

qu'on leur parle de se révolter avec une sûreté de succès, eh bien, marche-ront-ils? Non, ils craindront encore des malheurs. . . . Cependant ne perdons pas espérance, mon cher Monsieur, les Canadiens ne sont peut-être qu'en-

[20]F.-J. Audet, *Les Deputés de Montréal* (Montréal, 1943), p. 203.
[21]Papiers Duvernay, Perrault à Duvernay, 13 jan. 1840; Plinguet à Duvernay, 26 mai 1841.

dormis, à la moindre nouvelle de guerre avec les Etats-Unis, on verra nos compatriotes se rallier et remporter une victoire complète. Espérons et attendons cet instant, cette occasion, ce jour trois fois bienheureux.[22]

They intended to "tâcher d'éclairer encore plus nos habitants sur la justice anglaise" and continue the ferment: "La grande politique d'Oconnel [sic] et sa grande habilité, c'est l'agitation." From Burlington, Duvernay advised just that.[23] But the paper and the best-laid radical plans collapsed when Gauvin fell ill and died in March 1841. By then, of course, the Union bill was a *fait accompli*. Still, during the second half of 1840, Plinguet, Gauvin, and Duvernay had added their protests to the last great chorus against the Union.

In Quebec, meanwhile, Neilson resigned his seat on the Special Council, in opposition, it was thought, to its arbitrary policies, especially the Union. He thus regained the affection and influence he had lost back in 1838 when he accepted a chair at Colborne's table. And he continued to produce ever stronger editorials against the Union and responsible government.

LaFontaine disagreed, of course. He sympathized perhaps—and his letters from Hincks are full of reassurance and reminders that testify to the inner conflicts he must have suffered over his own plans—but he knew that however often Neilson and Leblanc de Marconnay repeated their arguments, whatever Viger said, whatever Duvernay wrote, they were all wasting their time. The Union must come. He realized too that he would be wasting his own time if he attempted to reason with them. Instead, he continued his noiseless, practical plans to circumvent the difficulties of the Union bill. In mid-May he welcomed to Montreal the Upper Canadian Reformer, William Hamilton Merritt, introduced him to Mondelet and others, and with them gratefully received reminders of how eager the Upper Canadians were to co-operate. "You may depend," Hincks summed up after hearing Merritt's report,

that the Reformers of U.C. will in the United Legislature act towards you and your friends in *perfect good faith*. . . . After what has taken place, your countrymen would never obtain their rights in a Lower Canadian Legislature. You want our help as much as we want yours. . . . Our liberties cannot be secured but by the Union. I know you think we shall never get responsible government, that the ministry are deceiving us—granted—*but we will make them give it whether they like it or not.*[24]

[22]*Ibid.*, 415, Plinguet à Duvernay, 19 juin 1840.
[23]*Ibid.*, Plinguet à Duvernay, 30 juin, 20 août 1840; Gaillardet à Duvernay, 7 sept. 1840; Bouthillier à Duvernay, 7 nov. 1840; 461, Côté à Duvernay, 15 nov. 1840; 469, Dumesnil à Duvernay, 9 jan. 1841.
[24]Papiers LaFontaine, Hincks to LaFontaine, June 17, 1840.

On June 30, LaFontaine left Montreal to return Merritt's visit. Yet so strong ran the anti-Union feeling that he dared not let his compatriots know the object of his trip. Even so, MacDonald in *La Gazette* of July 9 blamed him for being "renfermé avec MM. Baldwin et Hincks." *L'Aurore* commented on July 7 that the trip must be purely personal: "Mr. L. H. LAFONTAINE, Avocat de cette ville, est parti dernièrement pour Toronto. Le *Herald* suppose que c'est dans la vue de prendre des arrangements avec les réformistes du Haut-Canada *relativement à la tactique à suivre dans l'assemblée des provinces unies.* La supposition du *Herald* est hors de toute vraisemblance, vu que l'union législative des deux pays n'est pas encore effectuée et qu'il y a quelque probabilité qu'elle ne le sera pas du tout." Leblanc attacked more bitterly:

Le Herald tout en voulant attaquer M. Baldwin nous semble vouloir faire beaucoup trop d'honneur à M. Lafontaine [sic]; l'importance de ce dernier est totalement déchue, et la conduite tortueuse qu'il tint envers ses amis, les anciens chefs de la révolte, n'a pas été faite pour lui acquérir la popularité du parti. . . . Il a pu faire lui-même son panégyrique auprès du pouvoir, se donner de l'influence, et compromettre sur les destinées futures de sa patrie; mais le marché qu'on ferait avec lui serait une véritable duperie, dont il toucherait le prix sans en pouvoir la valeur. Personne ne voudrait se rallier sous son étendard, parce qu'il est plus sage de suivre un ennemi loyal qu'un faux ami. La carrière de M. LaFontaine doit être terminée et nous presumons qu'il doit être assez persuadé du dédain qu'on lui porte pour ne pas s'exposer à en recevoir publiquement l'avis. (*L'Ami du Peuple*, July 4)

Still, on his return, having won renewed promises that, as Hincks said, "the desire of all my friends will be to meet your wishes . . . and to act towards you in perfect sincerity and good faith,"[25] LaFontaine reported back to Toronto that the small nucleus who were aware of his policy felt "satisfied with the result" of his visit.[26] In September, Hincks came to Montreal himself. By then, LaFontaine, having made his views public, could give him an open welcome. Indeed, he entertained for him at a banquet in his own home, inviting Mondelet, Cherrier, Cartier, Lewis Thomas Drummond (another young lieutenant of great promise) and, most important, Denis-Benjamin Viger, who was impressed by Hincks and whose companionable urbanity made him, in turn, an instant hit with the Upper Canadian.

On August 18, however, when news arrived that Queen Victoria had finally signed the Union bill, the French-Canadian political community offered no overt signs of disunity. They had all signed their petitions, all strained against the hateful Union. Now all could deplore it together.

[25]*Ibid.* [26]*Ibid.*, Hincks to LaFontaine, July 18, 1840.

Having nursed the unity of the party by careful compromise, LaFontaine now had to persuade his fellow politicians to co-operate with his own project. He lost no time. On the front page of *L'Aurore* for August 28, 1840, his most celebrated manifesto, the Adresse aux Electeurs de Terrebonne, was published. In it he deplored the Union, and thereby bowed in the direction of the Neilson-Viger group. But, he went on to say that Lower Canadians should not therefore abdicate their rights and adopt a course which would inevitably lead to political suicide. Rather, they must play their rightful part, fight the next election, then unite with the Reformers of Upper Canada whose help they needed to win "le gouvernement responsable tel qu'on l'a avoué et promis à l'Assemblée du Haut-Canada." With this, "le principal moteur de la Constitution Anglaise," they could win back all they had lost. Without the Union, there could be no responsible government, no political liberty. The call was clear: accept the new constitution, join the Reformers from Upper Canada, win responsible government.

Before long, most politicians in the district of Montreal and many from Quebec agreed with LaFontaine. But not without reservations. As Antoine Gérin-Lajoie, soon to be one of LaFontaine's junior organizers, recalled years later: "Les plus violents allaient même jusqu'à proposer une abstention complète de toute participation à la chose publique; ils conseillaient aux électeurs des comtés canadiens français de s'abstenir de voter aux élections prochaines."[27] In *L'Aurore*, in the same issue that contained the Adresse, Barthe had attacked the bill. Yet slowly he began to come over to LaFontaine's view—by coincidence, perhaps, especially after Hincks' visit in mid-September. *L'Aurore* certainly could never admit the Union was good. "Les partisans de l'Union (car cette question est du domaine de toutes les conversations)," Barthe inquired bombastically on December 11:

savent-ils bien ce qu'ils approuvent? Ce soufflet machiavélique que la main du ministère a donné à la face du peuple colonial n'obtiendra-t-il qu'une lâche complaisance de la part de ceux qui se déclarent unionnaires? Peut-être ai-je tort de dire que ce soufflet a été donné à la face du peuple, car le régime qui le disloque et le désorganise ne lui a pas laissé de physionomie, et c'est dans cette époque de transition et de révolution morale surtout qu'il faut au peuple canadien du caractère et de la foi dans ses immunités sociales pour ne pas transiger avec les catastrophes qui l'entourent; car l'union renferme à la fois et la spoliation de la propriété et la violation des droits sacrés de la nationalité et de la religion.

[27]A. Gérin-Lajoie, *Dix Ans au Canada* (Québec, 1888), p. 68.

There were reasons, however, for not boycotting the Union. The *Canadiens* had been disenfranchised, gerrymandered, but abstention from voting might prove ruinous. As Barthe pointed out on September 4: "Une majorité tory dans la chambre d'assemblée de la législature unie pourrait être un événement sérieux pour cette colonie. Les Canadiens français surtout doivent le redouter." They should also respond to the sympathy of their fellow Reformers. They appreciated Hincks' editorials in the *Examiner* against the redistribution of seats in the Montreal and Quebec areas. They had nothing to lose, and, perhaps, much to gain: "La législature unie des Canadas sentant toute la dignité de sa mission va courageusement reprendre la défense des opprimés qui la députent, et comme elle se composera de l'élite des deux sociétés également intéressées dans les résultats, laissez-moi exprimer le vœu que le jour de la *Justice égale* va poindre à l'horizon" (*L'Aurore*, November 10).

L'Aurore's opinion carried weight. Since mid-August when *L'Ami du Peuple* had ceased publication and Leblanc de Marconnay had returned to France, it had been the only sizable French paper in the Montreal area. Also, in its measured approval of LaFontaine, it reflected the opinion of some of Duvernay's republican correspondents one of whom wrote:

Venons en directement à notre querelle—les Elections. Comme un républicain parle toujours la vérité—je vais vous donner franchement quoique vous ne me le demandiez pas mon opinion sur ce sujet important. . . . Je pense que le peuple doit prendre part aux élections, et élire des hommes sur les principes et l'indépendance desquels il peut compter. Il est vrai qu'il est peut-être difficile de trouver des hommes qui aient assez de magnanimité pour remplir aujourd'hui convenablement le beau rôle qui peut leur être assigné. Mais je crois qu'il y a encore quelques-uns de ces héros. . . .[28]

It also echoed LaFontaine's trusted friend, Jean-Joseph Girouard. On reading the Adresse, he wrote to LaFontaine: "En vérité il faut certainement beaucoup d'esprit pour écrire ainsi un morceau aussi difficile, où il fallait infiniment de l'habilité pour ne toucher que certaines questions, et pour ne dire que ce qu'il fallait dire, et comme il le fallait dire."[29] In Quebec, Parent reprinted the whole Adresse in *Le Canadien* on August 31 with strong approval: "L'on verra que M. Lafontaine [sic] en retour de l'appui qu'il offre aux réformistes du Haut-Canada attend d'eux qu'ils s'uniront aux réformistes du Bas-Canada, pour faire rendre au peuple du Bas-Canada la justice qu'on lui refuse dans l'acte d'union. Comme nous le disons ailleurs, en

[28]Papiers Duvernay, 454, A. P. R. Consigny à Duvernay, 25 oct. 1840.
[29]Papiers LaFontaine, Girouard à LaFontaine, 3 sept. 1840.

d'autres mots, il ne peut y avoir d'union sans confiance, et de confiance sans égalité."

Neilson, however, had thoughts of his own. He too printed the Adresse but he disagreed with it, with its approval of responsible government, and, implicitly, of a system in which, as he said on August 28, the Canadiens were "placés dans la position d'une caste dégradée sur la terre qui les a vu naître et qui renferme les tombeaux de leurs aïeux." He advised the Canadiens to boycott the election—an attitude that was not uncommon, especially in the columns of La Canadienne. "Pour ma part," wrote Perrault, an assiduous reader of the Gauvin-Plinguet newspaper, "que ça aille comme ça voudra. Je suis trop dégoûté."[30] And from Paris Papineau wrote a letter attacking the Union which was circulated among the young hot-heads in Montreal and Quebec. The Union was intended, he said, as a means to exclude the Canadiens from office. Now, "le parti Anglais" had triumphed and would hold on to the spoils "tant que durera le régime colonial." To acquiesce in the Union was to accept defeat, and this was treachery to the French-Canadian nation. But to renounce all co-operation with the Union and patiently to await "le jour indéterminé de l'émancipation" would be the height of disinterested patriotism.[31]

Neilson also reflected the views of the Church. Bishop Bourget, who had succeeded to the see of Montreal in April 1840, admitted that his only consolation on hearing the bill had been sanctioned was that "nous avons au moins la consolation d'avoir fait tout en notre pouvoir pour l'éviter."[32] He saw Union inevitably leading to the end of the British connection and of the liberties of the Church. He said no more, but other clerics did. From Three Rivers, Vicar-General Thomas Cooke wrote to Archbishop Signay that too many priests were speaking against the Union, a mistake which he thought could do great harm.[33] Morin wrote likewise to LaFontaine: "Je crains bien que le clergé ne se porte à des extravagances. Ce parti-là n'a certainement ni expérience, ni lumières; il compte trop sur sa propre importance."[34]

Backed by such unlikely partners as the republicans in Montreal and the clergy throughout the province, Neilson prepared an address of his own. Morin and Parent, seeing the threat of a split in the political community, began to negotiate a compromise. In mid-September

[30]Papiers Duvernay, 436, Perrault à Duvernay, 15 sept. 1840.
[31]Ibid., 443-4, A. Papineau à Duvernay, 3 oct. 1840.
[32]AAM, Lettres Bourget, II, 193-4, Bourget à Gosford, 25 août 1840.
[33]AAQ, VG XI, 30, Cooke à Signay, 20 oct. 1840.
[34]Papiers LaFontaine, Morin à LaFontaine, 18 sept. 1840.

Morin reported his success to LaFontaine: "Mr Neilson se trouve naturellement à la tête des affaires. Il va être publié une espèce de lettre qu'il a rédigée et à laquelle j'ai donné mon adhésion, parce que je la trouve correcte en principes. Il ne se prononce pas sur la principale question, qu'il laisse ouverte, savoir, celle d'essayer l'union ou la rejeter à la face de ceux qui l'ont faite."[35] Neilson had agreed to leave acceptance of the Union an open subject. With Morin, he called a meeting for October 14 but it was pouring rain and only 200 people appeared. Parent accordingly moved an adjournment until October 20 when over 1,000 people filled the Ecole des Glacis. Neilson presided, Glackmeyer acted as secretary, Aylwin, Parent, Vital Têtu, and Morin sat on the stage close by. Immediately after Neilson had explained in both languages that there could be no doubt of the opposition "que la masse du peuple de cette ville, comme de tout le pays, est déterminée à faire à l'Acte d'Union," as *Le Canadien* reported the following day, Morin rose to speak. First, he toned down the chairman's remarks, distinguishing carefully between the principle of Union and the bill. Then, he suggested that the bill could best be fought by active participation in the coming election. For, a strong reform contingent in the new Assembly could win much more for the French than complete isolation. Most important of all was "l'union entre les citoyens, le respect envers l'ordre légal, mais en même temps une fermeté inébranlable dans nos démarches pour obtenir justice."[36] The meeting then approved the motion that a Comité des Electeurs de Québec should be charged with drawing up an Adresse aux Electeurs de Toute la Province. The committee included Morin and Parent who made sure the address urged neither repeal nor boycott: rather, it agreed that "tout ce que nous pouvons faire maintenant, c'est d'en prévoir les suites fâcheuses en faisant un bon choix du peu de représentans qu'il nous laisse."[37]

The meeting broke up with a unanimous resolution calling for a united front in favour of common reform principles. Morin and Parent had won: the two addresses, that to the electors of Terrebonne and that to those of the province, said the same thing. LaFontaine had achieved the first of his victories.

French Canadians nevertheless greeted the actual day of Union with horror. "L'Union est proclamée demain," intoned Jacques Plinguet, "au son des canons et des trompettes des militaires et probablement au son des pleurs des Canadiens."[38] In Montreal on February

[35]*Ibid.*
[36]*Le Canadien,* 21 oct. 1840.
[37]*La Gazette de Québec,* 25 oct. 1840.
[38]Papiers Duvernay, 474, Plinguet à Duvernay, 8 fév. 1841.

10, 1841, Lord Sydenham took the oath at the Château amid the gold, the braid, and the plumes, while a salvo of nineteen cannon shots rang out from the Champ de Mars near by. But the large bilingual proclamations of the event posted "dans nos rues à tous les dix pas" were torn to bits and trampled under foot. By dawn of the fatal day, *L'Aurore* reported (February 11), not one of them remained. In Quebec Neilson sighed one last sigh for the separate state:

Consummatum est! La Constitution de 1791, l'œuvre des Pitt et des Fox, des plus grands hommes d'état de la Grande-Bretagne, cette Constitution qui en garantissant aux Canadiens les droits et privilèges qu'ils avaient hérités de leurs pères, ceux qu'ils avaient acquis par les capitulations de 1759, ceux qui avaient été stipulés en leur faveur par le traité de cession de 1763, et ceux qui avaient été assurés à toutes les colonies par l'Acte Déclaratoire de 1778, a conservé deux fois le Canada à l'Angleterre; cette constitution n'est plus, et nous entrons cette nuit dans une route obscure à l'entrée de laquelle sont le mensonge et la corruption, mais dont ceux qui nous y conduisent avouent qu'ils ne savent pas eux-mêmes qu'elle sera l'issu. (*La Gazette de Québec*, February 9)

Aubin noted ironically in *Le Fantasque* (February 11): "Le jour choisi pour nous installer dans l'union est un Mercredi. Les érudits vous diront que ce mot signifie: *jour de Mercure*; or Mercure est le dieu des marchands et des voleurs. Singulière coincidence." And Garneau published three columns in *Le Canadien* on February 22 mourning the abolition of French culture and reminding the British of "les principales inventions dûes au génie de la France, la gravure dite à *l'acqua tinta*, l'alun artificiel, les perles artificielles, les ponts-radeaux, le thermomètre double, le système de chimie moderne etc. etc. etc."

Five days after proclamation of the Union, the election writs, returnable on April 8, 1841, were issued in Montreal. The Neilson and LaFontaine groups campaigned in perfect unity, having lost none of their electioneering zeal against the pro-Union Tories and the Governor General. The Tories were the old enemy; now they had compounded their guilt by agreeing to the Union, by sitting on the detested Special Council. The Governor General (because he wanted the mercantile interests represented in the House) had gerrymandered the French population out of the city ridings in Montreal and Quebec; he had also insulted the two cities by proclaiming Kingston the new capital and offended the whole of *la nation canadienne* by including no French Canadian and only one Catholic on the new Executive Council. Against all this, the *Canadiens* reacted as one; all their candidates stood on the platform outlined in the two addresses. Yet Neilson and LaFontaine had a different stake in the results. For

LaFontaine, Morin, and their friends, the outcome might be the beginning of the grand alliance that would consecrate responsible government; for Neilson, it would be, at best, the opportunity to give public warning to the world of French Canada's greatest grievance, "obtenir justice pour le Bas-Canada, sans faire d'injustice au Haut: si non: Rappel!"[39] Each, accordingly, entertained preoccupations of his own as news came in from the different ridings.

In the Quebec district where nineteen seats were at stake, Neilson, with all his old spirit, wit, and eloquence, directed a smooth campaign. On February 16 he chaired an intimate strategy session at Glack-meyer's at which Morin, Aylwin, and other influential friends such as the merchants Louis Massue and François-Xavier Méthot dusted off and reissued the address adopted at the meeting last October. Sent to be posted conspicuously in every riding, it dominated the speeches of every candidate, and often the curé's sermon as well. "Quelques-uns des curés," wrote the Vicar-General from Three Rivers to Arch-bishop Signay, "se sont mêlés un peu trop d'élections. Celui de Saint-David a été interrompu pendant son sermon par un homme qui lui a crié qu'on ne devait pas parler d'élection dans l'église."[40]

In most constituencies, things went well. Eleven went by acclama-tion, all to candidates who had subscribed to the Adresse. In Rouville, one seat was lost by nine votes—377–368—when the *vendu*, Colonel Antoine de Salaberry, defeated Timothée Franchère in a contest so heated that Le Vrai Canadien reported (March 16) that one of Sala-berry's men was killed and two of Franchère's critically wounded. Neilson made up for this, however, in Saint-Maurice. There, his young friend Joseph-Edouard Turcotte, a rousing orator and a clever politician, ran against Colonel Gugy, a close friend of the returning officer who conducted the poll by asking "*que ceux qui sont pour Mr. Gugy ou pour Mr. Turcotte lèvent la main*" and then counting them all for Gugy— until Turcotte gathered a squad of his more extreme partisans and seized the poll to assure a majority.[41] In the dual riding of Quebec City Neilson's plans went amiss. Since redistribution, the English merchants controlled the election. In an effort to secure at least one of the seats, Neilson persuaded the sure winner, David Burnet, a highly popular merchant, otherwise politically independent but pro-Union, to agree to Louis Massue as his running mate against two strong *unionnaires*, Henry Black and James Gibb. The election was

[39]Papiers LaFontaine, Neilson à LaFontaine, 27 août 1842.
[40]AAQ, VG XI, 47, Cooke à Signay, 30 mars 1841.
[41]L'Aurore, 23, 27 avril 1841.

a quiet one lasting six days, but, instead of Massue, it was Black who was returned with Burnet. In Quebec County, however, Neilson himself triumphed by acclamation on March 22, and was escorted home through the cheering streets of his old city at the head of a fifty-carriage procession.

In the Montreal district, LaFontaine was faced with a much more complex situation. Except for the seven English-speaking ridings in the Eastern Townships where the Tories ruled unchallenged, he had a possible sixteen seats to win. But he did not dominate as Neilson did in Quebec. If anyone did, it was Sydenham. The Governor General, or "le Grand Electeur" as L'Aurore called him on October 13, had the power—and exercised it more than in any other district—to appoint his own men as returning officers and to place the polls in areas more easily accessible to the Tories. Besides, *les Anglais* were more numerous here, and, if possible, felt stronger anti-French prejudices. The Governor had a following real enough to find it worthwhile to fight a winter campaign in all but six ridings. Nor did LaFontaine command the organs of propaganda, or, indeed, the undivided allegiance of the *Canadiens* themselves. The clergy distrusted him. Viger and *L'Aurore* were last-minute, and as time would show, insecure converts to his views; another French paper, *Le Vrai Canadien*, started especially for the election, belonged to the Governor General. The young radicals suspected LaFontaine enough to circulate widely copies of an article by that old *vendu*, Léon Gosselin, in *Le Fantasque* as an answer to the Adresse aux Electeurs de Terrebonne:

Mr. Ménard qui se dit la fontaine a montré une versatilité de caractère qui doit retirer toute confiance dans son dévouement aux intérêts publics. . . . Si l'insurrection était un titre de patriotisme à ses yeux, Mr. Ménard devait se trouver à la tête de ses concitoyens; s'il ne l'approuvait point il aurait dû la blâmer tout haut. Il a donc perdu tout droit aujourd'hui à se dire véritablement patriote. Cet homme n'avait tout bonnement et n'a encore qu'une ambition démesurée, sans énergie pour la faire triompher; qu'une intrigue sourde pour supplanter ceux dont il se disait l'ami et pour se mettre à leur place. Il a plusieurs fois tenté de se débarrasser de Mr. Papineau pour vendre plus à son aise la popularité qu'il croyait avoir et à laquelle il n'arriva jamais. . . . Aujourd'hui . . . il recommence à crier patriotisme, à prétendre qu'il s'opposera au gouvernement; mais il a soin de mettre en avant "qu'il ne faut point demander le rappel de l'Union" afin de se laisser une porte de derrière ouverte si le pouvoir veut l'acheter.[42]

<hr>

[42]*Le Fantasque*, 16 nov. 1840. LaFontaine's first Canadian ancestor was called Jacques Ménard dit La fontaine, and Louis-Hippolyte was christened as a Ménard. His mother's name was Marie Fontaine. He signed his own name as a titled person would with a capital "F". As well as his natural aloofness, this might be a reason for his reputed snobbishness.

As a result, LaFontaine had difficulty finding candidates. "Fabre a refusé pour Verchères," commented Perrault, "vraiment on est en peine pour le comté de Montréal, pour Vaudreuil, Verchères, Laprairie [sic], L'Assomption, et plusieurs autres comtés."[43] In fact, by April 8, LaFontaine and his party could claim only one real victory in the whole district. That was in Berthier where, on March 18, David Armstrong, a good friend of LaFontaine's and an organizer whose partisans, said Le Vrai Canadien on March 19, conducted themselves "avec une extrême férocité," carried an upset election against Barthélémi Joliette, the seigneur and an influential business man who had sat on the Special Council. The Canadiens also took six seats by acclamation, among them Viger's Richelieu, Bouthillier's Saint-Hyacinthe, and Barthe's Yamaska. In the dual riding of Montreal, LaFontaine and his supporters were plagued by poor organization and personal conflicts. LaFontaine wanted James Leslie as a candidate, but could not find a running mate for him. Sydney Bellingham, undependable and ambitious, wanted to run, but could not possibly carry the Canadien vote: he had fought against the patriotes in a by-election in 1836 and under Colborne at Saint-Eustache, then had gone to Quebec to work with Neilson on the petitions against the Union, then taken the job of editor of the Canada Times, a new paper begun in Montreal in 1840 by William Walker, a good friend of the Upper Canadian Reformers. For Baldwin's sake, LaFontaine was about to agree to his running when Bellingham accepted from Lord Sydenham an emigration commissionership at £800 a year. The party having then decided that Leslie should run in Montreal County instead, the two Montreal seats went by acclamation to the prominent banker, Benjamin Holmes, and to the head of the Tory party in Lower Canada, George Moffatt.

In Montreal County, Leslie enjoyed better organization. With the help of Cherrier and Cartier, he conducted a heated campaign against Alexandre-Maurice DeLisle. Towards the end of the afternoon on election day, when Leslie had acquired 20 votes to DeLisle's 15, a mob of some 600 young men under Michel Coursol, Cherrier's stepson, seized the poll, but in the process they killed two of DeLisle's partisans, one victim being an Irish baker employed by Mayor Peter McGill. The bloody corpse was carried through the city. Somewhat predictably, on the next day, no 600 Canadiens were a match for the combined fury of the Tories and the avenging Irish. The poll fell to DeLisle. The band of youngsters had rioted in vain. Leslie quickly conceded.

[43]Papiers Duvernay, 477, Perrault à Duvernay, 19 fév. 1841.

In Terrebonne LaFontaine suffered somewhat the same experience. His campaign got off to a bad start when his opponent, Dr. Michael McCulloch, imported some three hundred copies of that article from *Le Fantasque* of November 16, in which, after the slander of LaFontaine, he was himself praised as "généralement connu dans le comté et n'y a laissé que des souvenirs honorables. . . . Le docteur n'est pas un homme passionné pour autre chose que pour la justice; . . . Il est demeuré étranger au fanatisme des partis." LaFontaine was also given what must have been intended as the kiss of death by *Le Vrai Canadien*. In its issue of January 12, 1841, it listed all the candidates in two columns headed: "ceux qui offriront à l'acte d'Union une opposition à outrance," and "ceux qui coopèrent avec les représentants du Haut Canada." LaFontaine's name appeared in the second column with such recognized enemies as George Moffatt and James Gibb, while Girouard, Morin, Barthe, Kimber, Armstrong, Turcotte, Massue, Neilson, and Aylwin were in the first. No wonder Hincks warned that "you will not be returned for Terrebonne, that you are suspected by your party."[44] By election day the Governor had fixed the poll at New Glasgow, far from the settlements of Sainte-Thérèse and Sainte-Rose where LaFontaine's organizers had their headquarters, and McCulloch had hired some two hundred bullies to march to the poll and make sure he won. Accordingly, when LaFontaine arrived in New Glasgow heading some 850 of his own partisans (armed with sticks, knives, and pitchforks), he discovered McCulloch's people, six or seven hundred strong and all carrying heavy cudgels studded with nails, lined up in the commanding position. Wisely, he declined the contest, returned to Montreal, and sent *L'Aurore* a tense seven-column censure of the Governor General, which appeared on March 30.

What else could he do? He was probably right in blaming the Governor. After all, he had stood for Terrebonne before and won large majorities there since 1830. And he would again in 1844. Yet he had his own enemies, and he was suspect to a number of *Canadiens*. He found the outcome discouraging. This was indeed his spring of disappointment. On April 8, when all the results had been tabulated, the *Canadiens* had only twenty seats out of the lower province's forty-two. LaFontaine had lost his own riding, and, as he looked over the list of returns, he could pick out only six or seven members whom he could trust to work for responsible government: Joseph-René Kimber from Champlain; Colonel Etienne-Pascal Taché, one of the dominant personalities of the Quebec area whom the electors in

44Papiers LaFontaine, Hincks to LaFontaine, Dec. 29, 1840.

L'Islet insisted on returning; the two friends, Morin, elected in Nicolet after a group of partisans put up the necessary £500 qualification for him, and Parent, the new member for Saguenay.

Yet this was the darkest hour before the dawn. The election had failed, but LaFontaine had achieved more than appeared. He had avoided a split and steered the *Canadien* party through what might have been its greatest crisis. Only two years before, he had come out of prison into a political wilderness, cut off from old friends, isolated from the two or three thinkers left in Quebec. Slowly, silently, he had appeased old enemies, made new friends, negotiated them and himself into a contest which, at the beginning, they had all refused. He had pointed the way to survival. Now he emerged from the election, defeated it is true, but at the head of a united, political organization determined to act.

5

"Les Epoux si mal en lune de miel" April-September 1841

The first session of the new parliament was summoned to meet in Kingston on June 14. The Governor General left Montreal for the new capital on May 26 and arrived the next day. He reported back to his friend, Lord John Russell, "I think we shall do very well at Kingston."[1] By the opening, he had completed moving and integrating the public records of the two former provinces, as well as all the arrangements for the new parliament, which was to meet in the spacious General Hospital, redecorated to receive the two Houses, the Assembly's room being fitted in green and furnished with eighty-four handsome stuffed armchairs of black walnut. "But," the Governor worried, "the fellows in these Colonies have been spoiled by all sorts of luxuries, large armchairs, desks with stationery before each man, & heaven knows what, so I suppose they will complain."[2]

The politicians were preparing more serious complaints. By his own manœuvres with the anti-Union petitions, and Morin's diplomacy with Neilson, LaFontaine had forged an incipient party unity and won the Viger-Neilson group, at least implicitly, over to acceptance of the Union. Now, in the weeks immediately after the election, he began to press on to the second objective he had proposed: the alliance with the Upper Canadian Reformers which he considered essential to circumvent all the evils placed in the Union bill by Russell and Sydenham.

Although they had agreed to fight the election, Neilson's and Viger's followers entertained serious reservations about merging with the Upper Canadian Reformers. Although LaFontaine and Parent believed national survival could best be assured if the government were in the hands of a single party representing the aspirations of both cultural

[1]Sydenham to Russell, June 12, 1841, in P. M. Knaplund, ed., *Letters from Lord Sydenham to Lord John Russell* (London, 1831), p. 143.
[2]*Ibid.*

groups in the province, Neilson and Viger feared this united party would precipitate precisely what they feared from the Union itself— absorption of *la nation canadienne* into the culture and interests of its neighbours. They suggested instead that the Lower Canadians remain firmly separate and practise what Morin disparagingly described as "the O'Connell-tail system, to unite with one party or another as momentary alliance or expediency may suggest."[3] Moreover Neilson and Viger distrusted the Upper Canadians who had, after all, voted for the hated bill. Napoléon Aubin expressed their thoughts in *Le Fantasque* (October 26):

Tous vos membres élus... doivent-ils d'emblée tendre la main aux réformistes du Haut-Canada? Moi, je dis non. . . . Ces réformistes s'occupent beaucoup plus de vous faire payer leurs dettes . . . qu'ils ne s'occupent de vous, de vos malheurs et du moyen de vous retirer d'où l'on vous a plongés. . . . Ce que je voudrais que vous fissiez, parbleu, il n'est pas difficile de vous le dire: vous placer là au milieu des partis et n'aider qu'à celui qui voudra vous aider.

L'Aurore agreed in several articles throughout April. And, for reasons which Morin referred to as "past disputes on the subject of responsible government,"[4] Neilson admitted his dislike for the Reformers of Upper Canada. He blamed them, among others, for the Union and all the attendant evils which he repeated again for William Hamilton Merritt.

The project originated in a desire to place the persons and property of the subject at the mercy of the office-holders and their connections; and it bears marks of being completed in that design. The sacrifices that the assembling of a representative body to treat of the common interest of a people extending over upwards of twelve hundred miles of territory, different in language, laws, religion, institutions, climate and circumstances, the manner in which the revenue of the country has been appropriated without its consent, and the Assembly bound down, leaves us only a mockery of free government and of the British Constitution.[5]

Parent accepted Neilson's challenge (*Le Canadien*, April 9):

Nous pouvons nous tromper, mais nous pensons, et le pensant nous devons le dire, que la position tranchée que prend *l'Aurore*, nous fermerait pour toujours la porte à la réhabilitation politique que nous avons à demander. Défions-nous de notre imagination, défions-nous de notre propre cœur même. . . . Avant de prendre une position décidée, immuable contre le

[3]PAC, MG 24, B 68, Hincks Papers, Morin to Hincks, May 8, 1841.
[4]*Ibid.*
[5]Neilson to Merritt, April 27, 1841, quoted in J. P. Merritt, *Biography of W. H. Merritt* (St. Catharines, 1875), p. 233.

gouvernement attendons que nous puissions sommer les réformistes du Haut-Canada . . . de s'unir à nous dans nos démarches.

But LaFontaine knew more than editorials would be required and he also knew how crucial it was that he succeed. "Be advised then My Dear Sir," Hincks encouraged, "and try and induce your friends to be so, no matter how deep the injuries you have sustained and God knows I admit them to be as great as you can, recollect that by taking an extreme course at present *you are playing the game of your enemies* and placing power in there [*sic*] hands to oppress you still more, whereas I think I see clearly that by good management the game is in your hands."[6] LaFontaine then began to manœuvre. First, he agreed to a move which would conciliate his opponents: the election of Augustin Cuvillier to the speakership.

Following the Lower Canadian precedent of electing the leader of the party as speaker, LaFontaine had first proposed Baldwin, but Hincks reminded him that since the latter sat on Sydenham's Executive Council, his election would be interpreted as a victory for the Governor.[7] Then, LaFontaine insisted on his faithful lieutenant, Morin. He certainly deserved a reward, needed the salary, and, most important since LaFontaine himself was without a seat in the House, could be depended upon to co-operate with Upper Canada. LaFontaine knew, of course, that Morin was the leader neither in fact, nor by temperament or inclination; yet he deliberately preferred him over men like Viger, Neilson, Quesnel, or Cuvillier. Was it because he knew that Morin, weak by nature, would be lost without orders from him? That with Morin as "House leader" he could continue to direct the party himself. Hincks had to write four letters to persuade him that Morin could not possibly carry the vote in the House and that the united Tories would then elect their own man. On the other hand, Cuvillier, a business man with connections and friends in all parts of the new province and among all parties, spoke fluent English, and could not possibly be rejected by the Tories. And, as he had campaigned against the Union, opposed the civil list, equal representation, the funding of the debt, and the proscription of the French language, his election would mean "an important triumph" for French Canada.[8] Besides, in an interesting interview with the Governor General that had somehow leaked out, Cuvillier had bluntly told Sydenham of his opposition.[9]

[6]Papiers LaFontaine, Hincks to LaFontaine, April 6, 1841.
[7]*Ibid.*, Hincks to LaFontaine, May 29, 1841.
[8]*Ibid.*, Hincks to LaFontaine, April 19, May 26, 29, 31, 1841.
[9]*Le Canadien* 2 juin, 1841.

LaFontaine hesitated, however. He distrusted the man who had broken with Papineau in 1834 and now professed close friendship with Neilson and Viger. However, he gave in. And thus Cuvillier, a member of the Neilson-Viger group, would be elected by the votes of the Upper Canadian Reformers and escorted to the dais by Baldwin himself—surely a fact likely to impress the diehards with the rewards of co-operating with *les unionnaires du Haut-Canada,* as *La Gazette de Québec* pointed out on June 17.

LaFontaine then began to press the *Canadien* members into a definite commitment to his friends in the sister province. Since he lacked a seat in the House, he again acted through Morin, so universally beloved, and now, in LaFontaine's view, the actual parliamentary leader. Morin and Parent had already pushed Neilson into fighting the election; perhaps now they could move him to soften his stand against the Upper Canadian Reformers. This was a formidable task. For Neilson was planning to propose (perhaps as a symbol of Lower Canada's particularism) an amendment to the Address in Reply to the Speech from the Throne, in which he would demand repeal of the Union and, by implication, condemn the Upper Canadians who had voted for it eighteen months earlier. According to Hincks, this would naturally strengthen "the conviction that you will yield nothing to produce harmony . . . by refusing to co-operate with them and going into determined hostility."[10] The amendment, LaFontaine feared, would not only waste time, but also force into the open the differences between his own friends (who were in the minority) and those of Neilson and Viger. Neilson unquestionably wielded the greatest influence. "If we were to support a Government," Morin sighed, "and he were to oppose it, we would not go on easily. . . . He is the leader and not I nor any other one."[11] With charm, care, and not a little talent, Morin accordingly set to work. At first, he continued in the same letter, "I almost believed I was alone in my way of thinking, and that unless I should modify it, I was not to consider myself as representing the general opinion here." But, within a few weeks, having "conversed with many of the Members and other Liberals," he had won over "a large portion of the members" to the conviction that "the Reformers of both provinces must and will act together, although circumstances particular to each Province put them respectively in a different position." Neilson himself made no definite commitment: "it is very difficult," Morin continued "to guess what he

[10]Papiers LaFontaine, Hincks to LaFontaine, April 6, 19, 1841.
[11]Hincks Papers, Morin to Hincks, May 8, 1841.

will or will not do, but when you meet him personally, you will find him very accommodating. I am sure he is not for violence or for creating difficulties." Neilson had at least listened. And his followers had succumbed to Morin's charms—or arguments. As Morin reported to Hincks, "Not two, perhaps not one, of the Quebec members would be for the line of policy recommended in those articles of the *Aurore*; as to the Montreal members I would be very much surprised if they thought otherwise than we do." And this Morin could count as victory enough.

Thus, when Neilson rose in the House to propose his long-feared amendment on June 23, he suggested a rather indefinite statement which refrained from attacking the Upper Canadians and included only a general condemnation of the Union. There was nothing in it which Morin, Parent, and even some six Upper Canadian Reformers could not approve easily enough. Indeed Morin seconded the motion. It was defeated, of course, but for the LaFontaine group it was a partial victory. Both factions had come to some kind of an agreement on how to conduct themselves towards their fellow Reformers from the west. But they had still not adjusted to trusting and working closely with them.

Hincks' communications, and the mildness of Neilson's amendment notwithstanding, the French-Canadian members remained unconvinced about the value of co-operation. They felt lost in the new capital, unimpressed by the reaction of the Upper Canadian Reformers, suspicious still that the Union must, after all, destroy them as a distinct nation. Kingston, "la ville bien aimée de milord Sydenham, le Grand Turc du Pays," as *Le Fantasque* described it on September 23, baffled them. They found it (*Le Canadien*, July 7, 1841) "une ville sans physionomie, sans caractère," and they wondered at its diseased climate in which "l'eau surtout [est] presqu'impotable; le jour un atmosphère de plomb qui vous tue, le soir une brise humide qui vous glace." Accustomed as he was to the enchantment of the Laurentians, Caron, in Kingston to attend the Legislative Council, wrote to Abbé Cazeau: "Pourquoi a-t-on choisi cette maussade place pour y faire le siège du gouvernement? La ville elle-même est passable, bien vite cependant vous en avez assez.[12]

The *Canadiens*, too, felt uneasy about the procedures of the new parliament—as if their own had since 1791 been a model of decorum. The day before the opening, when the Assembly met by proclamation to elect a speaker, instead of following the usual custom of summoning

[12]AAQ, G XI, 73, Caron à Cazeau, 12 juil. 1841.

the members to the bar of the Legislative Council, the Governor General met them—incredible!—on horseback outside. Was this, Neilson wondered (*La Gazette*, June 17), a "déviation de la part des usages établis qui pourrait frapper de nullité tous les actes de la Session." The *Canadien* members also complained about the manners of their colleagues. "Rien de plus curieux," *Le Fantasque* reported on September 27, "que l'intérieur de ce corps législatif. Les membres étaient juchés les uns sur les autres.... Tous parlaient ensemble, ... les cris, les rires, et quelques fois d'énergiques jurons faisaient retentir la salle, et ... une chaleur suffocante en chassait les personnes délicates ... cela ressemblait plus à une anti-chambre d'auberge."

But the new French members were disgusted by more than parliamentary bad manners. They found that the Upper Canadians, in their hurry to support Sydenham's "legislation unjust towards Lower Canada,"[13] presented a most unco-operative and unhopeful aspect. They counted, for instance, only six who dared support the amendment which Neilson had been persuaded to modify especially to avoid offending Upper Canada; they saw also how easily the Reformers agreed to Sydenham's Upper Canadian Municipal Council bill, a measure which did not really concern them, but whose Lower Canadian equivalent they themselves had vehemently protested in 1840. They concluded—not too surprisingly since they had considered in 1839 that the Upper Canadians had agreed to the Union only because their debt would be shared with Lower Canada—that the western Reformers had again sold their support to the Governor, this time for the promise of an imperial guarantee for a loan of £1,500,000, two-thirds of which would be spent in Upper Canada on a vast programme of public works. Even Hincks admitted: "I can hardly be surprized that the Lower Canadian members are disgusted at the conduct of our Reformers. I am so myself."[14]

Neilson's followers agreed. "Je n'ai pas grand espoir," wrote Glackmeyer, "que notre Province obtienne aucune justice. MM. du Haut Canada me paraissent si contents du fantôme de gouvernement responsable qu'ils ont qu'ils consentent à se passer de la réalité."[15] LaFontaine's friends had little to answer. "Les réformistes," wrote Quesnel with a touch of irony, "sont de fort bonnes gens et surtout très prudents; ils veulent être nos amis, ils sont ceux du gouvernement, et ne sont pas ennemis du million et demi qu'on leur propose, de sorte

[13]Neilson Collection, X, 271–3, Glackmeyer to Neilson, Sept. 1, 1841.
[14]Papiers LaFontaine, Hincks to LaFontaine, June 29, 1841.
[15]Neilson Collection, X, 197–9, Glackmeyer à Neilson, 30 juin 1841.

que tout ira le mieux du monde pour eux."[16] "Notre position est très difficile," Aylwin admitted, "il n'y a pas à se fier aux Hauts-Canadiens."[17]

The French began to fear that even their own pro-Union members might be bought. Amédée Papineau wrote to Duvernay:

Quant au Parlement de Thompson [sic], & le parti qui s'y dit réformiste (la section d'en haut surtout), c'est une infamie. Voyez la corruption. Morin même, Morin qui cherche à se vendre, qui est sur le marché de la corruption!!! O tempora! o Mores! Quel siècle! Quel monde! Quel Canadien qui peut désormais consentir à recevoir une charge des mains ensanglantées des bourreaux de ses frères? Honte! haine! & mépris éternel pour quiconque en acceptera! Qu'il soit infâme!!![18]

In fact, Morin had been summoned to the Governor's at Alwington House and offered the solicitor-generalship of Lower Canada. He had considered the offer, travelled to Montreal and Quebec to seek advice, and returned to Kingston on July 7, still unable to choose between the conflicting pressures from Parent—who suggested the *unionnaires* sign a collective statement promising support to any government that included Morin—and from the Neilson-Viger group who, naturally, looked upon any compromise as treason. Morin finally refused, "inquiet, obsédé" (as Caron reported it) "par les offres et propositions qu'on lui fait. Le cher homme, je le plains de tout mon cœur, il serait temps qu'il commençât à jouir de la vie."[19]

What a disillusionment, indeed, was the brave new tomorrow that LaFontaine, Morin, and Parent had planned. Denis-Emery Papineau had never believed in it, and now he gloated to his cousin Amédée about the parliament of minorities:

. . . des taxes générales à payer, des impositions locales à supporter; de mauvaises lois mal administrées, une chambre à la disposition du plus abominable gouverneur que le pays ait encore sur le dos. Maintenant que faire? Attendre et jusqu'à quand? Jusqu'à ce que les temps soient accomplis. Les membres libéraux du Bas Canada ne pressent pas les mesures populaires à cause de la *majorité Thomson* et celle-ci, ou plutôt les ministres ne présentent pas leurs mesures parce qu'ils craignent que leur majorité composée d'éléments étrangers ne se morcelle et donne la majorité aux libéraux. Voilà la position délicate et incertaine, douteuse, fausse où se trouve les partis.[20]

Barthe concluded in *L'Aurore* on July 13. "Il faut avouer encore que tout ce qui s'est passé dans le parlement-uni jusqu'à ce jour n'est pas

---

[16]Papiers LaFontaine, Quesnel à LaFontaine, 17 juin 1841.
[17]*Ibid.*, Aylwin à LaFontaine, 22 juin 1841.
[18]Papiers Duvernay, 512, A. Papineau à Duvernay, 9 juil. 1841.
[19]AAQ, G XI, 73, Caron à Cazeau, 12 juil. 1841.
[20]Collection Papineau-Bourassa, D.-E. Papineau à A. Papineau, 15 juil. 1841.

très propre à nous rassurer sur les sentimens qui animent les Hauts Canadiens à notre égard." And when one of the Upper Canadian members disclosed to him that he thought the Union could not last, La Gazette reported Barthe's reply (July 24): "que je désespérais beaucoup, en effet, de la longue amitié des époux qui se trouvaient déjà si mal en lune de miel." LaFontaine, Hincks, Parent, and the other unionnaires were certainly asking the Canadien politicians to show greater faith than is demanded of most.

Meanwhile the priests found their worst fears about the Union confirmed. On July 20, 1841, the Solicitor General (East), Charles Dewey Day, the Tory member for Ottawa County who despite his personal tact and smiling good temper was a special target of the Canadiens, introduced into the Assembly a bill for the establishment of common schools throughout the province. According to the project, a system of elementary education was to be set up, based on non-denominational primary schools administered by appointed (and the first ones were mainly English-speaking) district wardens and financed by taxes and by government grants taken from the funds of the Jesuit estates.[21] The French-Canadian bishops were, naturally, alarmed, but they were probably not surprised. For one thing, they had already studied and rejected Charles Buller's plan; for another, they had read a series of forty-seven articles by Charles Mondelet published during November and December 1840 in the new Montreal paper, the Canada Times.

In these articles, translated and sold in pamphlet form (1,700 copies) under the title Lettres sur l'éducation élémentaire et pratique, Mondelet had urged a school system in which, although French would be taught, English would dominate along with non-sectarian Bible classes designed to "faire disparaître les odieuses distinctions nationales" and "disposer ... à des sentiments de bienveillance mutuelle les différentes parties de la société."[22] He also proposed that the schools be financed by a fund made up of revenues gathered from government grants, taxes, the Crown lands, and the Jesuit estates. When the Solicitor General tabled his bill in July 1841, there seemed little doubt either that he had modelled it on Mondelet's plan or that Mondelet himself had seen the original draft a year earlier. The bishops may have

[21]J. C. Dent, The Last Forty Years (2 vols., Toronto, 1881), I, 145–6; L. P. Audet, "La Surintendance de l'éducation et la loi scolaire de 1841," Cahiers des Dix (1960), p. 147.
[22]Quoted in L. P. Audet, "Charles Mondelet et l'éducation," La Société Royale du Canada, Mémoires, IIIᵉ Série, LI (1957), s. 1, 1–28.

wondered, as many did then and since, whether or not Sydenham had invited Mondelet to write the articles.[23] Certainly they knew the latter had been a strong *unionnaire*, as was his publisher, the editor of the *Canada Times*, William Walker—another close friend of LaFontaine's and one of the few who had shared in the initial correspondence with Hincks. At all events the bishops felt the challenge, both to their schools and to their claim to the Jesuit estates.

As usual when they considered their rights imperilled, the bishops sought out the Governor General. From Rome, in the midst of his first European tour, Bishop Bourget reminded his Vicar-General back in Montreal: "Il semble que le gouvernement va s'occuper enfin de l'éducation. Vous veillerez soigneusement sur les intérêts de la religion."[24] The two administrators he left behind sent an official protest to Kingston asking that the bill not be sanctioned "avant que l'opinion des Catholiques et des autres dénominations religieuses ait eu le temps de se manifester."[25] In the old capital, Archbishop Signay wrote directly to Sydenham, underlining the "manque presqu'absolu de contrôle du clergé sur l'éducation" in the bill, and warning that "le projet proposé ne saurait atteindre le but pour lequel il a été dressé, et qu'il suscitera s'il devient loi un mécontentement général au grand préjudice de l'éducation."[26] Indeed, the priests were beginning to realize that the strength of public opinion might provide a telling argument. Mondelet had used the press; so would they.

In 1840, Bourget had fulfilled a long-cherished dream by arranging for the publication of a religious newspaper, *Les Mélanges Religieux*. With Abbé Jean-Charles Prince as editor, and, of all people, the anticlerical radical Jacques Plinguet as printer, it began regular publication on January 22, 1841. At first it had disseminated chatty clerical morals, pious pieces of advice, and ultramontane dissertations against Lamennais and for de Bonald. Now it found a new purpose. Beginning on July 23, 1841, three days after the education bill was introduced, it inaugurated a series: "Réponse aux lettres de M. Charles Mondelet sur l'éducation élémentaire." In these, over the signature "Un Catholique," the clergy's new organ attacked, among other items, the nonsectarian public school.

[23]T. Matheson, "Les Origines de la surintendance de l'éducation au Bas-Canada, 1830–42," *Bulletin de Recherches historiques*, 1957, pp. 93–7, argues that Mondelet had no connection with Sydenham. Audet argues that he did (see "La Surintendance de l'éducation" and "Charles Mondelet").
[24]AAM, Bourget, Lettres personnelles, 13, Bourget à Hudon, 22 juil. 1841.
[25]*Les Mélanges Religieux*, 20 août 1841.
[26]AAQ, Régistre des lettres, 19, 526, Signay à Sydenham, 17 août 1841.

Les écoles élémentaires ouvertes à toutes les croyances deviennent donc la destruction de toute croyance et par suite de toute morale individuelle et publique. . . . Partout où le clergé catholique instruit et dirige, il y a loyauté, moralité, progrès, paix, et bonheur. L'influence catholique ne crée ni fanatisme, ni querelle religieuse, ni désunion quelquonque. On le voit bien par la sympathie, la disposition amicale que lui conservent ceux-mêmes d'une religion différente qui ont fréquenté, quelque temps nos maisons d'éducation.

As to the use of monies from the Jesuit estates, the paper declared on August 13:

C'est avec l'argent pris au dépôt sacré, confié dès l'origine à l'Eglise catholique de ce pays, dépôt ravi, c'est bien vrai! depuis un demi-siècle à son légitime propriétaire, mais enfin, dépôt sacré et qui réclame sans cesse son maître . . . c'est l'héritage de l'Eglise Catholique que l'on distribue ainsi à qui l'on veut, à des ennemis peut-être! et dans la distribution de ces deniers l'on ne donne même pas un vote, une admission quelquonque aux chefs de cette Eglise.

Bishop Turgeon decided it would be even more practical to contact the members of parliament themselves. Shortly after the bill had gone to committee on August 10 he wrote to Neilson asking his aid; "nous sommes de mauvaise humeur, nous nous affligeons sur notre avenir; mais nous comptons sur vos efforts pour nous préserver des malheurs que nous appréhendons."[27] And Neilson agreed—as indeed he and Viger must, since, as the spokesmen for French-Canadian particularism, they apprehended more than most how essential to *la survivance* a French and Catholic education system was. In the House they became the main spokesmen against the bill; and in their newspapers they launched an editorial campaign. *L'Aurore* reprinted a number of articles in late July and early August, "Lettres sur l'éducation populaire," which the education expert, Jean-Baptiste Meilleur, had prepared for Arthur Buller in 1838. In these Meilleur struck a note more familiar and orthodox than Mondelet's: "Notre origine, notre foi, notre langue et notre nationalité sont trop intéressées à [l'éducation des enfants] pour nous permettre d'être un instant indifférents à ce qui peut y avoir trait."[28] *La Gazette de Québec* on July 17 groaned at the prospect of (educational) wars of religion: "Il s'amasse de nouveaux nuages sur notre horizon, nos malheureuses dissensions publiques vont se compliquer des questions religieuses qui agitent en ce moment l'Angleterre, l'Irlande, la France, la Belgique et les Etats-Unis: celle de l'exclusion de l'enseignement religieux proprement dit,

[27]*Ibid.*, 19, 531, Turgeon à Neilson, 17 août 1841.
[28]J.-B. Meilleur, "Mémorial sur l'éducation," quoted in A. Forget, *Histoire du Collège de l'Assomption* (Montréal, 1933), p. 24.

des écoles mixtes de Catholiques et de Protestants." It also sounded the theme of language and faith, blaming Mondelet for forgetting that the French Revolution was due to the decline of religious education on July 20 and for suggesting non-sectarian classes, "ce compromis entre toutes les croyances, cette apostasie de toutes les religions," on August 5.

Nevertheless the bill received royal assent on September 18, after several amendments had been passed, dealing especially with the office of superintendent and reserving the funds from the Jesuit estates to secondary education. The clergy had not succeeded entirely, but what it had accomplished it owed to the intervention of Viger and Neilson, to the influence of *L'Aurore* and *La Gazette*, as well as to its own *Mélanges*. Did the bishops wonder at the increasingly apparent connection between, on the one hand, those who inspired the law, like Buller and Mondelet, and the *unionnaires* like LaFontaine, Parent, and Morin; and, on the other hand, those who defended Catholic and French education and opposed the Union. LaFontaine himself may have wondered at this continuing alliance between the clergy and a political group which included such anti-clericals and/or independent thinkers such as Viger, Boucher de Belleville, and the young Papineaus. "Je suis sous le rapport religieux et politique ce que vous m'avez connu en 1837," the ex-editor of *L'Aurore*, who at the time of the rebellion had been one of the foremost anti-clericals, wrote to Duvernay, "mais notre position est tellement changée. . . . Je ne connais pas aujourd'hui un seul Canadien qui ne soit pas *patriote* au moins de cœur. Les prêtres le sont *tous*. Ceux mêmes que vous avez connu pour les plus violents torys sont aujourd'hui complètement changés."[29]

At the time when, despite LaFontaine's strategy and Morin's charm, most politicians continued sceptical about the Union, the propaganda of the Church against the education bill might easily dash all Parent's and LaFontaine's hopes. If a real alliance with the Upper Canadians were to materialize, LaFontaine needed a friendlier performance by the western Reformers themselves. He needed the intervention of Robert Baldwin.

Hincks had long ago convinced LaFontaine of Baldwin's sincere goodwill towards Lower Canada and of his desire to see justice done. "Come what will," he wrote, "I am anxious that you should believe what I know to be the case, that Mr. Baldwin is incorruptible."[30] LaFontaine knew it but his followers did not. Back in May 1841

[29]Papiers Duvernay, 489, Belleville à Duvernay, 9 mai 1841.
[30]Papiers LaFontaine, Hincks to LaFontaine, Feb. 22, 1841.

Baldwin had travelled to Montreal to plead for himself. While there, Sydenham had proposed to swear him in as a member of the Executive Council. Baldwin then seized the opportunity not only to demonstrate his "exceedingly strict principles" as the Governor noted, but also his sympathy for French-Canadian feelings and traditions. He objected to the oath of supremacy because it denied authority within the realm to any foreign prelate; he argued that in Canada the Pope exercised an authority recognized by the British government. Surely French Canadians would take to such a man, a man who declared that even "if he were sure of being deserted by the whole of Upper Canada, he would stand by the Reformers of Lower Canada."[31]

A month after this incident, Baldwin took a second step that pleased the *Canadiens*. He demanded of Sydenham that French politicians be included in the "cabinet," and, on being refused, resigned on the very day of the opening of parliament. Here was a champion for French Canada indeed! But Baldwin was to do more than resign. He arranged to have the defeated LaFontaine elected in the very heart of Upper Canada.

On August 15 Baldwin surprised LaFontaine with a note announcing that he had persuaded his constituents in the Fourth Riding of York (for he had himself been elected in two ridings) to elect LaFontaine in his place. "Under other circumstances," he explained, "I would not have taken this step without first having consulted yourself, but it appeared to me calculated to produce a better effect that you should have in no way been consulted beforehand."[32] LaFontaine answered as soon as he could, asking Baldwin to arrange for Morin to do anything necessary before his own arrival.[33] He was nominated at a meeting at Sharon on August 21 and reached Toronto a few days later to spend three weeks in the riding. Parent accompanied him, making sure, through regular reports to *Le Canadien* that Lower Canada could follow the details of LaFontaine's reception. Even before the final results were announced, he emphasized the significance of the victory. He needed to, for neither *La Gazette* nor *L'Aurore* gave it any attention. In particular, he drove home the message that LaFontaine, Baldwin, and all those who had nurtured the political marriage wanted the French to hear.

Que je vous dis un mot des braves gens que j'ai rencontré à New Market. Si tous les habitants du Haut-Canada leur ressemblent, je peux prédire les

[31]*Ibid.*, Hincks to LaFontaine, May 29, 1841.
[32]*Ibid.*, Baldwin to LaFontaine, Aug. 15, 1841.
[33]*Ibid.*, LaFontaine to Baldwin, Aug. 19, 1841.

plus brillants résultats de l'Union des Canadas. . . . Ils élisent M. Lafontaine [*sic*] pour montrer, disent-ils, leur sympathie envers les Bas-Canadiens, et leur détestation des mauvais traitements et des injustices auxquelles nous avons été exposés. (*Le Canadien*, September 27)

LaFontaine was returned for Fourth York on September 23, 1841, three days after Sydenham's death. The next day, he set out on the trip back to Lower Canada. Even as he travelled, Sydenham lay in state at St. George's in Kingston. LaFontaine might well have savoured his victory. Step by step, by judicial concession and clever manœuvring, he had drawn his people out of discouragement and isolation. Now, as a member from Upper Canada, he would melt down the *Canadiens'* distrust of their neighbours. But this, he knew, was only a beginning. The Union was still a fearful thing. Indeed, he could never truly win until the Union could be made to serve Lower Canada's interests.

At that very moment, the imperial cabinet was drawing up the Instructions of Sir Charles Bagot, the man who would deliver the last and most telling argument in the Union debate, and whose qualifications so to do had been excellently sketched by Charles Buller in a letter to Sir Robert Peel. He had written about the ideal governor:

He must be a humane just man who will have the liberality & good sense to raise up those, whom we have been forced to put down in Canada. I allude especially to the French. We have put down their rebellion, destroyed their nationality, & in doing this reduced them to a miserable state of social subjection. The governor that would raise them up to a social equality by mere justice & kindness would make them the instruments instead of the enemies of Government. The French Canadians, if rightly managed, are the natural instrument by which the Government could keep in check the democratic and American tendencies of Upper Canada.[34]

[34]C. Buller to Peel, Sept. 9, 1841, quoted in P. Knaplund, ed., "The Buller-Peel Correspondence Regarding Canada," *Canadian Historical Review*, VIII (1927), 43–4.

6

Sir Charles Bagot
January-September 1842

On January 10, 1842, two hundred sleighs, their riders bundled in buffalo robes, jingled into Kingston, while along the shore of frozen Lake Ontario, informal groups waved their greetings to the handsome, courtly, old diplomat arriving as their new governor general. Two days later, hundreds of people filled the drawing rooms of Alwington House where Sir Charles Bagot, splendid in his decorations and court uniform greeted the capital's leading citizens.

Bagot had been the centre of *Canadien* discussions for some months now. His appointment, announced in London on September 27, 1841, was reported in *Le Canadien* on October 8, and the Lower Canadians who had wasted no tears on Sydenham had begun immediately to speculate on his successor. What they knew did not impress them. In fact, they had never heard of him. "*L'Unicorn* qui vient d'arriver," commented Aubin on October 11 in *Le Fantasque*: "annonce comme définitive la nomination de Sir Charles. . . . nous ne savons encore qui, attendu que quelques journaux l'appellent Pageot, d'autres Pagot, d'autres Bagot; nous croyons que c'est un Fagot." They were told that he was a diplomat, not a good recommendation as *Le Canadien* noted (October 8): "Ainsi il paraît que d'une administration-loup nous allons passer dans une administration-renard." On October 21 *L'Aurore* declared that "dans la présente condition de cette colonie toute autre chose qu'un diplomate eut convenu."

Meanwhile officials and politicians converged on Quebec to greet the Governor General as he landed. Was it their sentiments which Aubin reflected in an open letter in *Le Fantasque* (October 25) which he directed to Sir Charles? In it he presented the usual catalogue of the country's wants—free elections, impartial distribution of patronage, public funds spent only with public approval, the return of the exiles and of the capital, the right of each citizen to "parler la langue qui lui plaît le plus"—concluding with a dramatic appeal not to "suivre la trace de vos devanciers, couper, tailler dans nos institutions, nous écraser, nous torturer," but "liez-nous ensemble et au char de votre souveraine par l'amitié, par la reconnaissance et soyez sûr que l'intérêt, c'est à dire l'amour du bien être, de la paix fera le reste. . . . Vous avez dans vos mains la verge du despotisme et la branche de l'olivier. Nous choisirons cette dernière si notre honneur n'y doit rien perdre." Be that as it may, state, church, and citizenry waited in vain. Bagot's ship was driven back by gales delaying his arrival.

Because it was now winter, he had to come by the American route, duly arriving in Kingston on January 10, 1842. Whatever feelings were hurt by the delay, he was soon deluged with the customary congratulations and praise. Archbishop Signay wrote nostalgically: "Aujourd'hui les citoyens de Québec se trouvent privés d'un honneur qu'ils ont toujours grandement apprécié, celui d'être les premiers à offrir leurs hommages au Représentant de l'Autorité Royale," but he prayed that the new Governor "contribuera à établir sur des bases solides l'harmonie qu'il est si désirable de voir régner parmi les sujets de Sa Majesté."[1] Bishop Bourget sent Jacques Viger to deliver personally his message of welcome. Addresses came from Quebec, Montreal, Three Rivers, from different patriotic societies, all entertaining bright hopes for a successful administration. The Tory press, of course, gave the Governor unqualified praise, but the French newspapers used his arrival as an excuse to repeat, with almost pathological insistence, all the old arguments against the Union.

When the news of Bagot's appointment had first reached Canada, L'Aurore had begun what became a six-month campaign for repeal. In a series which included titles such as "Du véritable patriotisme," "Du bon gouvernement," "Le gouvernement responsable," "L'avenir du Canada," Barthe, back in Montreal after the session and as discontented and rattlebrained as ever, repeated all the old points. The arrival of the new Governor, he claimed on October 30, this "homme nouveau, comme arbitrateur de nos inquiétantes destinées," should encourage the Canadiens once more to agitate against the Union. Perhaps, he suggested on October 26, they should organize another petition and send deputies to London to "solliciter, par tous les moyens imaginables, le rappel d'union, qui ne laisse rien à envisager que notre destruction politique. Si le pays se sent capable de sacrifices pour opérer son salut, c'est l'heure de les faire." For the Union was

[1]AAQ, Régistre des lettres, 19, 650, Signay à Bagot, 17 jan. 1842.

destined, need they be reminded, to assimilate them, and that in the name of an illogical principle, the impossibility of which this last session has amply shown: "Le résultat de la session législative, conduite par l'opération de Lord Sydenham dans *son Versailles Kingstonien,* est bien propre à nous faire prendre le gouvernement responsable dans les colonies pour une utopie parfaite (November 16). Nous fûmes frappés d'infériorité, brevetés d'incapacité par d'indignes représentans d'un souverain britannique" (November 11). Now, he saw a God-sent opportunity. With enthusiasm and renewed unity of purpose "devant la nouvelle vice-royauté qui s'élève," the *Canadiens* might succeed at last in bringing down the Union, or as he put it (October 30), "de faire triompher . . . la cause de la morale, de la vérité, de la justice, et de la liberté."

Denis-Benjamin Viger felt likewise. When the Governor arrived in January, he began a series in *L'Aurore*—"Le rappel de l'Union"—that continued regularly until March 1842 and began again that June. The strain he heard, however, was of a higher mood. He averred on January 25 that Bagot, "un homme habile, conciliateur généreux et éclairé . . . qui a été témoin de l'opération de l'union de la Hollande et de la Belgique, et qui contemple aujourd'hui les résultats de cette iniquité," must realize, and accordingly might well correct, the horrors of the Union, the venal and unrepresentative parliament it included, and most of all the flagrant violation of natural law.

Qui dit *anglification,* prêche sans déguisement la persécution la plus fanatique puisqu'elle s'attaque à ce qu'il y a de plus sacré dans la nature de l'homme, sa nationalité; qui dit *anglification* autorise et justifie les six siècles de martyre politique et religieux par lesquels l'Irlande, cette malheureuse entre toutes les nations, a passé; qui dit *anglification* invoque le bouleversement dans l'ordre établi par la Providence dans les arrangements sociaux de l'Univers, et médite d'intervertir toutes les règles du droit naturel et du droit public. Ce sont là les suites de l'Union. (June 21)

Indeed, if he really wished for "la paix et la prospérité de ce pays," the Governor must naturally become an ally of the *Canadiens* and their separate state: "le mot d'ordre de Sir Charles doit être RAPPEL DE L'UNION" (February 11). Barthe had called for a deputation to London; Viger recommended instead that the Governor might welcome a solemn national protest from French Canada, arrived at by the simultaneous passage by each municipal council of an identical resolution against the Union.[2] He also suggested that Bagot dissolve parliament

²*L'Aurore,* 18, 22 fév., 1842; see also *La Gazette de Québec,* 24 fév. 1842.

and call another general election on the constitutional issue, an election which would, this time, give a truer picture of *Canadien* sentiments: "Election—voilà le cri que nous voulons faire retentir d'un bout du Canada à l'autre."

Parent, who according to one of Neilson's correspondents "seems to be becoming quite a Government man,"[3] wrote more realistically. In an article about the incipient régime continuing through three issues (November 15, 17, and 19), he asked:

Que demandons-nous? que la Métropole passe l'éponge sur l'Acte d'Union des Canadas, qu'elle établisse le gouvernement de ces colonies sur de nouvelles bases? Non, le Bas-Canada n'exige pas cela; il sacrifiera ce point aux idées métropolitaines malgré les inconvénients pratiques du régime. Mais ce que nous voulons et ne cesserons jamais d'exiger, c'est que l'on fasse disparaître de la nouvelle constitution tout ce qui froisse le principe de l'égalité entre les deux populations et les deux pays.

He had little patience for Barthe's parochial escapism. He preferred to co-operate with the Governor, "s'il veut être juste, et respecter nos droits" (October 22). Neilson, on the other hand, reprinted Viger's articles from *L'Aurore* in the French *Gazette* on January 15 and 18 and February 24 and left no doubt whose side he favoured. But he wasted no time in writing articles of his own; instead he called a public meeting for March 15, 1842.

On the appointed night, the Ecole des Glacis was filled to capacity, and hundreds of people stood outside in the cold. Neilson chaired the meeting, Glackmeyer was secretary, and to waves of applause, speeches were delivered by Neilson's friends, the young lawyer from Dorchester, André Taschereau, and the well-known artist, Joseph Légaré, who had been one of the few active rebels in the district of Quebec in 1837. Parent, whom *La Gazette* had flayed five days earlier —"la tergiversation, la vénalité, la fourberie, et la mauvaise foi ont marqué ses traces"—attended, but Morin and Aylwin did not. Neilson proposed, and the enthusiastic crowd accepted, another Lettre des Electeurs de Québec aux Electeurs de la Province which asked for an avalanche of petitions against the Union and the retention of denominational schools. Unfortunately for Neilson, the appeal was not heard too widely. At Saint-Siméon-de-Rimouski on April 8 some habitants met and forwarded a petition asking for repeal, but in Portneuf on May 25 Aylwin chaired a meeting his constituents had called and made certain that the resolution attacking the Union and demanding an election also included two congratulatory messages, one to Robert

3Neilson Collection, X, 300–1, Wicksteed to Neilson, Dec. 28, 1841.

Baldwin for his conduct towards French Canada, and the other to the electors of Fourth York. There were few other meetings. Doubtless the *Canadiens* were bored by now with the old same arguments; also they were already feeling the effects of Bagot's new policies.

Although neither Parent, nor Neilson, nor Barthe, nor any other of those fierce debaters realized it until well into the late summer of 1842, "le règne de Charles Bagot" would conclude the Union debate. Even before his departure from the mother country, the new Governor had meditated seriously on the French-Canadian question, helped by a surprising number of letters on the subject from sources most varied but all in agreement on the solution they advised. From Lord Seaton, the man whom the *Canadiens* hated so deeply, he received a penetrating analysis of the present position of the French in Canada, advising him that "the population of French origin are to be recovered by attention to their wants, and that they will prove less troublesome than the Yankee classes settled in the Western districts. A few of the young Priests have been corrupted but the ecclesiastics generally of the R. Catholic community are very respectable, and will be found ready to work with a Governor inclined to improve the condition of the Seignories."[4] And in a letter from the Earl of Westmorland, Bagot read a memorandum to the effect that

the Canadians, as a nation, had resisted LaFayette & Washington. They had remained unvitiated through the great French Revolution & loyal to their new Dynasty under every change until the wandering, unguided Emigrants from Great Britain . . . in the form of Usurers, Missionaries, Demagogues, Paupers wandered without distinction, & intruded themselves amongst a people who were unable to cope with adventurers, as much their superiors in craft and subtilty [sic] as in Industry and enterprize.

To secure a return of this traditional loyalty, Westmorland suggested, Bagot must devote all his care to the *Canadiens'* "Ancestorial [sic] customs."[5] The Governor-elect even heard from LeBlanc de Marconnay, now in Paris: he offered his services, underlining that Bagot's mission should be "de concilier les esprits plutôt que de les aigrir."[6]

From all of these messages, there could be only one conclusion: if the Governor seriously intended to preserve the British connection, as indeed by his office he must, his first duty should be to recover the loyalty and sympathy of the French Canadians. And the best

[4]Bagot Papers, 10, Lord Seaton to Murray, Sept. 6, 1841; Murray to Bagot, Oct. 7, 1841.
[5]*Ibid.*, 10, Westmorland to Bagot, Nov. 7, 1841.
[6]*Ibid.*, 10, de Marconnay à Bagot, 23 oct. 1841.

means to achieve this, he was told, was to cater to their sensitivities, to treat them as true British subjects. He could not know it as yet, but this was very close to the advice which, had he asked, he might have received from LaFontaine or Parent.

Within a month after his arrival Bagot had come to the same conclusions; and, all unknowing of the price he would eventually have to pay, he set out immediately to heal the tensions and strains of the Union. At the end of January, when he received Mayor Caron, John Neilson, and William Walker, who had travelled from Quebec to present the old capital's address of welcome signed by 6,997 *Québecois*, he departed from the usual custom of acknowledgment. Instead of repeating the words of the address, he spoke of "my determination to know no distinctions of National or Religious creed,"[7] and told these proud men who still regretted the loss of the capital how sorry he was that he had been unable to land at the ancient port. To Archbishop Signay, he wrote in elegant French, in his own hand, a long letter in which he reiterated his intention to "vous prouver mon désir ardent d'établir et de maintenir sur des bases les plus solides et les plus égales, cette harmonie qui doit toujours régner parmi les sujets de notre Auguste Souveraine, et de cimenter de plus en plus les liens qui les attachent à Son Trône."[8] Indeed, he wanted to go to Lower Canada as soon as possible, "visiting Montreal, Quebec and other places," he wrote to the new Colonial Secretary, Lord Stanley, "making personal acquaintance with members for that part of the Colony, and using my endeavours to produce a good impression upon the French part of the population."[9] But even before this tour, he began to conciliate.

First he made a number of appointments, each a minor thing, but each of great symbolic value. Bagot, deeply human, understood what he described to his friend, Mr. Grenville, as "the universal thirst for place, every man in this land, no matter who—comes to my excellency and hopes it will please it to give him a small (he always means large) place in some public office."[10] He seems to have understood the importance of even the smallest political appointment to a nation rendered, by what it considered a policy of exclusion, extremely sensitive to the proportion of its representation in the public place. "It is

[7]*Ibid.*, 9, Bagot to Stanley, Jan. 25, 1842. See also G. P. Glazebrook, *Sir Charles Bagot in Canada* (Oxford, 1929).

[8]AAQ, G VII, 23, Bagot à Signay, 21 jan. 1841. Bagot's letters to the French Canadians were usually in French; Sydenham's were mostly in English.

[9]Bagot Papers, 7, Bagot to Stanley, Jan. 1842.

[10]PAC, MG 24, B 32, Grenville Papers, Bagot to Grenville, March 27, 1842.

despairing," he wrote in the same letter, "to see how they always take justice and kindness only as instalments of their own unreasonable pretensions wrung from our sense of their consequence, but it is none the less my duty and my policy to administer these ingredients to them as I propose to do as soon as I get amongst them."

When he arrived the Governor found that the Administrator, Sir Richard Jackson, had published a list of some one hundred and thirteen appointments (district court judges, syndics, clerks, customs inspectors, court treasurers, municipal council secretaries) completing the government reorganization of the new province. The *Canadiens*, for the first time, held a high proportion of the posts—district judgeships went to Morin, Mondelet, and the Quebec lawyer and friend of Parent's, M. Huot; and various clerkships to, among others, Taché, Turcotte, and Salaberry. Bagot could not take credit for this, but he shared much of it by adding more *Canadien* names himself and, despite editorials by the French-hating *Montreal Herald* and *Courier*, by confirming all the others. Parent exulted on January 10:

Les Canadiens français accoutumés jusqu'à présent à ne recevoir que les miettes qui tombaient de la table des enfants favoris ont été cette fois conviés au festin en nombre remarquable. . . . Les nominations de MM. Huot et Morin surtout en feront pardonner beaucoup d'autres. Nous devons rendre à l'exécutif la justice de dire qu'en choisissant ces deux hommes, il a non seulement assuré au public deux serviteurs capables et intègres, mais qu'en outre il a payé la dette du pays.

Later, in mid-February, Bagot acted himself. He conferred the title of Queen's Counsel on Cherrier, one well placed, as a partisan of LaFontaine and a cousin of most of the anti-*unionnaires*, to influence his compatriots toward what Bagot hoped would be "the commencement of a better feeling."[11] And, in fact, one of the cousins, T. Bruneau, reflected to another, Amédée Papineau: "la nomination de Côme est bonne, il est toujours le même homme, cette place d'honneur ne change pas ses principes, il pourra rendre des services importants au Pays."[12] The new Governor had apparently avoided the impression of trying to make *vendus*.

In May Bagot took two other steps designed to convince French Canada of his sincerity which were far more fundamental to *la survivance* than the appointment of a large number of French-sounding names to public posts. By the first, he settled the fears of the

[11]Bagot Papers, 9, Bagot to Stanley, Feb. 23, 1842; see also *La Gazette de Québec*, 15 fév. 1842.
[12]Collection Papineau-Bourassa, Bruneau à A. Papineau, 1 mai 1842.

French about the new education system; by the second, he ensured that French Canada's particular legal system would endure.

During the press campaign against the education bill the editors of *Les Mélanges*, *La Gazette de Québec*, and *L'Aurore* had all attacked the bill's provision to place the whole system of education under the control of a single superintendent. "La pensée mère de ce projet," *Les Mélanges* complained (August 13, 1841) "est de concentrer dans les mains d'un seul homme (qui peut être étranger aux Canadiens, étranger à leur religion) tous les pouvoirs nécessaires pour former à son goût la jeunesse du pays." But once the plan became law, the French bishops, like the heads of all other denominations, hurried to promote the appointment of their own candidate. Bishop Bourget wanted that erudite man of letters, Jacques Viger, and, having persuaded Archbishop Signay to agree, wrote a high recommendation to Sir Richard Jackson.[13] The Governor, of course, had to consider more than the fears of the Catholic bishops. "How is it possible," he wrote to Stanley, "without exciting, and very fairly, too, the apprehension of every sort and denomination in the country, except that to which the person appointed may belong, to fill up such an office?"[14] He did find it possible, however; and by spring he had solved the riddle by appointing a nominal superintendent whose duties would in reality be carried out by two deputies, one for each section of the province.

For Lower Canada, after having offered the post to Parent, he chose, not Bourget's nominee, but Jean-Baptiste Meilleur, the author of the series which *L'Aurore* had used against Mondelet's plan, and, as Bagot wrote, "a gentleman who was favourably recommended to my notice as a man of good abilities—of undoubted loyalty—and of great zeal in the diffusion of Education."[15] The Governor had done more than solve a ticklish problem. By placing in charge of Lower Canadian education a French-Canadian Catholic who was in close contact with the clergy, he had, whether he realized it or not, guaranteed that the schools would never be assimilated. By this one act, he had revoked one of the main purposes of the Union.

Did Bagot realize this? And did he also realize what he was doing when he determined against the publication of Sir James Stuart's ordinance reorganizing Lower Canadian courts along the lines of the English common law? In 1840, the Special Council had decreed the

[13]AAM, Bourget à Jackson, déc. 1841, 5 jan. 1842; AAQ, DM VIII, 63, Bourget à Signay, 3 jan. 1842; AAQ, Régistre des lettres, 19, 643, Signay à D. Daly, 15 jan. 1842.
[14]Bagot Papers, 7, Bagot to Stanley, Jan. 26, 1842.
[15]*Ibid.*, 9, Bagot to Stanley, May 11, 1842.

rearrangement of the ancient French system into that of the English courts of common pleas, stipulating, however, that a proclamation by the Governor General would be required to bring the new system into effect. Now, in May 1842, Bagot decided against it. He placated the Colonial Secretary by declaring that he had "by no means lost sight of the expediency of assimilating, hereafter, and when the fit time should arrive, the French to the English judicial practice";[16] but he did, nonetheless, postpone forever the enforcement and effects of the ordinance. And he made this decision public by appointing to the vacant chief justiceship of Montreal the first *Canadien* ever so honoured, Rémi Vallières de St. Réal, "who stands *consensu omnium* single and alone as the first lawyer in the country, and who is equally versed in the French and English laws and languages."[17] Perhaps only lawyers could measure the full import of the Governor's action—but then most *Canadien* politicians had studied law; however, all the French seem to have realized that another of the characteristics which differentiated them as a nation, their ancestral legal system, had been restored to them and their children. As one might expect, Parent, who subordinated his attachment for any particular French-Canadian institution to his longing for responsible government, commented rather flatly in *Le Canadien* on June 13: "Nous nous flattons que Sir Charles Bagot a conçu une idée assez favorable du caractère Canadien pour ne pas s'imaginer que quelques places d'honneur et de profit est tout ce que nous exigerons pour accorder pleine et entière confiance à son administration." But Neilson and Viger, so attached to all that segregated the *Canadiens* as a separate group, exulted unashamedly:

L'administration du jour a fait un acte éclatant de justice en honorant un homme du premier mérite et nous n'hésitons pas à le dire (parce que nous avons la confiance qu'il saura le justifier) un homme de génie qui depuis douze ans brillait sous le boisseau. C'est le premier Canadien qui ait encore été appelé à un poste aussi élevé et aussi digne de ses brillantes facultés. Que peuvent faire nos éloges quand les témoignages et les sympathies de tous les hommes éclairés du pays sont là pour attester de l'heureux coup-d'état que Sir Charles vient de faire? (*L'Aurore*, June 4)

Bagot had gone far to reconcile those who only two months earlier had sent around Lower Canada an anti-Union letter in which, as Bagot wrote, "all the old agitating and inflammatory topics are again brought forward, and urged as the proper munitions de guerre for all future Sessions of the Legislature."[18] Now he decided on direct diplomacy.

[16]*Ibid.*, 7, Bagot to Stanley, July 28, 1842.
[17]*Ibid.*, 7, Bagot to Stanley, June 12, 1842.
[18]*Ibid.*, 7, Bagot to Stanley, March 26, 1842.

His wife was to land at Quebec at the end of July and, in going to meet her, he would take the opportunity to continue personally what his measures had already begun to accomplish. He succeeded beyond his fondest hopes.

Bagot arrived in Montreal in the late spring. There, unfortunately, the Tories sought to monopolize his visit. The mayor, Peter McGill, had proclaimed plans for a procession of the three English-speaking benevolent and patriotic societies to escort the Governor to the Château de Ramezay. And, indeed, they formed a colourful sight, but the *Canadiens* happily refused to be left out. After all, they too must impress the Governor with the justice of their claims. Thus when the Governor arrived and proceeded, as *Le Canadien* reported (May 25), under triumphal arches "avec tout l'éclat qu'avaient fait espérer les préparatifs," the French Canadians, officially excluded, raised a universal shout of their own. And, the next day which was the Queen's birthday, when Sir Charles held his first levee, the *Canadien* politicians attended *en masse*. Bagot himself observed: "God knows what it may all be worth, but I am assured by those practised in such matters that my levee was unprecedented. All the Frondeurs, and the turbulent of the Province—the Vigers, the LaFontaines &c &c came to offer their homage and all was civil and smooth to the eye."[19] A few days later he brought into effect the appointment of Judge Vallières.

Bagot began to win more friends. He invited a number of locally important *Canadiens* to the Legislative Council, and offered Jean-Joseph Girouard, "beyond all comparison the best informed man on the subject," the office of commissioner for the seigneurial inquiry. Above all, he asked Cherrier to accept the solicitor-generalship. Cherrier refused, alleging ill health (an excuse he would use every time for the next fifteen years), but news of the proposal leaked out, and the Governor received all the acclaim due his generosity. "Si Sir Charles," commented *L'Aurore* on June 4, "continue à réaliser ces dignes espérances il fera presque autant de bien que son prédécesseur nous a fait de mal." When, a few days later, he renewed the commissions of a number of French justices of the peace that had been suspended during the "troubles," *L'Aurore* continued on June 14, "Sir Charles . . . veut fort et ferme entrer tout de bon dans la voie de la justice." And *Les Mélanges* agreed on June 11:

Il paraît que nous sommes tout de bon en bon chemin d'avoir justice; Que Dieu aide Son Excellence! On nous assure que C. S. Cherrier a refusé la

19*Ibid.*, 7, Bagot to Stanley, May 28, 1842.

place de Solliciteur-Général motivant son refus sur son mauvais état de santé. Si le fait est vrai il sera pour le pays le sujet de bien sincères regrets. . . . Ce sont de trop bonnes nouvelles pour que le pays n'en meure de joie! Ah! si ce n'est pas un beau rêve que nous faisons, Sir Charles veut donc se faire adorer du pays!

And from Paris, Papineau, who had heard of the offer to Cherrier and whose own opinion still took first place among the young radicals who had opposed the Union, wrote to Cherrier expressing his regret that his cousin had been unable to accept office. "Cette nomination," he said, "en même temps que celle du juge Vallières découragerait les méchants, donnait quelque confiance aux honnêtes gens. Mr Daly m'exprimait le chagrin que lui donnait ton refus, je lui ai dit, Mr Cherrier est si délicat sur l'honneur qu'il ne peut accepter un emploi qu'autant qu'il se sent la force d'en accomplir tous les devoirs dans les moindres détails."[20]

Soon, stories began to make the rounds. One reported in L'Aurore on June 11 went that "Son Excellence se promenait, l'autre jour, en habits séculiers et n'avait rien pour le distinguer que la dignité de son maintien et la noblesse de sa physionomie." When a man met him on the street, a man of the people, "le type national du pays," the man, "frappé de l'air distingué de ce personnage," tipped his hat. Sir Charles stopped and returned the greeting "avec tant de grace et d'urbanité" that the habitant ran to ask someone who the gentleman was. When told it was the Governor General, he exclaimed: "Celui-là, il ne nous trompera pas." Of such stuff are legends born.

By the time Bagot left Montreal on June 22 he might well have been content with his month's work. His fame preceded him to Quebec City. Here, René-Edouard Caron had tolerated no exclusions from the welcoming ceremony on racial grounds. And the Québecois decided to do the honours on this royal occasion as they alone could. They had begun to consider this man a friend.

Auspiciously on the morrow of Saint-Jean-Baptiste day, Bagot sailed down an avenue of flag-decked steamships into the ancient harbour. He disembarked to "des airs canadiens," met the mayor, and climbed into an open landau to ride through streets paved with pine needles and spruce branches, under rich triumphal arches of oak foliage, to Place d'Armes, where he reviewed the troops, resplendent in full dress, and the officers of the four benevolent societies. At the Hôtel-de-Ville he stepped out onto the balcony. From there he could see the fifteen hundred members of the Société Saint-Jean-Baptiste

[20]PAC, MG 24, B 46, Papiers Cherrier, L. J. Papineau à Cherrier, 30 juil. 1842.

who had been following his carriage, pour into the square below. Above them, along the three other sides of the square, he gave a courtly bow to "les Dames qui, dans leurs toilettes les plus élégantes, montrèrent leurs belles et riantes figures à toutes les fenêtres." At his feet, he watched as workingmen and professionals, rich and poor, crowded behind the green and white banner of Saint John the Baptist, the glory of French Canada shining on every face. From the whole square he could hear the joyous airs of "Vive la Canadienne." He seemed deeply moved. Turning to Mayor Caron, he whispered "Mais, c'est un peuple de gentilshommes."[21] He then drove smiling through the crowd to the apartments prepared for him in the north wing of the old Assembly House. Nearby, the students of the Séminaire de Québec broke into an enthusiastic "God Save the Queen." Then he mounted the stairs, according to Le Canadien on June 27, "au milieu des applaudissements de la foule qui avaient été presque continuels depuis son arrivée." Surely a day he would never forget, and one which the ancient city, with nostalgia for the old, good days, has long remembered.

Lady Mary Bagot arrived three weeks later, and finished the conquest. On July 28 she invited to a "circle" all those Quebec held most elegant. Le Canadien reported the next day: "Toutes les origines y étaient représentées par ce qu'elles avaient de plus notable. Nos dames sont revenues des plus enchantées des aimables qualités de Lady Bagot et des demoiselles Bagot qui toutes parlent le Français avec élégance et facilité."

Perhaps towards the end of his stay, Bagot read Le Fantasque for July 28. In it Aubin reminded him of "les trois routes politiques" open to him now that he knew his people. He could hold to the old line and "se jeter dans les mêmes voies de persécutions, d'ostracisme, qui ont fait le principal grief des dernières années." Or he could try to "s'aventurer sur une mer d'eau tiède; n'être ni chat ni rat; flatter tout le monde" and accomplish nothing. Or he could choose the way of honour and "oublier et faire oublier les injures passées; régner par la justice; se persuader qu'il est politique . . . de regarder les canadiens-français comme une nation adjointe à l'empire britannique et non point subjugée par lui; de leur garantir ce qui leur est cher, ce qui leur est dû; d'abandonner aux habitans du pays la juste direction de leurs propres affaires." It was a tribute to Bagot's great gifts that Aubin thought he would follow the third way.

The French Canadians soon realized that Bagot had chosen the way

21Bulletin des Recherches historiques, III (1897), 189.

of peace. They knew, of course, of the offer to Cherrier and of Val-lières' appointment. Now they also reflected that in the eight by-elections since prorogation they had experienced, for the first time perhaps since the turn of the century, no violence or pressure that could be traced to government influence. Of the eight contests, the *Canadiens* had carried seven, gaining two from the Tories: Rouville, where William Walker defeated Antoine de Salaberry by 476 to 376 on July 7, and Ottawa, where Denis-Benjamin Papineau carried a majority of 100 over Thomas Symes.[22] *La Gazette* underlined the moral on August 23: "Où est donc la cause de tout cela? Un homme de moins et un homme de plus; un homme de moins qui en 1841 s'était voué corps et âme au parti oligarchique à qui il promettait l'impunité et les récompenses; un homme de plus qui en 1842 a évité jusqu'à présent de tomber dans les tacs de ce parti, et qui au lieu de vouloir imposer sa volonté au peuple; paraît attendre du peuple l'ex-pression franche de ses sentiments." Rumours began to spread that testified to the *Canadiens'* impressions of the Governor's goodwill. One, reported in *Le Fantasque* on July 28, said "messieurs Caron, Parent et peut-être aussi Mr. Lafontaine [*sic*]" had been offered posts on the Executive Council. Others would have it that a general election was imminent, or even that "une amnistie générale et sans exception" would be proclaimed.

By the end of August it was clear that Bagot had succeeded in his efforts to convince the French Canadians both that they could trust him and that some good could come out of the Union. LaFontaine had been arguing the latter from the beginning, of course. Bagot, in using his charm to save the Union, had been reinforcing, however uncon-sciously, LaFontaine's argument against the Neilson-Viger group. Within a few weeks the two men—the aging, gracious diplomat, and the intense, sharp-willed young politician—would join forces. Bagot, under pressure from his Instructions and from Stanley to conciliate the French by "multiplying the vendus" and "playing the game of Divide et impera,"[23] and insistently urged on by his council in Canada to "introduce some members of the French Canadian party into my Gov't,"[24] realized that because of the changing pattern of politics in the Assembly, he must turn to LaFontaine. Indeed, since the French-Canadian bloc had gained three seats (LaFontaine in Fourth York, and

[22]For reports on the campaign and results, see *La Gazette de Québec*, 18 juin, 5, 9, juil., 23 août 1842.
[23]Bagot Papers, 9, Stanley to Bagot, Sept. 1, Oct. 3, 1842.
[24]*Ibid.*, 10, Bagot to Stanley, Sept. 26, 1842.

the two others in by-elections), and since a number of Upper Canadian Reformers were inclining more towards a direct alliance with the French, he became worried—quite apart from any consideration of responsible government—about whether he could even carry a legislative programme through the House. "It is impossible to disguise from oneself," he wrote to Stanley, "that the French members of the Assembly possess the power of the Country, and whoever directs that power, backed by the most efficient means of controlling it, is in a situation to govern the Province most effectually."[25] He needed the French.

LaFontaine also faced a crisis. During the spring of 1842, the whole theoretical debate about the Union had been revived. He knew that on this issue the Neilson-Viger group found its natural allies not among the Reformers, but among the Tories of Upper Canada who had also opposed the Union in principle. During the argument over the Durham proposals, Neilson had written against Parent in *La Gazette* (July 30, 1838): "Si le Bas-Canada échappe à cette Union mal assortie, il ne devra pas en remercier ses amis . . . de l'école soi-disant libérale; . . . il en sera plutôt redevable au rapport du Comité de l'Assemblée du Haut-Canada en réfutation de celui de Lord Durham." Now Neilson's friends and the Tories had in common not only their dislike for Sydenham's council but also a greater loyalty to the particularism of their respective groups than to the Union and/or responsible government. Unless LaFontaine could prove his claim that the Union could be made to serve the *Canadiens*, the goodwill Bagot had won would not likely be strong enough to prevent Neilson from leading them into an alliance which would bring all of LaFontaine's and Bagot's dreams to an end.

On September 10 LaFontaine received the summons to enter the Council, not as a *vendu*, but as the representative of French Canada. After painful negotiations resulting from Bagot's sense of what was due to his other councillors, and LaFontaine's eagerness to make it clear to his compatriots that he accepted office on his own, and not the Governor's terms, he took the oath as Attorney General for Canada East. On September 19, 1842, the "new ministry" won a vote of confidence from the House by 55 to 5, Neilson's lone Lower Canadian dissenting vote emphasizing the extent of LaFontaine's victory. He had won all he had hoped for, perhaps more than he had ever dreamed: he had won the Union debate.

[25]*Ibid.*, 7, Bagot to Stanley, July 28, 1842.

7

Thanksgiving
September 1842-March 1843

Bagot, having decided he had no choice but to turn to the French, wrote to Stanley, "and if it was to be done at all it was to be done confidently—largely—and by the instrument of those alone who could carry with them the general sentiment of their race."[1] Accordingly, he decided to negotiate with LaFontaine, the man who had believed all along that his people should accept the Union. But Bagot was still worried. What if LaFontaine was not strong enough to control his party? What, as he wrote to Stanley, if he could not bring with him "the consent and co-operation of the population"? Would Bagot's mission of winning over the French end in frustration? By summoning LaFontaine, had he merely acquired another *vendu*? He had, however, judged rightly. LaFontaine did deliver his party, and the press and the politicians outside the House accepted LaFontaine's leadership. As soon as he could, LaFontaine set to work to prove that he also had the wholehearted approval of the public, that he had indeed won the Union debate.

But first he had to form his "cabinet." There were five offices open on the Council: those of the two attorneys general which he and Baldwin filled, those of the two solicitors general, and that of the commissioner of Crown lands. As part of his agreement with Bagot, LaFontaine (aided and advised by Baldwin) suggested as solicitors general, the Upper Canadian Reformer, J. E. Small, and, for Lower Canada, his colleague Thomas Cushing Aylwin, "who combined," Bagot continued to Stanley,

with a good reputation for professional talent and knowledge high powers of debate, and two most important qualifications—he is an Anglo-Canadian by birth—and a representative of a county in the Province [District] of Quebec. Mr. LaFontaine laid great stress on this latter point, as he himself

[1]Bagot Papers, 7, Bagot to Stanley, Sept. 26, 1842.

is connected with Montreal, and under the circumstances of the jealousy which is known to exist between that Province and Quebec, it was essential that the latter Province should appear to participate in the advantages of the new arrangement.

As commissioner of Crown lands, LaFontaine had promised to choose Girouard, who possessed, Bagot averred to Stanley, "even greater influence with his countrymen than Mr. LaFontaine." Girouard refused, however, alleging in a formal letter to the man he termed "le premier ministre" that his health would not allow him to take on the responsibility.[2] Although LaFontaine insisted, and even got Parent to write and try again, Girouard still said no. Meanwhile, LaFontaine had asked Morin if he cared to exchange his district judgeship for the more lucrative post of clerk of the Council. He also offered him the Crown lands if Girouard persisted in his refusal. Generous Morin, whose place on the Bench had the advantage of being a permanent appointment, answered that "même si la question de places et de salaire est un embarras, je suis préparé à de nouveaux mais peut-être moins inutiles sacrifices. . . ."[3] Accordingly, when Girouard definitely turned down the office, Morin became Commissioner of Crown Lands on October 15. LaFontaine then pressed the clerkship of the Council on Parent, the thinker whose ideas he had been using for three years and who certainly deserved the reward. On October 21 Parent abandoned Le Canadien, taking leave of his readers of eleven years with an open letter stating "appelé à faire partie des nouveaux arrangements, j'ai cru dans la voix du représentant de ma souveraine, reconnaître la voix de mon pays: c'est à dire que j'ai obéi." The Council was now complete. And friends and former foes alike were not slow to raise a chorus of praise.

The first note came from LaFontaine's vivacious young aide-de-camp, George-Etienne Cartier. He wrote how he had rushed to LaFontaine's law office on first hearing the news, and with the new Attorney General's partner and close confidant, Amable Berthelot, "avons bu le champagne à votre santé. Nous avons mis notre [sic] estomacs en unison avec le cœur." He offered to drop everything in Montreal and come to Kingston immediately if he could be of any help and ended on a lyrical flight: "votre nomination a électriser [sic] nos cœurs et nos esprits. Nous commençons à nous raviver, à avoir de l'espoir et de la confiance. . . . Nous nous sentons éveillés de la torpeur et du dégoût

[2]Papiers LaFontaine, Girouard à LaFontaine, 19 sept. 1842.
[3]Ibid., Morin à LaFontaine, 27 sept. 1842.

qui nous tenaient à bas."[4] Mondelet, another friend whose encouragement had never wavered, repeated, "Je n'ai pas besoin de vous dire que je tiens à l'Union plus que jamais, sans laquelle nous n'aurions jamais eu le Gouv. responsable & sous l'empire de laquelle, je vous disais si souvent, que le Gouv. Métropolitain y penserait à deux fois avant de refuser une demande qui eut pu devenir sérieuse dans ses résultats."[5] And from Quebec Aylwin echoed happily that "nos gens sont tous contents et le parti opposé parait se soumettre de bonne grâce."[6] Indeed, even the anti-Unionists in Quebec and the young radicals in Montreal lent their voices to the concert.

There were, naturally, a few discordant notes. One was Neilson's own reluctance ("La conduite du père Neilson surprend beaucoup de personnes, c'est la seule chose qui nous nuise"—Aylwin had noted); another, the suspicions of LaFontaine's fine old enemy, the politician and seigneur, Marc-Pascal de Sales Laterrière, who wrote: "Je suis contre l'Union, même avec toutes les modifications que la nécessité arrache aujourd'hui à nos ennemis."[7] But, on first hearing the news, Glackmeyer had written to Neilson, admitting that "nous avons été extrèmement surpris de la tournure étrange que nos affaires ont prise; . . . les Canadiens-français sont au comble de la joie, moi je dis comme vous attendons: si Morin et Girouard joignent j'avoue que j'aurai confiance dans cette administration."[8] Morin did join; and in Montreal Denis-Emery Papineau could hardly believe it nor contain his joy: "Assurément si nous ne sommes pas au temps des miracles, nous n'en sommes pas très loin, ici, au Canada. Qui aurait jamais pu croire que sous le régime de l'Union on nous aurait donné un procureur-général Canadien français." Yet he too remained suspicious: "Le changement est si étrange qu'il faut qu'il y ait quelqu'anguille sous roche; c'est un revirement qui ne peut sans doute durer."[9] But Louis-Joseph Papineau seems to have trusted Bagot. "Je crois que les démarches importantes prises par Sir Charles Bagot l'ont été avec quelque sincérité," he wrote to Dr. O'Callaghan,[10] although he did not think so highly of the councillors themselves. Nor was he reconciled to the Union. He continued to O'Callaghan, "Je crois Mr Baldwin un honnête homme

[4]Ibid., Cartier à LaFontaine, 18 sept. 1842.
[5]Ibid., Mondelet à LaFontaine, 15 nov. 1842.
[6]Ibid., Aylwin à LaFontaine, 5 oct. 1842.
[7]Ibid., Laterrière à LaFontaine, 29 oct. 1842.
[8]Neilson Collection, X, 467–70, Glackmeyer à Neilson, 22 sept. 1842.
[9]Collection Papineau-Bourassa, D.-E. Papineau à L. J. Papineau, 12 oct. 1842.
[10]Ibid., 539, L. J. Papineau à O'Callaghan, 16 nov. 1842.

et éclairé. Sa nomination me donne plus de confiance que celle de tous les autres ensemble. Les autres sont honnêtes aussi, mais peu habiles. On pourrait facilement les amener à croire que les Canadiens ont plus obtenu par l'Union qu'ils n'auraient obtenu sans elle." Still, as he reiterated a month later, "Sir Charles Bagot a pris le système au sérieux, honnêtement avec un étonnant succès qui le justifie clairement."[11]

Surely this was as much as could be expected from those who had opposed the Union so strenuously and who now found that the old antagonisms were not as strong as the new pressures. The majority of Canadian politicians were becoming almost hysterical. This letter from LaFontaine's election agent in Yamaska is a good example:

Comment contenir plus longtemps la joie. . . . Je ne croyais plus que faiblement à une providence éloignée qui daignât peut-être un jour arracher nos arrières neveux de l'état d'ilotisme auquel je croyais la génération actuelle condamnée sans retour. Cette perspective même était bien sombre au fond du tableau d'un avenir obscurci par les nuages menaçants du malheur de la tyrannie. . . . La Providence nous a fait voir que nous ne devons jamais désespérer de Son secours, puisque souvent elle est d'autant plus près que nous la croyons plus éloignée. Qu'elle soit donc bénie à jamais, elle a daigné visiter le faible et l'opprimé. Bénie soit aussi celui dont elle a dirigé le cœur et l'esprit dans les sentiers de la justice qu'elle a envoyé à notre secours.[12]

The press echoed the fanfare. On September 20, 1842, *Le Canadien* put out an *extraordinaire* to announce the "REMODÈLLEMENT DU MINISTÈRE"; on the next day, it offered a soft I-told-you-so, mingled with further and higher hopes; "Le système de la responsabilité gouvernementale a donc eu, dès son début, pour résultat d'introduire dans l'administration des canadiens français possédant la confiance publique. Jamais le pays n'avait encore été témoin d'un événement aussi heureux. Il faut espérer que nous ne tarderons pas à en éprouver les salutaires effets." And it concluded by reiterating Parent's basic theme that by as much as the British constitution was frankly applied, by so much would French Canada's loyalty be strengthened:

Nous pouvons dire que Sir Charles Bagot, en ralliant les Canadiens à son administration, a fait un acte de haute politique qui aura l'effet le plus salutaire. Que par de pareils actes, et il y en a beaucoup à faire, le gouvernement nous rende pleine et entière justice, nous ne demandons que de la justice, et nous garantissons la possession du Canada à l'Angleterre aussi longtemps qu'elle voudra le conserver.

[11]*Ibid.*, 540, L. J. Papineau à Chapman, 26 déc. 1842.
[12]Papiers LaFontaine, Arcand à LaFontaine, 23 déc. 1842.

At *Le Fantasque*, Aubin agreed (September 22): "Après le gouvernement des Colborne et des Sydenham, ce simple retour vers une
politique moins exclusive fait revivre le Canada d'une vie nouvelle et
ramène le joie, la confiance et, le dirons-nous,—la loyauté dans le cœur,
depuis si long-tems ulcéré, de ses habitans." At *La Gazette de Québec*,
there was naturally more hesitation. On the day the news arrived,
Neilson's paper ran no banner headlines; it featured instead a guarded
note from the editor at Kingston to the effect that "il est difficile de dire
comment le nouvel arrangement opérera." On the twenty-second it
stressed, as another of the many illogical aspects it had formerly questioned about this "gouvernement responsable," that the members had
been asked to approve of the "nouveau ministère" on September 19,
that is several days before Aylwin, Small, and Morin had been sworn
in. However, after hearing that Morin might join, it allowed on the
twenty-seventh that "Mr Morin serait une des meilleures acquisitions
que pourrait faire le nouveau cabinet, et nous le croyons homme à
sacrifier ses intérêts personels en échangeant sa place de juge contre
une place moins assurée, s'il croyait par là servir la cause de ses
compatriotes." This was as much approbation as it ever gave. And *La
Gazette* continued throughout the autumn to refer disparagingly to the
"ministère racommodé," the "cabinet replâtré," and, always in quota-
tion marks, the "gouvernement responsable."

In Montreal where LaFontaine's control over the party waxed
stronger, *L'Aurore* came out squarely in favour of the new arrangement on September 27. "Il conviendrait que le peuple du Bas-Canada,"
Barthe wrote, "élevât la voix pour se prononcer sur la confiance qu'il
repose dans les hommes si justement aimés de lui que Son Excellence
vient d'appeler dans son Conseil Exécutif." Later, on November 26,
when Neilson's opposition had become more apparent, *L'Aurore*
disagreed with him for the first time since 1839 (although continuing
to stand guard over its old principles):

Il nous semble . . . que le vent paraît avoir un peu changé pour Mr. Neilson
depuis quelques tems, et nous avouons que ses hésitations, ses soupçons
contre le nouvel ordre de choses, cette espèce de puissance négative qu'il
oppose à toute amélioration pratique dans le gouvernement colonial, nous
effarouche un peu pour sa popularité. . . . Quand même il serait vrai que le
gouvernement responsable n'est rien qu'une autre forme de tyrannie, (et
certes nous n'avons jamais prétendu que dans une colonie surtout ce fut
un ordre de choses bien tangible) il ne serait pas moins vrai non plus qu'on
en dut tirer le parti le plus avantageux possible.

Then on December 1 Viger underlined how Bagot had healed those wounds which in 1838 had seemed to gape so wide: "L'administration de Sir Charles Bagot a déjà refermé les plaies et parlé au cœur du peuple; déjà il [le peuple] a entouré le pacifique et honnête administrateur de tout son dévouement . . . car le temps des martyrs est passé. Le temps est passé où l'on croyait qu'un peuple devait être l'esclave de l'autre." By February 28, 1843, Viger had conceded that for the time being *L'Aurore* would even cease to agitate for repeal of the Union, since responsible government should be given a chance to show how it could be made to serve French Canada.

LaFontaine's partisans (as all good politicians must) translated their joy into action. In fact, they had no alternative. They had to provide the Governor General with proof strong enough to convince the Colonial Office that his gallant gesture had also been the wise one. They had to offset the disturbing sounds they heard from the ancient enemy's quarters. They had to master those lingering anti-Unionists who still hesitated to rally to the party. And within three months they found an added reason to act quickly, fear that disease and death might rob them of their hero.

Bagot had realized that if the Union (and the British system in North America) was to be saved, he must guarantee the *Canadiens'* right to be themselves. He had acted accordingly. But Lord Stanley and the Colonial Office were less convinced of this necessity. As Colonel Murdoch reported to Bagot from London: "I very much doubt how far Lord Stanley is really alive to the true state of Canada. . . . I am afraid he is frightened at the French and at the apparent scandal of placing in high office men who have been more than suspected of treason."[13] In fact, Stanley had sent several instructions which all pointed against taking in the French as a party. And after hearing of the change, he dispatched what was at best a cold approval.[14] LaFontaine reasoned that unless the Governor could show how popular his measure was, how strongly it had reconciled the French to the Union, it might indeed be disallowed or Bagot recalled. Within two months, LaFontaine produced the necessary proof: he made certain that Baldwin was returned to the House, and he carried two election contests, one in Beauharnois, and another in the Montreal civic election.

Under the current constitutional practice, the new Executive Councillors had to resign from the legislature and seek re-election. Morin won in the Saguenay riding which Parent had just vacated, and all the others were returned in their own constituencies except Baldwin who,

13Bagot Papers, 4, Murdoch to Bagot, Oct. 18, 1842.
14Glazebrook, *Bagot in Canada*, pp. 79ff., 107ff.

for reasons best known to Upper Canadians, lost Hastings. This was on October 5, 1842. But already at the end of September, LaFontaine had suggested that, if things went badly in Hastings, the French were anxious to see Baldwin find a riding in Lower Canada. And the latter had accepted. Accordingly, on October 8, twenty-five members of the French party, including such outstanding anti-Unionists as Denis-Benjamin Viger and Denis-Benjamin Papineau, offered to resign in order to provide a seat for the Upper Canadian leader. "Ce serait une belle occasion," Lewis Drummond explained, "pour faire voir aux Hauts Canadiens que nous savons apprécier et rendre les bons services."[15]

Two weeks later, Michael Borne officially resigned in Rimouski and advised the electors there to send Baldwin a formal offer. LaFontaine, himself busy in Kingston, asked Louis-Michel Viger to hurry down to Rimouski "to do the needful."[16] Baldwin won by acclamation, as strong a proof as any that *la nation canadienne* was reconciled to the Union. And one which the people of Rimouski confirmed the following summer when, weather and business now permitting, the Upper Canadian leader came down with LaFontaine for a first visit with his new constituents who received him with great enthusiasm. Along the road from Quebec to Rimouski, every farm house had put out bunting, and as Baldwin's carriage passed the habitants ran behind it, shooting fireworks, unfurling banners, shouting their acclaim.

They might well. For Baldwin's return as member for Rimouski was heavy with meaning. It not only echoed the tribute paid to Lower Canada by the electors of Fourth York, but also served as a token of the new alliance with the Reformers of Upper Canada. It also came as some special kind of irony: as the Upper Canadians had first insulted them, so the French Canadians had ultimately been forced to find in the western Reformers their main source of hope. The earlier ignorance and prejudice of the debaters in Toronto had encouraged Neilson's isolationism and had even distracted Parent from his first fine enthusiasm for the Union. Yet, without the manœuvres of Hincks and the high principles of Baldwin, LaFontaine, and others, *la nation canadienne* could not now have taken their rightful place in directing their own national life. Moreover, because Baldwin, more than any other individual in Canada, symbolized the technique of responsible

[15]Papiers LaFontaine, Drummond à LaFontaine, 10 oct. 1842.
[16]Toronto Public Library (TPL), Baldwin Papers, A 55, 119, LaFontaine to Baldwin, Nov. 23, 1842; also Papiers LaFontaine, B.-N. Lemoyne to LaFontaine, Dec. 4, 1842.

government, his election in a totally French riding underlined how these people, alien in language and culture, nevertheless understood that their own future was best assured by this new idea.

More important, immediately, for LaFontaine's purposes than Baldwin's election was the successful election of Edward Gibbon Wakefield in Beauharnois on November 9. Wakefield had come to Canada as an attaché of Durham, and was a strong supporter of the latter's views on French Canada. At that time he believed "that M. Lafontaine [sic] and his friends were bent on pursuing a course which would be most injurious to the colony, and especially to the whole race of French Canadians. They appeared to be profoundly ignorant of their own position, and thoroughly devoid of judgment as leaders of their party."[17] Later, however, he seems to have changed his mind; for when he returned to Canada in 1841 as an agent of the North American Colonial Association of Ireland which had purchased the seigneury of Beauharnois and hoped to encourage settlement there by persuading the government to build its projected canal through this land, he soon became convinced that his scheme could best be furthered by co-operation with the French. He had long conversations with Girouard and remained in touch with Viger throughout the summer of 1842.

The by-election occasioned by the July resignation of John Dunscomb (a Sydenham Tory) had been called for November. Now the *Canadiens* were told the election had become, in Wakefield's words, a contest for "the purpose of showing the Colonial Office, as well as a single election could show it, that Sir Charles Bagot's policy of 'Justice to the French Canadians' is approved by the constituencies as well as by the Assembly."[18] LaFontaine's group chose Wakefield as candidate, but, since the riding was about evenly divided between English-Tory and French-speaking electors, they had a hard contest. However, the *habitants* had Drummond's and Barthe's assurances that a vote for Wakefield was a vote for the new appointments and gave him 1,688 votes to his opponent's 951, the majority coming almost exclusively from the French parishes. *Le Canadien* underlined the election's significance on November 11: "Ce qui donne à cette élection une grande importance politique, c'est que M. Wakefield, homme d'influence et de talent, s'étant constitué le défenseur de la population franco-canadienne, et ayant puissamment contribué par ses écrits à amener le nouvel ordre de choses inauguré dans ce pays par sir CHARLES BAGOT,

[17]Quoted in P. Bloomfield, *Edward Gibbon Wakefield* (London, 1961), p. 188.
[18]Quoted in *ibid.*, p. 261.

l'opposition avait, pour ainsi dire, personnifié cet ordre de choses en lui, et avait remué ciel et terre pour empêcher son élection."

The new representative, his canal now under way, left immediately for England, intending, so the French hoped, to enlighten the Colonial Office on Bagot's wisdom. In New York he received news from home and wrote a quick and intelligent note to Viger:

Since the receipt of letters from England by the last mail, I am taught that the circumstance likely to have the most weight in England as tending to consolidate the policy of Sir C. Bagot, is the *course pursued* in the Assembly by Dunscomb, Holmes and McCulloch. . . . I left Montreal with the hope that the old intolerant anti-Canadian party there must (if the Canadians manage well) be broken up by means of extensive *invitation* of Dunscomb, Holmes, and McCulloch. Therefore it seems to me of great importance that the Canadians in Montreal miss no opportunity of showing respect towards these gentlemen and acknowledging the importance of their public services during the late session. . . . It would be of great assistance to me in England if we should learn that the Canadian population of Montreal has done honour in some way to Dunscomb and Holmes.[19]

He went on to suggest that the municipal election then beginning in Montreal afforded the best opportunity of such a gesture. Indeed it did.

The first civic election to be held in Montreal since the Union was designed to replace the unpopular city council appointed by Sydenham. Benjamin Holmes, who sat as a Tory member in the House was one of the candidates. The LaFontaine group in Montreal had, of course, already appreciated that since most of the candidates and electors in the city were members of the traditionally Tory mercantile community, they had here a splendid opportunity of proving that Bagot had support from among the established classes. Even before Wakefield's letter arrived, they had selected a slate of candidates who would also be acceptable to the merchants. These included Lewis Thomas Drummond, just beginning his career but already trusted by the new Attorney General with dispensing patronage in Montreal, Joseph Bourret and Dr. Pierre Beaubien, both wealthy men, advocates of the Union since 1840, and business partners of LaFontaine, and Joseph Masson whom LaFontaine once described as "a merchant, proprietor of extensive *seigneuries*, reputed to be the wealthiest person in the two Canadas."[20] Whether because of Wakefield's advice or not, the *Canadiens* also endorsed Benjamin Holmes as one of their

[19]PAC, MG 24, B 6, Papiers Viger, Wakefield to Viger, Nov. 17, 1842.
[20]Papiers LaFontaine, LaFontaine to Rawson, March 15, 1843.

candidates. And by praise among their own, they made him worth the praising.

Although a Tory, Holmes was not completely unpopular among the French. He had been one of the administrators of the city before it secured municipal incorporation in 1832 and, since 1841, he had fought for denominational schools and divided his parliamentary salary between the Protestant and Catholic orphanages in his riding. On election day he easily carried the west ward. And when the new city council—in which LaFontaine's candidates had a majority of two —met to elect a mayor, Holmes voted with the majority for Bourret, against the Tory Sabrevois de Bleury, and was then, in turn, elected one of the six aldermen. He also seconded the first motion that the annual reports of the city auditor and surveyor be translated into French. Two months later, LaFontaine, perhaps wishing to seal the bargain, appointed James Holmes, Benjamin's brother, as a justice of the peace, "une nomination," wrote Cherrier, "qui nous aidera à attacher Benjamin Holmes, qui pourra lui-même détacher quelques autres du parti anglais."[21] LaFontaine's group had not only assured that Holmes would not oppose them, they had actually gained another member. During the next session Holmes voted with them on every important measure. Above all, they had added another proof of popular support for Bagot.

"The *Tories or destructives* are very much chagrined at the result of the Corporation elections here," one of LaFontaine's partisans concluded.[22] In fact, ever since September the Tories had been pouring on Bagot the same kind of invective the *Canadiens* themselves had thrown at Sydenham. The *Canadiens* decided therefore to hold a succession of public meetings to honour the Governor, hoping to console him for the Tories' insults, and perhaps also to help him regain the physical strength he needed to remain at his post (and keep LaFontaine in power). Soon after the new Council had been installed, Bagot had fallen mysteriously and seriously ill—enough for rumours to circulate that he had died. Prayers and expressions of sympathy, the good habitants decided, would restore him. "Les bons sujets canadiens," wrote Aubin in Le Fantasque on November 19, "tremblaient pour les jours de l'homme qui leur apporte un peu de justice. . . . La tranquillité, l'absence des tourmente-braves-gens, un air pur et sec, des témoignages d'estime et de respect, voilà ce qu'il faut à Sir CHR BAGOT." Since in most of their minds the Governor symbolized the

21*Ibid.*, Cherrier à LaFontaine, 3 mars 1843.
22*Ibid.*, Lemoyne to LaFontaine, Dec. 4, 1842.

Union (Sydenham had been hated precisely because of this), each meeting, each address of sympathy and congratulation, each prayer, would also, as far as LaFontaine was concerned, drown out any voices still speaking the thoughts of Neilson.

The press agreed. *Le Fantasque*, on November 12: "Puisque notre position réelle est si vile, nos avantages si précaires qu'ils dépendent presque d'un simple changement de gouverneur . . . il faut au plus tôt organiser des assemblées publiques afin d'exprimer noblement sans crainte, sans flatterie ce que nous pensons de ce qui a été fait." *Le Canadien*, on December 12: "Les voix des Canadiens français seront unanimes, et tous les Anglais raisonnables, tous ceux qui désirent la paix et la prospérité permanente du Canada sous l'égide de l'Angleterre . . . s'empresseront de se joindre à eux."

In Quebec Aylwin, already overworked with the solicitor-generalship, took charge of the preparations. He reported to LaFontaine: "Je me suis occupé de voir les gens les plus influents pour faire une assemblée publique, et pour adopter une adresse au Gouverneur. La chose est bien vue, et j'espère que Québec se montrera dans cette occasion."[23] When the day arrived, he might well have been proud of his success. The meeting, called in mid-afternoon on a week day, December 23, 1842, was nevertheless well attended. Mayor Caron presided, and politicians of such divers hues as Glackmeyer and Aylwin sat side by side to vote a resolution that offered, as *Le Fantasque* reported the next day, "de ferventes prières" for the Governor's well-being and continued residence in the colony, "où votre présence ne peut que tendre resserrer les liens qui nous unissent à la Grande-Bretagne." The country almost outdid the old capital. Aylwin travelled to Portneuf to organize a meeting there and to propose an address which *Le Canadien* described on December 7 as "un éclatant démenti à ceux qui prétendent que les canadiens français désirent une séparation d'avec l'Angleterre, ou qu'ils demandent autre chose qu'à vivre en paix et en harmonie avec leurs concitoyens." And in LaMalbaie, Sainte-Anne-de-la-Pérade, Rimouski, and L'Islet open meetings proposed similar addresses which were unanimously and enthusiastically adopted.

In Montreal Drummond began the groundwork that led to the triumphant rally of January 12, 1843, when the anti-Unionists Viger and Barthe, the former rebel and exile Wolfred Nelson, and even Alexandre-Maurice DeLisle, the *vendu* who had beaten Leslie in Montreal county and who had been the only French Canadian (save

[23]*Ibid.*, Aylwin à LaFontaine, 25 oct. 1842.

de Salaberry) to vote against the Neilson amendment of June 1841, shared the platform under the chairmanship of the arch-Tory Peter McGill before three thousand Montrealers—the largest public meeting since 1822—to sing the praises of Governor and Council and pray Divine Providence as *Le Canadien* reported on January 16 to "resserrer les liens qui unissent cette colonie à la métropole." This was an event for which *Les Mélanges Religieux* forgot its theoretical impartiality to describe on January 17 (in a paragraph that might have been written by a staunch follower of LaFontaine):

Cette démonstration solennelle . . . est un des événements les plus significatifs qui se soient passés ici depuis longtemps. Il doit avoir, il aura certainement un grand retentissement. Il dira donc à l'Angleterre ce que valent pour la mère-patrie des enfants qu'on lui a dénoncés si souvent comme dénaturés et indignes de toute affection; et par contrecoup ce que valent à leur tour ceux qui les ont ainsi constamment calomniés. . . . Espérons que Dieu conservera au pays un homme que le pays sait si bien apprécier, et qui comprend si bien lui-même ceux qui ont mis en lui leurs plus légitimes espérances.

From the country addresses and resolutions poured in, from Longueuil, and Saint-Denis, and Saint-Hyacinthe; everywhere, *Le Fantasque* reported on December 21, "le ralliement autour du noble homme d'état qui nous gouverne et de ses nouveaux conseillers est unanime."

The *ralliement* was unanimous because of good management by LaFontaine's party and because the Attorney General and his friends had known how to adjust politics to human nature. As soon as he had taken his place on the Executive Council, LaFontaine had begun to bind the *Canadiens* permanently to his party and to the Union by judicious allotment of the executive's favour. "Le patronage que vous aurez à exercer sera souvent un écueuil pour vous," Cherrier warned him,[24] but, despite his own personal and gradually increasing disgust at the need for such methods, LaFontaine knew that "patronage is power."[25] Accordingly, within six weeks he had appointed at least one judge, commissioners of all kinds, clerks for post offices, and an endless number of special magistrates empowered and paid to issue marriage licences. He also wrote to the *Canadien* members who had returned to their ridings and asked them to suggest candidates for posts as clerks, registrars, inspectors of potash, school commissioners, magistrates, customs inspectors, immigration doctors, justices of the peace. He advised nuns on how to apply for hospital grants, he instructed perplexed Legislative Councillors, and he listened patiently

[24]*Ibid.*, Cherrier à LaFontaine, 3 mars 1843.
[25]See Baldwin Papers, 64, 87, J. H. Price to Baldwin, Feb. 6, 1843.

to such complaints as that of Dr. René Kimber whose seniority in the medical corps had been questioned. In Montreal and Quebec so great was the press for emolument that he asked Drummond and Aylwin to take charge. They did, and handsomely, filling a widening variety of jobs with their partisans.

LaFontaine could not afford to forego this opportunity. He realized that although he had manœuvred his people step by step away from an extremist position, for most of the *Canadiens* the Union still remained, at best, the bonds of Ulysses, the only reasonable, unavoidable course. The sounds that enraptured them were those of the separate state. Since he could not make the Union lovable, he at least would make it profitable. Also by letting the flatteries and salaries of office percolate down to all classes of society—from merchants who wanted seats on the Legislative Council, through the poor professionals who could not earn a living without some government appointment, to the impoverished habitants on the crowded seigneuries—he gave the *Canadiens* the best proof that the government of the Union was their own, that it served their interests. He created among them, if not attachment to the new order, at least a psychology of consent.

While party stalwarts thus organized profitable meetings and welded party unity by patronage, the ordinary French Canadian responded with prayers. He arranged for masses of thanksgiving in honour of the Governor and of petition for the restoration of his rapidly declining health. Although an overflow of the enthusiasm generated by the rallies, the masses were more than the traditional ovation for the famous—especially since they continued after Bagot was obviously dying, and had been officially replaced. The habitant felt real sympathy for Bagot. At Saint-Nicolas, at Longueuil, at Saint-Eustache, at Sainte-Marie-de-Beauce, he attended solemn masses. At Saint-Louis-de-Kamouraska he added a collection for the poor, about which *Le Fantasque* commented on December 21: "C'est une belle action, digne du caractère canadien-français, que d'aller s'agenouiller aux pieds des autels, là prier pour l'avenir de la patrie, pour la conservation des jours d'un homme chéri et secourir nos frères en détresse." At Sainte-Anne-de-la-Pérade, at Saint-Hyacinthe, at Saint-Césaire, at Rimouski, in fact in all the French parishes the habitants offered what *La Minerve* called (February 20) "les prières les plus unanimes que jamais empereur ni roi n'ont vu sortir du cœur de leurs sujets consternés."

This river of pious concern for the Governor soon concerned the priests. Like all *Canadiens*, they admired the Governor personally and for his "great measure." Even before the September days, Bishop

Bourget had appreciated Bagot's kindness when he had agreed to have the government defray the expenses of a chaplain for the 2500 Irish Catholic workers on the Beauharnois canal.[26] Later, after the Council changes, he expressed his appreciation in public several times. Once, in a pastoral letter on the opening of a home for the aged by the Sisters of Providence, he referred to Bagot as the instrument of God's mercy to the *Canadiens*. "N'est-ce-pas," he asked, "depuis que des associations charitables ont commencé à se former dans les différentes parties de ce pays pour soulager les malheureux, visiter les malades, et bâtir un asile à la misère que le Seigneur a brisé les fers de notre captivité et changé nos habits de deuil en des vêtements de gloire et d'honneur?"[27] In Quebec, Archbishop Signay and his coadjutor felt likewise. They had golden reports from Bishop Gaulin of Kingston, who described Bagot and "toutes les qualités de son cœur et de son esprit";[28] and they heard from the new Bishop of Toronto, Michael Power, how the civil recognition of his see—always a sensitive question for the Catholic bishops because of the technicalities of British law—had been graciously and easily arranged "avec beaucoup de courtoisie par Son Excellence."[29]

However, because of the technicalities of canon law which then forbade public celebration of mass for a non-Catholic, the bishops had a problem. They worried about the overwhelming demand which the politicians and the habitants were making for public prayers. When approached by Mayor Caron and other leading citizens, Archbishop Signay persuaded them to rest content with an address. He explained that, quite apart from the point of canon law, he was embarrassed because "c'est établir un précédent dont on pourrait se prévaloir par la suite pour demander des prières en faveur d'un Gouverneur qui ne serait pas si aimé des Canadiens et dont la conduite ne serait pas si exemplaire."[30] The *Québecois* accordingly desisted but, a few days later, the Archbishop heard that the curés in the countryside were celebrating masses anyway. What were the bishops to do? In Montreal Bourget salved his conscience by telling his curés to go ahead, but to change the specific "intention" of the mass from Bagot's health to the spiritual and temporal welfare of the province, "si inté-

26AAM, Bourget à Bagot, 29 août 1842.
27*Ibid.*, Lettre pastorale pour recommander l'Asile de la Providence à la charité du clergé et des fidèles, 11 nov. 1842.
28AAQ, HC I, 154, Gaulin à Turgeon, 4 jan. 1843.
29*Ibid.*, 14, Power à Turgeon, 28 déc. 1842.
30AAM, Québec, 1842, Signay à Bourget, 15 déc. 1842.

ressé à ce qu'il n'y ait pas de changement dans l'administration."[31] And to show his own feelings, he had his clergy send a congratulatory address to Bagot "pour le féliciter de son sage gouvernement et des heureux succès qu'il a obtenu pendant son trop court séjour au milieu de nous."[32] The priests readily signed and in mid-March he forwarded the document, carrying the names of ninety-four diocesan clerics, all the canons of the cathedral, and the Sulpician and Oblate religious. In this he went farther than Archbishop Signay. The latter, on hearing of the Montreal address, assembled his councillors and was again advised against creating a precedent.[33] Instead, the Quebec priests sent a private letter, in which the Archbiship assured Bagot that "c'est donc avec une bien douce satisfaction que nous avons applaudi aux actes de justice qui ont signalé l'administration de Votre Excellence."[34]

Because of church law, Archbishop Signay may well have been right in his scruple about the masses. But since he had not hesitated to send a circulaire asking his priests to sign the petition against the Union in 1840, why did he worry that an address now might be interpreted as meddling in politics? Was he under the influence of Neilson and his friends—the only Canadiens who held reservations about Bagot's "great measure"? Bourget, on the other hand, took the risk of being identified with the LaFontaine group. Could he have realized it at the time—realized that, despite his agreement with the Neilson-Viger group on the questions of the Union and education, despite his suspicions of LaFontaine personally, he was really more in sympathy with the Attorney General than with Neilson or even Viger? Bourget and LaFontaine were both strong-willed men, unyielding in their principles, yet expert at manœuvring within the letter of the law. And they had this in common—each thought that he was in possession of the truth. Neither could accept from an adversary anything but complete conversion. They may still have disagreed on much, but at least since LaFontaine had forced the Governor to accept his terms, they understood each other as they never had before. Here also, in a way, LaFontaine had won the Union debate. And the Bishop of Montreal may also have divined that, despite appearances, it was within LaFontaine's group that the pulse of the clerico-conservative spirit had just begun, faintly, to beat.

[31]Ibid., Bourget à Archambault, 31 jan. 1843.
[32]AAQ, DM VIII, 121, Bourget à Signay, 10 mars 1843.
[33]AAM, Québec, 1842–3, Signay à Bourget, 16 mars 1843.
[34]AAQ, Régistre des lettres, 20, 299, Signay à Bagot, 29 mars 1843.

The editorials and the addresses, the political patronage, the masses and the meetings could not save Bagot's life. He died on May 19, 1843, amid the universal requiems of Lower Canada. Nor did they even quiet the Tories. One thing, however, they did achieve: they ended the debate on the Union. The *Canadiens* would be disappointed again; LaFontaine and his friends would realize that they had only won half as much as they thought. But by agreeing to work within the Union as a united political group, they had taken the first step towards circumventing Durham's sentence of death against their culture. Prodded by LaFontaine and wooed by Bagot's charm, they had actually sacrificed the dream of a separate state. Instead, they had chosen the evolving British system, and with it, had bent the Union towards the strengthening of their threatened nationality. Thus, according to the time-honoured theory, they had loyally guarded the British connection and opened up for themselves a wider, longer, richer, national life.

PART TWO

The Campaign for Responsible Government 1843-1848

8

The Great Awakening

"Les bruits les plus étranges circulent par le temps qui court," wrote Parent in *Le Canadien* on September 12, 1842, "et feraient croire que nous sommes enfin à la veille d'une nouvelle ère . . . de régénération." In fact, during 1842 and 1843 a new ferment, an awakened vitality had been generated among the *Canadiens*. They quickly came out of the *grand découragement* that had hung over them during the Union debate, and they joined the second critical battle of the decade, the argument over responsible government, in an enthusiastic and far more optimistic mood. For one thing the governor who provoked the new crisis was a man whose personal character, at least, had won their respect. For another, the disputing *Canadien* politicians had become more confident. They now argued, not as defeated rebels, the butt of Tory insults, but as actual or prospective members of the Governor's Council. Finally, during the next five years, 1843 to 1848, the climate in which they campaigned gradually changed: newspapers and writers caught the infectious nineteenth-century spirit of progress; Church leaders began to give a new, more assertive direction; and the economic depression slowly lifted. Above all the *Canadiens* revived in strength and spirit.

The *Canadiens* were themselves helping to create this new world. The great newspapers reorganized so that by 1843 the *Canadiens*, whose language and culture had been officially proscribed three years earlier, now had two large bi-weekly political newspapers in each of their main cities, *Le Canadien* and *Le Journal de Québec* in the old capital, *L'Aurore* and *La Minerve* in Montreal. Neilson was forced, regretfully, to discontinue the French *Gazette*. Ronald MacDonald, his assistant who had been in charge of the French edition, had decided to leave journalism and Neilson could find no replacement; he may also have been in financial difficulties. In all events, on October 29, 1842, a month after losing his five-year contest for French-Canadian particularism, he issued the last French number of French Canada's first newspaper. And with it, a bright flame was extinguished. Meanwhile, at *Le Canadien*, Parent having gone to the civil service, his associates offered his place to MacDonald, who then decided that he preferred to be an editor after all. On November 7 he took over Parent's chair.

Two days before MacDonald came to *Le Canadien*, a *circulaire* appeared announcing *Le Journal de Québec*. It was written by Joseph Cauchon, who had articled in Morin's law office, had then become a journalist under Parent, and, lately, had acted as editor of *Le Canadien*. A nervous and pugnacious little man, short, fiery, and thin, he had the energy of a born figher and a politician's lack of scruple. As a writer, he was easily Lower Canada's most witty and efficient muckraker. Through his flair for publicity, and by every innuendo he could conceive, he had made hundreds of enemies by 1850; yet he had become one of the surest political organizers in the colony. And throughout he kept one rare distinction: he was one of the few people who had a disinterested, deep, personal attachment for LaFontaine. On December 1, 1842, he declared the policy of the new paper: "Nous sommes ennemis de l'isolement qui serait funeste; nous voulons une politique large et généreuse, appelant au ralliement les hommes de tous les partis. . . . Nous tendrons donc de bon cœur la main à tous ceux qui désirent l'agrandissement et la prospérité de la patrie commune."

In Montreal meanwhile LaFontaine's organizers had successfully concluded a long series of negotiations that led to the re-founding of *La Minerve*. In the spring of 1841, when *L'Aurore* seemed at best a reluctant ally, they had decided that they needed a newspaper which they could control. John Ryan, who had edited the moderate *Le Libéral* in Quebec before the "troubles," then turned republican, and, later, returned from the United States to side with Parent and LaFontaine, offered to invest in such a paper; Morin was prepared to direct its editorial policy. After consultations, overtures were sent to Ludger Duvernay who was, after all, a good and penniless politician whose name and popularity, especially with the radicals, could be an asset to LaFontaine.[1] Duvernay had long been under pressure from his radical friends to return and revive his newspaper. Some, like Louis Perrault, wanted him to fight the republican battle; others, like Jacques Plinguet, longed for a permanent position at his press and, especially, for his political leadership against LaFontaine—whose own followers for their part seemed quite happy that the popular ex-editor of *La*

[1]Papiers Duvernay, 524, Dumesnil à Duvernay, 20 août 1841.

Minerve remained in Burlington. At first, Duvernay himself ostensibly preferred to stay in the United States, but as the months passed and his drinking grew worse, he sank further into insolvency. By the fall of 1840, his *Patriote Canadien* had failed, and the friends in Montreal whom he had asked to collect donations for his support, as well as arrears from ex-subscribers, reported less and less success! When one of them, for instance, approached LaFontaine for a £25 contribution, the latter turned away, briskly saying that Duvernay would be better advised to begin working than to "demander de l'argent aux uns et aux autres."[2] On March 13, 1839, *L'Ami du Peuple* reported he had been living for some time "dans un état très voisin de la misère," and two years later he himself admitted to Louis Perrault that "les choses sont tellement tendues que mon crédit en souffre, et je suis rendu à bout. . . . Je ne sais trop ce que je vais devenir. Mon moral en souffre au point de m'ôter le sommeil. Que faire? J'envoie quelques fois à tous les diables et la politique et tous ceux qui nous ont précipités dans ce gouffre."[3]

Duvernay may have been ready in private to send what principles he had to the devil, but when approached by the LaFontaine group, he announced (for the record perhaps) that he could not submit his editorials to a committee whose policies he did not approve.[4] Still, he came to Montreal to consider the idea. What he discussed at conferences there with Girouard, Drummond, and LaFontaine he did not divulge, but after them he—who had attracted the most radical republican correspondence known in the decade—never again attacked the Union or kept letters that impugned LaFontaine's policy on responsible government. Early in 1842, funds having been collected in Montreal to finance his move, he returned and put out *Le Journal du Peuple* which ceased in July when he announced that *La Minerve* would begin again.[5] On Friday, September 9, it did. Duvernay wrote in this first issue "qu'elle ne déviera pas de ses anciens principes et elle sera un actif champion des libertés populaires, mais elle se prêtera aux circonstances où se trouve le pays."[6] It did that too. Soon after, when LaFontaine took power and the politicians decreed congratulations for

[2]*Ibid.*, 393, 436, 477, 449, 485, 541, Perrault à Duvernay 13 jan., 15 sept. 1840, 19 fév. 1841, and Fortier à Duvernay, 20 fév. 1842; 525, Dumesnil à Duvernay, 31 août 1841.

[3]*Ibid.*, 510, Duvernay à Perrault, 6 juil. 1841.

[4]*Ibid.*, 525, Dumesnil à Duvernay, 31 août 1841.

[5]*Ibid.*, 533, 547, Amiot à Duvernay, 17 déc. 1841, 20 fév. 1842; *L'Aurore*, 22 mars, 7 juil. 1842.

[6]As cited by *Le Canadien*, 14 sept. 1842.

Bagot, Duvernay forgot all his separatist correspondence and by April 3, 1843, was intoning Parent's traditional theme that French-Canadian nationality and British dominion were concomitant.

In addition to these four great papers there were many short-lived, keen little papers that marked the new mood of the people, sheets such as Napoléon Aubin's *Le Castor*, Stanislas Drapeau's *L'Artisan* and *L'Ami de la Religion et de la Patrie*, and Amable Fortier's *Le Charivari Canadien* and *Le Citoyen*. And there were, finally, those two important anthologies, Michel Bibaud's *Encyclopédie Canadienne* and James Huston's *Répertoire National*.[7] From all of these the *Canadiens* became aware of their new opportunities: gone were the "morgue insolente et profond égoisme"[8] that had marked them three years ago. They marched ahead now, following the imaginative young writers, scholars, and statesmen who blossomed everywhere. They read Garneau's new national history and followed the steady stream of works from their own native authors: wild, romantic novels such as Joseph Doutre's *Les Fiancés de 1812*, Pierre Chauveau's *Charles Guérin*, and Georges Boucher de Boucherville's *Une de perdue, deux de trouvées*; and the first play, Antoine Gérin-Lajoie's *Le Jeune Latour*. All of these were involved, tangled, uneven, and often ugly, but, for all that, they were the first phase of what would be the *Canadiens'* national literature.[9] They conversed about it all wildly, discussing the weekly collections of current comment, immature verse, and unending, serialized plots which Louis-O. Létourneux served in his *Revue Canadienne*.

The *Canadiens* also listened to lectures, filling parish halls and hotel salons to hear people like Aubin, Mondelet, Huston, and Morin discuss the new ideas which both contributed and testified to the new mood of the nation. Particularly they listened to Etienne Parent. Parent had persuaded the *Canadiens* to agree to play their rightful role in the evolution of the colony's constitution towards greater freedom. The struggle for political liberty now won, Parent began to wonder how

[7]These papers appeared as follows: *Le Castor*, nov. 1843–juin 1845; *L'Artisan*, 9 jan.–17 oct. 1844; *L'Ami de la Religion et de la Patrie*, nov. 1847–?; *Le Charivari Canadien*, mai–oct. 1844; *Le Citoyen*, sept. 1844–?; J. Huston, *Le Répertoire National ou Recueil de Littérature Canadienne* (Montréal, 1848–50). See also S. Marion, *Les Lettres Canadiennes d'autrefois*, IV, *Phase préromantique* (Ottawa, 1944); D. M. Hayne, "Sur les Traces du préromantisme canadien," *Revue de l'Université d'Ottawa*, XXXI (1961), 142–3, and B. Bujela, "Michel Bibaud's *Encyclopédie Canadienne*," *Culture*, XXI (1960), 117–52.

[8]Papiers Duvernay, 471, Amiot à Duvernay, 3 fév. 1841.

[9]Chapters from Garneau appeared at intervals in *Le Canadien*. Chauveau's *Charles Guérin* came out in part in the *Album Littéraire et musicale de la Revue Canadienne* (1846), as did Boucher de Boucherville's *Une de perdue* (1847–50). *Le Jeune Latour* came out in sections in *L'Aurore* in 1844.

secure *la survivance* was without economic strength. In five great lectures,[10] delivered in Montreal between January 1846 and December 1848, he outlined a new social and economic philosophy in which he urged the *Canadiens* to assume their rights and responsibilities in the colony's social and economic life. Had they heeded Parent, the *Canadiens* might well have gained the key to the new economic order then being founded.

Parent questioned the classical educational system which prepared its students for nothing but the overcrowded professions. He criticized his compatriots' steady preoccupation with the purely political and the clergy's spirituality based on a premise of corrupt human nature, and he proposed sweeping reforms in all social, educational, and religious institutions, and, more important, in the habits of thought of the habitants. As in politics before 1840, so now in the economic and cultural spheres, Parent challenged the current doctrines, pointing the way to economic emancipation, exhorting his people to put themselves in the current of progress.[11] For, he concluded, in his first lecture, the *Canadiens* must awaken, so that "cette révolution qui s'est opérée de nos jours sous nos yeux, ne soit pas perdue pour nous, et qu'elle nous apprenne que l'empire du monde moderne a été donné au mouvement, à l'activité, à l'action vive, constante de l'homme sur la matière." He was not heard, of course, as fully as he would have wished. As late as February 21, 1848, *La Minerve*, commenting on recent progress in commerce and agriculture, deplored the average *Canadien's* lack of interest: "L'indifférence sur ces matières est impardonable, elle nous

[10]"L'Industrie comme moyen de conserver la Nationalité canadienne-française" (January 2, 1846); "Importance de l'étude de l'économie politique" (December 1, 1846); "Du Travail chez l'homme" (September 23, 1847); "Considérations sur notre système d'éducation populaire, sur l'éducation en général et les moyens législatifs d'y pouvoir" (February 19, 1848); "Du Prêtre et du spiritualisme" (December 16, 1848). The first of these lectures was published in *Répertoire National*, IV, 3–21, the second in *Les Mélanges Religieux* (9, 11, 15 déc. 1846) and the fifth in *L'Avenir* (27, 30 déc. 1848). Accounts and large extracts of the third and fourth lectures appeared respectively in *Les Mélanges Religieux* (28 sept. 1847), *L'Avenir* (2 oct. 1847), *La Minerve* (27 sept. 1847) and in *Les Mélanges Religieux* (22, 25, 29 fév. 1848), *L'Avenir* (26 fév. 1848), *La Minerve* (18 déc. 1848).

[11]M. Trudel, *L'Influence de Voltaire au Canada* (Montréal, 1945), p. 200; Emile Chartier, "La Vie de l'esprit au Canada français, 1792–1867, 3e étude," La Socété Royale du Canada, *Mémoires*, IIIe Série, XXVII (1933), s. 1, 49–61; Arthur St. Pierre, "La littérature sociale canadienne-française avant la Confédération," La Société Royale du Canada, *Mémoires*, IIIe Série, XLIV (1950), s. 1, 67–94; F. Ouellet, "Etienne Parent et le mouvement du catholicisme social," *Bulletin des Recherches historiques*, LXI (1955), 99–118; *Les Mélanges Religieux*, 4 déc. 1846, 28 sept. 1847, 9, 12, 16, 19 jan. 1849; *La Minerve*, 27 sept. 1847, 24, 28 fév., 18 déc. 1848.

ferait demeurer en arrière des autres peuples." Nevertheless, things were looking up: at least the leaders of French-Canadian opinion began to realize that economic activity was not a subordinate way of life and began to feel a sense of urgency.

Among the first to sniff the winds of change was young Denis-Emery Papineau. In a typically penetrating letter[12] he enumerated three "motifs d'espérance de rétablissement." First, the failure of so many harvests in the first years of the decade had brought long-needed improvements in the old agricultural methods and also had "forcé le peuple de changer sa manière dispendieuse de se nourrir pour en prendre une plus économique. Et lorsque les causes de disette auront cessé, il pourra facilement conserver ses habitudes d'économie et rétablir ses finances." Secondly, industry, which had suffered so much from "les déplorables et tragiques événements de 1837 et 1838," would benefit now from new skills and methods learned across the border by the refugees "dont bon nombre reviennent maintenant pour essayer de pratiquer ce qu'ils ont appris, ou bien ils donnent ces idées à leurs amis du Canada." And, he concluded, the many who remained abroad would leave more jobs for those at home.

There were other encouraging signs: the first Canadian protective agricultural tariff, the legislature's acts of 1844 and 1845 that raised grants to farmers to £150 for each *comté* in Lower Canada, the employment provided by the beginning of the Beauharnois canal, by the increase in shipbuilding in Quebec City, by the fleet of steamships sailing the St. Lawrence, and, above all, by the overriding interest in railroads.

In increasing numbers papers published stories of new ventures in which *Canadiens* were becoming involved. Cherrier and Cartier became proprietors, with George Moffatt and A.-M. DeLisle, of large blocks of shares in the St. Lawrence and Atlantic Railroad. A new steamship company, La Compagnie du Richelieu, was started with *Canadien* funds. The Banque d'Epargne founded by the *Canadiens* as a first step towards sharing in the return of prosperity and under the patronage of Bishop Bourget, chose as directors A.-N. Morin, Joseph Bourret, and Lewis Drummond. *La Minerve* commented on December 7, 1846: "il n'y a encore que peu d'années il n'existait que deux ou trois marchands canadiens qui se livrassent au commerce d'importation, et que maintenant il s'en trouve un grand nombre qui font d'excellentes affaires." Indeed, by December 31, 1846, *La Minerve* could pro-

---

[12]Collection Papineau-Bourassa, D.-E. Papineau à Lactance Papineau, 22 jan. 1843.

perly pronounce that "un grand progrès s'est accompli dans le pays vers les travaux qui facilitent les communications, et favorisent le commerce."

Nor was the church indifferent to the changes in the air. Shortly after his succession, Bishop Bourget had made it clear that he intended to renew the face of Catholicism in French Canada. During his first year he had organized a great mission throughout his diocese to be preached by one of the foremost orators in the Catholic world, Count Charles-Auguste-Marie-Joseph de Forbin-Janson, Bishop of Nancy and Toul, Primate of Lorraine. A member of one of the highest princely families of France, Monsignor de Nancy (as the *Canadiens* referred to him) was such a conservative royalist that he had been forced from his diocese by the revolution of 1830. But he was also absorbed in missionary activity and a master of rhetoric. In 1839, on a tour of the United States he became, rather surprisingly for a reactionary aristocrat, a fast friend of the liberal exile, Abbé Etienne Chartier, who probably suggested his visit to Canada. Between September 1840 and December 1841 Mgr. de Nancy traversed Lower Canada, visiting some sixty villages and preaching rousing sermons —two of which Sydenham attended in state in Montreal—before crowds sometimes numbering as many as 10,000 people.[13] Before he left, he had initiated the resumption of close and large-scale religious contacts with France.

While the Bishop of Nancy was still in Canada, Bishop Bourget travelled to France and Rome and returned carrying with him the reawakening energies of the Catholic revival. By 1845 he had arranged for the emigration from France of the Oblates and the Jesuits, the Dames du Sacré-Cœur and the Sisters of the Good Shepherd. He had also founded two Canadian religious congregations of his own, established the Saint-Vincent-de-Paul Society, erected a new cathedral chapter, carried out an extensive canonical visitation of his diocese, pressed Rome to establish an ecclesiastical province for the whole of British North America, and organized a whole series of parish missions and huge processions of holy pictures, relics, and statues of the madonna. In doing all this he was not only fostering Catholicism in Lower Canada; he had become one of the most powerful advocates of change, injecting into the *Canadien* mood the full fever of ultramontanism.

---

[13]*Le Vrai Canadien*, 18 déc. 1840; AAM, Bourget à Signay, 19 déc. 1840; N. E. Dionne, *Mgr de Forbin-Janson, sa vie, son œuvre en Canada* (Québec, 1895); W. Lebon, *Histoire, Collège de Ste-Anne*, I, 420–9.

The new orders, and especially the Jesuits who began in 1843 to
lay the foundations of the Collège Sainte-Marie that would train so
many energetic young *Canadiens*, were the main contributions to
this revolution. Another was *Les Mélanges Religieux*. Here, the *Canadiens* found long articles in praise of de Maistre and de Bonald,
copious excerpts from the works of Veuillot and of Montalembert,
attacks on Michelet and Victor Cousin, and discussions of the university question in France. They heard vibrant appeals exhorting their
youth to join the movement, like this of November 26, 1842: "Vous
voulez être de votre siècle, jeunes amis, vous voulez marcher avec lui?
Eh, suivez le donc dans les temples, au pied des chaires chrétiennes,
aux tribunaux de la pénitence, à la table sainte! Oui, c'est là qu'il vous
conduira à cette époque d'entraînement religieux, l'heureuse régénération, qui ne saurait plus être contestable." They were reminded of
how much they owed the Church, of how much *la survivance*
depended on it.

C'est ainsi que nous entendons la nationalité canadienne: la religion, le
catholicisme d'abord, puis la patrie. Car celle-ci ne prend de force et de
physionomie véritable que dans l'appui et la protection de celle-là: le
Canada sans catholicisme c'est un drapeau sans couleur. . . . Car ce ne sont
pas des frontières, ni même des lois et des administrations politiques
et civiles qui font une nationalité, c'est une religion, une langue, un caractère
national, en un mot; et si nous sommes de quelque valeur aux yeux de la
politique anglaise, soyez assurés que c'est parce que nous sommes catholiques et que nous parlons français.

And they received news of their fellow Catholics throughout the
world. "Pour parvenir à remplir leur mission," *Les Mélanges* noted on
March 31, 1846, "les Editeurs n'ont rien épargné; ils ont fait venir à
grands frais les meilleurs journaux d'Europe, l'Univers, l'Ami de la
Religion, le Journal des villes et des campagnes de France, le Tablet
de Londres, le Freeman's Journal de New York, le Cross d'Halifax,
le Catholic Magazine de Baltimore, le Catholic Herald de Philadelphie,
le Propagateur Catholique de la Nouvelle-Orléans." In a word, the
paper opened a window on the Catholic world for the *Canadiens*, and
through it there came the high ultramontane mood—aggressive,
assertive, almost intransigent—which was so much in keeping with
their own awakening.

As the climate of opinion in cultural, religious, and economic affairs
grew more enthusiastic, the *Canadiens* rediscovered their joyous and
hospitable sense of fellowship. Everywhere they began to join new
social and patriotic clubs. Napoléon Aubin's founding of the Société
Saint-Jean-Baptiste of Québec just prior to Bagot's 1842 visit seems

to have set the new tone. By the winter of 1843 Duvernay had decided to resurrect the parent society in Montreal; within the year several others were set up, all of them witness to the *Canadiens'* renewed interest in things cultural. As were the number of literary societies inaugurated between 1843 and 1845, most notably La Société Littéraire de Québec, founded by Aubin, and the Montreal Société des Amis which included the historian Garneau, a future political leader, A.-A. Dorion, and Cherrier's stepson, Charles-Joseph Coursol, and which sponsored the monthly *L'Album de La Revue Canadienne*. And on December 17, 1844, some two hundred young Montrealers met in the chambers of another recent foundation, La Société d'Histoire naturelle, to start the famous Institut Canadien.[14]

Although this was not, perhaps, the best of times, neither was it the worst. Everyone began to be happier and better fed. The elderly were dignified and respected. Men dealt with each other on equal terms. From commerce to literature, in the Church and in the salon, the *Canadiens* moved out of the depression, out of misery. They placed no limit on their enterprise. They had opened the Union debate in the drab, discouraging days of "POULET" Thomson. They now began the campaign for responsible government in a period of breathless activity, and under a governor general whose appointment and first actions gave rise to enthusiasm.

SIR CHARLES METCALFE

On February 25, 1843, while French Canada knelt in prayer for the dying Sir Charles Bagot, *Le Canadien* announced the appointment of his successor, Sir Charles Theophilus Metcalfe. The government in Kingston, however, had already heard the news, and with it, reports lavish with praise of the man. Bagot himself had confided to the Colonial Secretary that "often have I lain in my bed considering whom I should most desire to have as my successor and to play out my hand here. And Metcalfe has first invariably presented himself to me,"[15] a view which Bagot reiterated a month later when he wrote to Peel describing his successor-elect as "from all that I can learn of him the *unicus homo* for the post."[16] LaFontaine, in his turn, heard from Wakefield: "You have got a perfect new Governor-General. Falconer and I are quite delighted being sure that the new order of things in

[14]V. Morin, "Clubs et sociétés sociales notoires d'autrefois," *Cahiers des Dix* (1950), p. 206; see also *La Minerve*, 24 avril 1845.
[15]Bagot Papers, 7, Bagot to Stanley, Feb. 23, 1843.
[16]*Ibid.*, 7, Bagot to Peel, March 26, 1843.

Canada will be consolidated, not overturned, as some had hoped. . . . He is *all* that you can desire."[17] And Aylwin in Quebec received a letter from "une parente de Sir Robert Peel lui-même" reassuring him that "tout ira bien avec le nouveau."[18]

The press echoed these impressions. Cauchon told the readers of his *Journal* on March 24 that "une personne éminente d'Angleterre" had sent high acclaim for the new Governor, adding on his own behalf on April 11 that "les esprits les plus soupçonneux, s'appuyant sur le passé, sont forcés malgré eux de reconnaître en lui un homme d'une extrême justice et d'une grande habileté." *Le Canadien* commented on February 27: "D'après ce que nous connaissons des antécédents de sir Charles Metcalfe, il y a peu d'hommes plus propres à remplacer sir Charles Bagot. . . . On assure que Sir Charles Bagot est très satisfait du choix qu'on a fait de son successeur." It also reprinted on March 10 an encomium, which *La Minerve* had published in the question-and-answer technique of the catechism, describing "les qualifications de Sir Charles Metcalfe pour remplir le tâche difficile qui lui est imposée."

DEMANDE: Jugera-t-il par lui-même ou se laissera-t-il mener?
RÉPONSE: Il ne s'est jamais laissé mener.
D. Comment supporte-t-il la violence?
R. Jamais il ne la permet. . . .
D. Craint-il la responsabilité?
R. C'est tout le contraire.
D. Mais s'il fait erreur, comme il arrive aux plus sages et qu'un journal le rectifie?
R. Du moment qu'il apercevra l'erreur, il se corrigera avec empressement.
D. Trop confiant en lui-même, peut-être, et un peu aveugle sur ses propres erreurs?
R. Au contraire, il est modeste, exempt de toute fatuité mais ferme dans ses opinions, qu'il mûrit avec un soin exemplaire. . . .
D. Il n'est donc pas probable qu'il prenne en aversion les Canadiens-français.
R. Cette demande n'a pas besoin d'une réponse.
D. Il pourra sans doute s'apercevoir que Sir Charles Bagot a gagné le cœur des Franco-Canadiens par la justice et les bons procédés; et que ce peuple est placé dans les circonstances qui tendent à en faire le peuple le plus loyal entre les sujets de la reine d'Angleterre en Amérique.
R. Cela dépend de l'état des faits . . .
D. Quelle est sa règle de conduite?
R. C'est la conscience de son devoir, qu'il a forte.

17Papiers LaFontaine, Wakefield to LaFontaine, Feb. 2, 1843.
18*Ibid.*, Aylwin à LaFontaine, 8 mars 1843.

Little did Duvernay realize that within a year all these great qualities would be turned against his masters. But, for the time being, he seemed well satisfied with Metcalfe's unquestionable qualifications for canonization! So, apparently, was Aubin. He grew lyrical, writing in *Le Fantasque* on March 4 that

Il aime à juger par lui-même et ne se laisse jamais conduire.
Il ne souffre pas qu'on cherche à l'intimider. . . .
Il ne se laisse jamais surprendre par la flatterie. . . .
Il est modeste, point présomptueux, et ne s'aveugle pas sur lui-même.
Il est infatigable et saisit habilement toutes les parties d'une question. . . .
Un homme équitable dans toute la force du terme. . . .
Dites, Canadiens, avez-vous encore vu promesses aussi brillantes?

Meanwhile Metcalfe had sailed from Liverpool. He reached Kingston on March 29 and on the next day he went to Government House and met his councillors. Portly, moon-faced, and balding, he looked like Benjamin Franklin, noted *Le Canadien* on April 3, and showed all the signs of a good, firm, and prudent character. Moreover, "la conformation de son front indiquerait, suivant les phrénologistes, le siège d'une haute intelligence." Then began the usual testimonials, the rush to meetings of congratulation, and the hurried composition of loyal addresses. From Quebec Archbishop Signay wrote: "Si c'est avec douleur que nous voyons s'éloigner de nous Sir Charles Bagot dont le souvenir sera toujours si précieux aux Canadiens, cette douleur est tempérée par la satisfaction que nous éprouvons à le voir remplacé par un homme dont les vues libérales et la haute sagesse sont signalement appréciés dans la mère-patrie."[19] Bishop Bourget wrote likewise: "Ce que la renommée nous a appris des grandes qualités de Votre Excellence et de ses dispositions sincères à rendre justice à tous les loyaux sujets de notre Gracieuse Souveraine nous fait espérer que son administration fera le bonheur de cette Province."[20] And the Director of the Collège de Saint-Hyacinthe, Joseph LaRocque, expressed a hope which, according to *Les Mélanges Religieux*, the press and the politicians shared: "Votre Excellence a été précédée en cette Province par une telle réputation de sagesse, d'équité, et de Hauteur de Principes, que tous espèrent de son administration le bonheur et la prospérité générale."[21]

Accounts of public meetings and loyal addresses began to pour in. One of the first came from Quebec where, as *Le Canadien* reported

[19]AAQ, Régistre des lettres, 20, 300, Signay à Metcalfe, 29 mars 1843.
[20]PAC, MG 24, A 33, Metcalfe Papers, Bourget à Metcalfe, 7 avril 1843.
[21]Metcalfe Papers, LaRocque à Metcalfe, 15 avril 1843.

on April 10, "une assemblée très nombreuse" chaired by Caron met on April 8 and cheered a text prepared by Neilson—who had apparently forgotten his promise to Thomson that no French Canadian would ever co-operate with the Union. Another arrived from Montreal. There, on April 11, over five thousand people joined with a platform of orators to sing the praises of the new Governor. The address itself (published in *La Minerve* on April 13) was proposed by Cherrier, seconded by Cartier, repeating their "satisfaction de voir qu'un gouverneur cher au pays [est] remplacé par une personne dont la réputation est distinguée." And others came from Sainte-Elizabeth-de-Berthier, from Longueuil, from Saint-Hyacinthe, indeed from the home riding of every alert and astute politician.

In fact, Metcalfe deserved much of this praise. Born and trained in the Far East, he had developed into what Macaulay termed "the ablest civil servant that I ever knew in India."[22] Later, as governor of Jamaica, he had solved all problems and won all hearts by his kindness and generosity, earning from the Colonial Society in London the tribute that "Colonial Government could never thereafter be conducted on any other principles than those of his administration."[23] Now, in his late fifties, prematurely aged and afflicted with cancer of the face, he left his quiet retirement reluctantly, out of a sense of duty. And here in Canada, he continued, as ever, to make the best impression. Within the first five months of his tenure, he donated over £250 to various charitable (mostly religious) institutions in Lower Canada alone—thus initiating a habit which he would continue until his very last days, when, if there were two opinions of his policies, there still remained only one about his generosity.[24]

French Canada responded quickly. On the occasion of the Governor's pardoning a prisoner, *La Minerve* commented (June 19): "Chaque jour nous apporte la nouvelle d'un acte de miséricorde de la part de Sir Charles Metcalfe. C'est une grande puissance d'attraction que la miséricorde en politique. . . . Honneur donc, nous n'avons pas besoin de dire courage, à celui qui est juste et miséricordieux par principe et par caractère." Later, when Montreal celebrated Saint-Jean-Baptiste Day for the first time since its restoration as a holiday, Metcalfe's coat-of-arms appeared among the principal decorations. And in August 1843, when he came to Lower Canada, the French

---

[22]Quoted in G. E. Wilson, *The Life of Robert Baldwin* (Toronto, 1933), p. 169.
[23]Quoted in Dent, *Last Forty Years*, I, 264.
[24]*La Minerve*, 9 nov. 1843, claimed that Metcalfe's gifts in the colony amounted so far to over £2000.

Canadians gave him a more cordial personal welcome than they had ever accorded any other governor.

In Montreal men put up banners and bunting, women prepared their best dresses. In front of the City Hall, Mayor Bourret ordered a huge triumphal arch to proclaim the city's loyalty with big Union Jacks and allegorical designs of Britannia and Justice. And high in the newly completed towers of Notre-Dame, the Sulpicians installed a specially designed keyboard which *La Minerve* reported would connect with the great bells and "exécuter l'hymne national au passage de Son Excellence devant l'église paroissiale." Accordingly, at three o'clock in the afternoon of August 21, 1843, despite strong winds and thunder showers, an imposing procession traversed the ten miles out to the steamship landing to await the Governor. Behind it followed "une foule de gens impatients de témoigner leurs respects à Son Excellence." And, back inside the walls, the soldiers in full dress stood poised, large crowds waited impatiently in the wet streets, and "toutes les fenêtres sont garnies de dames." Unfortunately, they were all disappointed. *Son Excellence*, though he had been travelling since seven in the morning, was delayed by the storm. By six o'clock the tired troops had returned to their barracks, and the patient procession left the landing.[25] No one considered how much this might be an omen of future disappointments.

The Governor arrived quietly after seven. He rode directly to the Hotel Rasco. The next day, he apologized for the delay, and with great fanfare, visited the Port, Saint Ann's Market, the Mercantile Library, the new Notre-Dame "qu'il paraissait contempler avec beaucoup de satisfaction," McGill College, and the Hospital of the Grey Nuns. Everywhere, he received protests of devotion and made the best of impressions. Before sailing for Quebec, he finally conquered *le tout Montréal* by declaring, *La Minerve* reported on August 24, "que Montréal méritait de devenir le siège du gouvernement."

In Quebec, the city council and citizens organized an even more magnificent parade. On the evening of August 24, Mayor Caron and his council, all suitably robed, the whole array of the city's magistrates, General Sir James Hope, the Commanding Officer, the regimental bands, the Presidents of the Societies of Saints Andrew and Patrick, the companies of firemen, all the members of the Société Saint-Jean-Baptiste "avec sa musique, ses décorations, ses superbes bannières et les drapeaux de la milice," and whoever was left of the citizenry descended to the "quai de Gillespie and Co" to greet the

25*Les Mélanges Religieux*, 22 août 1843; *La Minerve*, 24 août 1843.

distinguished guest. He disembarked as a salvo of seventeen guns thundered from the Citadel, and took his place in the Mayor's official carriage. With R.-E. Caron he rode between rows of soldiers presenting arms, up Saint-Pierre Street and the Côte de la Montagne, under Prescott Gate "ornée de verdure et d'une couronne de baronet," and on to Place d'Armes where the Saint George Society stood cheering. Then, as he left the carriage, he received the usual addresses and answered "par des paroles gracieuses." Afterwards, the Société Saint-Jean-Baptiste, which had marched ahead "presqu'au complet et dans le meilleur ordre, bannières, flammes, étendards déployés," three times raised a universal shout of "Vive le Gouverneur." They had wanted, said Le Canadien, to show honour "à celui qui, tant par son caractère personnel que comme représentant de Sa Majesté, mérite si justement leurs respects et leurs hommages."[26]

In Three Rivers on August 28, there was the same story of salvos and pomp, of triumphal arches and streets lined with cheers. Metcalfe then travelled to Chambly and Sorel, and in both places the Canadiens repeated the same splendid, noisy, and popular welcome. They meant, of course, to impress him with the success of Bagot's policy, but they also admired in him the generous and dignified gentleman who continued on this trip, as usual, to shower them with kindness. As Le Canadien noted on September 1: "Il n'y a pas de souverain en Europe, nous pouvons le dire sans exagération, qui se montre aussi peu ménager de sa bourse que notre gouverneur-général Sir Charles Metcalfe. . . . Son Excellence a semé sur son passage dans sa promenade actuelle les largesses." "If grand receptions," Metcalfe confessed in a letter to his sister, "loyal addresses, banners displayed, and triumphal arches could afford comfort and assurance, I should have them."[27] The Canadiens meant that he should. In their new mood of energy and optimism they were welcoming Son Excellence into the brave new world they saw all about them. Above all, they were celebrating the arrival of the man who seemed to be bringing the promise of a better national life.

They did not yet know that in the council chamber approval rang with less wholehearted a note. For Metcalfe and his councillors were already disputing openly. And soon the personal and practical difficulties which divided them would explode from behind the cheers to stir the Canadiens into another profound national dispute.

[26]Le Canadien, 23, 25 août 1843.
[27]Metcalfe to Mrs. Smythe, Aug. 27, 1843, quoted in J. W. Kaye, The Life and Correspondence of Charles, Lord Metcalfe (2 vols., London, 1858), II, 354.

9

La Crise Metcalfe: Constitutional March 1843-March 1844

"I never undertook anything with so much reluctance, or so little hope of doing good," Sir Charles Metcalfe confided to a friend shortly before coming to Canada. "I fear that the little reputation that I have acquired is more likely to be damaged than improved in the troubled waters of Canada."[1] And, in fact, he soon encountered the constitutional dilemma which Lord John Russell had foreseen would arise out of the theories of those who were now Metcalfe's Executive Councillors. Worse, he also found himself temperamentally unable to interpret correctly the intentions of the men about him, and, judging them by the norms of his past experience, he was jolted by their ideas.

Metcalfe was not the only one to question the theory of responsible government in a colony. Neilson, Viger, Papineau had shared the difficulty stated by Lords John Russell and Sydenham. And even now no less a personage than Prince Albert repeated it to Lord Stanley:

I don't think the Crown of England could allow the establishment of a responsible government in Canada as that would be tantamount to a declaration of separation from the mother country. If the Governor General is constitutionally bound to act according to the advice of his responsible government, how is he to obey the instructions which the Queen's Government may think it proper to send to him? . . . The Queen thinks Sir Charles ought to be strongly backed by the Home Government in his resistance to the establishment of a responsible government.[2]

Even without this conflict on political theory, Metcalfe would probably have clashed with his Council. For one thing, he could not fathom party government; for another, he could not get along with

---

[1]Metcalfe to R. D. Mangles, Jan. 22, 1843, quoted in Dent, *Last Forty Years*, I, 274.

[2]PAC, MG 24, A 15, Derby Papers, Part I, Prince Albert to Stanley, May 31, 1843.

the particular party he found in office. Trained as a civil servant, he had always thought in only one dimension. He was not, like Bagot, a brilliant, civilized, highly trained diplomat; nor did he possess the same large humanity. He had none of the elasticity of mind with which Bagot had been able to translate so many intangibles. He was courageous, proper, an administrator of marked efficiency, a man brave in spirit, honourable, generous; but he could not accommodate the trimmings and compromises which mark the successful politician. He had too small a sense of humour and too great a sense of duty. Inevitably he did the wrong thing in the right way.

Following the Indian and Jamaican precedents that had built his reputation, he wanted a government of all the talents, one that "would bring into the public service the men of greatest merit and efficiency without party distinction."[3] "The idea of governing according to the interested views of a party, is odious to me," he confided to a friend, adding, in a despatch to Stanley, that he thought such a practice would be tantamount to "tearing up Her Majesty's Commission."[4] "He wants to conciliate all the parties," wrote George Wicksteed, law clerk of the legislature, to John Neilson, "and would like to have Mr. Cartwright [an Upper Canadian Tory] and Mr. Baldwin and Mr. Moffatt and Mr. Lafontaine [sic] excellent friends and fellow council-lors. He would persuade them and himself that there are no parties properly so-called in this country, and that they and the friends of all of them could form one great party anxious only for the good of this great and glorious colony &c &c &c."[5] Even if he had been able to adapt to the practice of party government, Metcalfe still would not have understood the group he found at the top in Canada. Indeed he reacted in the way which was all too typical: he considered the French rebels and the Upper Canadian Reformers republicans. He inclined towards the Tories whom he described as "the only party in the colony with which I can sympathize."[6] In LaFontaine he saw only "an Obstinate Man who will have his own way,"[7] and the other councillors were "men with whom it was impossible to cooperate satisfactorily."[8]

The Executive Councillors, on the other hand, expected what they

---

[3]PAC, C.O. 537/142, Metcalfe to Stanley, April 24, 1843.
[4]Metcalfe to a friend in India, as quoted in Kaye, Life of Metcalfe, II, 366; C.O. 537/142, Metcalfe to Stanley, May 10, 1843.
[5]Neilson Collection, II, 24–7, Wicksteed to Neilson, March 28, 1843.
[6]Metcalfe to Stanley, as quoted in Kaye, Life of Metcalfe, II, 360.
[7]C.O. 537/142, Metcalfe to Stanley, May 10, 1843.
[8]Derby Papers, Metcalfe to Stanley, Nov. 26, 1843.

thought Bagot had conceded, a responsible government in which they, and not the Governor, would rule through their party's majority in the Assembly. "Sir Charles Bagot's lamentable illness," Metcalfe complained, "favoured all their pretensions."[9] When he tried to right the practice, to administer as he, not they, thought best he learned from them, as he said, "that my attempts to conciliate all parties are criminal. . . . I am required to give myself up entirely to the Council, to submit entirely to their direction, to have no judgment of my own; to bestow the patronage of the Government exclusively on their partisans; to proscribe their opponents and to make some public and unequivocal declaration of my adhesion to those conditions."[10] He did not realize that their insistence on party government was in accordance with current practice at Westminister; but neither did the Council realize that, in theory at least, it was far ahead of current thinking there. As Peel noted, "The principle of the relation of the Sovereign to the Ministers here, is practically acted upon, it is recognized as the general constitutional rule—but what would be thought of the demand made by ministers that the Sovereign should formally and by stipulation admit it to be the rule? If this would be preposterous in the case of the Sovereign, it is much more so in the case of a servant of the Sovereign exercising a delegated authority."[11] And even if the theory had been accepted in the mother country, Queen Victoria exercised over her cabinet far more influence than the Canadian council were inclined to allow their governor.

Thus for reasons of both theory and temperament, a conflict was bound to come. It might have done so on any number of issues, on the question of the civil list,[12] or of an amnesty for the political exiles, or of moving the capital back to Lower Canada. On all of these LaFontaine and his people felt strongly enough to insist on their own way. But on these the Governor, whose mind was not wholly illiberal, tended to agree with them.[13] Instead, the break came over the question of patronage.

Since they had taken office, the Reformers from Upper Canada and the *Canadien* councillors had hardly had ears enough to hear all those seeking government appointments. To all the requests from

[9]C.O. 537/142, Metcalfe to Stanley, April 24, 1843.
[10]*Ibid.*, Metcalfe to Stanley, May 10, 1843.
[11]Derby Papers, Peel to Stanley, June 1, 1843.
[12]W. G. Ormsby, "The Civil List Question in the Province of Canada," *Canadian Historical Review*, XXXV (1954), 93–118.
[13]W. G. Ormsby, "Sir Charles Metcalfe and the Canadian Union," *Canadian Historical Association, Report* (1961), pp. 35–47.

his section LaFontaine had paid unwavering and unrelenting attention. And from Montreal and Quebec where they represented him, Drummond and Aylwin sent in an endless flow of requests, insisting on being heard. Aylwin, for instance, wrote rather acidly one day: "Je n'entends pas que l'Administration à laquelle j'appartiens me mette de côté lorsque je suis sur les lieux pour se consulter avec qui que ce soit, et je n'entends pas non plus qu'il se passe des affaires d'un intérêt local pour le district de Québec sans y mettre mon grain de sel."[14] LaFontaine and his people knew they had an obligation to do this. For they must win the *Canadiens* to the Union and to their own party. Without a united party they would have no practical way of assuring *la survivance*. On his part, the Governor General also required patronage. He had orders from the Colonial Secretary: "As the Head of the Government, and as the Representative of the Crown, the patronage of the Crown rests in your hands. . . . As long as you keep it in your hands, and refuse to apply it exclusively to party purposes, it will be felt that you have really substantial power."[15] Orders or not, he needed control of patronage if—as he had successfully done in Jamaica—he was to fill his Council with all the most able patriots. He resolved to keep his Council in its place. "The general course which I propose to pursue towards the Council," he wrote to a friend in England,

is to treat them with the confidence and cordiality due to the station which they occupy; to consult them not only when the law or established usage requires that process, but also whenever the importance of the occasion recommend it; and whenever I conceive that the public service will be benefitted [*sic*] by their aid and advice. At the same time, I must be on my guard against their encroachments.[16]

Metcalfe wanted talent; LaFontaine and his followers wanted a majority; and each needed patronage. And since LaFontaine's party held no monopoly on talent the Governor and the Council soon collided. In mid-April they were arguing about the appointment of a naval officer in Quebec. "Nommez un des nôtres," insisted Aylwin to LaFontaine, "il ne faut pas abandonner le patronage du gouvernement Provincial. Si Sir Charles Metcalfe veut faire le Sultan des Indes, il y aura moyen de l'amener à la raison. Courage, modération,

---

[14]Papiers LaFontaine, Aylwin à LaFontaine, 24 mars 1843; see also Aylwin à LaFontaine, 26 mars, 17 avril 1843.
[15]C.O. 537/141, Stanley to Metcalfe, May 29, 1843; Derby Papers, Stanley to Metcalfe, Nov. 1, 1843.
[16]Metcalfe to Normanby, April 24, 1843, quoted in E. Thompson, *The Life of Charles, Lord Metcalfe* (London, 1937), p. 361.

fermeté et le bon parti triomphera."[17] If necessary, he continued, LaFontaine should use strong language to impress the "nouveau venu" with the Council's unity. "Faites lui comprendre qu'il n'y a pas de dissidence entre les gens du Bas-Canada. S'il vous tarrabuste, il nous tarrabuste tous, et je vous donne ma procuration politique, vous ferez pour moi ce que vous ferez pour vous."

By the summer of 1843 they had reached an impasse. Metcalfe would not play a minor role. The French councillors and other *Canadiens* about him were disappointed. Had they celebrated responsible government ten months ago only to find now that what one governor had done his successor could undo? They grew increasingly suspicious and reserved. All sensed a threatening break. "On est dans un état d'ignorance complète quand aux procédés de Sir Charles," wrote Aylwin, "le Grand Mogul ou le Grand Sultan dans son Harem ne pourrait vivre plus à l'Asiatique."[18] "Now comes the tug of war," sighed Metcalfe,[19] unwilling, however, to ask outright for his Council's resignation. He wanted to conciliate everyone, not to antagonize the Reformers. And he had no wish to segregate the French or to gamble with that immense reserve of goodwill which he found during his tour of Lower Canada. "If the French Gentlemen now in the Council resigned," he continued to Stanley,

I should endeavour to bring in others of the same race, in order that the French Canadians may be fully represented in that body; but there is reason to fear, such is the blind following of nearly the whole of that party, that no influential members could be induced to accept office under those circumstances. The French Canadians generally and especially the Lower orders are supposed to take no interest in the question of "Responsible Government" but they are likely to follow their leader with implicit obedience.

Stanley suggested that Metcalfe attempt to retain LaFontaine, and even to bring him over to his views.

If he be, as I suspect him to be, merely a weak and vain man, fond of holding a conspicious Station, but unequal to the occupation of it, you may, through his vanity, and by great apparent deference to his advice, govern his Party whom it is essential to hold through him. If he be sincerely desirous of maintaining the interests, as he understands them, of his Compatriots, or, which comes to the same thing, afraid of being thought not sufficiently to maintain them, he may not be insensible to the argument, that the privilege which you now claim on behalf of the Crown, may,

[17]Papiers LaFontaine, Aylwin à LaFontaine, 17 avril 1843.
[18]Papiers LaFontaine, Aylwin à LaFontaine, 17 juil. 1843.
[19]C.O. 537/142, Metcalfe to Stanley, May 10, 1843.

under altered circumstances, be argued for the protection of a French, as now for a Conservative minority, and that it is more than possible that an overweening exercise of the powers of a numerical majority may, at some further time, recoil upon his own Countrymen, and the results of their disappointment fall upon him, who will have been found to have betrayed beyond their due limits, those rights which, as British Subjects, they now enjoy to the fullest extent.[20]

But Metcalfe could no longer put up with "the dictatorial Councillor."[21] He resolved instead to *"quarrel with the men, not with the great majority whom they represent for the time."*[22] Thus he thought to keep the French in the Council and rid himself of "the unreasonable pretensions on the part of Mr. LaFontaine."[23]

Metcalfe began a few discreet overtures to the Papineau group, realizing that to French Canadians the very name of Papineau was still a trumpet call—"Le nombre de tes amis augmente toujours," Denis-Benjamin wrote to his brother in August[24]—and that in the fall of 1842 there had been some intriguing by a number of *Canadien* politicians to have Papineau return to replace LaFontaine. "There are those who think his return very desirable," the Governor confided to Stanley in July, "and calculated to shake the exclusive ascendency of an Individual over the French party."[25] He may also have been aware that the Papineau clan had opposed the Union in 1840 precisely because they could not, like Metcalfe, reconcile party government with the legitimate authority of a colonial governor. In the fall, he approached Denis-Benjamin Papineau who reported that Metcalfe said, "J'ai eu occasion de savoir que votre frère est un ami ardent de son pays. J'espère qu'il sera le mien et je devrais le voir prochainement de retour.[26] And Dominick Daly, the only councillor whom Sir Charles trusted and with whom LaFontaine and Baldwin were already privately in disagreement, added that every hour which the great tribune spent in exile was "une heure de perdue et pour toi et pour ton pays."[27]

Soon after the session opened on September 28, 1843, Metcalfe also began to cultivate Denis-Benjamin Viger, the only *Canadien* in

[20]C.O. 537/141, Stanley to Metcalfe, June 2, 1843.
[21]C.O. 537/142, Metcalfe to Stanley, May 10, 1843.
[22]Wakefield to his London correspondent, Oct. 27, 1843, as quoted in F. Hincks, *Reminiscences of His Public Life* (Montreal, 1884), p. 114.
[23]C.O. 537/142, Stanley to Metcalfe, May 29, 1843.
[24]Collection Papineau-Bourassa, D.-B. Papineau à L.-J. Papineau, 7 août 1843.
[25]C.O. 537/142, Metcalfe to Stanley, July 26, 1843. See also Papiers LaFontaine, Wakefield to LaFontaine, Jan. 2, 1843.
[26]C.O. 537/142, Metcalfe to Stanley, July 26, 1843.
[27]Collection Papineau-Bourassa, D.-B. Papineau à L.-J. Papineau, 21 nov. 1843.

the province strong enough to influence his people. In May Metcalfe had written to Lord Stanley, "Mr. Viger is the only person in the French Canadian Party who is regarded as the rival of Mr. LaFontaine; and designations which are given of 'The Viger Party' and the 'Lafontaine party' are the only symptoms perceptible of a division among the French Canadian Party."[28] The Governor had seen through the still precarious unity which LaFontaine had taken such pains to forge and when he met Viger in September, he quickly "acquired a warm esteem for him,"[29] prizing the old man's qualities, not least of which must have been his hesitation about the LaFontaine version of responsible government and his vast knowledge of the niceties of British constitutional practice. Clearly the Governor had not only lost patience with his Council, but was beginning the search for another more to his liking, one composed of men who would agree to his "freeing himself of exclusive relations with this or that party, and of adopting the best measures, rendering equal justice to all, with councillors chosen in all the parties.[30]

But before he had concluded his arrangements, LaFontaine and Baldwin precipitated the clash. Their patience was also at an end. In July LaFontaine had threatened to resign unless the Governor extended to some Lower Canadian rebels (including Papineau) the same pardon he had, without consultation, granted two Upper Canadians.[31] In October Wakefield, who had returned to Kingston for some shadowy reason (probably financial) and had shifted his pen and brains to the service of the Governor, wrote that "I now *know* that Messrs. LaFontaine and Baldwin have got thoroughly into the Governor-General's bad graces. . . . I cannot doubt any longer that Sir Charles will come to an open rupture with them ere long."[32] Early in November LaFontaine found that the Governor had again acted without his "advice" in negotiating with Peter McGill, John Neilson, and René-Edouard Caron for the speakership of the Legislative Council.[33] But he

---

[28]C.O. 537/142, Metcalfe to Stanley, May 17, 1843.
[29]*Ibid.*, Metcalfe to Stanley, Nov. 10, 1843.
[30]Metcalfe to Stanley, June 25, 1843, as quoted in Wade, *French Canadians*, p. 243.
[31]Papiers LaFontaine, "Relation de mes entrevues avec Sir Charles Metcalfe au sujet du 'nolle prosequi'"; Daly to LaFontaine, Aug. 12, 1843; C.O. 537/142, Metcalfe to Stanley, Aug. 7, 1843; M. Boucher de la Bruyère, "LaFontaine, Rolph, Papineau, épisodes de 1838 et de 1843," Canadian Historical Association, *Report* (1923), pp. 56–64.
[32]Wakefield to his London correspondent, Oct. 27, 1843, as quoted in Hincks, *Reminiscences*, p. 114.
[33]C.O. 537/142, Metcalfe to Stanley, Nov. 10, 1843.

could hardly object then, since Caron had all the qualities for the post as well as being what *La Minerve* called (November 9, 1843) "un des nôtres." Two weeks later, however, the Governor appointed Francis Powell, son of an old-time Tory, as Clerk of the Peace for Dalhousie District in Upper Canada, a position Baldwin wanted for one of his followers. This was the end.

On November 24 the Attorneys General formally asked that Metcalfe not make appointments without consulting them and that these not prejudice their interests. The Governor, in an act which the whole of his life had gone to shape, refused absolutely. On November 25, at a council meeting, Governor and Councillors each repeated their arguments at length, but to no avail. The Council, except for Dominick Daly, decided to resign. The Governor accepted and, ever correct, entertained them for a dinner, after which they separated "en apparence les meilleurs amis du monde."[34]

Two days later *la crise Metcalfe* had come into the open.

News of the resignation, first announced in Kingston on November 27, reached Montreal two days later, and Quebec on December 1. Apparently the politicians in both cities had not suspected the mounting difficulties between the Governor and his Council. They were stunned. Duvernay published a straightforward account in *La Minerve* on November 30, adding simply: "Que va faire sir Charles dans une conjoncture aussi périlleuse? On l'ignore. . . . Encore quelques heures, et nous saurons tout." And at *L'Aurore* on December 2 word came from Barthe in Kingston that "on se perd en conjectures sur les causes de cette subite démarche." On December 1, *Les Mélanges Religieux* commented: "il n'est pas aisé de prévoir les éventualités de cette résignation"; and *Le Journal de Québec*, as yet without LaFontaine's version, merely said that "il n'y a encore rien de bien circonstancié." Only *Le Fantasque*, which could, of course, hardly wait to be in opposition again, sang a quick I-told-you-so on December 2: "Si ces résignations importantes . . . pouvaient achever de démontrer ce que nous avons toujours prêché, que la marche tranquille et efficace des affaires avec des hommes comme les Haut-Canadiens est chose impossible, alors nous nous en réjouirons." Otherwise the more serious editors, torn between belief and disbelief, seemed unable to voice an opinion for the next few weeks.

They realized that Metcalfe had just harassed to its resignation the

[34]Gérin-Lajoie, *Dix Ans au Canada*, p. 191.

first and only Executive Council of which French Canada had ever approved. Yet they heard conflicting accounts. At ten o'clock on the morning of November 27 LaFontaine, speaking in French and English, announced his "cabinet's" resignation and promised to give an explanation. Immediately Wakefield, whom most *Canadiens* still considered one of their own, moved up to sit with Daly in the places which LaFontaine and his friends had just vacated and proceeded to object on constitutional grounds to any further comments. To everyone's surprise, Viger agreed with him, and so did Neilson. On November 29, when Baldwin began to set forth his colleagues' reasons, Viger interrupted him, arguing at length from his copious fund of constitutional knowledge that attorneys general had no right to divulge in public what had passed in secret in the Council. The Assembly agreed with Baldwin by a vote of 46–23, after he assured everyone that he had Metcalfe's permission to speak; from that moment Viger became Metcalfe's main champion, assailing again and again with old and essential parliamentary quotations the unprecedented action of LaFontaine and his fellow councillors. When the Assembly nevertheless approved their resignation, Viger and Neilson and one other (obscure) *Canadien*, J.-B. Noël, voted against LaFontaine in favour of the Governor. More still: Viger soon passed from defending Metcalfe to speaking in his name.

The Lower Canadian newspapermen wondered at the whole incomprehensible performance. Used to writing about governors as either for or against their people, they could not now decide how to react. They were still more confused when they heard that as well as being supported by Viger, Metcalfe was also deep in negotiations with such unimpeachables as Caron, Neilson, Morin, and, they were told, even with Papineau.[35] They did not realize yet that the Governor and the Neilson-Viger-Papineau group shared far more than anyone had divined—especially, in recent months, a mounting aversion towards government based on "the exclusive ascendancy of an Individual." In their dilemma they sought refuge by serializing Jean-Baptiste Meilleur's endless and politically harmless report on education.

By mid-December the surprise began to wane. The Lower Canadian politicians received more details of the crisis, their newspapermen gradually recovered, and the two sides lined up. On December 13, four days after parliament had been prorogued and the ex-ministers had gone home, Viger agreed to enter the Council in their place along with

[35]*La Minerve*, 7, 14 déc. 1843; *Le Fantasque*, 2, 15, 30 déc. 1843; *Le Canadien*, 6, 15 déc. 1843.

the Upper Canadian William Henry Draper. Starting with Dominick Daly, who had not resigned, Viger set out to collect another set of ministers to represent Lower Canada. "Il dit qu'il travaille pour l'avantage de son pays et il le croit," Quesnel wrote to LaFontaine.[36] And truly Viger thought that the old forms were still the right ones. He was sincerely convinced that the resigning ministers had acted too hastily by giving "explanations" to the Assembly without the Governor's prior permission. They were young, inexperienced in the subtleties of the constitution with which he had been familiar for forty years. They had insulted the Crown. And they had jeopardized the immense goodwill which he knew Metcalfe entertained towards the French. He persuaded Parent, and the latter wrote soothingly to LaFontaine: "S'il y avait eu quelqu'irrégularité ou malentendu, il faudrait s'en prendre à la nouveauté de la chose et à l'entêtement du moment; mais il faudrait en justice reconnaître que le Père Viger n'est pas aussi fautif qu'on le pense."[37] Surely, Viger thought, patience and a long series of precedents would achieve more than sudden resignations and unparliamentary procedure.

The old *Canadien* leader had decided, *L'Aurore* reported on February 20, 1844, to remain at the Governor's elbow, and from there to defend French-Canadian claims to "leur part légitime dans l'administration du gouvernement."[38] He began his forward march through a maze of difficulties, approaching his friends, seeking who would join him. He asked Morin to continue as commissioner of Crown lands, promising as a reward to appoint him, later, as a district judge of Gaspé. Despite his poverty, Morin said no. Viger then contacted those two perennial refusers, Jean-Joseph Girouard and Côme-Séraphin Cherrier. "It is to you alone," Girouard was told, "that Lower Canada in particular can and ought to look up in so alarming a crisis. His Excellency needs your support, and I trust you will not withhold it from him."[39] He declined, however, and then sent to LaFontaine a copy of the offer and of his own answer with a note that left no doubt whose side he was on. Cherrier also refused, even though he owed Viger the expenses of his college education and the substantial grant that had formed the basis of his growing fortune. He refused as always on the grounds of ill health: but, like Girouard, he had written to congratulate LaFontaine on his resignation. The old man finally

[36]Papiers LaFontaine, Quesnel à LaFontaine, 10 jan. 1844.
[37]*Ibid.*, Parent à LaFontaine, jan. 1844.
[38]*Ibid.*, Quesnel à LaFontaine, 10 jan. 1844.
[39]*Ibid.*, Forbes to Girouard, Nov. 29, 1843.

called on Quesnel and summoned him to Kingston in virtue of his office as Queen's counsel. Before leaving, however, Quesnel also wrote LaFontaine promising him that he would do nothing of a political nature and from Government House he sent back several reports about Viger's negotiations. These and Viger's repeated failures all tended to confirm that the *Canadien* politicians were waiting to see what chance they had of keeping office before they accepted it.

Viger did not lose hope, however. For, whether the *Canadien* politicians at home supported him or not, he thoroughly expected that Papineau would rally the people to his cause. "Viger I think expects Papineau in May and that their family influence united will shove Lafontaine [*sic*] to one side," a friend reported to Baldwin,[40] while LaFontaine was told that rumours in Kingston had it "that Papineau's to be invited to take office" and that "Mr. Wakefield goes immediately to England to reconcile and get Lord Stanley's sanction for this scheme & carry out the arrangements with Mr. Papineau in Paris."[41] Denis-Benjamin Papineau took his brother's return for granted. When offered a post on the Council for himself, he declined on the grounds that with Viger and his brother already there, his appointment would turn the Executive Council into another Family Compact.[42] In fact, some six weeks before the resignation, Metcalfe, Viger, and Denis-Benjamin Papineau had all been discussing the hero's return. They were concerned with the question of the *arrérages*, Papineau's salary as speaker of the Lower Canadian Assembly amounting to £4500, which he had refused to touch during the agitation of the mid-'thirties. Through his brother, Papineau had billed the province, and Metcalfe apparently recognized that the day was coming when he would need Papineau. Although noting that Papineau had really forfeited any claim by refusing the salary when it was offered, and then by leading a rebellion, Metcalfe nevertheless forwarded the petition to Lord Stanley. He asked to be allowed to pay the "debt". "I conceive that it would be politic," he explained, "to show a ready disposition on the part of Her Majesty's Government to concur in it. . . . Acts of kindness and forgiveness which appear to be spontaneous are likely to have a better effect on the French party than those which seem to be extorted; and it is desirable that they should not attribute every act of that description to the influence of their Leaders. . . ."[43] On the

[40]Baldwin Papers, 38, Cameron to Baldwin, Dec. 21, 1843.
[41]Papiers LaFontaine, Dunn to LaFontaine, Dec. 27, 1843.
[42]Collection Papineau-Bourassa, D.-B. Papineau à Viger, 27 fév. 1844.
[43]C.O. 537/142, Metcalfe to Stanley, Nov. 11, 1843; Stanley to Metcalfe, Jan. 1, 1844.

night before the resignations Viger called Denis-Benjamin Papineau to his hotel, told him of the news and that he would side with the Governor, and then asked him to write quickly to Paris for the rebel leader's opinion.[44] He also put pressure on Amédée Papineau to insist on his father's return, and even tried to persuade Cherrier to help.[45] "Il n'y a que le brave et patriote Mr. Papineau qui pourrait nous tirer de cette fausse position," Viger's friend, E.-R. Fabre, told his sister, "il est le désiré de tout le monde, Anglais comme Canadiens."[46]

Neither Metcalfe nor Viger have left any indication of why they expected Papineau to support their administration. But they undoubtedly realized that he did not share LaFontaine's views on responsible government, that he would be gratified by the payment of his arrears, that, above all, he wished the particular rights of French-Canadian culture preserved by the separate action of the *Canadiens* themselves and not by what Neilson had called the "appui de l'extérieur" of a party united to Upper Canadians. And with all of this Metcalfe also fully agreed—he who could not tolerate party government but wished, on the other hand, "to do justice in every respect to the French Canadian people, and to consult their feelings as much as possible."[47] With reasons like these Sir Charles had won over Viger and D.-B. Papineau. Why not Louis-Joseph? At all events, the Governor and Viger expected to secure the great man's support. They were old men . . . they may be pardoned for dreaming dreams.

Viger was also certain that once "les hommes capables de réflexion" had grasped the whole of the "question soulevée par la résignation des ministres" they would agree with his stand.[48] He therefore set himself to compose another pamphlet: *La Crise ministérielle et M. Denis-Benjamin Viger*.[49] In it he dealt at length with the point of parliamentary etiquette, quoting constitutional chapter and verse to damn the impropriety of LaFontaine and Baldwin. But on the question of responsible government, he remained silent. Imbued as he was with the form and the law of the constitution, he seems not to have realized that the resignations attacked more than parliamentary decorum. Hence his pamphlet, which LaFontaine had feared enough to write twice to Baldwin for the list of precedents justifying their action,

---

[44]Papiers Viger, Daly to Viger, Feb. 6, 1844.
[45]Collection Papineau-Bourassa, 675, Julie Papineau à Lactance Papineau, 10 avril 1844; 692, Julie Papineau à L.-J. Papineau, 28 oct. 1844.
[46]APQ, Papiers Fabre, Fabre à Julie Bossange, 22 mars 1844.
[47]C.O. 537/142, Metcalfe to Stanley, May 10, 1843.
[48]Neilson Collection, II, Viger à Neilson, 2 jan. 1844.
[49]*La Crise ministérielle et M. Denis-Benjamin Viger* (Kingston, 1844).

turned out to be little more than a dry theoretical dissertation on "the proper and decent mode of dying, officially of course—so that all may fall with dignity."[50]

While Viger thus pursued his large concepts and high hopes LaFontaine manœuvred for the coming combat. Arriving in Montreal on December 15, he took advantage of Viger's absence in Kingston to tell his story first, holding several conferences with his political friends. He already had assurances from Girouard and Cherrier and within a week he could tell Baldwin that the others "all approve of the course we have taken."[51] At the same time Taché had gone to Quebec and held similar consultations with their followers. By the new year, with Viger still correcting the proofs of his pamphlet, they had made certain that despite Neilson their party held fast to LaFontaine's side of the story. Taché wrote: "Ici, silencieux, l'arme au bras on attend le jour du combat en colonnes sériées avec une noble assurance; la victoire ne sera pas un moment incertaine."[52]

The newspapers also took sides. "Les ci-devant ministres," as LaFontaine, Morin, and Aylwin were to be termed for the next five years, rallied Duvernay's *Minerve* and Cauchon's *Journal de Québec*; they could also rely, but with less assurance, on Aubin's clever *Fantasque*. Viger, on his side, controlled *L'Aurore* and held the sympathy of MacDonald's *Le Canadien*. He also had the respect of *Les Mélanges Religieux* which was finding it increasingly difficult to stay out of politics. Throughout December and January they all debated the protocol of *la crise*. According to *La Minerve* and *Le Journal de Québec*, the *ci-devants* had been right in demanding that the Governor agree to consult them and in resigning when he would not. Since they were "responsible" to the Assembly, they had also been absolutely correct in giving it the required "explanations." Besides, even if they had been wrong technically, *La Minerve* claimed (February 5) that Viger had acted even more unconstitutionally by taking office without the Assembly's support.

L'Aurore and *Le Canadien*, on the other hand, accepted Viger's argument that the ex-councillors had insulted the Crown by asking for a guarantee that Metcalfe never act against their political interests. They had compounded the insult by reporting their difficulties to the Assembly without written proof, thus forcing the members to choose between believing them or the representative of the Sovereign. Less

---

[50]Neilson Collection, I, Wicksteed to Neilson, March 7, 1844.
[51]Baldwin Papers, A 55, LaFontaine to Baldwin, Dec. 23, 1843.
[52]Papiers LaFontaine, Taché à LaFontaine, 20 jan. 1844.

inexperienced men, *L'Aurore* stated, and men less intent on their own ascendancy, would have ensured that the honour of the Crown could not be doubted. In two long, but tight and logical articles beginning on December 29, *Les Mélanges Religieux* reviewed the debate. It disagreed with the *ci-devants* for insisting on a formal guarantee that they be consulted. It deferred to Viger's opinion that they had shown bad constitutional manners, and it concluded by regretting that "la forme demandée par M. Viger n'ait pas été suivie. Elle aurait eu le bon effet d'arrêter l'espèce de division qui est la suite parmi les réformistes."

Unfortunately the division was permanent, and by the end of January, politicians, newspapermen, and the more discerning electors had deduced that *la crise Metcalfe* revolved around a far more fundamental point than parliamentary protocol, that it was based on different interpretations of responsible government. On these, for the next two months, they centred another round of discussions.

As reflected in *La Minerve* and *Le Journal*, the *ci-devant* position had all the force and merit of simplicity. To LaFontaine, responsible government meant government by the representatives of the majority who had the right to be consulted, to advise, and to expect the governor to do nothing prejudicial to their party's interests. For what *La Minerve* called on January 25 this "principe fondamental de la Constitution anglaise," the *Canadiens* had been struggling "depuis si longtemps avec tant de courage, de gloire, et de succès" (January 8). For this LaFontaine had three years ago agreed to work within the otherwise repugnant Union, and for this same principle now, the ex-ministers, as men of honour and conviction, had given up office and "courageusement immolé tous leurs intérêts et sacrifié leur amour propre et leur ambition" (January 25).

To Viger, on the other hand, and to Neilson, "responsibility" meant a "liberal" (that is non-Tory) government that honoured French-Canadian claims to a share in the administration. This type of government, they argued, did not depend upon a majority, but upon the goodwill of the governor. In a long series of complex articles which *L'Aurore* ran between the end of January and the beginning of April, Viger detailed the main points of his political creed. LaFontaine's principles of government by party majority, he posited, were inapplicable in a colony, but even if they were applicable, they would be unwise in Canada. For one thing, the governor enjoyed only "un pouvoir de délégation et nécessairement discrétionnel de la part de son souverain," and must confine himself to his instructions as well as to a rather vague "responsabilité impérieuse et redoutable pour sa réputation et les saintes obligations de son serment." Viger explained that the governor also held office as an executive councillor: "Ce qui doit lui permettre de jeter le poids de son opinion dans les délibérations du Cabinet. Ce n'est pas assez qu'il reçoive l'avis de ses conseillers pour qu'il s'y soumette, il a le droit incontestable de proposer et soutenir le sien." Thus burdened with "cette double responsabilité," Metcalfe could not then, as the *ci-devants* demanded so unreasonably "prendre sur lui de définir théoriquement un ordre de choses après tout si indéfinissable, et trancher d'un coup de trait de plume toutes les complications dont les rouages doivent nécessairement se modifier dans les diverses circonstances." Besides, French Canadians would be ill advised to demand that the governor put himself so completely at the disposal of the majority. First, because the British cabinet had approved "entièrement et sans réserves la conduite du gouverneur relativement à la résignation des ministres," and to insist now on his recalling the same men on their own terms would merely place the *Canadiens* once again, as in 1837, "en collision immédiate avec le gouvernement impérial" and perhaps even "jeter le pays dans un nouveau précipice." Second, as Stanley had remarked to Metcalfe, the French Canadians should remember the likelihood that emigration would soon make them a minority group. When this happened, LaFontaine's principle of majority rule would necessitate their abdication of any claim to "la mince part de pouvoir qu'on veut bien nous accorder." For all these reasons, then, Viger continued, the *ci-devant* position was untenable. How much more reasonable to support the governor and remain close to the source of power and influence. He concluded with his own definition of responsible government, "le plus sûr moyen de conserver un système de responsabilité dans le gouvernement pour tous ceux qui ne rêvent pas l'utopie de l'optimisme, est d'établir une douce et permanente prépondérance du principe libéral dans l'action gouvernementale."

Thus the press and the politicians re-argued and re-discussed in public the problem which LaFontaine and Baldwin and the Council on the other had debated the year before. Did responsible government mean the rule of the majority in parliament or simply a share in a liberal administration? In neither press, nor pamphlet, nor yet in the Colonial Office despatches had a clear answer been given or an opinion proved. Neither side had won. Ultimately, the only real answer had to be the one given by the electorate.

10

La Crise Metcalfe:
Party Platforms
March-December 1844

By March of 1844 neither the LaFontaine group nor the Viger party had succeeded in satisfying the other that it had the right attitude towards colonial rule, and each side began to realize that it must do more than provoke crises or write pamphlets. Each must turn to the electorate—either, as LaFontaine hoped, as a means to force his views upon the unwilling Governor or, as Viger thought, to rouse the *Canadiens* to his support. Since November both groups had busied themselves analysing the theory behind the constitution. Now they had to translate their conflict into terms which their constituents could understand, to devise the political platforms and electoral tactics which would make the *Canadiens* choose between them.

La Fontaine emphasized a single note: national unity against the ancient (Tory) enemy. And, practical as always, he allowed his propagandists at *La Minerve* and *Le Journal de Québec* to begin a stream of invective against his enemies. He also chose as his political organizers such efficient young managers as George-Etienne Cartier and Joseph Cauchon, both of whom he knew would neglect nothing that could ensure victory. Viger, on the other hand, decided on a more dignified (and, in the end, less effective) appeal to common sense and reason. For propaganda, he counted on his own record, on the reputation and good grace of the Governor General, and, above all, on the magic of the Papineau connection. Throughout 1844 each group contended for a majority.

Viger relied not only on what he considered the correctness of his constitutional position, but also on the learned, logical views about responsible government which he had outlined in his pamphlet and in his articles in *L'Aurore*. With these he had persuaded the editors of *Les Mélanges Religieux* who (among other signs of encouragement) had reprinted his pamphlet during February 1844 and agreed that on January 2 "la marche indiquée par Mr. D. B. Viger" was the better one. With his principles and his reputation Viger thought he could easily win over the *Canadiens*. In an explanation to his constituents published in *L'Aurore* on December 30, 1843—"Lettre écrite à quelques-uns de ses électeurs"—he appealed to his own popularity: "L'homme capable d'être resté dix-neuf mois derrière les verrous pour ne pas souscrire à des conditions qui n'étaient pas d'accord avec l'honneur de son pays, ni reconnaître un principe dangereux pour les droits comme pour les libertés de ses concitoyens, n'a pas souillé ses cheveux blancs par des démarches contraires à son devoir." His own followers had apparently persuaded him that his private character and public services would gain wide support. As an individual *le vénérable*[1] attracted; as a public figure he held an imposing fifty-year history of service. They planned therefore to herald the character of this "homme le plus vénérable et le plus digne de confiance qui soit en ce pays," and on January 13 *L'Aurore* stressed the long years of "les efforts de cette âme courageuse qui a passé par le creuset de toutes les épreuves possibles." His copious learning and vast experience, they argued on February 1, as well as "la dignité du style, des pensées et des sentimens de même que la grandeur des principes . . . [et] la position . . . la plus brillante qu'ait jamais eu aucun Canadien auparavant," should be enough to assure "le vénérable Président du Conseil Exécutif des suffrages de toutes les honnêtes gens." Whatever cause such a man supported, *L'Aurore* continued on February 15, must automatically become "la cause de la vérité, de la justice, et de la morale." And now, *L'Aurore* concluded on February 20, "l'homme le plus distingué du pays par sa lumière proclame hardiment que l'ex-ministère est dans l'erreur."

Besides this appeal of his person and record, Viger had another very important asset: his close family and political connection with the great Louis-Joseph Papineau—for all *Canadiens* the undoubted fount of patriotic inspiration. The private correspondence of every Lower Canadian politician between the years 1839 and 1845 as well as the editorial policy of every newspaperman in Lower Canada confirms Papineau's tremendous influence, which fifty years later French Canada's poet laureate, Louis Fréchette, recalled as "une popularité

---

[1] *L'Aurore* so often prefixed Viger's name with *le vénérable* that after a while *La Minerve*, *Le Journal de Québec*, and *Le Fantasque* capitalized it and used it instead of his name.

universelle, sans conteste et sans parallèle."[2] Viger and his followers, certain that Papineau was about to return, reasoned that a Papineau-Viger combination could carry the province.

They also considered the character of Sir Charles Metcalfe one of their main assets. They admired the courage with which he bore the agonies and misery of his cancer. Since the turn of the year the cancerous wound on his right cheek had grown steadily worse.[3] Yet, despite all this "pain inflammation and uneasiness, on the right side of the Face throughout . . . in an unabated degree," he continued in good humour, cheerful, and exact about all his business, punctual for audiences, a tragic figure, and one, as his and Viger's followers agreed, not without grandeur. Viger's followers also noted that although betrayed and insulted by his councillors, Metcalfe had continued his princely gifts to charity, proclaimed his intention to pardon some of the political exiles, and taken the first steps in the "repatriation" of the capital to the Lower Canadian section of the province. And to this series of "liberal" measures, they added the list of French-speaking functionaries which (with and without the advice of the ci-devants) he had appointed or maintained in office: some judges, the Clerk of the Council, the Superintendent of Education (East), the Speaker of the Legislative Council, and others. Hence, as a political tactic, they decided to emphasize Sir Charles' honourable character and his every "liberal" move. As a man "le bon, l'honnête, l'excellent Sir Charles," as L'Aurore described him on June 22, deserved confidence because of

[2]Louis Fréchette, Mémoires intimes, edited by G. A. Klinck (Montréal, 1961), p. 118. In 1840, for example, Denis-Emery Papineau wrote to his cousin Amédée, on February 20: "Chartier dit qu'il avait parcouru une grande partie du pays et que c'était étonnant quelle influence Papineau avait encore partout." Three years later on May 1, 1843, another cousin, T. Bruneau, reiterated to Amédée: "Il règne encore avec empire dans les cœurs Canadiens et plus d'un maudit Anglais voudrait le voir de retour." Edouard-Raymond Fabre told his son on August 28, 1843: "Mr. A.-N. Morin sort à l'instant de la maison. . . . Nous avons parlé de notre ami Mr. P. il désire son retour, afin de joindre ses efforts aux leurs." In 1839, the English official Stuart Derbyshire had noted a feeling "as general as that which pervaded France in 1814 of the return of Napoleon and Papineau seems to have inspired with the same devotional feeling towards himself the Canadiens as Napoleon did the French." The newspapers told the same story, printing every bit of gossip and news about the great man's life in exile. In 1843, at the second annual Saint-Jean-Baptiste celebration in Quebec, as Le Fantasque reported on July 3, Dr. Pierre-Martial Bardy, asked for the quick return of "le grand O'Connell Canadien, ce zélé défenseur, ce gardien vigilant des droits sacrés du peuple; cet homme dont la popularité [est] devenue proverbiale," and was greeted with "des applaudissements."

[3]Metcalfe's account of his illness to his sister Georgiana Smith is described in detail in Thompson, Metcalfe, pp. 394 ff.

"la pureté de ses intentions, l'heureux naturel qu'il a pour les doc-trines libérales et ses penchants particuliers pour la belle population franco-canadienne alliée par le sang à l'un de ses aieux." He was also to be praised for his generosity. In fact his charitable donations seemed to increase in direct proportion to the attacks by LaFontaine's group. It seemed that Metcalfe could never leave a worthy cause unaided. *L'Aurore* of course noted each contribution. As charities multiplied, so did the Vigerite acclaim for this "homme bienfaisant et généreux, . . . ami et protecteur du pauvre, de l'éducation, des sciences et des arts . . . homme tolérant, prodiguant ses richesses pour l'édifica-tion des temples au Grand Créateur" (November 27, 1845).

As admirable as they considered his private virtues, Viger's fol-lowers decided to give still more praise to the Governor's public acts. In fact, they gave him credit for every good that came out of Govern-ment House, especially the moving of the capital, the settlement of militia land claims from the war of 1812, and, most important of all, the pardon of the political exiles.

On October 6, 1843, some six weeks before the resignation, the Assembly had voted (over the objections of Montreal's own Tory member, George Moffatt) to transfer the capital from "cet enfer de Kingston"[4] to Montreal. The choice, however, had to have London's approval. It did. And on December 30 *L'Aurore* reported a proclama-tion by the Governor announcing the move. Barthe immediately gave all the credit to his heroes, Metcalfe and Viger. Later, in the February 8 issue of his *L'Aurore*, he did likewise with the news that the thirty-year problem of the lands promised to the veterans of 1812 had finally been solved: "Les miliciens de la guerre de 1812 sont à la veille d'obtenir enfin justice grâce à l'entremise de l'hon D. B. Viger dont l'arrivée au pouvoir a été marquée chaque jour par quelqu'acte éclatant de justice pour le pays." But much closer to the *Canadien* heart (and therefore politically much more profitable) was the solution to the old story of "nos compatriotes gémissant maintenant dans l'exil" (*Le Canadien*, November 26, 1841).

Since their banishment hardly a week had passed without some public mention of the political exiles, hardly a month without some petition for their recall. In fact, during the years between 1838 and 1843, virtually nothing, not the Act of Union, or the lost language and constitution, or the new school bill, or the forfeited and regained capital, was more described, discussed, and condemned than the fate

[4]Collection Papineau-Bourassa, D.-B. Papineau à ?, 14 août 1843.

of the exiles, both those who had been banished by Durham and those who had been deported to Australia. And from the beginning, those who were in close touch with these reports were the clergy and the Lower Canadian politicians who paid general allegiance to Viger and Neilson.

Earlier, in 1838, Bishop Bourget had shared with his superior, Bishop Lartigue, the duty of condemning the political theories of the rebels and meting out the punishment of the Church for their conduct. Yet he had given his heart to the defeated as individuals, visiting them in their cells, writing to their families, ordering their curés to come from the country parishes to give news at the prison, interceding for the condemned, and finally, after the exiles left Quebec, writing to Archbishop Polding of Sydney to recommend them warmly to his care.[5] Nor did he ever forget them.

In November 1841, when most of the civil dignitaries in the province converged on Quebec to welcome Bagot, Bishop Bourget joined them. As he wrote to Bishop Gaulin of Kingston, he wanted to confer with Archbishop Signay about a petition to the Queen for the return of the exiles. He wished also to be among the first to greet the new Governor and impress him with the need for an amnesty. With him, he brought Bishop de Forbin-Janson, who had just ended his tour of French Canada and was proving so enthusiastic about a pardon that he wrote to one of his compatriots in France:

Si je croyais qu'une visite à la Reine d'Angleterre pût obtenir quelques adoucissements au sort de plusieurs centaines de pauvres Canadiens, bannis à 6,000 lieues de leur patrie par suite de la dernière révolution, tentée, il y a deux ou trois ans, je n'hésiterais point à passer par Londres en revenant en France; mais il y aura peut-être des obstacles à ce désir de mon cœur pour un peuple que j'aime et dont je suis certain d'être aimé.[6]

Because Bagot's arrival was delayed, Bourget did not meet him until the following summer. But in April 1842 he commissioned Bishop Gaulin in Kingston to test the Governor's reactions to an amnesty for the exiles. And by July 1842 he could write in all sincerity to one of the prisoners at Botany Bay: "Je me suis employé autant que j'ai pu pour obtenir votre liberté et celle de vos compagnons. Je travaille et je travaillerai à votre libération."[7] In fact, he had convinced Bishop de Forbin-Janson to visit England, and in August 1842 the French prelate travelled to the Derby family estate in Lancashire to plead in person with Lord Stanley for an amnesty. Later Bourget persuaded all

[5]L. Pouliot, Mgr Bourget et son temps (2 vols., Montréal, 1955–6), I, 148–51.
[6]Dionne, Forbin-Janson, p. 118.
[7]AAM, Lettres Bourget, II, 560, Bourget à Lepailleur, 22 juil. 1842.

the Canadian bishops to reiterate the plea in writing; Les Mélanges Religieux, of course, repeatedly echoed it.

The politicians also concurred. The anti-*unionnaires*, especially after the Union, increasingly turned their attention to the subject of an amnesty. In June 1841 Glackmeyer wrote from Quebec that "the question of the exiles is exciting public feeling."[8] And a month later, he forwarded to Kingston a petition for their recall with 2,750 signatures. Dominick Daly, acting as provincial secretary, acknowledged receipt of the petition on July 31,[9] and on September 4 Neilson proposed an address of his own in the Assembly which Sydenham promised to forward to the Colonial Office.

After Thomson's death, and while the province awaited Bagot's arrival, Aubin published a moving plea to the new Governor:

Vous savez que beaucoup de nos frères sont absents; les uns sont libres; . . . . libres de ne pas revenir dans leur patrie! les autres sont couverts de chaînes, sans amis, sans parents. . . . Savez-vous ce qu'ils ont fait? Ils eurent le cœur trop haut placé; ils avaient dans le sang un peu trop de cette noble chaleur que l'égoiste ne connait pas . . . ils furent les plus faibles! S'il vous reste avec votre diplomatie, un peu de pitié, à défaut de pitié, un peu de raison, vous commencerez par nous rendre nos frères. (Le Fantasque, October 25, 1841)

Bagot heard the request (and the hundreds of others composed during the following months) at about the same time as he began negotiations with LaFontaine in September 1842. On the first day of the session that year, Neilson asked the government to table copies of any communications about the exiles with the Colonial Office. Bagot had to admit that Neilson's year-old address had never been transmitted to London, Sydenham having intended to do so on the day of his fatal accident. He himself forwarded it immediately, adding in a private letter to Stanley his personal recommendation that the Crown issue a general pardon. "The pressure upon me is great," he insisted, "and will increase."[10] A fortnight later, the new Council having taken office and LaFontaine insisting on quick action, he sent an official despatch to the Colonial Office, again declaring emphatically that "a general act of perfect oblivion of all that has passed . . . would tend beyond any other measure to complete the Union, to create a feeling of gratitude and confirm the attachment of the Canadians to the Mother Country; and to ensure the success of my recent policy."[11]

[8]Neilson Collection, II, Glackmeyer to Neilson, June 17, 1841.
[9]Ibid., Daly to Neilson, July 31, 1841.
[10]Bagot Papers, 7, Bagot to Stanley, Sept. 13, 1841.
[11]Ibid., Bagot to Stanley, Sept. 26, 1842.

But the matter was not quite as simple as Bagot and the *Canadiens* thought. The British government, then facing widespread discontent at home, had been forced into repressive measures against violence. It feared a general amnesty for Canada might weaken its policy at home and prove an embarrassing precedent for cases like that of the Chartists and other groups whose members had also been deported. Accordingly, in November, Stanley asked Bagot for more details and hinted at the necessary distinction that must be made between the exiles who had been legally condemned, those who had fled before being captured, and those who had been deported to Australia. He wanted to know the precise charges against each and detailed information that could provide a motive for his pardon. LaFontaine was disappointed. He wrote to Baldwin that "some more decided step must be taken, in relation to this question, so as to satisfy fully the just expectations of the People."[12] But Bagot could do nothing more than ask the Clerk of the Crown in Montreal to study the voluminous dossiers accumulated during the trials. On January 25, 1834, he discussed the results with his councillors and sent a report to London on the next day stressing that "I shall greatly grieve if the exigencies of British, as contra-distinguished from Canadian policy, or the difficulties inherent in the measure itself should prevent it."[13]

"Nous avons vainement attendu cette amnistie sans restriction qui eût donné trop de consolation à tout un peuple," Cauchon echoed in *Le Journal de Québec*, on March 21, 1843. "Que craint le gouvernement anglais? . . . Ne perdons pas pour tout cela courage: demandons toujours, demandons à grands cris, demandons spontanément." Indeed, beginning in December 1842, the French-Canadian press had waged a concerted, high-pressured campaign obviously designed to force the issue. Duvernay published more and more demands for an amnesty and Ronald MacDonald editorialized in *Le Canadien* on January 23: "AMNISTIE! AMNISTIE! . . . Sir CHARLES BAGOT, tout en servant habilement sa souveraine par sa politique libérale, s'est élevé dans le cœur de ce peuple un monument plus durable que l'airain. . . . Mais son œuvre n'est pas encore complète. . . . AMNISTIE donc, AMNISTIE GÉNÉRALE ET COMPLÈTE." Letters poured in to the editors: In the Lower Canadian section of the province (already well organized to pray for Bagot and welcome Metcalfe), politicians despatched a new set of addresses and called more meetings.

Shortly after his arrival in January 1843, Metcalfe, like his pre-

12Baldwin Papers, A 55, LaFontaine to Baldwin, Nov. 26, 1842.
13Bagot Papers, 10, Bagot to Stanley, Jan. 26, 1843.

decessor, had agreed with LaFontaine on the need for dispatch on the question. He had done so even before his personal and theoretical problems with his councillors had led him to realize that he could use the amnesty to reinforce his own position. At the beginning of May he sent Stanley "the fullest account of all persons" to be pardoned and pressed strongly to be given authority to do so.[14] In London, Prince Albert concurred, writing that "the General Amnesty strikes us [the Queen and himself] as a measure apart from its intrinsic merit, calculated to strengthen Sir Charles's hands opposite to the french and liberal party, with whom he will have next to contend."[15] Peel agreed, suggesting to Stanley that once Metcalfe had been given authority to announce the amnesty, he should weigh whether it would help him more to proclaim it before or after the rupture with his Council.[16] When the Colonial Secretary came to send the permission, however, he remembered his fears of complications at home and so hedged the concession with conditions that, from the Canadian point of view, it was useless. For one thing, he warned Metcalfe that "your authority does not extend to any degree to those who are suffering punishment of transportation." Secondly, he declared his hope that Metcalfe would use his discretion to pardon the others in the least ostentatious way possible, and only "if you should feel it absolutely essential to the peace of Canada and to the conduct of your Government." Thirdly, he warned

If the step be taken, it is important that it should be ostensibly the spontaneous Act of the Crown; and you will bear in mind that nothing would add more to the difficulties of such an act of grace than that it should be adopted upon the recommendations of a popular Assembly. You will indeed endeavour to impress Mr. LaFontaine that if he is sincerely desirous of a complete Amnesty for his misguided fellow countrymen, any Address upon the subject in the Legislature will only have the effect of placing an additional obstacle in the way of H.M.'s merciful disposition.[17]

Metcalfe was very disappointed. Where was the great magnanimous gesture that would raise his popularity enough to allow him to settle his contentions with LaFontaine? "The Act would be incomplete," he answered Stanley, "and a great disappointment if it were unaccompanied by the release of the French-Canadian convicts in Her Majesty's penal colonies. It is with regard to them that sympathy and

[14]C.O. 537/142, Metcalfe to Stanley, May 8, 1843.
[15]Derby Papers, Prince Albert to Stanley, May 31, 1843.
[16]Ibid., Peel to Stanley, June 1, 1843.
[17]C.O. 537/141, Stanley to Metcalfe, July 3, 1843.

anxiety are most strongly felt. The French population are probably unanimous in these feelings."[18] By August, in fact, the petitions and meetings had grown voluminous. "The French Canadians," wrote Metcalfe again, "pant for the return of their countrymen, and will not be satisfied without it."[19] Moreover, Neilson, whom the Governor knew to be "too independent and self-willed to be restrained by others," had resolved to propose a motion in the Assembly, and LaFontaine, wishing perhaps to force the issue, had told the Governor at a meeting of the Council that an address for a general amnesty could not be avoided.[20]

Late in September, however, Metcalfe met a man who told him it could be. When Viger came to intercede for two of the rebels, he assured the Governor "that the French party are not disposed to make any troublesome movement."[21] Metcalfe had hoped the amnesty would strengthen his position with the French-Canadian people in his quarrel with the Council. His hopes had been dashed. But now, unexpectedly, the issue introduced him to a French Canadian he could work with. Overjoyed, he told Viger of the Colonial Secretary's assurances that although there could be no general amnesty at least he could guarantee an individual pardon for each of the exiles who would petition for it. LaFontaine also knew this; he had filed a copy of Stanley's despatch in his own papers, but he had not published the news. Perhaps he thought that if pressure from the press and public continued, a genuine "amnistie absolue" might be granted after all. Or was he so attached to principle that he scorned a compromise which would have the same practical effect? At all events, he said nothing about the individual pardons and allowed rumours to continue that a general amnesty was imminent. Immediately after the resignation at the end of November, however, Viger lost no time in making public the news about the individual pardons.

Because of imperial policy, Viger could not capture the Lower Canadian imagination with a grand gesture and—as Metcalfe had fondly dreamed—show how he could succeed where LaFontaine had failed. Still, he expected that the return of the exiles by individual pardons would weigh heavily for him. Immediately after his announcement, a number of his followers organized the Association de la Délivrance and elected Edouard-Raymond Fabre its executive

[18]C.O. 537/142, Metcalfe to Stanley, July 23, 1843.
[19]Ibid., Metcalfe to Stanley, Aug. 7, 1843.
[20]Ibid., Metcalfe to Stanley, July 26, 1843.
[21]Ibid., Metcalfe to Stanley, Oct. 7, 1843.

secretary. In no time, Fabre saw to the printing and circulating of a quantity of petitions for each one of the exiles and began a publicity campaign to gather funds to finance their passage home. He worked well; and so did his team of young men headed by Amédée Papineau, now a practising notary in Montreal. Despite hard snowstorms, the young men travelled the countryside—Sainte-Geneviève, L'Acadie, LaMalbaie, Belœil, Saint-Jacques, Saint-Césaire, Maskinongé—to hold fund-raising meetings, as *La Minerve* reported on January 11, "pour procurer à nos compatriotes exilés les moyens de rentrer dans leurs foyers," while their elders held monster meetings in Quebec and Montreal.

Metcalfe, of course, headed the list of subscribers. He sent a much heralded £100 which drew from Aubin the comment (*Le Fantasque*, January 20) that "Son Excellence a donné £100. Voilà qui peut faire oublier pour des milliers de louis de peccadilles." Precisely! And other well-known contributors included Bishop de Forbin-Janson who also sent £100, Viger (£20), Dominick Daly (£15) and the Governor's private secretary, Captain Higgenson (£10). Actually the monies came quickly. By the end of February 1844 the Association proudly announced in *L'Aurore* that "sur les 58 de nos compatriotes qui ont été exilés, 25 ont maintenant reçu la permission de revenir." A month later, Fabre made it known that all fifty-eight of the exiles who wanted to return had been pardoned. And *L'Aurore* underlined the moral of the whole story on February 27: "Deux choses doivent frapper tous les yeux. . . . la première, l'empressement de Sa Majesté à se rendre au vœu si ardent de notre patrie; la seconde, . . . c'est grâce à la FORCE DE LA RECOMMENDATION DE SIR CHARLES METCALFE LUI-MÊME QUE CE PARDON A ÉTÉ ACCORDÉ."

As for Viger, rumours had been put in circulation for some time that the recall of the exiles had been the main reason for his co-operation with the Governor. His followers hoped by this popular measure, coupled with praise of Viger and the Governor, to capture the electorate.

While Viger and his followers were thus employed, LaFontaine and his followers resolved to highlight, not a person, but a principle: to face the electorate with a challenging plea for unity.

LaFontaine expected that Metcalfe's ill health would soon force his recall. The next governor, he thought, could not or would not attempt to govern without at least the semblance of a majority. To regain office, then, he must only keep the *Canadiens* united behind him. Moreover he understood the political practice which his people had evolved over the last two generations of voting *en bloc*. By stressing unity he would thus automatically acquire for his side the full force of the French Canadians' accumulated nationalist habits and by thus stressing his continuity with the past, he would put his opponents squarely on the defensive. Metcalfe also understood this. "One strong feature of the French-Canadian party," he wrote to Stanley, "is their determination to cling together. This increases the difficulty in obtaining aid from them, for unless they come over bodily they most probably will not come at all; and they are more likely to abandon Mr. LaFontaine and adhere to Mr. Viger, or to do the reverse, than to divide themselves between the two."[22] The Governor, therefore, had hesitations about Viger's reliance on the constitutional argument and on his own reputation. Neither was much understood by the mass of the *Canadien* politicians and people. But he decided for once to accept his advisor's advice. He continued to Stanley: "Mr. Viger is more sanguine than I am, and as he must know his countrymen better than I do, there would be some presumption in doubting the accuracy of his expectations." But Viger never seems to have understood that whatever the constitutional niceties or however "generally unpopular" LaFontaine might be personally because of what Metcalfe described in this same letter to Stanley as his "rude and overbearing demeanour," he had himself acted unwisely in breaking the traditional unity of his party. LaFontaine, although much younger, had been shrewd enough to realize the importance of this during the debate over the Union. And now, with complete self-confidence and all the ardour of embattled orthodoxy, he would make French unity the single theme of his party's propaganda.

Disunity was what his compatriots should fear most Duvernay wrote in *La Minerve* on January 8, 1844: "On ne saurait trop se pénétrer de cette grande vérité: que l'Union fait la Force. Que ce mot soit pour eux, dans ce moment surtout, leur cri de ralliement autour de leur vieux drapeau, le GOUVERNEMENT RESPONSABLE." It was unity, so *La Minerve* continued, that had won "le principe du gouvernement responsable auquel le pays est irrévocablement attaché" and only unity could restore it—especially since Viger had sold out to the traditional enemy by accepting office on their terms and against the will of the parliamentary majority.[23] "Mr. Viger et *l'Aurore*," Cauchon

[22]C.O. 537/143, Metcalfe to Stanley, Jan. 26, 1844.
[23]*La Minerve*, 1, 8 jan. 1844.

agreed in *Le Journal de Québec* on March 9, "veulent perdre le pays par le pays en le divisant, en le jettant ainsi affaibli entre les mains d'un ennemi acharné." All *Canadiens* must stand together as of old both to resist those who would thus "embrouiller, diviser le peuple sur cette question," and to restore "ce palladium de nos droits."

Towards Viger personally LaFontaine harboured mostly sentiments of respect. At the least, he feared that discourtesy would have a bad political effect, and he felt sincerely "qu'il est impossible de lui imputer des motifs malhonnêtes."[24] But his journalists and party agents thought otherwise. Though guarded at first and willing, as *La Minerve* put it on December 14, to "envisager sa conduite avec indulgence," they soon turned against the old man the full force of their invective. Cauchon, never discreet, wrote on December 16 that Viger was merely an ambitious jealous man: "M. Viger ne convoite pas des places pour en avoir les émoluments, tout le monde sait qu'il est très riche; mais il est des hommes qui aiment l'honneur pour l'honneur même.... Pourquoi ne pas dire que M. Viger et M. Lafontaine [*sic*] sont deux influences différentes qui se nuisent un peu et qui se font mutuellement ombrage." That he was also a *vendu*: "Qu'il ait trahi [son pays] par le désir du pouvoir ou par jalousie contre un homme public, ou qu'il l'ait fait pour l'une ou pour l'autre cause, il l'a trahi" (December 19). Later Cauchon even charged that Viger had taken a £40,000 bribe from the Provincial Treasury, ostensibly for a piece of his land in Montreal on which public buildings were to be built. When *L'Aurore* retorted that Viger had risked all his wealth and talents in the service of his country, *Le Fantasque* quipped on April 20: "*L'Aurore* dit que Mr Viger met jeu la première réputation et la première fortune du pays. Pour la réputation elle est risquée. Quant à la fortune, bernique!"

Then *Le Journal de Québec* and *La Minerve* began to throw names in earnest, calling Viger everything from a "mensonger de basses calomnies" to a "servile," "fanatique," "imposteur," "reptile qui lance son venin." For Barthe, who, as editor of *L'Aurore*, served as Viger's main spokesman, they made no pretence at respect. During May *La Minerve* called him "un atôme," "un fanatique," "un colporteur de basses calomnies," "infâme," "fourbe," "charlatan," "un allié du Toryism pur," "indigne de toute confiance." "Mr. Barthe bave de fureur," Cauchon wrote in a typical paragraph on December 30:

Il a ramassé sa plume de mépris et de dédain dans la bave ou auparavant, descendant de son trône intellectuel, il avait trempé son pied. Plongé lui-

[24]Papiers LaFontaine, Quesnel à LaFontaine, 20 jan. 1844.

même dans la fange épaisse où il paraît lui-même éprouver d'inéffables jouissances, il n'en tente pas moins audacieusement d'élever seul son arrogant orgueil vers les régions de la pensée et de la raison, comme le reptile hideux, se traînant dans la bave, rejette sa tête en arrière pour insulter et pour empoisonner.

Wakefield, among other things, was according to *La Minerve* (not too surprisingly) "un grand sorcier"; and Dominick Daly remained to *Le Fantasque* "l'inutile," or "l'honorable secrétaire extrèmement provincial."

All this ferocious journalism was designed by LaFontaine's agents to frighten any who might waver in their devotion to LaFontaine's cause. In June 1844 for example, Quesnel seemed to be weakening. Hincks, who, since March 5, 1844, had been editing the English-speaking pro-LaFontaine *Pilot* in Montreal, wrote to Baldwin: "Quesnel is much about the G.G.—a letter in La Minerve in which he is presumably alluded to as a 'rat' in Lord Gosford's time & my editorial yesterday will give him warning what he has to expect unless he is careful."[25] And a year later, in April 1845, Denis-Benjamin Papineau, by then Viger's only French-Canadian colleague in the Council and the one who had suffered more abuse than all the others, grudgingly admitted the success of this type of campaign. He wrote to his wife how several politicians "en diverses occasions ont essayé de me consoler des attaques violantes et personnelles dirigées contre moi; d'autres me disaient qu'ils se sépareraient assez souvent de l'Opposition mais que la manière dont j'étais traité les effrayait et qu'ils ne voulaient pas passer par la même étamine."[26] Against the Governor himself, however, LaFontaine's editors remained on their guard, since according to their view of responsible government, he could do no wrong. During the spring *Le Fantasque* managed none-theless to call him "Machiavel," "tyran," "Néron," "patron de l'Oran-gisme," "l'ennemi du peuple," and "le destructeur de la sécurité."

But LaFontaine's writers did better than abuse. They added ridicule to injury. Using the weapon he had sharpened so well against "POULET" Thomson, Aubin filled *Le Fantasque* with clever satires of the Execu-tive Council's meetings and scored the Governor's devotion to the Orange Order and Viger's endless and involved articles. He also made far from delicate references to the Governor's illness. Metcalfe took the satire to heart, unlike Sydenham who had ignored it, and Bagot who had enough sense of humour to have described it as "sometimes rather comical, always very wicked . . . and occasionally

[25]Baldwin Papers, 51, Hincks to Baldwin, July 2, 1844.
[26]Collection Papineau-Bourassa, D.-B. Papineau à sa femme, 1 avril 1845.

very good fun."[27] Metcalfe lowered himself to the point of having his secretary, Captain Higgenson, write to Aubin and denounce his "heartless vulgarity." Aubin was delighted at the publicity. He published the letter, then satirized it under the title "LA VÉRITÉ CHOQUE."

Aubin was not the only satirist. In Montreal *Le Charivari Canadien* began its short life in May 1844 and, like *Le Fantasque*, lampooned mercilessly. It also referred to the Governor's cancer: "Les journaux graves disent que Sir Charles Metcalfe riait avec beaucoup de difficulté à cause du *bobo* qu'il avait à la joue. Il est heureux pour Son Excellence qu'il se soit adonné dans un temps où les circonstances n'étaient pas tout à fait à faire rire" (May 10). But most often, it printed such good fun as this spoof of the Litany of the Saints on May 31,

Grand Denis Benjamin Viger Vénérable Patriarche Canadien Président de la Société Saint Jean Baptiste Qui avez souffert dix-huit mois en prison Qui avez des cheveux blancs Qui avez été de service pendant un demi-siècle Qui avez qualifié l'ex-docteur de L'Aurore Qui avez écrit le pamphlet sur la Belgique Qui avez publié *La Crise Ministérielle* Qui avez entraîné cette crise ministérielle Qui avez écrit le mémoire de votre emprisonnement Qui faites paraître l'Aurore Qui faites beaucoup de la forme Qui ne vous inquiétez pas du fond …	priez pour nous
Mânes de Sydenham Mânes du Conseil Spécial Mânes de la loi martiale Stanley, Peel Metcalfe Colborne, dit Lord Satan,· "Cheveux blancs" Sydney Bellingham Gésier Barthe Orangiste Gowan Ennemis des Canadiens Amis de l'Anglification Ennemis de l'éducation Lampeurs de whiskey Buveurs de bière Family Compact Ecrivains officiels Menteurs publics Tous les voleurs de deniers publics	priez pour l'administration

[27]Bagot Papers, 7, Bagot to Stanley, March 27, 1842.

PRIONS

Seigneur qui soutenez le faible et abandonnez le fort, soutenez les esprits faibles parmi nous et abaissez les esprits forts qui nous opposent; déliverez-nous de toutes tentations qui l'on pourrait nous offrir afin de nous faire trahir notre patrie; éloignez de nous ces représentants qui parlent beaucoup et ne font rien; purgez nos rangs et rendez-nous nos brebis égarés; donnez-nous la force de soutenir les épreuves qui nous visitent sans cesse, et faites que nous soyons tous de la société de tempérance et des bons patriotes. Ainsi-soit-il.

In addition to name-calling and ridicule, LaFontaine's strategists devised other tactics just as enjoyable, but more practical. One was to undersell *L'Aurore* and/or put pressure on its readers to cancel their subscriptions so that at the end of the eighteen months, they forced the paper to cease publication "pour des raisons toutes particulières,"[28] which LaFontaine spelled out to Baldwin as "Viger and Barthe have quarrelled; the latter has *resigned* the editorship of the 'Aurore'; and this publication is to be discontinued, for want of support."[29] Another tactic was to ignore the speeches and arguments of the Viger group and thus to keep the electorate in the dark about any good point they might make. "The *Aurore*," Hincks confided to Baldwin, "is edited by Barthe and Viger both good writers and it contains column after column on the political questions of the day all of which go unanswered. The doctrine is 'oh take no notice of the *Aurore*, it is not seen.' Duvernay of the *Minerve* always tells me that I write *too much*, that I ought not to notice what is said on the other side."[30] And, Hincks notwithstanding, the game worked. Denis-Benjamin Papineau testified that "il est bien certain que si la *Minerve* avait fidèlement rapporté les débats qui ont eu lieu en français durant la Session, j'aurais eu à gagner quelque chose dans l'opinion de mes concitoyens; c'est ce dont il fallait bien se garder, et dont en effet on s'est bien gardé."[31]

Thus, to their initial advantage of being the first to tell their side of the story, LaFontaine and his group had added a defiant plea for unity that linked them in the public mind with the struggles of the 1830's. With this single theme, and their careful plans to discredit and ignore the enemy, they stood ready to face the electorate. They had not emphasized their leader. They had not stressed theory. But whether they realized it or not, they had all but guaranteed their vic-

28*L'Aurore*, 2 déc. 1844.
29Baldwin Papers, A 55, LaFontaine to Baldwin, Dec. 2, 1845.
30*Ibid.*, 51, Hincks to Baldwin, Sept. 18, 1845.
31Collection Papineau-Bourassa, D.-B. Papineau à sa femme, 1 avril 1845.

tory by instinctively identifying their cause with the traditional nationalist doctrines which their electors had been brought up to revere. Perhaps they had also based their platform on the traditional principle that *la survivance* would best be served by evolving British institutions.

Although more intellectual in their approach, and certainly more narrowly nationalist, their opponents had let themselves be manœuvred onto a platform where they were forced to defend the British governor. Viger and Neilson prized the old constitution which was based on the governor's authority. Perhaps they did this from ingrained conservatism. But they also believed that the old order had succeeded in protecting the separate culture of the French-Canadian people. Indeed, ever since the Union, it had been the governor's authority, in their view, and not responsible government which had restored to them their distinctive institutions in education and civil law. And, as Viger clearly saw, it was Metcalfe, and not his "responsible" council, who could most practically and quickly effect the return of the exiles. They had therefore sprung to the defence of the old constitution and of the power which they considered could best preserve the uniqueness of French Canada. Their young radical followers believed less in the older order than in "l'émancipation qui n'est qu'une question de temps."[32] But they could see no harm in co-operating, meanwhile, with a "liberal" governor whose record offered so much promise of advantage for *la nation canadienne*. Nor by so acting did they commit themselves, as LaFontaine did, to a permanent belief in British institutions. They did not realize that in the eyes of most of the *Canadiens*, they had sold out to the traditional Tory opponent. Of this the electors would soon remind them.

[32]*Ibid.*, D.-B. Papineau à Viger, 27 fév. 1844.

11

La Crise Metcalfe: Elections
March-December 1844

The year 1844 was the decisive one for *la crise Metcalfe,* indeed for the whole future of French Canada. For the year showed how superior LaFontaine's political instinct was to Viger's intelligence. When the *Canadiens* delivered their electoral verdict, they rejected the niceties of the old man's constitutional philosophy to respond, almost automatically, to LaFontaine's appeal for national unity. They thus baffled the hopes of a hero and sacrificed the immediate advantages of co-operation with a generous governor. Instead they would choose the eventual achievement of permanent self-rule. By choosing LaFontaine rather than Viger, they also chose their future. For, behind the direct appeals for unity or advantageous co-operation with Metcalfe, LaFontaine and Viger implicitly called for a choice far more important. Thus, when they denied Viger, the French Canadians repudiated the particularist ideal by which they should stand alone, in direct and separate relation to the source of power, and await the day of final national independence. By electing LaFontaine, they entrusted themselves instead to Parent's doctrine that *la survivance* depended upon achieving genuine responsible government in union with the Reformers of Upper Canada and maintaining the ever-developing British institutions that would preserve the British connection.

They did not decide easily. In the spring both LaFontaine and Viger were still preparing what each thought would be the best approach to win his people. And as the months passed, the *Canadiens* seemed to smile on each alternately. In a by-election in Montreal in April, it was LaFontaine who won, but popular enthusiasm, in Montreal at least, seems later to have swung to Metcalfe and Viger. Viger scored again by bringing Denis-Benjamin Papineau into the Executive Council, only to have his thunder stolen by LaFontaine's resignation as Queen's counsel. Finally, in the general election LaFontaine carried the victory.

Indeed, he won so decisively that he found himself the undisputed leader of a people that had not made such a unanimous decision for over a decade.

THE MONTREAL BY-ELECTION

Having perfected their strategy, LaFontaine's agents decided to act quickly. They needed an early victory to establish the theme of political unity they had chosen as the basis of their platform. They knew their prompt success at the polls would also prove a great help to Baldwin who needed to prove to his electors that the French stood firm. They also hoped that an immediate victory would rob Viger of his prestige at the council table and render impossible any more successful bargaining with possible French colleagues. Moreover, success now would endorse the course LaFontaine, Morin, and Aylwin had taken at the time of the ministerial crisis in November and could be a decisive argument during the general election expected later in 1844.

They therefore made arrangements with Benjamin Holmes, the member from Montreal whom LaFontaine had converted to his party at the time of the municipal election in 1843 and whom Metcalfe now described as "one of the most active and unscrupulous opponents of the Governor . . . formerly a violent member of the British party in Lower Canada, but now apparently subservient to Mr. LaFontaine."[1] As his business had suffered from his absence in Kingston Holmes readily agreed to resign and thus open one of the Montreal seats. On February 5 the papers carried the news, and LaFontaine's politicians plunged into the by-election they wanted—an ideal one for them since their victory would be all the more striking, as LaFontaine said, in "that very place in which [our insolent] Tories always boasted of possessing exclusively intelligence, talents, wealth, influence."[2]

For the campaign, Viger, Barthe, and L'Aurore took the scholarly approach. They developed constitutional explanations, appealed to Viger's authority, and stressed the importance of a *Canadien* voice in the Governor's council. On February 15 they wrote: "Que nous importe, que doit nous importer à nous, entre les mains de quel ami du Pays la mince part de pouvoir que l'on veut bien nous accorder soit placée? Acceptons-la toujours." But for all this they acted like

[1]C.O. 537/143, Metcalfe to Stanley, Jan. 26, 1844.
[2]Baldwin Papers, A 55, LaFontaine to Baldwin, April 19, 1844.

political novices. Though even Hincks admitted that Mr. Viger and his friends "are much more industrious than ours,"[3] they lost precious time in bickering about a candidate. And in making their selection, they let themselves be manœuvred into supporting one of the old-school Tories.

At first Barthe thought Viger should run, for his personal popularity would almost certainly carry the French vote. Even LaFontaine admitted that many *Canadiens* would probably prefer to abstain than to vote against Viger. "It is evident," he wrote to Baldwin, "that the People of Richelieu would not like to hurt his feelings without being forced to do it."[4] But Viger, who had, literally, fallen on his face and suffered what *L'Aurore* called (February 10) "une grave contusion à la figure," wanted as the candidate his adopted heir, Cherrier, whom the Governor himself had picked for the Council. But Cherrier, who agreed with LaFontaine's version of *la crise*, pleaded "his bad state of health,"[5] thus provoking from Dominick Daly the worried comment: "Of Cherrier I will only repeat that his lamentable state of health makes your position a very painful one. . . . The question, then that always arises is—who will be Att. Genl. . . . Can nothing be done with Morin? In fact I know not what to suggest.[6]

Meanwhile suggestions came from the Tory merchant community. Like Viger but for their own reasons, the Montreal Tories also supported Metcalfe, and now were discussing the candidatures of such political nonentities as Duncan Fisher, prominent member of the Bar whose running, Daly averred, would only increase the *ci-devant* chances, and the highly uncertain Sydney Bellingham, who had changed sides twice since 1841 when he had first switched his support from Neilson to Sydenham. Bellingham was finally prevailed upon not to run. But when he declined the nomination, he did so in favour of Viger. Daly then again insisted to the old man: "What think you of accepting the President of Ex. Council place yourself & standing for Montreal. I am certain you would succeed. . . . as you may well imagine we are deeply anxious about the state of things in Montreal. Your coming forward for the city yourself would, I think, settle the issue."[7] Finally, on February 23, the divided Governor's party announced it had agreed on William Molson, notoriously Tory, a man who needed an interpreter to speak to his French electors and whose

3*Ibid.*, v51, Hincks to Baldwin, Feb. 19, 1844.
4*Ibid.*, A 55, LaFontaine to Baldwin, Feb. 15, 1844.
5*Ibid.*, LaFontaine to Baldwin, March 15, 1844.
6Papiers Viger, Daly to Viger, Feb. 14, 1844.
7*Ibid.*, Daly to Viger, Feb. 15, 1844.

very name, as *Les Mélanges Religieux* pointed out (April 12), was a challenge to the powerful *Canadien* Temperance Society. Twice, at least, Barthe felt the need to apologize, pointing out rather weakly on February 23 that "comme cette élection n'est que pour une session de Parlement, nous estimons que le succès de Mr. Molson sera un bienfait pour la ville et peut-être pour le pays," and on March 14 "qu'on se rappelle surtout que ce n'est point un homme qu'il s'agit d'élire, mais un principe qu'il faut soutenir." In Kingston, Daly tried, sadly, to be optimistic: "The *on dit* today is that Wm. Molson stands for Montreal, but I fear he is not the right man to secure success. . . . I look upon the present state of affairs & what it may lead to with apprehension and deep sorrow as regards the true interests and peace of the country. *Mais le Bon Dieu est Canadien, espérons!* I trust in Providence!!!"[8]

Of course, the choice of Molson was not completely foolish. During the bank crisis in 1837 the Molson firm had received permission to issue paper money, and the new notes had won immediate popularity in the *Canadien* parishes. The habitants apparently had unlimited confidence in the company which for years had bought all the grain they could produce. Not only were the notes never discredited, but they were favoured over those of some chartered banks. In addition to this reserve of goodwill, Molson could also count on what was still considered the important support of Viger. "Le Vénérable" might have rallied many French votes: "Bon nombre de Canadiens influents sont avec Mr. Viger, (et je suis de ce nombre quoique peu influent)," wrote Fabre to his sister late in March.[9] Instead he set out for his own riding, Richelieu, there to exhort assemblies of the already faithful.

After his return to Montreal, Viger stayed behind his desk piling up long involved articles on colonial and responsible government. He was ill. Perhaps he was reluctant, after thirty years of *patriote* activity, to mount the hustings in favour of such an outright Tory. Also, he counted heavily on the influence of Cherrier. After refusing the candidacy, the latter had agreed to publish a letter that vaguely supported the Viger version of *la crise*. Cherrier, after all, was highly in Viger's debt. But he let it be known privately that, as Hincks wrote, "he is heart and soul with us but he cannot bring himself into active opposition to Mr Viger."[10] At all events and whatever his reasons, Viger promised to come out only once and then the results were disastrous.

[8]*Ibid.*, Daly to Viger, Feb. 22, 1844.
[9]Papiers Fabre, Fabre à Julie Bossange, 22 mars 1844.
[10]Baldwin Papers, v51, Hincks to Baldwin, April 17, 1844.

He agreed to address a gathering at the Stellar Hotel on February 29 "pour donner des explications de sa conduite." But on the day appointed, when he discovered that Barthe, Bleury, Bellingham, Molson, and the others had (understandably) organized a popular fanfare and were asking for a well-timed entrance, he retreated to his library. At the last minute, while 1500 of Molson's *Canadien* partisans ("Les Canadiens formaient la plus grande partie de cette assemblée") chanted on cue in the street outside his home, he absolutely refused to appear in a political capacity, insisting on what *L'Aurore* reported on March 1 as "la délicatesse de ses sentiments" and his position as an executive councillor. Molson (and his interpreter) went out to the crowd, Barthe and others attempted explanations, and Bleury spoke feelingly for the candidate. But Montrealers retained a rather unfortunate impression. And Barthe, who might have preferred a leader more pliable and less scrupulous, went back to printing the essays on the constitution which continued to fall from Viger's table.

Perhaps Viger reasoned that the best contribution he could offer was his series on constitutional theory. Had he not consolidated the support of the clergy with it? In January Hincks had reported to Baldwin that "I saw Quesnel and Parent last evening. They both say that Viger has a party and that the priests are with him."[11] And at the end of the by-election campaign one of the Governor's *Canadien* supporters in Montreal wrote to Metcalfe that "the Church which is far-seeing—which is hierarchical and averse from Republican institutions is with us."[12] *Les Mélanges Religieux* claimed to be impartial, but all during the heat of the campaign it carried lengthy articles, probably written by priests from the Collège de Saint-Hyacinthe, which supported Viger's thesis. On March 5, for instance, it published a typical dissertation which summed up all the arguments.

The author first pointed out the error of those who, considering only "le droit absolu et ce qui devrait être," claimed that responsible government in Canada should be practised exactly as it was in Britain. "Il existe une différence de fait qui devrait se comprendre sans s'expliquer. Là, c'est un peuple puissant qui gouverne sans contrôle, ici c'est une puissance qui fait ses réserves. Là c'est une faible femme qui personnifie l'autorité, ici c'est une domination. De fait (nous faisons abstraction du droit) l'un est plus indépendant que l'autre. L'un est une ombre, l'autre une réalité." He went on to define his version of responsible government in a colony: "les rapports du

11*Ibid.*, Hincks to Baldwin, Jan. 28–31, 1844.
12Derby Papers, Metcalfe to Stanley, May 10, 1844.

gouverneur avec ses ministres, la combinaison des fonctions respectives des agents du gouvernement, co-ordonnée de telle sorte que les ministres puissent prendre, devant le peuple, la responsabilité des actes ou des omissions du gouverneur, *sans que celui-ci se départe en rien de sa dignité et de son autorité administrative absolue.*" The responsibility of the ministers, he claimed, did not originate in their office, but rather in their own will: "Ce n'est pas la *dignité du conseiller* qui le rend responsable, c'est *son acceptation des actes ou des omissions du gouverneur. . . .* La responsabilité ne s'encourt pas par l'acceptation de la place de conseiller, mais par l'acceptation des actes de l'administrateur." Hence, he concluded, Metcalfe's refusal to consult his councillors did not violate the theory of responsible government since the latter remained free to refuse responsibility for any of the Governor's actions or appointments of which they did not approve. Therefore any disagreement which might arise between a governor and his council should never be over a question of law, but always over a specific fact. Viger had clearly seen this and had been correct in asking the *ci-devants* to point out which particular incident they objected to. They, on their side, had answered only with their complaint at not being consulted. They took the responsibility for it before the people; on the other hand, if they disapproved, they were free to resign.

Mais le motif de la résignation porte alors, non sur la non-consultation, mais sur un fait dont ils ne peuvent prendre la responsabilité. Comme l'on voit la résignation doit toujours porter sur un fait, et c'est ce que demandait M. Viger. En voulant la faire porter sur une autre cause, il faudrait établir ou consacrer des principes qui amèneraient nécessairement des collisions entre la colonie et le gouvernement d'Angleterre.

A few days before this article (February 20), *Les Mélanges* had called for "l'abandon de tout esprit de parti, la recherche de la vérité et de la justice." But this piece looked suspiciously like an endorsement of Viger's reasoning—indeed it was like one of his own interminable articles. Duvernay was furious. On March 21 and April 1 he published two cold critical and cutting attacks against the priests (probably written by either LaFontaine or Morin) that set out an imposing series of constitutional precedents ranging from the disagreements between George III and William Pitt to the recent "bedchamber crises" in Britain and concluded that the question of distribution of patronage was as specific a fact as any of the issues involved in these incidents.

Like Viger, LaFontaine also hesitated to take too active a part in the campaign. Was he afraid of accentuating the split among the *Canadien* electors? He seemed to believe sincerely "that if they were of opinion that I was the cause of any division among them, I was ready to abandon public life."[13] Or did he think his participation really unnecessary? He had consulted with local leaders in January and still kept his finger on the political pulse. He knew that Viger's pamphlet had "not produced a good effect. I think many have been disappointed."[14] He also saw that Cherrier's much heralded letter had achieved "no effect or very little in L.C. It has been generally ascribed to pressure from Mr Viger."[15] Perhaps he feared that if he came out, Viger would also. And he surely realized that his own cold and distant manner which had earned him so few private friends, and even made him personally disliked by many who followed his policies, could never compete with the charm of the genial and genuinely popular old man. Whatever his motives, he kept his own counsel. Perhaps, also, he disapproved of his party's election methods. For while Viger's friends blundered so brilliantly, LaFontaine's had begun to build a first-class political machine.

First, on February 12—two weeks before the others, they published a challenging election manifesto and chose as their candidate the handsome Lewis Thomas Drummond, in the circumstances a candidate with every political asset. Irish-born, he had acted as defence counsel for the prisoners of 1838; as well he was a devout Catholic and fluent in both languages. Moreover, as the dispenser of LaFontaine's patronage in Montreal for some fifteen months he could probably count on many votes of thanks. Then, on the day after the announcement of Drummond's candidacy, his friends imported the best, and perhaps the cleverest election organizer in the country, Francis Hincks.

With icy calculation—and doubtless also a perfect sense of humour —Hincks immediately set out to forge a united party organization out of those two arch rivals: the *Canadiens* and the Irish canal and dock workers. Mounting every visible platform (sometimes with a brass band) as *La Minerve* reported on March 4 he harangued the French about the hereditary Tory enemy and the Irish about Molson's masonic past. Thus, and with the help of George-Etienne Cartier and what *L'Aurore* described (March 1) as "une manière fort peu édifiante avec toutes les ressources de la presse," he attracted both groups to bilingual meetings, fraternal drinking parties, and rowdy torchlight parades. He also bound the Irish vagrants of Griffintown into an effective striking force ("des bêtes féroces en guénilles au service de

13Baldwin Papers, A 55, LaFontaine to Baldwin, March 29, 1844.
14*Ibid.*, LaFontaine to Baldwin, Feb. 15, 1844.
15*Ibid.*, LaFontaine to Baldwin, March 29, 1844.

Francis Hincks," Barthe called them) that stood ever ready to break up meetings, cheer for Drummond, and/or beat up the Tories. "Nous sommes à la veille d'une élection," commented E.-R. Fabre, "et toute la ville est en émoi, & je crains que ça finisse mal."[16] "Hincks is playing the D—l in Montreal," Baldwin was told. "And the violence of the abuse of him is the measure of the harm he is doing the enemy."[17]

Lest Viger's formal constitutional defence convince some—and Les Mélanges seemed definitely persuaded—Hincks in English and Duvernay in French published some theoretical vindications of the Baldwin-LaFontaine resignation. But, in general, the ci-devant party seemed much happier in actual combat. One evening as L'Aurore reported on February 19 they arranged for the doors of the hall adjoining the cathedral to be left unlocked during the weekly Way of the Cross devotions. As the crowd poured out of the church, they bribed the children to enter the hall with candy; mothers followed children and husbands followed mothers. Drummond, Cartier, Hincks, et al., rushed onto the platform and before this churchful of people held one of their most successful meetings. How effortless their effort seemed! Just as smoothly organized was the one "glorious monster meeting"[18] which LaFontaine agreed to address on March 27. The Tories (no weaklings either) had made threats and sent bullies. But, "vers huit heures," gloated Duvernay in La Minerve the next day, "les Irlandais arrivèrent en colonne sérée, et force fut à ceux qui avaient pris possession de la place, de l'évacuer." With the band playing and flags flying, LaFontaine, Hincks, Drummond, and Cartier went up to the platform, and LaFontaine even "got three cheers for the Governor after having said that, as to our local affairs, my doctrine was that he could do no wrong."[19] Duvernay estimated that the mob of six to seven thousand which Hincks had marshalled was the largest in Montreal's history.

Yet Hincks ran into some difficulties. For door-to-door canvassing he had taken to distributing his Pilot among friend and foe alike. Big, burly Colonel Gugy waited for the newsboy one day and administered a good caning. Hincks sued and lost his case, but won still greater publicity for himself and Drummond.

On election day, April 11, Hincks had more trouble. When the

[16]Papiers Fabre, Fabre à Julie Bossange, 22 mars 1844.
[17]Baldwin Papers, A 41, S. Derbyshire to Baldwin, April 18, 1844.
[18]Ibid., v51, Hincks to Baldwin, March 27, 1844.
[19]Ibid., A 55, LaFontaine to Baldwin, March 29, 1844.

returning officer, A.-M. DeLisle, a Viger man, opened the main poll in Place d'Armes, Molson's faction had already occupied the square. Worse still, within fifteen minutes they had given, according to Barthe, some thousand votes to Molson. Hincks sent for his canallers. They came and both sides sprang at each other with sticks, pistols, "et autres armes meurtrières." DeLisle gallantly but vainly tried to separate the gangs. Finally he was forced to adjourn the election until April 16. Hincks at least had avoided defeat.[20]

For the next five days Montreal seemed to be in a state of siege while "les égorgeurs soudoyés par le parti de Drummond" roamed the streets, broke Tory windows, and spread such tactical rumours as "Mr. Molson avait résigné" or "Mr. Molson sera assassiné!" Hincks, Drummond, and Cartier, meanwhile, had done their best to buy the sympathy of the returning officer and his deputies. DeLisle absolutely refused, or said he did, but four of his deputies proved less scrupulous. Then, on the first day of the re-scheduled election, April 16, the Drummondites rose early, and this time, "on vit arriver [on Place d'Armes] les Irlandais par centaines . . . dans un horrible état de déguenillement et poussant des rugissements de fureur." When the poll opened at nine o'clock Molson's voters had also taken their stations, ready for anything. When one of Drummond's men named Dyer cast his vote, they immediately pounced on him and stripped him naked. Three of what Barthe called "les Irlandais" (Mollet, Champeau, and Charlebois by name) jumped to his rescue. The mêlée began. "Les Irlandais firent pleuvoir une grêle de pierre sur les électeurs," pistol shots rang out, and Champeau fell mortally wounded. But the contest continued. In the other polls, the deputy returning officers being more friendly to Drummond, less violence was needed. The second day, April 17, the returning officer noted that "the most desperate preparations are making [sic] by the Irish," who by now had been joined by new recruits from Lachine and numbered about 1200. DeLisle ordered troops to every poll and placed them, as the law required, under the command of the justices of the peace—who happened to be "the friends of Molson." Even so, "they could not save the voters from maltreatment." When, at five o'clock in the afternoon, DeLisle reluctantly tallied the vote, there was what Les Mé-

---

[20]Copious details on the election can be found in Derby Papers, Metcalfe–Stanley Correspondence, DeLisle to Daly, April 16, 17, 1844, and anonymous to Metcalfe, April 26, May 8, 1844; Baldwin Papers, A 51, Hincks to Baldwin, April 19, 1844; La Minerve, 12, 18 avril 1844; l'Aurore, 13, 18 avril 1844; Les Mélanges Religieux, 16, 19 avril 1844.

langes Religieux called "une majorité accablante de 920 voix" (1,383–463) for Drummond, owing, as DeLisle explained to Daly, to the fact that "Molson's friends had no organization."

After the whole mess was over, Duvernay ran a banner headline on April 18, "DÉROUTE COMPLÈTE DES TORIES," and Hincks (with tongue in cheek?) reported to Baldwin that "there was an attempt made by the Tory party to create an impression that we only succeeded by violence, and that there were French-Canadians in abundance to poll for Molson."[21] Indeed, publicly, Viger's friends blamed the defeat on "l'introduction dans la ville de cette troupe d'étrangers du canal qui n'avaient pas droit à voter" (*Les Mélanges Religieux*, April 23). But DeLisle admitted privately to Daly that "some of Molson's best friends and men of the first integrity have told me today that they were persuaded that D. had really a majority. Molson had not one Canadian voter in the St. Lawrence ward where he counted on many, and where they could have polled as much as they pleased on the second day."[22] The government saw to it that, as *Les Mélanges Religieux* noted on April 23, "les Irlandais du Canal de Lachine qui sont venus prendre part à la dernière élection ont été remerciés et se trouvent maintenant sans emploi." Molson also dismissed all those employees at his brewery who had voted against him. On his side, Drummond paid his debt to the canallers by turning young Champeau's funeral into a great political demonstration.

He might well do so. For Drummond, Hincks, and the other organization men had won by efficiency rather than on the merits of their cause. They had spoken little of principle, shown still less integrity. Viger and his French followers, on the other hand, had emphasized constitutional theory and counted on *Canadien* loyalty and good faith. Actually, however, the latter had agreed to work with Metcalfe on his own terms for a very practical (though on Viger's part, altruistic) reason: while awaiting permanent independence they would not give up what *L'Aurore* described (February 15) as "la mince part de pouvoir que l'on veut bien nous accorder." But LaFontaine had sacrificed office for the sake of principle, and for his sincere belief that only by true British institutions could he best secure *la survivance*. Indeed, quietly one night, without the publicity that attended Viger's compositions, and while Hincks was out conscripting his armed bands, the *Canadien* leader had written as much to Baldwin:

[21]Baldwin Papers, v51, Hincks to Baldwin, May 8, 1844.
[22]Derby Papers, Metcalfe–Stanley Correspondence, anonymous to Metcalfe, May 8, 1844.

"I do not hesitate in stating that I sincerely believe it to be the mutual interest both of England and Canada that the connection should subsist as long as possible—and a good government, based on our managing ourselves our local affairs, will secure the connection."[23]

VIGER GAINS

With the by-election won, LaFontaine had the advantage. But if Viger, Barthe, and *L'Aurore* could prevent it, he would not keep it for long. They planned two moves to increase their popularity. First, they decided on a great welcome for the Governor when he arrived in Montreal; then they set out to solve the nine-month-old constitutional crisis.

Soon after his party's defeat in Montreal, Barthe began to urge Montreal to give an enthusiastic reception to the Governor, who was about to take up residence in the new capital. As an admirer of the Governor, Barthe counted heavily on Metcalfe's ability to attract popular support and for the next six weeks he prepared for a great ceremonial entrance. To win popular support, he also included in every issue of *L'Aurore* some favourable anecdote about Metcalfe.

Duvernay attempted counter-propaganda and came up with one interesting spark. First, on May 13, he attacked the Governor's patronage of the United Empire Association—"Le caractère de cette association est palpablement orangiste"—and later, with horrified and copious editorials, he attacked Sir Charles' suspicious connection with the fiercely anti-French and anti-Catholic Orange Order. Indeed, LaFontaine's followers had fortunately happened upon a letter written by Ogle Gowan to his partner. Gowan served both as editor of the Tory *Statesman* in Kingston and as Grand Master of the Orange Order. In the letter, dated early in July 1843, he gave an account of an interview with the Governor General in which he had allegedly proposed a plan which Metcalfe had gratefully received whereby the Council could be dismissed without losing the support of the Assembly. Baldwin had been shown the letter in May 1844 and had immediately sent a copy to LaFontaine, declaring, however, that "it is expressly confidential and though I should feel justified in using it in every and any other way I am in doubt whether I can properly become a party to its publication in the newspapers."[24] LaFontaine

[23]Baldwin Papers, A 55, LaFontaine to Baldwin, Feb. 15, 1844.
[24]Papiers LaFontaine, Baldwin to LaFontaine, May 22, 1844.

agreed. But others did not. The letter was published in the Toronto *Globe* at the beginning of June, just in time for Duvernay to use it against Barthe.

On June 10 *La Minerve* highlighted a French translation of the letter under an article which began: "RÉVÉLATION EXTRAORDINAIRE. . . . Le voile qui couvrait la conduite mystérieuse du gouverneur-général envers ses ministres vient de se déchirer. . . . Quel est l'individu que Son Excellence avait choisi comme aviseur? . . . Un OGLE GOWAN, si tristement célèbre, *le grand chef des Orangistes en Canada*!!" "La lettre de Gowan a causé un grand scandale," Dr. Bouthillier wrote from Saint-Hyacinthe.[25] But *L'Aurore* published a statement saying the letter had been forged, and *Le Canadien* (June 12) like *Les Mélanges* (June 14), "plus enclins à croire le bien que le mal surtout d'un homme du caractère de Sir Charles Metcalfe," happily believed it. Apparently for once *La Minerve* was powerless. Duvernay could not prevent the success of Viger's and Barthe's planned triumph for their hero.

Nor could some of the others who tried. At the beginning of June, when Barthe called a meeting of his constituents at Saint-François-de-Yamaska, Turcotte and Drummond arrived with what Barthe later called "quelques individus gorgés de boisson." They started a brawl—but Barthe's group apparently won. By the end of the afternoon in which strenuous booing gradually turned into lusty cheers, Barthe had spoken for two hours "et mit à nu ses adversaires." His followers had also voted an address to Metcalfe and collected one hundred signatures, "parmi lesquelles se trouvent les plus respectables de toutes les parties du Comté." [26] Later in Terrebonne, a particularly sensitive riding for LaFontaine, another meeting voted another address to the Governor General "pour lui témoigner sa confiance et sa reconnaissance," as *Les Mélanges Religieux* reported on June 21. And at about the same time Viger was elected by acclamation for a second term as president of the Société Saint-Jean-Baptiste in Montreal. Obviously *La Minerve's* propaganda had a certain amount of effect.

On the great day all Viger's dreams seemed to come true. Metcalfe, who had been scheduled to make his official entry on June 21, was delayed until a far better day. He did arrive at Lachine late on the morning of the twenty-first, but after driving quietly to Monklands, his new official residence overlooking the western slope of Mount Royal, he asked that the state entrance be postponed. He was worried

[25]*Ibid.*, Bouthillier à LaFontaine, 25 juin 1844.
[26]*L'Aurore*, 5 juin 1844. See also *L'Aurore*, 8, 11 juin; *La Minerve*, 10, 13 juin; *Les Mélanges Religieux*, 21 juin 1844.

about the illness of Mrs. Higgenson, the wife of his private secretary and a lady who was taken by *Canadien* politicians to be the Governor's own natural daughter.[27] The Montreal city council agreed to the delay, and Barthe explained it in *L'Aurore* in an article on June 23 which concluded with this stirring note about the patient: "Fasse le ciel que cet être si intéressant à la félicité du vertueux et bienfaisant Metcalfe cesse de languir en reprenant la couleur des fleurs des champs qui l'entourent!"

The celebration accordingly took place on Saint-Jean-Baptiste day. "Tout concourrait à rendre ce jour mémorable," *Les Mélanges* noted on the twenty-fifth. When Metcalfe appeared, he was duly welcomed by mayor and council, then advanced into Montreal at the end of a line of landaus, brass bands, and flag-bearers. "Toutes les différentes sociétés," *Les Mélanges* continued, "revêtues de leurs costumes et à la suite de leurs bannières et de leurs drapeaux relevaient cette entrée triomphale. Par une heureuse disposition, la Société de Tempérance qui fermait la marche de toutes ces différentes associations se trouva à précéder le splendide équipage de Son Excellence. Le magnifique étendard de Saint Jean Baptiste flottait immédiatement devant la voiture de Sir Charles." As the procession turned into Great Saint-Antoine Street, the welcome became a tumult. Directly ahead of Sir Charles' carriage came Viger's and at a signal the crowd surged towards him and surrounded his carriage to cheer. After an interval of more singing and throwing of flowers the carriages inched forward between deep crowds past Notre-Dame (the new carillon loyally playing "God Save the Queen") to the Château de Ramezay where the higher clergy and notables awaited "au milieu d'un brillant état major et d'un peuple infini."[28] Duvernay gave the measure of Viger's success when he blamed Barthe on June 27 for putting "une couleur politique à tous les préparatifs qui ont été faits pour recevoir dignement le chef de l'administration." Still smarting under the reception given Viger, he fell back on criticism of the orange-coloured banners which had draped walls adjoining the parish church. Duvernay's sour comments notwithstanding, the *Canadiens*, though voting for LaFontaine, evidently preferred to cheer for Viger.

Metcalfe, Viger, and Barthe did not forget, however, that they had not solved the *Canadiens'* outstanding grievance against them—their

[27]PAC, MG 24, B 50, O'Callaghan Papers, Perrault à O'Callaghan, 11 june 1846.
[28]*L'Aurore*, 25 juin; *La Minerve*, 24, 27 juin; *Les Mélanges Religieux*, 25 juin 1844.

inability to complete the Executive Council. Now, as the election fever abated, their critics spoke louder. "Depuis [novembre]," *La Minerve* summed up on May 30, "à venir jusqu'à aujourd'hui . . . tous les départements du gouvernement sont privés de chefs, aucun n'est administré par des hommes ayant la confiance du peuple." And *Le Fantasque*, with clever allusion to Viger's long, involved articles, reiterated on June 15: "Dieu créa le monde en six jours; voilà bientôt neuf mois que Mr. Viger veut créer un ministère—il le fait sans doute à son image: interminable." Such complaints soon became so strong that Viger produced another series of essays for *L'Aurore* entitled "La Situation de la Province." Appearing between May 9 and September 12, they repeated the old arguments about Metcalfe's goodwill towards the *Canadiens*, and refuted the view that "le nombre de personnes dont le gouverneur devrait composer son ministère soit quelque chose de fixe et de sacramentel." In Britain, he explained, the Queen was satisfied with thirteen ministers out of some six hundred members, "soit un quarante-septième de la Chambre." Why could the *Canadiens* not be content with three out of eighty-four? Viger knew, however, that his critics were right. In May, Vallières de St. Réal had advised him privately that according to the constitution he should hurry to fill the Council.[29] And, of course, he was doing his best to do so. In June, the Governor had again offered Morin a post which Morin had again refused. Above all, Viger counted on a decision from his cousin in Paris.

But Papineau remained aloof. His life had not trained him to make concessions. Now, he could not bring himself even to seem to co-operate with the Union. He wrote to his wife, "un homme d'état éclairé et libéral ne peut pas approuver l'infâme acte d'Union et les conditions iniques dont il est tout saturé, imposé qu'il a été notoirement contre le gré connu et exprimé des majorités."[30] Moreover, he distrusted Metcalfe and his coalition policy. "Les vues et la conduite de Sir Charles sont pour moi une énigme indéchiffrable," he told Dr. O'Callaghan. "J'aime mieux la combinaison franchement avouée, naturelle et inévitable de deux partis, majorité et minorité. Je ne comprends pas de société rationnellement, équitablement administrée hors cette combinaison."[31] And he suspected the Governor's liberalism, observing that Metcalfe had not remedied the matter of unequal

[29]Papiers Viger, Barnard to Viger, May 14, 1844.
[30]Collection Papineau-Bourassa, 61, L.-J. Papineau à sa femme, 27 avril 1844.
[31]*Ibid.*, 544, L.-J. Papineau à O'Callaghan, 15 oct. 1844.

representation: "Tant que cela n'est pas concédé, il est très clair que l'on persiste dans les vues avouées que l'on a eues dans l'Acte d'Union, l'insulte et l'oppression pour nous au profit de l'autre section."[32]

Papineau wondered also at Viger's qualities as a leader. He questioned his cousin's break with the *Canadien* majority; he was shocked by the association with the Tories. If he returned, and remained true to his past, Papineau would have to oppose Viger. As he told Vicar-General Hudon who visited him in Paris, "l'état politique du Canada est la raison qui l'empêche de retourner: car il lui faudrait marcher en opposition avec Mr Viger, son parent, son ancien patron, et qu'en conséquence il se détermine à attendre de meilleures circonstances."[33] Yet another reason for not joining the government was that he still awaited his "arrérages," and he feared that if he co-operated, he would pass for a *vendu*. But he did not object to his son accepting the clerkship of the Court of Queen's Bench, a nomination which he called a "belle situation,"[34] and which Barthe, naturally, used for propaganda, describing it on July 9, 1844, as "un nouveau témoignage des sentimens de Son Excellence dont le pays a déjà eu tant de raison de s'applaudir."

Thus Viger had failed most where he had most hoped to succeed. Papineau would not return. Yet a full council must be put together. On August 26, it was completed. For the Lower Canadian section Viger had managed to press into service the unpretentious and unimportant lawyer, James Smith, and his own cousin, Denis-Benjamin Papineau. Smith took LaFontaine's office as attorney general (East), and Papineau took Morin's as commissioner of Crown lands.

When he heard of his brother's appointment, Louis-Joseph did not wonder. He realized that Denis-Benjamin's inclinations were the same as those of Viger and the younger members of the family. Like them, Denis-Benjamin Papineau entertained from the beginning to the end of his life high liberal and nationalist ideals. On accepting office, he stated categorically in a letter to a friend: "Vous n'êtes pas de ceux qui veulent croire qu'en acceptant un rôle dans la présente administration, j'ai renoncé aux principes de libéralité et de réforme que j'ai toujours professés. Je ne suis pas du tout changé."[35]

Denis-Benjamin Papineau believed strongly in the independence of French Canada. In fact, as a true nineteenth-century nationalist, he

[32]*Ibid.*, 63, L.-J. Papineau à sa femme, 31 déc. 1844.
[33]AAM, Hudon à Bourget, 1842-7, Hudon à Bourget, 8 sept. 1844.
[34]Collection Papineau-Bourassa, 61a, L.-J. Papineau à sa femme, 1 août 1844.
[35]*Ibid.*, D.-B. Papineau à Thibodeau, 20 sept. 1844.

considered it to be inevitable. "L'émancipation des colonies n'est qu'une question de temps parce que jamais une nation n'a été propre à en gouverner une autre," he wrote to Viger in February 1844,[36] reiterating the point later to his son Denis-Emery:

Les colonies ne peuvent rester telles que tant qu'elles ne sont pas assez fortes pour exiger leur indépendance, de manière à n'être pas reprises. Jamais nation n'ayant été propre à en gouverner une autre, l'Emancipation n'est qu'une question de temps, et lorsqu'elle arrive on fait justice de tous les inconvénients auxquels il a fallu se soumettre précédemment, et l'on corrige les abus en faisant alors table rase.[37]

Since independence was bound to come (and he was naturally an indolent man), why cause a stir and take unnecessary risks. "Il vaut mieux être décimé par la bourse que par la tête," he wrote to his cousin Viger. "Les métropoles cherchent dans leurs colonies leurs intérêts matériels; si les secondes résistent avant le temps, on les fusille et tout rentre dans l'ordre en vertu du droit naturel qui pour les animaux est le droit du plus fort."[38]

Why then did LaFontaine and Morin insist on a principle which could not work efficiently in a colony? "Quelque droit que l'on ait comme sujet britannique à un gouvernement vraiment responsable, cependant pour cette colonie c'est une chose nouvelle. . . . Surtout quand on voit que c'est encore la doctrine reçue dans toute l'Europe que les Colonies ne sont formées que pour l'intérêt de la métropole."[39] Since they had failed by their tactlessness to keep *Canadien* influence alive until the day of liberation, why should other men not be given a chance? "Je pense," he wrote, "que lorsqu'on ne peut obtenir d'une manière ce que l'on a le droit d'avoir il faut adopter d'autres moyens pour arriver à notre but commun. . . . Mon but en entrant dans le ministère actuel est d'employer d'autres moyens."[40] Later, as he experienced what *L'Aurore* (August 13, 1844) called Metcalfe's "conduite marquée chaque jour par des traits de sagesse, de bienfaisance et de justice," Denis-Benjamin also became a strong personal admirer of the Governor. Indeed, after four months in the Council, he wrote to his old friend, Pascal de Sales Laterrière:

Combien de fois ne me suis-je pas surpris à désirer que les Séances du Conseil Exécutif présidées par Son Excellence fussent publiques. Il ne faudrait que voir de quelle manière il agit tous les jours, pour se convaincre

[36]*Ibid.,* D.-B. Papineau à Viger, 27 fév. 1844.
[37]*Ibid.,* D.-B. Papineau à D.-E. Papineau, 17 juin 1844.
[38]*Ibid.,* D.-B. Papineau à Viger, 27 fév. 1844.
[39]*Ibid.,* D.-B. Papineau à D.-E. Papineau, 17 juin 1844.
[40]*Ibid.,* D.-B. Papineau à Thibodeau, 20 sept. 1844.

de sa bonté, de sa justice, de son intégrité, de son habileté, de son expérience dans les affaires. Il ne faudrait que cela pour le faire aimer de la
population Canadienne à l'égal des Prévost, des Sherbrooke, des Burton,
et des Bagot.[41]

Thus eager to serve so liberal a governor, and to press adroitly for
the gradual liberation of his people, Denis-Benjamin Papineau, par-
tially deaf, politically inexperienced, and fifty-five years of age, agreed
to join the government and lend Viger his name. L'Aurore immediately
underlined the implications on August 29:

Le nom de Papineau . . . se trouve une fois de plus côte-à-côte de celui de
Viger, quand c'est à l'union de ces deux noms si respectables pour le pays que
nous devons ce qui nous reste de libertés publiques. . . . Voilà que le frère, le
fils, les neveux et toute la famille du grand homme applaudissent à la conduite du vieil et fidèle ami des canadiens. . . . Sir Chs. Metcalfe est-il
l'ennemi du parti libéral, de l'origine canadienne et du gouvernement
responsable, quand il s'honore de pareils actes, quand il s'entoure de pareils
hommes?

With such high hopes and these great names the new councillors took
office on September 3. But within a week, LaFontaine, Morin,
Duvernay, and Hincks (still excellent propagandists) had succeeded
in pushing them right off the front pages. Ironically, it was Barthe
who provided the opening.

As an immediate proof of the new Council's popularity, Barthe
organized a huge meeting among the French-speaking voters of the
county of Drummond. On August 30, even before the new councillors
were actually sworn in, he led the Drummond delegation to Monklands and presented an address, in which Barthe (according to the
Montreal Gazette of August 31) accused the "late ministers" of
engaging in "measures and proceedings . . . tending directly, in our
opinion, to the terrible result of separation from British connexion and
rule." Perhaps Metcalfe himself had inspired the passage. At all
events, La Minerve reported his answer on September 9: "Having
abundant reason to know that you have accurately described the
designs of the late Executive Council, and the natural tendency of
such designs if they have been successful, it was my bounden duty
to resist them." LaFontaine and Morin lost not a minute. Addressing
the Provincial Secretary, Dominick Daly, they resigned their commissions as Queen's counsels and, as La Minerve reported, denounced
"le renouvellement d'un système qui tend à révoquer en doute la loyauté
et l'attachement des habitans du pays envers le gouvernement anglais.

[41]Ibid., D.-B. Papineau à Laterrière, 25 déc. 1844.

... Nous protestons avec toutes nos forces, et en notre nom, et au nom de ceux qui ont placé confiance en nous, contre toute imputation, de la part des Conseillers de Son Excellence, de la nature de celle que comporte l'accusation que nous repoussons aujourd'hui." Daly answered meekly that "His Excellency observes with equal surprise and regret" that the late councillors had misunderstood his words. They had not, they rejoined, and "nous regrettons d'avoir à dire qu'en donnant de nouveau toute notre attention au sujet, nous demeurons convaincus que nous sommes encore sous le poids de l'accusation qui a nécessité notre première lettre."[42]

What were LaFontaine's motives? Three months earlier he had written to Baldwin: "I wish they would cancel also the Letters Patent by which I was appointed Queen's Counsel. The fact is I do not like the silk gowns. I hate office more than ever."[43] But in reality and as his later career might indicate he appreciated honours more than he cared to admit. At the time he was created a baronet, his letter of thanks to Lord Elgin showed that he certainly appreciated the dignity: "Je serai le seul Canadien-français auquel cette dignité aura été conférée. Je suis le premier et de plus le seul Canadien-français qui ait été fait Procureur-Général et Juge-en-Chef de mon pays natal."[44]

In resigning the "silk gown" LaFontaine was, possibly, thinking less of his dislike of office and more of Baldwin's position, for in Upper Canada the disloyalty cry could be politically disastrous. He also knew that the move could do harm among his own people. Indeed, as La Minerve reported on September 9, he had written to Metcalfe that "cette accusation ... indique le renouvellement d'un système qui a déjà eu de funestes conséquences pour le pays, en ce qu'à l'aide de ce système, l'esprit du gouvernement et du peuple anglais avait été autrefois empoisonné contre nos compatriotes." Whatever his motives, he and his organizers succeeded in pushing the new Council out of the newspapers. For weeks La Minerve and Le Journal de Québec wrote of little other than LaFontaine's action: at the very time when D.-B. Papineau had "sold out" to the Governor, "les ex-ministres" had again shown their high calibre by resignation rather than subservience and on and on in the same vain. L'Aurore then had to abandon its paean for Papineau and take the defensive: LaFontaine and Morin were illogical and disrespectful; Metcalfe by

[42]La Minerve, 9 sept. 1844.
[43]Baldwin Papers, A 55, LaFontaine to Baldwin, June 2, 1844.
[44]Quoted in V. Jensen "LaFontaine and the Canadian Union," unpublished M.A. thesis, University of Toronto, 1943, p. ii.

his answer to them had given another example of "esprit de justice." Across the province many politicians, who perhaps thought like Aylwin that "la robe de soie en elle-même est peu de chose," had to admit, as Aylwin did to LaFontaine that "votre lettre a produit un excellent effet."[45]

Possibly the best comment on the whole tempest came from *La Fantasque* on September 21:

NOUVELLE CRISE DE LA CRISE.

c'est farceur!

Les gens de Drummond: Votre Excellence a bien fait d'arrêter à tems les ex-ministres; ce sont des rebelles qui nous menaient tout droit à la séparation.

Son Excellence: Je vous remercie sincèrement. En effet j'ai arrêté à tems les ministres; ce sont des rebelles qui nous menaient tout droit à la séparation.

Messieurs Morin et Lafontaine [sic]: Ah ça! dites donc, Mr. Daly, le gouverneur nous insulte; il nous traite de rebelles. Nous nous glorifions de ce titre il y a quelque cinq ou six ans; apprenez, qu'aujourd'hui nous ne sommes pas des rebelles, mais des ex-ministres. Allez vous faire lanlaire.

Mr. Daly: Eh non! Eh non! messieurs calmez-vous, vous n'êtes des rebelles, vous êtes d'honorables ex-ministres; restez-ainsi. Son Excellence n'a jamais dit ça; vous n'avez pas compris. . . .

Son Excellence: Ah ça dites donc, Higginson, il paraît que vous m'avez fait dire des choses désagréables à ces pauvres ministres. Voilà qui n'est pas bien.

Higginson: Eh non, votre Excellence, ces gens-là n'ont pas compris votre excellence!

Son Excellence: Ah c'est donc cela! Allons, tant mieux, car je ne voudrais pas leur faire de la peine; j'ai trop de bonnes intentions envers ces braves canadiens. A propos, envoyez vingt louis à une église catholique.

THE GENERAL ELECTION

Metcalfe and his councillors had looked upon the Montreal by-election as a test of strength. They had lost. But after the new appointments to the Council, especially of one with the name of Papineau, they had reason to feel confident. They wanted another test. Draper thought that the time was also ripe in Upper Canada. Accordingly, on September 23 Metcalfe's councillors announced a dissolution with writs returnable on November 12, 1844. In the lower part of the province (as in the upper) they went into the election crying "loyalty" to Crown and Governor. This helped in some of the English-speaking districts—in the traditionally Tory Eastern Townships, they carried all

[45]Papiers LaFontaine, Aylwin à LaFontaine, 9 sept. 1844.

eight seats. But among the *Canadiens*, they modified the cry. They knew that a majority of French Canadians feared above all else another Colborne or Sydenham. In consequence, and despite Metcalfe's answer to LaFontaine in the episode of the silk gowns, they disseminated the view that the attitude of the *ci-devants* would lead the province directly into another rebellion.

The LaFontaine people retorted without too much difficulty that Papineau and Viger, not LaFontaine, had caused the events of 1837. Cartier, for example, pointed out to a meeting at Saint-Denis that responsibility for the rebellion must weigh upon "ceux qui alors dirigeaient l'opinion publique; que lui, M. Viger, en était un."[46] And Duvernay (the founder of the Chasseurs!) produced several articles which pointed out squarely who was loyal and who was not. The *Canadiens*, not the Tories, had saved the empire in 1837. "Sans la loyauté inébranlable des Canadiens," he wrote on November 7, "sans leur attachement profond pour leur métropole, Dieu seul sait ce qu'il serait advenu de la colonie dans cette déplorable occurence." And, taking up Taché's theme of the "last cannon shot," he concluded that if the French stood squarely behind LaFontaine's programme, they would not only save themselves but prove once more "le boulevard contre la race Yankee et les idées républicaines" by which "l'Angleterre deviendra peut-être la dernière puissance européenne qui conserve un pied à terre en Amérique du Nord."

However, both French groups fought the election not so much on the issue of loyalty as on that of responsible government. And the electors had to choose between the principles of the *ci-devants* or those of Metcalfe and his new Council. Barthe in *L'Aurore* and MacDonald in *Le Canadien* urged Viger's reasons, pointing to the advantages in the old man's policy of co-operation. But LaFontaine was shrewd enough to identify his version of responsible government with *la survivance*. Only through responsible government—achieved by unity both among all the French-Canadian factions as well as with the Reformers of Upper Canada—could assimilation be averted. In an article in his new little paper, *Le Castor*, Aubin made the point most clearly on November 25:

Quelles garanties aurons-nous pour nos institutions nationales si nos institutions politiques ne sont point assises sur une base sûre? Quel contrôle aurons-nous sur le pouvoir lorsqu'il voudra attaquer nos institutions nationales, si

[46]*La Minerve*, 3 oct. 1844; see also A. Dansereau, *George-Etienne Cartier* (Montréal, 1914), p. 34.

nous n'avons point, par le moyen des institutions politiques, cette prépondérance que doit avoir la classe la plus intéressée au bon gouvernement, et que donnent seulement les institutions constitutionnelles et la responsabilité. . . . La question qui agite actuellement le pays est une question vitale de laquelle dépend notre existence comme peuple.

The whole point of the election, Cauchon added in *Le Journal de Québec* on September 26, "est une question de principe; et avec un pareil principe on ne peut pas transiger."

Both groups also hurled insults at each other—the *ci-devants* usually proving the more successful. To *L'Aurore* and the friends of Viger and Neilson, LaFontaine's whole policy rested purely on his own ambition and the belief that he alone could save the country. And *Les Mélanges Religieux* reflected that LaFontaine's position did not seem so altruistic. On October 22, it reprinted the old Lettre des Electeurs de Québec, which had played such an important part in the election of 1841, and pointed out that the question of the Union which had been so crucial then seemed to be relatively unimportant now. Perhaps, it hinted, LaFontaine's present principles might prove equally transitory: "C'était se déshonorer et déshonorer le pays en même temps que de voter pour un candidat favorable à l'Union, néanmoins rien n'a été changé, rien n'a été fait sur ce point; et personne n'a songé jusqu'à présent dans la présente élection à en faire mention. Voilà encore une fois ce que c'est que la volonté du peuple. Voilà ce que sont ces principes si précieux et si essentiels à la prospérité du pays."

In answer to all this the LaFontaine group, ever practical, enlisted the best candidates. In addition to LaFontaine, Morin, Aylwin, Drummond, and Taché, they collected all the names French Canadians knew best: Wolfred Nelson, Thomas Bouthillier (member for Saint-Hyacinthe since 1834), Jacob DeWitt (consistently re-elected since 1830), Joseph-Edouard Cauchon (never honourable but always a winner). And in Quebec Aylwin chose as the great Neilson's opponent twenty-four-year-old Pierre Chauveau, a fearless, versatile youth with classic features of mind and body.

Poor Viger was left to rally his clansmen. Among these, Denis-Benjamin Papineau of course agreed to run, as did André-Benjamin Papineau, an undistinguished cousin, and Louis-Antoine Dessaulles, Louis-Joseph's twenty-five-year-old nephew. The more popular Cherrier, however, again refused to be a candidate; so did another cousin, Louis-Michel Viger. John Neilson and Augustin Cuvillier both ran. So did Barthe who owed his 1841 election to LaFontaine, and that elegant man of the world and the government, Clément de

Sabrevois de Bleury. Otherwise Viger had to fall back on some five or six unknowns who had agreed to spend this brief, frustrating hour upon the stage.

Throughout the campaign the sounds of victory grew louder for LaFontaine. Four of his candidates won by acclamation in ridings where his group had been forced to fight a Tory or a Neilson man in 1841 (D.-M. Armstrong in Berthier, Pierre-Elzéar Taschereau in Dorchester, Morin in Saguenay, and J.-P. Lanthier in Vaudreuil). He also had been able to secure candidates to contest three of the eight English-speaking traditionally Tory Townships seats (Christopher Dunkin in Drummond, L. Brown in Missiquoi, and T. W. Lloyd in Megantic who lost by only 8 votes to Dominick Daly who had won there by acclamation in 1841). And, as another indication of his increasing influence, LaFontaine had managed, through Aylwin, to discourage Neilson's supporters as well as the English merchant community in the dual riding of Quebec from fielding candidates against his own men: Aylwin and Jean Chabot. In the election of 1841 the merchants had taken the two Quebec seats, and now *Le Canadien* gave its support to the outgoing member, Henry Black. But the latter refused to run. Consequently, on nomination day, over 3000 people, under the chairmanship of Dr. Pierre-M. Bardy, cheered Aylwin and Chabot to victory by acclamation.

Later, as the results began to arrive from other parts of Lower Canada, LaFontaine heard of mounting successes. Except for Denis-Benjamin Papineau in Ottawa and Sabrevois de Bleury in Montreal he had defeated every one of Viger's candidates. In the Quebec district, Aylwin, secure of his own election and with the constant, expert help of Cauchon, took such efficient charge of the organization that friends and foes alike dubbed him "l'électeur général." Eleven of the nineteen seats in the district were won by acclamation, one of these being Rouville which Alphonse de Salaberry had won by violence in 1841. In Lotbinière J.-B. Noël, the only other *Canadien* member who had voted with Neilson and Viger against the *ci-devants* in the crucial test after the resignation of November 1843, was easily defeated. In Nicolet where an unknown named Legendre ran against Aylwin's candidate, A.-P. Méthot, Aylwin and Cauchon encountered the full force of the Papineau problem. "Le comté de Nicolet est en feu," wrote a correspondent to *Le Canadien* on October 4:

Il paraîtrait que les amis de M. Lafontaine [*sic*] à Montréal auraient écrit à leurs amis du comté de faire élire un homme de leur parti, de bonne volonté, qui résignerait en faveur de M. LaFontaine dans le cas où ce dernier manquerait son élection à Terrebonne. Or le parti Viger . . . veut . . . faire élire l'ex-orateur Papineau, et le parti Lafontaine [sic] ne le veut pas, à moins que l'ex-orateur ne donne par écrit ses principes et qu'ils ne soient de soutenir les ex-ministres. Les autres répondent que M. Papineau ayant toujours été l'ami des Canadiens, vouloir cela, c'est lui faire l'injustice la plus odieuse; mais le parti Lafontaine [sic] craint que l'ex-orateur ne soit du parti Viger.

Still Méthot won. And so, after some difficulty, did Cauchon in Montmorency. He was nominated on October 22 to run against Viger's friend, André Taschereau, whose candidacy Glackmeyer had arranged although Taschereau should have been disqualified on the grounds that he was the superintendent of police in Quebec. Aylwin went out to Montmorency in person to fix the election, and he fully succeeded.

Most important of all, however, Aylwin and Cauchon managed to defeat Neilson, the man who in 1841 had stood unquestionably (as Morin had put it) "at the head of affairs." Aylwin blamed Neilson for the whole of la crise. "Le vieux traître," he told LaFontaine, "c'est lui qui a tramé tout ce qui est arrivé; il était au fond du sac et Viger est celui dont il s'est servi pour tirer les marrons du feu."[47] And he spared nothing to ensure his defeat. On October 1 he opened Pierre Chauveau's campaign on the steps of Saint-Roch Church with a vicious attack on the old veteran, and, two weeks later, on October 16, he and Cauchon, followed by "52 voitures dont un bon nombre à quatre roues" drove out to Charlesbourg to break up Neilson's nomination meeting. Under a slanting rain, they spoke for four hours and turned the seasoned old campaigner's own audience against him. Neilson fought desperately. Yet on election day, he whose fifty years of service to Canada had been until now almost a legend found himself with 1000 votes less than the twenty-four-year-old Chauveau. And from Charlesbourg he saw the young man set off, victorious, to return to the capital, "escorté d'un grand nombre de cavaliers et de voitures, accompagné d'un corps de musique pour célébrer . . . cette grande victoire du gouvernement responsable."[48] Here was one hero lost, another in the making.

In the district of Montreal LaFontaine left the management of the election to Duvernay, Drummond, and Cartier. They had proved their skill in the April by-election. Moreover he was facing a personal ordeal in the severe illness of his wife and the sudden death, in the

[47]Papiers LaFontaine, Aylwin à LaFontaine, 21 oct. 1844.
[48]Le Journal de Québec, 24 oct. 1844.

midst of the campaign, of his thirteen-year-old niece and adopted daughter, Corinne Wilbrenner.

Cartier concentrated first on defeating Viger in Richelieu, where Wolfred Nelson, certainly the strongest possible candidate, had agreed to run. The old man whose very name had once meant nationalism appealed to his constituents on a high plane: in an address which appeared in *La Minerve* on October 12, he said: "Me reposant sur les sentiments de justice et d'honneur des électeurs du Comté de Richelieu, j'ose me flatter d'obtenir une nouvelle marque de votre confiance, en recevant vos souffrages." And to convince them, he travelled across the riding with Cherrier. But, *La Minerve* noted on October 17, "l'*effort* ou le *sacrifice* du fils adoptif n'a pas plus servi au septuagénaire parent que le pamphlet sur la crise ministérielle." More important, Nelson and Cartier pursued them from village to village breaking up their meetings and making certain that Viger could never explain his position clearly. At the poll on October 15 Nelson carried the day. Humiliated, Viger decided to run in Montreal County which A.-M. DeLisle had won for the government by violence in 1841. D. M. McCulloch, who had won in Terrebonne against LaFontaine in 1841, stood there as Tory candidate against André Jobin who had taken the riding back from DeLisle in 1842. McCulloch generously resigned in favour of Viger. For once Viger seems to have decided to fight the *ci-devants* on their own terms. He arranged to have eighty sailors come up from Quebec by steamboat and seize the polls for his partisans. But Aylwin heard of the arrangement before the seamen left and sent a courier to warn LaFontaine in Montreal. The sailors were arrested on arrival. At the polls on October 28 Jobin won handsomely.

In Huntingdon, Cuvillier who had declared for Viger lost to the relatively unknown B.-H. LeMoyne and, like Viger, decided to run elsewhere. He chose Rimouski where Glackmeyer assured him of victory. But Cauchon secured his defeat by asking the electors there on October 19 "si le district de Québec peut, dans son intérêt, élire des hommes de Montréal qui perdent là leurs élections?" In Saint-Hyacinthe Dr. Bouthillier ran into some difficulty against Louis-Antoine Dessaulles because of the Papineau-Dessaulles ascendancy in that seigneury and the influence of the priests of the Collège. "Il y a eu ici, comme vous pensez bien, quelques sympathies pour M. Viger, et peut-être quelque chose de plus," he wrote.[49] But he carried the seat easily. André-Benjamin Papineau, the Viger candidate in Terrebonne, came as far as the poll, but could find only three sponsors out

[49]Papiers LaFontaine, Bouthillier à LaFontaine, 5 oct. 1844.

of the 200 electors gathered there. In Yamaska, LaFontaine's men hardly bothered to attack Barthe, for his own supporters had divided against him and had chosen Michel Fourquin to run in the Viger interest. Viger of course supported his protégé, but Louis Rousseau carried the riding for LaFontaine. By the end of October, therefore, except for Denis-Benjamin Papineau, every one of the former members of the Assembly who had declared for Metcalfe had been thoroughly defeated.

Only in Montreal, with its usual preference for violence over votes, did the wind blow towards Viger. Indeed, this time, perhaps because Hincks was in Europe, the canallers sold their services to the Tory side. Drummond and his running mate, Dr. Pierre Beaubien, went down to defeat before George Moffatt and Sabrevois de Bleury. Drummond ran again in Portneuf, near Quebec, where Cauchon this time said not a word about the different districts. Indeed, Cauchon managed to get the two candidates selected in Portneuf for the LaFontaine and Viger camps to resign in favour of Drummond, and the Montrealer carried the riding by acclamation.

In the end, the *ci-devants* counted up some twenty-nine seats. And LaFontaine who had come out of the election of 1841 under the shadow of Neilson and Viger, with only six or seven members on whose loyalty he could count, stood at thirty-seven, the undisputed leader of the French-Canadian people. Viger's campaign had made little difference. LaFontaine had been clever enough to identify his cause with that of *la survivance*. He had convinced the French that in unity alone could they achieve responsible government and their fulfilment as a nation. He had revived those years when *la nation canadienne* thought as one.

Yet the taste of victory was neither fresh nor sweet. The government had won in Upper Canada, and the Tories could claim a tenuous, over-all majority. LaFontaine was discouraged. Since his resignation, he had carried most of the burden of opposition in Lower Canada, he had persuaded the party chiefs to unite, he had won the first contest in Montreal, he had outmanœuvred Metcalfe by resigning as Queen's counsel. Now, he had won a decisive victory in Lower Canada. Yet he was robbed of the victory which he had hoped would vindicate his views. By superb political tactics he had carried the *Canadien* electorate, but he could not force himself upon Metcalfe and he would have to continue the fight within the Assembly.

12

Double Majority
November 1844-September 1845

On November 29, 1844, Sir Charles Metcalfe in his dark blue and gold ceremonial uniform rode in state to Saint Anne's Market and, enthroned under a huge high-vaulted canopy draped with dark red velvet, read the speech that opened the first session of the Province of Canada's second parliament—the first to meet in Montreal. He read the speech in English, then listened while the Clerk of the Legislative Council read a French translation. As he sat there on the dais, he may have felt satisfied that he had overcome a "very important crisis,"[1] that in this new parliament his followers would at last hold a majority. Indeed, a week or so before, he had claimed optimistically to Lord Stanley that he felt certain of mustering forty-six votes to the thirty-nine at the most which the LaFontaine-Baldwin alliance could command. Yet, Metcalfe must have known how tenuously he held his victory. By temperament, he was not good at winning people over, and by experience, he was unfitted for the situation. No Sydenham, he could not manage or manoeuvre hesitant partisans into concord—if he could there would have been no *crise Metcalfe*. Nor had he enough parliamentary experience for the ordinary tactics of party warfare which alone could allow him to consolidate his majority. Then, too, he was dying. Inexorably the unremitting pain from the cancer had spread to the whole right side of his face. "The complaint," he wrote at the beginning of January 1845, "appears to me to have taken possession of the whole of that side of the face, although the surface is not so much ulcerated as it has heretofore been. I feel pain and tenderness in the head, above the eye and down the right side of the face as far as the chin: the cheek towards the nose and mouth being permanently swelled. I cannot open my mouth to its usual

[1]Metcalfe to Stanley, Sept. 26, 1844, as quoted in Kaye, *Life of Metcalfe*, II, 389.

width, and have difficulty in inserting and masticating pieces of food."[2]

Not only did Metcalfe's government have only a token majority, but its most eloquent and shrewdest debaters were excluded from the Assembly. Viger had been twice defeated; Denis-Benjamin Papineau, with only two short sessions of parliamentary experience to his credit in any case, was growing deaf; Dominick Daly had never said a word in parliament; and the most dexterous of Metcalfe's supporters, the real leader of the government, "Sweet William" Draper, influential, fluent, and "le plus plausible des mortels,"[3] sat helpless in the Legislative Council. There remained—as far as the French were concerned—only Bleury, elegant, but hardly an oratorical or political match for the Governor's opposition.

From the other end of the chamber LaFontaine may also have speculated about the new turn which the crisis had taken. The two peoples of the united province had voted ambiguously, dividing almost entirely according to national interests. In the French section, he had carried a majority which was almost unparalleled, and the election had been a disaster for Viger. But because Metcalfe's followers had won in Upper Canada, LaFontaine himself was at a terrible disadvantage. He stood there, at the bar of the Legislative Council, the leader of every French-Canadian member but two, the head of a re-awakened, united people who had accepted from him the promise of responsible government, and, implicitly, a guarantee of la survivance. But because of the Reformers' defeat in Upper Canada he could not fulfil his pledge. Would the Canadiens conclude that Neilson and Viger had indeed been right in claiming that responsible government was impossible in practice, that the Union could never serve French Canada? Would the French be won over by the Viger-Papineau invitation to co-operate with the government, at least pending a more lasting constitutional arrangement? If Metcalfe's supporters managed to entice any number of his followers away from him, they would not only destroy LaFontaine's leadership and the unity of the Canadiens, they would also delay the advent of responsible government. Unless he acted vigorously, all might be lost.

Thus the Governor and the ci-devant Attorney General each held his majority without the power to enjoy it. For the next year they would manœuvre for position, the hopes of each group alternating

[2]Metcalfe to Martin, Jan. 3, 1845, as quoted in ibid., II, 402.
[3]Chapais, Cours d'histoire, V, 49, quotes a French-Canadian newspaper of the time as coining this nickname.

with the seasons. Throughout the winter session LaFontaine would fight a flamboyant offensive calculated to confirm the identity of his cause with *la survivance*; during the spring and summer months Viger would lead a massive theoretical assault which the *Canadiens* seemed, for a time, to endorse—as, throughout the autumn, did some of the politicians. But at the end of the year LaFontaine would still hold his majority, without its advantages, however. It would be a long, uneven year, without promise or bright prospect, without resolve, even without result.

WINTER

As soon as the session began, LaFontaine attacked, hoping he might topple the administration. His opponents were weak; the Governor was blind, the Commissioner of Crown Lands deaf, the Provincial Secretary virtually dumb, the President of the Council, Viger, still busy composing literary tracts. And on his side, LaFontaine had all French Canada's best spokesmen—such splendid orators as Aylwin whom *La Minerve's* reporter rated as "le plus sarcastique, le plus agressif, le plus mordant"; Drummond whose speeches, Cauchon claimed, joined "la richesse de l'imagination irlandaise à la froide raison de l'Allemand"; Cauchon himself, violent and feared—a terror to his enemies; Wolfred Nelson, the foremost critic left from among the great men in the old Assembly of Lower Canada; Taché, energetic and courageous, "orateur d'une force peu commune"; Pierre Chauveau who commanded the French language as few others have ever done. Even if these assets failed to force him back into office, LaFontaine could use them to save the unity of his party in the House and to reinforce it by keeping popular opinion outside in tune with his ideals.

As the symbol of his campaign for *la survivance*, LaFontaine chose the language question. Indeed it best suited his purposes for several reasons. The proscription of French as an official language for the united province had not only been one of the main points in the imperial policy of assimilation, but also among those most resented by the *Canadiens*. By identifying his cause with opposition to it, LaFontaine could add to the strength of his party the full emotional allegiance of his followers. And the language question had an added advantage in that, unlike the amnesty and the moving of the capital, it was more clearly LaFontaine's own.

Although during the debate on the Union the Lower Canadian politicians had assailed the restrictions imposed on the use of French, the *Canadiens* had soon come to realize that in practice the law had little meaning. They continued to speak French every day of their lives, their schools taught it, their newspapers maintained it. And even if it no longer held official status at the seat of government, such bilingual civil servants as Etienne Parent and Jean-Baptiste Meilleur wrote many of their reports in French, while Archbishop Signay and Bishop Bourget corresponded with successive governors general and their secretaries in their own language—and from Sir Charles Bagot, at least, received answers in French. Viger and Morin and, later, LaFontaine had delivered their first speeches at Kingston in French.[4] And now, in 1844, Metcalfe himself had reverted to the old Lower Canadian practice established in 1791 of having the Clerk of the Legislative Council read a formal translation of the Speech from the Throne. Indeed, concerned with the practical problems of securing the return of the exiles and beating the Tories in election contests, many *Canadiens* had probably forgotten the language issue.

LaFontaine had not. During his famous correspondence with Hincks he had complained specifically about the restrictions on his language, and he had emphasized the point again in his Adresse aux Electeurs de Terrebonne. During the September days in 1842 and subsequently, while he held office as Attorney General, he had made it a point to write many of his reports in his own language. He had even persuaded Metcalfe to ask the Colonial Office to repeal the obnoxious clause in the Act of Union. After consulting the cabinet, Lord Stanley had refused;[5] LaFontaine, increasingly preoccupied with the constitutional crisis, had postponed a fight over the language question for the time being. Now, as Leader of the Opposition, he revived it, making the issue (in Metcalfe's words) "a claptrap for popularity." Besides keeping his followers united, he hoped to succeed in what the Governor called "the double game of producing a feeling of hatred against the Government and of ruining in the estimation of . . . his Countrymen the French Canadian members of the Executive Council."[6]

As the session approached, therefore, LaFontaine's newspapers began to refer glowingly to their leader's first speech in Kingston on September 12, 1842. Rising to speak as the new member for the

[4]*La Gazette de Québec*, 17 juin 1841; *L'Aurore*, 27 sept. 1842.
[5]Derby Papers, Cabinet Memoranda, Aug. 10, 1843; C.O. 537/142, Stanley to Metcalfe, Aug. 18, 1843.
[6]C.O. 537/143, Metcalfe to Stanley, March 13, 1845.

Fourth Riding of York, LaFontaine had begun in French and been interrupted after a few phrases by Charles Day who asked, from his seat among the Tories, that the young member speak English. With all the dignity he could muster, as *L'Aurore* had reported, LaFontaine had grandly retorted:

L'honorable député a-t-il oublié que j'appartiens à la nationalité si injustement traitée par l'Acte d'Union? Il me demande de prononcer dans une autre langue que ma langue maternelle le premier discours que j'aie à prononcer dans cette Chambre. Je me défie de mon habileté à parler la langue anglaise, mais lors même que je la parlerais aussi facilement qu'un Anglais, je n'en ferais pas moins mon premier discours dans la langue de mes compatriotes canadiens-français, ne fût-ce pour protester solennellement contre cette cruelle injustice de cette partie de l'Acte d'Union qui tend à proscrire la langue maternelle d'une moitié de la population du Canada. Je dois cela à mes compatriotes, je le dois à moi-même. (September 27, 1842)

At the time, the incident had attracted little notice. Now Duvernay and Cauchon saw to it that no *Canadien* elector would ever forget it. And they succeeded. For that scene in the Assembly at Kingston was to become a source of song and story long after those who were gathered there had passed away. Thousands of young French-Canadian children have learnt the noble words which custom has not staled. The topic thus prepared by the press, LaFontaine stressed the language problem from the first day of the new session. And until the end, on March 29, 1845, he managed so to manœuvre the debates that in *Canadien* eyes a vote for the government came to mean a vote against French.

He delivered his first stroke when the new parliament met to discuss the election of its speaker. LaFontaine had again decided on Morin—as a tribute to his personal friend certainly but also as a political stratagem. "If we have any chance to carry the chair," he explained to Baldwin, "it is by putting Morin forward. I think Papineau will not dare to vote against him; and then the administration is paralysed. For us, it would be a victory to have one of the ex-ministers in the chair."[7] Denis-Benjamin Papineau was, after all, a close friend of Morin. And even *Les Mélanges Religieux* who had supported the Governor's cause since *la crise* agreed on November 15 that "les suffrages des différentes nuances politiques paraissent se réunir en faveur de l'hon. A. N. Morin. Pour nous cet accord de souffrages, dans une semblable circonstance, nous paraît la preuve la moins équivoque de la dignité et du mérite de l'hon. Monsieur et nous

[7]Baldwin Papers, A 55, LaFontaine to Baldwin, Nov. 12, 1844.

ne pourrions qu'applaudir à ce choix si judicieux." The government proposed the election of Sir Allan MacNab, the member for Hamilton and a gentleman whose story was well calculated to stir the antagonism of any *Canadien* nationalist. A Tory of the Tories, he had begun his chequered and fiercely loyalist career as a member of the Assembly of Upper Canada on the side of the Family Compact; in 1837 he had commanded the militia against the rebels, earning the enmity of all the Upper Canadian Reformers. For a French Canadian to vote for MacNab would be at the least embarrassing. LaFontaine's people contrived to make it impossible. Before the Assembly met, Duvernay had already noted (*La Minerve*, November 21) that the member for Hamilton could not understand or speak French and, worse still, that some Tory newspapers in Upper Canada were recommending his election as Speaker precisely for this reason—it would force the French members to speak English. When they proposed Morin, the Opposition members accordingly underlined the latter's bilingual qualities and stressed MacNab's deficiency. They then sat back as the Tories who championed the Upper Canadian began to argue that French was illegal in any case. When in fact the hearty, round, red-faced knight did carry the vote, it was by a bare thirty-nine to thirty-six.

The Opposition had lost Morin's cause, but happily it noted that among the three votes that had given MacNab the election were those of Denis-Benjamin Papineau and Sabrevois de Bleury. With scores of exclamations and italics, *La Minerve* left no doubt about who was a hero and who was not.

Le pays ne s'attendait pas à la désolante nouvelle que nous lui apprenons, que la présidence de la Chambre d'Assemblée, la place d'Orateur, a été remportée contre le parti libéral par une *majorité* de trois!!! . . . Mais ce que le pays apprendra avec douleur, c'est que cette élection a été remportée par le vote de deux Canadiens-Français!! Nous rougissons d'enrégistrer leurs noms. Ces deux individus ne sont rien moins que l'hon. D. B. Papineau et C. S. deBleury! (November 28)

Clearly on the defensive, *L'Aurore* made an attempt at rebuttal on December 7: "Le *Castor* . . . fait beaucoup de bruit à propos de la prétendue proscription de notre langue par l'hon. M. D. B. Papineau. . . . Comme s'il eut pu en décence et avec sens-commun supporter l'élection d'un des plus violens opposans du gouvernement, quel que soit d'ailleurs son mérite personnel et ses talens. . . . Ce n'est pas pour Sir Allan McNab [*sic*] que l'hon. M. Papineau a voté, mais pour un homme favorable à l'administration." But just as they had scored over Viger's support of Molson, LaFontaine and his orators succeeded again in branding Papineau with the hated *vendu* label. Nor did they give MacNab any quarter. On the day of the Opening of Parliament their papers attacked him furiously for sitting down at the bar of the Legislative Council when the Clerk began to read the French version of the Speech from the Throne. "On ne saurait appuyer l'administration actuelle," Aubin pronounced in *Le Castor* (December 19) "sans se joindre aux tories du Haut et du Bas-Canada. N'est-ce-point l'administration actuelle qui a *favorisé* l'élection de Messieurs Moffatt et De Bleury? L'un de ces Messieurs est la personnification du toryisme de Montréal, l'autre est politiquement la honte de la race canadienne-française; l'homme dont l'élection pouvait le plus insulter aux sentiments des réformistes canadiens-français."

LaFontaine immediately pressed his advantage. On December 9 he introduced an address to the Governor General asking him to table any communications with the Colonial Office about the language question. Of course, he knew the imperial government had refused eighteen months earlier to change Article 41 in the Act of Union; hence he must now have reasoned that his address would place Papineau, de Bleury, and their friends in another embarrassing position. It would prove at least that he had been the first to raise the issue. The Governor and Papineau reacted quickly and, for once, with political flair. On December 14, when the debate began on LaFontaine's motion, Papineau rose to announce that he would himself soon propose an address to the Queen begging as *La Minerve* reported on December 5 "que les deux langues fussent mises sur le même pied." He did so on December 20, and his address was accepted unanimously on January 31, 1845.

Metcalfe had disobeyed his instructions on the language question because he hoped to circumvent LaFontaine's plan "to incense the minds of the People."[8] He failed. For although *L'Aurore* and *Le Canadien* trumpeted Papineau's action throughout December and *Les Mélanges* printed two and one-half columns of his speech on December 17, the others paid no attention to his address. In fact, *La Minerve*, noting on December 5 that "c'est bien le moins qu'il fasse cette tentative après son vote en faveur d'un orateur qui ne sait pas le français," maintained an incessant attack against Papineau's vote for MacNab until all talk of the address to repeal Article 41 disappeared from the papers that supported the government. In a typical paragraph

---

[8] C.O. 537/143, Metcalfe to Stanley, March 13, 1845; see also Kaye, *Life of Metcalfe*, II, 392; Gérin-Lajoie, *Dix Ans au Canada*, p. 271; Ormsby, "Metcalfe and Canadian Union," pp. 43–4.

Duvernay even claimed (December 16) that the vote on the election of the speaker had been the more important one:

M. Papineau, fit ce qui, sans doute, devait être regardé comme *un coup de maître* . . . calculé, dans la pensée de son auteur, à produire un effet puissant et favorable à l'administration dont il est membre. . . . Mais . . . de grâce ne tombons pas dans les extrêmes, en prétendant, comme *Le Canadien*, que cette proposition de Mr D. B. Papineau "répond victorieusement" aux attaques que lui a values son vote de proscription de notre langue, à l'occasion du choix d'un Orateur de la Chambre. . . . Car le président est *le seul organe collectif de la Chambre;* et s'il ne parle pas, ou, ce qui est la même chose, ne professe pas de parler le français, comment peut-on dire qu'il serait l'organe de la majorité du Bas-Canada dont c'est la langue?

The pattern thus established, the Opposition members followed the same strategy for the whole season, devoting great energy to baiting the administration into impossible situations where they must appear to vote against the French language. Thus Papineau's address could do him no political good, and the Lower Canadians could be made to believe that, as Duvernay put it (December 26), "le nœud de l'alliance entre nos tories et M. D.B. Viger, paraît se resserrer tous les jours." To supervise the debates LaFontaine relied on Aylwin, who had become an unofficial House leader for the Opposition. Short, nearsighted, and (at this time at least) never quite sober, Aylwin commanded not by his physical presence as much as by his charming, genial bluffness and, above all, by his prodigious bilingual gift for words. With almost perfect skill, he organized tumultuous parliamentary scenes, and again and again manœuvred the debates onto the language question. He received able assistance at times from that tall, energetic hero, Wolfred Nelson (imitating LaFontaine in his contempt for Article 41, the old rebel took great pains to pronounce his first speech in French), and more often from Joseph Cauchon for whom the only honour was to succeed.

One night in December 1844 Aylwin almost came to blows in defence of French, and on February 4, 1845, he did. That cold night (27 below zero outside), in an unusually heated attack on Papineau, he called him "de la plus grossière et de la plus stupide ignorance." Bleury came to his friend's rescue and Cauchon to Aylwin's. Soon, in a "désordre . . . pire que jamais," members from both sides filled the aisle in a wild scramble. In the galleries citizens began to throw things at the members and at each other. Sir Allan MacNab ordered the visitors out, and the sergeant-at-arms threatened to expel Aylwin. Finally, LaFontaine who, according to *La Minerve* on February 6, "garda un sang-froid imperturbable pendant cet orage . . . cette scène, la

plus extraordinaire qu'on ait jamais vue dans nos fastes parlemen-
taires," calmly restored order. There seemed no doubt who was master.
L'Aurore blamed Aylwin and Cauchon for this "scène de cabaret"; so
did *Les Mélanges*. *La Minerve*, of course, blamed Bleury. A few
days later, on February 17, 1845, Joseph Laurin, the young notary
who had defeated J.-B. Noël in Lotbinière, rose, on cue, to make a
motion in French. The Speaker (with very little political instinct)
declared it out of order. Aylwin and Cauchon thundered. Marc-Pascal
de Sales Laterrière, newly elected in Saguenay, declared that "si nos
institutions sont ainsi à la merci d'une majorité fébrile, le rappel de
l'Union est notre seul recours." LaFontaine, declaring Article 41
immoral, appealed MacNab's ruling to the Assembly. Due to absences
that night, the Opposition all but outnumbered the government. As
the voting progressed, the *Canadiens* gleefully watched as poor Denis-
Benjamin Papineau twice rose to leave, then, apparently weighing
whether the administration absolutely needed his vote or not, twice
sat down again. When the Speaker's decision was upheld, it was by
one vote—Denis-Benjamin Papineau's. Of what use, the Opposition
railed, was his petition to restore the language if his single vote upheld
a decision against it?

And in this manner for another six weeks LaFontaine's orators were
forever on their feet. Day after day they branded Bleury and Papineau
as traitors, goading them into scenes that recalled the early 'thirties
when all true *Canadiens* stood together. By the end of March their
offensive had reached the stage where Dominick Daly challenged
Aylwin to a duel. Neither suffered from that meeting, but Daly was
encouraged. A few days later, he spoke in the Assembly for the first
time. During a flight of Taché's, he murmured through pursed lips:
"Your statement is false." This time, Taché challenged him. But on
the appointed morning, as they stood on snowshoes watching their
seconds try to count twenty paces in a field of deep snow, both
principals burst out laughing. The fights and the duels were not con-
fined to the parliamentarians. At the end of April, Duvernay spent
four days in jail for creeping up to Barthe on the street and hitting
him over the head with a club.

The newspapers supporting the Governor wasted their time attacking Aylwin and his tactics: "Le parti canadien a toujours été remarqué
pour son savoir vivre," *L'Aurore* stated on December 14; "de pareilles
avanies se réflètent injustement jusque sur lui." In mid-February, all the
members of the Opposition signed an address to Aylwin—"le cauche-
mar du parti ministériel," Aubin called him in *Le Castor* on February 20

—thanking him for his leadership. And after the end of the session, on April 17, 1845, a huge meeting of Aylwin's constituents met to adopt another address. They paraded through the streets of the old capital to his home carrying the vote of thanks they had signed individually on a sheet of paper twenty-five feet long. Aylwin deserved it. He had succeeded in preserving for LaFontaine and his party the united allegiance of the *Canadiens*.

SPRING

Aylwin's work in the House was essential. For despite the appeal of the language question and all the parliamentary (and extra-parliamentary) clamour, Viger quietly scored with some victories of his own—more silent perhaps but potentially more dangerous.

On January 19, 1845, the Lower Canadian *patriote* exiles, financed by the Association de la Délivrance, began to return. "Il y a 39 exilés canadiens d'arrivés," exulted Fabre with evident satisfaction, "après plus de six ans de captivité. . . . Quelle joie pour ces pauvres malheureux après une aussi longue captivité de revoir leurs femmes, leurs enfants, leurs Pères, leur Mères, enfin leur Pays, pour lequel ils ont tant souffert . . . comme dit Voltaire, à tous les cœurs bien nés, que la patrie est chère!"[9] In London they had been told by British officials that Metcalfe and Viger had negotiated their pardon. Shortly after arriving, a number of them accordingly went to Government House to thank the Governor and proceeded afterwards to Viger's for a reception. Barthe immediately seized upon the propaganda value of the visit and highlighted Viger's part in their release. Duvernay sprang into print on January 30, insisting that the *ci-devant* council, and not Viger, had done the real work: "Nous ne trouverions rien à redire à une expression de remerciemens de nos infortunés exilés si elle s'adressait à tous ceux qui ont travaillé pour obtenir leur retour, au lieu de s'adresser exclusivement à sir Charles Metcalfe et à 'son premier ministre', qui ne peuvent compter qu'après d'autres dans la liste de ceux qui ont un droit incontestable à la reconnaissance de nos exilés." A battle royal followed, with LaFontaine's agents urging the new arrivals to keep away from the Governor and Barthe pushing them into effusions of thanks to him. In Quebec, Ronald MacDonald wondered in *Le Canadien* on February 5: "*La Minerve* ne nie pas, elle cherche au contraire à justifier les tentatives . . . faites auprès des exilés

[9]Papiers Fabre, E.-R. Fabre à E.-C. Fabre, 25 jan. 1845.

rentrés dans le pays, pour les détourner d'aller . . . remercier Son Excellence. . . . Il nous semble qu'il n'y avait, au moins, rien d'inconvenant à ce que ceux-ci allassent tout d'abord remercier le représentant de notre très-gracieuse souveraine." And indeed Barthe continued for six weeks until he had led every one of the travellers regularly and with appropriate publicity to an audience at the Château.

While organizing the exiles Barthe also attempted to turn to good political account the Governor General's elevation to the peerage. There he was not as successful, however. At the end of December 1844 Metcalfe received four cordial letters from Stanley and Peel informing him of his summons to the House of Lords as a baron of the United Kingdom. By then the new peer had, in his own words, "lost the use of my eyes from the total blindness of one and the precarious condition of the other"[10] and would soon be reduced "to sit sheltered by screens, and when I go out, which I only do to attend business in town, I take every precaution in my power against the glare and dust."[11] Personally he felt the honour an empty one: it had been delayed till he was ill and could not enjoy it, till he was solitary and did not need it. But for his admirers it could, perhaps, be turned into a positive political asset. Barthe trumpeted the happy news in *L'Aurore* on December 31, 1844, with an invocation to the new Baron:

> Donc que ce nouvel an s'écoule pour ta gloire
> Et que ton nom Metcalfe, au temple de Mémoire,
> Retrace à l'univers tant d'actes de vertus
> Qui dans ce pays seul ont été méconnus.

And during the next few days, he led many *Canadiens* on a pilgrimage to the darkened room at Monklands where Lord Metcalfe, unsightly but cheerful, received their congratulations.

His opponents, however, refused to be impressed. Aubin thought the whole thing a joke and suggested that as the new peer had been born in the East he should adopt the exotic title of "Lord Mys-typhi-Léjan-Kosonta-Séphoupour-Selé-Séran-Bêter, Baron de Square-toes" [that is: Mystifie les gens qui sont assez fous pour se laisser embêter]. "Le titre est assez long," he explained on January 11, "mais il renfermerait bien les qualités qui distinguent la politique de Son Excellence." *La Minerve* reacted just as quickly, Duvernay denying on January 7 that Metcalfe could possibly have been rewarded for his services in Canada. Then on February 25, when an address of congratulations was moved in the Assembly, Aylwin claimed that the Governor should

[10]PAC, MG 24, C 5, Wallick Papers, Metcalfe to Wallick, Feb. 26, 1845.
[11]Metcalfe to Martin, as quoted in Kaye, *Life of Metcalfe*, II, 414.

have been recalled and tried for his crimes rather than honoured. And he led twenty-five members to vote against it. In general the press and the politicians paid little attention. Barthe had failed to capitalize on the peerage. He returned accordingly to his more successful theme: the gratitude of the exiles. For when he had finished introducing each of the latter to Lord Metcalfe, he began to lead their grateful wives to thank the Governor. Duvernay ranted and roared, but on this issue he was the loser.

Duvernay might well object. It could be dangerous for the unity of LaFontaine's forces if the public began to think the government party capable of some good. And in fact, as 1845 blossomed into spring, some people gave evidence of doing just that. For after Barthe's propaganda victory with the exiles, Viger and Papineau each made important points that not only underlined once again the basic particularist cast of their thought, but also impressed many *Canadiens*. Denis-Benjamin Papineau would finally guarantee the survival of French Canada's distinct system of education, and Viger would succeed in bringing to the forefront of discussion his proposal of "double majority"—an appealing new doctrine that was not really so new and could well split LaFontaine's party wide apart.

The discussion had begun quietly enough late in 1844 with a long, intelligent article on November 18 in *Le Canadien*. After reflecting that for all its majority in Lower Canada, the French party was unlikely ever to be called to office on its own terms, the anonymous author questioned whether the *ci-devant* policy of refusing to join the government might not lead to permanent exclusion from power.

Eh bien! nous, Canadiens-français, quel avenir nous faisons nous en nous mettant en opposition déterminée contre le ministère actuel, appuyé par une majorité du Haut-Canada et une minorité fort respectable du Bas-Canada, l'une et l'autre composée d'éléments Bretons? Nous leur apprenons ce que les évènements de 1842 leur avaient désappris, savoir: qu'il est possible de faire marcher le gouvernement sans nous et malgré nous; nous imprimons le cachet de l'expérience à l'inique pensée qui a présidé à l'acte d'Union; enfin, nous livrons notre pays, notre race à l'exploitation de la race Bretonne et cela pour toujours! Ce serait une faute irreparable. *Pensons y bien.*

Why, he asked them, could the French party not form a temporary coalition with whatever political group held a majority in Upper Canada, and work in a council formed of the two majorities, each in its own section for its own distinct interests?

Adoptons le principe que la majorité doit gouverner dans l'une et l'autre section de la Province respectivement: c'est pour nous un principe de salut pour l'avenir. Si nous étions, habitants du Haut et du Bas Canada, deux peuples homogènes, à la bonne heure; mais nous différons en tout; religion, langue, institutions, lois, usages, mœurs, tout diffère chez les peuples des deux sections de la Province. Or, qui doit légitimement être appelé à la législation et à l'administration pour chacun des deux peuples? la majorité ou la minorité?

This proposal seriously challenged the whole foundation of LaFontaine's dual doctrine that *la survivance* could best be assured by the working out of responsible government, which, in turn could alone be won by a strong political party uniting the French and the Reformers of Upper Canada. For the writer's plan implied that the French should agree to enter the Executive Council on the Governor's and not on their terms. What would then happen to responsible government? Moreover, it specifically stated that they should join the administration not as a political party, but as the representatives of a distinct national group: "Chacun a dû sentir déjà que pour nous la question nationale est la grande, la première question; la question politique ne vient qu'après."

Thus, apparently, began the notion (which would vex politicians for the next quarter-century) that executive councillors should take office not as representatives of the majority in the Assembly, but as delegates of the respective majorities from each section. The idea spread rapidly. On November 22, a few days after *Le Canadien*'s article, the editor of *Les Mélanges Religieux* completely endorsed the proposal. He reprinted the long article, approved of it, and added considerations of his own that carried the argument a step further. He underlined what *L'Aurore* had claimed all along, that Metcalfe's administration—whatever the technicalities of responsible government —had tended to favour French-Canadian aspirations far more than the old oligarchic régime of the Special Council. What about the capital, the exiles, the donations to churches, the repeated attempts to bring the *Canadiens* into the government? Were these not the work of a Governor and Council who must, indeed, be friendly to *la nation canadienne*? Why refuse then to support them? "Notre intérêt est donc d'appuyer l'administration de tous ceux dont la probité, les lumières, la fermeté, l'indépendance nous sont connues et dont le dévouement nous est acquis."

Three weeks later (*L'Aurore*, December 17), Viger summed up the new doctrine and, in one of his typical, involved articles, presented its final formulation. *Canadien* difficulties, he had always said, arose out of the Union. LaFontaine and his group had accepted it, and the political alliance with Baldwin, hoping to find "un auxiliaire puissant dans le parti réformiste du Haut-Canada." But the Upper Canadian Reformers had lost their majority, and the *Canadiens* had therefore been kept out of office. Four years ago he had himself warned against thus relying on support from outside. He had proposed the "O'Connell-tail system." Now that parliamentary circumstances had proved that French Canada's aspirations could not be fulfilled through a united political party, he asked again whether his people would not profit much more from co-operation at each new parliament with the current majority from Upper Canada: "Ne serait-ce pas un régime suicide pour le Bas-Canada que de renoncer à toute espèce d'alliance possible avec la majorité législative du Haut-Canada que l'événement électoral aura de fait réuni sous le toit parlementaire, quand le parti franco-canadien pourra en attendre sa part légitime de droits et l'exercise de ces mêmes droits?" He concluded that if they were ever to obtain this "part légitime de droits," they now had no alternative to an alliance of the two majorities.

LaFontaine's editors reacted true to type. They ignored the proposal. Yet *L'Aurore* and *Le Canadien* continued to discuss the double majority theory until Duvernay was forced to take notice. On thinking it over, he admitted on March 31 that the Tories of Upper Canada had a right to power, "car ils ont la confiance de la majorité du Haut Canada." Later, on May 2 he agreed that LaFontaine's own principles of responsible government could not be refused the Tories: "Quelle est donc notre doctrine? . . . C'est le maintien, c'est le triomphe du gouvernement responsable, ou représentatif . . . pour le Bas-Canada. Nous le désirons également pour le Haut-Canada, mais nous lui laissons le soin de le maintenir comme il l'entendra. . . . De quel droit pourrions-nous lui dire: Faites une telle majorité."

La Minerve was apparently won over. And, throughout April and May 1845 (the session and the language question having been prorogued), every Lower Canadian newspaper began to fill its columns with the advantages of double majority. Recalling Neilson's stand in 1841, *Le Canadien* stated (April 25): "Nous étions d'avis que les Canadiens français ne devaient attacher leur sort à celui d'aucun parti dans le Haut Canada, mais s'entendre avec le parti dominant quelqu'il fût, et laisser la majorité de cette section de la province gouverner chez elle comme elle l'entendrait, pourvu qu'elle nous rendit justice. . . ." *Le Castor* at first pointed out (May 8) that "quant au grand cri de nationalité et d'intérêts distincts; nous ne voyons pas que les tories aient de meilleures intentions pour nous que les autres," but later agreed that, after all, double majority did not essentially clash with their own theory of responsible government. Indeed, *Le Canadien* had taken unfair advantage of them by quoting on May 19 an old pre-Bagot speech by LaFontaine in which the French-Canadian leader had declared that "l'administration du Haut et du Bas-Canada devait être laissée à leurs conseillers respectifs." (In fact, whether *Le Canadien* knew it or not, LaFontaine had even intimated something vaguely like double majority to Hincks in 1839.[12])

Thus the double majority doctrine, which *Le Canadien* had tentatively suggested in November 1844, proved so attractive that by the end of 1845 every French-Canadian newspaper had accepted it. In years to come the term would hold a different appeal for different people. But in the spring of 1845 all French Canadians agreed with what *Le Canadien* would express on September 15: "L'administration du Haut et du Bas Canada doit être laissée aux conseillers de chaque province respectivement et la majorité du Bas Canada doit, s'il le faut dans l'intérêt général de la population, s'allier à la majorité du Haut Canada sans égard à sa couleur politique." And since LaFontaine's newspapers also acquiesced, Viger's began to ask why the Opposition leaders refused so adamantly to co-operate. Obviously it was not out of hatred of the Tories. Was it a question of personalities or LaFontaine's old dislike for Viger? "Après cela quoi penser de toutes les discussions de principes de la Minerve et compagnie," Denis-Emery Papineau averred, "lorsque les principes n'étaient que des prétextes et que le tout se réduisait à une pure question de personnes."[13] *L'Aurore* thought likewise. Or was it a question of ambition, of LaFontaine's stubborn refusal to share power with anyone? Metcalfe, the Papineaus, and Viger had suspected this all along. And so, now, did *Le Canadien*. Or was it, as *Le Canadien* also suggested, that the young leader's friendship for Baldwin blinded him to the interests of his own people?

Viger and his friends at *Le Canadien* and *Les Mélanges* had—happily for the government—succeeded in thoroughly confusing the issue. They were also being true to themselves. For their doctrine that the council should be made up of representatives from the majorities in each section, regardless of their political leanings, was based on the premise that their own national group profited best from isolation. In 1840 when Parent and LaFontaine had recognized in the Durham

[12]Ormsby, "Metcalfe and Canadian Union," p. 45.
[13]Collection Papineau-Bourassa, D.-E. Papineau à Casimir Papineau, 10 mai 1845.

Report an outlet for their national ambitions, Viger and Neilson had insisted on the restoration of the old constitution that had segregated the French. Again, after the Union, the Neilson-Viger group had first refused to fight the election, proposing the "O'Connell-tail system" that would keep them free of commitments to the politics of the united province. Again, at the time of the constitutional crisis in November 1843, they had supported the Governor who promised to uphold their particular interests without demanding adherence to a principle that implied a permanent commitment to the Union. However characteristic, their reasoning remained muddled.

Perhaps the old man's logic had grown weary. He apparently failed to see that in proposing a government formed of representatives of the respective majorities in Upper and Lower Canada, he was arguing himself out of office. (*Le Canadien* did mention on April 25 that if the double majority were adopted as a policy, LaFontaine and Morin would "reprendre la place que le vœu de leurs compatriotes leur assigne dans l'administration provinciale.") Viger had also forgotten that LaFontaine and Baldwin had resigned when each commanded a majority from his own section. And therefore he should not have implied that LaFontaine refused to allow his followers to re-enter the Council because of Baldwin's defeat. Viger may have purposely confused the whole question. But, consciously or not, he certainly struck at the two most vulnerable items in LaFontaine's defence: his personal stubbornness and intransigence and his alliance with the Upper Canadian Reformers. By mid-May, after press and politicians had said their say, Viger and his allies had so far softened Lower Canadian opinion that LaFontaine appeared to many as either perversely unyielding or stubbornly tied to Baldwin's minority group.

In fact LaFontaine was both. But no one, not even *La Minerve*, seemed to realize that this was hardly the point. There were, after all, essential differences between Viger's and LaFontaine's outlooks. For one thing, Viger thought of French Canada's problems only in national terms, whereas LaFontaine, at least since 1838, had decided that the solution for his people should be a political one. For another, Viger and Papineau had taken office on the Governor's terms, whereas LaFontaine would only do so on his own. Yet even LaFontaine's own editors were not graced with insight into their leader's mind or even into his view of responsible government. Double majority was not responsible government. It implied that the council would be composed of representatives taken from two majorities, but it did not guarantee that the governor would necessarily consult them. And this latter point had been the reason for the *ci-devants'* resignation. Because they did not fully realize this, Viger's newspapermen concluded that the whole difficulty lay in LaFontaine's personal obstinacy, and *Le Canadien* summed up their feelings in an article on May 12 which raised this old grievance against LaFontaine,

Le Canadien . . . s'occupe fort peu que les ministres représentant l'origine française et les intérêts de la population française du pays s'appellent Lafontaine [*sic*] ou Morin, Viger ou Papineau. *Le Canadien* s'occupe des principes et non des hommes; . . . il veut . . . que les Canadiens français et leurs intérêts soient représentés dans l'administration par des hommes de leur origine, méritant et possédant leur confiance, connaissant leurs intérêts et pouvant les soutenir.

So the old man's essays had produced something, after all.

Denis-Benjamin Papineau also contributed to the struggle. For while the politicians and the press debated double majority Papineau introduced in the Assembly a new school law which definitely established the distinctive structure of French-Canadian education. He did not claim full credit—in fact Morin and Meilleur had drafted much of the bill before *la crise*[14]—but he had put the final touches to it and took responsibility for piloting it through the Assembly. According to his project, all the obnoxious clauses of the law of 1841 would be repealed to make way for a school system which would be both independent of the municipal district councils set up by Sydenham and founded firmly on French Canada's traditional social unit, the parish. Each school was to be under the control of school commissioners elected on a denominational basis, its religious orthodoxy guaranteed by the curés or clergymen who were to serve *ex officio* as "visitor."[15]

Under Papineau's guidance the law passed easily through the Assembly. Although Morin and the Opposition forced some clarifications, they were all but committed to it themselves. *L'Aurore* and *Le Canadien* published it, but Duvernay, Cauchon, and the LaFontaine press followed their usual practice of ignoring whatever good came from the government. Yet Papineau's school law of 1845 was of far-reaching importance. For here at last was a system formulated by

[14]APQ, Fonds de l'Instruction Publique, Projets, 1843, Meilleur à Morin, 29 sept. 1843; L. J. Turcotte, *Le Canada sous l'Union* (Québec, 1871) I, 181; Gérin-Lajoie, *Dix ans au Canada*, p. 280.

[15]*Les Mélanges Religieux*, 11 avril 1845; *Le Canadien*, 17 fév. 1845; *L'Aurore*, 13 fév. 1845; L. Groulx, *L'Enseignement français au Canada* (Montréal, 1931), pp. 220 ff.

the French Canadians themselves and based on the religious theories and social order which they had evolved. Far into the future it would characterize them as a distinct people. And far more than any (purely symbolic) repeal of the language clause in the constitution, it definitely abrogated the threats to French-Canadian cultural survival inherent in the Act of Union.[16]

SUMMER

The school law would have profound consequences for the future. But for the moment Barthe's publicity for the exiles and, especially, Viger's principle of double majority seem to have succeeded in displacing LaFontaine's language issue in the popular mind. And during the summer, Viger and his group won two by-elections.

The first was Viger's own in Three Rivers. In mid-June 1845 over one hundred citizens whom *Le Canadien* qualified as "du parti libéral et canadien français" had offered him the seat left vacant by the death of their Tory representative, Edward Grieve. The old man was comforted, for since his double defeat in Richelieu and Montreal County in the general election of 1844, he had been under constant attack by *La Minerve* and *Le Journal* to resign. But he would not retire, and he could not find a riding. At first he thought of running in Saguenay, left vacant when Morin, elected in two constituencies, chose to sit for Bellechasse. But Marc-Pascal de Sales Laterrière, whose seigneury included part of the riding, wanted to run and even refused the offer of a summons to the Legislative Council which Denis-Benjamin Papineau made in exchange.

Now Viger felt relieved that Three Rivers was open. For it was a district controlled by the Saint-Maurice ironworks industry, which owed its prosperity, as Papineau noted from Paris, "à son bail des Forges que le gouvernement lui a donné et conservé par favoritisme."[17] Accordingly Three Rivers had almost invariably returned government candidates and so Viger felt secure. He made doubly certain by asking Bishop Bourget to get the opinion of Vicar-General Cooke, who had been curé in Three Rivers since 1835 and, presumably, knew the temper of his flock. "Comme il ne connaît personne dans votre ville, il m'est venu demandé s'il avait des chances d'être élu," the Bishop

---

[16]Cf. Albert Lévesque, *La Dualité culturelle au Canada* (Montréal, 1959), pp. 80 ff.
[17]Collection Papineau-Bourassa, 545, L.-J. Papineau à Roebuck, 16 juil. 1845.

wrote. "Je ne me mêle pas de politique mais je vous demande de vouloir bien répondre à cette question au plus tôt."[18]

Whatever the good curé answered, Viger accepted the nomination and travelled down to Three Rivers where, as *L'Aurore* said on June 19, "il a été accueilli avec enthousiasme surtout par les principaux libéraux canadiens de l'endroit qui de concert avec de leurs concitoyens d'une autre origine se sont fait un honneur et un devoir de l'accompagner." Then he returned to Montreal, leaving Joseph-Edouard Turcotte to arrange for victory over an unknown young lawyer named Burns. "Jamais la corruption n'avait été poussée aussi loin que dans cette dernière occasion," *La Minerve* claimed (July 14) of Turcotte's work: "d'un coté un jeune avocat sans fortune, et de l'autre un grand propriétaire qui pouvait répandre l'argent à pleines mains et de plus un premier ministre qui dispose des places à son gré." On July 7 Viger went back to see the results and, speaking to an audience representing "toute la respectabilité de la ville," he underlined the doctrine of the double majority. As *L'Aurore* reported on July 8: "Le vénérable M. Viger a parlé à émouvoir! Il a été sublime de cœur, d'âme et de patriotisme; il s'est montré ce qu'il a toujours été, grande patriote, homme éclairé et bien né." He carried the vote by a majority of fifty-two in a poll where (*La Minerve*, July 21) "l'intrigue et la corruption jouèrent un si grand rôle."

Writing to Baldwin before the results came in, LaFontaine anticipated Duvernay's estimate. "They talk of an opposition," he said, "but it is all nonsense. The Gov't influence in that little borough has always been powerful. . . . If, perchance, he was defeated, I would be very much surprised. . . . Alas! Poor Mr Viger! not able to find in L.C. another constituency than that of this rotten borough! How much fallen!"[19] Yet the offer of the candidacy had come from 108 French Canadians, and Viger's majority was surprisingly small for so rotten a borough. *L'Aurore* added on July 17:

La meilleure preuve que l'hon. Président du Conseil a été élu par la classe indépendante de Trois-Rivières et que la prétendue influence corruptrice du gouvernement n'a pas été mise en jeu, comme le prétend la pure et véridique *Minerve*, c'est qu'une quinzaine d'officiers publics et des gens en place au moins se sont abstenus de voter pour mieux démontrer que ce n'était nullement par l'influence des créatures du gouvernement que l'élection se fesait.

At all events Viger could now lay claim to some support, and, as Denis-Benjamin Papineau remarked, "nos adversaires acharnés ne

---

[18]AAM, Lettres Bourget, III, 624, Bourget à Cook 16 juin 1845.
[19]Baldwin Papers, A 55, LaFontaine to Baldwin, June 15, 1845.

pourront plus lui reprocher de rester dans l'administration sans appartenir à aucune des deux branches de la législature."[20] Viger may or may not have won the election by his discussion of double majority. But within three months his idea carried a significant majority in the riding of Dorchester.

Three weeks after the results in Three Rivers, one of LaFontaine's members, Pierre-Elzéar Taschereau, died leaving an opening in what *Le Canadien* called (September 15) the "comté le plus populeux de toute la province du Canada." Viger immediately approached the late member's elder brother, Joseph-André, promising to have him appointed solicitor general for Lower Canada if he could win Dorchester. Taschereau canvassed the riding and found more support than he had expected. After all, he belonged to a family whose ancestry, government contacts, and marriage connections made its influence second to none in the Quebec district.

LaFontaine claimed that he was not worried, but he sent his faithful Cauchon to investigate. Cauchon, who had taken Taschereau's candidacy against himself in Montmorency at the time of the general election as a personal insult, discovered that his enemy would win in Dorchester unless the LaFontaine people could find a candidate of high calibre to oppose him. For the big riding situated strategically on the populous south shore, just opposite Quebec, was seething with discontent. The young people whom Aylwin and Cauchon had organized so well to fight the general election in November 1844 were in open revolt. They had been won over by *Le Canadien*'s talk of double majority, and they wondered why LaFontaine would not enter a coalition with the Upper Canadians: "Ils ont compris avec un singulier désintéressement qui leur fait le plus grand honneur, que c'était folie et plus que folie de persister dans une ligne d'opposition sans base et sans portée" (*L'Aurore*, August 14). They complained, too, that LaFontaine had formed his policy without consulting them or the interests of their district. As one of them wrote to *Le Canadien* on September 1: "Le district de Québec a été constamment sacrifié jusqu'à ce jour. A quoi sert de s'entretenir exclusivement de disputes oiseuses et continuelles, d'utopies imaginaires, de s'attacher à des formes théoriques de gouvernement, tandis que nos opposants, nous laissant quereller sur la *forme*, nous emportent le *fond* et s'emparent des *fonds* à leur profit?"

"Une réaction à laquelle on devait s'attendre commence à s'opérer," MacDonald announced happily in that same issue of *Le Canadien*.

---

[20]Collection Papineau-Bourassa, D.-B. Papineau à sa femme, 10 juin 1845.

Cauchon became frantic. "Où est la réaction?" he thundered back. But it was all around him in Dorchester, and neither he nor Aylwin could find a candidate to fight Taschereau. "Comme ils sont aux abois les pauvres ex-ministériels," Barthe gloated in Montreal on September 2, "ils ne peuvent dans la ville, dans le District de Québec trouver un seul homme marquant." Of course almost all LaFontaine's possible candidates had been returned in the general election. But this was small consolation now. At last, Cauchon approached Joseph Légaré. But Légaré believed in Viger and refused. Finally, a locally popular gentleman named Horatio Patton did run, buttressed, according to *L'Aurore* on September 11 with "l'argent à flots." But against a Taschereau and double majority he did not stand a chance.

On September 1, 1845, Joseph-André Taschereau relinquished his duties as superintendent of police in Quebec, and took the oath of office as solicitor general. *L'Aurore* noted on September 4, "Cette nouvelle nomination rend l'administration du jour numériquement plus acceptable au Bas-Canada que l'ex-ministère dans lequel on ne comptait après tout que deux Canadiens Français, pendant qu'il s'en trouve trois dans celle d'aujourd'hui." And on September 9, after a straight fight on the double majority issue, Taschereau won 1,096 votes to Patton's 145. *Le Canadien* had already foreseen this on August 20:

Et quel mal qu'un Canadien soit solliciteur-général? quel mal que cet officier soit pris au barreau de Québec et qu'il représente un comté du district de Québec? N'est-ce-pas une garantie que d'avoir auprès du gouvernement un homme de votre origine, de votre localité, de votre choix, de vos principes? Et depuis quand les noms chers au pays des Viger et des Papineau sont-ils devenus si odieux qu'en s'associant à eux pour veiller aux intérêts de ses concitoyens, on se déshonore et on mérite d'être proscrit? Tant que la basse et vile jalousie présidera à la conduite des affaires publiques, et que tout Canadien appelé aux postes les plus honorables du gouvernement sera un homme qu'on dénoncera comme vendu, perdu d'honneur, traître à son pays, il n'est pas d'espérance pour nous; nous nous détruirons de nos propres mains.

And in Dorchester the victor celebrated what his partisans thought was the turning of the tide against LaFontaine. "Car il y eut un triomphe, s'il vous plaît, un triomphe immense:—quatre cents voitures pavoisées de drapeaux et empanachées de verdure, avec chevaux pomponnés, enrubannés et enguirlandés, à la suite d'un brillant équipage en quadrige, dans lequel, au milieu des hourrahs et des défis, trônait le nouvel élu, le front couronné d'un haut-de-forme gris."[21]

[21]Fréchette, *Mémoires*, p. 110.

La Correspondance: I

Viger may well have rejoiced. After a complete rout in the general election, he had managed to score highly with the returning exiles, and then go on to win a seat for himself and an indirect vote of confidence in the province's largest riding. Moreover, he had silently launched a revolution in his people's thinking.

By the late summer the district of Quebec seemed ready to co-operate with the government. Viger had sown the seed, and now the Attorney General from Canada West, William Henry Draper, came to reap the increase. On July 4, 1845, he had left Montreal with Viger and Papineau. Leaving Viger in Three Rivers where the by-election was in full swing, he had gone on to Quebec with Papineau. There he had confided to Mayor Caron that he would not be averse to bringing in to the Council French Canadians taken from the Opposition. A month or so later, with Viger elected and Taschereau virtually certain of winning in Dorchester, Draper wrote formally to Caron, reiterating his proposition of what seemed to the Mayor to be double majority. "Si je me rappelle bien notre conversation," Caron wrote, "après avoir observé qu'il y avait dans chacune des deux sections de la Province un parti puissant, celui auquel vous apparteniez par le Haut-Canada, et celui auquel j'appartiens par le Bas, vous avez insisté sur les avantages qui résulteraient à tout le pays de la réunion de ces deux partis, de laquelle résulterait une administration forte."[22]

Caron hurried to Montreal where, on August 1, he received more definite proposals: Draper was ready to replace Viger and Papineau with Morin and anyone but LaFontaine—preferably with Caron himself. LaFontaine he would appoint to the Bench. Caron, impressed, "appeared by his reasoning to lean to Draper's proposal."[23] On September 7 he transmitted to LaFontaine an outline of Draper's offer, adding, "Je dois vous dire que je suis d'avis que l'état dans lequel nous sommes ne peut pas durer. . . . Ce qu'on nous offre est peu de chose, mais ce pourrait être le commencement de quelque chose de mieux. . . . Il est très possible que je voie mal les choses, mais il me semble que

[22]Caron à Draper, 17 sept. 1845. All quotations from the Draper-Caron negotiations are from: *Correspondance entre l'hon. W. H. Draper et l'hon. R. E. Caron; et, entre l'hon. R.-E. Caron et les honbles. L.-H. LaFontaine et A.-N. Morin, dont il a été question dans un débat récent à l'Assemblée Législative; contenant plusieurs lettres supprimées* (Montréal, 1846). This thirty-six-page pamphlet was summarized and serialized in *Le Canadien*, beginning 10 avril 1846.
[23]Baldwin Papers, A 55, LaFontaine to Baldwin, Sept. 23, 1845.

cette ouverture vaut bien la peine qu'on y réfléchisse; je vous la com-
munique dans cette vue, afin que vous y pensiez."[24] LaFontaine was
annoyed. Of course, he did not want to keep his friends from office
and, indeed, he would have no reason to, if Draper really meant to
give the French control of their own section. But his clear logic and,
later, Hincks' shrewd political intuition warned him that Draper
intended less to practise double majority than to divide LaFontaine's
party. Moreover he was hurt that Caron and the *Québecois* should
be so eager, at a mere hint from Draper, to break with the Upper
Canadian Reformers. He admitted this to Baldwin, "I sincerely hope
I will never be placed in a situation to be obliged to take office
again. The more I see, the more I feel disgusted. It seems as if
duplicity, deceit, want of sincerity, selfishness, were virtues. It gives
me a poor idea of human nature."[25] He wrote Caron a blunt, even
contemptuous letter, "but Morin persuaded me that by doing so I would
not do justice to Caron."[26] He consulted Hincks. Hincks did not
believe in double majority even if it meant responsible government,
but he suggested that even if Draper did, Metcalfe would never allow
it. So with some traces of asperity still left, LaFontaine answered
Caron that as far as he was concerned, Caron and Morin should not
agree to take office except on their own terms.

Morin took the letter and hurried to Quebec overnight, spoke to
Caron on September 10, explaining that they must demand more than
the mere replacing of Viger and Papineau with themselves, since this
would merely turn them into *vendus*. They must insist on the
reorganization of the entire Lower Canadian section of the government. This Caron relayed in turn to Draper on September 17, also
sending a copy of his memorandum to LaFontaine. As Hincks had
guessed, Draper dropped the matter. And Caron, Morin, and Hincks
having each made several special trips between Montreal and Quebec,
and LaFontaine, Hincks, Baldwin, Caron, and Draper having
exchanged over a dozen complicated letters, the matter rested.

But not quite. For although he had not succeeded in splitting the
Canadien majority, Draper had nevertheless managed to stir up a
good deal of mischief. By cleverly having avoided answering Caron's
questions, and never actually defining his notion of double majority,
Draper kept his Quebec correspondent wondering whether the *Canadiens* had not been tricked out of office by LaFontaine's stubborn

[24]Caron à LaFontaine, 7 sept. 1845, *Correspondance Caron-LaFontaine-Morin.*
[25]Baldwin Papers, A 55, LaFontaine to Baldwin, Sept. 23, 1845.
[26]*Ibid.*

streak. Moreover, Caron could not help feeling that LaFontaine, whom he had treated properly as head of the party, had played him false by betraying his confidential letters to Baldwin, Hincks, and Duvernay. According to his own principles, however, LaFontaine had done the right thing. He had outmanœuvred Draper, and survived the first really serious challenge to the unity of his following. He could be satisfied that he had robbed Viger's propaganda and by-election victories of any practical parliamentary value. Yet he had done the right thing in the wrong way. Many of the *Canadien* politicians resented his stiff, unbending manner. They did not understand responsible government as clearly as he did. Hence they reserved lingering suspicions that his ambition, tactlessness, and/or reliance upon Baldwin were, as Viger had always said, at the root of the *Canadiens'* troubles.

Nor had the young leader's success cured the basic problem of the two majorities warring under the vaulted drapery of the Saint Ann Market. Yet, as fall approached, Viger's appeal faltered.

AUTUMN

In the autumn the *Canadiens* forgot politics to devote their attention to the details of the Anglo-American quarrel over the Oregon territory. "Le bruit de guerre est dans toutes les bouches," reported *L'Aurore* on November 15. And on the twenty-second: "Tous les esprits semblent ne s'occuper que de la question de l'Orégon." A month later on December 22, *La Minerve* observed:

L'humeur belliqueuse de nos citadins va toujours *crescendo*. On ne se demande plus en, s'abordant, qu'est-ce-que vous pensez de l'éventualité d'une guerre? mais tout d'abord: à quand la guerre? Tout le monde semble pret à se mettre dans les rangs, tout le monde veut se battre, et nous ne savons trop si la nouvelle de l'improbabilité, de l'impossibilité d'une lutte entre les deux grandes puissances, ne serait pas une nouvelle fort désagréable pour nos guerriers en herbe.

Obviously the people cared. Yet not one of the politicians seems to have related the warmongering to local affairs; at least none mentions it in the letters he left behind. Nor did the editors and politicians offer any opinion. They asked questions, like *Le Canadien* on December 22 —"Aurons-nous la paix, aurons-nous la guerre?"—but gave no answers, and complained with *L'Aurore* of November 11 that "la disette de la chronique politique se fait sentir avec tant de tenacité. . . .

La politique étrangère semble vouloir fournir ... des menaces de guerre! On ne parle plus que fortification par ici, fortification par là." Indeed, they seemed to feel that the crisis diverted attention from where it really belonged: on the struggle for political power.

"Notre monde politique" grew dull and was hardly noticed among the prophecies of war; Viger's party lost, in quick succession, the name that gave it prestige, its hero, and finally its newspaper.

The first loss came with the return of Louis-Joseph Papineau. On September 18, while LaFontaine, Caron, and the rest were still deep in correspondence, the greatest and last of the exiles finally returned to America. Nine days later, after a leisured cruise down the Richelieu, he touched Canadian soil at Saint Johns. It was a glorious, warm day, and a huge crowd, Denis-Benjamin Papineau (all in tears) at their head, had taken the thirty-mile trip from LaPrairie to welcome him. For hours, his right hand extended in all directions, he renewed old friendships. Then, with his family gathered about him, he rode on to Verchères and to Saint-Hyacinthe, finally reaching Montreal on October 9, where in his honour the Place de la Reine had been rechristened Place Papineau. After being carried shoulder high above a huge but surprisingly well-mannered crowd from the quay to his rented lodgings at the fashionable Hotel Rasco, Papineau met what L'Aurore described (October 11) as "l'élite de la société de Montréal [qui] s'est empressée de l'aller saluer [sic]." But even earlier, the cleverest party schemers on both sides had begun to wait upon him, each expecting that he would put his influence at their disposal, but each entertaining reasons for uneasiness.

Denis-Benjamin Papineau had been the very first to approach him. Since his own acceptance of office, the public had taken it for granted, as Julie Papineau wrote to her husband, "qu'il ne pouvait avoir accepté sans ton avis."[27] Surely his brother would support him. Now face to face, he rehearsed the family grievances against "ces ambitieux qui ont égaré le peuple" (as Julie had called them), against LaFontaine and the others "dont toutes les vues sont agrandissement personnel! A qui tous les moyens sont bons pour perdre dans l'opinion publique ceux de leurs concitoyens qui diffèrent d'opinion avec eux sur les moyens de travailler au bien-être commun."[28] They had seized leadership from the revered Viger back in 1840, and for the past two years had unleashed a flood of calumnies against him. How could Louis-Joseph

[27]Collection Papineau-Bourassa, 692, Julie Bruneau à L.-J. Papineau, 28 oct. 1844.
[28]Ibid., D.-B. Papineau à sa femme, 1 avril 1845.

side with them? But, as Denis-Benjamin very well knew, his great brother did not approve of the course he had taken. Indeed, he had refused his help, writing from Paris in 1844: "Le système dont vous feignez d'être engoués sera bien vite usé et répudié, et vous en reviendrez à demander les institutions électives. . . . A coté des Etats-Unis comme nous le sommes il n'y a qu'une libéralité sans bornes qui pourrait rendre tolérable le servage colonial, et le rendre un peu plus durable."[29] And Louis-Joseph Papineau was not one to change his mind lightly.

LaFontaine and his men also realized this. They knew that they had had Papineau's support as far back as June 1838 when LaFontaine, on his return from Paris, had conferred with him at Saratoga. Since then LaFontaine had been approved again several times, most recently in August 1845 when he had heard from the exiled leader through their mutual friend Amable Berthelot. He wrote to Baldwin: "Mr Papineau, the Ex-Speaker will return to Canada in Sept. next. . . . It appears that he approves of our course; but he gave Berthelot to understand that he will not interfere in politics any more. That is to say he won't be in active opposition to his cousin and brother."[30] Now, while "toute la presse du Canada s'est plus ou moins occupée de l'arrivée de l'hon. ex-orateur," *La Minerve* confidently asserted on October 16 that he would side with them. Hincks entertained some doubts, however, writing to Baldwin that "we know not what he intends to do."[31] And so did Cauchon and Duvernay. They betrayed their fears by beginning to direct against the great man what *L'Aurore* called on September 11 "toutes les batteries de l'intrigue sourde et de la calomnie." On April 21, 1845, in a lead article on double majority, Duvernay had let slip the ominous sentence: "Si M. Louis-Joseph Papineau revenait dans le pays et qu'il lui fut possible de reconquérir son ancienne popularité, ce qui ne se peut pas toutefois, il partagerait le sort de MM. Viger et Cie." And after this tentative beginning, he and Cauchon had set off on what five years later would become the greatest and most successful of their smear campaigns.

But for the time being, Dr. Bouthillier, the first of LaFontaine's friends to see Papineau, reported from Saint-Hyacinthe that "il est bien disposé envers vous personnellement et admire beaucoup *l'énergie* et la constance de ses compatriotes." (Papineau might well be disposed towards LaFontaine personally: LaFontaine had offered him

[29]*Ibid.*, 161, L.-J. Papineau à D.-B. Papineau, 15 oct. 1844.
[30]Baldwin Papers, A 55, LaFontaine to Baldwin, Aug. 16, 1845.
[31]*Ibid.*, v51, Hincks to Baldwin, Sept. 23, 1845.

unlimited credit during his exile in Paris.) Bouthillier warned however
that "peut-être serait-il prudent que La Minerve ne dise rien avant
votre entrevue."[32] LaFontaine himself hurried to the Hotel Rasco the
day after the exile's return; so did Wolfred Nelson. Five days later,
Bouthillier came again, this time with George-Etienne Cartier. "Notre
entrevue a été longue," he stated, "sa conversation franche et bien
affectueuse envers ses anciens amis."[33] This was good news. Later,
on December 5, Papineau himself brought better news still. On a
visit to LaFontaine, bedridden with rheumatism, he approved of all
LaFontaine's course "depuis notre entrevue à Saratoga en juin 1838
jusqu'à l'époque de ma résignation en 1843." Indeed, he seemed so
friendly that LaFontaine even trusted him with the Draper-Caron
correspondence, "d'une haute importance et d'un caractère tout confi-
dentiel."[34]

Yet the great tribune stuck to his decision to stay out of politics.
There was that embarrassing question of the "arrérages," and he
also hesitated to oppose in public his cousin, his brother, his son, and
his nephews. Besides, for all his outward approval of LaFontaine's
actions, he really distrusted him and his followers who continued to
insult his family. Perhaps there was another reason also. Despite
their apparent agreement, both Papineau and LaFontaine may have
sensed the irreconcilable difference which kept them apart: their
conflicting attitude towards the British connection. LaFontaine stubbornly refused to co-operate with Metcalfe because he would be
satisfied with nothing less than real British institutions. Papineau, on
the other hand, refused to co-operate because he awaited complete
independence. "Tu le dis bien," he wrote to his brother, "l'inévitable
séparation est une question de temps, ne soyez pas faux, & ne parlez
jamais d'union indissoluble."[35] Accordingly he thought LaFontaine
either a hypocrite or a *vendu*. As he wrote to O'Callaghan: "Vous
avez raison, c'est un contresens à LaFontaine et Morin d'avoir parlé
de leur loyauté et celle du pays lorsqu'ensemble ils souffrent persécution. C'est un mot qui devrait être rayé, quand il est si bien entendu
qu'il est de formule antique et non pas de sentiment actuel."[36] Poor
Papineau—a man not born to follow others. He both agreed and
disagreed with everyone. He agreed with his family on the inevitable

---

[32]Papiers LaFontaine, Bouthillier à LaFontaine, 3 oct. 1845.
[33]*Ibid.*, Bouthillier à LaFontaine, 17 oct. 1845.
[34]*Ibid.*, LaFontaine à L.-J. Papineau, 6 déc. 1845.
[35]Collection Papineau-Bourassa, D.-B. Papineau à J.-B.-N. Papineau, 10 fév.
1845.
[36]*Ibid.*, 544, L.-J. Papineau à O'Callaghan, 15 oct. 1845.

break with the empire but disapproved of their co-operation with Metcalfe. On the other hand, while he agreed with LaFontaine's opposition, he could not understand his loyalty. Unable to take sides, he retired to his seigneury, a hero from another age, a man at logger-heads with his time.

Papineau's retirement was a far more severe blow to his family's party than to LaFontaine's. The latter had never turned Papineau into a plank in his election platform; Viger had. And now that Papineau had actually returned and said nothing, the Viger group was severely shaken.

A few weeks later it suffered another shock when Metcalfe reached the end of his painful Canadian career. Throughout the summer and early fall he had undergone one delicate operation after another. Finally, on October 13, hardly able to talk and half blind, he dictated a letter to Stanley describing how he could no longer eat because of "a hole through the cheek into the interior of the mouth." He felt physically unable to continue. Still—had the pain driven him mad?—he would not resign, unwilling to inconvenience the ministry at home.[37] Then early in November he stopped driving from Monklands, even in his closed carriage, to his suite at the Château de Ramezay. On the tenth La Minerve reported,

Si on en croit des bruits qui circulent depuis hier, il paraît que lord Metcalfe est dans un état de faiblesse qui ne lui permet plus de s'occuper des affaires, par suite de la diète qu'il est forcé d'observer. On assure que Son Excellence n'a pris aucune nourriture solide depuis près de quinze jours. . . . Nous venons d'apprendre que Son Excellence a été hier recommandée aux prières dans toutes les églises protestantes de cette ville.

La Minerve, of course, could hardly wait to see him go. Indeed, it seemed almost happy to print the daily chronicle of his decline, as if the last obstacle to responsible government were rotting there before it. To the bulletins from Government House, Duvernay added such cold comfort, as for example on October 30, that officials were trying to "se justifier du retard qu'on a apporté à demander un successeur à Son Excellence." Even in death, La Minerve refused Metcalfe its respect. L'Aurore did not. Barthe ceased his partisan, political panegyrics and deferred to the Governor's illness. Viger, "avec une admiration idolâtre pour Sir Metcalfe,"[38] was still too much the gentleman to organize the performance LaFontaine had ordered for Bagot. He must have known

[37]Metcalfe to Stanley, Oct. 13, 1845, as quoted in Kaye, Life of Metcalfe, II, 418.
[38]Collection Papineau-Bourassa, 547, L.-J. Papineau à O'Callaghan, 12 mai 1846.

also that he no longer had the power to command the prayers and the masses.

By mid-November, even the high stoicism of Metcalfe could no longer bear the agony. Yet, he said, "I am tied to Canada by my duty."[39] Also, he knew how Viger, Papineau, and Taschereau had sacrificed their reputations for him, and he (who had blamed LaFontaine for thinking that he alone could save the country) would not leave them without the protection of his authority. Finally however, on November 23, he invited his faithful councillors to Monklands. Sitting in the dark, his head swathed in bandages, he asked them to decide his fate. Denis-Benjamin Papineau burst into tears. But all agreed that, on the chance of saving his life at home, he must go. On the twenty-sixth, the second anniversary of *la crise*, Papineau and Viger went out with the rest of the Council to escort the Governor to the steamer.

Troops lined the road. Behind them stood a vast, hushed crowd, made up of some of the hundreds who had personally experienced the Governor's many kindnesses. Lord Metcalfe and his councillors rode quietly past them; he was in agony, and they were close to tears. At the wharf, he descended and, true to type, stood to hear the short, sad civic address from the Mayor. Despite the great wound gnawing through his cheek, he answered graciously. Then, "très affecté, et sa suite aussi, il a versé des larmes et n'a pas été le seul," he boarded the *Prince Albert* to cross the river, his councillors following him as far as the train. Denis-Benjamin Papineau wept all the way. "Je n'en ai pas honte," he wrote, "et je n'en aurai jamais honte. Il faut avoir connu comme j'ai été à même de le faire la douceur et l'amitié de cet homme-là, son esprit de droiture, son tact dans les affaires, son affabilité, son esprit de condescendance, sa patience, et son assiduité dans les affaires, ses précautions et son attention pour ne pas s'en laisser imposer . . . pour pouvoir apprécier la perte que fait le pays en le perdant." At LaPrairie, after another tender parting scene, Papineau, still upset, waited to bid the last good-bye: "Je lui ai donné la main et à sa suite le dernier de tous."[40]

"Lord Metcalfe," Barthe eulogized on November 27, "emporte avec lui les regrets de tous les hommes bien nés et sensibles à la reconnaissance." But *La Minerve* remained unimpressed:

Quelques poignées d'or jetées à la face de tous les demandants ne doivent pas faire oublier que la bienveillance sociale n'a rien à démêler avec les devoirs

[39]Kaye, *Life of Metcalfe*, II, 121.
[40]Collection Papineau-Bourassa, D.-B. Papineau à sa femme, 27 nov. 1845.

attachés à l'administration de toute une province. . . . Les actes de bien-faisance annoncés journellement au son de la trompette et qui ne sont pas accompagnés d'une conduite sans reproches peuvent devenir suspects, c'est un manteau qui a couvert bien des fautes. (November 27)

And LaFontaine wrote a rather sour note to Baldwin. "Lord Metcalfe is gone!! Let his friends praise him as much as they please. But as to myself, I will always look upon him as a man who had no respect for truth, not to use a harsher word. I may forgive anything but a lie."[41]

When Metcalfe retired, Viger and Denis-Benjamin Papineau suffered a severe personal loss. They had worked many nights with him and come to understand his generous heart. Now he was gone, drawing to a sudden close their dreams. Nothing, for either of them, would be the same again.

As if to accentuate their loss and underscore the political rout, a week later, their party organ, L'Aurore, finally collapsed before the might of La Minerve's assault. For two years it had successfully thrown back in kind Duvernay's invective and slander. But it could not survive the massive cancellation of subscriptions, beginning with LaFontaine's in April 1845. "Si les meneurs ex-ministériels n'ont pas réussi dans leur projet de faire tomber l'Aurore," Barthe had written on April 19, 1845, "ce n'est sûrement pas faute d'ardeur ou de constance dans leurs efforts pour y parvenir." But by the turn of the year Duvernay had won. L'Aurore ceased its propaganda for Viger.

In a way L'Aurore deserved to die. For since la crise it had done Viger little service. It had published his essays on the constitution; it had praised Metcalfe and the Papineau connection. Yet during its long decline it had remained on the defensive, never attempting to explain its hero's political principles in terms which its readers could really understand and approve. It lacked political flair. And thus it had allowed Duvernay, Cauchon, Aubin, and the others to persude the Canadiens that the ci-devants and their view of responsible government could alone assure la survivance. L'Aurore never even mentioned, for example, that by the end of 1845 every legal threat to French-Canadian culture had actually been overcome without LaFontaine and without responsible government. The school system had been saved by Meilleur's appointment as superintendent in 1842, before Bagot's great geste royal, and it had been made independent of political control under Metcalfe after la crise. The particular jurisprudence which was the pride of Lower Canada had also been guaran-

[41]Baldwin Papers, A 55, LaFontaine to Baldwin, Dec. 2, 1845.

teed by Bagot's appointments to the Bench before LaFontaine came
to office. Again, it was in the Assembly directed by the Draper-Viger
faction that the address to repeal the anti-French clause in the Act
of Union was passed unanimously. It was the same administration
that had brought about the *Canadiens*' most desired measures. If it
had not entirely arranged the moving of the capital, it had at least
presided over it. And certainly the Governor General and Denis-
Benjamin Viger, more than any others, had achieved the return of
the exiles—undoubtedly, between 1839 and 1845, French Canada's
most constant and unanimous desire. Yet *L'Aurore*, even while herald-
ing each one of these actions, stumbled forward without ever making
an effort to relate them to the national theme. Had it done so, how
differently might Viger have fared!

LaFontaine and his propagandists had, nevertheless, been right.
However much Viger may have done to assure *la survivance*, he had
still left it dependent on the personal generosity of successive governors general or on the politics of the Colonial Office. With responsible
government as LaFontaine saw it, the French would control *la survivance* themselves. But no one in either group ever thought of pursuing
the discussion on so high a plane.

13

Politicians and Priests, II
1846

After bidding farewell to Metcalfe on November 26, 1845, Denis-Benjamin Papineau rode back to the Château de Ramezay, and there attended the quiet installation of Lieutenant-General Charles Murray Cathcart, eleventh Baron and third Earl Cathcart, as interim administrator of the province. Having taken his oath, the new Administrator spoke to his councillors, Papineau wrote to his wife, in a speech "remplie de bon sens et de sentiment. Il veut marcher sur les traces de son estimable prédécesseur, afin de gagner par là la part d'estime si bien méritée sous ses yeux à celui dont la santé précaire avait nécessité le départ si prompt."[1] Lord Cathcart, a tall, dark aristocrat of military bearing, had come out to Canada in June 1845 to serve as commander-in-chief. He shared with a great number of his contemporaries (and former colonial governors) the distinction of an enviable record in the Napoleonic wars. Now with Britain and the United States close to war over Oregon, he had been sent out to impress the North Americans with the empire's intention to fight.

In April 1846, after five months as administrator, Lord Cathcart received his commission as governor general in his own right. But, the Oregon threat having passed, he was recalled at the end of the year. A kindly, unassuming man, he had throughout his life taken little interest in politics; he paid no more attention to politics in Canada and was repaid in kind by the *Canadiens* who gave him little notice.

The people had evidently found other interests. And the editors who had, in 1845, considered the Oregon question a distraction from politics, now in 1846 discovered that they must indeed follow their public. The *Canadiens* continued to be absorbed with Oregon; *Les Mélanges Religieux*, for example, ran a special series on the Catholic missions there during October and November. Later, the French began

[1]Collection Papineau-Bourassa, D.-B. Papineau à sa femme, 27 nov. 1845.

to follow closely the historic debates in London over the repeal of the corn laws and the attitude of their fellow citizens in Canada to this question. They realized how deeply the issue concerned the British empire and, consequently, their own future. *La Minerve*, like a number of other newspapers, announced on February 26 the news of the first reading of the bill as "la nouvelle la plus importante qui ait, depuis bien des années, traversé l'Atlantique." Yet the editors wrote about it dispassionately, observing, as if it were none of their business, the reaction of *les Anglais*, the merchants and traders of Quebec, Montreal, and Upper Canada. On February 26, between reports on the debates in Congress over Oregon, *La Minerve* noted rather laconically about the corn laws: "Au Canada, l'opinion publique n'a pas encore eu le temps de se prononcer bien fortement. Cependant si nous nous en tenons aux premières impressions, cette réforme sera plus propre à y produire le mécontentement que la satisfaction." By July 2 Duvernay and the others were still filling their columns with editorials from "la presse anglaise du Haut et du Bas-Canada" adding merely as their opinion that "on voit, d'après ces citations, que la question est assez embarrassante et qu'on a besoin d'y réfléchir avant de se prononcer d'une manière ou d'une autre." Thus engrossed with Oregon and corn, remote excitements in far-off theatres, the *Canadiens* never realized how crucial 1846 would be for their own politics—apparently so monotonous, but about to undergo a momentous reversal of alliances.

At the general election in 1844 they had, as far as was in their power, decided the struggle for responsible government. Almost unanimously, they had made LaFontaine their leader. But among the more educated, it was Viger who continued to command allegiance. Parent had written: "Il faudrait reconnaître que le Père Viger n'est pas aussi fautif qu'on le pense." Fabre reflected that "le ministère est décidé à faire de la besogne, Mr D. B. Papineau dit beaucoup de bien du Gouverneur, il le trouve un homme d'affaires, poli, et Libéral."[2] And there were those who shared the thoughts voiced by *L'Aurore* on December 16, 1845: "Nous devons défendre . . . l'autorité légale sauve-garde des droits populaires et du pouvoir légitime." These people had continued throughout 1845 to look to the erudite Viger, to his theories, to his seasoned judgment, to his pamphlets. Most prominent among these were the Catholic priests and their organ, *Les Mélanges Religieux*.

Towards the end of 1846 Viger's group lost this powerful support—

[2]Papiers LaFontaine, Parent à LaFontaine, janvier 1844; O'Callaghan Papers, Fabre à O'Callaghan, 7 jan. 1845.

not from any shrewd diplomatic move by LaFontaine's followers, who continued, as usual, their questionable tactics of agitation and name-calling, but because of the emerging realization that there could be no alliance between Viger's ideas and those of the Catholic revival.

THE SESSION OF 1846

As the new year began, LaFontaine's group continued the tactics that had thus far served it so well. Immediately after the opening of parliament on March 20, the Opposition members decided that this year they must remain especially vigilant to prevent any move on Viger's part that might lead others to imitate "le noble exemple des électeurs canadiens des Trois-Rivières et du comté populeux de Dorchester, d'une réaction appuyée sur la justice et la raison" (*L'Aurore*, March 27).

Even before parliament met, they had captured the headlines. Late in 1845 the government had given orders for the militia to be reorganized. Accordingly on December 15, 1845, the Adjutant-General, Colonel Gugy, announced promotions from the ranks; but out of the one hundred and eighteen commissions, only sixteen were given to French Canadians. Duvernay and the politicians were furious—but happy. On the one hand, they were deprived of a number of posts that commanded a certain degree of prestige in the country parishes, but on the other, they had a new grievance with nationalist overtones like the language question of the previous year. They also had a perfect target in Gugy, an officer who in his forty-seven years had managed to do everything wrong. He spoke French, but he was a Huguenot; he had been elected to the old Assembly of Lower Canada by the loyalists of Sherbrooke, and there had eloquently (and worse still, successfully) opposed the great Papineau; in 1837 he had rushed to volunteer on Colborne's side, and then quartered his soldiers on the Dessaulles seigneury in Saint-Hyacinthe. "Gugy est le plus grand hypocrite de la terre," Amédée Papineau had written at the time.[3]

Duvernay began to assail Gugy and the government. He wondered (December 22) why Colonel de Salaberry, son of the hero of Château-guay, had not been appointed Adjutant-General instead of Gugy. He also suggested (December 18) that the *Canadien* officers protest the unfair number of British promotions by sending in their own com-

[3]P.-G. Roy, "Conrad-Auguste Gugy," *Bulletin des Recherches historiques*, XI (1904), 333.

missions. A month later, after Viger had incautiously and illogically admitted Gugy's wrongs and asked for more enlistments, the officers showed which newspaper they read and did exactly as Duvernay had suggested. "Les résignations pleuvent de tous côtés," wrote Duvernay on January 22. But Gugy only replaced the resigning captains with more Britons. Duvernay then suggested a petition to the Governor General. The government answered with statistics that the promotions were strictly according to representation by population: for example, out of 10 lieutenant colonels in the district of Montreal, there were 4 English-speaking Canadians, 4 French Canadians, 1 Irishman, and 1 Englishman; of 16 majors, there were 8 French Canadians, 4 Scots, 2 English-speaking Canadians, 1 Englishman, 1 Irishman, and so on. Duvernay, who had not himself returned his commission as captain, counted noses in the other ranks and came up with other figures, and more invective. Indeed, throughout January and February 1846 he continued his pressure: Gugy, unfortunately for Viger, continued to exclude *Canadiens*. (Compared with LaFontaine, how awkwardly Viger wielded patronage.) Finally, the Adjutant-General stopped making appointments. Duvernay wrote on March 9: "Il paraît que l'autorité qui fait mouvoir l'adjutant-général comme un ressort caché, lui a retiré le droit de faire de nouvaux officiers de milice." LaFontaine's group had scored again.

Shortly after the opening, with unfailing flair for publicity, they found another opportunity to attack the government and, incidentally, to proclaim their own basic doctrine that *la survivance* could only be guaranteed through the maintenance of British institutions. On April 18 all the members received the report of a commission which Draper and Denis-Benjamin Papineau (in an effort to gain French support) had set up the year before to investigate Lower Canadian claims for losses in the Rebellion—and also to reimburse the Papineaus, Cherriers, and Dessaulles whom the Rebellion had hit hard. In Quebec *Le Canadien* hoped for the best on May 13: "Nous sentons combien cette question est scabreuse, et combien de difficultés, d'obstacles, de résistances le gouvernement, avec la meilleure volonté du monde, aurait à surmonter pour satisfaire aux exigeances et de la justice et d'une saine politique. . . . [Il faut] chercher autant que possible à faire oublier le passé en réparant tous les maux et cicatrisant toutes les plaies." But when the politicians in the capital heard that the claims amounted to some £241,000, they returned to discussion rather than payment. Soon they were fighting the Rebellion all over again.

The government shelved the question, but not before a good deal of ill feeling had been created. This discussion, coming during a threat of war over Oregon and within a few weeks of the resignation of many French-Canadian officers from the militia, gave the government, and especially the Upper Canadian and Montreal Tories, pause. They chose to interpret as cowardice or disloyalty the French Canadians' pressure for an armed force as bicultural as the country it was called upon to defend. They also questioned the *Canadiens'* part in the War of 1812: "La presse de l'administration s'occupe beaucoup depuis quelque temps de la conduite des Canadiens durant la dernière guerre. . . . Est-ce pour reconnaître leur loyauté, leur courage, et les services qu'ils ont rendus à la mère-patrie? . . . C'est pour les insulter, pour diminuer, rabaisser le mérite qu'ils ont eu de conserver la colonie à l'Angleterre" (*La Minerve*, May 11). Duvernay, happy to have another grievance, reiterated with an air of injured innocence the usual theme that the *Canadiens* had saved the country at Châteauguay, and moreover had received congratulations for this from the Prince Regent himself. He also repeated his version of 1837: the *Canadiens* had remained loyal and peaceful, suffering "avec courage, avec résignation, les sentimens religieux qui les distinguent les ont soutenus, et leur ont permis d'attendre sans se livrer au désespoir," while under Colborne,

toutes les passions furent déchaînées et une guerre d'extermination commença. Nos campagnes furent éclairées à la lueur de l'incendie; les temples du Dieu de nos pères furent envahis et profanés par une soldatesque indisciplinée; les humbles demeures de nos malheureux habitans furent incendiées, pillées sans pitié, malgré les larmes, le désespoir des femmes, des enfans, des vieillards, que cette œuvre de destruction plongeait dans la plus affreuse misère.

The *Canadiens* had saved the colony for Britain, and indeed would continue so to do as long as Britain guaranteed their survival!

In the Assembly on April 24 Taché rose to make the same point. To packed galleries and what *La Minerve* described on the twenty-seventh as "des tonnerres d'applaudissements," he delivered the famous and impassioned speech which, like LaFontaine's on the French language in 1842, few French Canadians have since forgotten, and which, unlike LaFontaine's, the *Canadien* press immediately re-echoed. *Le Progrès*, for example, one of those little shortlived newspapers that proliferated in the middle of the decade, devoted its Saint-Jean-Baptiste day message on June 27 to *la nationalité*, explaining how this was connected with British rule:

Nous devons rendre justice à nos frères les Bretons, ils respectent les sentiments qui unissent la grande famille canadienne, car ils savent que les Canadiens Français ont été et seront encore les dévoués sujets de l'Angleterre; ils savent qu'au jour où les Anglo-Américains se sont séparés de la Mère-Patrie, les Canadiens sont restés fidèles à leur drapeau. . . . Nos frères les Bretons comprennent également que notre nationalité, notre attachement tout filial pour la Mère-Patrie, est un des liens les plus forts pour conserver la colonie, qu'attaquer ces sentiments, ce serait semer le trouble, la discorde, l'agitation parmi une population fidèle et dévouée.

But to maintain the unity of their forces, LaFontaine's followers had to do more than sustain agitation over the militia appointments and against the government. They needed to preserve the efficiency of their organization as well.

Hincks had continued to work among the Irish in Montreal. Early in January, he discovered (or said that he did) that one of his assistants named McKeon had agreed with Dominick Daly to act as *agent provocateur*. In an article in the *Pilot* which Duvernay repeated in *La Minerve*, Hincks claimed that while ostensibly recruiting his compatriots for the militia McKeon, to discredit Hincks, was in reality—incredible!—distributing arms for an uprising against the government. The night that the editorial appeared, McKeon waited outside the *Pilot*'s offices and, as Hincks emerged, hit him over the head with a stick. Duvernay claimed that Daly stood watching from a block or so down the street. Hincks had McKeon arrested. There was a trial, and the assailant was condemned to pay £3. But the matter did not end there. Hincks petitioned Cathcart to have McKeon discharged from the government service (he was an "agent surnuméraire" in Daly's office), and when the Provincial Secretary replied that McKeon's offence hardly deserved such punishment, Hincks stirred the Irish up to a meeting where they appeared 1500 strong and, after an address from Lewis Drummond, put on a demonstration to make any government pause. Nothing more happened. But as far as Hincks was concerned his organization had stood the test.

It enjoyed additional activity in the civic elections in Montreal. John Mills, a wealthy, American-born friend of LaFontaine's group, had Hincks' support and that of the canallers. The incumbent mayor, James Ferrier, had been elected in 1844 in the east ward mainly by French Canadians, but he was a member of the Tory merchant group and, in this election, the *Canadiens* wanted Mills to win. As mayor, Ferrier commanded the police, and on election day he rode out at their head to direct operations at the polls which Mills' partisans were likely to carry. The canallers came too. There were shots, sticks, stones, and blood staining the streets. By five o'clock bullies from both sides had run each other back and forth through the streets "poussant des cris féroces comme des sauvages" and, among other things, had broken into the medical school and thrown surgical instruments at each other. Dr. Wolfred Nelson alone cared for thirteen wounded, one with two bullet holes in his hand. Then, the following week when the new city councillors met to choose one of their number as mayor, Mills won by one vote: his own. Ferrier, who as retiring mayor had abstained, then decided that if Mills could vote for himself so could he. "L'affaire des deux maires" went to the courts. After six weeks Ferrier was declared elected. He then offered to resign if Mills did: but that is another story. Again LaFontaine's followers had shown that they had not relaxed the vigour of their organization.

They were not, however, making gains. Identifying themselves with *la survivance*, proclaiming their theory that they offered the best assurance for survival through the British connection, reviling Gugy, breaking bones, they had done all this before. And, if meanwhile they had remained united, they had still not substantially weakened the government. Cauchon admitted as much in a private letter to Chauveau: "Je ne crois maintenant qu'il soit possible de culbuter le ministère actuel avant les prochaines élections générales excepté dans le cas d'une guerre avec l'Angleterre ou d'une banqueroute."[4] And Duvernay testified to the boredom which the *Canadiens* felt by resorting to a trick reminiscent of Aubin. On September 2, 1846, he published and affixed to the main notice boards around the city a large "extra" that proclaimed:

> Arrivée du Britannia par estafette.
> Rappel de Lord Cathcart
> Duel entre le comte Grey et Lord Stanley;
>   ce dernier légèrement blessé.
> Marriage d'O'Connell avec la Duchesse de Kent.
>   Grande indignation dans toute l'Angleterre à
>   ce sujet.

If many believed such tales, he explained the next day, it was because of "la monotonie qui règne depuis quelque temps dans notre monde politique."

Although not necessarily because of LaFontaine's tactics, "notre monde politique," did lose one of its most notable figures. On June

[4]PAC, MG 24, B 26, Collection Meilleur, Cauchon à Chauveau, 22 mai 1846.

17, 1846, Viger wrote out in elegant, formal French his resignation from Lord Cathcart's Executive Council.

In accepting it, the Governor General replied how "fully sensible" he was "of the gratitude due to the generous impulse which led you to join the Administration under my predecessor, at a time of great difficulty and embarrassment which your example and valuable support contributed materially to remove." He assured Viger of "the lasting friendship of one who has learnt thoroughly to know and fully appreciate the many good and estimable qualities you possess and who will always feel it an honour to subscribe himself with the greatest truth your most sincere friend."[5] But from his peers, Viger received no such sympathy. How cruel they proved! And, without Papineau's support, without the inspiration of Metcalfe, without *L'Aurore*, how hateful he must have found his last session. Long accustomed only to words of affection, he had been treated to every indignity, and this from upstarts the age of his grandchildren, from youngsters like Cauchon and Chauveau, and, bitterest of all, from old friends like Wolfred Nelson.

Day after day, he had sat, white-maned and bent with age, apathetic to their nagging and pestering. How far away were the old days of popularity in 1827! Now, if he rose to speak, they shuffled their feet; when he sat down, they booed. He bore it all, even the apparent contempt of his colleagues with kind dignity, exhausted by the ordeal and increasingly detached from all human deeds. Now, with the Assembly prorogued, his rest could no longer be refused him. He passed out of politics into indomitable old age. Heartless to the end, Cauchon commented on June 20, "Comment! M. Viger a offert de résigner une situation où il se croyait si éminemment utile à son pays." And Duvernay declared in the same vein (June 18, 22): "On nous informe que l'hon. M. Viger s'est enfin *résigné* à résigner sa place de ministre. . . . Nous avons le plaisir au moins d'approuver ce dernier acte politique de la carrière ministérielle de M. Viger." Neither Cauchon nor Duvernay had ever raised their vision very far. They saw only the tired, defeated, old man.

Yet Viger had done the state some service—greater perhaps than he himself knew. In a moment of real crisis for his people, he had interposed himself, alone and almost unaided, between them and the imperial power. To Metcalfe he had given respect and even love, convincing the well-meaning Governor that at least some French

[5]Papiers Viger, Cathcart to Viger, June 17, 1846.

Canadians could qualify as "un peuple de gentilhommes," a compliment Bagot had paid to all of them, and an assertion which, with sorry results, Durham had questioned and Sydenham denied. For his own people, Viger had presided over the dissolution of the policy of assimilation. To those who never recognized this at the time, he had at least proved by his presence at the Governor's right hand that *les Anglais* (no matter who was governor and who was councillor) seriously meant to give the *Canadiens* a share in the administration of their own destiny, a fact which they had grown accustomed to deny. The Governor and the people he had served as interpreter of the one to the other. This was high service indeed. Ten years before, the imperial power and the *Canadiens* had clashed head on in bloody rebellion, among other reasons because of Papineau's intransigent contempt for the proposals of the governors general at the time. Now, when with equal stubbornness LaFontaine's followers refused Metcalfe's, both Governor and people surprisingly retained a good deal of their mutual trust, and in some instances at least their mutual affection. If LaFontaine's veto did not, like Papineau's, lead to an open and armed clash, Viger could justly claim most of the credit. This was, after all, what he had set out to do, and in his own clumsy way, this he had achieved.

But at the time, during the bleak summer of 1846, how could he believe any of this? Instead, he heard only the jeers of his unsparing opponents and looked around to see his shattered following divided, spiteful, disintegrating. He did not even seem to realize that the seed he had himself planted with the double majority idea, and which the Dorchester election had nurtured, was just beginning to bear fruit.

La Réaction

For LaFontaine all was not quiet in Quebec city. Pondering the theory of double majority, the *Québecois* had begun to grumble about being left out of policy-making, about being sacrificed to the Montreal interests. They recalled that LaFontaine had snubbed them in 1842 by appointing as their representative at the Council an Irishman, Thomas Cushing Aylwin—popular, yes, but not a *Canadien* by blood. LaFontaine, they felt, had also engineered the removal of the capital to his own Montreal; and now, because he was out of office, he obstinately refused "toutes améliorations et toute participation aux deniers publics" in the name of "des disputes oiseuses et continuelles d'utopies imaginaires" (*Le Canadien*, September 1). As 1846 progressed, they discovered more reasons to complain, prominent among these was the question of the Intercolonial Railroad.

Since the autumn of 1845 the *Québecois* had been organizing support for the Quebec to Halifax railway. Early in November Mayor Caron, Aylwin, Cauchon, Chauveau, and Neilson (emerging briefly from his twilight) had all met with prominent members of the merchant community to plan a public meeting "pour délibérer," as *Les Mélanges* explained (November 7), "sur cette question vitale et adopter des résolutions qui puissent inspirer de la confiance aux amis qui travaillent pour nous en Angleterre." Later, at the end of January 1846, they held a meeting attended by a large approving audience and by "Mr G. R. Young, Ecr., M.P.P. pour Halifax dont le voyage de Québec avait été entrepris dans les intérêts de cette importante mesure" (*Les Mélanges*, January 27). The project seemed to be going well when they heard that in Montreal LaFontaine was busy promoting a Montreal-Portland route, that on August 10 he would preside over a meeting of some six to seven thousand Montrealers in the Champ de Mars to approve the Portland line. Hincks, Cartier, and Drummond, as well as Holmes and Cherrier, addressed the crowd— a fact not likely to raise their favour in Quebec.

MacDonald at *Le Canadien* began the anti-Montreal campaign. "Alors commença la fameuse réaction," Louis Létourneux explained on May 22 in his *Revue Canadienne* in Montreal. "Tout le monde sait que *Le Canadien* est l'instrument choisi depuis longtemps par certaines personnes pour opérer dans le district de Québec ce qu'elles appellent une réaction, mais ce que nous appelons, nous, une division également fatale et aux intérêts nationaux de la population Française du pays, et aux intérêts sectionnaires du district de Québec." And gradually, under MacDonald's prodding, the minor politicians in the old capital began to raise the standard of rebellion. Naturally, they looked to Caron, the man with the most honour in their own country. MacDonald sought him out with all the stubborn perseverance of the man on the outside; but those among the *Québecois* who knew of Draper's offers in September 1845 rallied around Caron all the more readily because of LaFontaine's curt treatment of him. By the spring of 1846, Quebec's Mayor had decided to head *la réaction*.

On February 2, 1846, Caron had relinquished the mayoralty which he had held since 1834. A spontaneous generous man with every advantage and a chubby, smiling face, he had never known defeat. And when, on the afternoon of February 26, the *Québecois*, forming a "foule très nombreuse de citoyens de toutes origines, du clergé des deux paroisses et du séminaire," marched in enthusiastic procession from the Hôtel-de-Ville to his residence to present him with an address of gratitude for his decade of service, he seemed indeed to be the man to lead. From Montreal, so knowledgeable an observer as Parent commented to Abbé Cazeau: "Quant aux garanties de succès qu'il a, cela dépendra beaucoup de sa fermeté et des sacrifices pécuniers qu'il fera. . . . Rappelez-vous que Caron n'a jamais eu besoin de lutter; toutes les bonnes choses de ce monde lui sont tombées sur la tête presqu'en dormant. Par conséquent il n'a pas eu l'occasion de montrer son aptitude aux luttes politiques violentes." Parent wondered whether Caron could cope with all the earthy questions of politics which LaFontaine answered to easily, whether Caron realized the latter's strength in manœuvre and, especially, his "dispositions à riposter dur et ferme."[6] But in Quebec no one wondered. And soon the whole district would feel their sharpest grievance against the Montrealers, the publicity given to the secret Draper-Caron correspondence.

Since the turn of the year persistent and conflicting intimations had drifted down from Montreal. Some said that Caron had sold out to the Tories; others that he had been tricked out of office. In fact increasing numbers of politicians were fed different titbits of information about the Draper overtures. LaFontaine himself had talked to Morin, Hincks, Baldwin, and Papineau. In mid-October, Duvernay knew, and by the new year so did Etienne-Pascal Taché. During February Draper let it be known that he had done his best by the French. At the same time Caron himself sent judicious selections of the confidential letters to Montreal, asking for more discretion, but obviously aware of their circulation. Indeed, LaFontaine had already decided to publish the correspondence, hoping, perhaps, not so much to repay Draper's own mischief in kind, as to prove that he also adhered to "the principle of the *two* majorities and to the Federal system," as Hincks said.[7] Early in March, in a brief encounter at the Court House in Montreal, he casually mentioned this to Caron. Caron was thoroughly alarmed at such a breach of confidence and categorically forbade publication. But a few days later, LaFontaine made a special trip to Quebec with the ever diplomatic Morin, and won permission to use the letters if it were necessary "selon les usages constitutionnels."[8] Had he already planned to publish the letters? At all events, after parliament met and while the private members

[6]AAQ, DM H-255, Parent à Cazeau, 22 avril 1846.
[7]Baldwin Papers, v51, Hincks to Baldwin, Sept. 23, 1845.
[8]Papiers LaFontaine, Caron à LaFontaine, 16 mars 1846.

gossiped and speculated of nothing else, he continued to press Caron. On March 27, Malcolm Cameron, a front-bench Reformer from Upper Canada, rose to direct an embarrassing question about the letters. Draper denied everything. Then inevitably, at the next caucus, the Reformers from both sections, intrigued now past curiosity's endurance, insisted that a very unreluctant LaFontaine read the correspondence.

Infuriated, Caron realized what had happened: the party leader had cleverly managed the "usages constitutionnels" according to which he could honourably read the letters in public. He also suspected that LaFontaine's version would probably highlight too much of LaFontaine. He decided "pour sa propre justification et dans l'intérêt de tous ceux qui y avaient pris part" (*Le Canadien*, April 10) to publish the correspondence himself and sent a vexed note to the party leader telling him so. Overjoyed, LaFontaine claimed that Caron's decision released him from his own earlier promise not to publish. He rushed to the Assembly and at last read the famous (and probably disappointing) documents.

Whatever he had intended, LaFontaine mainly achieved disunity and ill feeling, for he soon found himself at the centre of a controversy. Draper blamed Caron for being indiscreet; Caron accused LaFontaine of revealing confidences without permission and of sharing the secret so widely in the first place; LaFontaine ingeniously replied that Caron had acted as an intermediary, and hence the documents really belonged to him. Besides, he continued, Caron's obligation to secrecy had ceased when Draper refused to reshuffle his cabinet. Whatever anyone said, the result was the same: furious party leaders rushed to the printing presses and throughout April this battle raged in all the papers! Caron wrote an indignant pamphlet; LaFontaine reviewed it to crush his arguments. Caron answered with a "Revue de la Revue du pamphlet de M. Caron." And on and on the brochures and editorials went, ransacking British history for precedents about political organization, about the duties of the Opposition, about party caucuses and, after a few days, inevitably concentrating on local personalities. "Nous regrettons," wrote *Le Canadien* on April 22, "que dans cette polémique, les journaux, au lieu d'examiner, de discuter froidement . . . se soient laissés entraîner à des personnalités qui n'ont pour résultat que de faire perdre de vue la question maintenant soumise au tribunal de l'opinion publique."

LaFontaine's editors, who seemed always to consider that their best defence was slander, began their usual attacks. At first, they kept them for the government, as in *La Revue Canadienne* on April 17:

"Quel est le résultat de la fameuse correspondance? Rien autre chose que des admissions de faiblesse et des preuves d'incapacité du Cabinet actuel, et aussi la fourberie des uns et la niaiserie des autres." But as *Le Canadien* increased its attacks on LaFontaine, and as opinion in Quebec seemed to side with Caron, they turned their invective from Draper to Draper's correspondent. *Le Journal de Québec* began in April (13, 18): "M. Caron fausse entièrement son rôle à l'égard de ses amis de l'Opposition. C'est dommage . . . M. Caron n'aurait jamais dû s'imaginer qu'il allait écraser d'un seul coup de plume toute la représentation du Bas-Canada. . . ." Létourneux took up the theme on May 1: "Le Canadien de Québec a entrepris une croisade au bénéfice de l'honorable M. Caron contre M. LaFontaine. Un de ses derniers numéros est en partie consacré à cette guerre sainte contre le chef de l'Opposition. On veut en vain faire sortir M. Caron pur et immaculé de cette affaire. L'opinion publique ne sera pas trompée." Cauchon knew that Caron was genuinely popular and was purposely mild with what *Le Canadien* had called (April 29) those "suppositions les plus gratuites, les plus malignes et les plus attentatoires" against Caron. But against Ronald MacDonald he showed no pity. He called him stubborn, iniquitous, contemptible, and, when the editor of *Le Canadien* retorted by calling LaFontaine "un entêté," "un tyran," "un hypocrite," Cauchon made fun of MacDonald's personal tragedy. On June 12, 1846, in a disastrous fire at the Théâtre Royal, the latter lost his wife and daughter, barely escaping with his own life. The next day, in his account of the accident, Cauchon wrote: "M. McDonald [sic], le rédacteur du *Canadien* eut aussi le bonheur d'échapper à cette calamité. Dès qu'on l'aperçut et qu'on l'entendit, plusieurs bras s'attachèrent à lui, et on le retira; dans les efforts qu'on avait faits pour le dégager, il avait perdu ses bottes. Ce serait peu si c'était là sa seule perte, mais il pleure la perte de son épouse et de sa fille aînée . . . qui ont péri dans les flammes."

Cauchon ought to have known better. "En tout cas," Louis Fréchette later recalled, "M. Cauchon eut beaucoup de peine à se faire pardonner cet impair par le sentiment public révolté."[9] He floundered, too, in his campaign against Caron. The majority of the *Québecois* knew that Caron was an honourable man. And Caron said LaFontaine was ambitious; that he had played fast and loose with a gentleman's trust. Moreover, the leader of the Opposition was led by Upper Canada. Was it not a member from the upper section, Malcolm Cameron, who had first mentioned the correspondence in parliament? Was it

9Fréchette, *Mémoires*, p. 113–14.

not Baldwin who had presided over the caucus that had demanded the reading? "Les *vauriens* du Haut Canada ne respectent rien," Caron wrote from the Legislative Council to Abbé Cazeau in June, "ils n'ont ni foi, ni loi. Jugez des autres par l'immaculé Baldwin."[10]

Even Montrealers seemed to waver—though not too obviously. *L'Aurore* had reappeared shortly after its bankruptcy in December 1845, in a different format and with a different publisher, T. L. Doutney. But it came out irregularly and suffered from such poverty that even an old friend like Louis Perrault wrote to protest that his mill should not be held responsible for the cheap paper on which it was printed. It continued to support Viger and sometimes carried an article that was unmistakably his; but in the main it restricted its news to short, simple items with an anti-LaFontaine bias. Thus, when *la réaction* began in Quebec, it sided with Caron, printing his interpretation of *la fameuse correspondance* on April 10 and later, on May 9, protesting the *ci-devant* tactic "d'incriminations personnelles contre ceux qui sont l'objet de leurs préjugés." Neither *La Minerve* nor *La Revue Canadienne* bothered to answer. Still, Denis-Benjamin Papineau, no impartial witness to be sure, reported to his wife that "il y a grande diversité d'opinion parmi les gens de Montréal sur le mérite des deux hommes [LaFontaine and Caron] néanmoins ils inclinent comme de raison en faveur de Mr. LaFontaine. On ne sait encore ce que pensent les gens de Québec. Il est certain que là Mr. Caron est très populaire et avec raison." He left no doubt about his own sentiments. "Je ne puis m'empêcher de voir un honnête homme, Mr. Caron faisant ses efforts pour faire entrer ses amis au pouvoir, franchement et honorablement et les autres le sacrifier aux vues ambitieuses d'un seul homme."[11]

Did Papineau ever wonder about what might have been, had the widening division between Quebec and Montreal occurred eighteen months sooner—before the collapse of Viger's energy, before Metcalfe's departure, while his own brother's return still held high promise. But now of what use was *la réaction?*

La Correspondance: II

Draper thought the reaction could help him. The Upper Canadian leader, to whom LaFontaine would refer seven years later as "le plus habile et le plus éloquent, et par conséquent le plus formidable de mes

[10]AAQ, DM G XI, 90, Caron à Cazeau, 3 juin 1846.
[11]Collection Papineau-Bourassa, D.-B. Papineau à sa femme, 13 avril 1846.

adversaires,"[12] wondered whether the time had not now come to shatter LaFontaine's following. He had lost heavily in his attempt in September 1845 but he had revealed LaFontaine's weakness. Since then Metcalfe had gone and Viger had resigned. This time he might succeed. He accordingly began a second correspondence with the Speaker of the Legislative Council.

Towards the middle of July 1846 Draper asked Caron to come to Montreal. Caron, who by now had completely broken with LaFontaine, came and agreed to help Draper bring three *Canadiens* into the Council, although he himself preferred not to be one of them. He called first on Chief Justice Rémi Vallières de Saint-Réal to offer him the presidency of the Council. Vallières, older than his sixty years and within six months of death, lived up to his reputation for repartee. He laughed in Caron's face and, referring to the government's bid to retire him last year for ill health, observed "that he was very glad to see that the Ministry had now a better opinion of his health." When he heard of the offer, LaFontaine commented:

This proposition made to Vallières is indecent, imprudent, and cruel; indecent because it is choosing political characters among Judges; imprudent because the accusation preferred against Mr Vallières by the Ministry last session, is still pending; and cruel, because the state of his health would not allow him, without risking his life, to assume the duties of a Parliamentary leader, even in the Legislative Council. At the same time it shows a great want of judgment on Mr Caron's part.[13]

Four days later, on July 30, Duvernay reported rumours that Vallières had been offered the post and asked "Aurons-nous bientôt un ministère? Voilà la grande question dont se préoccupe et la presse et le pays entier." He added pertinent suspicions about Caron's intentions. In fact, Caron was busy on his second visit: an attempt to pry Morin away from LaFontaine. Although living in Montreal, Morin was really a *Québecois* and not unimpressed by their grievances. "A split between Morin and LaFontaine is to be made," wrote Hincks. "I am very apprehensive of it. At this moment I am convinced that each is dissatisfied with the other and I fear lest a cooling may spring up."[14] But Morin, never able to make up his own mind unaided, went to consult LaFontaine who, intransigent, aloof, and stoic as usual, refused to have anything to do with Caron's proposals. He had been the scapegoat last time and he had no intention of being involved again. Poor melancholy Morin—Caron had returned to Quebec, leaving him with

[12]Papiers LaFontaine, LaFontaine à Draper, 26 août 1853.
[13]Baldwin Papers, A 55, LaFontaine to Baldwin, July 26, 1846.
[14]*Ibid.*, v51, Hincks to Baldwin, Aug. 16, 1846.

the responsibility. As *Le Canadien* reported on August 21: "C'était à lui à voir les chefs de son parti, à les consulter et à prendre leur opinion sur l'acceptation ou la non acceptation des offres." Caron had also promised (now that Cauchon and Duvernay had shown him what was in store for him) that this was to be his last effort, that he would not accept unless Morin did.

In a sad state of indecision, Morin called in everybody: Cartier, Taché, Drummond, DeWitt, Nelson, Holmes. They sat loudly deciding between them the whole course of future history, the Montrealers hesitating to join the Tories but Taché and "the Quebec influence generally" pressing for more explicit details from Draper. If Draper meant to offer them control of the Lower Canadian section, Taché could not see why they should refuse. Then Hincks walked in and (according to Hincks) "found everything to sixes and sevens." He had no patience with double majority, and, at his expert politician's best, he pulled Morin into the back room. The group, he told him, had been wasting its time on hypothetical cases; it would do better to refuse outright and give no reasons to Caron or anyone else.[15] Relieved to have some definite orders at last, Morin agreed.

Meanwhile, people were talking, and Duvernay, sensitive to every whiff of opposition to LaFontaine, called upon his readers on August 17 to notice that "Malgré ces antécédents [last year's negotiations], M. Caron se charge encore de faire des ouvertures pour le replâtrage du ministère, et il est inutile de le répéter, il n'a pas mieux réussi dans cette dernière tentative que dans l'autre. Nous n'avons qu'un mot à ajouter pour aujourd'hui, c'est que M. Draper et ses amis doivent perdre tout espoir de diviser les Canadiens. Ils ont fait leur preuve de fidélité à leurs principes." In Quebec *Le Canadien* (August 21) jumped to Caron's defence blaming Duvernay's "exposition menson-gère et calomnieuse de ces faits dans le but de noircir un personnage honorable sous tous les rapports, et qui n'a d'autres torts aux yeux de certains journaux de Montréal, que d'avoir osé lever la tête devant un célèbre personnage, et aussi d'être Québecois." *L'Aurore* on July 17 had tried to encourage Morin to accept the proposals: "Nous croyons que l'on pourrait trouver ici des hommes ... sans même avoir recours au *grand homme* LaFontaine et aux autres membres de la clique dont il est le chef." But Morin had already decided. And *La Revue Cana-dienne* claimed on August 31 that the whole thing was mainly a question of Caron's pique: "M. Caron voulait faire de la *réaction* l'automne dernier, il en veut faire encore aujourd'hui; M. Caron ne

[15]*Ibid.*

peut pardonner à M. LaFontaine d'avoir publié la fameuse correspondance, et c'est encore sous l'influence de ces sentiments d'hostilité personnelle à ce monsieur qu'il agit aujourd'hui, qu'il voudrait former un cabinet dont M. LaFontaine ne serait pas etc. etc. . . . Les Canadiens sans cause ne se sépareront pas de leurs chefs."

Draper had failed again. And to proclaim the party's unity (and also to make sure that both sides told the same story this time), Morin wrote an open letter which *La Minerve* and *Le Canadien* published simultaneously on August 31. He defended Caron against any suspicions—"Je regretterais . . . que l'on fit en aucune manière contraster sa conduite et ses vues avec les miennes"—and added, with an obvious reference to LaFontaine, that there could be no differences between a party and its leader. He had assumed leadership at this time, not in opposition to LaFontaine—"non contre lui mais sans lui"—but out of a sense of duty "et par mon vif désir de voir régner l'union."

Draper had come close to breaking LaFontaine's party, for who could foretell the outcome if Morin had been able to make up his mind, or if Hincks had not walked in at the right moment? Yet the very nearness of Draper's success underlines the unity LaFontaine had achieved. For over a year the people had been distracted by war stories and corn laws; for eighteen months the press had been discussing double majority and the politicians in the Quebec district rising to a heat of *réaction*. But no less gifted a personage than the leader of the dissidents, the Speaker of the Legislative Council, the ex-mayor of Quebec, René-Edouard Caron, did not dare on two occasions to accept Draper's offer without first feeling certain of the acquiescence of the leader in Montreal.

If he were sensible to that kind of thought (and his many enemies said he was) LaFontaine, strong and silent in his lonely study and curtly refusing even his faithful Morin the benefit of his advice about Caron's proposals, may indeed have been reflecting upon how manifestly the will of the country had, in fact, become the will of one man—himself.

THE ALLEGIANCE OF THE PRIESTS

Draper's second overture to Caron was a crucial test which LaFontaine and his dedicated lieutenants, Hincks and Drummond, Cauchon and Cartier, passed, if barely, at least effectively. It confirmed the victory of 1844, and it testified to the young leader's greatest achievement:

the education of his politicians to sacrifice an immediate gain in return for a distant advantage. In this sense 1846 was momentous, and to LaFontaine and his men, as victors, goes the credit. Unknown to LaFontaine, however, 1846 would be significant for another reason as well: it brought his party the allegiance of the priests.

LaFontaine was a practical politician. In 1844 he had succeeded in persuading his people to follow him. In 1846 he confirmed the unity of his party. And for none of this had he needed the priests. Nor had he attempted to convince them—in fact he had won despite, or at least without them. Yet in a future he could not then foresee, their support would make all the difference.

By 1846 LaFontaine's followers and the priests had for some time been moving imperceptibly towards each other. The debate on the Union was settled, the quarrel over the Mondelet–C. D. Day education bill had been resolved, and ever since Bishop Bourget had, in effect, allowed masses for Bagot, there had been some understanding between the two groups. Although *Les Mélanges* publicly sided with Viger over *la crise Metcalfe*, on a personal level new friendships were being forged between the clergy and LaFontaine's politicians. In Quebec, Jean Chabot and Joseph-Edouard Cauchon increasingly enjoyed the hospitality Neilson had once received at the Séminaire. Moreover, Cauchon was becoming a close correspondent of Abbé Cazeau. Also, since the suspension of the religious page of *La Gazette de Québec*, and later of the whole French edition, contact between Curé Baillargeon, the priests, and Neilson's staff had declined. In Montreal, Morin also received a cordial welcome at the bishop's palace, especially from Vicar-General Hudon. So did people like Lewis Drummond and Joseph Coursol. Gradually they came to counterbalance the influence which Viger still enjoyed there. In addition, the priests were hearing disturbing reports about the Governor General which tended to confirm the stories told by their new friends. From Toronto, for example, Bishop Power wrote of Metcalfe's connection with the Orange Order:

Que pensez-vous de ce brave homme le Gouverneur-Général? S'il avait osé, il aurait persécuté la Religion Catholique. Il est l'ennemi acharné des Canadiens-français, des Irlandais Catholiques, et l'ami de tout ce qui nous est opposé, des orangistes, des francs-maçons, des *odd fellows*, et de toutes les sociétés secrètes. Il nous a fait dans le Haut Canada un mal qui aurait été irréparable, si le siège du gouvernement n'avait pas été transféré à Montréal. L'Evêque Anglican me disait dernièrement "c'est un homme sans religion."[16]

[16]AAQ, HC VI, 25, Power à Turgeon, 2 sept. 1846.

None of these things alone was sufficient to bring the priests into LaFontaine's party, but they did prepare the way. Then, in 1846, in the public discussion over the new education bill and over the funds from the Jesuit estates, the clergy found that their natural allies were among the official Opposition; and in the theoretical discussion that followed, they discovered the full extent of their differences with Viger's government.

Denis-Benjamin Papineau's Education Act of 1845 had established the independence and distinctive character of French-Canadian education and for this reason it was of the greatest political and cultural significance. But it did not satisfy the clergy. Although it provided for the curés to be *ex officio* visitors to the schools, it did not give them the control they wished. Therefore they continued in and out of the public eye the campaign they had begun in 1841 to have the law changed in their favour. On March 11, 1842, *Les Mélanges* had made the position clear in emphasizing the intimate link between education and religion: "Observez combien il est important d'entourer la jeunesse de précautions pour la préserver du souffle empesté d'une éducation fausse; étudiez l'histoire de tous les pays et de tous les siècles, et vous en serez convaincus. . . . Voilà pourquoi dans tous les pays on a toujours confié l'éducation de la jeunesse aux ministres et à la religion."

By the fall of 1843, when the *Canadiens* had taken office and Morin was engaged in preparing a new education bill, the bishops despatched to Kingston the capable and efficient Monsignor Hyacinthe Hudon, Vicar-General of Montreal, to act as their representative and *chargé d'affaires*. He served his cause well; after three weeks of tactful lobbying he could report that in conversations with Morin and "plusieurs membres de l'exécutif," he had secured that "le bill d'éducation ne sera pas mauvais."[17] However, when Denis-Benjamin Papineau finally introduced the bill eighteen months later in the spring of 1845, the clergy found that a number of the Morin-Hudon clauses had been dropped, especially those which had conferred powers on the curé at the local level. "M. Papineau auquel j'ai eu le plaisir d'administrer quelque dure médecine pour lui faire digérer son *bill* d'éducation, ne veut pas que l'éducation soit religieuse," Cauchon wrote to Abbé Cazeau.[18] And from the Opposition benches Morin introduced the amendment which gave the right of visitation to the curés *ex officio*.

17AAM, Lettres Hudon, 1842–7, Hudon à Prince, 3 nov. 1843; AAQ, HC VI, 22, Power à Turgeon, 6 nov. 1843.
18Groulx, *L'Enseignement français au Canada*, p. 227.

But when it was finally passed the bill still did not entirely satisfy the bishops. *Les Mélanges* explained on May 6:

Tant que l'acte refusera de lui accorder [au clergé] cette surveillance efficace, c'est-à-dire tant que la loi n'exigera pas que LA MORALITÉ DE L'INSTITUTEUR ET L'ORTHODOXIE DE L'ENSEIGNEMENT RELIGIEUX ET MORAL SOIENT CONSTATÉES PAR UN CERTIFICAT AUQUEL L'AUTORITÉ ECCLESIASTIQUE OU LE MINISTRE DE LA RELIGION AURA NÉCESSAIREMENT PRIS PART, COMME UNE CONDITION SINE QUA NON, le clergé réclamera et sera obligé de réclamer.

For the next year *Les Mélanges* campaigned for the law's amendment, and in its fight found great support in the influence of Morin: "ce monsieur dont le cœur est droit," as one curé wrote.[19] Indeed, on December 18, 1845, Morin's address to a capacity audience at the new Institut Canadien pleaded for a system of education which would happily unite clerical authority on the local level with centralized control by the superintendent at the education department. He ended with a remarkable plea for religious freedom:

Si ma voix pouvait être entendue partout où règne la charité publique et la bienveillance chrétienne, je conseillerais de ne pas paralyser l'efficacité des écoles en les divisant inutilement. . . . A tous je ferais remarquer que ceux qui sont majorité dans un endroit, sont minorité quelque part; que quand à l'oppression par le bras de la loi, elle est inutile et dangereuse. . . . L'homme sans religion serait un monstre; l'homme persécuteur ne serait guère mieux. . . . Unissons avec un esprit chrétien toute notre énergie et notre charité pour instruire, relever, nourrir, au moral comme au matériel, la société telle que Dieu l'a constituée et dont il a voulu que nous formions utilement partie. (*Les Mélanges Religieux*, January 16, 1846)

In mid-1846, Denis-Benjamin Papineau bowed to the pressure. By a series of amendments to his law of the year before, he provided that elections to the school commissions would be strictly by denomination and, the point on which *Les Mélanges* had been insisting, that the curé or minister in each parish would hold a veto power in the hiring of teachers and in the selection of textbooks. On this last point *Les Mélanges* had been quite emphatic as far back as November 28, 1843: "Le choix des livres . . . devra être fait avec le plus grand soin, pour empêcher que nos campagnes, encore si morales, ne soient innondées d'un déluge de livres impies et immoraux. A cette occasion, nous dirons que ceux qui ont reçu la mission divine de veiller sur la doctrine et les mœurs, devraient, suivant nous, être chargés de surveiller ce choix afin de détourner ce fleau."

[19]APQ, Fonds de l'Instruction Publique, Lettres reçues, Davignon à Meilleur, 23 nov. 1843.

If the bishops felt relatively happier at the law, they owed it to the campaign waged by *Les Mélanges*, but also in great part to the support, in and out of the House, of politicians like Drummond, Cauchon, Taché, and, above all, Morin. By the time Papineau's amendments became law, the clergy had turned their attention, however, to another burning interest, the funds from the Jesuit estates.

The Jesuit estates had been vexing the Colonial Office, the Lower Canadian legislature, and the Catholic church for over half a century. These lands and the properties which were granted throughout the French régime to the Jesuit Order by a succession of kings and nobles to serve as an endowment for education and missionary work among the Indians had passed to the British Crown in stages at the time of the conquest in 1763, the suppression of the Jesuits in 1774, and the death of the last Jesuit in Canada in 1800. After 1792 they had served mainly as another of the Lower Canadian Assembly's grievances against the executive power. In the Assembly's view, their revenues, which the Colonial Office was using for any number of government sinecures, ought to come under its control. After years of bickering the Colonial Office, as a gesture of conciliation, agreed in 1832 that the estates should be administered by the Assembly. But then began another struggle with the Catholic bishops who claimed that they and not the Assembly were the true heirs of the Jesuits and thus the only ones who could fulfil the intentions of the donors of the estates: Catholic education and missions. By the time of the Union, the revenue had accumulated to some £20,000. With his usual vitality, Bishop Bourget set out to acquire the funds for the Church.

In 1838, during Arthur Buller's commission on education, all the bishops of Lower Canada had presented a petition to Durham urging "que les biens des anciens Jésuites soient affectés suivant l'intention des donateurs."[20] They had received no answer to this plea. But after the Union they felt the need all the more, since the government's policy of non-denominational education might force them to found private schools which must, somehow, be endowed. At all events, early in 1843, Bishop Bourget found out from LaFontaine that as part of their general policy of reform the executive councillors had decided to settle the issue. He wrote immediately to Quebec and organized another petition which he read privately to the Attorney General when the latter visited Montreal briefly at the end of May 1843. LaFontaine seemed embarrassed at the petition "parce qu'il craint

---

[20]AAM, Lartigue à Signay, 23 juil. 1838; Requête de Mgr Signay, Mgr Turgeon, Mgr Lartigue à Lord Durham, 20 oct. 1838.

qu'elle n'entrave leurs mesures pour se mettre en possession de ces riches propriétés. . . . Il ne m'a pas caché que les Protestants auraient leur part à ce gâteau," Bishop Bourget reported to Archbishop Signay.[21] Yet he continued to press the government. In July he travelled himself to Kingston on Church business—Bishop Gaulin had gone mad—and visited LaFontaine again. So did Monsignor Hudon, several times. Indeed, Hudon reported that Metcalfe himself "s'est montré sympathique."[22] Soon, however, *la crise* exploded, and the politicians all forgot about the estates.

Bishop Bourget did not. In the summer of 1844 he prepared another petition. And to give it all possible weight, he asked Hudon on a trip to Paris to find out legal opinion there on the Church's claim. Late in 1844, while LaFontaine was winning the general election in Lower Canada, Hudon returned with a brochure—*Note sur les biens que les Jésuites possédaient au Canada, et sur l'affectation que ces biens doivent recevoir aujourd'hui*—prepared by M. de Vatismenil, a Parisian jurist who had been Minister of Education under Charles X. As if an opinion on such a subject from such a source could be different, M. de Vatismenil concluded, after ten pages of argument, that "c'est exclusivement à l'éducation catholique qu'ils doivent être employés aujourd'hui."[23] Bourget had the memorandum printed in French and English for distribution among the members of parliament, and it was published in *Les Mélanges* during May and June. Then, together with Morin (who, among other services, suggested the use of the word "spoliation" to describe the Church's loss of the estates revenues), he prepared another petition to the Governor General and, in February 1846, had a personal interview with Lord Cathcart. In sending the petition in at the end of March, he wrote Viger a personal letter in which he promised to make good use of the funds:

Si donc ces biens sont laissés à la disposition de l'Eglise Catholique à laquelle ils appartiennent, les Evêques ne manqueront pas, sous la protection d'un Gouvernement aussi juste qu'équitable, de travailler à promouvoir le grand bien de l'Education et des Missions. Il existe déjà dans cette Province huit Séminaire ou Collèges qui pourraient être selon leurs besoins, encouragés dans la belle cause qu'ils se sont imposée, celle de répandre l'Education dans ce Pays.[24]

[21]*Ibid.*, Lettres Bourget, III, 119–20, Bourget à Signay, 30 mai 1843.
[22]AAQ, HC VI, 22, Power à Turgeon, 6 nov. 1843; AAM, Lettres Hudon, 1842–7, Hudon à Prince, 3 nov. 1843.
[23]"Notes sur les Biens" published in *Les Mélanges Religieux*, 19, 26, 29 mai, 2 juin 1846.
[24]Papiers Viger, Bourget à Viger, 30 mais 1846.

The bishops' petition was finally tabled in the House on May 14, 1846. It was turned down. Basing its judgment on the Lower Canadian precedent of 1832, the government decided to apply the revenues from the estates to the cost of education in Lower Canada. Education in Upper Canada, on the other hand, would be financed from the consolidated treasury of the united province. This meant, in effect, that the funds would go to the Protestant schools in Lower Canada as well as to the Catholic ones and that Upper Canada would also profit, since that section would now enjoy alone the budget which had been applied before to the whole province. Above all, the government refused any claim by the bishops. Morin, who had been acting as confidential adviser to the clergy, sprang to his feet. So, in turn, did LaFontaine, Drummond, Taché, and Chauveau, each delivering impassioned speeches against the "spoliation" of French Canada's heritage. Morin proposed an amendment that the funds be transferred entirely to the Church, which was, naturally, defeated. Then Viger rose to defend the government's policy on the grounds of precedent and parliamentary supremacy.

And outside, as they read the newspapers, the *Canadiens* discovered interesting new connections. *Le Canadien* and *L'Aurore*, defending Viger's speech, began to attack the Church's position, while *La Minerve*, *Le Journal de Québec*, and *La Revue Canadienne* became defenders of the faith. "Le Canadien attaque MM. LaFontaine, Taché et autres membres de l'Opposition," wrote *La Revue* (June 12), "pour avoir après tous leurs amendements perdus, et malheureusement nous le craignons que trop perdus pour toujours, voté pour sauver du nauffrage une partie de l'héritage de leurs compatriotes, et les Viger, les Papineau, les Taschereau livraient à l'ennemi sans raison aucune, si ce n'est celle de tout sacrifier pour rester ministres quand même." Cauchon could hardly hide his glee at Viger's discomfiture: "Aujourd'hui, bien différent de ce qu'il était autrefois, il se trouve, pour ainsi dire, en guerre ouverte avec les chefs de l'Eglise catholique du Bas Canada pour leur contester un droit qu'ils réclament" (*Le Journal de Québec*, June 18). And when he resigned a few days later, Cauchon claimed (June 20): "Nous étions bien sûr que M. Viger ne pourrait pas *digérer les Jésuites*, et qu'ils causeraient inévitablement sa mort. Si M. Viger et M. Papineau, ainsi que M. Taschereau, eussent résigné sur la question importante des Jésuites, importante en fait, mais en principe surtout, ils laisseraient la vie publique avec plus de considération et d'affection populaires qu'ils n'en emporteront maintenant avec eux dans leur tombe politique." LaFontaine's supporters, already masters of the "défenseur de la langue" thesis, had begun to practise the "défenseur de la foi." Before long the two themes would run in myriad variations through their propaganda.

The disappointed bishops sent a solemn protest to Cathcart. And before they knew it they were involved in a disagreeable controversy with *L'Aurore*, a discussion which made them realize how wide a gulf divided them from Viger.

The discussion, which ran for over two months and covered pages of *L'Aurore* and *Les Mélanges Religieux*, began when *L'Aurore*, naturally enough, defended Viger's stand. "Les feuilles ex-ministérielles," it averred on June 3:

sont remplies de déclamations contre le président du conseil qu'on représente comme un bon vieillard à voix débile, dont on ne peut presque jamais saisir un seul argument. . . . Nous ne savons que penser de la requête qu'on publie comme étant celle de nos évêques au sujet des biens des Jésuites. Ce document ferait supposer qu'ils ont perdu de vue quelques considérations d'une grande importance relative à ce sujet.

In a series of articles during June which could hardly have been written by anyone but Viger, *L'Aurore* insisted that the bishops had at most a tenuous claim to these funds which had never, in fact, belonged to them and which, if the intentions of the donors were really to be the criterion, should be applied to the whole territory of what had once been New France. Since they were being spent exclusively in Lower Canada, as the bishops themselves agreed (in fact the Lower Canadian bishops had quickly closed ranks to deny a claim from Bishop Power of Toronto), the revenues derived their title from the imperial decision of 1832 which put them at the disposal of the "volontés réunies des pouvoirs Exécutif, Législatif, Administratif" of the Lower Canadian parliament, and hence of the Union government which was its heir.

When *Les Mélanges*, *La Minerve*, *Le Journal de Québec*, and *La Revue Canadienne* all replied that taking the property from the Church in the first place had been a sacrilege, the argument rose to another level. Running through precedents that went back to pre-Revolutionary France, *L'Aurore* retorted on June 16 that since the Church's possession of property derived from civil law, any change by the state could hardly be a sacrilege. Besides, the estates had been given to the Jesuits and at their demise the Crown had merely exercised its duty to protect private property until it could be returned to its "destination primitive." To this, in its best scholastic manner, *Les Mélanges* retorted, on June 26 in syllogistic form, that since the

Church possessed property by divine and natural right, civil recognition added nothing: "L'Eglise du Canada possédait donc les Biens des Jésuites par le droit divin, le droit naturel et le droit civil. On lui enlève ce dernier droit; il s'en suit donc, d'après les deux premiers, que ce n'est qu'une injustice que l'on commet contre elle." And to this L'Aurore, in the best liberal tradition, replied on June 30 that since nature knew only individuals, no corporate body such as the Church could claim existence by natural law. And so the controversy went.

Unlike other quarrels between newspapers, this discussion never descended to personalities. But neither could it be resolved. For while Les Mélanges reasserted the doctrine, so dear to nineteenth-century ultramontanes, that the Church by natural and divine right was autonomous with respect to the state, Viger, brimming with the liberal's faith in the individual, denied any natural right to a corporate body. It was an argument which would not be settled for generations, but at the time it marked a turning point in the relations between the politicians and priests.

This was not the first issue which had brought L'Aurore and Les Mélanges into conflict. In 1842 they had blasted each other over the interpretation of Bishop Lartigue's famous mandement against the rebels in 1837; then too they had been quarrelling, fundamentally, from the opposing viewpoints of the ultramontane and liberal doctrines.

The conflict, that time, had been occasioned by Abbé Chartier's letter retracting his statements of the rebellion years. Late in 1841, Chartier had returned from exile in the United States and asked to be received into the diocese of Quebec. Before the censures against him could be lifted, however, he was asked to publish a statement of obedience to the doctrines of the Lartigue mandement of 1837 which he had questioned at the time. Accordingly, he wrote an abject recantation of his own patriote theories and, probably on the advice of Bishop Turgeon, sent a copy to the French edition of the Quebec Gazette, where it appeared on December 14. In Montreal, Bishop Bourget refused to let Les Mélanges publish it. But on December 24 L'Aurore carried a note distinctly sympathetic to Chartier's old ideas, blaming him for "se jeter à genoux pour adorer l'idole du despotisme en Canada." The Abbé soon found that he had launched his friends once more into the whirl of controversy.

A group of Chartier's former parishioners from Saint-Benoît, well-read patriotes certainly, wrote to L'Aurore on December 24 protesting his recantation, assailing his repudiation of his former sermons— "Voulez-vous donc imiter vos supérieurs, que vous avez tant blamés de s'être faits les trop complaisans étais d'un pouvoir persécuteur et cruel?"—and reproaching him for adhering to the *mandement* which they likened to "ces mandements, calqués sur un certain bref liberticide adressé aux Evêques de l'intéressante et malheureuse Pologne. Si ce but fut pour ainsi dire, dicté et commandé par l'autocrate Russe, nous savons quelle part eut le général Anglais aux manifestes de l'épiscopat Canadien, et quel partie on en a tiré." On reading what it considered to be slanders against Pope Gregory XVI and Bishop Lartigue, *Les Mélanges* bristled. It dared the correspondents of *L'Aurore* to prove their statements about the Czar and the Pope, about Colborne and the Bishop. Then—and he did not have to—Viger himself entered the fray. On January 11, 1842, a paragraph appeared that not only firmly established his own liberal cast of thought, but also indicated how bitterly he must have resented his cousin's *mandement* five years before.

Il est trop absurde, à l'époque de raison éclairée où nous vivons, d'entendre soutenir encore des doctrines dans lesquelles d'abord l'Eglise ne doit, ne peut pas intervenir. . . . Nous nous réjouirions d'entrer en lice avec qui voudra, parce que nous savons d'avance que le mandement qu'on défend si fort, et dont on se plaît à sanctionner bien inconsidérément l'étonnante et sophistique déraison, ne paraîtra plus en effet que le fruit de quelque influence étrangère au *sentiment de conviction* d'un homme qui était trop éclairé pour ne pas estimer tout le contraste qu'il fesait avec la vérité. Nous ne sommes plus au tems où Galilée était déclaré hérétique.

Les Mélanges retorted on January 15, accusing Viger of casting "l'injure et la calomnie sur cet évêque" and denying the teaching authority of the Church. Viger answered in *L'Aurore* on January 18 that "les matières politiques sont de ces sujets 'que Dieu laisse aux disputes des hommes.'"

Thus both *L'Aurore* and *Les Mélanges* began to blind their readers with theologizing. The latter claimed throughout that the insult to the memory of Bishop Lartigue had never been proved. Viger, on the other hand, claimed that the insult to the Bishop was rather the belief that he would have written such a *mandement* of his own free will. Within a few days the controversy had moved on to the more fundamental questions of infallibility, passive obedience, the separation of church and state, œcumenical councils; the historical points, Canossa, John Lackland, usury, Galileo, Frederick II, the anointing of Napoleon; and finally, Gallicanism, liberalism, ultramontanism.[25] By March, neither

---

[25]Cf. F. Ouellet, "Le Mandement de Mgr Lartigue de 1837 et la réaction libérale," *Bulletin des Recherches historiques*, LVIII (1952), 97–104; L. Pouliot, *Bourget*, II, 205–8.

could entertain any doubts about the other's erudition, or indeed about *Les Mélanges'* ultramontanism or Viger's liberalism. Radicals such as Louis Perrault rejoiced. "Il s'est élevé une querelle récemment," he wrote to Duvernay, "entre le Journal Ecclésiastique les Mélanges et l'Aurore. C'est une querelle qui ne paraît pas s'éteindre, l'un et l'autre sont dans le tort; car l'Aurore aurait du accabler les Mélanges dès le début au lieu d'avoir entamé une discussion religieuse."[26] But Bishop Bourget lamented the quarrel. "Ce n'est à coup sûr," he wrote, "qu'avec beaucoup de répugnance que le Journal ecclésiastique s'est lancé dans cette arène. L'obligation de soutenir les droits de l'église et de venger l'honneur de son chef, si honteusement outragé par cette feuille, a semblé à l'Editeur une raison bien puissante pour rompre le silence."[27] And despite their differences in outlook which could hardly be reconciled, *Les Mélanges* continued to support Viger and *L'Aurore* in all their political attitudes, reprinting many of their articles, and once, on February 10, 1843, writing about Viger an homage it never gave to any other individual:

La haute érudition dont fait preuve si souvent M. l'Editeur de l'Aurore, le caractère de profonde vérité dont sont empreints la plupart de ses écrits, joint à l'éloquence du style, nous porte à le féliciter au nom de tous les bons esprits, au nom du Catholicisme et de l'ordre social dont il est devenu un puissant et intelligent défenseur. Puisse toute la presse catholique de ce pays comprendre ainsi ce qu'il y a de noble, d'utile, de vital, dans des questions qui tiennent si essentiellement à l'existence et au bonheur de la société.

It took four years for the priests at *Les Mélanges* to grasp *L'Aurore's* essential radicalism. Of course, during that time, they came to appreciate new friends like Drummond and Cauchon and increasingly to admire the piety of Morin. After *la crise*, too, they may have felt a new regard for LaFontaine's attitude which, like the priests' embattled orthodoxy, demanded total surrender from its adversaries. They reflected, perhaps, upon his pressing of the language issue and Cauchon's incipient doctrine that language was the best guardian of the faith. After the session of 1846, after Denis-Benjamin Papineau's performance on the education bill, after Viger's decision about the estates, and especially after the quarrel about the Church's right to property, the clergy never again supported Viger's friends.

For LaFontaine, as for the priests and Viger, the events of 1846 had not been insignificant. During the session he had kept the government on the defensive; outside, by complete intransigence, by never swerv-

26Papiers Duvernay, 538, Perrault à Duvernay, 4 fév. 1842.
27AAM, Lettres Bourget, II, 505, Bourget à Gagnon, 16 mars 1842.

ing from his aim, he had confirmed his leadership and the unity of his following. Finally, he had witnessed a change in the political attitude of the Church. Then, on September 7, he read of the appointment as governor general of Lord Elgin, of whom Denis-Benjamin Papineau would presently write, "chacun l'attend comme devant apporter avec lui la panacée politique universelle."[28] Now began the end of the long inconclusive years. The political pace quickened and the winning of the struggle for responsible government was within the sight of the *Canadien* leader.

[28]Collection Papineau-Bourassa, D.-B. Papineau à J.-B. Papineau, nov. 1846.

14

Lord Elgin
September 1846-March 1848

When answering Caron's letter about the first Draper offer in September 1845, LaFontaine had written: "Lord Metcalfe est le Lord Sydenham et son successeur sera le Sir Charles Bagot."[1] Thus with his keen intuition into the political struggle he was waging, the young leader had foreseen that once the battle between the governor's party —be it Sydenham's or Metcalfe's—and the *Canadiens* was drawn, a new governor must win it for the *Canadiens*. Now, with Draper's overtures twice refused and LaFontaine's Lower Canadians still united, the battle was drawn. And, on September 7, 1846, *La Minerve* announced that "Lord Elgin, qui fut successeur de lord Metcalfe au gouvernement de la Jamaïque, a été nommé gouverneur-general." Even in the manner of his arrival, Lord Elgin imitated Bagot. While the government and people prepared to receive him, he was delayed; and when he did arrive, again like Bagot, he did not immediately side with LaFontaine.

At first the *Canadien* press was guarded. "Lord Elgin est un *conservateur*," wrote *Les Mélanges* in a typical comment on September 11, "et comme tel opposé au ministère de lord John Russell. Ce choix fait donc honneur à ce dernier, qui en choisissant cet officier a témoigné par là ne point agir par esprit de parti, mais il l'a uniquement choisi à cause de son habileté et de son grand discernement pour les affaires publiques." And Duvernay added in *La Minerve* on September 14: "La presse anglaise approuve généralement sa nomination, sans distinction de parti politique, à cause de son aptitude particulière. Il va sans dire que nous ne pouvons prononcer aucune opinion. . . . Nous pouvons sans doute espérer que tous ceux qui auront été gouverneurs de la Jamaïque ne seront pas nécessairement des tyrans." But at least there was hope, for the new Governor possessed "de grandes et

[1]Papiers LaFontaine, LaFontaine à Caron, sept. 1845.

éminentes qualités" and had been named by Lord John Russell, despite his known opposition to Russell's colonial policy in the days of Thomson. In a way his appointment underlined the extent of the change in colonial policy that had taken place in Britain since 1839.

During the decade Russell—about whom it had been said that Euclid himself would have had a poor chance, had he happened to have decided that the interior angles of a triangle were *not* equal to two right angles—had had second thoughts about the British empire. He had to accommodate a welter of opinions in Britain and, after leaving the Colonial Office in 1841, he had been influenced, indeed persuaded, by the new ideas of the *laissez-faire* radicals and the colonial reformers like Wakefield and Buller. And when Russell formed his government after the defeat of Peel's conservative administration in July 1846, he offered Buller a cabinet post and placed in his own old office as Colonial Secretary a man who happily blended the theories of the colonial reformers and the economic radicals.

Sir Henry George Grey, third Earl Grey, had the great mind that went with a great empire. A brother-in-law and kindred spirit of Durham, he had a passion for *laissez-faire*. A friend of Buller, he was an outspoken free trader. And to these liberal ideas in trade and government, he added the imperial theme. He saw the empire as a fountain of honour and glory, as a potent instrument for peace and fair play, as a solemn trust committed by Providence to British hands. "The authority of the British Crown," he wrote, "is at this moment the most powerful instrument, under Providence, of maintaining peace and order in many extensive regions of the earth, and thereby assists in diffusing among millions of the human race, the blessings of Christianity and civilization."[2] The empire must be saved, he thought, for the good of humanity. It must be built on the firm rock of liberty and fraternity, on those famous ties which though light as air are as strong as links of iron. And thus responsible government, as Baldwin, Durham, and LaFontaine had explained it, must follow quickly. In November 1846, consulted about the difficulties facing the governor and council of Nova Scotia, Grey despatched to Sir John Harvey the famous instruction which, in effect, inaugurated the new system. But already, late in the summer of 1846, he had appointed the Earl of Elgin to Canada.

Aware of the changes at the Colonial Office, some of LaFontaine's friends thought Lord Elgin would dissolve parliament as soon as he

[2]Quoted in J. L. Morison, *British Supremacy and Canadian Self-Government, 1839–1854* (Toronto, 1916), p. 276.

arrived and call their leader to office. Létourneux wrote in *La Revue Canadienne* on September 18: "Le Conseil Exécutif est l'âme du gouvernement constitutionnel (ministère responsable); notre gouvernement est donc un corps sans âme. Nous espérons que lord Elgin va de suite lui donner la vie, en refondant son ministère. Peut-il avoir une autre marche à suivre que d'appeler auprès de lui un homme qui puisse parmi les hommes de son parti choisir un certain nombre de personnes intelligentes."

Meanwhile the province prepared to receive the new Governor. On November 3 Cathcart vacated Monklands, and on December 21 *La Minerve* reported that the political leaders had petitioned Mayor Ferrier to summon a public meeting to adopt an address of congratulation. They had their meeting, but on December 28 they were disappointed to read in *La Minerve* that "Son Excellence lord Elgin ne doit s'embarquer que le 4 de janvier." On January 13, 1847, under pressure from Francis Hincks, they met again to adopt an address of welcome composed by Morin. By now, after three months of waiting, they were very anxious.

At first LaFontaine had been wary. Perhaps his predictions would not come true. In July 1846, on hearing rumours that Arthur Buller might be appointed governor, he wrote to Baldwin that "as governor I would prefer some nobleman older than him, and not connected with any party."[3] So when he heard that the new appointee was instead "a young man, since he is younger than you and myself," he confessed: "I have some apprehension. I have so little confidence in the Whigs, in relation to colonial matters, that I have an idea that the new governor was chosen, because of his being, like lord Metcalfe, supposed to be a man to act in opposition to what we do, and must consider to be our constitution."[4] Baldwin, answering from Toronto, concurred: "You speak of the opinions entertained by some of our friends in England of our new Gr Gl. I confess I am inclined to place little importance on them. We had no such commendations of poor Sir Charles Bagot, but abundance of them with respect to his successor." But he added some words of encouragement. Lord Elgin was poor—an advantage when compared to the use "the last specimen we had" had made of his fortune. He also had good Reform connections: "You saw what I said in one of my late speeches on the advantage of having relations and political friends of Lord Durham's in political office. I think Lord Elgin's marriage to his daughter is an advantage of the like

[3]Baldwin Papers, A 55, LaFontaine to Baldwin, July 26, 1846.
[4]*Ibid.*, LaFontaine to Baldwin, Sept. 25, 1846.

description."[5] LaFontaine took heart. He was seriously ill at the time—"in a very precarious state," Hincks said[6]—but he eagerly anticipated being called to office. "Here is a case," he wrote to Baldwin, "for your opinion: Suppose I have an interview with lord Elgin, and he asks my advice. I respectfully enquire before replying: Am I to understand, My Lord, that your Ministry have resigned? Oh! no, says he, but I would like to have your opinions. Then, My Lord, I wish and I feel it my duty to abstain from expressing any such opinion, so long as you have any constitutional and responsible advisers. What do you say to that?"[7]

Meanwhile Denis-Benjamin Papineau, the only *Canadien* left among the "constitutional and responsible advisers," wondered "quel changement l'arrivée d'un nouveau Gouverneur fera dans nos affaires,"[8] though he left no doubt about his own hopes: "Si Lord Elgin fait maison nette je suis remplacé tu peux bien penser que je ne penserai ni à demeurer en ville ni à aller vivre à Maska [Saint-Hyacinthe]."[9]

Finally on January 25, 1847, James Bruce, eighth Earl of Elgin and twelfth Earl of Kincardine, landed in Boston to begin a trip to Montreal every bit as brilliant as Bagot's tour of Lower Canada. A cold coming he had had of it, buffeted by Atlantic gales and the fatigues of a three-week journey at the worst time of the year. But he set out over huge snowbanks and made it in three days to Phillipsburg, "premier village qui se trouve de ce côté-ci des lignes," where hundreds of sleighs came out to welcome him and form a steaming caravan for him all the way to Saint Johns. After the new Governor charmed the crowds there with a "réponse toute gracieuse" (*La Minerve*, February 1) in French to their loyal address, he went on to LaPrairie ("les citoyens . . . ne sont pas demeurés en arrière") and arrived at Monklands by mid-afternoon on the twenty-ninth. The next day he made his official entry into the capital.

The decorations set up earlier were in ruins and an abundant snowfall fanned by high west winds blocked the roads into the city with tall drifts. But Lord Elgin, wrapped in buffalo robes, arrived punctually at one o'clock. *La Minerve* described the welcome on February 1: "Une garde d'honneur était stationnée en face de la maison du gouvernement; une brigade des pompiers bordait la rue de chaque côté; venait ensuite la société des Odd Fellows, puis la

[5]Papiers LaFontaine, Baldwin to LaFontaine, Dec. 17, 1846.
[6]Baldwin Papers, v51, Hincks to Baldwin, Dec. 16, 1846.
[7]*Ibid.*, A 55, LaFontaine to Baldwin, Dec. 29, 1846.
[8]Collection Papineau-Bourassa, D.-B. Papineau à sa femme, 15 sept. 1846.
[9]*Ibid.*, D.-B. Papineau à J. Papineau, nov. 1846.

société de St Andrews; la société des Allemands; l'Institut Canadien; la société de Tempérance de l'évêché; l'association St. Jean Baptiste; la société St. George et enfin la société de St. Patrice." And behind all these "une foule de citoyens" filled Notre-Dame Street from Place d'Armes to the Château. Mayor John Mills welcomed the new Governor at the Porte Saint-Antoine with Morin's address. *La Minerve* continued: "Après la lecture de l'adresse et de la réponse, le cortège se mit en route, Son Honneur le Maire ayant pris place dans la voiture de lord Elgin. A son passage où stationnaient les différentes sociétés, Son Excellence fut saluée par de bruyantes acclamations et les bandes de musique jouèrent le *God save the Queen*." Then the crowds lining the streets moved in to join the procession, "avec des acclamations et des applaudissements sans cesse répétés" (*Les Mélanges*, February 2). At the Château de Ramezay, Elgin descended, and the majority of the *Canadiens* saw him for the first time:

Sa taille est au-dessous de la moyenne et il paraît prendre de l'embonpoint. Quoiqu'agé que de 37 ans, il est un peu chauve, et a des cheveux et des favoris très gris, le teint brun et méridional, les traits fins et délicats, les yeux noirs et animés, une bouche petite et indiquant la fermeté et la décision de caractère. Sur le tout c'est une physionomie agréable et intelligente et on le dit doué de beaucoup d'éloquence. (*La Minerve*, February 4)

The Governor definitely made a good impression. "La réponse de lord Elgin," Duvernay continued,

à l'adresse des habitans de Montréal a été appréciée comme elle devait l'être, on ne pouvait desirer rien de mieux, et le *Pilot* a raison lorsqu'il dit que cette réponse de Son Excellence nous permet d'anticiper que lord Elgin sera le gouverneur du peuple canadien et non celui d'un parti. Son discours s'adressait à toute la population du pays, à toutes les nuances d'opinion, et personne ne peut mettre en doute la sincérité de ses paroles.

"Il faut avouer," Cauchon concluded in Quebec on February 4, "qu'il s'annonce par de bien favorables augures."

Within a few days the Governor started to conciliate the French. Early in January 1847, he had despatched his younger brother, Colonel Robert Bruce, to deliver to Hincks an *exposé* of his views on responsible government. These must have gone far to inspire the *Pilot's* happy anticipations and encourage LaFontaine on his sickbed. Shortly after his arrival he delivered his views personally to "a very well-bred intelligent man," the great Papineau himself, whom he entertained at dinner.[10] Later, on February 8, he turned down a proposal

[10]Elgin to Lady Elgin, as quoted in J. L. Morison, *The Eighth Earl of Elgin, A Chapter in Nineteenth Century Imperial History* (London, 1928), p. 89.

by Draper to dismiss Caron from the speakership of the Legislative Council. Draper wanted to make that office a political one, both to consolidate his fast deteriorating position in Upper Canada and to show Lower Canadians that their alliance with Baldwin "in no way favours them politically or personally."[11] But Elgin refused to revoke Caron's commission, precisely on the grounds that it would make him seem unfriendly to the French and, in his own words, "a partizan Governor, at the head of a British Anti Gallic party—a Position alike repugnant to my Principles & inconsistent with my Professions."[12]

Elgin first tried to conciliate the French by offering them more seats in his Council. He did not, however, summon their party leader; instead he tried, as Draper had before him, to bring in a number of influential politicians "as individuals." Was this because his views on responsible government obliged him to support the cabinet he found in power? However tenuous its hold, it had not lost its majority in the Assembly, and he had no constitutional reason to call in LaFontaine or anyone else. Or was it because he misunderstood the Canadian situation? He claimed to Lord Grey that bringing the French leaders in as representatives of their race would hurt national unity. Too new in Canada to know better, he may have made the same mistake as Durham who had seen "two nations warring in the bosom of a single state" instead of two political parties fighting for or against reform. In 1847, Lord Elgin, no more able to see through the nationalist overtones of LaFontaine's party propaganda, may have seen a French and an English party instead of a party for and a party against responsible government. In fact most of the French Canadians did belong to one party, but their allegiance to it was political rather than national, and they stood united mostly because of the continuing efforts of LaFontaine, Morin, Hincks, Duvernay, and Cauchon. Elgin apparently thought the division was a national one, and so to achieve national unity he felt he must split the French along political lines. "I believe," he wrote to Grey, "that the problem of how to govern United Canada would be solved if the French w^d split into a Liberal & Conservative Party and join the Upper Canadian Parties."[13] Had he been successful, he might or might not have achieved national unity, but he certainly would have routed LaFontaine's forces, and, perhaps, unwittingly delayed his own policy of responsible government.

[11]Sir A. G. Doughty, ed., *The Elgin-Grey Papers* (Ottawa, 1937), I, 15, Elgin to Grey, Feb. 10, 1847.
[12]*Ibid.*, I, 17, Elgin to Grey, Feb. 10, 1847.
[13]*Ibid.*, I, 20, Elgin to Grey, March 27, 1847.

On February 23 the Governor sent his brother on another mission, this time to Morin's residence with a secret memorandum stating his sincere wish that "the interests & feelings of that important Section of the inhabitants, which is of French Origin, should meet with the fullest attention, & consideration," and asking "to have the means of including in his Executive Council, Some of those Gentlemen, who enjoy in a high degree their Esteem & confidence."[14] Four days later Morin returned it. In words which echoed both his own rejection of the "O'Connell-tail system" five years before and LaFontaine's basic doctrine that the *Canadiens* should form a political and not a national party, he refused politely while underscoring his attachment to British institutions: "L'idée d'un Conseil Exécutif où ne régneraient pas une parfaite confiance et une entière unité de Sentimens et d'action, Serait Contraire à celle d'un Gouvernement fondé Sur l'opinion publique, présentant dans sa marche toute l'harmonie et la force que donne cette opinion, et calqué ainsi Sur les bases mêmes d'institutions . . . auxquelles nous Sommes fermement attachés."[15] Disappointed, Elgin decided to try elsewhere. Indeed, he suspected that despite his request that he "bring it under the Consideration of his friends," Morin had not mentioned the offer to the *Québecois*. Accordingly, he sent for Etienne-Pascal Taché on March 11, and showed him the memorandum. Taché seemed unimpressed, declaring (with a mental reservation at least) "that he had not found among his Countrymen any disposition to enter into an alliance with the Existing Ministry—that they Seemed to expect there would Soon be a break up of the administration, after which they would have it all their own way, & that with this idea in their heads they were So 'exaltés' that he did not consider it prudent to put my memorandum into their hands."[16] But Taché had exaggerated. On the same day, Denis-Benjamin Papineau, accompanied by, of all people, Etienne Parent, was on his way to Quebec to tell Caron of the Governor's offer and to tempt him with the chief justiceship of Montreal as a reward for securing some *Québecois* for the Council. When Caron heard of the Governor's offer and of Morin's answer, he was furious. He castigated the "intolerable tyranny" of the Montreal leaders, prompting Elgin to comment that "the Quebec French seem very indignant with their friends here for rejecting my proposals without taking any measures to ascertain their views."[17]

[14]*Ibid.*, I, 19, Elgin to Grey, Feb. 23, 1847.
[15]*Ibid.*, I, 22, Morin à Elgin, 27 fév. 1847.
[16]*Ibid.*, I, 23, Elgin to Grey, March 27, 1847.
[17]*Ibid.*, I, 20, Elgin to Grey, March 27, 1847.

Meanwhile "many false rumours" had spread to the streets. Indeed, as Draper informed the Governor, "they, (meaning the Canadian Party, & their Upper Canada ally Mr Hincks) are getting very uneasy. They fully Expected that they would have been Sent for by Lord Elgin . . . and they now begin to doubt whether they have any present chance."[18] Many were accusing Morin of refusing again merely because LaFontaine had not been asked. "Pour nous," corrected Duvernay on March 29, "nous exprimons notre intime conviction en disant que l'offre faite à M. Morin paraît absolument identique avec les deux précédentes; que sa réponse a dû être de même conforme à celles d'alors." Hincks wrote in a panic to Baldwin about LaFontaine's followers: "His country-men are panting for office, and it is difficult to keep them in temper."[19] Aylwin noted impatiently to LaFontaine: "Le pays ne comprend pas nos abstractions, questions de forme, etc. Il ne verra que le fait patent de votre refus et que le temps arrive où la réaction se fera sentir si vous ne consentez pas à prendre les rennes";[20] and he repeated the same to Morin:

Néanmoins vous ne pouvez que voir l'ingratitude se montrer au grand jour, et que des misérables osent critiquer un homme qu'ils ne comprennent pas. On dit "Que LaFontaine et Morin ne croient pas que le pays puisse marcher sans eux"! Une bête . . . l'écrira dans son journal et cent autres le répéteront. Ils [sic] est bien vrai que sans vous il ne se fera pas et ne peut se faire rien de bon ni de solide dans les affaires publiques, "and fools walk in where angels fear to tread". . . . Je crois que vous avez eu tort de refuser les offres du gouverneur. Vous auriez du passer outre si ce que D B Papineau et Parent ont dit ici est vrai.[21]

Thus, instead of winning over the French as a nation, the Governor seemed on the verge of breaking them as a party. Caron appeared to be about to accept even less than double majority. On April 1 Denis-Benjamin Papineau pressed him once again to accept the presidency of the Council, threatening him with the loss of the speakership if he did not. Harassed, the poor man prepared immediately to leave for Montreal and start bargaining. But he ran into Aylwin and "l'ami Morin" who had hurried down to Quebec to intercede. As LaFontaine wrote to Cauchon, the melancholy Morin was upset again by the Governor's offer and by the attitude of the Québecois. "Morin comme vous savez est très impressionnable, et fut jeté dans un état d'excitation

18*Ibid.*, I, 18, Draper to Elgin, Feb. 14, 1847.
19Baldwin Papers, v51, Hincks to Baldwin, March 25, 1847.
20Papiers LaFontaine, Aylwin à LaFontaine, 5 avril 1847.
21PAC, MG 24, B 54, Correspondance Chauveau, Aylwin à Morin, 26 mars 1847.

assez vive. . . . Je vous assure qu'il est profondément affligé et dans un
état fébrile. Je vous conjure de le traiter amicablement [sic]."²² Upset
or not, Morin apparently recalled Caron to reality, and on April 5
Aylwin reported happily to LaFontaine:

Caron est parti ce matin après avoir vu Morin. . . . Je sais qu'il demandera
des explications, et que dans le cas où le gouverneur fasse offre du système
des deux majorités, sans indemnité, ni tour de baton, aux ministres sortans,
il lui dira que la chose est possible et fesable, mais que quant à lui il ne
peut l'entreprendre. . . . S'il lui est permis de suggérer il recommandera
un appel de nouveau au parti libéral. Je crois sincèrement que Caron veut
faire quelque chose de bon, et qu'il désire votre rappel au pouvoir.²³

Caron had been awakened from his dream that double majority was
possible or that Draper really intended to offer it. Besides, on arriving
in Montreal, the Speaker was snubbed. He was received not by Denis-
Benjamin Papineau who had invited him, nor by his old friend and
enemy, Draper, nor by the Governor General who had personally
interviewed Morin and Taché. Instead he found himself ushered in
to see the Inspector General, William Cayley, who had prepared
terms, as LaFontaine later wrote to Baldwin, "with a precaution and
cunningness such as to make the proposals appeal to the eyes of the
Mass of the people, particularly in the District of Quebec, as being
equivalent to the adoption, practice, of the system of the double
majority and calculated to create, in that District . . . a great excitement
against us."²⁴

On his guard, Caron consulted Morin. Morin called in Leslie,
DeWitt, Nelson, Drummond, Hincks, and others. They decided that
Cayley's terms were unacceptable, but that Caron should have the
responsibility of refusing. Caron therefore returned to Quebec to
summon a meeting of his own. As it opened, the quick-witted Cauchon
who was chairman asked pointedly whether all those attending
belonged to the same party. Caron (probably recalling the columns
of slander printed against him the previous year in Cauchon's paper)
answered, yes. And from then on, the division between the two
districts was healed. Caron even wrote to LaFontaine apologizing for
his part in the dispute over the publication of the Draper-Caron
correspondence two years before. And Drummond commented that
"la double majorité, ce monstre à deux figures dont l'un regarde le
passé et l'autre l'avenir," had been buried forever. Draper's ruses

²²Ibid., Drummond à Chauveau, 19 avril 1847.
²³Papiers LaFontaine, Aylwin à LaFontaine, 5 avril 1847.
²⁴Baldwin Papers, A 55, LaFontaine to Baldwin, April 11, 1847.

had had "l'heureux effet de nous réunir tous comme autrefois dans une phalange invincible."[25]

Once again LaFontaine, fiercely independent, sharp-willed, uncompromising, had carried his party, this time more easily than the last. With the help of Taché, Morin, and Cauchon, he had not only maintained its outward unity, but healed its internal wounds. However, he had also been shaken from his dream rehearsals of the magic summons to Government House. Victory, he realized, would come only when constitutionally proper. LaFontaine had come to see that the Governor had acted in perfect accord with LaFontaine's own principles of responsible government throughout the negotiations. If he had almost split the party, his intentions had been of the highest. "There appears to be a genuine disposition," Lord Elgin wrote with satisfaction, "to give me credit for acting constitutionally, notwithstanding the support I have given to my Ministers, and the severe censures passed upon them."[26] In fact, at the height of the discussion on March 16, La Revue Canadienne printed a translation of a speech given by Lord Elgin, then Lord Bruce, in 1841, approving Durham's recommendation of responsible government. At the same time on March 29 La Minerve wrote a paragraph which contrasted sharply with its articles about Metcalfe and concluded: "Nous exonérons entièrement de blâme le noble personnage qui est à la tête du gouvernement."

Lord Elgin had at least persuaded the Canadiens of his goodwill. And he himself had learned that he must wait to bring the French into office, not as individuals who would represent la nation canadienne, but as political leaders whom the Canadiens themselves had chosen. Meanwhile he would practise responsible government. "My course in these circumstances," he wrote to Lord Grey, "is I think clear & plain. . . . I give to my Ministers all constitutional support frankly and without reserve, & the benefit of the best advice, such as it is, that I can afford them in their difficulties."[27]

"My Ministers," tired and increasingly out of touch, were fast losing support in Upper Canada as well. Having failed to split the French in the lower section, they set themselves to reshuffle as best they could the chairs around the council table. On April 22, 1847, James Smith left to go to the Court of Queen's Bench. He had been a minister as long as Denis-Benjamin Papineau and had done much

---

[25]Correspondance Chauveau, Drummond à Chauveau, 19 avril 1847.
[26]Doughty, ed., Elgin-Grey Papers, I, 50, Elgin to Grey, June 13, 1847.
[27]Ibid., I, 46, Elgin to Grey, May 27, 1847.

less. Taschereau also resigned, a disappointed man now that *la réaction* which his election had symbolized had led nowhere. He was angry, also, at being passed over as attorney general. "Dans les circonstances," wrote *La Minerve* on April 29, "cette résignation fait honneur à M. Taschereau." A few days later he accepted a judgeship, and Duvernay changed his tone on May 6: "La conduite de M. Taschereau rappelle celle de ce saint homme de rat de la fable qui s'était *retiré du monde* en se logeant bien commodément dans une meule de fromage. M. Taschereau a *résigné* sa place de solliciteur-général pour accepter celle de juge! ce qui n'est pas trop mal viser."

On May 28 Draper himself left the Council whose main ornament he had been; and four days earlier Caron had been told that the speakership would henceforth be political and that he too must go. To replace them the ultimate parade of Tory pensioners appeared, making a state appearance positively for the last time. William Badgley took Smith's place as Attorney General for Lower Canada; his counterpart for the upper section of the province was Henry Sherwood, curly-haired, assertive, learned in constitutional practice, and boasting the bluest loyalist blood in Upper Canada. Peter McGill, president of the Bank of Montreal in the Château Clique's heyday and mayor of Montreal in Sydenham's, became speaker of the Legislative Council. Denis-Benjamin Papineau, despite himself, remained; so did "l'immuable M. Daly" and William Cayley. Hence, as far as the *Canadiens* were concerned, the government included only Denis-Benjamin Papineau, the bruised leader of a very lonely little group.

Lord Elgin opened parliament on June 2 and launched a dull, uninteresting session. The Executive Councillors (*La Minerve*, June 16) "sont dans un état à exciter la compassion. Ils sont mornes, taciturnes, on dirait qu'ils redoutent quelque grande calamité. M. Daly surtout paraît plus mort que vif." For the next six weeks they hardly dared raise one debatable point while, on their side, the *Canadiens* did not bother to offer any serious challenge. LaFontaine had not yet recovered his health; also, he no longer needed the headlines. He knew his party was united behind him and that responsible government was only a question of time. The old autocratic years of Canada's story were coming to an end, not with a bang but a whimper.

As the summer crept by people were concerned with more vital things than politics. Business affairs, wrote E.-R. Fabre, "sont bien mauvaises ici."[28] Commerce, the timber trade, and agriculture were all in serious recession. During June the temperature rose to intolerable

28Papiers Fabre, Fabre à H. Bossange, 28 juin 1847.

heights, and three people died of heat in the streets of Montreal. More anxious still were the long sick lists, and the daily chronicle of death. "L'année 1847," mused Duvernay on January 3, 1848, "sera nommée dans notre histoire, l'année de l'émigration. Prés de cent mille malheureux, ont quitté l'Irlande pour venir chercher du pain sur le rivage du St. Laurent; pour comble de malheur, la fièvre les a décimés." "La fièvre" was the dreaded typhus. Before autumn, 13,000 Irish immigrants (1100 in Quebec and 3800 in Montreal alone) would die of it, and thousands of the native population be infected. The newspapers in Quebec and in Montreal listed new deaths in each issue. In the week of August 10, for example, Monsignor Hudon, "one of the most eminent men in the Canadian Church,"[29] died, Bishop Bourget was sent, gravely ill, to the Hôtel-Dieu, and the curé of Notre-Dame blessed one hundred and sixty-five graves in the parish cemetery. The politicians left Montreal, LaFontaine travelling to Rhode Island for his health, and the others to their ridings for politics. Denis-Benjamin Papineau resigned with little fanfare on July 29 and went home to his estate at Petite-Nation.

When the members returned in late autumn they brought rumours of a general election. In fact the government could not stand the humiliation of another session. "L'opposition libérale," commented La Revue Canadienne on November 9, "qui représente fidèlement les intérêts et les besoins de la majorité du peuple canadien, poursuit sans relâche depuis quatre ans la réalisation sincère et sérieuse de la vérité du gouvernement responsable. Le moment est favorable pour organiser une agitation sage, modérée, énergique. Le ministère actuel a bravé, dédaigné, révolté le bon sens du peuple canadien." After some weeks of agonizing indecision, of "struggling for existence—Catching at straws—living from hand to mouth,"[30] they advised a dissolution. On December 6, 1847, the Governor proclaimed the election, with writs to be returned on January 24, 1848.

The election was the calmest of the decade in Lower Canada, and, of course, a triumph for LaFontaine. For one thing, he had no serious challenger and for another, there was no pressure from Government House. La Minerve reported on December 16 that "les nouvelles les plus rassurantes" came in from all political quarters. On December 21 Aylwin and his running mate, Jean Chabot, carried Quebec with a large majority and by January 10 some twenty-one seats had already gone to LaFontaine. The party leader himself, running in Montreal

[29]Doughty, ed., Elgin-Grey Papers, I, 65, Elgin to Grey, Aug. 13, 1847.
[30]Ibid., I, 128, Elgin to Grey, March 2, 1847.

with Benjamin Holmes, carried his riding by over 1400 votes. On January 16 he wrote to Baldwin that reports from the whole province assured him "that the liberal party have now a great majority, it is beyond all doubts."[31] Even an old enemy like Colonel Gugy, elected from Sherbrooke, promised his support. Indeed, by January 24, except for some five or six irreconcilables in the English ridings, LaFontaine could count on practically every Lower Canadian member. With the Upper Canadian contingent—for Baldwin had avenged 1844 —the united Reformers could count on some fifty-four seats to the Tories' twenty odd. The election also marked the high point in the Governor's campaign to conciliate the French.

During the deadly summer of 1847 he had done more than practise responsible government; he had finally convinced the *Canadiens* of his intentions. During the dismal round of death, they had come increasingly to feel his solicitude for the sick, his concern for the healthy. They saw him risk his life in visits to the impoverished hospital sheds where he talked to everyone as if he mattered; they appreciated his sympathy at Monsignor Hudon's funeral; they were honoured when he personally led the mourning for Mayor Mills. Besides, schooled as he was in every grace, he had thoroughly charmed them. He impressed everyone with his elegant French, and with the "courtesy and attention paid to every sort of visitor."[32] In June 1847 he had marked the anniversary of the coronation by "une brillante réception . . . à Monklands" that according to the report in *La Minerve* of June 24 attracted, in pouring rain, a "foule . . . immense, au point qu'il était difficile de circuler." They had come out to be captivated by "Son Excellence en grand uniforme" and by *Madame la comtesse d'Elgin* ("On ne pouvait s'empêcher d'admirer ses manières pleines de dignité, sa pose gracieuse, et son aimable sourire"). Later, in July, at the end of the short, sad session, he entertained again, this time for the politicians, and was "successful in bringing men of all Parties together and dismissing them well pleased."[33]

In the fall Elgin sailed down to Quebec to celebrate a triumph perhaps greater than Bagot's memorable visit in 1842. "On eût dit," wrote *La Minerve* (September 27), "que la vielle capitale reprenait son rôle naturel, retrouvait son ancienne vie." He came up to the sound of cannon and under the traditional spruce arches "accompagné du maire dans la voiture à quatre chevaux aux armes de Son Excellence." The

[31]Baldwin Papers, A 55, LaFontaine to Baldwin, Jan. 16, 1848.
[32]Doughty, ed., *Elgin-Grey Papers*, I, 54, Elgin to Grey, June 28, 1847.
[33]*Ibid.*, I, 61, Elgin to Grey, July 27, 1847.

streets overflowed with joyous, cheering *Québecois* who had turned out in pouring rain. In front of the Hôtel du Payne were "the St George's and St Jean Baptiste societies turning out together for the first time and the president of the former wearing the maple leaf, the Canadian French Emblem."[34] *Leurs Excellences* appeared on the rain-drenched balcony, and, that most renowned *Québecois* of them all, John Neilson, President of the Saint Andrew's Society, read the loyal address. The Governor and the *Québecois* had adjusted to one another perfectly. "What a magnificent site for a seat of government!" Elgin exclaimed to Grey, "How wonderful that Montreal s^d ever have supplanted it!" What more gracious sentiments could he have found to win this ancient sceptred city?

Thus, by tactful interviews and brilliant receptions, Elgin persuaded the *Canadiens* that he was on their side. Thus also, when the election came in December, it was more than LaFontaine's inevitable political victory: it became a triumph for Lord Elgin. It had, of course, been called on the advice of the Council, but the *Canadiens* liked to think of Elgin as mainly responsible. On November 15, while the rumours of the impending dissolution circulated, *La Minerve* had claimed the Governor was daily pressing his councillors for a resignation which they daily refused.

Furthermore, as the results came in the *Canadiens* also realized that the Governor had left them free from the usual pressures. LaFontaine had heard "that Major Campbell [Lord Elgin's secretary], in reply to an observation made to him as to the great influence which a Governor may exercise in our elections, had stated that Lord Elgin had expressed himself on the subject that, not only he would take no part in elections, but would take good care that the elections should be free from gov't influence."[35] As the election progressed, the *Canadiens* increasingly sang his praises. On January 15, when LaFontaine and Holmes were proclaimed in Place d'Armes in Montreal before "une foule très nombreuse," the old rebel, Dr. Wolfred Nelson, called for "trois cheers pour la Reine qui furent poussés avec un vif enthousiasme," and George-Etienne Cartier (himself soon to be returned from Ver-chères) ended his speech by proposing "trois hourras en honneur de Son Excellence le Gouverneur-Général."

Lord Elgin and the *Canadiens* now understood each other. The election over, parliament was summoned for February 25. The Governor General had reached the constitutional position from which he

[34]*Ibid.*, I, 69–70, Elgin to Grey, Sept. 27, 1847.
[35]Baldwin Papers, A 55, LaFontaine to Baldwin, May 13, 1847.

could bring in the French as a political party and, as he put it, commit to their trust "the flag of Britain." During the election, he had seen "on their part a desire to prove . . . that they were libelled when they were accused of impracticability and antimonarchical tendencies."[36] And he had also come to understand that he and LaFontaine, although perhaps speaking different words, both thought the same thoughts, both saw the same vision. The *Canadien* leader fought for responsible government because he saw it as the best guarantee of his people's survival as a nation. He knew that, if successful, he would save the British connection as well. On his part, the Governor General, who as a colonial reformer yearned to save the British empire by means of responsible government, gradually realized that, if he succeeded, he would be assuring *la survivance*. In the short year since his arrival in Canada Lord Elgin had learned the lesson of "the last cannon shot" well. As he wrote to Lord Grey,

I must confess . . . that I for one am deeply convinced of the impolicy of all such attempts to denationalize the French. Generally speaking they produce the opposite effect from that intended, causing the flame of national prejudice and animosity to burn more fiercely—But suppose them to be successful what w^d be the result? You may perhaps *americanise*, but, depend upon it, by methods of this description, you will never *anglicise* the French inhabitants of the Province.—.Let them feel on the other hand that their religion, their habits, their preposessions, their prejudices if you will, are more considered and respected here than in other portions of this vast continent . . . and who will venture to say that the last hand which waves the British flag on American ground may not be that of a French Canadian?[37]

Now with the election over, he could send for LaFontaine and for Baldwin, speak to them "in a candid and friendly tone," and tell them "that they might count on all proper support and assistance from me."[38]

For LaFontaine, this was the golden moment, the victory. A few weeks later at a party caucus, he asked his victorious followers for their choice of a speaker for the Assembly and rejoiced to hear their universal shout: "Morin! Morin!" Then a few minutes later, he at last conducted his loyal lieutenant of ten years to the chair. Later, at the beginning of March 1848, he was summoned to form, along with Robert Baldwin ("the man whom I always considered one of my

[36]Doughty, ed., *Elgin-Grey Papers*, I, 135, Elgin to Grey, March 17, 1848.
[37]*Ibid.*, I, 149, Elgin to Grey, March 4, 1848.
[38]*Ibid.*, I, 135, Elgin to Grey, March 17, 1848.

happiest days to have become acquainted with"[39]), the first Canadian administration based on the principle of responsible government. He had dreamed the impossible dream, and now at last he saw his people "devenus par les traités sujets anglais . . . traités comme tels." He had fought the unbeatable foe, outwitted Sydenham, conquered Metcalfe, destroyed Viger, persuaded Caron. He had exasperated many, even his closest friends. He had kept secrets, manœuvred in silence, and, refusing explanations, demanded obedience. Perhaps, at times, he had been hurt by his compatriots' distrust. Yet he had never stopped dreaming and fighting. He could not be loved, but how difficult he made it for those who would not admire him.

Among the Canadiens, there was none of the spontaneous overflow of joy that marked LaFontaine's earlier victory in the Union debate. This election had been quiet, the victory subdued. There were no Te Deums, no popular meetings, no loyal addresses. For this time triumph did not come quickly in the golden days of autumn. Now death was knocking on every door, and the papers still published lists of the dead rather than political news. The French-Canadian politicians, no longer young, had lost their first enthusiasm. They were weary of their five-year struggle, of the two general elections, of three serious assaults against their unity, of slander, of duels, of oratorical contests.

Yet, whether they marked the day or not, the Canadiens, having accepted the Union and won responsible government, had saved "notre langue, nos institutions, et nos droits." In so doing, they had consecrated the banner of Saint George flying over Quebec's ancient citadel. Soon they would be foremost among its defenders.

[39]Baldwin Papers, A 55, LaFontaine to Baldwin, Sept. 25, 1846.

PART THREE

The Crises over Repeal and Annexation 1848-1850

15

Les Eléments de la crise

On April 19, 1848, Louis-Joseph Papineau wrote to his old friend, Dr. E. B. O'Callaghan. All during October, with the arrival of each new steamer from Europe, he had been rejoicing in the news of how those whom he considered kindred spirits had lit the spark of liberty. In every great capital from Paris to Budapest, they had fought a dozen revolutions and toppled as many crowns, and the lightning from their storm had illumined the world. But as he looked at his own country in the new light, Papineau found little to encourage him. "Tout est gloire, bonheur, progrès dans le reste du monde entier," he wrote. "Tout est bassesse, oppression, mouvement retrograde dans la société canadienne."[1] For in Canada he was living through years of disaster and misery. He was disgusted by the politics and the patronage, repelled by the power of the priests. Especially, he suffered at being forced to witness his people's final commitment to the British connection.

LaFontaine also found these difficult years, times when, as Morin noted, "les mauvaises passions et le mépris des lois en général vont leur chemin . . . le retentissement du socialisme en France, l'écho des idées de liberté illimitée qui se propagent en Angleterre."[2] Yet they were also years of solid, lasting achievement. On March 19, 1847, *La Revue Canadienne* noted how "nous touchons à l'époque la plus importante de notre existence coloniale. Après des jours de misère, de servage et d'inaction, les colonies anglaises sont appelées véritablement à prendre part au bienfait du gouvernement représentatif. Le vieux régime tombe et croule sous les coups de liberté constitutionnelle." And although the "jours de misère" continued until the early 1850's, LaFontaine and his agents did succeed in putting the crowning touches to their decade's work: they not only initiated the French

[1] Collection Papineau-Bourassa, 548, L.-J. Papineau à O'Callaghan, 19 avril 1848.
[2] Papiers LaFontaine, Morin à LaFontaine, 9 mars 1850.

Canadians into the responsibilities of self-rule, they gave proof to the world of how richly they deserved it.

THE DEPRESSION

Occupied and thrilled as they were by the new challenge, the French politicians could not avoid the misery all about them, the agitation, the depression. The *Canadiens* felt disturbed and insecure. The plague continued a constant threat each summer until 1851. No wonder that the city dwellers left *en masse* for the clean air of the country, or that some 2000 *Québecois* rioted in July 1849 when they heard that the customs building in the port was to be turned into a refuge for cholera victims. The *Canadiens* also heard menacing sounds from across the border. One day it was that those visionary lunatics called Young Irelanders were infiltrating key posts in Montreal; and another, "that 50,000 Irish were ready to march into Canada from the States at a moment's notice";[3] or later, that in Boston the Irish Republican Union had been formed "to raise men & money for the invasion of the Canadas—Already 5000 men have joined headed by men of education and property . . . Similar proceedings are going forward in New York 15000 having subscribed the rules in a few days."[4] If these were only rumours, some facts about the Irish the French knew for certain.

For one thing, the sickly but quarrelsome immigrants had definitely brought with them to North America the problems of Ireland. For another, 1848 was a quadrennial year in the United States: "the Presidential contest is going on & no party can afford to lose the Irish ticket."[5] In Montreal the government made plans to raise two regiments of volunteers (one French, one English) to garrison the capital while the regular army went to the border. And societies founded to agitate for repeal of the Irish union held meetings as *La Minerve* reported on May 4, 1848, "pour fins hostiles au gouvernement" or gathered, 2000–3000 strong, to stir up public attention. In the end, the French passed through the crisis "without explosions" (as Lord Elgin put it),[6] but what with disease and turmoil, the Irish had certainly added much to the *Canadiens'* share of disaster and misery.

Nor would the depression lift. Although the doctrine of free trade

[3]Doughty, ed., *Elgin-Grey Papers*, I, 209, Elgin to Grey, July 18, 1848.
[4]*Ibid.*, I, 281, Elgin to Grey, Dec. 26, 1848.
[5]*Ibid.*, I, 224, Elgin to Grey, Aug. 16, 1848.
[6]Elgin to Grey, May 4, 1848, as quoted in C. Martin, *Empire and Commonwealth* (Oxford, 1929), pp. 312–13.

had allowed the British statesmen to reconcile colonial independence with imperial dominion, it had loosened the bonds of the economic order that gave Canada its prosperity. And particularly since 1843, when the Canada Corn Act had allowed Canadian wheat and milled flour free entry into the British market, the well-being of the colonial merchants and farmers rested more than ever on British protection. Thus, with the abolition of the corn laws in 1846, an unparalleled financial failure in milling followed. And the end of the British railway boom in 1846 brought abysmal losses for the timber merchants whose investments had been based on the all-time highs of the previous years. "Stanley's Bill of 1843," Lord Elgin explained to the Colonial Secretary,

attracted all the Produce of the West to the St Lawrence, and fixed all the disposable capital of the Province in Grinding mills, Warehouses, and forwarding establishments—Peel's Bill of 1846 drives the whole of this Produce down the New York channels of communication, destroying the Revenue which Canada expected to derive from Canal dues, & ruining at once Mill owners, Forwarders, & Merchants. The consequence is that Private Property is unsaleable in Canada, and not a shilling can be raised on the credit of the Province. We are actually reduced to the disagreeable necessity of paying all Public officers, from the Govr Genl downwards, in debentures, which are not exchangeable at par.[7]

Because they lived almost entirely on what their own farms produced, the habitants were not as gravely stricken by the repeal of the corn laws as were their opposite numbers in the upper section of the province. Still, they suffered heavy privations, and they had to face another succession of bad crops, due in great part, as *La Minerve* noted on December 11, 1849, "au manque de connaissances pratiques parmi les cultivateurs canadiens-français et leur peu d'entreprise." The *Canadiens* in the Quebec district also shared in the collapse of the timber trade. For the merchants there ceased to invest and began to collect their credit. In Montreal, always in a most vulnerable economic position, the businessmen who counted on the St. Lawrence carrying trade declared bankruptcy one after another, and "property in most of the Canadian towns, and more especially in the Capital has fallen 50 pc^t in value within the last three Years."[8] Inevitably the professional people and farmers shared in the misery.

"Les affaires sont bien mauvaises ici et l'argent rare," E.-R. Fabre had written earlier in June 1847,[9] thus beginning a refrain that would

[7]Doughty, ed., *Elgin-Grey Papers*, I, 256, Elgin to Grey, Nov. 16, 1848.
[8]*Ibid.*, I, 349, Elgin to Grey, April 23, 1849.
[9]Papiers Fabre, Fabre à H. Bossange, 23 juin 1847.

continue for four years, and be picked up on February 19, 1849, by Duvernay—"Jamais les affaires n'ont été aussi stagnantes que cette année . . . tout est arrêté comme au temps des épidémies"—and by young François-Xavier Garneau who wrote to Dr. O'Callaghan in May: "Malgré le retour de la belle saison, les affaires ont beaucoup de peine à reprendre. Le commerce est presque nul à l'heure qu'il est; et le Seigneur choléra qu'on attend d'un jour à l'autre laisse peu d'espoir de le voir reprendre une grande activité. Cette année sera donc en toute probabilité encore fort chétive."[10] In October 1849 Fabre described how, despondent and discouraged, "les Canadiens émigrent par milliers, la population de Montréal est diminuée de 8 à 10,000 âmes depuis 2 ans."[11] They were tempted by the stories they heard of the wealth of California. And by January 1850 Fabre wondered whether he should not go himself:

Il en est parti un grand nombre pour la Californie tant de la ville que de la campagne; les affaires ici sont si mortes que réellement c'est alarmant. Nos demandes cette année ne seront presque rien, notre fonds est encore si con-sidérable: nos ventes ont été moitié moins cette année que l'année dernière et l'année dernière un bon tiers moins que l'année d'avant; si ça continue il nous faudra aussi gagner la Californie.[12]

To solve this situation, the new Council, sworn in on March 11, 1848, commissioned the Inspector General, Francis Hincks. And with his noted efficiency, he set himself to the unenviable task. First, he forwarded to the Colonial Office a deluge of petitions, addresses, and memorials demanding the repeal of the Navigation Laws by which Canadians were forced to receive only British manufactured goods and load their own produce on British vessels alone. Then, in mid-June he organized a monster meeting of some 2000 Montrealers who listened to Morin, Cartier, and George Moffatt explain the benefits Canada would reap by opening its ports to the shipping of other nations. In 1847 he had been gratified by a temporary suspension of the restric-tive regulations, and, in June 1849 he witnessed their final repeal. Secondly, he began to work on public opinion at home, and, through William Hamilton Merritt, on officials of the American government, to enter into negotiations for a reciprocity treaty. The treaty did not come about until 1854, but it finally did allow Canadian merchants and businessmen to share the profits of the American railway and settlement boom. Thirdly, Hincks spent himself in encouraging a policy of railroad development at home which would bring into the

[10]O'Callaghan Papers, Garneau à O'Callaghan, 9 mai 1849.
[11]Papiers Fabre, Fabre à H. Bossange, 1 oct. 1849.
[12]Ibid., Fabre à Julie Bossange, 19 jan. 1850.

colony the capital to convert it from a minor, staple-producing area into an integrated "metropolitan" area. Thus with the same adroitness which had won him so many elections, Hincks worked to transform his diseased and depressed country into a prosperous land suffused with national pride.

RESPONSIBLE GOVERNMENT AND PATRONAGE

While Hincks worked at solving the deep economic wounds of the colony, LaFontaine took charge of Lower Canadian politics. He found much to be done, for, except in the sphere of education, most of the reforms which he had begun in the municipal system, in land settlement, and in the judiciary had remained as he had left them at the time of *la crise Metcalfe*. And in addition to these he intended other reforms in the electoral laws and the registries, as well as a reorganization of the Lower Canadian courts. Between 1848 and 1851 he worked steadily at these projects, and by filling the hundreds of posts he thus created, he provided at last the outlet which the *Canadien* professional class had been struggling to secure for the last two generations. As leader of the French group in the united Reform party, however, his first responsibility was to organize his section of the Council.

"La tâche . . . sera difficile, laborieuse et probablement ingrate," *Le Canadien* warned him on January 28, 1848, and Aylwin reiterated from Quebec: "Il y aura beaucoup de manigances à apporter pour ne pas blesser l'amour propre des uns ni les intérêts des autres."[13] Discussing the candidates with Baldwin, LaFontaine narrowed down "those who are desired by themselves and others . . . whom I think likely to feel disappointment at not finding themselves the subjects of consideration" to some ten or eleven: Morin, Cauchon, Holmes, Aylwin, Chabot, Chauveau, Drummond, Leslie, Caron, and Louis-Michel Viger. Among these, he gave first recognition to those who had held office with him in 1842. Thus he returned to Caron his office as president of the Legislative Council and to Aylwin his post as solicitor general. But he could not persuade Morin to return to the Crown lands. "Morin desires to be made nothing else but Speaker," he told Baldwin. "He pleads his ill health, his incapacity to use his right hand in writing [arthritis], and the want of rest during a great portion of the year."[14] So at the party caucus on the day before the opening, he arranged for his old friend's election. But as the assembled members

[13]Papiers LaFontaine, Aylwin à LaFontaine, 12 fév. 1848.
[14]Baldwin Papers, A 55, LaFontaine to Baldwin, Feb. 2, 1848.

cheered Morin, LaFontaine noticed Louis-Joseph Papineau walk swiftly out of the room. The great man, returned for Saint-Maurice, had apparently been expecting the chair he had occupied so conspicuously for twenty years before the rebellion. Here was one enemy reconfirmed.

Since Morin refused it, LaFontaine let Baldwin have the Crown lands for an Upper Canadian. In return he accepted the commissionership of public works which he gave to Taché. But in doing so he created another enemy, for Chauveau had expected to be chosen as representative of the French electors of the Quebec district. When he heard of Taché's appointment, Chauveau threatened to resign his seat and made such a scene that LaFontaine's friends had to stay up for twenty-four hours pleading with him not to make a fool of himself. To sit for the commercial community, LaFontaine selected as receiver general Louis-Michel Viger, the rich president of the Banque du Peuple whom Papineau called "mon frère d'âme" but who had remained uncommitted to his cousins' interpretation of *la crise Metcalfe* and had lived in retirement from politics on his seigneury at L'Assomption, where, as *Le Canadien* put it on April 17, 1848, "les charmes de son manoir et son immense fortune avaient réuni tant de molles jouissances." To James Leslie, who had been a faithful lieutenant for years, he gave the presidency of the Executive Council with, at the same time, a life appointment to the Legislative Council. Thus he opened up Verchères riding for another worthy lieutenant, George-Etienne Cartier, though he disappointed a powerful friend, Benjamin Holmes, who had expected to be the one chosen to speak for the Montreal merchants. In any event, by March 1848, LaFontaine had finished his first task.

But not quite. Baldwin who had had similar difficulties for the western section had not been so successful. He could not find a place for William Hume Blake whom he considered essential. LaFontaine dropped a hint to Aylwin, but the Solicitor General (East) refused to take it. As two solicitors general could not hold a seat in the Council, there remained only the solution offered by Hincks: "If Aylwin were to go to the Bench, I think it would remove the difficulty with Blake."[15] Accordingly, on April 20, 1848, *La Minerve* announced Aylwin's appointment as a judge of the Court of Queen's Bench, and a few days later, Blake's accession to the solicitor generalship (West). As Lower Canadian solicitor general, but without a seat at the Council, LaFontaine chose Drummond, thus happily rewarding another col-

[15]Papiers LaFontaine, Hincks to LaFontaine, April 13, 1848.

league. Aylwin blessed the day, writing to LaFontaine: "Je m'estime heureux, trois fois heureux d'être sorti de la vie politique. C'est de vous que je tiens ce bonheur, et je vous en serai toujours reconnaissant, ainsi que de la confiance et de l'amitié que vous m'avez toujours témoignées par le passé."[16] But the *Québecois* were furious. Cauchon wrote, "La population de nos faubourgs, si bien disposée d'ordinaire est irritée contre Aylwin."[17] And, indeed, *Le Canadien* complained on April 26 that the appointment deprived the citizens of the old capital "d'un de leurs plus illustres appuis." Besides, the paper remarked on April 21: "Nous protestons . . . contre la coutume qui devient un abus criant, de tirer presque tous les hauts fonctionnaires du sein même du corps qui les nomme." LaFontaine must have realized, however, that the complaints would cease in proportion to the largesse he distributed. And for years he spent hours every day, as he had in 1842, selecting from among the endless stream of favour-seekers a long list of judges, Queen's counsels, justices of the peace, medical examiners, school inspectors, militia captains, postal clerks, mail conductors, census commissioners, and so on.

After Aylwin became a judge LaFontaine distributed patronage in the Quebec district according to the advice he received from Caron and Cauchon. Through the first he could hold those who had sympathized with *la réaction*; through the second he could reward the faithful. And from both he received a constant flow of supplications for appointments to everything from coroners in back seigneuries to clerkships in customs houses. Caron made recommendations indiscriminately. Cauchon, however, was politician enough to have worked out priorities. First, he considered appointments should either reward or serve to encourage friends who had worked for the party. In December 1848, for instance, he opposed a nominee to a judgeship in Saguenay district: "Si vous faites cette nomination vous allez indubitablement décourager et attiédir ceux qui ont travaillé sincèrement et activement pour la cause. . . . J'ai exprès sans faire semblant de rien sondé l'opinion des travailleurs et des hommes de profession. La suggestion seule leur a fait jeter des hauts cris." Secondly, he thought some jobs should go to friends when their allegiance began to waver. "Les vrais amis," he explained to Taché on Christmas day 1849, "les amis de la bonne souche n'ont pas besoin de surveillance ni de bons offices, quoique cela ne leur fait [sic] pas de mal; mais les autres ont besoin de petits soins que vous négligez suivant moi." Thirdly, he

---

[16]*Ibid.*, Aylwin à LaFontaine, 1 juin 1848.
[17]*Ibid.*, Cauchon à LaFontaine, 24 avril 1848.

preferred French Canadians. In November 1850, when there was question of making one H. Gowan a member of a road inspection commission in Quebec, Cauchon insisted to Taché: "J'ai répondu à LaFontaine qu'il fallait tâcher d'infiltrer dans cette commission comme partout ailleurs un peu d'influence française, de cette influence exclue jusqu'ici. . . . Si nous n'amassons pas nous-même pour les mauvaises années, nos ennemis le feront-ils pour nous?" Finally, he thought appointments should go to those who had useful connections: "M. le Grand-Vicaire Cazeau me parle de son frère qui est au bureau de poste avec un salaire de £.90. Il ne demande pas une augmentation de salaire; mais comme il est obligé de remuer des ballots . . . cela le rend extrèmement malade. Si donc il était transporté aux douanes avec un salaire du même calibre on vous en aurait une obligation marquée."[18]

From Montreal, LaFontaine heard the same refrain from Drummond. Indeed, sometimes he heard it by telegraph in code. Because he was often in a hurry, Drummond explained in December 1849, he thought it best to "établir une correspondance par voie de télégraphe." "Pour mettre ce plan à éxécution, j'ai mis toutes les lettres de l'alphabet dans un chapeau et après les avoir mêlées je les ai tirées au hazard mettant devant chacune lettre de l'alphabet en usage celle qui doit la représenter dans notre alphabet de convention. Cet alphabet ayant été formé par le hazard ne pourra jamais devenir intelligible à d'autres." Code or not, the messages insisted on the same things, clerkships, magistracies, court reporters. And, like Cauchon, Drummond set priorities; appointments should go, first to "des fermes appuis du ministère actuel," and, secondly, they should be made without mixing nationalities. "Autant que possible," he wrote, "on doit éviter de nommer des Canadiens dans les comtés Anglais, et des Anglais dans des Comtés Canadiens." He thought, too, that if nominations had to go to people who did not have "des droits acquis depuis longtemps au souvenir de ceux qui contrôlent la distribution des emplois," then they should go to the lesser of the two enemies. Thus he opposed the granting of a judgeship to Joseph-André Taschereau who had accepted the solicitor-generalship at the time of *la réaction*. When he read of the latter's nomination in *Le Journal de Québec*, he wrote hurriedly to LaFontaine: "Il est impossible que Cauchon ait été autorisé à faire

[18]For Cauchon's views on patronage, see *ibid.*, Cauchon à LaFontaine, 17 déc. 1848, and APQ, Papiers Taché, A 43, A 45, A 50, Cauchon à Taché, 25 déc. 1849, 9 jan., 14 nov. 1850.

cette annonce. Quand à moi j'espère que la nomination n'aura pas lieu. Il s'agit de choisir entre deux adversaires politiques. Je regarde la défection de Mr. Taschereau dans un moment de crise comme celle de notre lutte avec les disciples de Metcalfe comme infiniment plus injurieuse à notre parti que toutes les erreurs de Duval."[19]

To LaFontaine's enemies all this seemed like bribery and the worst kind of corruption. "Il paraît que les douanes vont être mises sous le contrôle du gouvernement," Fabre wrote to O'Callaghan as he surveyed the government's legislative programme,

Dans ce cas le Ministère aura une vingtaine de places à donner & si le Bill de Judicature passe, encore des places à donner, c'est tout son bonheur, on dirait qu'il ne vit que pour cela, enfin c'est dégoûtant. . . . Cartier a à ce qu'il paraît refusé la place de Juge, Chs Mondelet sera nommé à son refus. LaFontaine fait son possible pour corrompre, il a placé un certain nombre de Jeunes Canadiens dans les bureaux du Gouvernement.[20]

But patronage was more than bribery. On the political level, it was the most effective means of strengthening the bonds which held the party together—no easy thing in a time when only vague views and family connections united most politicians. On the emotional level—and one not without its political rewards—the system served as a symbol that *la nation canadienne* had truly come into its own. Then, too, on a sociological level of which neither LaFontaine nor any of his contemporaries was aware, the appointments he made in every branch of the government service allowed the members of the *Canadien* professional bourgeoisie to escape at last from their frustration. For fifty years the graduates of the collèges had been pouring into the professions only to find, once they were established, that election to the Assembly offered the only hope of any further advancement. And this slim hope only the more talented could entertain and fewer still fulfil. By creating and opening up other avenues LaFontaine provided an opportunity for those who had no other talent to recommend them than a bit of local political influence. And thus by his appointments he served more than his party: he guaranteed political stability. For he proved to the *Canadien* political community that through the British system of responsible government there would now be the possibility of room at the top for all *Canadiens*.

LaFontaine also worked at controlling his journalists. Some he

[19]For Drummond's views on patronage see Papiers LaFontaine, Drummond à LaFontaine, 8, 13, 28 nov., 15 déc. 1849, 23 jan. 1850.
[20]O'Callaghan Papers, Fabre à O'Callaghan, 19 avril 1848.

managed by personal friendships. "La Minerve," Louis-Joseph Papineau said in 1848, "est sous la surveillance plus spéciale de Drummond et Cartier; les mélanges religieux sous la surveillance plus spéciale de Morin."[21] Others he helped by allowing them to publish the official government announcements. Indeed, as the system progressed, "les annonces" soon came to make the difference between survival and practical extinction. Without support except for the occasional contribution from Viger, L'Aurore stumbled forward with fewer than 200 subscribers, while Le Canadien, which Aubin had taken over from MacDonald and brought into the LaFontaine camp in May 1847, blossomed until by May 1848 its circulation had increased by some 250 per cent to about 1200, and it had surpassed every other paper in the Quebec district. But when Aubin began to criticize the government in the spring of 1848, he lost the official announcements and found his costs rising so fast that the owner, Jean-Baptiste (Edouard) Fréchette, had to let him go. As Luc Letellier, a young political agent of Chauveau, wrote to his member: "Le Canadien est vendu au ministère! Saches, mon cher ami, que Edouard Fréchette était propriétaire du fond d'imprimerie et que son frère . . . était associé sans acte de société et qu'il a plu à Monsieur Edouard de dire à son frère qu'il eut à filer qu'il ne voulait plus le garder. Et qu'il a ensuite dit à M. Aubin qu'il n'avait plus besoin de ses services ayant pris d'autres engagements plus profitables."[22] Ronald MacDonald then returned as editor, if not as a supporter of the administration, at least as a neutral observer. Cauchon reported to LaFontaine: "Le Canadien se comporte bien et c'est heureux pour le moment. Il y a entente cordiale entre McDonald [sic] et moi. Nous sommes convenus de nous entendre sur les questions politiques."[23]

La Revue Canadienne with a circulation of only 400 closed down when Létourneux returned to his law practice, but the other newspapers that supported the party prospered. At La Minerve, Duvernay, who had taken on the young littérateur Antoine Gérin-Lajoie as an assistant editor in 1845 and hired a second one, Raphaël Bellemarre, in 1847, saw his paper climb to some 1500 subscriptions and become the undisputed master of the French reading public in the Montreal district. It not only profited from announcement fees, but also became indispensable reading for the lawyers who needed to follow official

21Collection Papineau-Bourassa, 548, L.-J. Papineau à O'Callaghan, 19 avril 1848.
22APQ, Collection Chapais, Papiers Langevin (henceforth Chapais-Langevin), Letellier à Chauveau, 10 mars 1849.
23Papiers LaFontaine, Cauchon à LaFontaine, 24 oct. 1849.

court decisions, for farmers who awaited the publication of auction sales, or for notaries, justices of the peace, militia captains, school inspectors, and all those who must be conversant with the latest departmental decisions or legal enactments. In the Quebec district, Le Journal de Québec grew likewise, especially after it also became the only repository of official information. In June 1848 Cauchon warned LaFontaine that by sending advertisements to the (English) Quebec Gazette "vous engraissez ainsi vos ennemis et les rendez forts pour vous combattre."[24] After that his own paper thrived so successfully that by October 1849, with 1200 regular subscribers, he began to plan a daily edition (the first in French Canada) and in February 1850 a weekend supplement for the country. If LaFontaine's accession to office had transformed the future of the professional political classes, it had also begun a new era of prosperity for the press.

PROGRESS IN THE CHURCH

Though not necessarily because of the transformations in the political world, the Church was also working to consolidate its hold on public opinion. Over the decade it drew inspiration and strength from the renewal of spirit initiated by Bishops Bourget and Forbin-Janson, from the multiplication of religious houses and charitable foundations, and from the gradual extension of its mission field to new dioceses in Toronto, British Columbia, and Oregon, "cette vaste chaîne de sièges épiscopaux qui doit s'étendre un jour nous l'espérons de la mer jusqu'à la mer: a mari usque ad mare."[25] The Church also began imperceptibly and, at first, only intuitively, to realize the mission it had to revive the religious practice of the people at large. As the end of the decade approached the Church was helped in this task largely by Les Mélanges Religieux and by the preaching of Abbé Charles Chiniquy.

While curé at Beauport in the late 'thirties, Chiniquy had become obsessed with the problem of alcoholism and decided that he had the power to solve it. He was a small man, but his manner attracted. He walked slowly, his head at an angle, somehow projecting an impression of modesty, self-controlled shyness, and, to many, holiness. His eyes looked both sympathetic and intense, his smile was meant to charm. His long, darkish hair was soft as a woman's, his gestures as

24Ibid., Cauchon à LaFontaine, 23 juin, 1848.
25Les Mélanges Religieux, 13 mai 1842.

delicate. His voice, it was said, melted the hardest hearts. When he began to preach he fast became feverish, staring eagerly at his audience, and, alternating between tones that now recalled the angels, now their opposites, he would send his words splashing out in an uncontrolled stream that drowned his listeners in fear and hope. Then, when he ceased, he once more put on his modest mien, and charmed again. A perfect hypocrite.

"Le petit père Chiniquy" (as he came to be called) began his crusade at Beauport in March 1840 when he enrolled some 1300 of his parishioners in a Temperance Society.[26] From there he progressed across the Quebec diocese, leaving temperance groups behind him wherever he went. At the same time he composed a small 158-page booklet, Le Manuel de la Tempérance. The first edition of 4000 was sold out in a few years; a second of 10,000 copies (prefaced by four bishops) sold out in eighteen months. Still, at the end of 1846, he had been forced to move to the diocese of Montreal for reasons which Archbishop Signay was anxious to keep secret: the orator had pursued a housewife from a neighbouring parish with attentions that were far from temperate.

He then burst upon the Montreal district, lighting a fire of enthusiasm. Sometimes he enrolled as many as 17,000 people in one month. "Le Père Chiniquy est comme le choléra, il faut qu'il pénètre partout," complained one beer merchant (Les Mélanges, October 10). But 1849 was even more dazzling. Chiniquy gave some five hundred sermons in one hundred and twenty parishes to over 200,000 people. Finally, on July 5, retiring briefly to Longueuil to prepare the third edition of his Manuel, he celebrated what must have been his life's supreme moment. On the South Shore, bright banners blowing and tall tapers held against the sun, a procession of several thousand people moved through the village to the door of the church. There some two to three thousand more waited in reverent (and temperate) fervour. When the crowd settled, "le petit Père Chiniquy" appeared at the door of the presbytère and, with an expression of embarrassed humility and surprise, came over to the church steps "au milieu des acclamations et des hourras de cette foule de pas moins de 8 à 9,000 personnes." The cheering subsided and Charles Mondelet began a long panegyric, at the end of which he presented the priest with a gold medal inscribed "Au R.P. Chiniquy, Apôtre de la Tempérance. Hommage à ses vertus, à son zèle, à son patriotisme." Chiniquy later averred the medal was

[26]These and many more details on Chiniquy's influence are described in M. Trudel, Chiniquy (Trois-Rivières, 1955).

also wrapped up in four one-hundred dollar bills. "C'était," concluded *Les Mélanges* on July 17, "pour l'Apôtre de la Tempérance un bien beau jour qu'il méritait aussi depuis longtemps." Indeed, no French Canadian, not even Papineau in all his glory, had ever been granted such a triumph.

When the third edition of the *Manuel* came out in 1849, it contained a rather flowery preface which linked Chiniquy with the great theme of *la survivance.* "Le sort des armes," it began,

avait fait passer le Canada sous la domination anglaise. Les Canadiens peu nombreux pouvaient craindre dès lors pour leurs Institutions, pour leur Langue, pour leur Religion; mais on veillait là haut. Trois quarts de siècle après, ce petit peuple a grandi, il compte plus d'un demi-million d'hommes; sa langue et ses mœurs ne périront pas. Mais un danger plus grand le menace: cette fois, il ne s'agit plus d'anglification; c'est le chancre de l'Intempérance qui le dévore. . . . Pour ce chancre hideux, pour ce cancer infect, pour cette plaie dégoûtante, le ciel nous réserve un grand médecin; et . . . desseins adorables! . . . c'est au milieu de nous qu'il le trouvera, c'est au sein même du pauvre peuple qu'il viendra le chercher. Il le nommera son Envoyé, son Représentant, son Messager de Paix, et les hommes l'appelleront le Prêtre du Seigneur, l'apôtre de la Tempérance, le RÉVÉREND PÈRE CHINIQUY.[27]

Not too surprisingly, the author was a disciple of LaFontaine: Hector-Louis Langevin. A well-connected law student (his father had been an undersecretary of Lord Gosford) who was articling in the offices of Morin and Cartier, he had taken over the editorship of *Les Mélanges Religieux* in July 1847.

Since 1842, when it had a mere 450 subscribers, the diocesan paper had been in financial trouble. Of course it enjoyed no government largesse, and because it refused to make any political comment other than vague generalities opposing the Union and approving Lord Metcalfe, it seemed rather dull to most lay people. "Quant à la politique," it admitted on September 29, 1843, "nous avons compris combien il était difficile et dangereux pour nous d'aborder cette nouvelle carrière." A month later it was forced to close down for several weeks until it was purchased with the relatively small inheritance of Abbé Janvier Vinet, curé of Rigaud. Within two years, it had to stop again because, it said, people seemed indifferent to a nonpolitical publication. This time a group of priests met at the Collège de Saint-Hyacinthe to devise some means of rescue. In February 1846 Abbés Jean-Marie Bellenger and André-Toussaint Lagarde pooled what money they had to buy the paper. But they too refused to make

---

[27]C. Chiniquy, *Mes Combats: autobiographie de Charles Chiniquy* (Montréal, 1946), préface par Hector Langevin, pp. 5–6.

it interesting. When readers complained, for instance, that *Les Mélanges* had not carried news of the turbulent municipal election of 1846, the editors asked on March 31, 1846: "Conviendrait-il à des Editeurs-Prêtres d'aller se mêler au milieu des assomeurs au beau milieu des bâtons et des manches de haches pour avoir le plaisir de rapporter les premiers l'histoire peu édifiante de la mairie?" By such reasoning they too failed. And finally, in July 1847, they felt obliged to hand over the directorship to young Langevin whose religious orthodoxy they felt well guaranteed by his two brothers in Quebec: Jean, a priest since 1844 and a professor at the Séminaire, and Edmond who was to be ordained in September 1847 and become secretary to Vicar-General Cazeau at the Archbishop's office.

With mentors like Morin and Cartier, the youthful editor soon threw his paper into the thick of the political fight. *Les Mélanges* became a voice to be heeded. Subscriptions rose, and, in true journalistic tradition, Langevin took to assaulting the dying *L'Aurore* and its main supporter by calling "le Vénérable" names and making malicious comments about feeble old age.

Nor did he forget more abstract speculations. In a series of articles during his first months at the paper, the new editor poured out his developing talent in discussing "L'Avenir du Canada." Since Lord Grey's despatch to Sir John Harvey about responsible government had brought up the question of the future of Canada as an independent colony, he wanted to give his own views. "Pour notre part," he began on October 5, ". . . nous croyons sincèrement qu'une union fédérale par laquelle l'on voudrait rendre justice à TOUS les partis, est ce que nous pouvons désirer de mieux." He rejected the idea of annexation to the United States which some had proposed, for, he held, it could be of no advantage to French Canada. As a nationality, the *Canadiens* would be lost in the American union:

Placé tout-à-fait dans le Nord de l'Union Américaine, le Bas-Canada dont la grande majorité de la population est d'origine française, ne pourrait trouver des peuples qui pussent avoir des intérêts semblables aux siens, que dans le Sud de l'Union, dans la Louisiane. Or, à la Louisiane, si nous pouvons en croire l'histoire et les faits de tous les jours, la population française n'a plus l'usage de ses lois, elle n'a plus l'usage de sa langue dans les tribunaux et ailleurs; sa langue en un mot est proscrite.

Religiously, he thought, they would be drowned in the anti-clerical republican atmosphere that had drifted over from Europe: "il est notoire que les mauvais principes de notre ancienne Mère-Patrie y ont été transplantés avec l'immigration Française." Besides, he continued, the whole tradition of French Canada rejected the proposition.

Quand bien même l'Angleterre voudrait abandonner le Canada pour le joindre à la république américaine, ce ne serait pas encore une chose à faire. Car le peuple du Bas-Canada, le peuple Canadien-français ne voudrait pas entendre parler de pareille chose. Il se demanderait pourquoi tant de fois, à tant de reprises, et à des époques éloignées les unes des autres il a pris les armes? n'était-ce pas toujours pour repousser le joug américain.

On the other hand, he felt the *Canadiens* owed it to themselves to retain the British connection by joining the other British colonies in a federation. In such a union, Lower Canada could enjoy all the benefits of local autonomy that would accrue to it as a distinct state—"le gouvernement projeté aura le gouvernement américain ou plutôt la constitution américaine pour modèle"—and at the same time preserve on the larger scene the influence it now exerted in the united province. Indeed, in the new order, the *Canadiens* would share in creating a new nation where, as Parent and LaFontaine also fondly dreamed, the divisions would be along political, not racial lines.

Nous ne devons point envisager cette Union avec des regards craintifs; tout est rassurant dans cet évènement que l'avenir nous réserve. C'est un acte, un grand acte, nous dirions un acte de sublime réparation qui se prépare. Cette Union telle qu'il nous semble que nous devons l'entendre, cette Union doit amener les résultats suivants. Elle doit faire disparaître les distinctions d'origine, de langue, de mœurs, de religions, elle doit établir comme nous l'a dit récemment un homme distingué de notre pays, elle doit établir une seule division dans l'Amérique anglaise, et cette distinction ce sera celle "des libéraux et des rétrogrades."

Thus the young editor caught sight of the vision which would inspire politicians twenty years later. But for the moment he concentrated on defending his party. *L'Aurore* and what was left of the Viger group complained bitterly of *Les Mélanges'* descent into practical politics. To have lost its support after the affair of the Jesuit estates was one thing; to see it defending LaFontaine was another. Langevin was not the only vigorous young writer on the Montreal scene that year, however.

RENEWED RADICALISM

Also in July 1847, another youthful group headed by twenty-two-year-old Georges Batchelor—a *Canadien* despite his surname—founded *L'Avenir*. This group of a half dozen or so youths formed the nucleus of the Institut Canadien, the most successful of the many patriotic and social clubs founded in the mid-forties. After spending three years in sponsoring lectures and debates and building a public library which by April 1845 already included some four hundred volumes, they started their newspaper in Montreal to assure a permanent repository for their ideas and debates. Batchelor acted as editor until he moved to New York in November 1847. Then the others took charge under the general direction of twenty-one-year-old Jean-Baptiste-Eric Dorion.

"L'enfant terrible," as Cauchon tagged him, young Dorion was small, nervous, and brilliant. He earned his nickname because of his ferocious journalism, and at L'Avenir he was surrounded by friends worthy of his talent. There were Rodolphe LaFlamme and Joseph Doutre, two law students who had just graduated from the Collège de Montréal: both with incisive minds and impetuous characters. There was the inseparable pair of Charles Laberge and Joseph Papin—the first a retiring, pale, little youth of nineteen with a huge, black, bushy head of hair and delicate, feminine gestures, the other a square-shouldered, handsome giant of over six feet, with a heavy, pointed beard and long brown hair. "Danton" his friends called Papin, and he revelled in the name. He wrote as powerfully as he spoke, and he shared with his friend Laberge a vibrant imagination and probably the soundest judgment of the whole group. There were four members of the Papineau-Viger family: intelligent Denis-Emery (Denis-Benjamin Papineau's son); Gustave (Louis-Joseph's son), a remarkably mature teenager; Louis Labrèche, a stranger to the clan by blood, but not by talent, and an adopted son of Denis-Benjamin Viger; and finally, Louis-Antoine Dessaulles, Louis-Joseph's nephew, the oldest of the whole L'Avenir group, probably the most intelligent and certainly the most free thinking. All of them had listened to the rebel leader's philosophy and heard of deeds which their eager hearts burned to emulate. If it only depended on them, they would win through the sharpness of their minds what he could not by sharpness of sword.

Together these enthusiastic young people revived—but in a much more effective manner—the old nationalist, radical ambition that had inspired the youthful ex-Chasseurs François Lemaître and Pierre Lefebvre to found La Quotidienne and Le Courrier Canadien back in 1838, and, later in 1840, had led Henri Gauvin and Jacques-Alexis Plinguet to publish La Canadienne and Le Jean-Baptiste. In the days of le grand découragement they had failed because they had been too few and too divided. They had no leader and they lived under martial law. But in 1847, at a time of national if not economic prosperity, enjoying the patronage of the main French-Canadian councillor, Denis-Benjamin Papineau, and of the "venerable" Viger, and reflecting the nationalist fervour which LaFontaine's party had spread while in Opposition, the youngsters achieved a performance of uncommon excellence. At first, *L'Avenir* supported LaFontaine. But after Batchelor's departure it increasingly turned its energies towards extreme solutions, pressing for measures which would lead inevitably to an anti-clerical republic. Especially—and with a vengeance which the immature ex-*patriotes* of 1838 and 1840 would have envied—it pressed for repeal of the Union and annexation to the United States.

As if to celebrate (or bedevil) the final accession of the French Canadians to political power, all these forces—economic stagnation, the triumphant and ever stronger party of the politicians and the press, a reinvigorated and militant Catholicism, and, finally, an extremist group that had rediscovered its vigour after ten years—contradictory as they were, merged to put the times out of joint.

16

The Re-Emergence of Papineau
November 1847-May 1848

It was the evening of March 14, 1848. The front desks at the right side of the Speaker were empty. A week before, Lord Elgin had sent for LaFontaine and Baldwin; on March 11, they had resigned their seats in the Assembly, taken their oath of office, and advised the Governor General to prorogue parliament. They wanted a breathing spell—an opportunity first to win the re-election then demanded by constitutional practice, and, secondly, to prepare the details of the legislative programme they had promised their electors. Before prorogation, however, they needed to ask for the routine vote of the usual supplies. Tonight, therefore, Drummond rose to put forward the motion. He did so briefly, explaining to the House that once its legislation was ready, the new administration intended to recall parliament as soon as possible. He asked for a rapid vote, bowed to the Speaker, and sat down. Then he noticed an unusual stillness had fallen. At the far end of the Chamber where Neilson used to sit, Louis-Joseph Papineau rose to speak.

Word had spread quickly that the most renowned orator in French Canada had, unexpectedly, chosen this moment to make his first speech. And there was no *Canadien* who did not remember "le temps du refus des subsides," the days in the 'thirties when Papineau had translated all their national aspirations into a refusal to vote supplies. Tonight, he stood there again, still tall, still wearing his hair, now white, brushed straight up to a point at the front. His face looked tired, but his handsome features had not changed, and his eyes shone with all the energy of the past.

Then Papineau began, slowly at first—he had always had this habit of hesitating as if to hold back the national destiny bursting on the tip of his tongue. Then, his rich evocative tones swelling, he rolled out the impassioned words. He had trusted the new men until now, he said. But what did they mean by responsible government if they expected the House to vote credits before it appraised their programme? Were they no better than the old oligarchy? What need was there to prepare legislation? Why did they not immediately propose the repeal of the Union? Or, having finally achieved power, had they decided to forget all justice, all right? He would not forget; he would lead the movement for repeal.[1]

Two years before, as Papineau was being fêted on his return, he had answered an English friend who congratulated him on having kept his fine features that "I am the same in all."[2] Now he proved it. He could not break his habit of looking for battle. He must be in opposition. He must battle against all those who would imperil the attainment of true democratic institutions as he alone knew them. He would fight the Union. He would struggle to found a democratic republic. Indeed, he had been clarifying this intention for five months now. Ever since his return, his family had pressed him to re-enter politics. He resisted as long as he could. "Ici point de changement," his old friend Fabre reported to O'Callaghan, "toujours de la cabale," and Papineau "ne voulant pas être la cause d'une plus grande division entre ses Compatriotes."[3] "Mon oncle, je pense, ne rentrera pas au moins actuellement dans les affaires pour bien des raisons," Denis-Emery Papineau explained. "La principale est, je crois, qu'il ne s'accorderait avec personne sur l'idée mère (autour de laquelle toutes les autres devront se grouper), qui devra être la base de la politique du pays. Cette idée, je crois, est celle-ci: que tant que nous serons avec l'Angleterre, nous ne ferons rien; qu'il n'y a qu'avec les Etats-Unis que nous ferons quelque chose."[4]

But by November 1847 his refusals grew weaker. When the general election began, he received invitations from two important ridings, Saint-Maurice and Huntingdon. He wavered. His brother had resigned; his cousin, Denis-Benjamin Viger, had retired to the relative impotence of the Legislative Council. In Quebec, John Neilson lay dying. Those who still wanted a separate state—and there were many —had no guide. Those who looked to the United States—and as financial losses deepened these also were many—had no one to lead them. If all those who had never believed in responsible government

[1]*La Minerve*, 16 mars 1848; *L'Aurore*, 24 mars, 8 avril 1848.
[2]Quoted in Gérin-Lajoie, *Dix ans au Canada*, p. 314.
[3]O'Callaghan Papers, Fabre à O'Callaghan, 19 jan. 1847.
[4]Collection Papineau-Bourassa, D.-E. Papineau à J.-B.-N. Papineau, 24 mars 1847.

were to be rallied together, he alone could do it, and he must do it now. In mid-December, he issued what Lord Elgin called "a pretty frank declaration of republicanism"[5]: the Adresse aux Electeurs des Comtés de Huntingdon et de Saint-Maurice.

He began by declaring his reluctance to return and his fear to divide the *Canadiens* who since 1844 had given their trust to LaFontaine:

Il faut que vous vous efforciez de reporter les mêmes hommes au pouvoir. Si le gouvernement responsable est une vérité, le temps est venu où ils pourront faire beaucoup plus de bien que je n'en espère, moi, qui le regarde comme une tromperie. . . . Puissent-ils réussir; personne ne les applaudira plus sincèrement que moi. Ils pensent que le jour n'est pas venu où ils doivent se reporter à 1836, et redemander dès aujourd'hui les réformes que nous demandions alors: moi je pense que ce jour est venu. A raison seulement de cette diversité d'opinion, je vous déclare donc ma pensée sincère et entière; non seulement je ne désire pas entrer dans la vie publique, mais je désire n'y pas entrer. Je crains de n'y pas faire de bien.

But, he continued, he could not share the party leaders' platform. He was against the Union which had been imposed against the will of French Canadians, which forced upon them the debt of Upper Canada, and the injustice of equal representation. Nor did he believe it could be made acceptable by the doctrine of responsible government, "un mot jeté au hazard, une vaine théorie nullifiée par la pratique et par les explications des lords Russell, Sydenham et Metcalfe." He did not believe that even LaFontaine's followers knew what they meant by it: "Ils ont dit ce qu'elle [la responsabilité] n'était pas, et ils n'ont pas dit ce qu'elle était. Elle est donc une énigme interprétée diversement par celui qui l'offre et par celui qui la reçoit: dès lors, une source fertile de malentendus, de plaintes et de récriminations entre les gouverneurs et les représentants." Instead, Papineau proposed the restoration of Lower Canada as a separate state, with an elective government modelled on "les sages institutions des Etats Unis, les plus parfaites dont ait jusqu'à présent été dotée l'humanité." But, he insisted again in closing, he did not want to divide the *Canadien* party:

Les probabilités sont si grandes que nos amis politiques vont se trouver plus forts dans le prochain parlement qu'ils ne l'étaient numériquement dans le dernier, que je les vois au pouvoir et à l'œuvre. S'ils réussissent à faire le bien pour lequel vous, eux, et moi, soupirons, leur marche aura été la meilleure. S'ils n'y réussissent pas, alors ce sera tous ensemble, peuple et représentants, constituants et constitués, qu'il n'y aura plus à différer de délibérer sur les moyens d'organiser l'opposition la plus vigoureuse possible.[6]

[5]Doughty, ed., *Elgin-Grey Papers*, I, 102, Elgin to Grey, Dec. 24, 1847.
[6]*La Minerve*, 20 déc. 1847; *La Revue Canadienne*, 21 déc. 1847; *L'Avenir*, 24 déc. 1847.

La Minerve, La Revue Canadienne, and *L'Avenir* all published the Adresse and separate copies printed on Duvernay's press flooded the two ridings. On January 3 Papineau was returned unopposed in Saint-Maurice. "Ce document a créé une vive sensation dans le pays," Duvernay said in *La Minerve* on the twenty-seventh echoing Lord Elgin's private estimate that "considerable excitement has been produced."[7]

The hero had re-emerged fully armed but he had not challenged LaFontaine's position openly. In fact, as he wrote to O'Callaghan, "Si mon nom et mes opinions ont conservé quelqu'autorité auprès de mes compatriotes, elle [l'Adresse] disait assez de bien d'eux pour fortifier leur influence populaire."[8] Yet, by his attacks on the Union and responsible government, he obviously undermined the party's position. And in private, as he continued to O'Callaghan, "ma conversation de chaque jour est sans réticence aucune quand à mes prédilections pour les intitutions [sic] & les pays démocratiques, mes antipathies pour les institutions Aristocratiques, et mes plaintes contre l'injuste traitement imposé à mon pays par l'Angleterre." LaFontaine's followers were embarrassed. They were unhappy over Papineau's address, they feared his influence. But since he had praised them, they could hardly attack him openly. Also, some of their number rejoiced at what Lord Elgin called "his introduction into public life at this moment."[9] Before the Adresse, Cauchon confided to LaFontaine that "pour ma part, j'aimerais à voir Mr. P. dans la Chambre parce que ses talents si ses opinions n'étaient pas extrèmes pourraient nous être utiles."[10] And even after it came out, Hincks wrote Baldwin that

I do not think he will do us harm. He takes a *radical* position. He does not want office. He will support us against the Tories, and in fact it is in my opinion no harm for a party to have others taking a more extreme course than themselves. The Whigs did not *abuse* their radical supporters. Of course I believe in the full efficacy of Responsible Government, but I cannot but admit that there is even yet strong ground to doubt the sincerity of the Imperial Gov't.[11]

However, LaFontaine did care. "It is an ill-advised and uncalled-for Manifesto," he wrote,[12] agreeing later with Baldwin's assessment that

[7]Doughty, ed., *Elgin-Grey Papers,* I, 102, Elgin to Grey, Dec. 24, 1847.
[8]Collection Papineau-Bourassa, 547a, L.-J. Papineau à O'Callaghan, 22 fév. 1848.
[9]Doughty, ed., *Elgin-Grey Papers,* I, 117, Elgin to Grey, Jan. 7, 1848.
[10]Papiers LaFontaine, Cauchon à LaFontaine, 3 nov. 1847.
[11]Baldwin Papers, v51, Hincks to Baldwin, jan. 14, 1848.
[12]*Ibid.,* A 55, LaFontaine to Baldwin, Jan. 16, 1848.

"I see nothing but embarrassment from his being in Parliament after such a manifesto."[13]

Thus, when Papineau rose to oppose the motion of supply, he surprised LaFontaine's party only in the moment and manner he chose to make the break, not in the fact. In open opposition, and around the nucleus of young radicals at *L'Avenir*, he planned to rally to his cause the politicians LaFontaine had twice defeated, in the debate against the Union and at the time of *la crise Metcalfe*. To do this, he took the offensive in three directions, and by the end of June, Papineau had spelled out his doctrine, moved into active support of a popular colonization scheme, and finally made a political tour of the province. His Adresse soon became known as *le manifeste Papineau* and during May, he issued two others.

The second appeared as a supplement to *L'Avenir* on May 15. Cast in the form of a dialogue between himself and two Irishmen who came ostensibly to invite him to chair a public meeting calling for the repeal of the union of Ireland and Great Britain, it was an expression of

mon mécontentement, et mon dédain pour l'ordre politique forcément imposé à mon pays, dans le même but hostile, par les mêmes moyens pervers, qui ont enchaîné le vôtre, par une Union, meurtrière et dégradante pour l'Irlande, comme la nôtre nous est hostile et plus dégradante encore pour le Bas-Canada, colonie deux fois assujeti à deux Métropoles, celle de l'Angleterre qui nous opprime par antipathie, celle du Haut-Canada, qui nous exploite par cupidité.

Unlike the Adresse it made an overt attempt to divide the *Canadien* party by praising the *Québecois* who had resisted the Union in 1840 and contrasting them to the Montrealers under LaFontaine who had not:

Il y a de la vie et de l'honneur dans Québec. Il y en a eu quand, sous le règne de la terreur, et sous l'inspiration de la liberté, en présence de lord Durham, l'on y a flétri sa tyrannie, exercée contre les exilés de la Bermude; ... quand le *Fantasque* édifiait ses lecteurs, sur les folies quotidiennes des actes de la dictature d'alors (celle du moment, pourrait bien le ressusciter avec toute sa verve); quand on y a protesté et pétitionné contre l'acte d'Union. ... Oui, il y a à Québec de la vie et de l'honneur. A Montréal c'est autre chose. Nous y avons le siège du gouvernement responsable. Nous y avons des hommes d'état, politiques profonds comme l'abyme et muets comme la tombe, qui étouffent toutes les mesures qui naissent dans Québec.

A week later, May 24, 1848, a third manifesto, also published in *L'Avenir*, repeated all Papineau's old ideas, but this time his attack

13Papiers LaFontaine, Baldwin to LaFontaine, Jan. 25, 1848.

was explicit. He knew LaFontaine better now, he began, and could testify to his ambition and corruption. "Il y a deux camps séparés bien distincts," he continued, contrasting the government's followers with those he claimed for himself.

Les Unionistes qui ne font appel qu'aux passions basses at cupides, la peur et l'avarice. Ils disent . . . ne regardez qu'aux quelques mille piastres, qu'une demie douzaine de Canadiens-Français nommés aux emplois, de plus qu'en 1837, reçoivent aujourd'hui. Ne vous plaignez pas constitutionnellement par des assemblées, des écrits, des protestations, contre les iniquités de l'acte d'Union. . . . Nous sommes au pouvoir, et nous sommes le gouvernement responsable. Il y a le camp des Anti-Unionistes toujours, qui font appel aux sentiments généreux, et disent soyez fiers et fermes sans être violents.

Then he attacked the Union itself. Conceived in iniquity and carried out in injustice, nothing could ever set it right. He recalled all the old grievances—undemocratic representation, the clause against the language, the shared debt of Upper Canada. "Des intérêts vitaux sont détruits par ces dispositions, et l'honneur national est outragé au vif." Repeal of the Union was a question of "l'honneur national." Finally, he summoned all true patriots to join his camp:

Il y a le camp des Anti-Unionistes toujours, dont le cœur est trop noble, la raison trop juste et trop élevée pour séparer le *libéralisme* de la *nationalité*, pour sacrifier celle-ci à celui-là: et qui sait qu'il est dupe ou menteur le *"libéralisme pratique"* de ceux qui veulent donner double représentation, double puissance, doubles droits à la population Canadienne, *d'origine anglaise*, comparativement à ce qu'ils en accordent à la population Cana-dienne, *d'origine française*, et qui ne cessera de combattre sous le drapeau de la *nationalité*, tant que celle-ci sera proscrite et persécutée; tant que le *vrai* libéralisme n'aura pas placé toutes les nationalités, sur le pied de la plus complète égalité.

Having launched this major propaganda assault Papineau went on to direct political action by joining in a new land settlement society.[14] In the fall of 1847 an Irish missionary in Sherbrooke, Father Bernard O'Reilly, suggested in a series of letters to Le Canadien that the French Canadians found a land settlement company like those which were attracting immigrants for Upper Canada, with the aim of funnelling to the Eastern Townships at least part of the great flow of emigrants to the United States. By March 1848, Les Mélanges Religieux and La Minerve having shown sympathy for the proposal, the young men of the Institut Canadien decided to act. They drafted a constitution of an Association des Etablissements Canadiens des Townships. Using

[14]L. Pouliot, "L'Institut Canadien, Papineau, Mgr Bourget et la Colonisation des Townships," a ms article graciously lent to me by the author.

the organization of the Society for the Propagation of the Faith as a model, they planned for a membership of 600 and offered the presidency to Bishop Bourget who accepted. Then they called a public meeting.

On April 5 some 8000 Montrealers crowded into Bonsecours Square to witness the founding of the Association. About 2000 more were turned away from the gate. On the stage, Bishop Bourget presided and the young executives from the Institut sat with such notable elders as Papineau and Cherrier. Morin did not attend; he sent an excuse at the last minute. But Bishop Bourget and Cherrier praised the scheme; and the members approved a slate of officers chosen from among the Institut members. When Papineau rose to speak, he mentioned the new Association only in passing. Instead, he went on once again to repeat the substance of the *manifestes*: the iniquity of the Union, and the long series of British crimes against the *Canadien* nationality from the deportation of the Acadians to the deception that was responsible government. Lord Elgin described the scene to Lord Grey: "At a great meeting convened at Montreal he held forth for three hours to the multitude (the Bishop in the chair) ascribing this [lack of land settlement] and all other French Canadian ills, real or supposed, to the selfish Policy of Great Britain and her persevering efforts to deprive them of their nationality and every other blessing."[15] Eventually Papineau caused the plan's failure. But he did not seem to care so much about the settlement of the Sherbrooke area as he did (as Lord Elgin said) about "making himself of importance in the eyes of his countrymen and of gratifying his ruling passion by abusing England."[16] So much the better if he could influence settlement, but in truth he could not have worried much about emigration to the United States when he had ended his first manifesto with a paragraph encouraging American travel. Possibly Papineau hoped that the progress of the Association would disguise his own glaring lack of positive accomplishments.

The Association petitioned the new government for assistance and, while waiting for an answer, the President, Bishop Bourget, prepared a pastoral letter. Meanwhile Papineau left on a tour of the province to spread the gospel against the Union. He went first to Quebec, the scene of so many of his parliamentary triumphs. The old capital had been foremost in its resistance to the Union in 1840 and had become the centre of *la réaction* in 1845. Now, in the spring of 1848, it still

---

[15]Doughty, ed., *Elgin-Grey Papers*, I, 191, Elgin to Grey, June 29, 1848.
[16]*Ibid.*

seethed with what Caron described as "l'esprit de fermentation."[17] And, luckily for Papineau, it was now without a leader. Aylwin had gone to the Bench. Chauveau remained on the point of breaking with LaFontaine but hardly wielded enough personal influence to direct a revolt—besides, he was too young, as was Cauchon. Caron himself, as speaker of the Legislative Council, was restrained by what was already the beginning of cabinet solidarity. Above all, any hopes the anti-*unionistes* may still have entertained were broken by the death of John Neilson on February 1: "une perte réelle, un événement regrettable pour le pays qui l'a possédé, bien que ses vues aient pu généralement venir en contact pénible avec celles de la majorité de ses contemporains . . . Il serait difficile de peser impartialement aujourd'hui la conduite publique de cet homme, l'un des plus marquants sans contredit qu'ait produits le Canada" (*Le Canadien*, February 2).

Neilson's funeral was one of the most impressive ceremonies ever held in Quebec. And it may well have given Papineau some confidence. It was a cold and leaden day. The old, steep streets and grey buildings were blanketed in snow. Against the white, black drapes drooped starkly from almost every window. The stores were closed, the presses at *Le Journal*, at *Le Canadien*, and at the English papers halted. From Saint Andrew's Presbyterian Church up narrow Sainte-Anne Street to the Protestant cemetery, the *Québecois* stood in quiet rows along which the only sound was the occasional muffled voice whispering, now in French, now in English, a well-known anecdote about the man whom none could recall without pride and sorrow. If they had not gathered to acclaim all his life, at least they had come to mourn his death. And as the long procession moved sadly and slowly past, they bowed in grief. As it turned into the cemetery, as it laid the great man in his grave, many in this vast, silent, sorrowing crowd may have realized that they had just witnessed the final passing of politics in the grand manner.

With Neilson gone, the *Québecois* who had been among his most faithful followers rejoiced at Papineau's call for repeal. At the beginning of April they met in private consultation and decided to invite him to take over the leadership. They must surely have realized how horrified Neilson would have been at Papineau's attacks against the British connection, but they knew for certain, as Glackmeyer wrote (*Le Canadien*, May 17), that "ce grand citoyen est mort avec le regret que l'on eut jamais abandonné cette question du rappel de l'Union." And, after all, Papineau shared with Neilson the belief

[17]Papiers LaFontaine, Caron à LaFontaine, 1 mai 1848.

that repeal would, somehow, automatically bring with it efficient, humane, and just government. They wrote, therefore, asking Papineau to come to a rally on May 11, 1848. He accepted and on May 9 left Montreal, travelling with his nephew, Louis-Antoine Dessaulles.

It took less than a day for the news of his coming to sweep the valley of the St. Lawrence. For over a decade few *Canadiens* outside Montreal had had the opportunity to see the man whose legend "comme une héroïque fanfare . . retentissait d'un bout à l'autre du pays, et . . . trouvait des échos enthousiastes dans les villages les plus reculés, et même au fond des cœurs les moins belliqueux."[18] When the tidings spread from village to village that he was coming, they went into a fever of excitement. Tales of his golden oratory, the stories of his escape, and the poverty of his exile, all were repeated. Around Lévis, children began picking fights with their English-speaking neighbours by crying "Hourrah pour Papineau"; and in more remote areas, mothers examined their newborn sons to make certain they did have "la tête à Papineau." "Un Papineau," Louis Fréchette later recalled, "c'était le summum de tout ce qui pouvait être grand, noble, intelligent et beau."[19] As Papineau sailed down the river with the first warm wind of spring, bonfires were lit on the shore and salvos of musketry cracked through the air in salutation.

On May 11 it poured rain, but by noon thousands waited in the crowded stalls of the Marché Saint-Paul where the meeting was to start at two. Another huge crowd gathered outside Papineau's hotel to escort him to the hustings. There he met the leaders of the new-found party, Glackmeyer, Joseph Légaré, Dr. Bardy, Chauveau, and Aubin, a recent convert to repeal. Jean Chabot presided (but cautioned his audience that although he admired Papineau, he was against repeal). The rain continued, but Papineau walked resolutely to centre stage. "Il était beau à contempler," an eyewitness remembered years later, "ce grand orateur au port majesteux, aux nobles manières, à la voix sonore. Pour moi, il me semblait entendre un de ces illustres orateurs de l'antiquité, harranguer sur le forum romain en présence du peuple roi."[20] He spoke for three hours, waving before the crowd of 8000 the splendour of one idea: repeal of the Union. And over and over, by calling on them to notice an apparently unlimited gamut of conspiracies against their nationality, he brought the *Canadiens* to a fever of cheers against the Union. It was almost dark when the meeting ended. From Montreal, Lord Elgin wrote to Lord Grey his description of the meeting, and included a good summary of Papineau's themes: "M.

[18]Fréchette, *Mémoires*, pp. 117–18.
[19]*Ibid.*, p. 119.   [20]APQ, O. Robitaille, "Mes Mémoires," p. 213.

Papineau has had his monster meeting at Quebec and held forth for nearly four hours in the rain to an assembly rather numerous than select. His topics—'English oppression of Ireland & Canada— in both cases by means of Acts of Union'—'glories of revolutions, especially French'.—'Superiority of Quebec & its inhabitants to Montreal'— 'Humbug of responsible Gov^{t}.'[21]

On his way back to Montreal, Papineau stopped in Three Rivers to relate before another enthusiastic crowd his now familiar list of grievances. A few days later, he began a visit in his own riding of Saint-Maurice which came to a climax at Yamachiche on June 6 when he delivered another three-hour speech, which the reporters from *L'Avenir* recorded "au moyen de la phonographie." His foes said he had attracted only 750 people, but his friends estimated the crowd at closer to 2500. At all events, he left behind him, especially in the district about Quebec, the beginnings of what might become another serious challenge to LaFontaine.

For there were many who accepted Papineau's rhetoric as evidence. In Quebec, Glackmeyer organized several meetings at which hundreds of electors approved resolutions demanding repeal. And in Montmorency riding on the outskirts of the city, another anti-*unioniste*, Jacques Rhéaume, a youngish lawyer who practised in Quebec and whom Cauchon called "le plus influent du comté de Montmorency,"[22] set out to bring Cauchon's riding into the repeal camp. He had been on the platform with Papineau at the great meeting and soon after began to agitate. To all who would listen he repeated the substance of Papineau's *manifestes*, adding a particular invitation of his own to attend a meeting at Château Richer on August 1. There he intended to unmask the corruption of Cauchon and all the *unionnaires*. When the day came, some hundred or so habitants turned up. So did Cauchon— the last man in Quebec to allow himself to be criticized, but who was, this time, about to be surprised.

The meeting was convened at noon. By three o'clock the fistfights had not yet ended. As soon as the chairman called for order, Cauchon appeared with a group of some twenty young men, including Narcisse Belleau and Jean-Charles Taché (a cousin of Etienne-Pascal Taché), and ran up to the platform. However, before he reached the top step, one of Rhéaume's men tripped him. Cauchon kicked him off, jumped down, and began to fight. But he was fast overwhelmed. Rhéaume cried out: "En avant les gars! Frappez, frappez!" Out came sticks and pitchforks, and one of Cauchon's men named O'Brien

[21]Doughty, ed., *Elgin-Grey Papers*, I, 166, Elgin to Grey, May 18, 1848.
[22]Papiers LaFontaine, Cauchon à LaFontaine, 13 juil. 1848.

grabbed first an iron axle, then a horsewhip, and began to hit in all directions. Rhéaume shouted: "Ils sont armés. . . . Ils ont armés les Irlandais pour nous battre." Belleau and O'Brien cleared a path to rescue little Cauchon who was being beaten practically to death. They managed to get him into a nearby farmhouse, but Rhéaume's rioters stayed on guard outside, threatening to kill him if he emerged. About five o'clock, some of Cauchon's friends, reasoning that the barricade might last all night, rode into Quebec and brought back Joseph Légaré, who was fast becoming the local leader of the repealers. He persuaded Rhéaume and his men to let Cauchon through. "Il fut admis par tout le monde des deux partis," Cauchon laconically told the readers of Le Journal, on August 2 "qu'une telle assemblée ne pouvait être l'expression de l'opinion du comté de Montmorency." Still, the little editor may well have reflected that Papineau certainly had a following at Quebec, and one which had learned his own tricks well. In fact, six weeks later, two meetings on the Island of Orleans passed strong resolutions congratulating the old *patriote* leader on his re-emergence in politics.

In April 1848 Cauchon admitted to LaFontaine: "Je regrette infiniment les démarches de Papineau et de la jeunesse de l'Avenir. . . . Les mots rappel de l'Union est [sic] un talisman dans notre population. . . . Je vous dirai qu'à Québec cette agitation prend de la consistence, la nomination d'Aylwin y aide puissamment, mais encore plus les évènements d'Europe."[23] In June, writing from Quebec, Caron concurred about the "mécontentement qui existe même parmi nos meilleurs amis et les personnes les plus raisonnables."[24] By December there was trouble in Montreal. And the politicians there began to realize it could become dangerous. Hector Langevin, for one, wrote to his brothers in Quebec:

Il n'y a pas à se le dissimuler, il règne une scission parmi les Canadiens-Français. . . . Pour moi en particulier, je defends le ministère actuel car je le crois le pouvoir nécessaire à l'état actuel: s'il réussit, nous sommes pour longtemps encore sous la protection de l'Angleterre; s'il ne réussit pas, nous sommes Américains avant cinq ans. . . . Je n'ose penser à l'avenir, car j'y entrevois alors pour nous des malheurs et des troubles, et le Canada se jettera de désespoir entre les bras des Yankees.[25]

In only a few months Papineau had made his point. He had attracted the habitants and a score of politicians; he had also rallied important newspapers.

[23]*Ibid.*, Cauchon à LaFontaine, 24 avril 1848.
[24]*Ibid.*, Caron à LaFontaine, 1 juin 1848.
[25]Chapais-Langevin, 246, H. Langevin à Edmond et Jean Langevin, 8 déc. 1848.

Le Canadien had gradually moved over to Papineau's camp. Few were really surprised. Since Ronald MacDonald had taken over in 1842 French Canada's oldest newspaper had supported the separatist leanings of Neilson and Viger. In 1845 it had sided prominently with *la réaction* and had printed the first definition of the doctrine of the double majority. True, after Aubin became editor, it defended LaFontaine. But earlier, as editor of *Le Fantasque* in 1840, the Frenchman had lent the aid of his satire for Neilson's great campaign against Thomson's Union. And if, after September 1842, Aubin praised LaFontaine's policies, he always continued to glory in being a French liberal. After the Paris February Revolution, he filled *Le Canadien* with accounts of its heroic deeds, claiming on March 24 that "cet événement . . . a effacé complètement l'importance et l'actualité de nos petites affaires *provinciales.*" He was therefore naturally in sympathy with Papineau. During the spring he printed the long speech at the Townships meeting, for instance, and a series of letters against Cauchon from Jacques Rhéaume. After the great Quebec meeting where Papineau praised him by name, he officially joined the repeal party. By September his shift had become so obvious that *Le Canadien* lost the government announcements, and LaFontaine's Quebec politicians began a campaign which eventually led to a sharp drop in subscriptions. Of course, Aubin remained henceforth immovable in his opinion that Papineau's arguments "démontrent qu'il n'y a désormais pour le Bas-Canada, pour *ses institutions*, pour *sa langue*, pour *ses lois*, d'autre voie de salut que dans le rappel immédiat de l'acte d'Union" (June 16).

And, on Papineau's invitation, Aubin resurrected *Le Fantasque*. He was better at satire, and also, by using the little paper for his political crudities, he could keep *Le Canadien* on the more dignified level that might persuade some people it was really impartial. "Depuis quelque temps," Luc Letellier told Chauveau at the beginning of 1849, "j'essaye de persuader aux propriétaires du Canadien qu'ils feront bien de dire une fois pour toutes 'qu'à l'avenir ils ne répondront à aucun article du Journal de Québec.' Si Aubin veut *turlupiner* M. Cauchon Le Fantasque est là et Le Fantasque peut faire beaucoup de politique au dépens du Journal de Québec et le Fantasque serait un aide au Canadien qui lui paraîtrait en dehors de ces petitesses."[26] The new *Fantasque* came out on June 10, 1848, and continued until the end of the year. Aubin filled its pages with articles poking fun at LaFontaine, at Cauchon, at the capital in Montreal. He continued his old practice of parody on supposed despatches of the Governor General to the Colonial Office. But in general, his satire had lost its bloom. Instead

[26]*Ibid.*, Letellier à Chauveau, 10 fév. 1849.

of playing on words, he harped on the glories of the French Revolution or of annexation to the United States. He became lost in the perennial (and slightly boring?) search for conspiracies against *la nation canadienne*. In a long article on *l'anglomanie* on November 18 he railed against the *Canadiens* themselves:

"En désirant l'annexion du Canada aux Etats-Unis, disent certains Canadiens-français, vous ne réfléchissez pas que vous renoncez *à nos institutions, à notre langue et à nos lois!* Si jamais l'annexion avait lieu, c'est pour le coup que nous perdrions notre langue française, que nous serions *anglifiés!"* . . . Pensez-y un instant, et vous me direz si vous devez craindre d'être anglifiés plus que vous l'êtes. . . . Dans les faubourgs surtout, où la population est toute canadienne-française, chaque marchand-épicier ou autre a son enseigne en langue anglaise. Et quel anglais, grand Dieu!—de l'anglais qui ferait rougir un Chinois. . . . L'Anglomanie est à l'ordre du jour, c'est la mode de 1848–9; vous la trouvez dans toutes les maisons, à chaque coin de rue, à la campagne, chez les petits et chez les grands, chez les savants et chez les ignorants. . . . Les beaux parlent presque toujours la langue anglaise, singent aussi bien qu'ils peuvent le *dandy* de Londres. . . . Chacun son goût: pour moi, je ne serai jamais anglomane; car à l'épais *John Bull* à l'abdomen proéminent, à mine renfrognée et hargneuse, à l'air hautain et aristocratique, je préfère *Brother Jonathan* à l'œil intelligent, à manières sans gène et à principes d'égalité.

Sometimes he managed to recapture some of the freshness of his 1840 days—as on August 26 when he suggested abolishing the death penalty and condemning murderers instead to eating any three issues of *Le Journal de Québec*. But these flashes were too rare, perhaps inevitably. For the young, uncompromising, often bitter separatists who now followed Papineau were men without humour.

L'Avenir proved this. It was intelligent, but as it moved over into the Papineau party it grew tiresome with its continual warnings of national disaster. Now, it alluded to the "cruelles injustices faites aux Canadiens" (February 19) or to the "MOYENS DÉSHONNÊTES *par lesquels l'Union a été imposée*" (April 26). During June it carried long articles on how England had always tried to defraud French Canada of its liberty, on the injustice of the shared debt of Upper Canada, on Lord Sydenham, or, most often, on the illusion that was responsible government. At first the bold young writers had included interesting literary criticisms and accounts of erudite lectures at the Institut Canadien. They were genuinely and generously concerned with bringing their countrymen up to the new standards of the century of progress. But by mid-1848 they were wasting their talents on the dark misdeeds of the British. However, while Papineau trotted out his manifestos against the Union, the young editors of *L'Avenir* did provoke a magnificent theoretical discussion about the Union and responsible government.

17

"L'Union et la Nationalité" 1848

"Je n'ai pas jusqu'ici développer [sic] ma pensée au sujet de notre position actuelle; mais M. Papineau et son neveu ne perdent rien pour attendre," Joseph Cauchon wrote to LaFontaine at the beginning of April 1848.[1] Papineau had just broken with LaFontaine's party and begun his agitation for repeal of the Union. Things were going badly. There were the Irish; there was the depression; there were dissatisfied *Canadiens* suing for patronage. And now, as Lord Elgin said, there was "Guy Fawkes Papineau, actuated by the most malignant passions, irritated vanity,—disappointed ambition, and national hatred . . . waving a lighted torch among these combustibles."[2] Cauchon thought that Papineau himself could be taken care of, though perhaps with difficulty. But now *L'Avenir* had begun to publish a serious theoretical argument in favour of repeal.

The new discussion on the merits of the Union began early in 1848 with a few letters in *L'Avenir* and became serious in April when the young editors published a set of editorials on "L'Union et la Nationalité." In these they marshalled all their best arguments and soon launched the press of the eastern section of the province into heated debate. Indeed, before the year was out, *Le Canadien* in Quebec had also issued a series, "La Position," and *La Revue Canadienne*, *Les Mélanges Religieux*, and *Le Journal de Québec* had each replied. Taken together, the articles showed that the nascent political parties had each developed a substantial doctrine.

The case for repeal began with two letters in *L'Avenir*, one on December 31, 1847, the other on February 5, 1848. They bore the signature "Anti-Union," and appeared just as Papineau began his break with LaFontaine's party. Like the address to the electors of

---

[1]Papiers LaFontaine, Cauchon à LaFontaine, 8 avril 1848.
[2]Doughty, ed., *Elgin-Grey Papers*, I, 149, Elgin to Grey, May 4, 1848.

Saint-Maurice and Huntingdon, these letters castigated responsible government as an imposture, and the Union itself as a piece of nonsense. Responsible government had not yet corrected the injustice of the shared Upper Canadian debt or of the unfair representation. The Union had been imposed without the consent of the *Canadiens*, indeed against their expressed wish. This made it unjust. But, in fact, the Union was also unreasonable: "La réunion des deux provinces est un acte contre nature et qui n'aura jamais son exécution franche et entière." Geographically, it was stupid, for it joined two large territories in each of which communications remained difficult. Culturally it brought together two peoples whose "diversité des lois, du language, de la religion, des coutumes et des usages" had forced the building of a "système d'administration *à deux faces.*" How much simpler it would be to divide the province back into its natural parts. The letters concluded, perhaps not so illogically, with "A bas l'Union et Vive la Reine." "Anti-Union" thus repeated substantially the arguments Neilson and Viger had used in 1840. But when the editors of *L'Avenir* began their series, in April 1848, they added a new dimension which the tolerant, eighteenth-century minds of the older men had barely been able to glimpse—the argument based on nationality. To the young men of the Institut, the main objection to the Union was that it prevented the *Canadiens* from achieving the natural destiny of every nation, a separate national state. And therefore they entitled their series "L'Union et la Nationalité."

"La nationalité est le principe de vie des peuples," the articles began, and the Canadian union, "faite dans le but de nous perdre," was killing this nationality: "Nous nous trouvons dans un état tel que nous n'osons plus rappeler au peuple qu'il a une nationalité à soutenir; que c'est son devoir, que c'est son droit; que cette nationalité . . . finira par se détruire au contact des nationalités étrangères, comme *l'acier* se détruit par l'action lente mais continue du tems" (April 29). The Union must therefore be repealed. And now more than ever was the time. Since 1840 the *Canadiens* had struggled to achieve responsible government, hoping to "parer les inconvénients et les mauvaises conséquences [de l'Union] pour en obtenir plus tard les avantages." But responsible government had been in operation since 1842 (they said) and in five years had done nothing about the unjust representation and the Upper Canada debt. Indeed, the articles pointed out (with a dubious interpretation of the facts): "L'Angleterre a réservé plus de bills, a donné de plus fréquentes et minutieuses instructions sur des détails de législation intérieure qu'elle ne l'a fait sous la constitution antérieure" (June 28). The system had proved wrong and must be repealed before it could do more damage:

Ne nous a-t-on pas vu pendant cinq ans condamnés à jouer le rôle d'une faction. . . . cela après avoir formé seuls une société parfaitement organisée, avec unité de language, de mœurs, de religion, de lois, d'institutions qui composaient la nationalité canadienne, condamnés à être la minorité lorsqu'il s'agissait d'exercer des droits politiques, condamnés à ne plus entendre la langue dans nos assemblées législatives, quoique ces institutions politiques et cette langue fussent celles de la majorité.

The choice, "l'Union ou la nationalité," must be made now. Besides— the international situation favoured them: "Ces évènements qui éclatent sans cesse en Europe lui donnent des garanties de succès. La révolution française doit bouleverser le monde . . . Il faut que le peuple du Bas-Canada puisse être prêt . . . lorsque son heure arrivera" (April 15).

The authors made few specific suggestions about how separation was to be achieved. They merely kept insisting on the need to be themselves, presuming, apparently, that repeal would come for the asking: "Il est tems que le peuple connaise tous les maux que lui a faits *l'Union*; il est tems qu'on lui indique ceux dont il est menacé; il est temps qu'il en connaisse, qu'il en mesure toute la grandeur pour en demander la fin. S'il est unanime, on ne la lui refusera pas" (April 15). They denied that responsible government had been worth the effort. "Les avantages prétendus" of the Union would have come "par la seule force des choses, par la marche irrésistible des idées." And in any event it could not be repealed. For if responsible government could serve the nation "attaché au Haut-Canada par des *liens dégradans*," how much more valuable it would be to a people "séparé et chez lui, maître comme doit l'être la majorité" (April 29).

To reinforce the argument, *L'Avenir* continued throughout May to repeat it in various forms. At the same time it ran a series of five letters by Louis-Antoine Dessaulles signed "Campagnard." Dessaulles added no new ideas, but in his passionate style repeated those in the original series in different terms and at great length. All supported one dominant idea: "L'Union est sans contredit la plus flagrante injustice, le plus infâme attentat à nos droits naturels et politiques qui pût être commis" (May 3).

L'Avenir's series had not been concluded when Louis Létourneux began his answer. On April 18, *La Revue Canadienne* printed its own article called "L'Union et la Nationalité." In it Létourneux deplored the agitation begun by Papineau and his young followers. They had claimed that the most propitious time to achieve repeal was at hand, that responsible government had just been inaugurated "après une lutte longue et pénible, après des efforts puissants et bien dirigés" to correct the injustices of 1840. Now at last "le peuple qui n'était rien avant l'Union, et qui se voit roi et maître aujourd'hui" would begin to rule. Hence "le moment en est on ne peut plus mal choisi pour révolutionner le Canada." He went on to deal with the nationality argument. *L'Avenir* claimed the Union and nationality could not co-exist. But, Létourneux asked pointedly, "est-ce que quand nous avons un premier ministre de la couronne, des orateurs des deux Chambres, des juges-en-chef notre nationalité est nullifiée et jetée sur un pied d'infériorité?" *L'Avenir's* stress on national distinction would bring ruin to the *Canadiens.* For years, Létourneux recalled, the French had complained of the odious "distinctions d'origine." Since 1840 they had succeeded in winning over to their side liberal-minded politicians of other races and with them had been able to achieve what they could not secure alone. They should not now be the ones to raise the same cry.

L'Union fut faite dans le but de nous perdre. Mais l'Union nous a sauvés. . . . Ce n'est pas après que notre parti a recruté dans ses rangs des hommes de toute origine, que nos amis les libéraux du Haut-Canada et ceux du Bas qui sont d'origine étrangère, ont fait des efforts prodigieux pour remporter les élections, et que tous ensemble nous avons remporté la victoire la plus signalée, ce n'est pas maintenant qu'il faut faire appel aux préjugés.

Finally, Létourneux declared, *L'Avenir's* articles never proved their contention that once the separate national state had been established, every benefit would follow.

Si nos jeunes et ardents confrères nous faisaient voir l'avantage que nous aurions à quitter le port et à nous lancer sur la haute mer de la politique; s'ils nous prouvaient comment notre nationalité grandira et se fortifiera plus exposée aux vents et aux injures de la tourmente qu'à l'ombre d'un gouvernement libéral, sage et éclairé, qui la protégera et la fera chérir de plus en plus, à la bonne heure! Nous pourrions vous écouter.

At *Les Mélanges,* Hector Langevin agreed, reprinting the article from *La Revue* on April 25 and adding two others of his own on the twenty-second and twenty-eighth. In the first of these he deplored the growth of agitation now, just when the *Canadiens* had finally achieved their goal:

Pourquoi cette opposition? car il faut bien le remarquer, la nouvelle politique que propose l'*Avenir*, ce n'est autre chose, quoiqu'il en dise, qu'une opposition systématique au système gouvernemental existant. . . . Et que veut-on mettre en place? que veut-on substituer à l'ordre de choses qui existe à l'heure qu'il est? *L'Avenir* ne nous le dit pas; ce n'est pas son affaire; ce qu'il veut c'est détruire. Or, tout le monde le sait: détruire, est facile, mais reconstituer ne l'est pas. D'ailleurs quelles garanties d'ordre, de stabilité, de bon gouvernement nous donne l'*Avenir*? Aucunes.

In his second article he drew a dark picture of what *L'Avenir*'s trouble-making could mean:

Vouloir le rappel immédiat de l'Union, c'est refuser la libre navigation du St. Laurent, c'est refuser la réforme des postes et des douanes, c'est refuser la réforme des lois d'éducation, de municipalités, etc.; en un mot, c'est refuser ce que nous tenons déjà. Vouloir le rappel immédiat de l'Union, c'est échanger notre état de prospérité, d'activité, de richesse et de bonheur, tel que nous le prépare la concession des grandes mesures de réforme et de progrès énumérées plus haut, pour nous plonger dans une agitation sans fin et une opposition systématique à toutes autres mesures, et nous engager dans une longue suite d'années de misères, de tourments et de troubles sans nombre.

And he concluded by expressing his fears about the lack of balance of people like the self-absorbed young editors who considered themselves the agents of history and subordinated every natural consideration to their one dominant idea: "Comme on le voit, notre confrère persiste dans sa doctrine. Rien ne saurait réussir auprès de lui. La religion, la patrie, l'égalité, la concorde, la fraternité, tout cela n'a aucune signification à ses yeux; il n'envisage que le rappel: voilà son Dieu du jour."

On May 5 Aubin, who had not yet transferred his pen to Papineau's service, published an editorial in *Le Canadien* in which he too disagreed with *L'Avenir*. While agreeing that the Union was perverse and that even now it continued "encore fausse, dangereuse, critique puisque [le Bas-Canada] n'a pas obtenu réellement le rappel d'une seule de ses clauses iniques," he believed that agitation and division among the French would be worse, for they might lead to another rebellion— "circonstance," Aubin mentioned with a reference to the tender years of the editors of *L'Avenir*, "qu'oublient ceux qui n'ont pas souffert." Besides, he agreed with Létourneux that it was impractical to rely on different and difficult solutions when with responsible government the *Canadiens* had "à notre disposition les moyens de nous faire justice nous-mêmes au lieu d'user sans fin nos forces et nos moyens à la demander à d'autres." He concluded with an unfortunate example which in the next few years would be used on both sides of the discussion. Unions usually harmed nationality, he said, citing the examples of Poland, Belgium, Ireland, and Sicily-Naples, but in

Louisiana where the French continued to elect their own state government and administer their own civil code and education system, union with the United States had proved to be an exception.

La Louisiane française unie, noyée au milieu d'une nationalité d'hommes d'une nationalité rivale partout ailleurs, ne se plaint pas de domination, d'envahissement. La raison en est simple: cette union bien que forcée, est fondée sur l'égalité. Les hommes traités en égaux ne se plaignent pas pour être pris pour ce qu'ils valent, et tant qu'on ne les persécute pas *pour* leur origine, on ne les voit pas se réunir et s'allier pour dominer *par* leur origine.

If there could be justice to all "origines nationales," as seemed possible with the LaFontaine-Baldwin party, then why could the Canadian union not succeed in the same way?

Thus *La Revue Canadienne, Les Mélanges Religieux,* and *Le Canadien* answered *L'Avenir's* challenge. Together they emphasized the argument used earlier during *la crise Metcalfe*: that division among themselves must always be the *Canadiens'* main enemy. They questioned the wisdom of agitation at the very moment when the French, precisely because of their co-operation with another nationality, had just won the struggle which Papineau himself had initiated a generation earlier.

At *Le Journal de Québec,* Cauchon had finished preparing his arguments in favour of LaFontaine's policy. In May, while Papineau toured the Quebec district, he published three major articles entitled "Le Rappel de l'Union." In these he showed that when he wished he could make a serious and thorough examination of a problem.

His first article (May 4) covered the same ground as the other journalists. Division among the French Canadians was a form of political suicide, especially when they had at last achieved power: "A peine, après cinquante ans de luttes orageuses, possédons nous un pouvoir qu'ont fécondé notre sang et les cendres de nos ruines chaudes encore, que nos jalousies et nos ambitions poussent des cris de colère et de vengeance, et morcellent nos forces à l'infini. L'histoire est là pour dire que l'anéantissement est la destinée certaine de la société travaillée par de pareils éléments." Agitation for repeal now would inevitably lead to an armed clash, which the *Canadiens* would inevitably lose:

Si d'autres considérations ne peuvent valoir à nos yeux, calculons du moins notre force, car la lutte arrivera au moment que nous n'aurons pas prévu. Ne nous a-t-elle pas déjà surpris une fois il y a onze ans, lorsque nous étions loin de l'attendre, si tôt du moins? n'a-t-elle pas dégoûté tous nos calculs et toutes nos espérances, si toutefois nous avons calculé et nous avons espéré? Vous aurez beau dire, comme on disait alors, que vous ne voulez pas la lutte, vous l'aurez malgré vous à cause de la nature même et du but avoué de votre agitation.

And the cry for a national state was a serious error. In an area like Lower Canada, where citizens of so many different origins lived so close together, a government based on distinctions of race could not last. Indeed, was this not precisely what the *Canadiens* had opposed before the Union? And, at that time, when some of their leaders had begun to use the national cry, they had driven many of their allies away, thus delaying the achievement of their own political ambitions. "On comprend," he concluded, "ce que signifie ce cri de nationalité": used by one group, it must inevitably cause an echoing prejudice in the other. And, of the two, the *Canadiens* would probably be the losers.

In his second article on May 13, Cauchon reiterated in a flowery passage the dangers of "une agitation ayant pour base la nationalité, surtout au milieu d'un population hétérogène":

Nous avons signalé la folie d'une politique qui tend à tracer des démarcations profondes entre les nationalités enlacées les unes dans les autres et qui, avec un petit peu de sagesse et de direction, pourraient vivre et croître sans se nuire sur le sol généreux de la patrie; qui proclame comme un principe fécond de prospérité et de régénération du libéralisme, ou ce qui revient au même, de la justice universelle des droits égaux pour tous au plein midi de la civilization annonçant aux hommes, au nom de l'Evangile porté sur la foudre et sur le feu, qu'ils sont tous frères et tous membres de la même grande famille humaine, et qu'ils doivent se réunir sous la banière des principes et des opinions plutôt que sous celle des langues et des limites territoriales.

He pointed out the contradiction in the argument concerning the need of further reforms, of the debt, for instance, and of the system of representation. If the present councillors adopted a platform of repeal, they would have to resign their posts in the administration and would, therefore, not oversee the passage of reform measures. To remain in control of further legislation, on the other hand, they could not permit the growth of a movement for repeal. Also, if the new council resigned, the Tories would take over, basing their power on "l'exclusivisme national" and once more isolating the *Canadiens*. "Tels seront les faits inévitables," he warned, "de votre politique d'isolement."

In his third article, on May 27, Cauchon looked at the province's economic position. He noted that the English-speaking commercial classes of Lower Canada would object to repeal, as would the Upper Canadians. He hinted that the French-Canadian population of the

Montreal district would too. The Montreal region was economically dependent on Upper Canada for its prosperity. Montreal *Canadiens* might grow tired of a nationalist cry which would lead to the sacrifice of their prosperity to "la vie galvanique et la surexcitation qui tue."

Ne devez-vous pas craindre que la population franco-canadienne du district de Montréal, c'est à dire la population la plus nombreuse de cette population pour laquelle on veut faire de la nationalité aux dépens de son existence politique et sociale . . . ne se fatigue à la fin et ne finisse pas par désirer ou au moins accepter sans murmurer, au préjudice d'une nationalité aussi morcelée et travaillée par des guerres intestines, une annexion qui augmenterait immensément sa richesse et sa prospérité.

Finally, he asked, why agitate for repeal in the name of a democracy which must come inevitably if left to its normal development: "Personne ne doute quels que soit ses goûts ou la théorie gouvernementale de sa conviction, que l'avenir du Canada ainsi que de l'Amérique du Nord ne soit acquis à la démocratie."

In Montreal both *La Revue Canadienne* and *Les Mélanges* reprinted Cauchon's articles. And in *Les Mélanges* Langevin added a summary of his own views (July 18):

L'adoption du rappel de l'acte d'Union en entier comme principe d'action politique par la population française du Bas-Canada, doit avoir pour conséquences: 1. l'opposition absolue à cette mesure par la population britannique du Bas-Canada; et conditionnelle de la part de celle du Haut-Canada; 2. la réunion de la masse entière de cette population sans distinctions de partis politiques, contre la population française; 3. l'isolement de cette dernière dans la lutte et par suite la minorité; 4. la résignation forcée de ses chefs et sa non-participation dans la conduite des affaires; 5. l'antagonisme de l'Angleterre qui naturellement devra préférer les intérêts de sa propre population, aux nôtres; 6. enfin la lutte, lutte de nationalté et par conséquent de haine et de vengeance.

Some six weeks later, he amplified these points. On September 1 he explained how responsible government had initiated a new age in which the *Canadiens* could, for the first time, act as a free people. To want a change signalled a lack of faith: "La Providence, qui a veillé d'une manière si spéciale sur les destinées du Canada, ne peut que nous réserver un avenir glorieux et magnifique. Secondons donc ses vues, et pour cela n'aidons pas à nos ennemis, par nos divisions, à retarder notre avancement et nos progrès."

Langevin did not have the last word, however. Aubin, now a repealer, published another editorial two days after he had lost the government announcements on September 22. It began with a scathing attack on responsible government and party patronage. The government, Aubin declared, "a déserté la grande cause des libertés canadiennes pour se rétrécir aux proportions d'une faction ennemie de toute institution équitable et agissant par et pour les intérêts du petit nombre au détriment du grand nombre." And what, he asked, was all this talk about the *Canadiens* having come to power? There were more English-speaking councillors in the administration than French, and these same Upper Canadian Reformers held office on the basis of an unjust representation. Responsible government was government of a majority by the minority, the Union a "rêve antisocial vide de justice politique."

Thus, as 1848 drew to a close, the arguments for and against repeal had been stated. In Quebec Cauchon's *Journal de Quebéc* had scored better and more serious arguments against *Le Canadien's* article in favour of repeal. For while Aubin attacked what he considered the corruption of party politics that seemed inseparable from responsible government, *Le Journal* stressed the dangers of political disunity among the French and politics based on nationality. In Montreal, Létourneux and Langevin had led the assault on *L'Avenir's* doctrine. They had pointed out the new opportunities for *la survivance* provided by responsible government and, like Cauchon, rejected any agitation founded on "les odieuses distinctions nationales." Among all the journalists, the strongest opposition to *L'Avenir* came from Cauchon and the transplanted *Québecois*, Langevin; the weakest came from *La Minerve.*

Throughout the theoretical discussion on repeal Duvernay had kept his counsel. He must have felt in a delicate position. At heart a republican, he had been one of the most hostile opponents of the Union in 1840. He had returned to Quebec in 1842 to support LaFontaine only because he had been practically reduced to begging on the streets of Burlington. In addition, his assistant was now Raphaël Bellemarre, a young man much closer to *L'Avenir's* ideas than to Langevin's. Yet Duvernay knew how much *La Minerve* depended on government advertisements, and LaFontaine and Cartier kept a close watch over its editorial policy. Also, Duvernay seems to have entertained a personal animosity towards Papineau. Torn between the two sides, he chose neither. During April and May, he avoided the topic of repeal, filling *La Minerve* with comments about the navigation laws and the revolutions in Europe. On May 1 Duvernay at last gave in and published one short comment on "L'Union et la Nationalité," a moderate, reserved, noncommittal article which he promised would be the last: "Nous ne prendrons pas de part [à cette discussion], tant qu'on n'aura pas un but un peu mieux défini. . . . Nous ne comprenons pas dans quel but on veut en occuper le public dans le temps actuel."

LaFontaine may have been just as happy that *La Minerve* ignored the discussion. With its circulation of over 1500 readers, Duvernay's paper reached as many people as *Les Mélanges Religieux, La Revue Canadienne*, and *L'Avenir* together. Thus many *Canadiens* in the district of Montreal must have remained relatively unaware of the whole discussion. As long as the French Canadians believed *la survivance* to be inseparable from responsible government, there would be no political trouble for LaFontaine and his party. In the Quebec district, of course, the two large circulation papers had taken part in the debate, but again luckily for LaFontaine, Cauchon's "pensée au sujet de notre position actuelle" seemed to carry the most weight.

In any event, victory in this theoretical discussion was not that important. For if the readers of the newspapers reacted like the editors, they were convinced only by the theories that supported their chosen political allegiance. The journalists that supported repeal had generally opposed LaFontaine since 1839, and those who now found arguments to defend the Union had fought Viger since 1843. The *Canadiens* at large, however, still worshipped "le roi Louis-Joseph 1ᵉʳ," and if repeal was to be defeated it would have to be not by political theories, but by the destruction of Papineau.

18

The Destruction of Papineau
1848

"Vous n'êtes pas au courant, mon cher Dr de toutes les intrigues de la Clique contre L. Joe, c'est épouvantable," E.-R. Fabre wrote to Dr. O'Callaghan in February 1848. "Je crois qu'aujourd'hui il pense comme moi, que ces gens-là veulent le perdre comme ils ont perdu son cousin Mr. Viger et son frère M.D.B.P."[1] He was right. However well they might score against the theory of repeal, LaFontaine and his partisans realized that they must also destroy Papineau's personal prestige. It was not so much his arguments that would turn electors against them, as the spell of his personality. As long as this man, the most powerful influence in the province, stood out against them, they would never be safe. And so they must destroy him.

They had begun quietly in 1847 when the rumours that Papineau intended to re-enter public life first started. Then, after his sortie in the House in March 1848, they increased the momentum and bitterness of their attack. They assailed his character and his motives; they revived all their old tricks to beat his candidate in a by-election and to nullify his efficiency in the Townships colonization scheme, particularly. They called him names, and they persuaded Dr. Wolfred Nelson to cast doubts on his integrity. By the end of 1848 they had really destroyed his power and popularity.

THE FIRST ATTACKS

When the address to the Electors of Saint-Maurice and Huntingdon came out in December 1847, LaFontaine and his politicians hesitated. Cauchon had already hinted privately to LaFontaine that Papineau would be an asset, and on November 6 he declared in *Le Journal* that

[1]O'Callaghan Papers, Fabre à O'Callaghan, 11 fév. 1848.

if the old Speaker entered the House, "il y trouverait sa place naturelle et l'accueuil auxquels ont droit ses services et ses talents." But LaFontaine feared the worst. While the proofs of Papineau's document were still in Duvernay's office, the party leader called his friends together. "We had a Council of War on Papineau's address before it was published," Hincks wrote to Baldwin, "and Holmes and I went to see him about it. I felt then that he could not suppress it consistently with self-respect. He had no desire however to do so. I think him quite sincere. . . . Lafontaine [sic] and Holmes were strongly urged to denounce the address but my advice was ultimately adopted viz to treat him kindly and say nothing to irritate."[2]

La Minerve accordingly published the address on December 20 with a note emphasizing the section where Papineau claimed his reluctance to re-enter public life. "En général," Duvernay added on December 27, "on regarde comme bien fortes les raisons qui ont déterminé M. Papineau à désirer la retraite." At La Revue Canadienne and Les Mélanges, Létourneux and Langevin took the same attitude. They wished him well but thought Papineau himself would rather not be returned. Létourneux' own change of attitude was striking. Before he had seen the address, he wrote (La Revue, December 17): "Nous apprenons avec un vif plaisir que l'Hon. Louis-Joseph Papineau, l'éloquent, le formidable champion d'autrefois, se rendra aux vœux des électeurs . . . et qu'il s'est décidé à consacrer le reste de ses jours au service de son pays." But four days later, after printing Papineau's text, he added:

M. Papineau approuve ses anciens amis politiques, les ex-ministres, dans tout ce qu'ils ont fait. Il recommande aux populations de reporter les mêmes hommes au pouvoir. . . . Mais quant au gouvernement responsable, il souhaite se tromper, mais enfin il n'y croit pas. C'est là ce que nous regrettons. Les choses étant ainsi, nous croyons que les électeurs de Saint-Maurice et Huntingdon auraient dû se rendre au désir de M. Papineau et de ne pas le forcer à prendre maintenant un siège dans la chambre d'assemblée contre ses sentiments.

Létourneux' reaction was fairly typical. "I have searched in vain I regret to say, through the French organs of public opinion," Lord Elgin wrote,

for a frank and decided expression of hostility to the anti-British sentiments propounded in M. P's address—A commentary on this document, couched in almost all cases in the same or similar terms, has gone the round of the French Press,—"regretting that M[r] P. s[d] have so bad an opinion of the British Gov[t] and of Responsible Gov[t]"—"hoping that he may be mistaken—" and "recommending that a further trial should be given to the system before

2Baldwin Papers, v51, Hincks to Baldwin, Jan. 14, 1848.

extreme measures are resorted to"—Deprecating in short M^r P's present appearance on the stage, but intimating that if the General Election does not bring their Party into power, it will be proper to rally round him and espouse his political creed.[3]

The only exception was a penetrating article in *Le Journal de Québec* of January 4 many suspected had been written by Morin. It probably had, for it was the most outspoken (although polite) attack on Papineau in the whole Lower Canadian press since even Cauchon still held to the common declaration of approval. In substance the article made three points. First, it reminded everyone that Papineau did not seem to understand the real nature of French Canada's position in the Union. He had returned from exile in 1845 to find his own family in a most compromising situation:

Il avait vu son cousin et son frère donner la main à l'oppresseur de son pays, et, par vanité et par ambition, monter ignominieusement les degrés d'un pouvoir qui venait de prouver qu'il était l'ennemi de tout droit populaire et de toute liberté constitutionnelle. Il arriva au milieu de nous au plein midi de la corruption et du despotisme auxquels son nom, sinon sa pensée, était intimement lié dans sa famille.

Papineau might well have been depressed by what the new régime had done, the article continued. He had been unable, apparently, to discern not only that the Union carried within itself the seeds of reform, but that by active, positive measures, the most crucial of which had been the alliance with the Reformers of Upper Canada, these could be made to bear fruit:

Ce n'est pas, il faut y songer, avec nos forces seules, surtout avec les forces que l'Union nous a faites, que nous pouvons remporter la victoire, mais avec ces forces combinées avec d'autres qui nous manqueront si nous acceptons l'état de choses auquel M. Papineau veut nous amener. Si nous voulions revenir à 1836, dans ce moment tous les hommes sincères qui se rallient à notre cause nous abandonneraient de suite pour nous laisser dans l'isolement.

Secondly, Papineau did not understand responsible government. The actions of Sydenham and Metcalfe and of Papineau's own relatives had not weakened the strength of the principles which Durham had proposed and which Elgin was now beginning to put into practice. Had not the dissolution of parliament, just now, been effected "par et de l'avis et *consentement* de notre conseil exécutif?" The very reforms which Papineau himself urged—changes in the judiciary, the civil list, the electoral law—would soon be effected by a new council

[3]Doughty, ed., *Elgin-Grey Papers*, I, 117, Elgin to Grey, Jan. 7, 1848.

in which the French would be well represented. And even though responsible government had not been observed since 1840, the opinion of the *Canadiens*, expressed by the united Reform party in Opposition, had exerted much influence—on the restoration of the French language for instance and on the school law. In Papineau's time, before the Union, the French had had little chance to influence their own future: "Quelqu'excellent et désirable que fut le régime ancien, cette opinion n'exerçait son influence que sur le peuple de la colonie sans pénétrer les conseils du souverain. La représentation populaire etait complètement isolée des deux autres branches de la constitution et en lutte ouverte avec elles. . . . "

The author then continued to deprecate Papineau's agitation. He apologized for opposing the ex-Speaker's emergence into politics, "car Papineau est un grand homme et glorieux . . . et nous ne voulons censurer son passé." But now Papineau proposed a leap in the dark and denied the only practical hope for the future of his people: "Est-il opportun d'agiter? peut-on à l'heure qu'il est, sans danger et avec quelques chances de succès, agiter le rappel d'une mesure dont nous nous accordons avec lui à reconnaître l'injustice et la tendance mauvaise? C'est l'unique problème dont nous devons en ce moment demander la solution aux hommes réfléchis! . . . protester toujours eut été une absurdité, un suicide."

Unlike the other editorials that merely expressed regret, this studious and thoughtful work presented solid arguments against Papineau's comeback. It also spoke with a certain assured calm about the hero. This calm did not last. By February 1848 Duvernay refused to publish articles favouring Papineau, and in March, on the day the ex-Speaker rose to attack the motion of supply, all LaFontaine's press unleashed its pent-up invective. The journalists felt they had no alternative. "Quand on voit un misérable comme Papineau se créer des sympathies qu'on refuse à des cœurs sincères et vraiment patriotiques, il est difficile de se taire," Aylwin wrote to the Attorney General.[4] And throughout May, as the manifestos kept falling from Papineau's table, each editor took his position.

In Montreal, *La Revue* and *Les Mélanges* condemned the whole commotion and offered as explanation Papineau's own dishonourable motives. Létourneux said (May 16) that the second manifesto had a "tendance et but de jeter au milieu d'une société paisible et tranquille la discorde, les haines, les divergences, les tempêtes." He added (May 19) that Papineau had "déblatérer avec un fanatisme démagogique . . .

4Papiers LaFontaine, Aylwin à LaFontaine, 1 juin 1848.

avec si peu de réserve . . . des absurdités, des mensonges, fausses représentations, paroles insidieuses." And he wondered whether the manifesto was not the product of "les libéraux exaltés, les mécontents et les envieux," since it seemed filled with "des expressions qui peuvent convenir à un COMMUNISTE ou à aucun membre des clubs exaltés de Paris." Langevin, on his part, said (May 19) that he rejoiced that "M. Papineau jette enfin le masque. . . . Il lui tardait de quitter . . . le rôle qu'il joue depuis quatre ou cinq mois pour reprendre celui d'un agitateur." He reprinted Létourneux' comments, and wrote a long refutation of the third manifesto filled with statements like "il est le plus dangereux ennemi du peuple," "cet ancien défenseur de nos droits se retourne aujourd'hui contre son pays," "ses attaques aussi peu mesurées qu'elles sont impolitiques et anti-patriotiques," and ending on May 26 with this thrust: "En parlant aussi indépendemment que nous le faisons, nous montrons encore que, lors même que nous reviendrions de l'exil, et que nous trouverions au pouvoir quelques-uns de nos parents qui trahiraient notre pays, nous ne consentirions jamais à nous taire pendant des mois et des mois, quand ce serait même pour recevoir la jolie somme de £4,500!"

In Quebec, Cauchon also reprinted the articles from La Revue and also denounced Papineau as a dangerous agitator led by personal ambition. In a typical paragraph on May 20, he wrote:

Tout lecteur lisant avec sang-froid le nouveau manifeste jugera si avec de pareilles idées l'avenir du pays est en sûreté. Une haine profonde et des paroles de vengeance constituent ce long récit. Il est évident que M. Papineau veut démolir l'administration que le pays a pris tant de temps à édifier. Il accuse de sentiments mercenaires des hommes (les ministres) que, dans son premier manifeste du mois de décembre, il préconisait de toute la puissance de sa parole. Nous comprenons bien sa pensée. Haine, haine, haine profonde de l'Angleterre! Mais où va nous conduire cette haine.

This time, La Minerve joined in. Duvernay now had no hesitation in attacking Papineau personally. Like his colleagues, he lamented the agitation and questioned Papineau's motives. When the second manifesto came out in May, condemning the councillors whom the December address had praised moderately, he published both statements with the comment:

Tout le monde a été surpris et contrarié par le dernier écrit de l'hon. L. J. Papineau; ses plus chauds partisans y trouvent à redire, personne ne l'approuve. . . . Nous avons fait le dépouillement des deux manifestes pour en faire voir l'esprit et les contradictions. . . . M. Papineau d'aujourd'hui est réfuté complètement . . . par M. Papineau de décembre dernier. Est-ce le patriotisme qui le ronge et le change ou quelqu'autre sentiment?" (May 22)

A week later, when the third manifesto appeared, he added that although he agreed with Papineau about the excellence "des institutions électives républicaines," he nevertheless considered it unwise to raise further turmoil for the present. "On commence à panser nos plaies," he wrote on May 29. "Nous n'aimons pas l'Union, mais nous l'aimons mieux que la dévastation!"

Except for *L'Avenir* and *Le Canadien*, the Lower Canadian press, therefore, was unanimously opposed to the manifestos. The politicians soon proved that the editorials reflected the views of the electors. The seat in the dual riding of Quebec City which Aylwin had resigned when he went to the Bench was to be filled at a by-election on June 7, 1848. LaFontaine's followers determined to give Papineau's manifestos the most practical of possible answers.

But they had to work hard. The *ministériels*, as the LaFontaine party was already being called, first chose as their candidate Dunbar Ross, a lawyer of Irish extraction who had the double qualification of a good record of service to the party (in 1844 he had written a pamphlet, *The "crise" Metcalfe and the LaFontaine-Baldwin Cabinet defended*) and an English name, and so would continue the custom of having one member for the dual riding chosen from each of the English and French groups. The repealers put forward Joseph Légaré, a separatist since the 1830's and a passionate partisan of Papineau since December. Realizing that the election would be fought on the question of repeal, the *ministériels* decided to change their candidate. For one thing Cauchon had discovered that Ross did not have the support of the Irish; for another, he felt that in a contest on the repeal issue, they should have a French name. The party accordingly selected a popular Quebec merchant, François-Xavier Méthot. Ross, however, had been promised the candidacy by Aylwin and refused to step down. Meanwhile, in the repeal camp, Glackmeyer had declared that the nomination should by rights come to him. Had he not been Neilson's second-in-command? At a meeting on May 18 the splits in both groups became public. Neither Ross nor Méthot would abdicate, and each seemed to have some backing. Glackmeyer also remained stubborn, but he was booed by the other repealers. On the following Sunday, when Glackmeyer tried to recapture support by a speech after mass on the steps of Saint-Roch church, he was shouted down. He then retired from the contest. Thus, when the nomination meeting took place, the *Québecois* were presented with a choice of three: Ross, an independent, Méthot for LaFontaine, and Légaré for Papineau.

Légaré and his followers hoped to profit from the dissatisfaction aroused by Aylwin's appointment so soon after his election. But they concentrated particularly on the question of repeal, attacking the alliance with the Upper Canadian Reformers and calling on Papineau's influence. On May 26 *Le Canadien* complained about the instability of Upper Canadian politics and the consequent disadvantage for the *Canadiens*:

Il leur [the *Canadiens*] faudra, eux dont l'opinion ne varie pas, subir, sans moyen de se protéger, toutes les vicissitudes politiques auxquelles les exposera toujours l'instabilité de l'opinion publique dans le Haut-Canada. Il leur faudra se soumettre sans murmure à tout ce que voudront leurs *frères* libéraux lorsqu'ils seront en majorité et combattre avec eux dans l'opposition lorsque les tories du Haut-Canada auront remporté une victoire électorale; exploités par les uns, écrasés par les autres.

A vote for Légaré was a vote against the Union. Méthot's supporters answered, as *Les Mélanges* reported on June 6, that their candidate "désire le rappel de l'union des Canadas à défaut des justes concessions que le Bas-Canada réclame et qui lui sont dues, mais il est opposé au système de l'agitation immédiate, voulue par M. Papineau." They stressed the need for the political calm that would give the new ministers the opportunity to make responsible government serve. But Cauchon who had never lost an election was worried about this one.[5] So was Caron.[6] By May 25 he was a bit more encouraging, however:

Nos affaires politiques s'améliorent un peu. . . . l'on me donne à espérer que l'on pourrait venir à un entendement. . . . Le parti Légaré serait, dit-on, disposé à se réunir à celui de Ross, ou plutôt à se retirer de la lutte si le parti Méthot en fesait autant; il n'y a rien de décider [*sic*]. Mais il pourrait y avoir plus de calme—Glackmeyer malgré ses lectures en plein air ne gagne rien, si ce n'est de faire rire de lui.[7]

In the end Méthot won by 1,669 votes to Légaré's 1,196. His election was a valuable step towards the frustration of Papineau since, in the midst of the campaign, the hero had come down and harangued 4000 *Québecois* for three hours in the rain and his second and third manifestos had been printed and distributed free in the Quebec district by the young men of *L'Avenir*. Thus Méthot's election could be seen as a telling blow against Papineau himself. "Le beau résultat d'hier," Cauchon declared in *Le Journal* on June 8, "a consolé tous les amis de la paix. L'effet et l'influence morale de ce résultat sont incalculables, incommensurables; et sauvent le pays de la plus désastreuse

[5]*Ibid.*, Cauchon à LaFontaine, 26 avril 1848.
[6]*Ibid.*, Caron à LaFontaine, 1 mai 1848.
[7]*Ibid.*, Caron à LaFontaine, 25 mai 1848.

des agitations. La vieille métropole du Canada a compris l'importance de sa mission."

Meanwhile the *unionnaires* in Montreal were also at work to restrain Papineau's sway. And since he seemed to have chosen it as his instrument, they first set out to neutralize his influence over the Association des Townships. In this LaFontaine's party received considerable help from the Governor General. On April 19, 1848, Bishop Bourget, Papineau, and other leaders of the Association attended Lord Elgin at the Château de Ramezay to request government support. "In dealing with them," Elgin recounted to Lord Grey,

I had one of two courses to choose from . . . either, on the one hand, to give the promoters of the scheme a cold shoulder—point out its objectionable features—& dwell upon difficulties of execution,—in which case, (use what tact I might)—I should have dismissed the Bishop and his friends discontented, and given Mr P. an opportunity of asserting that I had lent a quasi sanction to his calumnies.—or, on the other, to identify myself with the movement, put myself in so far as might be, at its head, impart to it as salutary a direction as possible, and thus wrest from M Papineau's hands a potent instrument of agitation—.[8]

Elgin chose the second alternative, and among the reasons he described in this same letter, one testified again to the belief which he shared with Parent, LaFontaine, and Taché that *la nation canadienne* treated justly stood as the strongest guarantee of Canadian independence of the United States.

No one object in my opinion is so important, whether you seek to retain Canada as a Colony, or to fit her for independence and make her instinct with national life & vigor, (a result by no means less desirable than the former in so far as the interests of Great Britain are concerned) as the filling up of her vacant lands with a resident agricultural population. More especially is it of moment that the inhabitants of French origin should feel that every facility of settling on the land of their Fathers is given them with the cordial assent and concurrence of the British Gov^t and its Representative.—and that in the plans of settlement . . . French Canadian nationality which Papineau endeavors to pervert to purposes of faction, may yet perhaps if properly improved furnish the best remaining security against annexation to the States. Was it, think you, love for England or hatred for those *sacrés Bostonais* which stirred the French Canadian mind in the Revolutionary war and again in 1812?

Nor does it matter when you are dealing with Frenchmen how near the Yankee line you locate them. An English man, Scotchman or Irishman when he is outwitted by his Yankee neighbour may be tempted to admire his superior sagacity, and to curse the Gov^t and constitution of Great Britain for the consequences of his own stupidity or apathy. But it is not so with

[8]Doughty, ed., *Elgin-Grey Papers*, I, 191, Elgin to Grey, June 29, 1848.

the Habitans. Contact with those precious specimens of Anglo Saxondom, who are ignorant of his language, despise his intellect, ridicule his customs, and swindle him in every transaction in which he is engaged with them, is by no means provocative of affection in his breast.

In his hope to "keep the good side uppermost and defeat M. P's object,"[9] he sent the Association a personal gift of £20 and promised that the government would act quickly. Meanwhile he multiplied requests to London for a special grant from the imperial government to cover the extraordinary expenses incurred by the province at the time of the typhus epidemic of 1847. And in May he received assurances that London would pay £20,000.

Meanwhile, LaFontaine and the government had announced that Crown lands in the Saguenay and Ottawa regions would be made available under favourable conditions and that the Association would soon be hearing excellent news about the Townships. "Tout canaille que M. Papineau veuille bien faire nos ministres," Duvernay noted on June 8, "ils auront donc fait plus que tous leurs dévanciers pour la colonisation des terres incultes. Quand nous disons dévanciers, nous ne parlons seulement de nos représentants depuis 37 . . . mais aussi de l'ancienne chambre d'assemblée." Then, on June 10, in a much publicized letter to Bishop Bourget (as president of the Association) the Executive Council announced that the £20,000 received from London would go to opening up roads and providing the necessary facilities to guarantee the Association's scheme. After such a princely gift, there could be no doubt about who, Papineau or the councillors, had done more to assure the prosperity of (as the Council was quoted in La Revue on June 10) "les descendants des premiers colons dont les patients et persévérents travaux en temps de paix et la bravoure en temps de guerre ont tant fait pour l'avancement et la défense de cette partie des domaines de Sa Majesté."

The Canadiens seemed to take the hint. LaFontaine and his colleagues gladly allowed their press to exploit the Governor's actions in favour of the Association. La Revue immediately underlined the "dispositions bienveillantes des autorités Impériales et Provinciales" (June 16). Langevin added a statement on July 11 which robbed the Institut Canadien of any credit by suggesting that the government had acted, not according to the petition of April 19 which had been composed by Papineau, but really upon the advice of a secret memorandum from Bishop Bourget. The Bishop himself issued a pastoral letter on June 17, the day after the Executive Council's answer was published, in which he sought to remove the colonization scheme from

[9]Ibid., I, 145, Elgin to Grey, April 26, 1848.

politics. But on June 20 *Le Journal de Québec* published a letter which put the plan right back in the anti-Papineau context. The letter, reprinted by *Les Mélanges*, and *La Minerve*, was from Father O'Reilly, the originator of the plan, and it left no doubt about who was the greater benefactor:

Puissent tous ceux qui affligent le pays par des discussions qui ne produisent que l'animosité et la division, se taire pour unir leurs voix et leurs efforts aux nôtres, afin de promouvoir l'œuvre de la colonisation des Townships. . . . Unissons-nous pour rappeler des bords de l'Hudson, et des villes des Etats voisins, tant de milliers de nos compatriotes qui y végètent dans un avilissement pire que la mort. Ramenons par nos efforts, ces canadiens égarés au double bercail de leur patrie et de leur religion; nous aurons par là accompli une révolution plus utiles que le rappel de l'union; et qui nous mettra plus tard en état, de conquérir avec plus de certitude et de facilité nos droits légitimes.

When *L'Avenir* replied on June 28 by attacking the priest for involving himself in politics, Father O'Reilly wrote a second letter, ostensibly to offer excuses for sending the missive to Cauchon, but in reality underlining his devotion to LaFontaine. *La Minerve* published it on June 30.

M. Cauchon connaissait mieux que personne mes sentiments et mes convictions. . . . Aujourd'hui je n'ai pas honte de me ranger de son côté. J'ai toujours blâmé l'Union; mais j'aime trop les Canadiens-français pour les exciter dans ce moment-ci, à compromettre la magnifique position qu'ils occupent, afin de les engager dans une agitation politique, qui les plongerait infailliblement dans l'infériorité sociale dont M. LaFontaine . . . les voudrait préserver.

LaFontaine's propagandists and political agents had done good work. By the autumn of 1848, Papineau's manifestos had been answered point by point and his active enterprises ruined. They had only begun, however, for they still had to demolish his reputation.

WOLFRED NELSON

In June 1848 Aylwin wrote to reassure LaFontaine about Papineau. "Il doit rencontrer," he prophesied, "le mépris qu'il mérite, et comme je l'ai prédit il y a douze ans son nom sera détesté et honni par tout le Canada."[10] LaFontaine, more pessimistic, told Elgin that he feared "Papineau would draw away all Lower Canada and leave me and my Ministry powerless."[11] Aylwin proved the better prophet—but only

[10]Papiers LaFontaine, Aylwin à LaFontaine, 1 juin 1848.
[11]Doughty, ed., *Elgin-Grey Papers*, I, 290, Elgin to Grey, Jan. 29, 1849.

after a miserable campaign against the *patriote* hero's honour. During the last half of 1848 those seasoned demolition experts, Duvernay and Cauchon, successfully destroyed the most prestigious reputation in their province. They expressed regret at having to do so, but they convinced their people that Papineau was an impatient demagogue stimulated only by ambition.

In 1845, when Viger's faction was using Papineau's name as a drawing card, *La Minerve* and *Le Journal* had begun to circulate suspicious intimations about him. But when Papineau had retired to his seigneury on his return, the journalists turned to other things. Now, on March 17, 1848, Langevin began the smear campaign with a column which recurred with increasing frequency as the months passed. Headed "L. J. PAPINEAU" in the largest and blackest letters his typesetters could devise, it recounted anecdotes from the tribune's past, or flagrant contradictions in his present statements, each seasoned with unsavoury innuendos about his character. Létourneux imitated the process at *La Revue Canadienne*, but less regularly. He underscored Papineau's impatience, attacked *L'Avenir* as "ce journal ... aux doctrines erronées, hors de saison et suicide," and insinuated that the clergy disapproved of the "agitation intempestive, dangereuse et mal intentionnée" (May 2).

At *La Minerve* Duvernay varied the fare. At times he wrote of how "Notre ... intention ... est de mettre Papineau en contradiction avec lui-même" (May 18); at others of the man's speeches as "fondés sur le préjugé, la haine, l'orgueuil, le ressentiment, l'ambition et l'esprit de vengeance" (May 29). By mid-June Papineau was commonly "le grand agitateur," or the leader of a "clique de turbulents, de mécontents, de désappointés et d'une parenté prétentieuse et égoiste qui veut que le pays lui obéisse"; by December, he was among the "fanatiques aveugles ... des esprits troublés" (December 7) who "ne sont montés au pouvoir que dans le but d'y obtenir de l'argent ou des honneurs" (December 28). But, *La Minerve* insisted, the French would certainly not let themselves be led "ni par un nom ni par une famille, quelqu'éclatant que soit ce nom, quelque puissante que soit cette famille" (December 28).

In Quebec, Cauchon improved on Cauchon. He told his readers on November 7 that he had long hesitated, out of courtesy (!), to attack Papineau's "plattes allusions et égoisme profondément blessé, style incorrect et language ignoble. Nous voulions oublier les erreurs pour ne voir que le bon côté de cette gloire de l'ancien régime. ... Mais quand nous avons vu qu'il fallait choisir entre l'homme et le pays, entre l'homme ambitieux qui veut démolir parce qu'il n'a pas édifié lui-même, et la société toute entière . . . nous n'avons pas hésité un instant." And, in truth, he had waited until the autumn of 1848; when he did begin the quality of his slander left the Montrealers' far behind. He referred repeatedly to "la personnalité de l'ancien régime" and to Papineau's followers as "les jeunes qui nous conduisent aux barricades." "Papineau," he wrote "jette le poids de sa parole haineuse dans l'urne électorale avec ses écrits dégoûtants de mensonges et d'injures" (November 18). Sometimes he attacked Papineau's press in Quebec: Le Canadien was filled with "des doctrines insaisissables" (November 18) and Le Fantasque was an "adultère héritière de la vieille haine Voltérienne qui ne mérite plus que le sourire du mépris" (December 5). Meanwhile, LaFontaine carried on "l'action intelligente et persévérante de la raison et de la vérité qui ont cicatrisé les blessures et miné les fondements du despotisme" (December 5). But most of the time Cauchon concentrated on the head of the "prétendus libéraux qui ne rèvent que despotisme et asservissement" (December 19) and wove into his invective insinuations that the Church was against the man who was using "les aimables procédés du passé, la haine entre le peuple et ses chefs religieux pour assurer le triomphe des doctrines pernicieuses et antinationales" (February 6). By January 1849 he stated that the great agitator was "un homme dont la voix fut puissante autrefois et qui malheureusement court aujourd'hui s'abimer dans la banqueroute de ses idées ou surannées ou extravagantes" (January 23). And after continuing his denunciation of the "opposition haineuse et injuste . . . et l'injure, l'invective, les récriminations, les insinuations, et les accusations sans motif, sans décence, et sans vérité" (January 25), he concluded on January 30: "M. Papineau a compté ses jours de gloire et de triomphe; ces jours sont passés sans retour. La Haine, la rancune, et l'invective ne sont ni de la gloire, ni du triomphe."

Like the earlier demolition of Viger, the destruction of Papineau could not be complete without a duel. This took place in mid-summer 1848 between Joseph Doutre and George-Etienne Cartier. By then Cartier had been elected member for Verchères. Short, self-assured, and pugnacious, smart with a small gold figure of Napoleon always on his lapel, and with his hair brushed straight up on his forehead, he was just the man to attract a thrust from L'Avenir.

At the beginning of August 1848 the paper published an anonymous and not very funny little comedy called "La Tuque bleue," about the engagement at Saint-Charles in 1837. In it a character, unmistakably Cartier, began in mid-battle to quake with fear and run for his life. Cartier, who had taken a conspicuous part in the battle, was not likely to tolerate this. Bursting into L'Avenir's offices he challenged the unknown author, one Charles Daoust. Jean-Baptiste-Eric Dorion, "l'enfant terrible," picked up the invitation. But the short Cartier drew himself up to his full height, looked down at the shorter Dorion, and declared that he did not duel with children. The next day Joseph Doutre answered. At the meeting on Mount Royal, just as the pistols were about to go off, the two antagonists were stopped by the police who had been summoned by Damien Cartier, George's brother. A few days later, they met again, this time without interruption. Doutre's bullet could never be found and Cartier's pierced a hole through Doutre's hat hanging on a branch of a tree behind him. Then the two men departed unreconciled.

Much the most important move in the crusade to destroy Papineau was the verbal duel between the "grand agitateur" and Wolfred Nelson, the hero of Saint-Denis. Since at least 1840 Nelson and Papineau had been engaged in some kind of feud. By the beginning of 1847 Papineau suspected that Nelson had something to do with the animosity which his family felt LaFontaine's supporters had for them; and a year later, when LaFontaine's group held their "council of war" about the Saint-Maurice address, Nelson was foremost in advocating a strong stand against Papineau. "Nelson has a strong personal feeling against him," Hincks wrote Baldwin, "and will I fear commit himself in the House."[12] Accordingly, after Papineau's great speech on the supply motion in March of 1848, Nelson sprang up to charge that Papineau had fled cowardly from the sound of cannon at Saint-Denis. A duel royal was on, for in the vilification campaign against the *patriote* leader, what stronger ammunition could LaFontaine's journalists use than charges of cowardice by "le seul des chefs révolutionnaires qui ait livré un combat glorieux en 1837?"[13]

As the offensive against Papineau intensified, Nelson began a tour of his own riding. On May 21 he spoke in three villages after mass— Saint-Aimé, Saint-Barnabé, and Saint-Jude. In each speech he repeated his charge that Papineau had fled in the moment of trial. Four days later Duvernay published Nelson's charges in La Minerve under the title "Le Manifeste du Dr. Nelson," and a week later, Cauchon did the same on the front page of Le Journal de Québec. Le Canadien also ran it on May 31, but "tout en regrettant vivement la publication

[12]Baldwin Papers, v51, Hincks to Baldwin, Jan. 14, 1848.
[13]Le Journal de Québec, 30 mai 1848; see also Les Mélanges Religieux, 9 juin 1848, Le Canadien, 24 mars 1848, La Minerve, 16 mars 1848.

et pour l'auteur et pour le pays." Naturally, Papineau answered. If he had left the battle at Saint-Denis, he had done so on the orders of Nelson who was in command. From then on until September the two old rebels issued charges and counter-charges which repeated the same points in different terms: either Papineau was a coward or Nelson was a liar. The journalists, of course, believed the hero of their choice.

By the beginning of June others had joined in the hue and cry. La Revue Canadienne began to publish letters from witnesses who declared Nelson was right. Then L'Avenir produced affidavits attesting to Papineau. As the months passed, after an avalanche of details from a score of minor ex-patriotes, Cartier and Dessaulles each began a series of their own, the first in Les Mélanges defending Nelson's version, the latter in Le Canadien supporting Papineau's. Dessaulles followed this with a little book, entitled Papineau et Nelson: blanc et noir et la lumière fut faite, in which he charged that those who had wanted to support Papineau had been warned by agents of the Attorney General that they would be arrested if they spoke out against Nelson. Then someone who preferred to remain anonymous put out a Résumé impartial de la discussion Papineau-Nelson. He argued that even if Nelson had ordered Papineau to go, the tribune should have refused. "Que les amis de M. Papineau," he wrote, "citent un seul précédent d'une conduite aussi extraordinaire! Dans l'histoire de toutes les insurrections du monde qu'ils nous trouvent un seul chef qui ait abandonné ainsi ses partisans, au moment d'un combat décisif." Besides, he declared with some knowledge of character, he could not imagine Papineau obeying an order: "Mr. Papineau soumis! Mr. Papineau obéissant comme un enfant! Mr. Papineau cédant aux sollicitations d'un seul ami: oh! non, ce n'est pas là le caractère de cet homme; il n'a jamais rien cédé, il n'a jamais fait preuve de soumission, d'abnégation. . . ." In this last argument, the anonymous author came very close to an opinion expressed as far back as 1838 by a man who never forgot possible political implications. In a letter dated June 1838, LaFontaine had written: "Il paraît qu'au commence-ment de l'affaire de St-Denis lui O'Callaghan et Papineau se sont sauvés de la maison de Nelson où ils étaient. . . . il paraît que tous deux désapprouvaient cette résistance. Papineau aurait pu l'empêcher. Ne l'ayant pas fait, il aurait dû se battre."[14]

Late in January 1849 Nelson went on another tour to repeat charges, followed by the young men of L'Avenir who afterwards

[14]LaFontaine à Chapman, as quoted in F. Ouellet, "Papineau dans la Révolu-tion de 1837–8," Canadian Historical Association, Report (1958), p. 25.

claimed, as on January 31, that "nous sommes prêts à prouver que le Dr. n'a jamais dit grand nombre des choses que la *Minerve* lui met dans la bouche et qu'il en a dit d'autres qu'elle ne reproduit pas." In the end, the true story was too complicated: no one could be sure of anything about Saint-Denis, except perhaps that much could be said on both sides. Yet, and this was precisely what Nelson, Duvernay, Cauchon, and the rest must have intended, as Papineau appeared more human, the legend which had enveloped him began to dissipate.

At Monklands, Elgin, writing to Grey, surveyed the issue with a touch of humour. "It is not easy to foretell how this struggle may terminate but in the mean time it is very ludicrous, and must be *nuts* to the old loyalists to see that more than one half of the space of the French Papers is occupied with the controversy which is going on between two sections of the Rebel army of 1837 & 1838."[15] Ludicrous or not, the campaign against Papineau proved successful. Cauchon reported to LaFontaine that, "Le jeune Cazeau, l'avocat, qui arrive de Rimouski nous dit que les esprits sont partout montés contre M. Papineau, il se sert du langage de notre ami M. Chiniquy, prêtre, qui m'écrivant sur la tempérance me disait l'autre jour 'que les amis de Mr. P. dans toutes les grandes paroisses qu'il avait récemment visitées, étaient aussi rares que les épis après la moisson'."[16] And a year later, he referred to his victory with evident self-satisfaction in another letter to LaFontaine. At the time, Malcolm Cameron was threatening to resign from the Council and begin an agitation against the government in Upper Canada. Cauchon told LaFontaine not to worry as long as the press was on the right side: "Si le *Globe* est prudent et la chose est indispensable (j'espère le contraire) il peut le démolir, car son influence peut faire dans le Haut ce que j'ai réussi à faire à l'endroit d'une influence bien autrement colossale dans le Bas-Canada. Les Bas-Canadiens n'affectionnaient pas Papineau, ils l'adoraient, ils le regardaient comme l'envoyé, le Sauveur."[17]

The spell of the hero had been broken forever.

THE ELGINS

The destruction of Papineau involved more than name-calling. It was accomplished in part by Lord and Lady Elgin who spent several months of 1848 following (at a dignified distance in time) after the

[15]Doughty, ed., *Elgin-Grey Papers*, I, 227, Elgin to Grey, Aug. 28, 1848.
[16]Papiers LaFontaine, Cauchon à LaFontaine, 26 juin 1848.
[17]*Ibid.*, Cauchon à LaFontaine, 2 déc. 1848.

disaffected tribune. Between June 1848 and January 1849 they paid several visits to Quebec and the Richelieu Valley and their warm, winning manners quickly provided the *Canadiens* with an alternative focus of loyalty.

Early in the summer they spent a few days in Quebec, just time for Lady Elgin to visit a number of the local convents and for the Governor to show his personal concern for the Irish immigrants and the priests, nuns, and officials who had cared for them so zealously last summer by "drop[ping] down among them some fine morning unexpectedly."[18] On the way back to Montreal, they stopped to celebrate Saint-Jean-Baptiste day at Chambly, where they delighted the populace by holding an informal levée at the *presbytère*. They even pushed thoughtfulness to the point of congratulating the curé for serving them water—a gesture which later won praise from Abbé Chiniquy and the whole Temperance Union. Back in Montreal the Governor General distinguished another (postponed) Saint-Jean-Baptiste celebration by attending the banquet sponsored by the Institut Canadien. Then, on July 19, he climaxed his summer tour by attending the closing exercises of the Collège de Saint-Hyacinthe.

It was one of those great royal occasions. Lord Elgin had wanted it so, partly because it was "the most populous and I believe not long ago most disaffected rural district of Lower Canada,"[19] partly because it might give some moral support to the campaign being waged just then in the same area by Nelson, about whom the Governor wrote that he was "the conqueror of Gen Gore at St Denis, a really fine brave fellow, who fought like a man when he was in arms against the Gov^t."[20] The Governor rode in state through the Richelieu Valley, his carriage preceded by his equerries in the livery of the House of Elgin and followed by his official escort. At the entrance to the town (population 2,700) he passed under a remarkable triumphal arch erected out of spruce branches and spangled with hoes, pitchforks, bags of grain, and an allegorical plough. And as the vice-regal party appeared, *Le Journal* reported on July 25 "sa vue souleva l'enthousiasme et des démonstrations de respect et d'estime." At the Collège Elgin was welcomed by Bishop Bourget, Morin, Cauchon, Parent, Bouthillier, and the seigneur de Saint-Hyacinthe, Papineau's brother-in-law, Louis Dessaulles. Before the day was over, he had presided at the academic exercises, questioned the students in Latin and Greek,

[18]Doughty, ed., *Elgin-Grey Papers*, I, 205, Elgin to Grey, July 5, 1848.
[19]*Ibid.*, I, 216, Elgin to Grey, Aug. 2, 1848.
[20]*Ibid.*, I, 181, Elgin to Grey, June 6, 1849.

delighted the priests with his knowledge of their problems, and delivered a speech in French (*Le Journal* continued) "avec une facilité, une aisance, qui indique qu'il est loin d'être étranger à la langue." A few days later the Governor sent the Colonial Secretary a copy of the Saint-Hyacinthe address. It contained a paragraph expressing thanks for "la libéralité avec la quelle [*sic*] votre Gouvernement a préparé, dans les Townships de l'est, pour nos industrieux cultivateurs, qui manquent de terres, un système de Colonisation très large et conforme à leurs besoins et habitudes."[21] Lord Elgin could be well pleased. He had received an unprecedented triumph in a Catholic institution that had been noted a decade ago for its *patriote* sympathies. Not only was Papineau outshone in his own district, but the Governor and LaFontaine party were reaping the credit for the colonization of the Townships.

In August Lady Elgin, her sister, Lady Alice Lampton, and the little Lady Elma Bruce, Lord Elgin's daughter by his first marriage, all moved to Beaumont in the country near Quebec. There they lived close to the people, Lord Elgin coming down frequently to join them and losing no opportunity to meet the habitants informally. In October he returned to the Richelieu Valley, visiting Longueuil, Chambly, and Saint-Hilaire, where "tout s'est fait avec la plus parfaite cordialité et la meilleure entente possible" and where the reception accorded him, Duvernay hoped on October 23, "convaincra sans doute de la popularité que ce gouverneur s'est acquise dans nos campagnes." Indeed, even Denis-Benjamin Papineau, who in 1844 had been predicting an imminent dissolution of the British empire, admitted to Bouthillier that "à coup sûr le Gouvernement Impérial pourrait faire pire que de le laisser ici. . . . Lord Elgin m'a toujours paru être un homme comme le Gouvernement Impérial devrait s'efforcer d'en avoir à la tête de toutes ses colonies."[22] And by the new year, the *Canadiens* in Montreal bought up in two days the whole supply of a new daguerreotype which *La Minerve* called (January 8) "une ressemblance fidèle du gouverneur le plus populaire que nous ayons eu en Canada."

At the beginning of the new year Lord Elgin put the crowning touch to his conquest of the *Canadiens*. He reinstated the official use of their mother tongue, and he did so in the grand manner. By ignoring the restrictions against French, he was, of course, merely carrying out the wishes of the Assembly's resolutions of 1845, but he now wanted

21*Ibid.*, I, 218.
22Collection Papineau-Bourassa, D.-B. Papineau à Bouthillier, 30 nov. 1848.

to reinforce LaFontaine against Papineau. And he knew that the language issue, unlike the earlier grievances over the exiles, the capital, the unequal representation, and the public debt of Upper Canada, was particularly LaFontaine's. Accordingly, he chose to highlight the event and his councillor's power in a symbolic gesture at the opening of parliament.

On January 18, 1849, amid traditional pomp, Lord Elgin slid smartly in a large sleigh down Notre-Dame Street to the Marché Sainte-Anne. There, splendid in his dark blue and silver tunic, he read his speech in English, paused, and, his courtly diction filling the chamber, repeated it in elegant French. Thus, in one fine, royal, unprecedented gesture, he wiped out forever and for all *Canadiens* to hear, the last national iniquity of the Union. And as he stepped out a few minutes later into the open air, the fanfare seemed to ring out with greater sound, and in the distance, the bells of Notre-Dame proclaimed in clearer tones, perhaps, their ceremonial "God Save the Queen." As the vice-regal procession receded, *Le Journal* reported (January 23) that Denis-Benjamin Viger in tears exclaimed: "Que je me sens soulagé d'entendre dans ma langue les paroles du trône!" And Cauchon went on to praise "ce fait inouie dans les fastes de notre histoire parlementaire." Langevin noted proudly for his readers on January 19 that "Lord Elgin prononce le français aussi purement qu'un Parisien." Duvernay could not resist chiding the editors of *L'Avenir*, who like *Le Canadien*'s in Quebec, said nothing about the French speech: "Les jeunes et fougueux apôtres de notre nationalité, qui ont fait tant de bruit depuis un an, qui ont poussé tant de fois l'heureux cri de réveil national n'ont pas dit un mot (les honnêtes gens!) ... sur ce fait assez intéressant, ce nous semble. ... Quand notre nationalité a-t-elle été plus respectée, plus honorée" (*La Minerve*, January 22).

In this epoch-making speech the Governor General had inserted a paragraph congratulating the province on the peace, order, and tranquillity which prevailed throughout the year of revolutions. He saw this as a proof "de l'amour de l'ordre et de l'attachement des Canadiens à leurs institutions" and went on to declare that "le peuple Canadien voit tous les jours l'avantage de l'ordre de choses actuel." When the time came for the Assembly to debate this paragraph in the Address in Reply to the Speech, Papineau gave LaFontaine the opportunity which the Attorney General had been waiting for to complete his enemy's destruction.

LAFONTAINE

On the night of January 22 the member for Leinster moved the Address in Reply to the Speech from the Throne in a motion seconded by one of the members from Upper Canada. There were a few other short speeches and then Papineau sprang up. Specifically, he objected to the paragraph attributing to the excellence of Canada's institutions the order which had prevailed since the last session, and he introduced an alternative paragraph which was quoted in the press on January 25 as ending

jusqu'à ce que nos constitutions aient été réformées par l'extension du principe d'élection à beaucoup d'autres charges et départements que ceux où il prévaut; au point de nous rien laisser à envier à nos voisins, nous n'avons pas plus de chance dans l'avenir que nous n'en avons eu durant un long et pénible passé, d'obtenir le bon gouvernement de la province, . . . la prospérité générale et le contentement de ses habitants.

But in reality he had risen to express all the anguish of the last twelve months. He had been shocked by the treatment he had received. For when he began to attack the new councillors last March, he had spoken against their ideas and principles. He had questioned their theories, tried to shake their premises. But they had answered by personal invective, slander, disparagement, malicious gossip. They had examined his motives, insulted his family, blackened his reputation. They had defeated his candidate in Quebec; they had ruined his influence in the Townships Association. They had crushed him. And in his own heart he must have realized that all was finished.

The words burst from him, uncontrolled, fierce, interminable. Passing from French to English and back again, he struck out in every direction, at the Governor, at LaFontaine, at the press, at the Union. When the Assembly adjourned past midnight, he had to be stopped, and the next day, he started again for another three hours, and the next day, and the next until he had spoken for over twelve hours. He was making his last apologia, his ultimate effort.

Beginning with the clause about *Canadien* institutions, he assailed responsible government and the unequal representation. Then, repeating himself over and over, he lashed out at LaFontaine and his colleagues, comparing them to the worst of the old oligarchs: "quant à moi je dois l'avouer, je ne vois pas de différence essentielle, de différence marquée entre ces deux partis politiques, entre les torys et les libéraux." Indeed, he preferred the Tories—"Nous avons plus à craindre avec un ministère libéral fort qu'avec un ministère tory faible"—and would join them if they agreed to repeal. He complained of the press and of its calumnies against Viger and his brother, especially the abuse against them at the time of the Jesuit estates debate: "Ceux qui publiaient ces calomnies savaient très bien que M. Viger était plus catholique et plus religieux que plusieurs de ceux pour le plaisir et le profit desquels on publiait ces indignes reproches." At the end of four sittings, having censured the British and acclaimed the Americans, having called on the revolutionary spirit, having blamed all the nation's woes on patronage, he moved on to repeal of the Union:

Tous les hommes de bon sens sentent que cette mesure est désirable, sentent la difficulté qu'il y a de législater pour deux pays si différents en tous points. Cette union a été fournie dans le but avoué de nuire au peuple canadien. De quel prétexte s'est-on servi, pour nous l'imposer? C'est qu'elle devait nécessairement emmener l'extension du commerce. On doit voir aujourd'hui qu'on s'était trompé, si c'était là l'idée qu'on avait; que le pays n'a jamais été plus souffrant qu'il ne l'a été depuis l'Union.

Papineau's friends at *L'Avenir* edited the four speeches and published them as one on January 31. *Le Canadien* printed most of the French parts on January 31 and February 25. But LaFontaine's press naturally answered this speech as they had Papineau's other outbursts, with ridicule and more invective. *La Minerve* denounced "ses manifestes et ses écrits incendiaires et révolutionnaires, sa conduite et ses discours . . . [son] opposition violente, factieuse, acharnée" (January 25). Langevin published two long articles in *Les Mélanges* oozing with innuendos about Saint-Denis and Papineau's cowardice. Cauchon in *Le Journal* spoke of Papineau's "opposition haineuse et injuste, l'injure, l'invective, les insinuations, et les accusations sans motif, sans license et sans vérité" (January 25), before describing the different speeches as "parfaitement identiques les uns aux autres. Les injures seules dont ils étaient parsemées ont pu varier de forme, ou d'intensité. Il a été plus injurieux, plus insultant, plus riche d'accusations et d'insinuations perfides dans la langue de ses pères, la belle langue française, si chaste d'habitude" (January 27).

During Papineau's speeches in the Assembly, Cauchon had tried several times to interrupt him, so had Wolfred Nelson—"la terrible voix du chef, du héros de Saint-Denis, prennant la solennité du tonnerre adressa une foudroyante apostrophe," *Le Journal* said. But LaFontaine had sat motionless, his arms folded, his expression severe, letting Papineau empty himself of all his anger. Then he gave notice that on the next day he would himself address the Assembly.

It was a cold night, January 23, but the chamber was packed—not a seat was vacant on the floor of the Assembly, or in the galleries. Public, journalists, intruding Legislative Councillors crowded every inch. In the government lobby, Cauchon, Cartier, and Nelson waited with a number of their colleagues. Then the leader came in briskly, nodding recognition in several directions. He had never evoked much spontaneous affection, and until now he may, perhaps, have never felt the need for it. But tonight they knew he appreciated their presence. In a few minutes he would have to enter the chamber and measure his limited rhetorical talents against the most splendid orator his nation had ever produced. LaFontaine knew he was no match for Papineau; in fact he could hardly even rival Taché's emotional appeal. Nor could he rely on the daring verve which made Cauchon so effective. Yet, although his own studious personality showed so few signs of endowment, among all of these he was the leader.

There was a stir as LaFontaine came into the House. For a few minutes he sat, his eyes gleaming sternly, his face unsmiling, conscious of the multitude of eyes upon him. Close by was Baldwin who had brought him back into the politics of the Union in 1841 and Hincks who had saved so many situations. Above, in the gallery, he could see Parent, a beacon in the days of dark discouragement, and beside him some Legislative Councillors who had come knowing that the elected chamber would be far more interesting tonight: Taché who had so moved the House four years ago, Leslie who had written to him about the Union during his trip to Europe back in 1838, Bourret, his business associate and now mayor of Montreal, Viger. To his left Morin sat, the most loyal of his friends, now honoured with the most distinguished office the electors of the province could bestow. And across the green carpet, to his far right, LaFontaine saw Papineau, attentive, waiting. Because of his own decisions a decade ago, because of his chosen policies since, all these lives had had new meanings. The discouraged and the ruined had come into influence and power. And thousands more outside now enjoyed what they had only craved before.

Tonight, he must account to all of them. He must explain how, despite appearances, the Union which had been meant to destroy the *Canadien* way of life had actually brought salvation; he must remind them how he had found a nation divided, quarrelsome, and weak, and made it stronger than it had ever been before; he must show how he had opened up for posterity a limitless horizon. He must unravel all the decade's political tangle to show the wisdom of his own choice. He must stand here tonight, before an audience already entranced by Papineau, without the brilliance of Aylwin or the forcefulness of Nelson, without Drummond's power or Morin's tact, and justify his stewardship of his people's trust. He must measure up to the past, convince the present, and speak to the future.

He opened in a matter-of-fact tone.[23]

Je ne suivrai pas l'hon. Membre sur les terrains des personnalités qu'il semble avoir parcouru avec tant de satisfaction pour lui-même; le respect que je porte à cette chambre, le respect que j'ai pour mon propre caractère, le respect que je suis obligé de porter à la qualité de représentant de l'honorable membre, me font un devoir de m'abstenir d'imiter sous ce rapport celui dont les déclamations acerbes et virulentes n'ont pas duré moins de trois heures.

And then, beginning with the rebellions and the Union debate, he explained each of his actions. He had taken office under Bagot on his own terms ("je dictai mes conditions avant d'accepter un siège dans le ministère") and with the full approval of the House. He had resigned in 1843 rather than surrender one item of his people's rights, and now, if he accepted office again, it was as the head of a party dedicated to *la survivance* by means of constitutional practice. Already he had achieved the repeal of the unjust clauses in the Union, he had brought the capital back to Lower Canada, and now he was opening up new lands for *Canadiens* to settle. Above all, by his conduct, LaFontaine had saved the nation:

Dans la pensée du gouverneur qui l'a suggérée, dans la pensée de celui qui en a rédigé l'acte, l'Union de deux provinces devait écraser les Canadiens-français! ce but a-t-il été atteint? La pensée de Lord Sydenham a-t-elle été realisée? Tous mes compatriotes à l'exception de l'hon membre, répondront d'une voix unanime, non! Mais ils diront aussi, et tout homme sensé le dira, que si le système d'opposition à outrance que préconisait l'hon membre eut été adopté, il aurait accompli dès à présent le but de lord Sydenham et les Canadiens seraient écrasés! Voilà où nous aurait conduit le système de l'hon Membre, et où il nous conduirait infail-liblement encore, si les représentants du peuple étaient assez peu judicieux que de le suivre.

He had co-operated with the Union in order to "lui faire produire un résultat tout opposé à celui qu'en attendait son auteur." If he had not done so, "où en serait notre langue?" If he had kept aloof as some

[23]*Le Journal de Québec*, 8 fév. 1849; Chapais, *Cours d'histoire*, VI, 286–307.

suggested in 1840, or if, having taken part in the elections, he had agreed on a policy of non-alignment, the French might now be lost. And where would Papineau himself be? "Il serait encore à Paris, fraternisant sans doute avec les républicains rouges, ou les républicains blancs, ou les républicains noirs, et approuvant tour à tour les constitutions qui se succèdent si rapidement en France."

No cheers interrupted LaFontaine. He was not that kind of speaker. He argued logically in sharp and precise terms, his voice even. He did not make passionate appeals, yet, as he talked, he grew more confident and forceful. As he spoke, his hearers must have contrasted the two men, the passionate tribune of the night before so overwhelmed by his vision of life as it was not, and the other, now methodically demonstrating how co-operation could do more than rebellion, how hope could take the place of despair. Papineau had ranted for hours, tossing out words that masqueraded as principles; LaFontaine in ninety minutes was candidly reviewing the tireless dedication of a decade. He did not exaggerate; he refused to offer his antagonist the hostage of even one mis-statement. He satisfied his listeners that Papineau presented only symbolic and powerless opposition while he offered the promise of reason and truth. With a last apostrophe to the great man whom he had once genuinely admired, he looked back to those glorious days when the tribune's every sentence had mobilized the nation. But he stressed that times had changed, that Papineau belonged to the past. "Que l'honorable membre," he exclaimed, "ne se laisse pas abuser par d'anciens souvenirs."

Papineau's power had been reduced to an ineffectual nuisance.

19

Annexation 1849

The duel between LaFontaine and Papineau was not the only high-light of that year's session. In February, there was the great debate over the Rebellion Losses bill, an event which impelled many English-speaking Tories to begin discussing annexation to the United States and thus, indirectly, to supply Papineau's followers with strange new allies in their efforts to overthrow the Union. Indeed, before the fretful winter and spring were over, the repealers had shifted their enthu-siasm for repeal to a new demand: annexation.

THE RISE OF ANNEXATION

Among the *Canadiens*, the question of annexation had come up before—briefly. On the occasion of Lord Grey's despatch to Sir John Harvey in 1847, when Langevin had written his articles proposing the confederation of British North America, two French newspapers in the United States had suggested that Canada should join the United States instead. In Montreal *L'Avenir* and the *Canadiens'* old Tory enemy, the *Gazette*, had replied that annexation might be the better solution. *L'Avenir* had declared (December 4, 1847) that it preferred annexation to Langevin's proposed confederation of Britain's North American colonies, for in the latter the *Canadiens* would find only "un piège de plus tendu à nationalité canadienne-française, entouré de fleurs magnifiques, et dont il nous est presque impossible de prévoir tout le fracas." As for the *Gazette*, as Duvernay summed up on December 2, it "n'a pas hésité à proclamer que toutes les tendances des habitants d'origine britannique du Canada, que toutes les sympa-thies des Canadiens sont pour les Etats."

At *Les Mélanges*, Langevin answered that his series of articles "viennent de démontrer l'inconvénient, l'impossibilité pour le Bas-Canada de s'annexer aux Etats-Unis; ils ont montré que tout s'oppose à cet événement, et que si l'on voulait goûter de ce nouveau régime, ce serait vouloir perdre sa langue, perdre ses lois, perdre ses mœurs, perdre ses institutions, perdre tout ce qui distingue le Canadien de ceux qui seraient alors ses co-sujets" (October 19). But he could not prevent the discussion from continuing through several more issues. Then, on December 2, La Minerve put a stop to the argument. It admitted much could be said on both sides. If anything, La Minerve took the part of annexation, but only to the extent of refuting the point Langevin kept reiterating—that by joining the United States the Canadiens would suffer the same assimilation that had befallen the French in Louisiana:

Si nous ne voyons l'histoire de Louisiane que pour la période qui a précédé son annexion, nous avouerons qu'elle a été une colonie plus malheureuse que la nôtre, mais cela sert à prouver que son annexion lui a été fort avantageuse. D'ailleurs nous ne demanderions pas d'autre preuve en sa faveur que son état de prosperité actuelle, et l'opinion de ses habitants. Quant à notre langue et notre religion, nous pouvons affirmer qu'elles sont pour le moins aussi respectées et protégées dans la Louisiane que dans le Canada.

Still, La Minerve felt this was not the time to discuss this issue. And for the moment—what with the general election, the new cabinet, and Papineau's agitation—this was the last word. The question was not revived for fifteen months and when it was, it was as a result of the Tory reaction to the introduction of the Rebellion Losses bill.

LaFontaine himself proposed the first reading of the bill on February 13, 1849. In his speech he explained how the government meant to proceed at once with the recommendations made in 1846 by the commission set up to compensate those loyal Lower Canadians whose property had been destroyed during the rebellion by persons acting in support of the civil authority. Going over the story, he pointed out that the Assembly of Upper Canada had voted a similar compensation for its section before the Union and that in 1841 the legislature of the united province had carried out the provisions of that law. However, very little had been done for Lower Canada until 1845 when Metcalfe, acting on a petition of the Assembly, had appointed a commission to investigate the Canadien claims. The report had been tabled in April 1846, but shelved during the political crisis which followed. Now, LaFontaine concluded hopefully, this bill would rectify the omission. And he hoped it would be passed promptly.

It was not. The Tory leaders were in no mood to vote monies to the Canadiens. First, their politicians reasoned that they had lost office because of the French: they had courted them under Metcalfe, only to have them repudiate Viger and Papineau. The Tory merchants, suffering the pangs of financial ruin, concluded that the new government of lawyers and professional French politicians was to blame for the economic crisis. And now—crowning indignity—that same government intended to use their taxes to reimburse rebels. On this point the Tories probably had a case. In February 1846 the commissioners appointed by Draper had asked the government how they should distinguish among the myriad claims those of persons who had aided rebellion and those of loyal citizens. Dominick Daly had advised them to be guided by the verdict of the courts. Yet the rebels of 1837 who had been pardoned by Lord Durham's amnesty and those of 1838 who had never been captured had never been convicted for treason; and, for example, there was a claim for £1200 from that famous rebel, Wolfred Nelson! Exasperated and deeply suspicious, the Tories resolved to fight the bill at every stage of its passage through both houses. The Rebellion Losses bill thus became a test of the true meaning of responsible government.

The opposition put forth all its strength—especially Sir Allan MacNab and Colonel Gugy. The government answered with its own best speakers, and as each side summoned its followers to fill the galleries for support, the debate grew bitter. On February 15, Sir Allan MacNab and William Blake called each other traitor and rebel and nearly came to blows on the floor of the House. That same day Morin felt obliged to order the galleries cleared because the "strangers" were arguing more loudly than the members. On February 20 LaFontaine spoke for over an hour; on February 22 the Assembly sat continuously for twenty hours trying to outlast the shouts and whistles from the thronged galleries. Finally, on February 27, the bill passed first reading. After another tumultuous week it passed second reading on March 2, and on March 9 by a vote of 47–18 it was finally sent to the Legislative Council. There, Caron, Quesnel, and Taché piloted it through another avalanche of stale words until it passed on March 15. (Viger voted against it.) "A good deal of excitement and bad feeling has been stirred," Lord Elgin summed up in an understatement for Grey: "The opposition leaders who are very low in the World at present, have taken advantage of the circumstance to work upon the feelings of the old loyalists as opposed to Rebels, of British as opposed to French, and of Upper Canadians as opposed to Lower, and thus to provoke from various parts of the Province the expression of not very temperate or measured discontent."[1] "La question de l'indemnité,"

[1]Doughty, ed., Elgin-Grey Papers, I, 299, Elgin to Grey, March 1, 1849.

La Minerve confirmed on February 19, "absorbe en ce moment toute l'attention. . . . Depuis plusieurs jours le ton des journaux tories tient de la fureur." "Les journaux du Haut Canada surtout," it added, "sont dégoûtants de préjugés nationaux, on dirait des chefs Iroquois qui préparent leur tribu à venir combattre les Hurons."

After the Legislative Council had voted on the bill, the Tories expected the Governor General to refuse assent. How could British authority sanction an indemnity to rebels? How could the Queen's representative turn his back on his own people to confirm the power of an alien race? Personally, the Governor doubted the timing of the bill. But he understood the meaning of responsible government well enough to refuse to interfere. He showed that henceforth there could be no conflict between the will of French Canada and the functioning of the British constitution. And he did this at the risk of his life. For when he drove into Montreal on April 25 to give royal assent to the bill, the Tories' resentment overflowed in a dangerous attack on his person.

No sooner had the Governor General performed the rite in the Legislative Council than a groan broke out in the galleries, thronged as seldom before but with no women in attendance ("ce qui laisse à douter qu'il y avait eu préméditation," *La Minerve* observed). Then, as Elgin rose to retire, the visitors rushed out into the square, where a crowd of respectably dressed citizens began to shout insults as soon as he appeared. Elgin had barely entered his carriage when a shower of débris broke against the door. As the outriders dodged to avoid the missiles, the horses galloped towards Monklands taking Elgin out of the Tories' reach. The Tories remained, distracted momentarily by the fire bells ringing out an alarm and by the appearance of a herald who announced a meeting at the Champ de Mars at eight that evening. At that time some 1500 gathered carrying torches and brickbats. Then Alfred Perry, the chief of the fire brigade now turned mischief-maker, trampled out the torch illuminating the speakers' text and shouted: "The time for speeches is past: follow me to the Parliament House." The excited crowd streamed towards the Marché Sainte-Anne.

The Assembly was still sitting at nine o'clock when a volley of stones came crashing into the chamber through the vaulted windows and a dozen ruffians erupted into the hall, swinging sticks at the gaslights. In a moment, the chamber floor was crowded with rioters. One threw rocks at the clock; another, mounting the steps of the Speaker's chair right under Morin's nose, pronounced, "I dissolve this French House"; another began to hack the throne to pieces. Perry pulled down a portrait of Papineau and trampled it under foot; someone else seized the splendid mace and hurled it out a window to the excited crowd. Some members, who had hurried out to the library, now ran back to announce that fire had broken out. Whipped by the wind blowing through the broken windows, and feeding on the escaping gas, the flames, already out of control, soon reached the velvet drapes at the front of the Assembly. Instinctively the members gathered about Morin, who had sat impassive, waiting to leave his chair until the House had duly adjourned. Then behind the Speaker, the members walked gravely down the stairs to the main entrance and —just as the chamber burst into flames—out into the street. At the other end of the building the Legislative Councillors were trapped and forced to escape by climbing over the railing and sliding down the wooden pillars of the second-storey balcony. This they did, one at a time, a single, stout legislator losing his hold and crashing ponderously into the crowd below. Last to come was Sir Allan MacNab, emerging out of the flames carrying the portrait of Queen Victoria that had been hanging in the Assembly.

By then the flames were licking the walls about the roof while the rioters were running around the building, singing, and yelling, celebrating the ruin of French domination. They had turned away the firemen and cut their hose. At midnight the huge fire still raged high into the black sky.

The next morning, April 26, Tory Montreal was in the streets, storming about the business district and finally collecting before Bonsecours Market, where the dispossessed Assembly and Council had met, the Executive Council sitting all night and on into the afternoon. Perry and other notable Tories had been arrested, and the air was charged with threats, as soldiers of the Montreal garrison patrolled the streets. At suppertime the crowd pounced on Benjamin Holmes and LaFontaine as they left the building, injuring Holmes and letting the Attorney General go only after soldiers intervened.

At seven o'clock a new demonstration began, when the police decided to move Perry to the jail at the east end of Notre-Dame Street. As the police cab appeared, the crowd surged upon it and sent the terrified horses off through the streets. Perry appealed to his supporters to stop, stating he had given his word to go to jail peacefully. However, the demonstrators refused to disperse, realizing they could rush the police. Amid a volley of stones, bricks, wood, and hard clay, they stripped their uniforms from the unfortunate constables, and, as bells rang in alarm, the fire brigade charged through the soldiery to carry Perry off. On the prisoner's reiterating that he had given his word to go peacefully, the riot became a triumphal procession. Escorted by his own firemen, friendly soldiers, and the cheering crowd, Perry marched to jail. There, by orders of the sheriff (another angry Tory), he was put in the most comfortable wing of the building, and with four other Tory prisoners allowed the services of Montreal's most popular chef, the owner of Dolly's Chop House.

Meanwhile another group of embattled Tories had begun a second demonstration. Gathered in the Champ de Mars, they encouraged each other to rebel against "French domination" until someone cried out "to Hincks." They then dashed to the offices of the *Pilot* where they broke all the windows, but hesitated to light a fire because friendly Tories owned the property next door. They swept on to the homes of Hincks and Benjamin Holmes. Mrs. Hincks, warned by a young friend-of-the-moment, just had had time to hide a few valuables and flee to the Blakes' house nearby when the crowd tore into her lodgings. It did likewise at the Holmes' where the ladies escaped by the back door as the mob stormed in the front.

Then, the rabble rushed to LaFontaine's house. The Attorney General was about to move into a new cutstone home decorated with delicate wood carvings and costly period furnishings. The house was empty. The rioters broke in, ransacked the furniture, smashed the woodwork and chairs, pulled off the window sills and shutters, ripped up the floors, and shattered the china and glass. They set fire to the stables, burned several coaches, and pulled up a dozen saplings from the orchard. By midnight, they had gone on to break windows at Wolfred Nelson's and Lewis Drummond's (but at Drummond's they found an armed guard and did no damage). At several other spots they hacked at shutters or broke windows until at last they retired, their forces spent, but their fury—as tomorrow would prove—not yet exhausted.

At dawn on Friday, the twenty-seventh, posters summoned the Tories to the Champ de Mars at two. But by noon, a mob had gathered before the jail to demand the release of Perry and his fellow inmates. At one, it had grown so fierce that Perry was allowed to mount the prison walls and (to cries of "Jump! Jump!") calm his friends. At the same time, militiamen were being brought across the river from Sorel, and some 3000 Montrealers were converging on the militia depot to volunteer as extra policemen. Another Tory group attacked these volunteers, but was dispersed. At two o'clock George Moffatt presided over another assembly of several thousand Tories,

who heard Michael Murray regret that Lord Elgin was also a Scot, and
Thomas Wilson of the Bank of Upper Canada summon all Englishmen,
Scots, and Irishmen to join forces against the French. Colonel Gugy
also spoke, rousing his audience to such a pitch that it ended the
meeting by rushing to the rostrum to seize the Colonel and carry him
in triumph to Dolly's Chop House. The next day, after another night
of clamour, the Tories massed outside Bonsecours Market. Troops
surrounded the building. Shortly before noon, an order was read
announcing the liberation of the prisoners, and, with much cheering,
the mob rushed to the jail and escorted the prisoners back to the
city.[2]

Meanwhile the Tories of Three Rivers and Quebec had also mani-
fested their discontent. In Three Rivers they burned Lord Elgin in
effigy, and in the old capital, on the night of April 27, a large con-
course met on Place d'Armes to do likewise with dummies of the
Governor General and LaFontaine. But before the effigies could be set
on fire a squad of Irish and French-Canadian shipyard workers
erupted into the crowd. After an hour's brawl the soldiers of the
garrison surrounded the mob without intervening, while the shipyard
workers captured the effigies and paraded them boisterously through
the city to the strains of an Irish- and French-accented "God Save the
Queen."[3]

While the Tories were thus proving, in the words of La Minerve
(May 1), "qu'ils ne savent pas même qui a fait le soleil et la terre, et
à qui ils auront à rendre compte de leurs actes," the government had
not been inactive. On the morning after the burning of the legislature,
a great book had been placed in the lobby of the Château de Ramezay
for citizens to sign their names in appreciation of Lord Elgin. Within
half a day, it was filled with names and with the Xs of those thousands
of Canadiens whose loyalty was apparently greater than their knowledge of writing. The government decided to refuse the offers of
Canadiens volunteering to guard the peace: "the great object," Lord
Elgin explained, "is to keep them quiet and to prevent collision
between the races."[4] The Assembly, meanwhile, adopted an address to

[2]The details of the Montreal riots can be found in all the newspapers of the
time and in Sir James Alexander, Passages in the Life of a Soldier (London,
1857); E. A. Collard, "Memoir of Alfred Perry on the Montreal Riots of 1849,"
Montreal Gazette, 9, 16, 23, 30 April 1960; L. Groulx, "L'Emeute de 1849 à
Montréal," in Ville, ô ma ville (Montréal, 1942); W. Weir, Sixty Years in Canada
(Montreal, 1903).

[3]Le Canadien, 30 avril 1849; Le Journal de Québec, 1 mai 1849; La Minerve,
1 mai 1849.

[4]Doughty, ed., Elgin-Grey Papers, I, 352, Elgin to Grey, May 5, 1849.

the Governor reaffirming its loyalty and expressing its indignation at the events of the twenty-fifth. *Noblesse oblige*: Lord Elgin announced he would receive the address publicly at the Château de Ramezay, his official residence in the heart of the city, at noon on Monday, April 30.

On that day the frantic Tories were up earlier than the government. By mid-morning agitators swarmed about the streets near the Château and blocked the open space before Bonsecours Market. Around noon when the members emerged from their improvised legislature to walk the block to the Château, they were greeted with hooting and a shower of vegetables, dead rats, and garbage. A military escort was lined up to protect them. Yet they arrived at the corner of Notre-Dame Street dripping with slimy matter. When a municipal official began to read the Riot Act, he was struck in the mouth by an onion. Then, exactly at noon, a troop of cavalry galloped up Saint James Street followed by the Governor General, riding in a closed brougham. Like the walk of the politicians up Bonsecours Street, his drive was greeted with an ominous hoot.

The sidewalks were impassable as the escort passed between the crowds. The Governor had to keep his hat before his eyes as stones and bricks glanced off the carriage. Once past Place d'Armes, however, the vice-regal party dashed up onto the lawn in front of the Château and the gates were slammed against the pressing tumult. Lord Elgin rushed up the steps and entered the state apartments carrying a two-pound stone which he had retrieved from the floor of his carriage.

During the ceremony inside, troops moved in around the Château to insure the Governor's safety. The Tories, determined he should not escape, barricaded Notre-Dame Street. But Elgin left by a side gate, and, as his escort galloped down Bonsecours Hill and up Saint-Denis towards Sherbrooke, he wisely returned to Monklands by another way. The mob went wild and took chase after the flying Governor, with hundreds of rioters racing up the side streets to intercept the carriage. At the corner of St. Lawrence and Sherbrooke, rebellious Toryism and the Crown met head on. Stones were ripped up from the pavement, and the vice-regal carriage battered until its sides broke. Colonel Bruce, sitting beside his brother, was injured on the head. And, under a shower of stones, with the coachman lashing the horses on through Côte-des-Neiges, Lord Elgin escaped to Monklands. He had held his honour higher than his ease. He had saved responsible government; and more than any single individual, he had assured the right of French Canadians to be themselves. For this he had been insulted, but he emerged from the experience drenched in glory.

It took another three months for Tory fury to abate. Tory merchants left their stores, and learned gentlemen of the bar turned their backs on the law. Industry paused while hundreds of ordinary men and women paraded like fanatics in the streets of the capital with one pent-up objective: finding *Canadiens* to insult. On the evening of the attack against the Governor General, a minor gang tried to burn down the hospital of the Grey Nuns, but were prevented by another horde of what *Les Mélanges Religieux* called on May 1 "les braves habitants de Griffintown." The next day, another group gathered at the dock to attack the *John Munn* as it arrived bearing a delegation of *Québecois* come to show support for Lord Elgin. On May 9, a similar group rushed at the Hotel Têtu where a delegation of Upper Canadian Reformers was dining. The rioters knocked down the door, broke chairs, glasses, and windows, exchanged pistol shots, and wounded three guests before troops arrived to disperse them. Six weeks later, on July 18, the agitators were still active enough to erupt into violence in the salons of the Donegana Hotel at a concert given by the European artists, Toffanelli and Laborde. When Laborde appeared with a tricolour flag to sing "La Marseillaise," the Tories interrupted with whistles and catcalls, and the *Canadiens* fought back, the fight lasting long into the night.

Less than a month later, on hearing that the leaders of the April demonstrations had been arrested, the Tories rioted again for three, final violent days. By mid-afternoon of August 15, protest groups were forming in the streets; by early evening barricades had gone up once more in Notre-Dame Street. At ten o'clock the Tories were again at LaFontaine's, chanting "God Save the Queen" and battering down the gate. This time the Attorney General was ready: his house was in darkness and a group of friends that included Etienne-Pascal Taché and his son-in-law, Charles-Joseph Coursol, waited behind the shutters with guns. As the rabble moved towards the front door, shots rang out on both sides (LaFontaine's group claimed the Tories started the firing), and before the rioters had fled, six were wounded, and one, William Mason, killed. For the next three days "le trouble et le tumulte ont régné tous les soirs." On the seventeenth, about 530 young Tories followed Mason's red-draped casket to the cemetery attired in red shirts and with red bands attached to their hats as *La Minerve* commented on August 20, "un fait qui ne s'est jamais vu en Canada et dans bien des pays sans doute." That night, there were beatings and fist fights and smashing of gaslights until Mayor Fabre and Colonel Gugy rode through the streets in an attempt to bring calm. On the morning of Monday, August 20, rumours filled the city that LaFontaine would be assassinated as he arrived to testify at the inquest into Mason's death. He was not. But the hotel and two other buildings were set ablaze, and again flames roared until late into the night.

Thus the Tories reacted to the Rebellion Losses bill with the primitive, panic-stricken, almost standard response of a dispossessed political class. And to the French it appeared a revealing counterpart of their own rebellion ten years earlier. For if not in lives lost, at least in national bitterness and property damage, the reaction of the Montreal mob had several parallels to the "troubles." It even had its own "rebellion losses" aftermath, when LaFontaine's supporters claimed damages for the destruction of their property: Morin, £34; Francis Hincks, £34; J.-L. Têtu, £66; Charles Wilson, £71; the Grey Nuns, £65; and LaFontaine himself, £716. (They did not claim from the provincial government, however, but from the municipal adminis-tration of Montreal—headed by the Papineau partisan, E.-R. Fabre.) Henceforth, neither of the national groups could claim a monopoly of loyalty; and one would have on its conscience an outrage aimed directly at the Crown.

On second thought, the Tories turned to more practical means of regaining control of the colony. And according to the degree of discouragement with the present situation which each individual felt, they tended to join one of two political movements, the young British North American League or the Annexation Association.

The original branch of the British North American League was formed at Brockville early in 1849, but the organization only began to prosper in Montreal during the debate over the Rebellion Losses bill. On April 19 George Moffatt chaired the first meeting and three days later announced the election of local executive officers and a political programme based on a policy of uniting the Anglo-Saxon population against the "domination" of the *Canadiens*.[5] On May 7 another branch began in Quebec "qui a pour objet ostensible," noted *Le Canadien* on May 11, "d'*anglifier* le Bas-Canada par des procédés analogues à ceux que l'empereur Nicolas a employés pour *russifier* la Pologne." In Upper Canada and the English-speaking Townships, local associations multiplied until by July the League represented almost every colour of conservative public opinion in the colony

[5]C. D. Allin, "The British North America League, 1849," Ontario Historical Society, *Papers and Records*, XIII (1915), 79; C. D. Allin and G. M. Jones, *Annexation, Preferential Trade and Reciprocity* (Toronto, 1905), pp. 53–61.

except the French, their main bond being opposition to the LaFontaine-Baldwin administration. At a grand convention held in Kingston on July 26, the League proposed a confederation of all the colonies of British North America as the best means of overcoming "French domination" and of opening up wider markets for the distressed businessmen of Montreal and Quebec. However, the idea seemed premature for serious discussion, and after another general assembly in November in Toronto, the League died a natural death.

On the subject of the British connection, the British North American League had been uncompromising. In its original address to the public it left little doubt as to who would be the last to defend the Union flag: "If there be, as some have said, a time when all colonies must, in the course of human events, throw off their dependence on the parent state, and if, in our generation, that time should be destined to arise, we predict that, if true to ourselves, it will not come until no British hands remain able to hoist the flag of England on the rock of Quebec, and no British voices survive able to shout 'God Save the Queen.'"[6] But the second Tory organization, the Annexation Association, concluded that French domination could not be destroyed within the British empire, but only by annexing the Canadian province to the United States. If the British government abandoned them to the tender mercies of a vehemently hostile French faction, then why not join the English-speaking republicans to the south?

Thus, in the summer of 1849, the Montreal merchants and prominent Tories found themselves entangled in an annexation campaign. They were determined to remain English even if they had to sacrifice being British. On May 28 La Minerve reported that "plusieurs dames travaillent activement à broder un drapeau étoilé qui doit servir à proclamer l'indépendance," and on July 4 many Montreal business houses flaunted the star-spangled banner. By the beginning of October the leaders of the four principal English newspapers in the capital, having openly declared themselves annexationist, held a meeting of some 150 people at Temperance Hall to elect John Redpath, the sugar manufacturer, president of the mother association. On October 11 they published their manifesto which bore the signatures of some of the most prominent of the capital's Tory community and a sprinkling of LaFontaine's own followers among the commercial class—Benjamin Holmes and Jacob DeWitt, for instance. It also included the names of the French-Canadian vendus, like Sabrevois de Bleury, and all the young radicals of L'Avenir.

[6]Quoted in Allin and Jones, Annexation, pp. 54–5.

Since the turmoil over the Rebellion Losses bill, *L'Avenir* had shown new life. Earlier in the year it had run out of arguments for repeal of the Union, but now the debate over rebellion losses and the ensuing violence seemed to prove that the Union could never work. "Un seul mot à nos confrères," *L'Avenir* mocked on April 28,

mais un mot franc et loyal. Vous avez cru réussir dans votre politique de conciliation, vous avez tû les intérêts de votre nationalité pour ne pas blesser les farouches susceptibilités de vos *frères* (comme vous les appelez) d'origine étrangère. Depuis huit ans vous suivez la même marche. Qu'avez-vous obtenu? Les partis sont-ils conciliés? La haine des Anglais contre la race française est-elle diminuée . . . ? C'est l'Union qui est la source de tous nos maux.

And, after the annexation manifesto, the leading republican of all, Papineau, rejoiced at the reversal that gave him allies among the very men who had served as Colborne's volunteers in 1837. He wrote to Dr. O'Callaghan: "Voilà un mouvement tout nouveau, tout imprévu, celui de la demande de la séparation d'avec la métropole et de l'Annexion aux Etats-Unis, par les volontaires de '37. . . . Cette démarche imprévue d'annexion semble être un secours providentiel qui nous advient."[7] He did not himself join the annexation association. He probably found it unnecessary: there could be no one who would not know his feelings. Perhaps he had finally realized his political days were over; certainly he knew how much he had been discredited by the propaganda of LaFontaine's press. But his youthful disciples, who had earlier failed in their assault against the Union, now set out again to stir the emotions of French Canada.

"LA COLOSSALE RÉPUBLIQUE DU NOUVEAU-MONDE"

L'Avenir led the French-Canadian discussion in favour of annexation as it had the recent debate over repeal, but the young republicans also founded two more newspapers, *Le Moniteur Canadien* in the capital and *Le Canadien Indépendant* in Quebec. The latter put out its first issue in the third week of May 1849, under Napoléon Aubin's name and "dans les intérêts politiques de M. Papineau et en opposition aux ministres actuels." Although generously subsidized (by Fabre among others) it lasted only until November. *Le Moniteur* proved much more successful. Edited by J.-G. de Montigny, it repeated most of the ideas expressed in *L'Avenir* but in a far more contentious (and often vulgar) spirit. Begun in May 1849, it appeared three times a week in winter

[7]O'Callaghan Papers, L.-J. Papineau à O'Callaghan, 1 fév. 1850.

and daily in summer. Although without advertisers in the beginning, it managed, by September, to afford a special weekend edition for the country, the Edition des Campagnes "contenant la matière éditoriale du petit format." As the discussion over annexation continued into 1850, Le Moniteur became increasingly important, but L'Avenir continued to set the tone.

On December 2, 1848, it reprinted an article which had appeared in Aubin's temporarily resurrected Le Fantasque on November 18, and reopened the annexationist debate. Later, on February 24, 1849, Louis-Antoine Dessaulles published his first serious article on annexation. Writing under the pseudonym of "Le Campagnard" which he had used in the "Union et Nationalité" argument, he added a new point to the nationality argument: why could French Canada not imitate Louisiana and enjoy both separate statehood and the advantages of American prosperity?

In mentioning Louisiana, Dessaulles had introduced a new idea into the repeal debate, but, for the moment, the repealers seem not to have noticed it. They continued to build their hopes on the influence of Papineau, without even bothering to make plans for their state once it was separated. After the violence, however, and the Tory endorsement of annexation, L'Avenir began to spotlight the Louisiana story. True, the English merchants wanted to join the United States to be rid of "French domination"; but, the revolutionaries of L'Avenir reasoned, the American union would really serve the French by insuring a separate French state as it did in Louisiana. In a long article on July 28 they compared their situation with that of the Louisiana French. Canada had been conquered; Louisiana had passed peacefully to the Americans without need of even "un peloton de soldats." Canada had been entangled in seventy years of parliaments and charters; Louisiana in one simple transaction had been guaranteed freedom of religion and "la jouissance paisible de toutes ses anciennes lois." How was it, they asked, that "avec un gouvernement si mauvais, si dangeureux, . . . les citoyens de chaque état sont-ils plus instruits que les sujets canadiens?—Comment, sans revenus de douanes, de la vente des terres publiques, ont-ils réussi à faire du peuple Américain le peuple le plus instruit de l'Univers?—Comment avec des taxes directes à payer, le peuple y est-il plus riche qu'ici?" Later, on September 4, they addressed those who might fear that la survivance would be impossible without British institutions: "La Louisiane est là qui vous répond qu'elle n'est pas passée elle par le creuset de la dénationalisation comme l'Irlande . . . . mais qu'elle est encore française et catholique parce qu'elle est démocratique."

As the annexation movement grew, the *nationaliste* arguments varied, but they always included the comparison with Louisiana. *Le Moniteur Canadien*, in a typical article on October 26, underlined how simple repeal of the Union would not be enough: "L'Union des Canadas, certes, est bien une des causes principales de nos maux; mais son rappel, quoique peut-être désirable comme mesure préparative ne ferait que remédier en partie à la maladie qui nous ronge jusque dans la moelle des os, et le seul remède capable de nous guérir complètement, c'est notre entrée dans la confédération américaine." Then, in addition to these articles in favour of nationality and prosperity, the annexationist papers also carried a number of special series.

One of these, a set of articles by Charles Laberge signed "34 Etoiles," and running in *L'Avenir* from June 2 through October 30, carried the discussion several steps further by setting out with precision the philosophical necessity for annexation. The young republicans, Laberge protested, formed a party, "qui veut l'indépendance du pays, non par la violence, mais en le préparant peu à peu et activement à l'avenir de liberté qui s'approche avec une vitesse dont les myopes politiques seuls ne peuvent s'apercevoir." For, he continued, it was in the nature of every nation to evolve towards republican democracy: "Les peuples appellent la démocratie comme la terre promise. C'est que la liberté est à la fois le premier besoin, le premier devoir et le premier droit de l'homme; c'est le soleil commun, la patrie commune: hors de là, l'homme et la société languissent, puis meurent." France and England had thus progressed, passing from anarchy to the colonialism "du colosse romain," and thence through feudalism to "l'unité dans l'absolutisme d'un roi." Then came the revolutions, 1688, 1789, and the birth of democratic nationality. In England there still remained "le regime bâtard que l'on appelle monarchie constitutionnelle, qui n'est ni entièrement républicain ni entièrement monarchique, mais qui tient des deux par leurs plus mauvais côtés." But, in the nature of things, the advent of the British republic could only be a matter of time.

Canada, on its side, had also passed through the classical stages, and then, after the American Revolution had forced Britain to grant Canada a constitution, to the colonial system which "la liberté de commerce achève de ruiner." Now, Laberge concluded, "nous sommes arrivés à l'époque où le Canada doit devenir république, où notre étoile doit aller prendre place au ciel américain." The *Canadiens* must allow nothing to deter them from breaking with the British connection. Certainly not affection; certainly not interest. Once there may have been commercial advantages to the British connection, but now "la magnifique conquête de Cobden sur l'aristocratie anglaise les a réduits au néant"; indeed, without the corn laws, "c'est une tyrannie que de nous restreindre à commercer exclusivement avec elle." Canada must be free to regulate commerce, to open banks, to build railroads and bridges. There may also once have been military advantages. But now "contre quelle puissance l'Angleterre nous protégerait-elle?" Not against the Indians, or against the Russians—"Nous n'avons jamais eu de démêlés avec l'Amérique Russe [Alaska]"—or against the Americans. In fact, on two occasions, it was the Canadian militia that had protected British interests from the United States. Besides, the French no longer needed to be protected from the south: "Après être échappés aux griffes du lion britannique qui nous tient à terre, notre destinée est de nous élever dans les serres de l'aigle américain." Nothing could bind the *Canadiens* to Britain: on the contrary everything should obligate them to the United States. For with annexation would come an end to the national injustice of the Union: "Il faut toujours se rappeller [*sic*] que le Canada s'unissant à la confédération américaine, formerait plusieurs Etats, que la confédération américaine se compose d'un certain nombre d'Etats ou de pays, qui ont chacun leur gouvernement séparé . . . qui a la direction entière et absolue de l'Etat . . . que le gouvernement fédéral n'intervient jamais dans les affaires d'un Etat." Thus "34 Etoiles" sought to convince everyone that annexation was preordained by an everlasting wisdom![8]

For those whose intellectual activity flourished on a less Olympian level, the annexationists ran another series: "Le Bon sens du peuple, ou Dialogue entre Jean-Baptiste père et Jean-Baptiste fils." Published concurrently in *Le Canadien Indépendant, Le Moniteur*, and *L'Avenir* and designed for the man on the farm, it ran from the end of August to the end of October 1849. Throughout each instalment Jean-Baptiste, père, gave all the worst arguments against annexation: "Ah! monsieur le raisonneur, le communiste, le socialiste, je suis partisan du gouvernement qui nous rend justice qui donne des places à nos messieurs"; and each time Jean-Baptiste, fils, defended all the best reasons for it: "[L'Annexion sera] l'effet de la réflexion, et le désir sincère de voir améliorer le sort de notre cher pays, qui si l'on n'y prend garde à tems s'appauvrira peu-à-peu; de notre race qui si on ne la tire pas de sa léthargie deviendra la proie d'hommes . . . qui l'exploiteront, s'enrichiront à ses dépens, absorberont nos propriétés et nous réduiront sur notre propre sol à l'état d'ignorants et supersti- tieux ilotes." The son naturally won every time. He spoke of the

8*L'Avenir*, 2, 5, 14 juin, 26 juil., 18, 30 oct., 1849.

injustice of the *Canadiens'* present position and enumerated the "abuses" in the present system: the qualifications for candidacy to the Assembly, which were so high that only two or three "agriculteurs" were members although ⅚ of the French population were habitants; the expenses of the Legislative Council; the position of the Governor General who was paid too much and knew neither "notre pays ni nos affaires, ni nos hommes publics" whereas in the United States, "le peuple élit l'homme qui lui plait et . . . leur donne un tout petit salaire parce que l'honneur d'être le plus aimer [*sic*] de par tout un grand peuple est compté pour beaucoup"; the present poverty of the people due to the high cost of responsible government—"Nous sommes pauvres . . . parceque dans un pays où l'homme ne travaille guère que six mois de l'année il paie ses officiers publics beaucoup plus cher que dans les pays riches."

Jean-Baptiste, fils, also answered the two objections his father brought forward against union with the Americans. First, Great Britain certainly would not oppose Canadian secession because British statesmen knew that all colonies must become independent some day. All the *Canadiens* needed to do was ask. Secondly, complete independence, as an alternative to responsible government or annexation, would be harmful for the French Canadians: "Je craindrais que l'indépendance après les grandes querelles qui ont eu lieu entre nos partis ne fut plus dangeureuses qu'utile, car il me semble que laissés à eux-mêmes, nos politiques seraient trop violents pour s'entendre." Throughout the whole dialogue lay the underlying theme that those who opposed annexation did so only from personal ambition and for the rewards of office. "L'Union continue à nous ruiner plus que jamais," the son concluded, "mais nos membres ne protestent plus, parce-qu'ils ont peur de gater ce qu'ils appellent leur belle position. . . . autrefois tous les hommes instruits et énergiques visaient à conduire le peuple à la liberté et à l'indépendance. Aujourd'hui on leur a ouvert quelques unes des portes du gouvernement et ils s'y jettent avec avidité."[9]

In addition to these two serials, the annexationist papers published daily articles reiterating all their main ideas. Apart from the arguments based on natural law and the abuses of party government, they frequently compared the high cost of administering Canada with that of governing the United States: "Le gouvernement du Canada coûte deux fois plus cher que celui de l'Etat de New York, et cinq fois plus cher que celui de l'Ohio" (*Le Moniteur*, September 28). They also stressed

[9]*Ibid.*, 30 août, 1, 15, 20, 27, 29 sept., 2, 4, 6, 23 oct. 1849.

the positive side, advantages such as American democracy, free trade, canals, the abolition of seigneurial tenure, tithing, and the clergy reserves, a better postal department, an end to the flow of emigration from Canada, "l'accroissement rapide de la valeur de toutes nos propriétés; Le travail en abondance, et l'aisance et le bonheur pour toutes les classes de notre population" (*Le Moniteur*, November 16). They ran instalments from François-Xavier Garneau's *Histoire* on such episodes as the deportation of the Acadians and the "despotisme militaire" of the years 1759–91. They published flattering accounts of the benefits which independence from Austria had brought to northern Italy. For some time they stressed the proposed constitution of California, a territory like Lower Canada with a Latin population. Above all, they stressed the ease with which good things could come to the *Canadiens* as in *Le Moniteur* of October 26:

Ce n'est pas la guerre ni la révolution que nous voulons, c'est *une séparation paisible et amicale de notre pays d'avec l'Angleterre*, et il n'y a pas moyen de l'obtenir autrement qu'en démontrant . . . à la mère patrie que la majorité du peuple le veut. Alors l'Angleterre qui attache peu d'importance au Canada, ne saura se refuser à une demande si légitime et elle nous déchargera, sans aucun doute de notre loyauté, puis nous entrerons dans la confédération d'une des premières puissances du monde, où le soleil de la liberté répand ses rayons bienfaisans dans toutes les classes de la société, où la misère et la gène sont pour ainsi dire inconnues, mais où règnent en revanche le bonheur et les richesses.

And all this evidence they restated in the second annexation manifesto addressed to the people of Canada and published in *L'Avenir* on December 15, 1849.

Meanwhile, the annexationists had also been campaigning. In Montreal some 1500 people, although English-speaking, had signed the first manifesto in October. Satisfied with this showing, the young *Canadien* radicals decided to bring the document to Quebec City to win adherents there. They called a meeting on October 27 and on the day appointed a large crowd gathered under the direction of most of the repealers of 1848: Dr. P.-M. Bardy, Napoléon Aubin, J.-P. Rhéaume, Joseph Légaré, Antoine Plamondon, and others. But when Dr. Bardy began to speak, he was interrupted by a group of Cauchon's friends sent to break up the meeting. After order was restored, there remained only forty to fifty gathered around a candle (the lights had been broken) to vote resolutions which were then circulated around the city for signatures. Within a few days, they had about 600 signatures, but Dr. Bardy resigned the leadership of the movement and retired from public life (for reasons which he said had nothing to do with annexation). Happy with this relative success—they had been disappointed that Papineau and Bleury had declined to come to Quebec—the young republicans returned to Montreal to call an annexationist meeting there.

On November 8, 150 to 200 people, again mostly English-speaking, came to Temperance Hall to listen to speeches from John Redpath, William Molson, Benjamin Holmes, and J.-B.-E. Dorion. *L'Avenir* reported (November 10) their resolution that their association "ne terminera sa tâche que du jour où en présence de Dieu et des hommes, la première assemblée nationale canadienne, proclamera l'indépendance du Canada, et décrétera au nom et en présence de tout un peuple-roi, la constitution d'un nouvel état souverain qui viendra s'allier, sous le beau nom d'état du Canada, à la colossale République du Nouveau-Monde." Later, they carried the message to Rouville County, and then to Saint-Edouard, where Charles Laberge and Louis-Antoine Dessaulles gave erudite lectures between speeches by English Tories . . .

SUCCESS

Despite all their magnificent principles, the *rouge* politicians—for so they had begun to be designated—were weakest when they were talking to the people. They could not speak plain words on plain things. And apparently the *Canadiens* saw the young radicals for exactly what they were: a very small intellectual French head attached to a large English Tory body. And they could hardly be attracted to the monster. "Le gouvernement soutenu par les amis du bon ordre est bien assez fort," Hector Langevin told his brother, "pour déjouer les projets de dix fois autant de Tories qu'il y en a dans le pays."[10] LaFontaine's agents in both Montreal and Quebec confirmed this judgment. Drummond reported: "There is a split in the Annexts. . . . Parmi mes partisans aujourd'hui plus nombreux même qu'à l'époque de ma dernière élection, deux seulement se sont déclarés annexionnistes."[11] From the old capital, Cauchon reassured the Attorney General: "Il n'y a pas une élection que nous ne puissions faire dans le district de Québec."[12] "Annex: does not at all take in the parishes," Wolfred Nelson wrote,[13] echoing Morin's "L'Annexion ne fleurit pas."[14]

[10]Chapais-Langevin, 249, H. Langevin à E. Langevin, 4 juil. 1849.
[11]Papiers LaFontaine, Drummond à LaFontaine, 7 fév., 1 mars 1850.
[12]*Ibid.*, Cauchon à LaFontaine, 14 mars 1850.
[13]*Ibid.*, W. Nelson to LaFontaine, Feb. 26, 1850.
[14]*Ibid.*, Morin à LaFontaine, 9 mars 1850.

Still, in March 1850, the annexationists captured the municipal election in Montreal. Edouard-Raymond Fabre, the mayor of the capital since March 1849, made no secret of his sympathy for the *rouges*, although he had declined to sign the annexation manifesto out of fear of prejudicing a case of his before the Privy Council. "Je sais," he protested to O'Callaghan, "que mon nom aurait engagé un certain nombre de Canadiens, tous Républicains, à signer."[15] In January 1850 he decided to run again for the mayoralty and hoped to carry the vote: "J'espère que les annexionnistes auront le dessus; quant au maire, je crois que j'ai une grande chance d'être élu."[16] Benjamin Holmes, Jacob DeWitt, and Henry Atwater, all LaFontaine supporters who had switched to the other camp, also decided to run, each in a different ward. Drummond immediately realized what political capital the *rouges* could make of such an annexationist sweep. Wolfred Nelson agreed, writing that Fabre was "aiming at the mayoralty and in this position hopes to have given annexation a good lift."[17]

Drummond set out to seek LaFontaine supporters as candidates against Fabre and the turncoats. But he could find none. He reported: "J'ai fait *sub rosa* tout en mon pouvoir pour mettre en avant d'autres candidats, mais je dois dire que nos amis m'ont paru très indifférents."[18] Were most of his political friends too busy invading the provincial administration to bother about municipal politics? In all events, the only two last-minute candidates he discovered were Duncan Fisher and Colonel Gugy, both repentant Tories who had switched to LaFontaine precisely because of annexation. Drummond was far too experienced a politician to expect a victory in such circumstances and on such short notice. Here were two traditional enemies, Fisher and Gugy, running against a slate of adversaries who had been traditional friends. "Les Franco-Canadiens, nos amis," Etienne-Pascal Taché explained afterwards to Gugy, "n'ont vu que le *ministère* dans cette élection, représenté dans la personne de Holmes, un du parti qui a placé ce ministère au pouvoir; dans Mr. Gugy un individu qui dans toutes les circonstances s'est trouvé dans les rangs de leurs ennemis. Le fait est qu'il n'y a pas assez longtemps que les nouvaux éléments luttent pour que les partis qui les composent aient appris à se caser."[19] Fabre and Holmes won, though not without a hard

15O'Callaghan Papers, Fabre à O'Callaghan, 24 nov. 1849.
16Papiers Fabre, Fabre à Julie Bossange, 19 jan. 1850.
17Papiers LaFontaine, W. Nelson to LaFontaine, Feb. 26, 1850.
18*Ibid.*, Drummond à LaFontaine, 7 mars 1850.
19Papiers Taché, E 2, Taché à Gugy, 19 mars 1850.

fight in which several shots were fired and several people wounded. Holmes carried the vote by only a dozen of 110 voters. Then, on March 14, his fellow aldermen re-elected Fabre. "Les Annexionnistes crient au triomphe," Drummond concluded, disappointed.[20]

Besides taking the Montreal council, the annexationists also made a deep impression on the politicians, indeed on many of LaFontaine's own friends. Fabre had been a radical since the 'twenties, Chauveau was a repealer, at least since Papineau re-entered public life in December 1847. Their adherence to *L'Avenir* was no surprise. But it was a loss to LaFontaine's party that Joseph Masson should not only become an annexationist but use his vast wealth to subsidize *L'Avenir*, becoming for it "une vraie Californie."[21] It was cause for anxiety that Louis-Michel Viger confided to intimates how uncomfortable he felt in a council that was not annexationist. And it was significant that Jean-Joseph Girouard, an intimate friend of LaFontaine and Morin and a man of much influence behind the scenes, should be so serious about it. Morin worried in a letter to LaFontaine:

Vers Noël, J'allai faire ma visite ordinaire à notre bonne [sic] ami. Tout en témoignant comme d'ordinaire son aversion pour les luttes et même pour les discussions politiques, il me communiqua une lettre qu'il vous avait écrite. . . . Cette lettre qui allait à vous conseiller de prendre l'initiative pour agiter le rappel de l'Union me surprit. Il voyait le moment favorable pour cela. Je lui dis, à première vue, que je ne voyais le temps propice ni dans les moyens à votre disposition ni même dans l'état des partis et des esprits après la séparation si elle était obtenue. . . . Je ne sais si je fus intelligible, s'il me comprit, mais moi je ne comprends nullement les raisonnements au moyen desquels il a pu en arriver là, ni les résultats qu'il attend.[22]

It was also dangerous that Duvernay and *La Minerve* were about to declare their republicanism openly. If such leaders turned, the people might begin to respond to the new demand. Realizing this, Drummond, Langevin, Cauchon, and others were careful from the beginning to make sure that they would kill the monster.

[20]Papiers LaFontaine, Drummond à LaFontaine, 7 mars 1850.
[21]Chapais-Langevin, 601, H. Langevin à J. Langevin, 19 jan. 1850.
[22]Papiers LaFontaine, Morin à LaFontaine, 12 fév. 1850.

Politicians and Priests, III

The Tory reaction stirred the *Canadiens*. The angry debate in parliament over the Rebellion Losses bill had made abundantly clear the anti-French motives that animated most of its adversaries. "Ils n'ont plus ni réserve, ni pudeur," *La Minerve* commented on February 13, "tout ce qu'il y a . . . de plus respectable dans notre société ne saurait trouver grâce à leurs yeux." Consequently, when the attack broke out against Lord Elgin they understood that every insult and every rotten egg hurled at him was really directed at them. Once again the honour of French Canada had become inseparable from that of the British crown and every French-language newspaper in the country underlined the fact.

L'Avenir—being republican—naturally expressed itself more discreetly; its main headlines on April 28 said "Le Gouverneur insulté par les loyaux! . . . Menaces des Tories!" And on May 2 it merely commented: "nous suspendrons notre jugement sur la conduite des autorités jusqu'après le rétablissement de la tranquillité." But *La Minerve, Le Canadien*, and *Les Mélanges* lost not a day. All three wrote as one, embellishing three central themes, that it was the French who were the real objects of Tory fury, that the rioters had shown the true feelings of the loyalists of 1837, and, finally, that Lord Elgin deserved the affectionate gratitude of every true *Canadien*. On April 26, the day after the burning of the parliament buildings, *La Minerve* considered the riots too horrible for even the Tories to be held responsible. "Qu'on juge de l'éducation de ce parti, nous ne voulons pas dire tory, car nous savons qu'il y a chez ce parti des hommes respectables qui rougissent de ces excès," it said, also praising the conduct of "notre noble et magnanime Gouverneur-Général." Later, on May 10, "au milieu de tous nos regrets et de l'indignation profonde sous laquelle nous gémissons encore, à l'aspect des insultes et des outrages qu'une poignée de vagabonds soldés vient de faire au pays," it rejoiced in announcing that the Queen had honoured Lord Elgin by agreeing to be godmother to his first son, born at Monklands shortly after the riots and called Victor Alexander after her. All the Executive Councillors attended the christening.

In Quebec on April 26, *Le Journal's* typesetter broke into the middle of a front-page article to announce: "un député a dépêché par le télégraphe à 2 heures que Montréal etait dans un état d'insurrection; il confirme la nouvelle de l'incendie du Parlement." In subsequent issues the paper carried more detailed accounts, stressing the courage of the Governor and wondering how far the Tories were willing to go: "A la lecture de tant d'outrages impies, tout Québec est saisi d'indignation, et l'on se demande avec clameurs quelle est cette puissance occulte qui glace, qui paralyse, qui rend inutile l'arme du devoir" (May 1).

At *Le Canadien*, meanwhile, Napoléon Aubin (in one of the last issues he edited before going to *Le Canadien Indépendant*) wrote what is a good summary of the reaction of the French press:

C'est avec les sentiments de la plus vive indignation que nous avons appris hier, par une dépêche télégraphique, l'infâme conduite des tories de Montréal . . . un échantillon de la *loyauté*, de l'honneur de certaines Anglais de Montréal, qui. . . lèvent audacieusement l'etendard de la révolte contre le représentant de leur souveraine. . . . Qu'on le remarque bien, ces émeutiers sont les mêmes qui ont reproché et reprochent encore aux Canadiens-français un mouvement motivé par des circonstances, excusables sous plusieurs rapports. (April 27)

A week later, Ronald MacDonald, back at his old chair at *Le Canadien*, continued in the same vein. Writing about the cry of "French domination" raised by the Tories, he said:

Ce cri n'est qu'un prétexte imaginé par ceux dont la loyauté s'étant évanouie avec leurs rêves de domination perpétuelle, n'en trouvent point d'autre pour justifier leur dessein de s'annexer aux Etats-Unis, on se flatte peut être encore, qu'en excitant les antipathies et les jalousies nationales entre les habitants des deux sections de la Province, ils parviendront à se rallier une majorité de leur propre origine et à ressaisir ainsi le pouvoir qui leur est échappé. (May 9)

At *Les Mélanges* in Montreal Hector Langevin stressed on May 4 the need for counteraction:

Nous sommes à un moment critique. Il s'agit de défendre nos droits, il s'agit de défendre notre religion, il s'agit de nous défendre nous-mêmes. Il nous faut seconder les efforts de nos représentants, soutenir le ministère de notre choix, et approuver la conduite du noble Lord qui représente parmi nous notre auguste Souveraine, et qui se fait le gardien de nos droits constitutionels. . . . Agissons constitutionnellement. Assemblons-nous, passons des résolutions, adoptons des adresses à Son Excellence Lord Elgin pour approuver sa conduite et celle de ses habiles ministres.

The politicians had not waited for the call of the journalists to act. Even before the ashes of the Parliament Buildings had cooled, LaFontaine paid visits to Bishop Bourget and other notables in the capital to enlist their support. At the same time Drummond and Cartier drew up an address to be circulated among the citizens at large. In haste Caron despatched Parent to Quebec to organize an address there and wrote himself to Abbé Cazeau to urge the clergy's aid: "Je considère comme de la plus grande importance que tous les gens qui veulent maintenir la paix dans le pays et la connexion avec l'Empire fassent une démonstration énergique désapprouvant les scènes qui viennent d'avoir lieu à Montréal, approuvant le gouverneur et son gouvernement et exprimant de la confiance dans l'administration."[1] And before the unhappy session had been prorogued on May 30, practically every member of the united Reform party had commanded meetings and addresses of loyalty from his constituents. They all wanted a show of strength, the French Canadians probably more than anyone. The latter felt the need to reassure the Colonial Office: "Il est important," Caron continued to Cazeau, "que l'on ne crée pas en Angleterre contre le Gouverneur une impression défavorable qu'il serait difficile de détruire." For, if the Governor's action was reversed, the struggles of the last decade would be in vain and, in LaFontaine's mind, *la survivance* would be hopeless. Then, as the Tory reaction took on more annexationist overtones, the addresses, as in 1842–3, became an important bond of French-Canadian political unity.

On the very afternoon of LaFontaine's visit, Bourget summoned the leaders of the clergy, told them to support the *adresses* in each parish, and then rode out with them to pay a personal call on Lord Elgin. Other leaders in the capital went to the Château de Ramezay to sign the book opened there, and ordinary citizens signed the *adresse* prepared by LaFontaine's agents. By May 2 Langevin was ecstatic: "je pense qu'hier soir nous n'avions pas moins de dix mille noms!"[2] And, in fact, a few days later, there were 7,686 signatures. On May 9 a delegation headed by Holmes (not yet an annexationist), Cartier, Cherrier, and Nelson read it to the Governor. On the same day a delegation from Three Rivers presented a similar address signed by 638 loyalists there.

[1]AAQ, G XI, 95, Caron à Cazeau, 29 avril 1849.
[2]Chapais-Langevin, 248, H. Langevin à E. et J. Langevin, 3 mai 1849.

The *Québecois* also reacted quickly. In record time, the priests composed and signed two addresses, one to the Governor and one to the Queen. And less than four days after his letter to Abbé Cazeau, Caron was already writing to his friend: "Tout ce que vous avez fait est excellent, votre adresse au gouverneur ne pourrait être meilleure, votre adresse à la Reine aura un excellent effet."[3] The laity, meanwhile, called a meeting for Sunday afternoon, April 29. It was, according to *Le Canadien* (April 30), "une assemblée des plus nombreuses qui se soient jamais tenues à Québec," some 7000–8000 people attending, among them even such outstanding repealers and soon-to-be annexationists as Aubin and Légaré, *Québecois* also attended two other assemblies a few days later, one in the suburbs of Charlevoix and the other at Lévis.

Then there began a veritable storm of glory for the Crown, each parish in the eastern section rivalling its neighbour in paying homage. Beginning on May 8, and continuing until July 20, 1849, the front page of *Les Mélanges Religieux* featured, in a column or two headed "Ce que pense le Peuple," a practically endless roll call of the addresses received at Monklands, thus: Répentigny, the curé and 60 habitants; LaMalbaie, the curé and 795 habitants; Longue Pointe, the curé and 1,287; LaPrairie, the curé and 959; L'Assomption, the curé and 1,110; Belœil, the curé and 773; Berthier, the curé and 2,985 habitants; Côte-des-Neiges, the curé and 197. On and on went the litany. *Le Journal de Québec* did likewise with a similar census entitled "La Voix du Peuple," beginning on May 10 and going on until mid-July, when Cauchon bravely declared that "les adresses continuent d'arriver de tous côtés," but ceased to list them. In fact, by July 2, counting those from Upper Canada, *Le Journal's* lists contained 310 addresses expressing the temper of 169,547 people.

The few who did not express their loyalty encountered difficulties. Jean-Baptiste-Eric Dorion, for instance, met Langevin on St. Vincent Street late one night, and after a glorious fist fight (which each claimed the other started) ended the day in court. Others suffered more severely—they were left off the Council's patronage list. In Quebec, Cauchon wanted no appointments for annexationists. "On dit qu'un nommé L. Falardeau, fils, de S. Ambroise va être fait magistrat. C'est un *annexioniste*," he cried, "n'allez pas le nommer."[4] To one Dr.

[3]AAQ, G XI, 97, Caron à Cazeau, 3 mai 1849; G VII, 30, Elgin à Signay, mai 1849.

[4]Papiers Taché, A 48, Cauchon à Taché, 11 jan. 1850.

Thomas Michaud of Kamouraska, Etienne-Pascal Taché explained government policy: the doctor had lost his chances for an appointment "par l'information qui a été reçue que vous étiez *annexionniste* et à peu près le seul annexionniste respectable dans la Cité! J'ignore comment on a pu connaître vos opinions ni si le rapport est bien ou mal fondé; mais en attendant vous sentez, que, dans une semblable conjoncture, je ne pourrais pas même faire mention de votre nom."[5] In Montreal, Drummond felt the same way. He wanted nothing done "sans m'avertir d'avance," for "il faut écarter les amis de l'Avenir . . . et j'aurai toujours des renseignements positifs que vous ne pouvez avoir," he told LaFontaine.[6] Sometimes though, he thought a waverer could be converted: "Il ne faudra rien faire pour indisposer ceux qui tiennent encore au ministère dont le parti est aujourd'hui beaucoup moins fort à Montréal que dans les campagnes. . . . pourquoi dans des momens aussi critiques que ceux où se trouve le ministère dans le Bas-Canada persister à faire des ennemis là où on pourrait s'assurer au contraire d'un certain appui!"[7]

Others who had not pledged their loyalty forfeited the benefits they already enjoyed. Many of the republican sympathizers among the new magistrates, justices of the peace, Queen's counsels, postal clerks, and militia officers lost their offices and commissions. Hincks insisted on this. "It was *agreed* in Cabinet that the Queen's counsels sh'd be dismissed," he reminded Baldwin. "*I* am strongly of opinion that unless we dismiss these annexationists we are ruined."[8] And LaFontaine's agents applied the policy so well that Denis-Emery Papineau feared the worst. He wrote to his uncle:

Beaucoup de personnes ici sont en faveur de l'Annexion, même parmi ceux qui sont considérés comme partisans dévoués au Ministère ou plutôt des gâteaux qu'il est en pouvoir de distribuer à droite et à gauche; malheureusement un grand nombre de ces personnes hésitent à se prononcer ouvertement; elles veulent laisser faire, attendre, puis voilà maintenant les destitutions dans la milice et dans la magistrature qui vont commencées contre les signataires de l'adresse.[9]

In another move to check the republicans, the government decided to remove the capital from Montreal. Indeed, they had little choice: there were no parliament buildings, and even Bonsecours Market could only be used under the continued protection of the infantry.

5*Ibid.*, E 2, Taché à Michaud, 29 jan. 1850.
6Papiers LaFontaine, Drummond à LaFontaine, 13 nov. 1849.
7*Ibid.*, Drummond à LaFontaine, 9 jan. 1850.
8Baldwin Papers, v51, Hincks to Baldwin, Oct. 29, 1849.
9Collection Papineau-Bourassa, D.-E. Papineau à L.-J. Papineau, 2 nov. 1849.

Also, they reasoned that since the Tory-annexationist movement was strongest in Montreal, members and civil servants would be less influenced elsewhere. Immediately after the riots, therefore, the Assembly voted to move. But where? The Upper Canadians wanted the capital at home—where, they claimed, there were never riots. Besides, they argued, since both Upper and Lower Canada had to date held the capital in turn, they should have it next. The *Québecois* disagreed. On May 4, during the debate in the Assembly, Marc Pascal de Sales Laterrière summed up all their best arguments with a paragraph quoted in *La Minerve* on May 7:

Québec est essentiellement anglaise, ne peut prospérer que par ses relations anglaises; toutes ses affections sont anglaises; elle ne peut en avoir d'autres. . . . Toutes nos habitudes, tous nos intérêts sont anglais. Il n'y a pas un Canadien français qui ne versa son sang pour la défense du pavillon britannique comme en 1775, 1812, et même en 37, époque des malheurs attribuables à la même faction qui alors, comme aujourd'hui, cherche par tous les moyens possibles à troubler l'ordre des choses, à renverser le gouvernement pour satisfaire sa cupidité et son ambition désordonnées.

The House voted to move, but left the choice of place to the government. Lord Elgin and the western Reformers favoured Toronto. LaFontaine and the French were in a quandary. They must leave Montreal or the *rouges* might win over more of their members. Yet if they left, they antagonized their own electors in the Montreal area, and LaFontaine himself represented the city of Montreal. In addition, if they departed for Upper Canada, they might alienate their friends in Quebec. As the summer wore on, they delayed deciding. In July Caron wrote from Quebec: "Je suis d'avis que la translation du siège du gouvernement à Toronto pour commencer créera beaucoup de mécontentement dans le Bas-Canada sans compensation équivalente dans le Haut."[10] In Montreal, even as faithful a partisan as Langevin insisted in *Les Mélanges* on October 16 that "la translation du gouvernement hors de Montréal tiendrait en ce moment à agiter de plus en plus l'esprit public." Finally the Council agreed to alternate the capital, moving to Toronto until the end of the present parliament. Thus Upper Canada could be satisfied, and Quebec reassured (by *Le Journal de Québec*) that Toronto would enjoy the honour for only two years and the seat of government would then return to Quebec City for the next four. Among the Montrealers, only Louis-Michel Viger resigned from the Council, but he had been restless since the annexation crisis had begun, and took the opportunity to leave

[10]Papiers LaFontaine, Caron à LaFontaine, 21 juil. 1849.

because he could not "partager les vues de mes collègues sur la question du siège du gouvernement."[11] The others blamed their loss on the Tories and, by association, on the *rouges*. From Toronto LaFontaine reported that the next session would be able to work peacefully: "Les Annexionnistes n'auront pas de chance dans cette partie du pays."[12] The members would be free from any *rouge* contagion.

By the time the Council left Montreal at the end of October 1849 the annexation manifesto had come out, and the *Canadien* politicians were occupied in counteracting it with a loyalist manifesto: Protêt Contre la Séparation du Canada d'avec l'Angleterre et son Annexion aux Etats-Unis. Appearing in *La Minerve* on October 15, four days after the Tory document, it began solemnly:

Sincèrement attachés aux institutions que la mère-patrie a depuis peu reconnues et convaincus que ces institutions sont suffisantes pour nous assurer, au moyen d'une législation sage et judicieuse, un remède prompt et efficace à tous nos maux dont la province puisse se plaindre, nous croyons devoir nous empresser à protester d'une manière publique et solennelle contre les opinions énoncées dans ce document.

It was signed by most of the *Canadien* politicians in the Montreal area. A copy was despatched to Quebec where Caron, Louis Méthot, Louis Massue, Bouthillier, and others joined the Montrealers. By November 2 over 1000 names had been collected in the old capital. One man refused to sign it, as Cauchon reported: "Chauveau a refuser [*sic*] de signer notre contre manifeste qui lui a été présenté par M. Massue en disant: 'Si les annexionnistes allaient avoir le dessus, nous nous serons placés dans une situation compromettante.'"[13] But, he continued, it was encouraging that the annexation manifesto, circulating at the same time, received little attention: "Les signataires ont presque tous été pris dans Brisseauville où s'est réfugiée la population la plus pauvre et la plus crapuleuse depuis les incendies de 1845. La grande masse des bons citoyens de nos faubourgs n'a pas signé. Il va falloir marcher contre avec main forte."[14] "Le temps est favorable," Caron confirmed, "les rouges sont en déroute, les annexionnistes n'osent plus se montrer."[15]

[11]*Ibid.*, L.-M. Viger à LaFontaine, 26 nov. 1849.
[12]LaFontaine à Amable Berthelot, 16 nov. 1849, as quoted in O. Maurault, "LaFontaine à travers ses lettres à Amable Berthelot," *Cahiers des Dix*, 1954, p. 154.
[13]Papiers LaFontaine, Cauchon à LaFontaine, 24 oct. 1849.
[14]*Ibid.*, Cauchon à LaFontaine, 26 oct. 1849.
[15]*Ibid.*, Caron à LaFontaine, 13 nov. 1849.

In Montreal, the *rouges* campaigned against the countermanifesto, underlining how most of its signatories had profited from the Union. They compared each one's situation in 1837 with his profits from the government now, and they asked their readers to draw their own conclusions. James Leslie who had no salary in 1837 now received $4000 a year; A.-N. Morin who also had nothing in 1837 now enjoyed $4400 a year as Speaker; L. T. Drummond, described as a "Démocrate" in 1837, was earning $2400 now; Wolfred Nelson the "général en chef" in 1837 now received $8 a day; Joseph Bourret, "rien" in 1837, now had $4 a day; and George-Etienne Cartier, a rebel in 1837 and "un homme *qui prêche l'annexion depuis des années*," now according to *L'Avenir* (October 18), was a "juge ou ministre en perspective."[16] Nevertheless, Montrealers signed in such numbers that a dozen days after its publication the Protêt had 1100 signatures.

One of the annexationists' most telling arguments, apparently, was that separation from the mother country would be peaceful. In fact, *L'Avenir* and *Le Moniteur* claimed that the British themselves wanted to be rid of the colony, highlighting various anticolonial English opinions like Cobden's (*Le Moniteur*, February 1). And they reproduced tendentious articles from the London *Times and Morning Advertiser*, which, as Drummond reported, caused "une grande joie aux annexionistes puisque l'on y annonce que le Cabinet Anglais s'est décidé à consentir à l'annexion."[17]

LaFontaine and Drummond were furious. Writing about the article from the *Times*, Drummond commented on December 3:

Les hommes d'état qui sont à la tête des affaires en Angleterre ont moins à cœur la conservation de la colonie aujourd'hui qu'autrefois. Ils auraient fait infiniment mieux s'ils eussent envoyés une dépêche dans laquelle ils auraient prononcé fortement leur détermination à prêter main forte à ceux qui ayant lutté depuis un quart de siècle pour obtenir l'extension de la constitution britannique au Canada sont disposés à se rallier sous le drapeau de cette constitution pour résister à ceux qui s'y opposent, qu'ils s'appellent Tories ou annexionistes. Ils auraient beaucoup mieux fait de rencontrer le mouvement en faveur de l'annexion par un envoi de troupes.[18]

By the beginning of November Drummond had already insisted with LaFontaine that "il faut ce me semble que Lord Elgin suggère à Milord Grey la nécessité de dissiper sans délai tout doute . . . que le mouvement annexioniste serait accueilli probablement ou même d'un œil

[16]*L'Avenir*, 18 oct. 1849.
[17]Papiers LaFontaine, Drummond à LaFontaine, 17 jan. 1850.
[18]*Ibid.*, Drummond à LaFontaine, 3 déc., 1849.

indifférent par les hommes d'état de la métropole."[19] And in January 1850 he insisted again. Finally, on February 2, *Le Journal* flashed the news: it had just heard by telegraph from Montreal that Lord Grey had sent a formal condemnation of annexation. *Les Mélanges* and *La Minerve* carried the latest despatch from the Colonial Office in full, *La Minerve* commenting on February 4: "Ceux qui ont signé de bonne foi, l'adresse intempestive au peuple du Canada, en seront certainement étonnés." Drummond breathed more easily. He wrote: "Je conçois que la dépêche de Lord Grey est de la plus haute importance et pour le ministère et pour le gouvernement impérial. . . . En conséquence j'ai fait imprimer cette dépêche . . . pour faire voir à la population qu'elle a tout à perdre et rien à gagner en poursuivant le fantôme de l'annexion."[20] And on February 7, *La Minerve* described the effect on the annexationists: "Les journaux qui ont favorisé le mouvement, les organes des agitateurs, se sont laissé aller tout d'abord à un mouvement de colère et de dépit, mais ils semblent s'être un peu pacifiés depuis, sans doute parce qu'ils entendent dire à tous les signataires de bonne foi du manifeste annexionniste qu'ils s'en tiennent à leur promesse de ne plus *désirer* l'annexion, si la Grande-Bretagne s'y oppose."

The Tories had been discredited, and late in the winter of 1850 many of them began to see themselves as others saw them: a group of solid businessmen who held their fortunes and interests above their loyalty to their country and their sovereign. Their tarnished allies, the *rouges*, had had other motives and possibly, higher hopes, but they, too, were losing support. Their party had always been held together by emotion rather than organization. Their little manifesto looked silly next to the daily lists of loyal addresses to Lord Elgin. Their meeting at Quebec at the end of October had failed, and their leader in the old capital had been forced out of public life. Despite his sympathy for them, Papineau had refused open aid. When a relatively small newspaper, *L'Echo des Campagnes* began to print annexationist articles in December 1849, the subscribers protested so strongly (so Cauchon said) that the editor felt obliged to resign in favour of Langevin, who, on taking over, printed an editorial in *Les Mélanges* on January 25 thanking those who had protested.

Had the *rouge* annexationist movement been nothing but the daydream of desperate romantics? At the end of January 1850, they again tried to revive their spirit by calling a public assembly at Saint-

---

[19]*Ibid.*, Drummond à LaFontaine, 8 nov. 1850.
[20]*Ibid.*, Drummond à LaFontaine, 6 fév., 1850.

Edouard, the *chef-lieu* of one of the safer radical ridings, Huntingdon. But they had overreached themselves. Scheduled for Sunday, January 28, after a high mass, the meeting was soon disrupted by fights and heckling. For the *rouges* it resulted in nothing more than a special address sent a week later by 1100 electors to their member urging him to have nothing to do with annexation.

According to *L'Avenir* on January 31, the outcome of the meeting had been settled on the morning before it began: at the neighbouring village of Saint-Isidore, the curé had told a group of parishioners who had come to consult him in the sacristy that *"s'ils se mêlaient d'annexion, la reine les chasserait hors du pays."* And according to *La Minerve* (February 11) at Saint-Rémi, another parish nearby, curé Bédard had allegedly declared from the pulpit: "S'il y a une assemblée à St-Edouard, vous pouvez y aller si vous le voulez, vous êtes libres, mais quant à moi, je n'y vais point. Je ne suis pas prophète, mais tout ce que je puis vous dire, c'est qu'avant deux ou trois mois, j'irai vous faire sortir de prison, comme je l'ai fait en 1837." In short, if the young radicals failed to capture support, it was not so much because of the exertions of the politicians as because they had been under attack from the clergy.

PRIESTS

Between 1842 and 1846 most priests had gradually come to realize that the anti-clerical radicalism of 1837 now survived among the followers of Viger and Papineau rather than the supporters of LaFontaine. Since the 1846 debate over the education bill and the dogmatic disputes with *L'Aurore*, the priests had tended to sympathize with the advocates of responsible government. They watched with growing pain when Papineau re-entered public life on a platform that included the abolition of tithing. By the time of the tribune's split with the ministers they were convinced. Before the debate over repeal was far advanced they had decided to fight, and by the time of *la crise annexioniste* they had become one of the great forces on the side of responsible government in French Canada.

It could have been anticipated that the French-Canadian clergy would play an increasingly political role during the closing years of the decade. With responsible government, the *Canadiens* had for the first time in their long national life taken over the direction of their own destiny. And as the Church had always had an important role in fashioning their thought, it was natural for most of those on the political stage to welcome its support. As the general election of 1847–8 swept LaFontaine to victory, reports from different parts of Lower Canada had come in that "certains prêtres, même à Montréal ont prononcé en chaire des discours presqu'exclusivement politiques."[21] Then, after the formation of the Reform cabinet in March 1848 and the Papineau manifestos for repeal, the clergy had become more and more involved, behind the scenes, with important government plans.

Among these, railroads held priority, for they had become a symbol of the struggle against annexation—especially in the Quebec district where economic prosperity seemed to depend so much on the projected Halifax Intercolonial. One of the young radicals, Luc Letellier, explained: "Depuis que les nouvelles d'Europe nous portent à croire avec certitude que le chemin de fer d'Halifax ne reçoit aucun encouragement de la Mère Patrie les habitans de Québec songent de plus en plus à l'Annexion, voire même à l'indépendance."[22] Among those who assured the scheme's promoters of their interest and co-operation was Archbishop Signay, who personally told the company director, Timmins, that he would be happy to "encourager de son nom les aspirations du comité" as soon as it was organized.[23] Another of the government's important policies concerned repeal of the Navigation Laws. And in Montreal, none knew better their significance than the editor of Les Mélanges Religieux. He wrote to his priest brother in Quebec: "Il est surtout une mesure particulière dont la passation ou le refus influencera immensément sur les destinées futures du pays; c'est la libre navigation. Si on nous l'accorde, nous obtenons par là tous les avantages du gouvernement américain sans en avoir le mauvais côté: mais si on nous le refuse absolument, je n'ose penser à l'avenir."[24] He endorsed the administration's plans and during the autumn of 1848 filled his newspaper with articles and notices on the "Lois de Navigation."

In the Quebec district, the politicians gave great weight to the suggestions of Abbé Cazeau. For instance, Cazeau seems to have influenced Caron's decision when his family insisted that he resign the speakership of the Legislative Council in the fall of 1849. Cauchon tried to persuade Caron to stay on: a by-election in Quebec at that moment might be dangerous. "Comme je le laissais," Cauchon

[21]Les Mélanges Religieux, 14 déc. 1847; J. Barnard, Mémoires Chapais, II, 1848–75 (Montréal, 1961), pp. 17ff.
[22]Chapais-Langevin, Letellier à Chauveau, 10 mars 1849.
[23]AAQ, Régistre des lettres 22, 808, Cazeau à Timmins, 17 août 1849.
[24]Chapais-Langevin, 246, H. Langevin à E. Langevin, 8 déc. 1848.

reported to LaFontaine, "M. Cazeau le secrétaire de l'archevêché entrait pour l'engager de ne pas vous abandonner, il aura fait tout son possible en ce sens."[25] Caron remained another month. When he did leave, he and Cauchon again consulted Cazeau who suggested Jean Chabot as his successor. LaFontaine recommended Chabot as head of the Department of Public Works. The new executive councillor unfortunately turned out to be a hopeless alcoholic who had to resign in March 1850 after spending a night in the Toronto jail—to LaFontaine's and Cazeau's great embarrassment. Cazeau then recommended another successor.

More important, however, than such private advice, was the influence wielded on behalf of LaFontaine by Les Mélanges Religieux in Montreal and by its junior associate in Quebec, L'Ami de la Religion et de la Patrie. Edited by Jacques Crémazie, L'Ami first appeared early in 1848 under the interesting motto: "Le Trône chancelle quand l'honneur, la religion, et la bonne foi ne l'environnent pas." It endorsed LaFontaine's party so unequivocally that on October 24, 1849, Cauchon reminded the party leader: "Il ne faudra pas oublier quand vous donnez des annonces d'en donner aussi à l'Ami de la Religion, qui je crois ne peut pas vivre bien longtemps, mais qui, malgré qu'il sort à présent, bien mal écrit, montre de bonnes dispositions et fait tout le bien qu'il peut."[26] Later LaFontaine's agent again reported that friends in the old capital "disent tous . . . que Crémazie a rendu contre Papineau, par L'Ami de la Religion, d'importants services à l'administration."[27] Like its model in Montreal, the Quebec religious newspaper had taken an active part in the "Union et Nationalité" debate and in the campaign of vilification against Papineau.

In that particular campaign, Les Mélanges had injected a clerical note all its own. At the height of the controversy between Nelson and Papineau, it had published a letter supporting Nelson from the rebel priest, Abbé Etienne Chartier. In 1842 Chartier's retraction of his 1837 speeches had sparked a bitter polemic over the relations of Church and state—the first serious disagreement between the priests and the members of the Neilson-Viger-Papineau faction. Now, Les Mélanges decided to use him against the revolutionaries. On January 26, 1849, it ran an article of his in which—and as the patriotes' chaplain he ought to know the facts—he accused Papineau of a whole series of crimes: of having "voulu et causé l'insurrection de 1837" and

[25]Papiers LaFontaine, Cauchon à LaFontaine, 15 nov. 1849.
[26]Ibid., Cauchon à LaFontaine, 24 oct. 1849.
[27]Ibid., Cauchon à LaFontaine, 17 déc. 1849.

yet having prepared no defence; of having "lâchement abandonné les Canadiens" in the thick of the fight; of having spent his time in the United States hiding instead of trying to help the other exiles (Chartier, presumably); of having interrupted negotiations with three American generals who were ready to come to the *Canadiens'* assistance. "Hélas! M. Papineau," he concluded, "que la nature ne vous a-t-elle donné autant de courage que d'éloquence. . . . Il est incroyable que l'Amérique aurait produit deux Arnold!" To which the editor of *Les Mélanges* added: "C'est le document le plus fort que nous ayons encore lu contre M. Louis-Joseph Papineau." And certainly it helped Nelson's cause.

As the months went on *Les Mélanges* became so involved in politics that at last the priests felt they had to warn Langevin to tone down his enthusiasm for LaFontaine. He did not. And, on July 20, 1849, he announced that he was therefore resigning. Still, the priests could not comfortably abandon their subscribers to *L'Avenir* and, before long, Langevin returned, not as editor, but as political commentator. Then, in the fall of 1849, when he left to take over *L'Echo des Campagnes*, *Les Mélanges* hired Louis Létourneux to continue the political comment against the *rouges*.

During his time as editor, Langevin did his greatest service, perhaps, in publicizing the clergy's support of Elgin and its opposition to annexation. On May 4, 1849, he issued the rallying call:

En présence de cette activité des gens turbulents et ennemis de la constitution, on se demande ce qu'ont à faire les libéraux. La réponse n'est pas difficile à faire. Il faut de l'union parmi nous. . . . Regardons enfin nos évêques, regardons nos prêtres, regardons tout notre clergé; il vient de nous montrer l'exemple en présentant lui-même des adresses à S.E. Lord Elgin, et en envoyant d'autres à notre gracieuse souveraine. Après cela, hésiterons-nous à agir avec vigueur, promptitude et énergie? Hésiterons-nous à suivre la route que nous trace notre episcopat, que nous trace notre clergé tout entier.

And throughout the summer of 1849 the daily recital of loyal addresses reminded his readers that the curés had signed at the top of every list.

In 1840 the priests had organized and signed petitions against the Union. Nine years later they now took a leading part in guiding public opinion to oppose its repeal. Much, of course, had happened in the meantime. But what must have impressed the priests most was the *rouge* propaganda against the Church. All during 1848 and 1849 *L'Avenir* and *Le Moniteur* maintained a continuous anti-clerical offensive. During 1849 alone, the two newspapers attacked the temporal power of the Pope, the Lower Canadian system of tithing, and the clergy's involvement in the seigneurial and educational systems.

The attack against the Papal States began on March 14. *L'Avenir* published and commented on extracts from the European liberal press on the revolution which had forced Pius IX into exile and proclaimed Mazzini's republic. The articles were bitter: and it was clear where the sympathies of the Lower Canadian republicans lay. *Les Mélanges* took up the challenge, publishing several series of learned articles during March. Langevin hoped, he said on the thirtieth, that in reading these, "les Messieurs de *L'Avenir* devront comprendre maintenant toute l'injustice et la faute qu'ils ont commises, spécialement par leur article au sujet du Souverain-Pontife." The young editors did not understand. They continued to insult the Pope, and at their Saint-Jean-Baptiste banquet that year, they replaced the traditional toast to the sovereign with a defiant speech by Charles Laberge on "Rome Régénérée". *Les Mélanges* protested:

"A Rome Régénérée"! c'est à dire, aux assassins de Rossi, au poignard démocratique, aux misérables qui ont insulté Pie IX et l'ont forcé à quitter sa capitale, aux oppresseurs de la presse honnête, aux prêtres apostats, aux spoliateurs des temples et des maisons religieuses, aux vandales qui pillent les musées et vendent à l'étranger les monuments de leur pays, aux assassins du curé de la Minerve et de plusieurs jésuites, aux démagogues qui fusillent 25 citoyens parce qu'ils ne veulent pas prendre la défense du gouvernement intru de Rome, aux oppresseurs enfin du St. Siège et de l'Eglise!! (June 28)

From *L'Avenir*'s side, Gustave Papineau rejoined unrepentant: "Quant à la santé de la reine, il nous semble absurde de vouloir forcer les *nationaux* réunis le jour de leur fête *nationale* à s'occuper d'autres sujets que ceux qui touchent leur nationalité ou leurs sentiments démocratiques" (June 30). "Les journaux socialistes et anti-religieux sont sans cesse à vanter les *hauts faits* de MM. les Rouges à Rome," Langevin continued on July 6, while *L'Avenir* carried on its praise for the *carbonari* throughout July. In June, Joseph-Guillaume Barthe, writing under the pseudonym "Trépassé," began another series in *L'Avenir* against the Pope's temporal power, provoking from Langevin the comment (September 21) that "la manie d'aboyer contre la soutane semble être devenue à la mode." *L'Avenir*, of course, was striking at one of the great problems of the Catholic Church at that time, but one with little relevance to Canadian politics. Soon it struck closer to home.

On July 21 it carried an article by Dessaulles on the revenues of the curé of Saint-Hyacinthe. It began: "La dime, suivant moi, est un abus encore bien plus grand que la tenure seigneuriale." And for three months the journalists were absorbed in another debate, this time on tithing. "Tantale se désespérait de pouvoir atteindre à une seule goutte d'eau," Langevin commented on September 11; "les Républicains-Rouges se tirent les cheveux de ne pouvoir mettre tout à feu et à sang et trôner sur des ruines et des cadavres." Both *L'Avenir* and *Le Moniteur* started their assault on the *Canadien* Church with a special series calling for the repeal of tithing. On October 20 *Les Mélanges* regretted that Protestants rejoiced: "ils trouvent une sanction non suspecte aux préjugés déjà si forts et si peu rationnels qui leur sont inspirés dès l'enfance." *Le Moniteur* observed ominously (November 16) that tithing would cease automatically with annexation. Langevin rebuked them all: "Est-ce donc si odieux, si exorbitant qu'un Catholique paie 30 sols par année à son Curé pour tous les services qu'il en reçoit? Un médecin en exige deux et quatre fois autant pour administrer un simple purgatif, sans parler ici de ce qui se pratique par les Avocats et des hommes des autres professions" (October 5).

"L'Avenir et le Moniteur préparent les esprits à la suppression des dimes," Bishop Bourget wrote to Bishop Turgeon at the end of October.[28] The two papers had also begun to demand the abolition of seigneurial tenure, and in the process, to attack the Church's owner-ship of seigneurial lands. In fact, *L'Avenir* averred, one of the main weaknesses of the system was the amount of revenue which accrued from it to the Séminaire de Québec and other religious institutions. *Le Moniteur* claimed (September 22) to have the public on its side: "*L'Avenir* en ayant le courage d'attaquer les mauvaises tendances du clergé canadien, s'est attiré la sympathie et l'estime de tous les hommes de cœur." And thus the two journals continued throughout 1849. On the clergy's influence on popular opinion, for example, *Le Moniteur* declared in the spring:

A qui la faute si le peuple manque d'éducation politique? C'est au parti clérical, ou, si vous l'aimez mieux, au parti tonsuré . . . une véritable Inquisition politique d'un rigorisme absolu. . . . Quel est le principe politique du clergé? "Obéir au pouvoir", le grand, l'unique, l'immuable principe politique que le clergé enseigne au Peuple, c'est l'obéissance au pouvoir, mais une obéissance passive, mais une obéissance illimitée. N'essayez pas de dire le contraire, notre malheureuse histoire vous démentirait. (May 24)

To all of this *Les Mélanges* answered in kind; ordinary citizens reeled in shock, it claimed: " 'Impossible maintenant, nous ont-ils dit, de se dissimuler qu'il y ait de l'irreligion, de la haine et de la mauvaise foi cachées sous ces écrits. Si ce n'est pas absolument du *voltaire*, c'est au moins de l'*ex-constitutionnel* de Paris tout pur' " (September 14). *Le*

28AAM, Lettres Bourget, V, 332–5, Bourget à Turgeon, fin octobre 1849.

Moniteur mocked: "Paraissant à l'heure actuelle dans les états de l'Eglise romaine, nous serions immanquablement tombés avec les héros du brave Garibaldi sous les coups indulgenciés de la Tiare sanglante du successeur de St Pierre" (September 11). And—displaying a clever sense of humour—the young radical editor bought advertising space for *Le Moniteur* in *Les Mélanges* for three weeks, to Langevin's and the priests' great embarrassment. "Nous voulons dire que nous ne voulons en aucune manière recommander les doctrines de ce journal," they put rather starchily above the advertisement on January 8, 1850.

As 1849 progressed *Les Mélanges* contained an increasing number of articles culled from the European ultramontane press: speeches by the Spanish conservative Donoso Cortès, Montalembert's great oration on the roman question, de Bonald's pastoral letter "contre les erreurs de son temps," and a long book review condemning Eugène Sue's salacious *Les Mystères de Paris* which *L'Avenir* was praising in an attempt, said *Les Mélanges*, "de répandre sur la religion et ses pratiques tout l'odieux possible."

On September 14 *Les Mélanges* warned the two republican papers: "Nos adversaires ne doivent pas se dissimuler que, par leur conduite et leurs écrits, ils se font plus de tort qu'ils ne nous en font à nous mêmes. Il est peu de catholiques impartiaux et sensés qui ne se lassent et s'indignent de tels procédés." The *rouges* should have heeded the advice. Instead, shortly after the publication of the annexation manifesto, Joseph Doutre had *L'Avenir* make the following announcement on November 24, which *Le Moniteur* repeated (November 30) under the heading "Quel affreux tripotage":

Nous devons aujourd'hui pour répondre à une haute confidence, annoncer au peuple du Canada un fait qui révèle toute la faiblesse du gouvernement et toute la corruption dont il est capable, pour conserver la position qui lui échappe.

Il ne s'agit de rien moins que d'une lettre autographe de Son Excellence Lord Elgin, proposant aux évêques catholiques du Canada le parti suivant:

Les évêques catholiques travailleraient au moyen de mandements, de circulaires, à étouffer le mouvement annexioniste parmi leur population et en retour le gouvernement restituerait les biens des Jésuites, et même ferait dépendre la question de la translation du siège du gouvernement dans le Bas-Canada, du plus ou moins d'ardeur que mettraient les évêques dans cette propagande.

Unfortunately the news was false. "Le bruit est absurde," Drummond said to himself as he wrote immediately to LaFontaine to ask: "existe-t-il quelque correspondance qui ait pu donner lieu à cette histoire?"[29] Cauchon also enquired from the government and then went straight

[29]Papiers LaFontaine, Drummond à LaFontaine, 24 nov. 1849.

to Abbé Cazeau to get a denial. The whole *presse ministérielle* joined *Les Mélanges* to challenge the republicans.

L'Avenir put on a brave front: "Nous comprenons votre colère, et nous vous la pardonnons; car si elle n'est pas légitime, elle est au moins bien excusable," wrote Joseph Papin on November 29. But, once assured by LaFontaine and Cazeau that there was no such thing, LaFontaine's journalists pressed their advantage. "[Le] mensonge le plus détestable que les écrivains puissent imaginer. . . ." (November 26.) "Ce bruit n'a d'autre fondement que le cerveau de personnes mal disposées contre toutes les autorités civiles et religieuses," wrote *La Minerve* on December 3. "Voilà des journaux qui ont une singulière tactique," *Le Canadien* commented on December 7: "ils avancent des faits et au lieu de prouver leur existence, ils nous chargent de prouver qu'ils n'existent pas." On December 1 Cauchon printed Cazeau's firm denial, and well on into February 1850 *Le Journal* carried on its front page a challenge to *L'Avenir* ("organe mourant de la démagogie expirante") to prove its assertion. But as early as December 6, *L'Avenir* had already backed down: "La nouvelle que nous annoncions nous avait été communiquée par une personne dont la respectabilité ne nous laissait aucun doute sur le fait de la proposition." *Les Mélanges* gloated on December 18: "*L'Avenir* et le *Moniteur* avaient osé publier que les chefs vénérés de notre Eglise devaient trafiquer leur pouvoir spirituel pour des terrains. C'était bien certainement l'assertion la plus effrontée qui soit jamais sortie de la presse. Calomnier les personnes sacrées les plus haut placées dans la hiérarchie de l'Eglise, voilà ce que peuvent ces journaux."

For the *rouges* the lie about Lord Elgin and the bishops had been a tactical mistake. But they had not erred in this any more than in all their other attacks on the Church. The republicans hurt their own cause. On repeal and annexation they might conceivably have been able to succeed in weakening LaFontaine if they had continued to emphasize the threat to nationality and the defects of the Union, but by challenging the clerics of a revered Church they merely confused the issue. Instead of fighting for repeal, they fought against the Church, thus cementing the alliance between LaFontaine and the priests.

As both were being attacked from the same source, LaFontaine's publicists quickly came to the rescue of the priests. All during 1849 *Le Journal de Québec*, *Le Canadien*, and *La Minerve* joined *Les Mélanges* as if they themselves had been directly attacked. During March, while the dispute raged over the Pope's temporal sovereignty,

Cauchon's *Journal* featured a serial on the subject by Bishop Dupanloup of Orléans; another series the same month assailed *L'Avenir* for "la prétention qu'il entretient de catéchiser le clergé sur ses devoirs." So also on the issue of tithing in October. Cauchon defended the Church's rights and underlined the connection between anticlericalism and the republicans: "Ce sont les aimables procédés du passé, la haine entre le peuple et ses chefs religieux pour assurer le triomphe des doctrines pernicieuses et anti-nationales." *Le Moniteur* which criticized the clergy's role in the schools and blamed it for keeping the populace in ignorance, was answered by Cauchon who asked why lay educators did not work:

Qui vous empêche d'appliquer vos connaissances et vos talents à l'encouragement et au perfectionnement de l'agriculture? . . . Qui vous empêche de former des sociétés de commerce pour vous protéger contre les étreintes du monopole; pour vous soutenir mutuellement au lieu de vous envier vos succès; pour vous faire des protecteurs en pays étrangers comme ont fait les Cuvillier, les Méthot, les Langevin, les Maçons [*sic*] les Fabre et autres noms honorables? Il faut au pays des hommes de cœur et d'action, mais non des calomniateurs et des pourfendeurs de prêtres. (*Le Journal de Québec*, March 2)

He went on to give the clergy credit for *la survivance*:

D'où vient cette haute portée d'intelligence, ce caractère si beau, si noble, si grand de franchise, d'honneur, de grandeur d'âme et de religieuse honnêteté qui distingue nos premiers citoyens et qui contraste si étonnement avec cette populace de banqueroutiers qui soudoient les incendiaires, les parjures, les voleurs et la lie des villes pour commettre en leur nom, pour eux, et à leur profit des crimes dignes des Vandales? Du clergé national.

Finally, when the *rouges* hurled insults, the editor of *Le Journal* answered as he alone could.

Détrôner le Dieu de nos pères et lui substituer l'infâme idole du sensualisme, voilà leur but; vilipender le prêtre, calomnier son enseignement, couvrir d'un noir venin ses actions les plus louables, voilà leur moyen. . . . Quel but, quelle fin vous proposez-vous en livrant à l'ignominie le prêtre du Canada, votre concitoyen, votre ami d'enfance, l'ami dévoué de notre commune patrie! Aurez-vous relevé bien haut la gloire de notre pays lorsque vous aurez avili aux yeux de l'étranger ses institutions les plus précieuses, couvert de boue ses hommes les plus éminents dans l'ordre religieux et civil, enseveli sous un noir manteau de calomnies le corps le plus respectable de la société comme un cadavre sous un drap mortuaire. (December 6)

Le Canadien wrote less lyrically, but like *Le Journal*, it too came to the defence of the priests, and struck back at *L'Avenir*. During *la crise Metcalfe* it had opposed LaFontaine, and when Papineau had returned to public life it had supported him, but it could not support the *rouge* attack on the Church. On May 31, 1848, it found their articles "représentent trop de passion et par conséquent une notable injustice envers des hommes en qui le pays a confiance." And at the height of the dispute over the Papal States, it noted how the same republicans who now praised Mazzini's revolution had supported the Canadian Tories who had founded the British North American League, "un parti dont les organes prêchent ouvertement la guerre civile, une guerre ayant pour objet l'extermination de ce peuple, et dont les chefs organisent à grand bruit une LIGUE de leurs adhérents dans le but avoué de proscrire et d'anéantir sa langue, ses lois, et toutes les institutions qui lui sont chères." "Plus je songe à l'article de *l'Avenir*," Luc Letellier complained to Chauveau who refused to protest against annexation, "plus je regrette une aussi sotte sortie contre le Saint Père."[30]

To all the insults they usually flung at their enemies, Duvernay and Cauchon could now add "socialiste, communiste, prud'hommiste," and could blame them for their "orages d'injures énumérées sur le clergé catholique" or for having "confondre tout le clergé catholique avec l'ordre des Jésuites." *La Minerve* concentrated on the alliance between the Tories and the anticlericals. Commenting on *L'Avenir*'s charge that priests should be forbidden to express political opinions, it declared:

On se rappelle que M. Papineau a déclaré en pleine chambre et en face du pays "qu'il se réservait, à lui, le droit indépendant de ne rendre compte de ses actes à aucune autorité sur la terre" et cela, en matières religieuses, puisqu'il fesait cette déclaration, en parlant des doctrines immorales, suivant lui, du clergé français sous Louis XIV. . . . Tout le monde peut juger de l'orthodoxie de ce principe démocratique au suprême degré. . . . il s'est emporté en déblatérations haineuses contre le clergé catholique du Canada, avec une malice qui lui a valu des applaudissements de la part de nos ennemis. (May 14)

But when Duvernay accused Dessaulles of being an atheist, the latter sued for libel and £12,000. The trial became a *cause célèbre* for it involved all the leading personalities of both the LaFontaine and *L'Avenir* factions. But for Duvernay it was a lost cause. Drummond defended him, although he knew he would lose. (As he left for the Court House he told LaFontaine, "J'aimerais autant aller prendre un bains dans le Saint Laurent" [it was December 17].[31]) He pleaded for over an hour basing his argument on the right of free speech, and

---

[30]Chapais-Langevin, Letellier à Chauveau, 4 avril 1849.
[31]Papiers LaFontaine, Drummond à LaFontaine, 17 déc. 1849.

Duvernay was condemned to pay £100. Drummond regretted the incident and Les Mélanges reported on January 26 his comment: "L'Avenir ne manquera pas de crier victoire, non pas sur le propriétaire du journal mais sur le ministère." It did, indeed. But, lacking the patience of the law, most Canadiens had by then believed Duvernay.

By joining the clergy and its two journals in opposing L'Avenir, LaFontaine's agents and their newspapers had clearly put themselves on the side of the angels. And if they needed to prove it, they had the word of French Canada's most influential personality, for 1849 was the year of Chiniquy's triumph. And, in the spring, the new hero interrupted his sparkling season to join the campaign against L'Avenir. For three months he assailed the rouges with a constant stream of erudite articles in Les Mélanges. In March he wrote "Les Principes de L'Avenir," five long monographs defending the temporal sovereignty. In May, he returned to the fray with a set of open letters to the editors of L'Avenir in which he not only defended papal supremacy but also attacked the whole doctrine of the young republicans: "L'Avenir a insulté la religion et le prêtre, en Canada, il a insulté les évêques, il a insulté le Pape, au nom de sa démocratie. Et voilà pourquoi je ne puis être démocrate à la façon de l'Avenir. . . . L'Avenir est l'organe d'une fausse et mauvaise démocratie . . . et voilà pourquoi un catholique ne peut soutenir ce journal s'il ne change pas, sans trahir sa conscience" (May 29). The young editors answered back. They had already insulted the Pope—a bad tactic. Now, at the peak of his popularity they turned upon Chiniquy—an even worse tactic. Langevin, Cauchon, La Minerve, and Le Canadien all came to the priest's defence.

The apostle of temperance had mentioned republicanism only by implication in his religious tracts. But he soon took the short step from condemnation of L'Avenir's religious views to approval of the political ideas of his own friends and began to preach against annexation in May and appear at political meetings. His superiors feared the worst,[32] for he had that embarrassing episode in his past which L'Avenir's editors would certainly not hesitate to produce. Whether he knew of the scandal or not, LaFontaine also worried. He wrote from Toronto: "Je vois que l'abbé Chiniqui [sic] figure dans les assemblées publiques. Ses intentions peuvent être bonnes, mais il n'a pas de jugement. En outre, il devrait se borner à son métier."[33] Others

[32]AAM, Lettres Bourget, V, 279–80, Bourget à Turgeon, 21 août 1849.
[33]LaFontaine à Amable Berthelot, 1 avril 1850, quoted in Maurault, "LaFontaine à travers ses lettres," p. 141.

were scandalized by a priest being so overtly involved in politics. Recalling this period some time later, Jean-Baptiste Meilleur declared:

Je l'ai entendu moi-même . . . adresser en face de l'autel, les paroles les plus onctueuses, à l'administration du jour . . . et faire à son antagoniste, les allusions les plus flétrissantes. Alors, l'Administration du jour était son dieu et Papineau son démon à . . . abattre. . . . Je ne fus pas le seul qui eut à gémir sur l'intervention scandaleuse d'un prêtre entre deux champinions [sic] politiques, habitants d'une sphère que sa qualité d'Apôtre devait lui [faire] dédaigner.[34]

Dangerous or not, Chiniquy attracted crowds. Indeed LaFontaine's politicians had succeeded in gaining for their cause the only popular orator who ever matched Papineau. And his presence on the hustings beside the anti-annexationist orators proved for all to see that the *rouges* had finally assured what had been in the making since 1846— although it was not yet openly recognized—the *bleu* alliance of priest and politician. It was an alliance which coupled the faith with the doctrine of nationality preached by Cauchon since 1842, and which Hector Langevin repeated to his brother in January, 1850: "si les rouges avaient l'autorité en mains, prêtres, églises, religion, etc. etc. devraient disparaître de la face du Canada. Le moment est critique. Il faut que le ministère continue à être libéral tel qu'à présent, ou bien on est Américain, et puis alors adieu à notre langue et à notre nationalité."[35]

[34]Meilleur à l'abbé Bois, as quoted in Trudel, *Chiniquy*, p. 110.
[35]Chapais-Langevin, 253, H. Langevin à E. Langevin, 25 jan. 1850.

21

The Defeat of Annexation

LaFontaine's politicians probably gained a great deal from Chiniquy's support, for they could now use the full force of the religious argument against *L'Avenir*'s idealism. They defended their "petit père," "ce prêtre au regard et à la voix douce," as Langevin wrote in *Les Mélanges* (September 4, 1849), "que vous avez vu mille fois jetant du haut de la chaire des paroles de paix et de charité, paroles dont l'onction a pénétré vos cœurs et vous a convaincus que vous ne seriez heureux que par la sobriété et la paix et le bien-être qu'elles donneraient à la famille, ce prêtre, qui prêche l'amour, le pardon et les sacrifices, qui se sacrifie lui-même chaque jour *pour vous*." And, thus they could lead their readers to conclude that just as its religious opinions were suspect so *L'Avenir*'s political ideas were also anathema. *Les Mélanges* declared on October 5: "Ceux qui portent leurs mains impies sur l'autel pour en arracher la divinité; ceux qui traînent le sacerdoce dans la boue du chemin, pour le conduire aux gémonies, sont les mêmes qui ont fait monter la patrie sur l'échafaud ou qui l'y feraient monter pour sauver 'leur principe,' sans se sentir émus!" However, the politicians did not depend entirely on the clergy to defeat the opposition. While the priests, both in private and in the press, were becoming increasingly involved with *le parti ministériel*, LaFontaine's journalists and agents worked diligently at their own refutation of the *rouge* theories.

They founded their refutation of the annexationist doctrine on two principles. First, the republicans confused the French Canadian's problem of survival with one of constitutional form, thus proving their own inexperience and impractical idealism. For in the minds of LaFontaine's theorists *la survivance* depended not on abstract systems but on practice, on the daily, vigorous effort of the whole nation. And this effort the British constitution had already invoked, even guaranteed. Responsible government gave the *Canadiens* all they needed to be great—certainly more opportunity than they could ever reap from American institutions or any liberal republican arrangement. Secondly, LaFontaine's journalists claimed annexation would be an unmitigated disaster. Practically, it might ruin Lower Canada's economy, and, Louisiana notwithstanding, it would bring an end to French Canada's institutions and nationality. In addition to these two basic arguments, LaFontaine's agents urged all *Canadiens* to beware of annexation propaganda as a stratagem of malevolent Tories intent on robbing them of influence and position.

Langevin and Cauchon led the debate. They insisted that *la survivance* did not depend on the form of government. Writing a guest article in *La Minerve* on January 2, 1849, Langevin stressed what was essential and what was not:

Quant à la masse du peuple, elle a appris à ses dépens que la politique doit être moins turbulente et plus pratique; le peuple commence à sentir qu'il doit se préparer pour toutes les éventualités quelles qu'elles soient, que son intérêt est de profiter de tout ce qui peut le protéger et lui donner de la force, en s'emparant miette à miette, pouce par pouce, de tous les avantages matériels que procurent le pouvoir et l'autorité; le peuple commence à sentir que la politique sentimentale n'est plus de saison; que le système du tout ou rien est destructeur.

And in his own *Mélanges* a year later, he spelled out how the needs of education, for example, were far more important than a change in the constitution:

Quant à la Province que nous habitons, ceux qui croient faire la prospérité de 600,000 Canadiens-français qui la peuplent, en procurant à ce pays des institutions républicaines par son annexion aux Etats-Unis, se taisent pour la plupart sur l'état arriéré de l'enseignement populaire qui est la véritable cause de la lenteur des progrès industriels en Canada, et oublient en même temps que le remède à ce mal transitoire est à notre portée. (March 8, 1850)

In reply to the *rouge* demand for an elected national leader chosen from among themselves, Langevin explained that under responsible government the *Canadiens* could no longer complain of being governed by aliens.

Cauchon made the same point in *Le Journal*. What mattered since 1838 had not been abstract forms of government but rather "l'action intelligente et persévérante de la raison et de la vérité qui a cicatrisé les blessures et miné les fondements du despotisme." "Que nous importe à nous," he had asked as early as December 5, 1848, "que nous vivions sous une monarchie constitutionnelle ou sous une démocratie pure, pourvu que le peuple soit heureux et content et qu'il jouisse d'une douce et paisible liberté." And it was a pity, Langevin agreed at the end of the debate on April 19, 1850, that serious adults had had to waste their time on the propositions of youngsters so unenlightened about politics that they did not know that "on ne prouve point l'avenir par des calculs, on ne convainct pas par des espérances." Revolutions may be exhilarating for ambitious youths, but not for responsible men, and in Canada some more fundamental thinking was needed. The inexperienced radicals put their faith in the American union, but, Cauchon corrected, the slavery issue, to name but one, seemed about to split the United States apart. And for those who believed in the liberal republican creed as such, he explained in more detail on March 20, 1849:

Il y a 60 ans que l'Europe assiste à l'école des révolutions. . . . Le peuple français qui a le plus dévié dans cette débâcle générale des anciennes mœurs et des principes qui en étaient la sauvegarde ne sait plus aujourd'hui à quoi s'en tenir, à qui croire en fait d'autorités politiques et de gouvernement stable. Il n'y a plus chez lui de conscience, de respect, de religion, à l'égard des choses fondamentales, il a perdu le sens social sur les bases mêmes de la société. . . . Et vous voulez faire croire . . . que le peuple canadien, avec ses mœurs douces et son bon sens, est prêt pour ces combats de cannibales!

When the annexation manifesto appeared in October 1849, Le Journal de Québec ran a special series of articles to refute its claims. But ever since the previous spring, Cauchon and Langevin had been publicizing the arguments they summed up then. From the practical point of view, they had decided, the union of the Canadian province with the United States would be a disaster for the prosperity of both the agricultural and commercial interests of Lower Canada. "L'annexion serait-elle Avantageuse pour le Cultivateur du Canada?" So Cauchon headlined two long articles on October 16 and December 27 which Les Mélanges reprinted on January 11 and 15. He stressed the higher taxes which Canadian farmers would have to pay and gave a record of the present Canadian and American tariffs on goods essential to the agricultural community. The American ones, naturally, came out much higher, while the Canadian list, he claimed, might even decline "lorsque nos canaux seront terminés et que les lois de la navigation ne restreindront plus notre commerce, les frais et coûts de transport sur le Saint-Laurent seront probablement à des taux plus réduits que sur la voie américaine."

Annexation must surely be harmful for the commercial class as well. He admitted that business was low just then, but how could the republican system improve it? Had the republican constitution in the United States avoided the great depression between 1830 and 1842? What about the bank war between the federal government and the

states? What about the many bankrupt American railroads? "Allez,"
he taunted on October 27, "annexionnistes, ou menteurs, ou insensés,
dire maintenant que notre dépression commerciale est due à notre
condition coloniale." In fact, Cauchon pointed out on October 23, the
Canadian colony obtained loans on the London market far more easily
than individual American states were able to borrow from Washington. And what of the timber industry so highly favoured in Britain?
And all the money spent in the colony by the British government and
troops? He concluded on December 27:

Faisons de profondes réflexions et laissons-nous guider par les vérités
salutaires qui suivent:
—Que le Canada sous la connexion britannique a avancé dans les voies de
    la prospérité plus rapidement et plus sûrement qu'aucun autre pays sur
    la terre.
—Que nous connaissons ce que nous possédons, mais nous ne prévoyons
    jamais ce qui est réservé dans l'avenir.
—Que nous perdrions £400,000 par année par le rappel des troupes.
—Que nous perdrions £200,000 par année par le rappel de tous les autres
    départements du gouvernement Impérial.
—Que nous aurions à payer en impôts directs additionnels la somme de
    £750,000 par année.
—Et que toutes ces sommes que nous aurions à payer formeraient un
    montant d'environ sept millions de piastres par année.
—Tout ce mouvement annexionniste est sans contredit une évidente folie.
    Il n'y a jamais eu de peuple si prospère que les Canadiens quand ils
    savent seulement comment jouir de leurs avantages.

There were other expenses. Le Journal warned that after annexation
Canada would no longer enjoy revenues from customs—at that time
the main source of government funds. Direct taxation would therefore
have to be introduced and indirect taxation would go up. Then, when
L'Avenir began publishing comparative tables of the high salaries of
Canadian government officials and the low salaries of the Americans,
Langevin cut them short on November 6 with the comment: "Le
Canada exerce aujourd'hui plus des attributs de la souveraineté qu'aucun des trente états de l'Union Américaine, sans en supporter les
charges." La Minerve denied L'Avenir's figures outright on November
19: "Vous vous servez de chiffres pour faire impression, pour faire
croire que vous faites 'des travaux longs et vraiment pénibles' et vous
avez le talent d'exagérer 'dans une proportion effrayante,' ou suivant
le principe de votre 'campagnard', la finesse de 'mentir énormément et
sans limites.' " And Les Mélanges summed up on April 16, 1850, arguing that even if Canadian salaries were higher, "l'annexion est inutile
pour opérer une réforme qui nous regarde seule, et que nous avons les

moyens d'effectuer autant qu'il est nécessaire. . . . D'ailleurs il y a bien autre chose à considérer que les chiffres dans une question de finances, surtout lorsque l'on parle d'effectuer les ressources et par là même la position des fonctionnaires publics."

Above all, LaFontaine's journalists opposed annexation because of the tragedy it would be for *la survivance*. The party leader himself confided to his friend Berthelot: "Les Canadiens annexionnistes sont ou bien aveugles ou de mauvaise foi. Annexion et nationalité sont une contradiction." Cauchon, of course, thought likewise. He challenged *L'Avenir* in *Le Journal* as early as March 20, 1849: "Je ne vois pas quel degré de liberté plus large, nous posséderions pour la pleine action de nos institutions, de notre langue et de nos lois. . . . Mais qui sait, une fois le drapeau britannique abattu sur le cap illustre du religieux Champlain, quel serait le sort de la religion en ce pays de foi?"

Louisiana confirmed their view. "Le sort de la Louisiane ci-devant française est là pour servir de leçon à nos compatriotes," Langevin noted on December 4, 1849. True, the American state had its French laws and had elected a French governor, but for years it had been a territory under federal administration, a prey to every Yankee speculator. As a result, its economy had been ruined, and even before the third generation since the Purchase, French culture was fast becoming assimilated. How could *L'Avenir* guarantee a better chance for Lower Canadian survival under the Americans?

In addition to all these practical and nationalist arguments against annexation, the journalists reminded the *Canadiens* that whatever the merit of the views for or against such an action, they should guard against two dangers: trusting Tories and jeopardizing the concrete gains already acquired. When the manifesto appeared in 1849, Langevin explained in *Les Mélanges* on October 12:

Il faut en effet que les libéraux prennent garde à eux; ce manifeste est un piège dans lequel on semble vouloir les prendre. On dit que l'on veut la séparation *amicable* et *paisible* d'avec l'Angleterre, et que sans le consentement de celle-ci, cette séparation n'est nullement praticable. On veut par là engager les Canadiens à signer cette adresse; et quand l'Angleterre aura dit qu'elle ne consent pas à cette séparation (ce qui est bien certain), c'est alors que le parti Tory attend les libéraux. . . . Dès ce moment les Tories nous tourneraient le dos, ils se serreraient sous l'étendard anglais, et ils crieraient Vive la Reine. Les libéraux, eux, en seraient pour des coups de fusils et les échafauds élevés pour les y faire traîner comme en 1837. Voilà le beau tour qu'on semble vouloir jouer aux Canadiens.

The Tory party, after all, "ne cessera jamais d'être pour les Canadiens

Français leur ennemi le plus à craindre" (*Les Mélanges*, May 7, 1850). In *Le Journal*, Cauchon concurred. On October 23, 1849, he blamed *L'Avenir* for its "alliance monstrueuse et criminelle avec les Tories," and on February 14, 1850, concluded:

Nous avons dit plus d'une fois que l'annexion avait pris son origine dans les cendres brûlantes de la maison du Parlement et que les Annexionnistes n'étaient que des Tories déguisés, au désespoir d'avoir perdu le pouvoir et jetant un cri ardent de démocratie pour surprendre et pour attirer à eux les Canadiens-français qui, croyant à la sincérité de leurs paroles, donneraient avec eux le coup d'épaule pour renverser une administration qui les offusque et les placer eux-mêmes sur le pavois.

When *L'Avenir* asserted on July 19, 1849, that ideas and principles, not party labels should count—"de cette propagande annexioniste naîtra au moins un parti ami de la liberté"—*Les Mélanges* declared emphatically (August 7): "Nous sommes bien décidés à n'encourager en aucune façon les efforts des tories pour se relever, non plus que ceux des ultra-radicaux qui voudraient marcher sur les traces des révolutionnaires de Paris et de Rome."

The warning proved successful. As Langevin had told his brothers, the *Canadiens* would readily believe that "si aujourd'hui pour demain le ministère tombait, le pouvoir tomberait aux mains des Tories et alors les échafauds et les pendaisons renaîtraient."[1] And Edouard-R. Fabre complained to his friend O'Callaghan in New York in November: "Le projet d'annexion va son train, les ministres et leurs amis font des efforts pour empêcher les gens de signer en les arrarmants [*sic*] ici à Montréal, les Canadiens ne signent pas comme ils le feraient s'ils voyaient plus d'anciens noms Canadiens quoiqu'ils soient tous républicains de cœur, cependant ils se rappellent les misères de 37 & 38."[2] Nor did *Canadiens* want to block the steady stream of appointments beginning to flow their way. "Le plus grand argument des partisans du ministère," *L'Avenir* complained on July 25, 1849,

l'argument derrière lequel finissent toujours par se retrancher les défenseurs de notre système de gouvernement . . . pour faire apprécier les avantages du gouvernement responsable, . . . c'est que . . . les ministres sont maîtres de tout, ont à leur disposition un patronage considérable, sont à même de favoriser leurs partisans comme bon leur semble, et ont par là le moyen de mettre leurs compatriotes et leurs amis dans une position supérieure à celle des tories.

And indeed, *la presse ministérielle* continually reminded its readers that "les meilleurs et les plus beaux postes seront occupés par les

---

[1]Chapais-Langevin, 253, H. Langevin à E. Langevin, 25 jan. 1850.
[2]O'Callaghan Papers, Fabre à O'Callaghan, 24 nov. 1849.

Américains et les places les plus lucratives perdues pour les Canadiens, si l'annexion arrive" (Les Mélanges, February 25, 1850). From Montreal in March, 1850 Morin sent LaFontaine in Toronto a wise summary of all the arguments being used:

Ce que Je puis vous dire, après mûre considération et avoir conversé avec des personnes de différentes localités, c'est que l'annexion ne fait pas de prosélytes; elle en fera peut-être occasionnellement dans des circonstances particulières qu'on ne peut prévoir, comme toute chose nouvelle et en opposition à ce qui est, comme point de ralliement. Pour moi l'état de nos compatriotes à présent, leur position probable sous le système américain, le manque de contrôle ou au moins d'épouvantail sous ce système contre les fauteurs du meurtre des violences, et de l'oppression, la question de division dans l'union américaine, l'absurdité de croire pouvoir obtenir l'annexion par les moyens prétendus, l'union entre les perturbateurs de toute nuance, sont des motifs d'une telle force que j'ai une répugnance invincible pour les annexionistes qui ne peuvent suivant moi agir seulement par aveuglement.[3]

In Quebec Le Canadien also published a good summary of the debate on August 15, 1849. Imitating L'Avenir's serial, it published a "Dialogue entre Jean-Baptiste et son représentant," in which a member of parliament and his elector discussed the arguments point by point. First, le représentant reminded Jean-Baptiste that with all this annexation agitation, the Tories wanted to "entacher ton caractère de désaffection et de déloyauté par le leurre de la république," and thus "te jeter sur les bras toutes les forces de l'Angleterre." Would annexation bring prosperity and happiness? No, Jean-Baptiste answered with true peasant wisdom, the habitants' prosperity derived from agriculture; if the country did not prosper now it was because the citizens had not been economical enough during the good years. It was silly to expect that the Americans would come and feed the Canadien farmers for nothing. But, the member objected, playing the devil's advocate, once the colony was annexed Canadian manufactures could be sold to Americans who would thus open up new possibilities.

What if Canada joined the United States, retorted Jean-Baptiste, and Americans did not buy: "Nous sommes bien, tenons-nous y. Peut-être ailleurs serions-nous pis." Furthermore, he continued, once the colony became a part of the union, the revenues from its customs and Crown lands would go to Washington and the Canadiens would have to pay taxes to support themselves. Besides, the member passed to another point, even if Lower Canada did become a state of the Union, the habitants would probably continue to elect the same men to govern them. "Aurions-nous plus d'influence sur notre gouvernement,

[3]Papiers LaFontaine, Morin à LaFontaine, 9 mars 1850.

aurions-nous d'autres et de meilleurs hommes pour nous gouverner?"
And he added another argument: at present the British government
spent over a million pounds a year in Canada for defence. "Il n'est pas
besoin de te dire que cette poule aux œufs d'or sera perdue pour
toi du moment que le drapeau britannique cessera de flotter sur la
citadelle de Québec." The Americans would send few soldiers and
spend little in Canada on supplies. Annexation, therefore, would mean
a million pounds less from Britain yearly, and in addition a half
million sent to Washington from Canada's customs and land. How
could it be, therefore, Jean-Baptiste asked in amazement, that "des
hommes de talents, de bons patriotes, de bons Canadiens . . . en petit
nombre il est vrai" could support annexation. From motives of revenge,
or jealousy, le représentant concluded, or perhaps from inexperience:
"Nos jeunes gens, une belle et brave jeunesse certes, m'ont paru faire
de la politique comme ils font souvent de l'amour. Ils s'enmourachent
de la première petite folle venue . . . le cœur l'emporte. On se marie . . .
le repentir ne se fait pas attendre mais, le mal est fait. . . . Les mots de
République et d'Indépendance les fascinent."

During the whole debate over annexation, it was Les Mélanges that
carried LaFontaine's message to the Montreal district. The party
organ, La Minerve, remained silent. "Il faut avouer que vous avez une
presse qui vous défend mal à Montréal," Cauchon complained to
Lafontaine. "Duvernay est annexionniste et il reste entre deux eaux.
D'ailleurs la rédaction de la Minerve est excessivement factice et
souvent compromettante."[4] Cauchon was right. When it came to
attacking Papineau or L'Avenir, Duvernay agreed with the rest of la
presse ministérielle; when it came to supporting railroads, or the
repeal of the Navigation Laws, when the change of the capital needed
explanation, La Minerve met the challenge as well as Le Journal. It
even supported the proposition that the whole commotion over
annexation was a Tory trick. But neither Duvernay nor his assistant,
Raphaël Bellemarre, would join the fight against annexation. For
LaFontaine's party this was a grievous blow. Luckily Les Mélanges
did its best, and, in private, Langevin did even better.

Duvernay readily admitted as early as July 27, 1848, that the
annexationist group "se compose de turbulents, de mécontents, de
désappointés et d'une parenté prétentieuse et égoïste qui veut que le
pays lui obéisse et soit sous elle," and during May of 1849 he joined Les
Mélanges in assailing L'Avenir for its anticlericalism. When L'Avenir

[4]Ibid., Cauchon à LaFontaine, 24 oct. 1949.

used the economic situation as an argument for annexation, *La Minerve* corrected on November 29: "Il n'y a peut-être jamais eu dans le Canada plus d'entreprises publiques en voie de progrès ou en contemplation que dans le temps actuel." Duvernay also helped to rally support for the government's move to Toronto. But throughout 1849 he composed his editorial page as if he were desperately trying to think of something else to write about. He covered most of his front pages with a non-political *revue européenne*, with articles on economics, or sometimes with dissertations on public health. At the beginning of June most Lower Canadian politicians had begun to draw the correct conclusions about *La Minerve*'s silence. On June 12 *L'Avenir* recalled in print that in the autumn of 1847 when annexation had first been mentioned, Duvernay had been the one to put an end to the discussion. And it revelled now in quoting excerpts from his own articles and others written against the Union before Bagot's great measure in 1842.

On July 9, 1849, *La Minerve* finally spoke. Taking note of the British North American League and the incipient annexation movement, it clearly avoided criticism. Then in its next issue (July 12) it explained that although it would continue to support the ministry for the time being, it considered annexation a valid alternative. "Nous avons toujours regardé notre existence coloniale comme transitoire," it admitted,

et nous avons toujours travaillé à nous préparer aux éventualités, aux changements de condition que le temps et les circonstances amèneront. . . . Si nous soutenons encore aujourd'hui un ministère choisi par le pays, l'administration libérale et réformatrice de lord Elgin, ce n'est pas en sacrifiant nos principes mais par ce qu'elle était indispensable à notre salut, et qu'elle nous a déjà fait faire un pas immense dans la voix des libertés.

It did not fear annexation: "L'annexion ne nous a jamais effrayé. . . . On peut croire et démontrer que l'annexion *serait* une chose avantageuse et avoir en même temps confiance dans l'administration du jour, et être fermement déterminé à respecter les lois."

L'Avenir delighted in Duvernay's dilemma. On July 17 Joseph Papin delivered a dissertation, partly rejoicing, partly challenging. "Nous sommes extrèmement flattés," he began, "de voir que la *Minerve* ait adopté une ligne de conduite aussi en harmonie, suivant nous, avec les vrais intérêts du pays." If *La Minerve* was sincere, he continued, it would immediately set to work "instruire le peuple sur les avantages moraux et matériels [de l'annexion] et . . . dépouiller des préjugés qui existent [contre la mesure]." *Les Mélanges* and *Le Journal* said nothing. But *Le Canadien* ran a headline "La Minerve et l'Annexion" on July 16. It had not been surprised at the Tories' disloyalty, or at *L'Avenir's* propaganda which, it claimed, could never hurt LaFontaine. But, MacDonald noted, *La Minerve* could do harm, and its article of July 12 could well become "quelque chose dont on ne manquera pas de se servir . . . comme d'une pièce de conviction contre le ministère du jour et le peuple canadien-français en masse." Duvernay retracted. "Nous n'avons pas prétendu nous faire les apôtres de l'annexion," he declared on July 16: "ni la mettre à l'ordre du jour comme sujet de discussion ou de calcul. Encore moins avons-nous cru représenter les vues de l'administration. . . . Nous sommes bien prêts à admettre que tous ceux qui veulent l'ordre, la liberté et la sécurité, soutiennent et doivent soutenir comme une même doctrine et le ministère libéral et la liaison avec la Grande-Bretagne, et cela franchement et sans arrière-pensée." He hardly mentioned the question again, although he lost no opportunity to praise the United States, its railroads, its prosperity.

When the annexation manifesto came out, and then the *Canadien* members' Protet, Duvernay published them on October 11 and 15 with no other comment than that "nous donnons plus bas comme pièce historique, le manifeste que viennent de lancer. . . ." Later, on November 26 he took part in the castigation of *L'Avenir* for printing Elgin's alleged letter to the bishops. He also seemed willing to attack *L'Avenir's* reasons for supporting annexation (whatever he was, Duvernay did not belong to a generation of self-pitying cry-babies):

Le "Manifeste" de la Ligue que M. Papineau trouve si sage et si habile représente le Canada comme ruiné et en banqueroute sous tous les rapports, comme un pauvre malheureux, dépouillé de tout, réduit à mendier le secours de ses voisins. Au lieu de représenter noblement le Canada comme un enfant majeur qui n'a plus besoin de la tutelle de ses parents, qui a des ressources par lui-même et est capable de les faire valoir, comme un enfant majeur qui demande des droits et non des faveurs, ce manifeste implore la pitié de l'univers sur le Canada ruiné et dans la voie de la banqueroute. Ce manque de noblesse et de fierté dans les motifs . . . ont fait mépriser souverainement une agitation qui aurait peut-être eu quelque succès si on s'était tenu dans les justes bornes de la vérité. . . . Le manifeste est donc évidemment mensonger, et le mensonge ne saurait jamais servir même une bonne cause. (November 5, 1849)

And LaFontaine's agents were relieved that Duvernay went that far, and that he did not openly support the movement.

Langevin saw to that. Throughout the autumn of 1849 he visited "les gens de la Minerve" twice a day and, as he told his brother, developed "une assez bonne opinion de leurs intentions." He understood their dilemma. On the one hand, "Duvernay et Bellemarre sont annexionnistes de cœur"; on the other, "ils ne veulent pas paraître soutenir les annexionnistes d'aujourd'hui parce que ces annexionnistes sont Tories et papineautistes pour le plus grand nombre." Over and over again, he discussed the crisis with them, trying to win the editors over to attacking the republicans, but they would not capitulate. At last he achieved an agreement that he would at least be allowed to write anti-American guest columns for their paper and that they, on their part, would refrain from actually advocating annexation. Thus, he explained in the same letter:

c'est les rendre ennemis de l'annexion, et voici pourquoi: avant quelques années la position des Canadiens sera certainement meilleure que celle de tout autre peuple; ce sera le peuple le moins taxé et le plus libre. Nous aurons la libre navigation . . . le gouvernement responsable, la liste civile à notre disposition et discrétion; l'Angleterre ne conservera que la nomination du gouverneur et le *veto*, que du reste le Président des Etats-Unis lui-même possède. Avec de pareils avantages *la Minerve* ne pourra pas se prononcer pour l'Annexion.

"J'aime mieux," he concluded in another letter, "voir la Minerve telle qu'elle est que de la voir favoriser l'annexion . . . et j'ai lieu de croire qu'en allant avec eux, comme je le fais, j'en obtiens bien des concessions pour la bonne cause."[5]

LaFontaine showed less indulgence. When, for example, he saw a large advertisement in *La Minerve* urging people to attend the annexationist meeting at Saint-Edouard in January 1850, he complained to Berthelot "Duvernay ne s'aperçoit pas que, pour l'amour d'un avertissement, il se met dans une fausse position vis-à-vis des deux partis, et que, sans se faire du bien à lui-même, il compromait l'Administration. Je ne sais ce que fait Morin. Il avait promis de mieux diriger cette presse. Vous ferez bien de lui en dire un mot."[6] Morin commented that "ces annonces m'avaient à moi-même déplu," but "ne croyez pas, mon cher ami que nous ayons été ici sur un lit de roses et maîtres de diriger à notre gré l'opinion." He too had done all he could, and with some success, to keep *La Minerve* from fully endorsing the republicans. "J'ai réussi aussi bien souvent à donner la couleur que je désirais." In all events, he went on, "je crois que dès à présent la

---

[5]Chapais-Langevin, 253, 255, H. Langevin à E. Langevin, 25 jan., 11 fév. 1850.
[6]LaFontaine à Berthelot, 14 jan. 1850, quoted in Maurault, "LaFontaine à travers ses lettres," p. 154.

tournure est au mieux."[7] Indeed it was: from an unexpected quarter unforeseen and unsolicited support arrived.

As it continued its campaign for annexation, Le Moniteur Canadien published a series of letters from Denis-Benjamin Viger who opposed his friends' policy of union with the United States.[8] Not surprisingly, perhaps, for Viger was too wise to believe that a republican constitution automatically established efficient, just, and perfect government. With Neilson he had fought LaFontaine and Parent in 1840 for the very reason that he feared they expected such automatic perfection from responsible government. In 1843 he had again opposed LaFontaine for his intransigence. He was of the temper that trusted men rather than doctrines. And now, with all the authority of his experience and long meditation, he spoke out against the republicanism of the rouges.

In the past, Viger had marvelled at American institutions. He still did. But admiration was one thing, annexation another. Now, in October and November 1849, he asked the rouges to recall a few stark facts. What made them so certain that England could afford to cede so rich and strategic a colony as Canada to a potential rival? They should bear in mind that for Britain the United States constituted "celle des puissances qui plus que tout autre peut d'un jour à l'autre devenir une rivale dangereuse, même hostile" (October 30). Would the United States want Canada? Lately, the republic had become involved in an increasingly irrepressible conflict over the extension of slavery. If Canada applied for statehood, Viger averred, "Les citoyens du Sud qui tiennent à la propriété de leurs nègres repousseraient le projet d'annexion dans la crainte que ces nouvelles provinces n'ajoutassent un nouveau poids contre eux dans les délibérations relatives à l'abolition de l'esclavage" (November 8).

Viger did not think Britain would let Canada go easily, or that the United States would easily welcome it. For his part, he agreed with LaFontaine's journalists: Lower Canada would suffer from American control. It would also, as part of the United States, lose its distinctive nationality. What would happen to the French if Canada became a territory under an appointed governor who knew nothing of its traditions, religion, and laws? Louisiana provided a horrible precedent. Why not then be realistic, he taunted the young men who had once been his followers, why not agree that la survivance and the

[7]Papiers LaFontaine, Morin à LaFontaine, 12 fév. 1850.

[8]F. Ouellet, "Denis-Benjamin Viger et le problème de l'annexion," Bulletin de Recherches historiques, LVII (1951), 195–205.

British connection were indeed interconnected? Instead of seeking to join the republic, he would rather see them toil at securing from Britain "une indépendance plus complète sous sa protection, chose qui serait dans les règles d'une saine politique puisqu'elle serait fondée sur leur avantage réciproque" (October 30).

Just as Viger had, the electors had also been convinced. When a by-election became necessary in Quebec because of Jean Chabot's appointment to the council, both the annexationists and LaFontaine's faction decided to make it the decisive test of strength. It became one of the few elections held in Lower Canada which focussed on the issue of annexation. And despite tempting invitations from the republicans, the *Québecois* confirmed their traditional commitment to the British connection.

Jean Chabot officially accepted his appointment to head the Department of Public Works on December 13, 1849. The writs for his by-election were immediately sent out, returnable at the end of January 1850. In November Caron had reported that "tout le monde ici est de bonne humeur. . . . Chabot se fera élire facilement."[9] And Cauchon had agreed: "il n'y a pas de candidate à opposer à Chabot."[10] But soon afterwards the annexationists realized what vitality a victory in Quebec could inject into their party. "In my opinion," Antoine-Aimé Dorion wrote to a Tory friend in Montreal, "this election is of the greatest importance at the present moment as it would have great influence . . . in case of a general election."[11] By Christmas they had decided to run Joseph Légaré again. He had won some 1200 votes against F.-X. Méthot in the same (dual) riding in June 1848, and was, Dorion continued, "the most popular man among the suburban population of Quebec."

Cauchon remained certain of victory. "N'ayez aucune crainte," he told Taché, "vous savez que je ne me suis pas encore trompé sur le résultat d'une élection."[12] But he sought more than victory. He wanted a large majority. "La majorité sera de 900 à 1000 voix au moins," he promised. "Nous travaillons comme des géants afin de faire le triomphe le plus éclatant possible et le plus accablant."[13] Unfortunately, he had a poor candidate. Chabot spent more time in

[9]Papiers LaFontaine, Caron à LaFontaine, 12 nov. 1849.
[10]*Ibid.*, Cauchon à LaFontaine, 2 déc. 1849.
[11]A. A. Dorion à R. McKay, 2 jan. 1850, as quoted in A. G. Penny, "The Annexation Movement of 1849–50," *Canadian Historical Review*, V (1924), 236–63.
[12]Papiers Taché, A 46, Cauchon à Taché, 11 jan. 1850.
[13]Papiers LaFontaine, Cauchon à LaFontaine, 11 jan. 1850.

the taverns of the *basse ville* than he did working on his own election. From Montreal Drummond warned LaFontaine that "il ne possède ni la dignité personnelle ni la position politique qu'il faudrait."[14] And Cauchon likewise explained: "Je vous dis franchement que pour ma part il me faut une forte considération d'intérêt public pour soutenir Chabot."[15] Indeed, on the very day that the offer of the Public Works appointment arrived in Quebec, Cauchon had been obliged to look for the appointee all over the city, finding him at last "fortement sous l'influence" and "en plein midi" at that.[16] But whether the candidate was drunk or sober, Cauchon intended to keep his record of electoral success. He wanted to defeat annexation. And he put forth his greatest effort and action.

He had many advantages. As one of Légaré's friends told the editor of the *Montreal Herald*, "The leaders of the ministerialists, having office, money, religious and civil influence on their side, are heavy odds against the orators of *Jeune Canada*. The only three French newspapers are with them."[17] Also, with a dozen eager young men, Cauchon set up a first-rate team. "J'ai autour de moi," he reported, "une phalange de jeunes gens de talent . . . prêts pour les luttes électorales. Ce qui manquait auparavant à ces jeunes était un centre. A défaut de mieux je me suis fait ce centre et dans l'intérêt du parti."[18] Chabot volunteered some £500 for campaign expenses, and Cauchon's young men collected another £150 in contributions. But before their victory was complete, they had to spend over £800 and exert what Cauchon called "des efforts prodigieux."[19]

One of the youths working for Cauchon was the bookdealer, Pierre Crémazie. From his back room Cauchon decided the party strategy and supervised the organization. The election would be fought on annexation and on the record of the ministry. ("Pas un n'a supporté Chabot pour lui-même et ça été une question purement ministérielle," he wrote LaFontaine.[20]) The election would be won by addresses and meetings and by hard fighting. From the populous Saint-Roch ward there came in to headquarters an address declaring, as *Le Journal*

[14]*Ibid.*, Drummond à LaFontaine, 8 déc. 1849.
[15]*Ibid.*, Cauchon à LaFontaine, 15 déc. 1849.
[16]LaF., Cauchon à LaFontaine, 7 avril 1850.
[17]J. Bouvery to E. G. Penny, Jan. 11, 1850, as quoted in Penny, "Annexation," p. 257.
[18]Papiers LaFontaine, Cauchon à LaFontaine, 17 déc. 1849, 11 jan. 1850.
[19]*Ibid.*, Cauchon à LaFontaine, 8 mars 1850.
[20]*Ibid.*

reported on November 13, that "nous désirons demeurer fermement attachés à l'Empire Britannique, et nous sommes prêts à maintenir la connexion par tous les moyens possibles." To answer, Cauchon and his group went down the next Sunday after high mass to thank the good citizens. It rained, but *Le Journal* noted on November 13 that "les citoyens sont restés exposés pendant trois heures à la pluie pour prouver qu'ils comprenaient l'importance de la question qui les réunissait." Cauchon spoke against annexation for over an hour and a half. During the speech, Augustin Soulard, one of Légaré's organizers arrived with a few of his own partisans. The artist-annexationist was being heralded throughout this campaign as "le candidat du peuple," and now Soulard began interrupting Cauchon with cries of "nous le peuple," "nous souffrons pendant que les ministres ont des gros salaires." Cauchon retorted by pointing to Soulard's clothes: he wore a dandy's apparel—a huge red cravat, white suit coat, and yellow gloves. The crowd roared with laughter and before the day was over there were three enthusiastic "hourras pour la Reine."

Légaré's aides nevertheless felt confident. "Mr. Légaré's friends," the Tories in Montreal were told in a private letter, "are sanguine as to the result of the election; M. Aubin who is the most active among the annexationists of French origin, seems quite confident of success."[21] They had no newspaper in Quebec, but they distributed thousands of free copies of *L'Avenir*. And at the traditional "assemblée contradic-toire" on nomination day, they literally stole the show. That day Cauchon had gathered about 2000 supporters while Légaré (according to Cauchon) came "entouré de 3 ou 4 annexionnistes—banqueroutiers, et d'une centaine d'individus plusieurs d'entr'eux ivres et brandissant des bâtons." While the candidates were being nominated Légaré's supporters distributed thousands of leaflets which looked like news-paper extras with the news that the British parliament had just voted to cede Canada to the United States. For the remainder of the after-noon Légaré became the rising sun. By evening he had drawn Cau-chon's crowd away to escort him home in a candlelight procession.

But Cauchon had other methods to keep the initiative. He continued to laugh at the annexationists. And he contrived the destruction of one of Légaré's agents, Jacques Rhéaume, whom Cauchon had detested ever since Rhéaume's agitation for repeal in 1848 when, as he told LaFontaine, "il avait réussi à tourner contre moi une population qui

[21]Bouvery to Penny, Jan. 11, 1850, as quoted in Penny, "Annexation," p. 257.

jusque-là me donnait sa confiance." As the election drew near, he published two articles in *Le Journal*, one a vicious political attack called "Confession de Jacques," the other a conscientious-sounding censure of duelling as an immoral practice. In this last Cauchon claimed that he himself would never accept "un duel qui était opposé à mes principes religieux." Rhéaume fell into the trap. Banking on Cauchon's refusal, he challenged the editor. Cauchon accepted, and chose as his second Louis Fiset, one of his campaign helpers. Later, he gave LaFontaine a detailed description of the comedy that followed:

> Dès que Rhéaume appris que j'avais accepté il fit tous les efforts possibles pour se faire prendre par la police et il y réussit à la fin. Les seconds furent obligés de changer trois fois le lieu du rendez-vous dans l'espace d'une heure, car aussitôt le lieu fixé qu'il était connu. Les parents de Rhéaume voulurent me compromettre en engageant mon beau père à me faire prendre, et il allait le faire si je ne l'avais menacé d'une haine à vie. Le beau père de Rhéaume alla trouver deux fois ma femme pour lui dire que nous battions à 3 heures, et ma femme éperdue courrait en toute hâte au devant de moi. Elle ne me trouva pas car je m'étais caché. Quand je vis qu'il y avait un warrant contre moi, je me hâtai de me rendre avec Fiset au lieu du rendez vous; c'était 1¼ heure avant le moment fixé. Rhéaume se promenait dans les rues. Il avait été dire adieu à son frère en lui disant qu'il se battait à 3 heures. . . . Or c'était à 4¼ mais il ne voulait pas que la police arriva trop tard. Il avait un rendez-vous préalable avec son second Okill Plamondon, il ne s'y trouva pas et Plamondon nous rejoignit seul. Rhéaume . . . arriva enfin et se promena dans le chemin afin d'être pris, il le fut en effet car son beau-frère arriva avec la police. Plamondon dressa un procès-verbal où il déclarait que Rhéaume avait forfait à l'honneur et s'était rendu indigne du titre de gentilhomme, ce procès verbal étant signé par les deux témoins. Puis Plamondon sur l'effet de l'enthousiasme me donna au bas du procès verbal un certificat à moi adressé: "M. Cauchon—M.R. s'est conduit en insigne poltron dans son affaire d'honneur avec vous, et je regrette d'avoir été si longtemps la dupe d'un homme sans cœur". Cette affaire a eu et a encore un immense retentissement et les annexionistes déclarent qu'elle les perd à jamais, car c'étaient eux qui avait aiguillonné Rhéaume.

Like Soulard in his dandy clothes, another annexationist had been ridiculed—and disposed of as a threat. Before the day ended, Cauchon warned Rhéaume that he would print Plamondon's note the next time he heard another political word from him. Poor Rhéaume: he sent his father-in-law "pour implorer miséricorde." But the little editor of *Le Journal* treasured his scrap of paper and concluded his letter to LaFontaine with the assurance: "Nous en sommes débarrassé pour toujours et . . . j'ai reconquis d'un coup toute l'influence qu'il m'avait fait perdre."[22]

[22]Papiers LaFontaine, Cauchon à LaFontaine, 15 nov. 1849.

Cauchon also brought in the priests, "le clergé catholique étant," in Abbé Cazeau's own words, "le principal boulevard de la loyauté canadienne contre les projets de nos démagogues . . . qui cherchent à le spolier précisément à cause de sa fidélité au gouvernement et puisqu'il s'oppose à leur projet de faire annexer le Canada à l'Union Américaine."[23] During the campaign, the Archbishop's secretary made no secret of his high regard for Chabot—who, incidentally, was his cousin. Just before the election, he went with another priest for a well-publicized supper at the candidate's home and subsequently (according to Papineau) went

plusieurs jours successivement bras dessus bras dessous, de maison en maison avec Cauchon et hoc omne genus, solliciter des voix pour Chabot, en assurant que les annexionnistes étaient convenus que s'ils pouvaient constater qu'ils auraient la majorité dans les deux villes, ils commenceraient à persécuter leurs adversaires et à amener par ces provocations le recours aux armes, et la répétition des malheurs de 37 et 38.[24]

Naturally Chabot won. On election day (January 26) the city took the precaution of swearing in five hundred extra policemen and the sheriff forbade anyone carrying a stick to approach the poll. But the *Québecois* voted peacefully, 1,207 of them for Légaré, 2,011 for Chabot. Cauchon had not obtained his 900-vote majority, but the British connection had been vindicated. He could run a banner across *Le Journal* on January 29: "Grand et Glorieux Triomphe pour l'Administration," and in private, he assured LaFontaine "l'annexion est morte à Québec."[25]

It was, and also throughout the French section of the province. The French Canadians had realized that the annexationists were inspired by hatred, not by true love of their country. The Tories wanted to crush "French domination," the *rouges* the British connection and the Church. Both were destructive, neither offered any promise for the future. The *Canadiens* knew they had entered a new era. If they looked back, they saw great things accomplished: dangers overthrown and difficulties vanquished. They saw they had finally become masters in their own house. Now, under leaders in whom they had faith, they were strong—too strong for any leap in the dark. For to-morrow, they knew they could again do great things together. Often, late into the night, Colonel Etienne-Pascal Taché would ponder over his nation's

[23]*Ibid.*, Cazeau à Caron, 22 mars 1850.
[24]O'Callaghan Papers, L.-J. Papineau à O'Callaghan, 1 fév. 1850.
[25]Papiers LaFontaine, Cauchon à LaFontaine, 8 mars 1850.

fate and future. At the beginning of April 1850, he confided to his friend, Colonel Gugy,

De grands évènements se préparent. . . . Les habitants du Canada devront se regarder en face: que tous . . . se donnent la main. . . . Encore une fois, je ne vois que deux choses, ou il faut l'arme au bras demeurer anglais coûte-que-coûte, ou tout doucement s'amalgamer aux républiques voisines, il n'y a pas d'autre alternative, la crise approche. . . . Pour tous ceux de la population anglaise qui veulent tenir à leur allégeance, ils ne peuvent faire mieux que de s'allier à nous: car comme je l'ai prévu et prédit depuis longtemps (pardonnez-moi si je vous le rappelle) les Canadiens seront les derniers à tenir à la connexion.[26]

[26]Papiers Taché, E 2, Taché à Gugy, 7, 10, avril 1850.

Conclusion

"Je me souviens." So boasts the armorial bearing of the French Canadians. And for many of them the best memories are those which derive from the eventful days which followed the rebellions of 1837 and 1838. During those years, some of the most momentous in the long history of French Canada, their lay and clerical leaders, working closely with the imperial envoys, committed their future to "les institutions britanniques auxquelles nous sommes fortement attachés," and thereby saved their own national identity and possibly the British connection as well.

This national and imperial triumph was to a large extent determined by the four men who served during those years "in the image and transcript" of the British monarchy to link the imperial interests with those of the *Canadiens*. Varied in character and background, these four governors also differed in their achievements. But coming in the order in which they did they slowly led the politicians from an avowed hostility to any British governor, through discussion and respect, to open confidence, esteem, and even reverence.

Lord Sydenham, the efficient and enterprising businessman who had no patience for the economically backward, misunderstood the *Canadiens*, and all but told them so. He earned in return their hatred, and, worse still, their sarcasm. Lord Metcalfe, kindly, honourable, and trained to autocracy, was unable to accommodate himself to changing political circumstances. Nevertheless, he respected the French. He gave financial support to their cultural projects, recalled their loved ones from exile, and sought counsel from the most radical of their leaders; in fact he gave them everything except the one concession they really wanted. And generally they responded with respect, honour, even friendship, everything except the political victory the Governor strove for almost to his dying breath. Sir Charles Bagot, on the other hand, and the Earl of Elgin—both diplomats, and men of culture—gave the *Canadiens* both the respect Metcalfe had shown and the understanding Sydenham had refused. They received in return universal adulation and sincere affection. Indeed the failures and achievements of the four governors of the 1840's show how important it is that he who represents the Crown should understand and respect the "religion, habits, prepossessions, prejudices" of the people he governs.

The successes and failures of these four men also point to the importance of a governor's background. Sydenham and Metcalfe failed, but they had far more in common than their failure. Both sprang from a bourgeois liberal *milieu* and neither had married; consequently their horizons seem to have been limited, for the one, to business contacts and trade agreements, and, for the other, to colonial administration. They had courage and were not without talent. But they devoted their qualities to long office hours rather than to the more intangible methods of inspiring loyalty. Besides, they were both ill. Sydenham was gouty, impatient, and, on occasion, bedridden for weeks at a time; Metcalfe was dying of cancer. And neither gave much evidence of an ability to speak French, or even of any particular desire to conciliate the crowds, who, even in those days, played an important part in deciding the course of politicians. In contrast, Bagot and Elgin inspired tremendous loyalty. And they too had much in common. Their aristocratic birth gave them an hereditary vocation to govern. These men knew how to reign as well as how to rule. And both were humanists of wide culture. Bagot, a man of the world, fluent in French, moved through Lower Canada conversing with *jeux d'esprit* and wit. Elgin, a graduate of Eton and Oxford, enjoyed a reputation for splendid oratory in two languages. Both were happily married to ladies of rank, dignity, and beauty; and both had made an art of entertaining society at a *levée* or captivating a crowd in the street. They were helped in their success, of course, because they eventually conceded the demands of the *Canadiens*. But in each instance, they had won the loyalty of the people and the politicians before making their concessions.

This same decade saw a significant change in attitude on the part of the priests. At the beginning, they hardly conceived that practical politics could be their concern, nor did they stress the nationalist theme. They worked behind the scenes, and, in 1838, for instance, when they decided to oppose the Union, they sent an unpublicized petition directly to London. But eight years later, they openly sided with LaFontaine, and during the repeal and annexation crises, allowed their unofficial press to give public approval to Lord Elgin's administration. Furthermore, they openly supported the idea that the Catholic faith, French nationality, and the British connection depended on one another.

This different attitude stemmed partly from the influence of the Catholic revival in Europe where the clergy sought with some success for new ways of re-integrating the Church into the educational life and social services of the restoration period. Through publication in *Les Mélanges Religieux* of the articles and speeches of Montalembert, Donoso Cortès, and other European ultramontane politicians, the *Canadien* priests developed a new respect for lay politicians and adopted new ideas on how they could assist them. But this European influence aside, they owed their new attitude more particularly to the historic changes in local political conditions. With the coming of responsible government, effective political power passed from the governor general, who had normally favoured Catholic influence, to the *Canadien* electors. If the Church was to exercise the influence which the priests felt in conscience it must, then the clergy, like Sir Charles Bagot and Lord Elgin, must deal directly with the people. They soon found politicians who gladly accepted the powerful help they could offer.

The politicians of the 1840's were a diverse lot. On one side was Louis-Joseph Papineau, powerful even when absent, idealistic and idolized, highly intelligent, but unable to compromise. By 1840 he had come to hate all things British and stood by waiting for the great moment when Lower Canada must inevitably become the thirty-fourth state of the American union. In his shadow sat John Neilson and Denis-Benjamin Viger, the one stubborn and able, the other a courtly scholar, and once an impassioned national hero. Both were sincere nationalists. They were also too logical in their thinking to understand the true nature of the British constitution. Now old, and a little divorced from reality, they were content to await the inevitable dissolution of the colonial bond, striving all the while to save for the day of liberation as much as possible of French Canada's heritage. Separatists to the end, they refused, at first, to participate in the Union, fearing it would destroy their national identity. They preferred splendid isolation, the building of a compact national group, ready at most (O'Connell-like) to throw the strength of its votes temporarily to whoever offered the most concessions. Later, they proposed double majority, another device that would keep them separate, restricted to mere formal co-operation with the British. Behind them there followed a host of ardent intellectuals who shared their particularism. Later, after Neilson's death spared him one of the consequences of his ideas, the younger radicals improved upon separation by promoting the founding of a Louisiana of the north. Oddly enough—like the radical nationalists of a later day—all of them, Papineau, Neilson, Viger, and the *rouges* soon found themselves allied with the Tories, their traditional enemy.

On the other side was Louis-Hippolyte LaFontaine, ardently patriotic, stubborn, introverted, and a supreme realist: "Les Canadiens sont devenus par les traités sujets Anglais. Ils doivent être traités comme tels." No deep thinker, he grasped that French Canadians were best served by the British constitution and that he had in the Union parliament the means to forward its evolution. A practical man, he accordingly set out with consummate political skill to win responsible government for his people. In fact, as the decade passed, he came more and more, all unwittingly, to personify British institutions. His ideal, of course, was responsible government, but he was very British in his political methods and in his reliance on party politics. He also excelled at choosing the most advantageous political stance. Under the influence of Etienne Parent, for instance, he aimed first for political and economic reforms and sought accordingly to form a united party with the Reformers of Upper Canada. In his address to the electors of Terrebonne (as in his letters to Edward Ellice in 1838) he described his people's problems in political terms alone. Yet, gradually, under pressure from his opposition, and such followers as Cauchon and Langevin, he became more of a nationalist and sought alliance with the Church. By January 1849 he could declare with truth that his course of action was guided by one pole star: national survival. By such means, he achieved both reform and survival. Incidentally, he also became one of the godfathers of the Commonwealth.

Apart from this basic theoretical difference, the conflict between the factions had strong personal roots. LaFontaine, for one, tried the patience of many who might otherwise have followed him. Aubin and Louis Perrault, to name but two, thoroughly disliked him, as did most members of the Papineau clan. Duvernay and de Bleury despised Papineau and each other; so did Wolfred Nelson. Cauchon and Chauveau could hardly stay in the same room; and Edouard-Raymond Fabre, who also detested LaFontaine, found it difficult to remain on speaking terms with his son-in-law, George-Etienne Cartier.

An additional complication was the traditional rivalry between Quebec and Montreal. In 1840 the *Québecois* led the opposition to the project of Union and thus directed against LaFontaine's Montrealers much of the resentment that broke out during *la crise Metcalfe* against the alliance with the Upper Canadian Reformers. Ironically, after having lost out to the Montreal politicians, on the first two issues, the Quebeckers became LaFontaine's strongest champions, once the separatist strength moved to the leader's own district. Of course, the economic prosperity of each city (the one dependent on the timber industry and shipbuilding, the other relying on the Upper Canadian hinterland) tended to prejudice Montrealers towards the Union during the first two disputes, and likewise dictated the *Québecois* attitude during the third conflict for the preservation of the British connection, imperial preference, and some, at least, of the Navigation Acts.

The Neilson-Viger, *rouge* faction thus lost all of the three conflicts. Judging by the eventual fate of Louisiana, this was probably most fortunate for French-Canadian culture. Nevertheless the group made a profound mark upon *Canadien* nationalism. The younger members— Barthe, the Papineau cousins, Dessaulles, and the Dorions—left behind a radical separatist tradition that has been a recurring phenomenon. The older members, Neilson and Viger, equally particularist although never republican, bequeathed to their intellectual descendants both a belief in the primacy of parties based on nationality (rather than policy) and a lingering respect for a kind of *ancien régime* paternalism. After all, the *Canadiens'* most urgent demands after 1840 (the return of the exiles, an independent school system, the maintenance of a particularist French judiciary) had been achieved not by political action or "responsible" party government, but by the good-will of Governors General Bagot and Metcalfe. To them, party government and democracy became synonymous with political trickery and patronage—an impression which LaFontaine's actions did little to correct. For their followers the Crown has always stood not so much for liberty and self-government (which it does in the British tradition) but as a symbol of authority and integrity. This authoritarian, paternalist, national tradition has also been a recurrent theme in French-Canadian history.

LaFontaine's party won. And the magnitude of their victory gave a lasting strength to most of the themes they contributed to *Canadien* nationalism. There is the theme that *la survivance* can be achieved only by the united effort of all *Canadiens*; the theme of the struggle to win the right to speak French; and the multitudinous variations on the theme of the language as the guardian of the faith. Many of these LaFontaine originated in the 1840's—it was Joseph Cauchon, for instance, who brought in Abbés O'Reilly, Chartier, and Chiniquy to add a religious note to the national chorus he was directing against Papineau. But, above all, it was with the theme of the last cannon shot that LaFontaine placed himself and his followers directly in the mainstream of nineteenth-century French-Canadian nationalist thought.

Indeed, the theme was a recurrent one at least a generation before Colonel Taché put it into marmoreal phrase in April 1846. As early as 1823 the rising and still pro-British, Louis-Joseph Papineau objected to a proposed union bill on the grounds, among others, that it would destroy his people's civil rights, customs, habits, religion, and prejudices. He warned Britain that these same prejudices, and especially the French language, "a été sans contredit, une des causes qui ont le plus contribué à conserver cette colonie à la Grande-Bretagne à l'époque de la rébellion des Américains."[1] Later, François-Xavier Garneau said as much when welcoming Lord Durham in 1838:

> Durham, l'avenir le verra,
> Sur ce grand continent le Canadien sera
> Le dernier combattant de la vieille Angleterre.[2]

This fundamental idea that just as British dominion depended on French Canada so the national aspirations of French Canada could not be adequately fulfilled unless linked with the British connection, that just as a non-American, non-republican state could not exist in northern North America without a self-governing French Canada, so without British North America there could be no *Canadiens*, this theory of mutual dependence, begun years before Parent's and LaFontaine's era of power, has continued long since in the thunder of oratory and the sweep of history. It survived under the guise that greeted the Commandant de Belvèse in 1855: "Nos cœurs sont à la France mais nos bras sont à l'Angleterre." And in George-Etienne Cartier's claim in 1869 that "les Canadiens Français sont des citoyens anglais parlant le Français." It was present in Henri Bourassa's admiration for what he called "the illogical but so broad and so humane British Constitution." Indeed, Louis-Joseph Papineau's grandson based his opposition to militant imperialism on his fear of a reaction whose "résultante inévitable en Amérique sera l'annexion du Canada aux Etats-Unis." "Le raisonnement et l'étude," he declared, "m'ont fortement attaché aux admirables traditions de la vie nationale britannique et je les considère nécessaires à la conservation de notre propre

---

[1]Quoted in F. Ouellet, *Papineau*, Cahier de l'Institut d'Histoire de l'Université Laval, 1 (Québec, 1958), p. 27.
[2]*Le Canadien*, 8 juin 1838.

caractère national, menacé par l'infiltration des idées et des mœurs américaines."[3] The same theme is implicit in Premier Jean Lesage's declaration in April 1963 that "the French-Canadians on the whole have always looked to the Crown as their protector. The French Canadians would be the last to join the United States. They will stay in the Commonwealth."

LaFontaine accepted the Union, and by winning responsible government, guaranteed for the *Canadiens* their right to be themselves. He then went on, by defeating annexation, to guarantee the British connection. Of such stuff then did French Canadians fashion their nationalism. They insisted on their right to be themselves. Convinced that this right was best redeemed in a British North America, they remained firmly loyal. An unemotional loyalty, true; one founded not on sentiment, or quick-lived stirring passion. Indeed, this is its strength, that it is securely rooted in self-interest. If allowed to remain himself the French Canadian will be the last to defend what Etienne Parent described in 1840 when he approved the uniting of the two Canadian peoples, "une grande nationalité Canadienne assez forte pour se protéger elle-même et vivre de sa propre vie."[4]

[3]Bourassa's statements quoted here are in House of Commons, *Debates*, 1899, p. 1332 (March 28); "Les Canadiens-français et l'Empire britannique," *Revue de la Nouvelle France* (1903), p. 8; and *Le Devoir*, 28 oct. 1912. They were pointed out to me by M. Jean Amyot, who graciously lent me the fruits of his research on Bourassa and imperialism.

[4]*Le Canadien*, 6 juil. 1840, See *supra*, 63.

Bibliographical Note

No really useful purpose would be served by listing all the secondary published sources which have gone into the making of this book. The footnotes in which I have inscribed my more obvious and direct intellectual borrowings should be enough to indicate the extent of my debts. I have also consulted all the available primary source material that has been published about the psychology and the policies, about the politicians, the priests, and the press of mid-nineteenth–century French Canada. In addition, I was fortunate in being able to make use of three valuable studies, Fr. V. Jensen's "LaFontaine and Canadian Union," and George Metcalf's "The Political Career of William Henry Draper," two M.A. theses completed at the University of Toronto in 1943 and 1960 respectively, and W. G. Ormsby's "Canadian Union, 1839–45: The Emergence of a Federal Concept," an M.A. thesis presented at Carleton University in 1960.

My two main primary unpublished sources—as the footnotes throughout the book have doubtless made obvious—have been the whole of the French-Canadian press from 1838 to 1851 on the one hand, and, on the other, the private papers of the main *Canadien* politicians, British officials, and Catholic religious leaders during the same decade. Of the private papers I made more special use of the correspondence collected in Manuscript Group 24 of the Public Archives of Canada and of the Collection Papineau-Bourassa in the Archives of the Province of Quebec. The latter are discussed and published here by special arrangement with Miss Anne Bourassa of Montreal. I examined the Colonial Office despatches on microfilm copies in the Public Archives in Ottawa, and I wish to acknowledge, that this unpublished Crown copyright material from the Public Record Office, London, has been reproduced by permission of the Controller of H.M. Stationery Office. C.O. 537/141–3 contains very useful confidential despatches between Lords Metcalfe and Stanley about the questions of the French language and the amnesty for the exiles: I would not have found them but for Mr. W. G. Ormsby who pointed them out to me outside their regular place in the order of Colonial Office papers. In the Archdiocesan Archives of Quebec and of Montreal, I consulted all the available correspondence between 1838 and 1851, part of which has already been calendared in the *Rapports* of the Quebec Archives for 1938/9, 1945/6, 1946/7, and 1948/9; at the Toronto Public Library I read the Baldwin Papers.

Among the newspapers, there are not many complete collections. *La Minerve* for 1842–50 and *L'Avenir* for 1847–50 were consulted from the Canadian Library Association microfilm copies at the University of Toronto Library. Marginal notations on many of the original numbers of *L'Avenir* indicate that the film was made from copies belonging to Amédée Papineau. *Le Canadien* (1837–50), *La Gazette de Québec* (1839–oct. 1842), and *Les Mélanges Religieux* (1841–50) were consulted from the complete, bound collections at the Archives of the Collège Sainte-Marie in Montreal. *L'Aurore* was consulted for 1839–42, 1845–6, and 1847 from incomplete collections in the Archives of the Province of Quebec, the Bibliothèque Saint-Sulpice in Montreal, and the Public Archives of Canada, and for 1842–5 from the collection kept at the University of Western Ontario and forwarded to the University of Toronto Library by courtesy of Interlibrary Loan. *Le Fantasque* (1837–44, 1845, 1848–9) is fairly complete in the Archives of the Province of Quebec and the Library of the University of Toronto. *Le Journal de Québec* (1842–50) was consulted from another fairly complete collection at the Bibliothèque Saint-Sulpice, where marginal notations on many of the issues indicate that they belonged to Denis-Benjamin Viger. The minor newspapers, *La Revue Canadienne*, *Le Populaire*, *La Quotidienne*, *La Canadienne*, *Le Jean-Baptiste*, *Le Vrai Canadien*, *Le Castor*, *Le Charivari Canadien*, *Le Progrès*, *L'Ami de la Religion et de la Patrie*, *Le Moniteur Canadien*, were consulted from incomplete collections in the Public Archives of Canada, the Archives of the Province of Quebec, the Bibliothèque Saint-Sulpice, and the Salle Gagnon of the Montreal City Library.

Index

election, 187; and double majority, 204–5, 206, 207; on Rebellion losses, 227; begins *la réaction*, 233, 239; attacks LaFontaine's publication of Draper-Caron correspondence, 236; supports Viger view of Jesuit estates funds, 246; on LaFontaine's choice of Executive Council, 275, 277; Aubin's brief tenure (1847), 280; supports Townships association, 293; gradually moves into Papineau camp, 299, 301, 305–6; attacked by Cauchon, 322; supports Papineau view of Saint-Denis, 323–4; publishes Papineau's assembly speech, 330; on Montreal riots, 354–5; supports Church against *L'Avenir* attacks, 370–2, 373; summarizes arguments against annexation, 381–2

Le Canadien Indépendant (Quebec), 345, 355

Le Castor (Quebec), 126, 199; supports LaFontaine in 1844, 187–8; supports double majority, 207

Le Charivari Canadien (Montreal), 126, 165

L'Echo des Campagnes, 362; Langevin takes over, 366

Le Citoyen (Montreal), 126

Le Courrier Canadien (Montreal), 15, 286

Le Fantasque (Quebec), 17; on Durham, 18–19; on Colborne, 21; on exiles, 22; on Sydenham, 36–41 *passim*; distrusts Reformers, 79; letter to Bagot, 91–2; on LaFontaine *ministère*, 109; on Bagot, 115, 116; on Metcalfe, 133; on LaFontaine resignation, 144; weak support for LaFontaine, 149; attacks Viger and Metcalfe, 163, 164, 181; on LaFontaine and Morin resignations as Queen's counsels, 186; resurrected, 299; attacked by Cauchon, 322

Lefebvre, Pierre, 15, 286

Légaré, Joseph, 94, 213, 357; supports Papineau and repeal, 296, 298; loses 1848 Quebec City by-election, 316–18; supports annexation, 350; loses 1850 Quebec City by-election, 387–91

Legislative Council, 43, 53; Bagot appoints *Canadiens* to, 100; Caron as speaker, 143–4, 262, 275, 364–5

Le Jean-Baptiste, 65, 286; collapses, 66. *See also La Canadienne*

Le Journal de Québec, 123, 299; founded, 124; on LaFontaine resignation, 144; supports LaFontaine view of *la crise Metcalfe*, 149; attacks Viger and his group, 152, 163–4; on exiles, 158; supports LaFontaine call for unity, 162–3; and LaFontaine's resignation as Queen's counsel, 185–6; supports LaFontaine in 1844 election, 188; attacks Caron and MacDonald over correspondence with Draper, 236; "defender of the faith," 246–7; first daily paper in French Canada, 281; rejects repeal, 301; "Le Rappel de l'Union", 306–8; on Papineau's reemergence, 311–12, 313–14; attacks Papineau, 315, 321, 330; on 1848 Quebec City by-election, 317–18; publishes O'Reilly letter, 320; attacks *Le Canadien* and *Le Fantasque*, 322; supports Nelson version of Saint-Denis, 323; on Montreal riots, 355; lists loyal addresses sent to Elgin, 357; supports Church against *L'Avenir*, 370–2, 373; attacks annexationist doctrine, 376–82

Le Journal du Peuple (Montreal), 125

Le Libéral (Quebec), 124

Lemaître, François, 15, 286

Le manifeste Papineau. See Adresse aux Electeurs des Comtés de Huntingdon et de Saint-Maurice

Le Moniteur Canadien (Montreal): founded, 345–6; supports annexation, 346–50; claims Britain anxious to be rid of colony, 361; attacks Church, 366–72; publishes Viger letters against annexation, 386–7

Le Populaire (Montreal), 11, 15, 31

Le Progrès (Montreal), 228

Les Fils de la Liberté, 14

Leslie, James, 44, 51, 115, 260, 275, 331, 361; advises study of Norway-Sweden union, 46; supports LaFontaine decision to co-operate with Union, 49; defeated 1841, 75; president of Executive Council, 276

Les Mélanges Religieux: founded, 86; replies to Mondelet articles on education, 86–7; part of Catholic revival, 130; on LaFontaine resig-